The Virginiad

The Virginiad

400 Years of Virginia History in Poetry

by
Tim Lewis

Limited First Edition

This is not an epic of one hero,
But of countless borrowed spirits
Who have roamed our woods and rivers
Unacknowledged, without trace,
Often unwilling, forced, forgotten,
Despairing in their seemed disgrace,
Yet in their silent, gleaming rise,
Unswerving, marching, hoping,
Their heads towards the well-cared prize
That is our shared inheritance.

ISBN 1-4392-0526-4

With thanks to Karen, my muse,
without whom this work would never have been written.

With thanks to the Poetry Society of Virginia, which awarded First Prizes
to three poems included in this history.

Cover design by Tim Lewis.

Published by The PWI Press, 311 5th Street SW, Charlottesville, Virginia.

Please send comments to the author at the above address.

Printed and bound in the United States by BookSurge, South Carolina.

Contents

My Sweet Virginia

For Karen

Oh, my sweet Virginia,
How you raise within my blood
Such depth of loving heart
And breadth of mutual suffering...

I look with you
Crooked within my arm,
Towards an Atlantic breeze
And eastern shore remembrances
Of clam-crammed estuaries,
Wild Chincoteague horses,
Spartina and
A tern-skreeked mazery
Of crazy silhouettes upon
A quilted assateague of sky,
For you are my sweet Virginia
And I am trying to merge
Into the soft surge of your beauty.

You are my paneled fabric,
Virginia,
Stitched from rags and refugees
Of every dream and pedigree,
And sewn with such a supple thread
That thrills our pattern's dread emerge
From your people's will –
And there are many times, Virginia,
When you and I have oft rethreaded
The comfort of our lives,
And morals of our future mysteries,
Yours in mine in yours...

Oh, Virginia,
How humility embraces
As I snuggle in my face
To your body, protection from the wind,
And listen to your breathing
Stop, divine, and redefine your self
To some surrendered fall,
As we seek your tendered soul
In our entwined identity.

For is it not true, Virginia,

That as we stroll the old ridge road,
We are tossed alike
From our chesapeake of estuaries,
Marked by oft-lost memories,
And recall, recall...

...the voices...

...of names you whisper me...

...names across the veils...

...of the simple centuries...

...As a wefting softness
– Such a wefting softness! –
Enwraps my caring search
To caress the red-earthed heart
Of your most verdant nature, Virginia,
Springing from that sanguined soil
Of our drift-reflective history.

I have only recent understood,
Virginia,
Your past, your words, your destiny,
And how you entwine with me
So subtly,
And within such noble warmth;
We interflow, you and I,
Blood in blood,
Within a merge of be becoming
Caring, sharing, democracy –
And I have fixed continually,
– Joyous every time –
Within the silver-soft informity
Of your ethereal wing,
Borne upon the wind
Of our kind-departed destiny...

...As now I ring within my heart
The beat of Richmond's pulse,
To linger-sing the rulsing James,
While skipping rocks and rills
And let its thrill encompass me,
Then move west, to snuggle
The press-furled hills
Of your mountain-laurel slips,
Shenadoahs of curve and waist,
And surrender to your oak-flecked hair,
Dark-browed temples hoving to the wind,
Eyes staring over hollow, ridge and cove,
O'er the heaves and rhythmic skies

Of soft-set slopes and danville vales,
Piedmont breaths and sighs,
My only sweet Virginia.

Oh,
I never understood
The nature of return,
Of return to me,
Until I lay with you each night,
Breathing in your summer-seasoned hair
And drank such smiles of sacred-hearted stares;
I had lost my way, my essence, my self-belonging
Until your upland curls and undulations,
Your blue-ridged hips and appalachian eyes
Seduced me and forced me to proclaim,
"I am a Virginian!"
Yes,
"I am a Virginian!"

You and I are one, Virginia,
I am you and you are me,
And there is no I between us,
Anymore, anymore, anymore...

Oh, how I hear the voices...!

...names across the veils...

...As I die in your sweetness,
Ringing in your voice of heart
And laughing in the ecstasy
Of rejoicing country lanes...

But more, Virginia –
You have brought me back to me,
To my soul, my heart and spirit,
To the person I long to be...

New from old; new; old; forms, merged...

...new into old into new...

And I hear the voices,
Hear them now,
Rejoicing from ancestral soils
That mark our graves and hopes,
The suffered toil of all.

And so,
What is our destiny, Virginia,
You and I,
What choices shall we seam together

With our tree-stroked needlereams
Of mutual folk and seed?
And what do ancestors of our soul
Cry out to us,
If only we had ears to tell
The retelling of their tale?

I listen to their heartbeat,
Residing, as it does, in you...

Each age, it seems,
Is faced with some morality
It must piece into design,
And is defined by its success;
So what is ours, Virginia,
And will the cloth of futured generations
Deem us harshly?
Can we join in mutual care,
In sharing being, responsibility,
Empathy and community,
Where love for this land, this country,
And all its people equally
Can rise upon the shoulders
Of our shared humanity?

It can be done, Virginia,
For I have rebirthed my soul
In your mist-wisped woodland groves,
Rebordered my love
Within your deep-rooted honesty,
Refound myself
In the finish of your sanctity,
In your slow-mirrored current,
In your squares of soy and pasture,
Your corn and chickens, that chattled forestry,
That has repatterned our symmetry.

All rebirth is hard, Virginia,
New from old from new,
And you have recast me, Virginia,
Within your verdant hue;
You are from dawn to dusk, Virginia,
From first blush to evening blue;
You are my all, Virginia,
As I let my search subdue
Into that love and soft serenity
That *is* our eternal due.

Note on the Text

The Virginiad comprises nine books, each covering about thirty to sixty years of Virginia history. Each book is divided into about ten sections. And each section consists of a mixture of short and long poems interwoven with poetic conjunctions and interruptions, songs and brief historical notes about key events.

Most Indian words used in the text are based on Captain John Smith's tiny list and William Strachey's more complete *A Dictionarie of the Indian Language*. When used by the colonists, they are written as recorded, but when used by Indians, they are broken into phonemes with glottal stops, to distinguish them from their Anglicized originals. In the later books, they employ modern American spellings. Thus, an Indian name may be spelt up to three different ways, depending on who is using it at the time.

Prior to the Declaration of Independence on July 4th 1776, the poem uses modern British English spelling and grammar; after then, it uses modern American English. While this change is not historically accurate for a variety of reasons, it symbolizes the emergence of the new nation and emphasizes the transformation in Virginia's status at the time from colony to independent commonwealth.

In general, the linguistic structure of the poetry is present-day English – without "ye" or "thee" or "thou," etc. Nowhere does it use archaic English forms, old spellings, punctuation or the antiquated use of uppercase for nouns, except in a few songs, hymns and quotes from the period.

This raises the issue of anachronisms and whether or not the poetry should use the language structure and concepts of today or the past. I decided to keep strictly to the language forms of today because this is a *contemporary* poem that uses modern language and understanding to reflect upon the completeness of Virginia's history. It is a present-day poet's attempt to cast a contemporary eye upon the lessons of our past. But they are *our* lessons, not the past's. In fact, the past may have viewed them quiet differently.

While the poem attempts to be historically, philosophically, socially and technologically accurate, the poetry itself is written by a modern poet with modern things to say. The punctuation and spelling is modern and it is obviously designed to be read by a modern audience. It is a personal exploration of our past that challenges accepted ideas of who we once were and who we are today.

Note:

The Virginiad contains clues to a valuable treasure
located somewhere within the landscape. Find the clues and
follow the directions to the treasure. The clues will also
tell you what the treasure is.

Use this code to help you decipher the clues:
ABBC DBAD EFGH AIJH GHED E–KE DLEH

Book I

James Towne:
Struggle for Survival, 1607-1646

I

'Tis time, 'tis time
To ring the circle of ten thousand years[1]
And mark the passing of four hundred
With an abundance of our mercied tears
And harsh truth of our inheritance;
So come with me, soft wanderers,
And listen to the whispers
Of those veiled and visioned ancestors
Who wish to tell their silenced tale
And give some deeper insight
Into whom we are today...

Come Callings, call unto the MindWeavers,
The Wefts of our ancestral souls
Who whisper words of spirit realms
Where the enchanted Sufferers dwell.

"Au-ma-umer! Coh-qwa'ivwhe As'pa-mu!"
With open arms towards the dawn:
"Ken'kut-ema-um Ke'show-tse!
Ough! Ne'tap-ewhe!"

Such is our strength,
Our power, the power
Of our many and our one...

But hush...hush...hush...for
As I stand upon the eastern shore
A dark rise irks us be gone,
And with a trepidatious glance,
Drop up'po-woc upon the lurking sun.

Awwaaaiiieeeee!
Awwaaaiiieeeee!

---

[1] By 1607, Native Americans had lived in Virginia for at least 11,000 years. This poem begins with a call for the calm earth to awake, welcoming Ke'show-tse, the sun; up'po-woc is sacred tobacco.

I hold the strength of this land
In my embracéd arms!

Awwaaaiiieeeee!

Ten thousand times
Upon Asa'teeg's weeping shore,
We have raised our highstretched arms
– Upon Ra-pa-han-o'k, Pot'au-ma'k,
Upon the rilting A'po-ma'tu'k,
Upon the confluence of Pa-mun'ki
And deep-soft Ma'ta-po-ni,
Upon the Ma-na'ho'ac forest hills
And the Mo-na-su'ka-pa-no[2] rills,
Upon chestnut dales of Mo-no'kans,
Rift-rivered vales of Tu'te-lo,
And far-clouded Sha-wan-wa ranges
That echo to the eagled rage
Of the uninterrupted ages!

Awwaaaiiieeeee!

Ten thousand times
We have raised our sage to that same orb
That shines across our peoples,
And thanked it for the calm of earth
We sit-absorb upon;
And we beg you listen careful now,
Great Ke'show-tse, in your blood-red shift,
To that forgotten heritage
We will lose so tenderly,
So silently,
– To the drifts the past will spell,
Preserved despite our cavedwell fall –
Lessons of a common cast,
As humans, within all that is past that is all.

Awwaaaiiieeeee!

Ten thousand times
We have crossed our legs
And pierced our arms,
And drawn ten thousand circles
With a scent of out'haman-goyt'he[3]
To u'ero-an'ts the welcome born
Of the Great Sun's fierce adorn,
Pow'ha-'tan, Chi-'ka-hom-ini,
Nan-se-mand and Chero-en'ha'ka,

---

[2] The Saponi. The Sha-wan-wa are the Shawnee; the Chero-en'ha'ka are the Nottoway.
[3] A tobacco pouch; a u'ero-an'ts (werowance) is a chief or spiritual leader of a tribe;
a ka-wa-so is a feathered cape; and ka'nti-ka'nti is to dance.

Ani-Ki'tu-hwa-gi...a-gi...a-gi...,[4]
Imbibing sacred herbs, the sage,
Wis-a-'kan and ma-u'ha-san
Playing the reedy, dourful flute
That tunes the songs of yesterways
And lets our minds revolve within
Those lost ancestral tears
We have called as long our breath upon,
Aye, ten thousand years.

Awwaaaiiieeeee!

My ka-wa-so of feathers, hair and fur
Blurs the ancient, spectral wind
– For the elegies of our mothers' past
And kan'ti-kan'ti of our fathers' fast
Are the spirit ways of learning
The confrontations of today –
Yet there is no one here to listen,
No one to display the glisten-pipe,
No one to dance the o'erwhelméd dance,
To trance our fathers into the realm
Of the Great Spirit, who no longer hears
The calling of ten thousand years!

Awwaaaiiieeeee!
Awwaaaiiieeeee!
Awwaaaiiieeeee!

Burn me, Great Sun, burn me,
Shave my head in sacrifice...

Awwaaaiiieeeee...!
Awwaaaiiieeeee...!

Oh, let us sway in curling disobey
With torches bearing high our arms,
And circle-circle the kettled grave,
The crypt of marshy veils and charms
That folds within the water's edge
And harbours those entrapéd souls
We wish to free from swirling spite,
But who can only rise from dire despite
When red and black and white unite...

...As
A cardinal merry chirrups
Upon a boneset vine,
Believing all the world is quietly his
And none of it is mine – or thine –

---

[4] Cherokee; wis-a-'kan is a healing herb; ma-u'ha-san is the nettle, also a herbal remedy.

And a skitting swallowtail gently flits
Across the souls of time...

So hush, my ravened babe,
Lie soft and take your time,
For the journey is bare bemoaned,
And there lurks a sultry-lisping gloam
Upon this linger-fingered land
Of wind-green, waving growth
And aroma of lush decay, as a
Storm of start-sparked pigeons
Darkens the dawnlit skray
Of ibis-washed spartina marsh,
Crab-sifted, spawning oyster bank,
Corded egrets, terns and cormorants,
Carolina parakeets, cypresses and gums,
And the shad-sunned maple creeks
That harbour-teem a continent's sad rim.

Hark, listen, shroud
Within the slow-drift cloud of tupelos,
Black-lipped to the bullfrog's call,
Stagnant hillocks of moccasin grass,
Trillium-fern and dying scent,
Cougar, black bear, bobcat snarl,
An ivory-bill's stark-raspéd krill.

Hark, listen, observe,
As the thin-robed sisters four,
SylvanVeil, beauty of the forest dales,
SkyDawn, caller of the bright-lit morn,
RippleDeep, of stream and lake and keep,
And AltaMont, who sprinkles silver dust
Upon the distant mountain vales
Of this resplendent dylan land,
Fourfold feed and fourfold care
And fourfold lay into their breast
The rituals of the hooded chest
That feeds and succour-dwells within
A tortured nest of secret rest,
There to hide, outcast-purged,
'Til 'tis time for ralliant call.

Oh, mourn with me
The rose-rise rush of fall-line hush
And slow-drift, langoured stream
That pulls the silvered mountain dew
Past humus a million years in brew,
And cycle flows the clear-aired rain
As it glows within
The primal gleam's gulf stream.

Mourn with me
The wind-warbled trees of chestnut,
Roiling once the singing breeze,
Swish-wooshing tops that tristle down
Faint soothing, upturned faces
Of sweet, bee-buzzéd, raggéd balm,
Soft-mistling leaves' rushling frown,
Dribbles of an early-autumned rain...

And look,
There, at a glimpse of freakish clouds
Upon the blue-hazed peaks
That harbinge a cooling, even pour
And question the sunset-riding ships
Waiting beyond the dipping shore
To inquire:
"Will tomorrow presage a day's-end storm
Or some new-cast, unagéd dawn?"
– And begs us ask this of ourselves:
"Do we, with hope and joy, presume
To celebrate four hundred years
Of our inheritance of this womb,
Or should we hide in entombed grief
At the many silent genocides
That mighty calls to liberty
Have thiefed from out our sight?"

II

Hush,
Hush,
For thus it begins,
WindTeller,
Watcher of the veils...

Let the night-time breezes drop a-while,
The eyes await amid the trees,
As we hold our breath and try foretell
Whether they bring us happiness
Of hope, or the sharp poke
Of dark, enspited years,
To which we alone are uninvited...

...As OakCrow calls to GlimmerGleam
The song of Harbinger's waking dream:
As the singer sings and the drummer plays
And the fiddler sparks the night,
Their spirits waft across the waves
As dawn becomes the night,
As dawn becomes the night...

17

So, yes, my innocent one,
Bubbling in your turmoiled brew,
As the east's fresh rays refill your sails
And hushness dews upon your rails
Amid a mist of morned expectancy
And rush of off-shore breeze
That drifts the scent of opportunity
And fears of nameless gifts –
For one cries of witches, ghosts,
Lost spirits come to haunt your masts
And cast your sundew-risen hopes
Into the mire of past oblivion,
Another quilts a silent sail,
While one more dour hums
Hymns of native Sussex downs.

There is an anxious quietness here,
As lonely seagulls mewl their names,
Susan Constant, Godspeed and *Discovery*,
To the creaking strains of lanyard pulls,
Reefs flapping on the crossing blow,
A sailor's shout, another's taut reply,
Orders to heave-to, drop swift anchor,
Ready the shallop, dip its intent oars,
And grimly arm themselves against
This rim of golden continent.

For
We come this fourteenth day of May[5]
With arms not opened, but closed stiff tight
Upon pikes and swords and musket bars,
Intent on fortress-building and stern fight;
We come, not as freedmen buoyant
Upon a tide of swift democracy,
But as fortune-grubbing gentlemen,
Plus valets bonded unto us
In such ready-makéd hierarchy
Of class and tightly leashed desire
That replicates our English serf and sire;
We come to learn, but only to survive,
And deceive with promises, not respect,
To better plunder, toil and neglect
This verdant-splendoured trophy;
We come to construct a fortress to our fears
And deceive the trinket-musing Indians
With copper, beads and coloured cloth

---

[5] On 14th May 1607, after spending several weeks searching for a good harbour, 160 (eight score) pioneers land on an island in the James River. Of those, 104 remain when, on June 22nd, Captain Newport sets sail for England, one week after James Fort is completed.
Note: By the modern calendar, the landing took place on 24th May.

Into surrendering us their common worth;
We come, we say, for God – to convert
This Satan-rattled land from darkness
To the glory light of His stark hand,
But 'tis mere excuse of our nature
That stealths our short-breathed selves,
To win for us alone such wealth
As can open-quarry a ready-taken continent
With hopes of imposéd feudal dreams,
Advance through societal esteem,
Gentlemen sharing barely aught,
Intent each on each in each for each
Within the bound of soliloquyed thought,
On titled influence and unjust connections
That grant them all prestigious land,
And hands us poorer servant men
– From most intent beginning –
A song to sing our menial need
And dependence on our masters' greed.

Indeed,
Their enticement is to see
How they can keep us sober men
From our intended liberty,
And *from* that sun of shaded tree
Upon which we seek to silent hang
Our own dear-hoped autonomy.

Aye, we come
Unburdened of justice or fair play,
Harbouring no standing of compassion,
No mutuality, acceptance of another's sway,
Mere notions of a common way and
Thinly veiled desire;
Indeed, we have left as much as come,
Pushed as much as fortune pulled,
Quitted an isle of landless lack,
Where abuse of energy's hard-worked back,
Plague and overcrowding dysentery
Linger in bubonic sanctity,
Here to build divided destinies
And satiate a desperate need
For gold and passaged spice
Upon occupants unready to concede.

Oh,
But halt!
Stay a moment, stay!
For am I not the Muse of Hindsight
And do I not see through my trail
Of myth and hailed expectancy,
No war, no strife, no difficulty,

No rife division, no infamy –
Only a sure and steady stream
Towards freedom and democracy,
And the just American Dream?

Oh yes, I see it all already there –
The philosophy of the USA,
The seeds of legality, God and liberty,
Planted by those first shore-bound feet –
I see it all preplanned, dreamed out,
A natural progression without reverie,
No interruptions, struggles, doubts,
No evils to betray the curse
That has beset this common land.

And then she's gone,
Lost within the mists
Of truth-succumbing mystery…

…As, marking with untimely dirge,
I immerse the starkness of our pain
Within the dark, unurging earth.

So come, let us sink our feet
Within the bloodened sand
Of this ensanguined shore
And remember our ten-thousand lives
And ten-thousand come before,
Recall their tear-lacked, juried stance,
For we have not been let to cry
The fury of our inheritance.

Come! 'Tis final time for tears, in truth,
Not the mockery of souring lies
That have canalled our dourful past
– From the first unto the last!

Ah, the raven calls and the lion howls
And the drowning sward does shed a tear
For the pillage of four hundred years,
As the Hood and Rattle, Rabbit and the sun,
The Callings borne upon the ocean's spate,
Rush upon this late-blessed land
With a lust of fearful squalling
That they call their godly calling…

…As a second cardinal intrudes upon
The first's long-lived domain…

So sing, my boys, sing,
As we reef the canvas in
And set the hawsers firm;

Sing, my boys, sing,
As we strain to the oars
And search the nearing shore
Within the estuaries of Chesapeake;
Sing, my boys, sing,
As we rush upon the beach
And hide behind the reach
Of our musketry and cannon;
Sing, my boys, sing,
With fear our first emotion,
And hew into position
A palisade for halberd, sword,
To startle savage vultures
Into terror, harsh and bare,
And haul our sicklied culture
Across this newland's ravished care.

Oh, and thus…

…We build our well-planked walls
Against a bowflight continent
And the philosopher's dream lies shattered
Upon the need of mere eight score,
Who scamper-point their readied guns
Landward from the prickléd shore
And hurry axe and saw and adze,
Hack and seize the round-fit trees
To frame a prison for our liberties.

III

Shlink, sklink, shkling, shklangk…

Within a few days of the landing at James Fort, Sir Christopher Newton sails up
the King's River to the falls, lands near the site of present-day Richmond, and
plants a cross in the name of King James of England. Along the way, his party
meets Pow'ha-'tan, leader of several Tidewater tribes that pay him allegiance.

And seeing, Lord,
The highest end of our plantation here
Is to set up the standard and display
The banner of Jesus Christ,
Even here where Satan's throne is,
Lord let our labour be blessed in labouring
The conversion of the heathen;
And because thou usest not to work
Such mighty works by unholy means,
Lord sanctify our spirits and give us
Holy hearts that so we may be
Thy instruments

In this most glorious work.[6]

These early days of encounter are dominated by the colonists building their fort, planting two small fields of wheat, exploring, and trading with the Indians, some of whom are friendly, but some of whom, especially the Pas-pa-heegs – in whose territory the settlers have landed – attack the colonists repeatedly.

We come! We come!

We see them come,
Ghosteyes, heavy-dorned and filthy clad,
Suicide in their strangely smiles,
Thund'rous canoes, yi-hakans[7] afloat,
With billowed branches of the clouds
And magic spears that gloat our death
Upon threads that spurt of caverned blood...

We come! We come!

And so they come, and so they come!
...Oh, such foreboding heart!

But then *we* come, we come,
With warriored ta-ma-'hak,
Remembrance in our brows and chests
Of pithy Jesuit and Roanoake;
We capture Captain Smith
Straying the Chi-'ka-hom-ini,
Kill companions, Cassen flayed alive,
Disgusted at his lack of fight,
But let sweet Ma'to'aka[8] reprieve
Their enspited leader, now relieved
And in our plightful debt.

Hiieee – flash!
No! Hiieee!

So we sit in m'seta-'qwa-ish and co'ka-ro's,[9]

---

[6] This prayer was said in James Towne at the time. According to Capt John Smith, services were held twice a day under a canvas tarpaulin, with more on Sundays. Logs and an old canvass awning were used when it rained.

[7] A house or dwelling made of saplings and reed mats, often covered with a bark roof. The Indians interpreted the settlers' ships variously as floating islands, houses on the water or giant canoes bearing the spirits of their ancestors from the land of dawn across the eastern ocean, come to reclaim this land for themselves; a ta-ma-'hak is a tomahawk, or hatchet.

[8] Pocahontas.

[9] A m'seta-'qwa-ish is a circle; to co'ka-ro's is to sit in council; a kwi-o'ko-su'k is a shaman-priest; ne'tus-pus and hus-pis-aan both mean to leap; a shim'ga-won-a'k is a rattle; a ma'sha'ca-ma'k is a great house, temple; a pe'ku'tsa is a prayer; an u'ta-a'k'a is a sacrifice; ma-un-o'mo-ma'un is the act of prayer; a mara-po'u is an enemy; Ke'show-tse is the sun; A'ro'ko'te, As'pa-mu and I'a-pam are the sky, earth and sea; A'ho-ne is a

Tossing round the staff of talk,
The central walk of fire,
Sun plucked by our kwi-o'ko-su'k,
Women, children, sundry friends
Squatting close about, bending
To shout, ne'tus-pus and hus-pis-aan,
The dancing man of thanking thoughts,
In fox and weasel, red and black,
Our kwi-o'ko-su'k tack-entranced
As he ka'ntis up the spirit guides
With beat and flashing song,
To ride their thoughts and pride,
Shake within his shim'ga-won-a'k
Racked bones of divination
Taken from the ma'sha'ca-ma'k,
Place of pe'ku'tsa and u'ta-a'k'a
Temple of far reeds, smoke,
Where lie, in well-dried rows,
Our great fathers, and
Burrows from trancing spin and roll,
Within rhythmic beat of foot and soul,
As we sing in ma-un-o'mo-ma'un,
In flash of horn and bead and skin,
Howls and yowls and chanting beat
That will defeat untrusty devils
And don us strength of sprinkled dust
To resist their evil threads of death.

Oh, Great Ke'show-tse! Awake!
A'ro'ko'te! As'pa-mu! I'a-pam!
We must kill them, drive them back!
They are mara-po'u, thru' and thru'...!

No!
We must trade, buy copper, guns,
Wrest power from the Mo-no'kan –
They have promised us alliance
To conquer all our foesmen!

No!
Let our warriors, one-by-one, wait
In fake ambuscade, capture, take
A few, prove their great bravery!

No!
We need their guns and ta-ma-'haks,
To learn their skillful ways,
Watch, observe, discern their wares,

---

great god. The Mo-no'kan are the dominant tribe of the southern Virginia Piedmont; and, finally, Tsena'ko-ma'ka is the Tidewater area of Virginia and North Carolina dominated by the Powhatan peoples and their immediate neighbours.

Search out how they dare behave –
Let us trade with them and save
For us
Their history and their ways.

No!
Drive them back – they bring disease,
Lies and violence in their wake,
Have awoken from the Underworld
To take from us Tsena'ko-ma'ka–
More will come and more and more,
Until they ream us from our lands
And we are lies within their dreams!
Mara-po'u! Mara-po'u! Mara-po'u!

No!
Our wives demand their beads and pins,
Their needles for their tattooings,
Entice them in with tricks, pretend
To trade, to honour-feed and fill, bend,
Then kill their leaders, debowel and smoke,
To erect them on our sacred stones,
For A'ho-ne's dedication, sacrifice
And memorials to our countryfolk!

All.
Let us do all.
Let those who will trade, trade;
Let those who are brave to go, bring down a man
And return with hair upon his belt;
And let us see whose way is best,
As we slowly starve them, sure deplete
Their scared and fleeting force...

...While, click, click, click, the fleeing light
Echoes, off and on, about our newbled night...

...And SelfSearch wanders by,
The Sufferers standing tight round
In studied, lowered sanctity,
Praying for the night to shift
Its drifting shroud from off this land,
Their heads in touching threesome arc,
Fla'ed Weaver and The Sadness,
Maid Marion meditating stark
Upon the minioned prayer
Of our lost communion.

...But
There may be more to it than this,
More to the truth of lies
And the circle curves of testimony

That heart us in as energy
To the flailing mists-deceive
Of how we seek to know-believe
And how we deem to understand
This world-beset, distorting glass
That mirrors our desiring needs
Much clearer than the bleeding of reality…

Oh, the singer sings and the drummer plays
And the fiddler sparks the light,
Their spirits waft across the dawn
As the sun becomes the night,
As the sun becomes the night…

…While we sit in circled fear to face
The setting of the sun, cry out
And grace grains of corn upon the ground,
Tobacco, water from our tears,
Wail and wave our arms about,
To call Great Ke'show-tse back again.

Within ten days of the two larger ships leaving in mid-June, the remaining 104 men start to fall sick. They blame the foul tidal water they have to drink – they have no well – the over-bearing heat, the constant work building the fort and guarding against Indian raids, and the acute shortage of food – "half a pint of wheat and as much barley boiled with water for a man a day" according to Capt Smith – while he accuses Winfield, the leader of the Council, of hoarding supplies. Men are dying nearly every day of "flux",[10] "swelling", Indian arrows and exhaustion, and are "very bare and scanty of victuals" (Percy). Forty-six rapidly die.

…shlink, sklink, shkling, shklangk…

The screams, the nightly screams
Of famine dying, streaming flux,
Of gore-taut swelling, starvation, war,
Shrieks ringing 'round our hollowed fort,
Leering from our shallowed graves,
Brought by the saline-sliméd water
Of our reach's tidal flow,
And by God's own swiftly carrier,
Typhoid Parson Hunt,
To this fly-infested bar.

And so we creep our braves upon
Their fly-infested bar,
Long by us abandoned
For its worthlessness,
Harass them in arrowed flight
And might of ta-ma'hak and knife,

---

[10] Many thoughts and images on the next pages are based on reports of the time. "Flux" was probably typhoid or dysentery; maybe a combination of both.

Slashing, swarming, dashing
To persuade them from our sight,
And from our rapid-hearted fears.

…shlank, sklink, shlink…

With Spanish Florida, buccaneers,
Roanoake and Croatan strong
Upon our rapid-hearted fears,
We day-on-day-on-day engage
In a blood-for-blood dispute
With Powhatan and werowance
Of deceit and counter-play
Against those idolatrous Satan-men,
Tense-bled, red-clawed, bared,
Our survival devilishly pared
Dark against an impish sea
Of palisaded oblivion,
Crab-clinging to the fringe
Of a wish-ensuckled bay, until,
At once, they nip their braves
And meekly turn to parlay
For our copper-tingéd clips – saviours
Of our rough-besiegéd souls.

Aie, we do clip our braves,
Rough observe and trade
The copper they most crafty nip,
Parlay of the gloried Sun,
Our storied soul personified,
Seek its savioured status,
Crave knowledge of their ways –
Their powers, stronger hold
Worthy counterweight
To our bold inland enemies;
And so we welcome, shut-pretend our eyes,
Watch and market, to understand
Those angry, desperate, starving-seized
Who crowd upon their anxious isle,
Swampy, waterless and diseased.

…shlink, sklink, shlank, shling…Ha!

Aie, so we do,
We crowd upon our isle,
Swampy, waterless and diseased,
A few gardens grown, wheat patches sown,
And wait anxiously upon, but
Are unprepared, in our ambition,
To abandon cankered feudal sores
Of refined hierarchy and mores,
Near sixty of our lords mere sneering

Lacéd gentlemen
Who will not embrace
A hint of demeaning chores
– Though they soldier well –
The rest of us fearful
Bonded valets, labourers,
Not farmers, though we pull the plough,
Blacksmith, surgeons, drummer boy,
Unfit to hoe or weed or sow;
Instead,
The honoured laze, eat unreplenished stores,
Gorge, play bowls, mock duel,
Leave their tasks undone, fuel ungathered,
Unless their servants 'mong us, overworked,
Sickly, exhausted, throng them to ourselves
To do...

...sklink, shlink...

Sickly they lie, exhausted,
Yet a few do all the women's work
While others shirk in idleness and play –
Strange be it those gaudy loungers
Who guard and eat the rationed food
And let their workers fade away;
'Tis weird, those savage drones,
Who share nothing, smoke and lurk,
'Gentlemen' in name alone.

...shlink, sklank...Ha!

Shared stores? Don't make me smirk.
We share nothing. We workers own
Nothing. Gentlemen in name alone
Lay claim to all. So, I say,
Why work at their praise and call
When they pout and laze,
And our share is nothing,
Nothing of barely nowt at all?

...sklink, sklank, shlink...

The wealth-lined purses of their promises
Are not worth a deaf flea's ear. Enough!
I say, enough!

Enough!
These fleas promised us a temporary stay,
But the ghost-eyes bear no trust,
Even amongst themselves, where
They have built a lusty palisade,
And stray up our rivered heart

And veins of fingered bay…

Sklink, sklink, scklack, sklink…
Yes! Ha!
– The sounds of dueling practice
And laughter as we cruel await
Our lazy-terrored, alleyed fate…

Enough!
Dig faster, fellow, or I'll whip
You within a breath of our life!

Aie, we do indeed extend our stay,
Splay fingers out to the southern shore,
Musket drill, desport timber, redefine our fort,
Negotiate with sly old Powhatan,
Trade for corn, talk and pinnace fly,
And must most guarded walk
Our hot and swampy refuge –
Yet still we seek some western passage,
Creek-weaving, trading geographic news,
Allow smiling Indians in,
Children, women greeting, trading,
But braiding uncalm consternation
As we treat our dying hands
With tinctures and soft balming lotions,
Lay up omens and satanic notions,
And forebodings of our Judgement Day,
For God hath interceded many trials,
From which we must take final heart
– Tho' are we not by Apostles' words
Reported that tribulation shall precede
The majestic Kingdom of the Lord
And banishment of the Devil's might
From this savage-bred and suckled land
Of idolaters – casters of black potions
In Satanic passages of the night?

Their gods are so strange –
Of greed clothed in righteousness…

But, for us we wait
And cast ourselves to rites of passage,
Within the realms of brotherhood,
And the lotions of our suffering,
As we whisper to the teller of the wind
The graceful notions of our sanctity
And resit in circled co'ka-ro's
Within a spirit-facing round,
In pearl and shell and coppered piece,
Pass apo-'kan, up'po-woc and lighted coal
And upsoul the spirits of our ancestors,

The mon'to-ac[11] and Ke'sh-ow'tse, Great Sun,
To run of strange and markéd things,
Mirrors, books and feathered scripts,
Their ways of sparking fire within
A box, and other things magic-tipped
That stamp scares of death upon our people
Of blood and suppurating sores,
Of coughing-fevered shakes,
Blackened bowels and stomach aches.

Within our crampéd quarters, blackened walls
We hear them sing their curdled dance
Around their strange-faced poles,
As we fancy-face scares of more deaths
From blood and suppurating sores,
Of coughing-fevered shakes,
Blackened bowels and stomach aches.

Thus we shrill sing the dance around
Our circled poles of mon'to-ac,
To call upon our curdled Mystery
Of stream and lake and destiny,
To request the animals and sacred plants
Aid in our endeavour
To keep this resting land
For our children's sake,
And not take their heritage forever;
So sing, my brothers, dance the rounds
Of circled bark and agéd tree,
Call on M'i-sha'bo, his profound canoe,
Dawn Creator, morn-dew hare,
Guardian of the ancestral ground!

Ccchhh! Ccchhh! Ccchhh!

Awwwaaiieeeee!
'Tis time to raise
The staff of our hunting vow,
When we must praise the spirits
Of the calf and bull and cow
For them
To feed us through the moons
Of pun-sa-osh[12] somehow,
And so must prance the lunared loop
To dance the humpbacked buffalo,
Rattles, hoops and flutes of drums,
Our makers thrummed in sacred suits

---

[11] Lesser deities, spirits.

[12] Winter; a kwi-o'ko-su'k is a shaman-priest; po'to-po'ta-taw is the red dye Indians wear on their skins; No-ko-mish is Mother Earth: a u'ero-na-us'qua is a female leader; Mo-un-sha'qwa'tu-whe is the abode of the spirits, translated by the early settlers as 'heaven'.

Of skins and furs, pawing at
The hallowed ground and bellowing,
Snorting,
Chewing at the clawing grass,
Shaking heavy-manéd heads,
As our kwi-o'ko-su'k raise crying prayers
To end these years of trying drought,
Entice their spirits near to us,
And make them willing sacrifice.

So, daubing each with po'to-po'ta-taw,
Arms and calves with sooted fats,
We briskly hoof into the woods
And dance upon our moonlit route
To surround and shoot with feathered darts,
Until their hearts surrender
To our welcome sustenance.

…come, oracle, come…!

No-ko-mish, u'ero-na-us'qua
Within the circle-sacred fray,
Of three-in-one to our endeavour,
Cries to Mo-un-sha'qwa'tu-whe
To stall the earth's fine breath
From the flooding stink of death
That links with such disturbéd birth
And sheds the blood of all…

…While still the echoes ring
Of death about the fort,
Sklink-sklank, shlink-shlank, shlink-shling…

IV

Then first winter freeze descends,
Sneezing airs and mists portend
More sickly deaths, starvation now,
Though,
To our saving grace and good,
The Indians rescind and thankful trade
Us much-needed banks of food…[13]
Our u'ero-an'ts tell us to deed our crop
To these strangers in their frozen need,
To succour and forgive, in hope
They will, most grateful, leave.

---

[13] This proves to be a bitterly cold winter, so cold that the rivers freeze over and the colonists suffer intensely from frostbite and starvation.

But still our fate is grim, for,
With First Supply have come
A hundred gullets more to feed
From our dwindle-festered stock;
Though they bring we-need supplies,
The mariners trade our copper 'til
'Tis made worthless and we
Must over-barter for our grain
With wily Powhatan,
As stores are lost to sudden fire,
And of the rest, the gentlemen
Do keep the best,
And sailors drain our meat and cheese,
Plundered for their treat and ease
Of voyage here and back again.
Then come winter frosts, extreme, intense,
And bitter loss of gangrened limb,
As stinking faeces stench our woods
And bickering wrenchs out our ranks,
With Kendall shot for Spanish thanks,
While drought and fire and wilting corn
Mock our meager, forlorn fields,
Bare ploughed, untended, dire.

Oh,
The passageway is dark and tight,
The rituals unlearnt and feared,
As we cling upon this beach's hold
With fingertips of blackened pain
And scold to lift our lives again
Upon Our Mother's lighted gift.

The *Phoenix*, part of the First Supply, finally arrives in the spring of 1608 with much-needed stores. Then the Second Supply arrives in late 1608, bringing seventy more colonists, including the first two women. Soon, James Towne witnesses its first marriage, between Ann Burras and John Laydon. Its first child, Virginia, is born in 1609. (She is the second English child born in North America – the first was another Virginia, born in the lost colony of Roanoke).

Our second year proves less affray,
As we plant this time the Indian way,
Fish with nets, lay stores well in,
Explore, trade greatly with old Powhatan,
Have new men, swell-suited, skilled,
Some Deutschmen and some Poles,
Hogs and chickens, goats awhile.
With the hunting good, the Indians' smile,
As Captain Smith takes stern command,
Orders dug a new, sweet well,
Logs for houses, guard posts, sentries too,
Imposes true will and due punishments,
That he who does not work

Will not eat, in a first-hand victory
For stronger minds who, till now,
Have planned long hours for the glow
Of an idle-enshirkéd gentry
We care not for a curse nor vow.

But we soon hear in disbelief,
A call that,
In a far and distant squall,
A tempest's fearsome cast
Has smashed our Third Supply[14]
Upon the blast of some
Dismal-tided Bermudan reef,
Yet brings to us survivors,
Four hundred desperates wracked
By yellow fever, hurricane,
Their food spoiled or lacked or lost,
Driving us to count the cost
In redwindled scant supplies,
No time to plant before
A frost descends once more.

And then there's worse, as,
In capricious planned intent,
The Powhatans vicious slay
Ratcliffe and his thirty comrades
Upon the lay of trustful trade,
Massacred in guesting huts
Under a smothered friendship flag,
– Seduced and dragged and butchered in,
Helled up, flailed
By shelling, scraping women –
Who then refuse us more communion,
Glutted with our trifles,
And instead rifle boats and hogs,
Hunt away our deer and game,
And lie within the ambushed woods
To murder singly as we tamely come,
Our hopes now darkly beached upon
The pithy fire that burnt and leached
The thigh of valiant Captain Smith.

Thus we plunge once more
Upon starvation, strife and war,
Our birth aborted, stifle-stilled,
The cuts resown in bloodied disarray,
As we mark our first remembered sight
Of WindTeller within the mighty boughs
Of mocking trees above our plight,
Watching, orbs of timeless grey,

---

[14] Arrived the summer of 1609.

The passing of our desperate night
At the darkest time of day,[15]
Alone, conflicted, constantly betrayed
By those cutlass-curséd gentlemen
Who brought us thus to disrepair –
That class of imbrewed idlers
Who have divided rich and poor,
And deserted hope of brotherhood,
Now Captain Smith is gone,
Then destroyed our voyaged pact
By succouring unto themselves
All meat and herbs, all salt and grain,
Till we are but sickly-starving faults
Of their most venomous game.

Oh, the cardinals chip
In harsh reply,
And the swallowtail does flitter by...

Kan'ti-kan'ti, sisters, kanti-dance,
In your most delirious midnight trance,
Rattle-gourd the circles high,
Pound the drums to piping sky
And call the Great One sweet hello
As we sit in circled ma'tcha-co-mico[16]
To chuckle-muse those muted men
Who hand
Disease and poverty, servitude,
To this great and verdant land.

Aie, we bring class and privilege
To this great and verdant land,
Even in the starving time,
As sailors extort our rancid food
Priced too high for desperate men,
Bakers coarsen poor men's loaves
To better supply the gentlemen,
Cooks steal oft our succoured victuals,
Gardeners thieve our roots and herbs,
Soldiers turn-desert and pirate flee,
While others sail our hope-blazed skiff
To trade our precious copper off,
Then set to sea with an impunity
And the desperate-fled provisions
That our brazen values sanctify.

---

[15] The winter of 1609-10; this was the most desperate period for the new colony, nearly destroying it. Its problems were partially due to the climate and Indians, but largely due to inherent issues; the anger and accusations expressed here are based on contemporary accounts by the colonists.

[16] A sacred council circle.

So too, now, all discipline of sharing tasks
Is denied in unshared pride,
And weakened, sickened labourers
Demur to side with lazy scum,[17]
Refuse to mend the fishing nets
Or guard the skulking river boats,
Spurn to salt the sturgeon rotting,
To hoe or plough or seed
The unmanured and dying earth
As the foetus starves within the womb
Of its once-proclaiméd birth.

And still we do not learn,
As ambitious discord, private needs,
Tear the colony to placental shreds,
And the gentlemen trade away
Our priceless swords and musketry,
While two of our poor company
Are tied to posts and left 'til ghosts
For raiding slender-stocked supplies,
Now privateered monopoly.

Yet, in the long-drought winter moons,
The Horseman, grey-clad, leaves
In hibernation now upon his brow,
Watches from a briared tree
As we who suffer venture out
To starving woods and creeks
For private root and shellfish meal,
Acorns, berries, seeking nuts,
Now and then a little fish,
While yet we flail in foul despair
At the desolation, muck and filth
Of our fumed and putrid lurking,
Eat dogs and rats, exhume a grave,
And take recourse to thrice the boiled
And scrapéd skin
Of a one-time slaughtered horse.

Thus do four hundred of us die,
Before we have the chance to live,
Torn from our newborn hopes
And tossed upon the rivered dreams
Of those who sent us here, destroyed
By self-starvation, Indian wiles,
And are forced, in such despair,
To build a new-laid craft and try
To weave our stormy voyage back,
As wracked upon a mythic scream
That defines the human ages,

---

[17] The over-worked servantmen, treated as feudal chattel, go on strike.

Down the river to the cape
That was once a welcome sight,
Only to be mighty saved
And be rebound by De La Warr's
Last-gasp arrival
And the sudden turning of our fate
To aggression from survival.

V

From the sanctity of hidden boughs
SelfSearch watches the cardinals now
Avow in bloody red array,
Their pregnant dames awaiting
The outcome of the day, flailing
In flashing stabs the other's skin,
Remorseless, unflinching in their fray,
Death preferred to another's win
In the sun-filled glade of a summer's day,
In which neither is well displayed.

Oh, let us ring our praising fears
Upon this pagan, Satan land...

Oh, kwi-o'ko-su'k, dressed in fox,
Snake-eyed ferret dripping skins
And horns upon your blackened face,
Raise and play your shim'ga-won-a'k,[18]
And erase the mystery of this day...

...For
That awful day will surely come,
The appointed hour make haste,
When I must stand before my Judge,
And pass the solemn test.[19]

Oh, enter-dance in shifting trance
The step-step skip and leaping jacks
Of yowling calls that raise the dead
To hear us in the dreadful halls
Of our templed ma'sha'ca-ma'k!

Thou lovely chief of all my joys,

---

[18] A kwi-o'ko-su'k is a shaman-priest; a shim'ga-won-a'k is his rattle; a ma'sha'ca-ma'k is a great house, as for a chief or a temple for the bodies of the ancestors; an u'ta-a'k'a is a sacrifice; up'po-woc is sacred tobacco; net-shet-su'nh is 'soul', or breath of life.

[19] Taken from the popular hymn *Windsor* written ca. 1591 by Isaac Watts. One of the prime objectives of the colonists is to convert the Indians to Christianity; to this end, they plan a college and churches for their edification.

Thou sovereign of my heart,
How could I bear to hear thy voice
Pronounce the sound – depart?

Drop the cornseeds into circled rows,
Then carve them up with sticks,
To foretell the coming vows
And dispel the white-eyes' tricks!

The thunder of that dismal word
Would so torment my ear,
'Twould tear my soul asunder, Lord,
With most tormenting fear.

Oh, Ke'show-tse, Okee, M'i-sha'bo,
Take our u'ta-a'k'a and our prayers,
Reglow within our ochred dance,
And entrance up'po-woc upon its smoke
To our ancestral net-shet-su'nh!

…but it is too late…too late…

…As,
With martial law and swift campaign
Of ruthless, bloody imagery
We smack-respond to red attacks
By slaughtering in our savagery,
And they in train kill more of us,
Until, in our bouts of escalation,
We burn the huts of Paspaheghs
And massacre them out,
Toss Indian babes from bobbing boats
And butcher their struggled bones
In a cardinal-foamed and fretted tide
We hope will pride us from our anger,
But only re-empowers our augered sin,
Sends Appomattuck to in-kin reply,
Then us to avenge ourselves on them –
As sudden-plucked from out the womb
Of our terrored pain as smacked
And loomed back in again.

'Twould tear my soul asunder, Lord,
With most tormenting fear…

But the tide is turning, as
The colony at last does germ,
With yet another strong supply,
Sir Thomas Dale, firm leader,
Women, farmers, cattle sent,
Artisans of a more needed bent
Than useless gentlemen,

In the narrow glint of strife
That hints, at last, at a more permanent life,
And lets us run to husbandry
And trade with cunning Indian.

Oh, the circle, the circle – and the oracle…!

With more settlers and newly confident aggression towards the Indians, recent-arrived and surviving gentlemen begin the process of consolidating the land between themselves and reintroducing the English class system to the colony.

Under the shadow of the MusicMen,
Servants of a harsher toil,
We and Indians, new-enslavéd,
Boil in steamy field and row,
While invigorated masters plot
To self-divide the best-carved lots,
– No acres for us servantmen –
And settle new-sown, planted fields
With stakes of their despotic wealth,
At Henricus and 'cross the James' flow.

In these early years, servantmen and women have no hope of setting up on their own; they are *not* indentured for a set number of years, nor can they look forward to any land for themselves. They are expected to spend their entire lives as *de facto* slaves of the gentlemen, who are planning how to use a 'plantation' system to corral their workforce behind heavy palisades. Meanwhile, captured Indians are enslaved and work side-by-side with white servants – both men and women – in the fields.

Oh, the Conjure Man and women three
Of the welling's deepmost sanctity…

…ah, yes, the well…

Let me tumble down and drown
Within the darkness of surround
That is painless, spelled and true…

Thus does Sir Thomas Dale impose
A tyranny that's deft and needful close,
Theft and usury harsh repressed,
Of baker, cook and sailored pest,
Prices fixed, as he now forbids
Individual trade with Indian foes,
Protects our tools and prime weapons,
Bans blasphemy, comes down hard on crime,
But also shreds our rightful speech,
Impeaching further and embedding
The superior wiles of gentlemen,
Jibing us to sanctity of church,
To abide the sermons he prescribes,
In a religious-run morality

Of a strictly royal, English kind,
Where God is Truth in this, His land,
We His servants manorally,
And speaking out 'gainst lord or king,
Or our most sovereign governor's wish,
Is dashed by a swift, un'giving death
– As is that short-sucked gift of life
We had, till now, been left to pluck.

*"But ye shall receive power after the Holy Ghost is come upon you, and ye shall
be witness unto me both in Jerusalem, and in all Judea, and in Samaria, and unto
the uttermost part of the earth."* – Acts 1.8

Aie, they are the *acts* of the Apostles...

...And for good reason, not the words,
For, as the Apostles spread the news
Of Jesus shedding His sea of blood,
So must we share the Gospel of the Lord
In this blasphemed, unlistened world,
Even to its utmost parts,
And be a light unto the darkest hearts.

"Oh, Halleluiah! Lord!
Grant us the strength
To cultivate this Eden
Into a Garden unto Thee,
And convert the pagan Heathen
To Thy Love and Prosperity!"

Yea,
When Man was so woeful fallen,
God hath him fairly clothed;
When the earth was ashamed in flood,
God hath given him safest berth,
And housed him in His redemption;
And thus He hath provided us the ships
To bring us bearing His saving Word,
And on our shoulders placed the duty
To clothe these savages, teach them to pray,
And serve Him in the manner of the Way,
By building unto them Houses of the Lord
And witnessing unto Him, as in the Holy Land,
His new Jerusalem, and our Promised Land.[20]

We come! We come!

Oh, I know not whom to blame...

Where are you, M'i-sha'bo, sunrise,

---

[20] Closely based on a sermon of the time.

Shifting, changing hare, Creator,
Trickster saviour of the earth and men,
From the flood of ancient times?
Where is your dawnrise canoe, your songs
Of ancestors to guide us through these brooding wrongs?

Why are the voices quiet?

Drive away these eaters of our lives,
With neither woman nor brindled child,
Who must be born of forebears spectral
Made to take this temporal land
For their final-trumped inheritance!

We come! We come!

...As The Horseman, green-clad, leafed,
Watches from a briared, distant tree
SelfSearch feeling close the binds,
– First closed binds –
Of loss of individuality.

Not only is the Church of England used to enforce a strict regimen on the colony, including very harsh punishments, but part of the remit of the colony is to establish a religious college, in part to educate the Indians in 'civilised, Christian ways'. To this end, a parcel of 10,000 acres is set aside in the new plantation of Henricus, close to the falls on the James.

We rise before the rapping dawn
And hasten down, as before,
To the shrouded waters lapping,
Plunge within and dunk ourselves,
Then raise our arms to the sunken sun,
And offer up our last few shreds
Of sage and sacred up'po-woc,
Begging Him remember us
To our taking enemies,
And not let the circle break.

The circle – it is breaking!

Oh, SelfSearch, ere they came,
You were strong and proud
In health and name,
Resilient, confident and sure,
Resting in communal lore
And the empowering call of love
Of fame in one and all –
But you are breaking,
As the circle breaks,
For you *are* the circle,
Are who the circle makes...

...oh, but...hope...

In a merge of woodland grove,
A young woman, verged on marriage,
Lies upon unagéd back,
As elder women speak and sit,
Wipe her forehead, chin and cheeks,
Then tweak her firm and start to prick
With fishbone dipped in magic bark,
Mushroom dye and worming root,
To pock and needle curling rings
Of dots and lined imaginings
That mark entranced fecundity
And new-won status in her tribe –
She will bear two sons, three daughters,
One of whom shall survive to seed
The centuries
And keep the thread
Of our circle's memories,
Until all are ready to attend
Its power and its mysteries...

It will live forever!

Hush! For now
We swiftly oar towards the shore
From the safety of our brigantine,
Land, hurry tie and hie
Upon the wooded bank, disperse,
Watch, first guards there,
Spread, debark, unlade our stores,
Axes, weapons, tents, supplies,
Then raise our camp and rapid-set
To girdle trees and fast commence
Our palisaded plans
For a new plantation fanned
Beside the river's tidal course.

So now, thwack and thwack,
Timber cracks and crashes, echoes
Across the cormoranted flow
As terns glide their angled wings
From side to startled side,
And great herons stare anxious back
To hear their silence hacked away.

As new plantations are established up and down the James, settlers clear fields
and construct fortified houses surrounded by palisades. All are close to the river,
in case of Indian attack.

'Tis strange, history...

...For, when
Old Rolfe quietly steals, and soft,
Those fateful first tobacco seeds,
Crafts them back and plants them swift,
Tends and hoes, piles soil around,
To toil Virginia's prime-tamed crop,
We *all* crazy hop insatiably insane,
And plant all strips we craven may
With Indian slaves and bonded men
To maximize intensive gain,
Ignoring fences, houses, stores of grain,
In our haste for an immediate prize,
As we desprize our ministries
In scrit and scramble to acquire
– And in the process uninspire –
The feudal realm our gentlemen
Are so determined to claw and retain
– The spread of wealth deploring
Law and undermined litany
In our first unplannéd lesson
In tobacco-harvest liberty.

VI

Nu-ma'sha! Nu-ma'sha! Nu-ma'sha...[21]

Are they gods, these reeking, sickly gentlemen
From the ocean of the dawn,
Where the Great Sun pleasures ancestors
And grants them angered morn?
Or are they ghosts of our forebears,
Tearing disease and famine, war,
To kill us with those thunder crashes
That froth upon our shore
And spurt my people's matted blood
With their threads of fatted wrath?
Are they moonshine magicians,
Dark-bearded u'ero-an'tsa,
Whose stinking smell offends,
Cannot tend their corn,
And are not of women born?

Oh, I,
Ma'to'aka
In my playful joy,
Call to No-ko-mish, Mother of the Earth,
And the strength of her coy

---

[21] Go home! Go home! Go home...
From here to ** comprises *The Song of Ma'to'aka* (Pocahontas).

Fertility to enmesh us, spare us
From our fated history, for
I am terrored with my people
And fear the hearted white demise
That plagues each village touched
By ri-apo'ke[22] lies.

Nu-ma'sha! Nu-ma'sha! Nu-ma'sha…

My father names me Playful One,
To smile and deal with them well,
Spy upon their sorcered lives
And spell their magic herbs,
In hope they will surrender
Their raging to our tragic soul –
Thus, I stroll within their fort,
Gambol for their fun,
Offer as-a'pan and a'po-ans
And observe with breezy eye
Their strange and loathsome habits,
As we all fall tired of warring's din
And drift into some peaceful ease
Of shiftful drum and flute,
And games mute beneath the sun.

Yet my people are too impatient,
My brothers steal and kill,
I am wedded to Ko'co-um,
Then am wrenched by a captain
To ride aboard his stenching isle
As ransom and a bargain ploy,
Until I am left to roam and toy
Their houses, palisades and bakeries
And learn their sacred-charmèd ways,
Until once more I am to march
With angry-armèd men
Who slash and burn our crying homes,
Our huts and corn and stores,
And finally abandon me
To my brothers on the shore.
Nu-ma'sha! Nu-ma'sha! Nu-ma'sha,
Oh, please, Nu-ma'sha…

Caught between two peoples,
Used of both somehow,
I am told to delve and ken
The kewas-o-wok of these men,

---

[22] Bad, harmful, terrible; as-a'pan is a type of pudding; a'po-ans is bread; kewas-o-wok
are sacred images in human form; mon'to-ac are minor gods, spirits; Po-po-gu'so is the
underworld, a hellish pit towards the sunset, from which the local Indians believed the
English had come – thus, it also came to mean the land of the English – England.

Their temples' secret malevolence,
Where they receive in silence,
Pray and dwell to mon'to-ac,
Crosses, books and spells,
To hook us for reprieve.

So great father Pow'ha-'tan
Has ordered me to briar-bind,
Marry them to us in a peace,
Enter into their sacrifice
And their ceremony,
Carry a quill-scratch given,
Travel into the mouth of the sun,
Unravel how it is they're born,
Where their ancestors turn, sob,
And mourn
For the ghosts of so many left
To bob the grand and rivered glow
Of our birthrite's ebbing flow.

Thus I join with one termed Rolfe
And am taken on a floating isle,
Its creaking sways and tossing
Bearing me and Tom to Po-po-gu'so,
Land of hell and blackened eyes,
Whitened faces, filth and theft,
Of jewelled kings and courtiers,
Deathly John Smith, my father roamed,
And a sickness for my ancestral home.

Oh, Nu-ma'sha,
Is this our to-come?
Are these the slow-eyed faces
Of our futured generations?
Is this what we are to be,
White man, red man, wife and son?

"Ka-peshe-ma-pa-an'gu'un!" They say,
"Ka-peshe-ma-pa-an'gu'un!"
Then demand, "'Tan-go-a!" [23]

Aiiieee!
Ma-la-com'ne-ir!
Ma-la-com'ne-ir!
Nu-ma'sha! Nu-ma'sha! Nu-ma'sha... [24]

---

[23] "Give me a little piece!" They say,
  "Give me a little piece!"
  Then demand, "Give it to me!"
[24] I will not give it!
  I will not give it!
  Go home! Go home! Go home!

Let me call the earth to our womb,
To the energy of our women as they hoe
The beans and squash and pushing corn,
As they sow us potions, scan for herbs
And roots and barks to mark
Our power and our common strength
To protect our yi-hakan and our way,
The bereft circle and the hoop,
From the white-eyes' stooping theft.

Oh,
Nu-ma'sha! Nu-ma'sha! Nu-ma'sha…
Go back! Go back! Go back!
Will we ever rest in peace again? [25]

                                              **

No, I don't want to go back!
Don't send me back,
I have no choice but here,
Convict, orphan, derelict
Of my home's rejected care!

As I roll and curl in my musty bunk
'Tween decks of this stinking hulk,
The cattle moaning and pigs distressed
With the rush and buckle of the storm's protest,
I rise, my sicklied stomach roused,
Lest we cast on some swift-sudden reef
By Bermuda's coral-cutting shores,
Praying as I clamber up
In grief and suicidal terror,
Through spraying hatch to sea-blown air,
To watch the tars clew out the sails
As we turn steady to the wind
And I grab a halyard tight against
This passage to the caverned night
Of paralysed reluctance, swept
By a man who's bought my life,
Kept until the dawn's sweet rise
Below the lifting, haloed skies
That herald a crow's nest cry of sight
Against the dark horizon's sighs.

I want to return, but then say no,
Am glad and relieved to start anew,
Recall a family left behind, belief,
Responsibilities, culture, people I knew,
And tremble in my vacillating grief

---

[25] Pow'ha-'tan, grief-stricken at the news of Ma'to'aka's death in England, rescinds his position of leadership and spends the rest of his life "visiting his country". The next year, 1618, he dies, succeeded by his second brother, Opi-tha-'pam. Several months later, O'pe-shan'ka-no assumes control.

As I cramp my stomach and press my brow
In a womb-told bundle of helpless joy
At what my future urges bold,
My past no more, present yet to unfold,
Changed utterly from the girl I was
In England's sold, good-riddance land...

Don't let me go back!
I don't want to go back!
But, oh, to rest within the womb
And my mother's soft-sensated breast!

I must go back.

Don't let me, don't let me, don't let me...

And so I
Pace the anxious, keeling deck,
Pressed hard before the onshore wind,
And then the tears, too blind for words,
Other than to raise a cry
To the diminished rain's soft beat,
Directionless, friendless, lost,
Cast not with glory nor desire,
But wrenched of all displacéd fire,
Powerless to reface myself,
Or wipe the fears from off my cheek,
In some hope-seeking final joy...

...of my new-buoyed home.

VII

By 1616, there are 351 surviving Virginia colonists, including sixty-five women
and children, plus a number of enslaved Indians, as well as 144 cattle, 6 horses,
216 goats and too many pigs, dogs and chickens to count. There are a number of
plantations up and down the James, the college in Henricus is under construction,
and there are plans to build churches and an iron forge on one of the creeks
coming over the fall-line.

Now, each year comes new supply,
Hundreds of souls, plus holds of animals,
Strong leadership and firm control,
And our community healthy grows,
Lays bold roots and stretches boughs
Either side the Royal River's tree,
Spreading up its tributaries,
Hampton, Bermuda, Digges,
Shirley, West and Flowerdew,
Timbered hundreds palisaded

Against native lands we stealthy frame
In contempt for their intent or will.

"'Tan-go-a!"[26]

The lord's cattle, goats, poultry, swine
Are reproducing handsomely,
Released, allowed to grunt and roam,
Then slaughtered for our delicacy;
We erect homes of logs, clear forest well,
Build chapels, wharfs and skitting skiffs
To ply the waters and communicate,
As mutual help aids private wealth
And all contribute to the communal health
Of individuals in tight conspiracy.

"'Tan-go-a!"

While newcomers settle up and down,
James Towne prospers and expands,
Is more generous in its standards,
With two rows of houses now,
Cabined blocks, warehoused stores,
A churchyard, farms outlying,
Fields fenced, yearly planted corn,
A wharf new built, a dock for ships
That regularly supply our homes,
Take our timber, naval goods,
And bring us animals, furniture and tools,
Craftsmen, millers, farmers, maids,
Masons, wainwrights, carpenters,
Tailors, brewers and physicians,
All skills for our necessary trades.

"'Tan-go-a!"

And so,
In the soft and subtle sentiment
Of a moment's forgotten sigh,
We turn from 'we' to 'I'...

...as SelfSearch wanders on...

...And we come, the orphans,
Paupers, prostitutes and criminals,
Side-by-side with masons, millers,
Craftsmen of a higher mien,
All pressed to the Company's keen cause
And need for hard-worked lien and toil
To finance aristocratic dreams
Of gentleman and new élite,

---

[26] "Give it to me!"

As yet they still most firm negate
All effete lies of liberty.

Aie, for we, the bought and sold,
Once debarked, descend
To cold and chattelled service
As slaves of private destiny,
Martial laws so strict applied
That men are hanged and ready-flayed,
Staked out, broken, burned alive,
For mostly minor crimes –
And now, too, we must strive
To find quick-limed taxes
And have lost all Company grain
That kept us once aloft – though,
In some soft heart of recompense,
Dale grants us, as for necessity,
A glimpse allowed of self-sensed land,
A mere three-acred pittance scratched,
No great allotments matched until
Years of servile bondsmanship
Have ploughed us to the bone.

And so are laid, by lieutenant
Governor, councilmen and courts,
Not fast roots of liberty,
But the old-world seeds of class,
Of thoughts as feudal property,
A ruler's godly, eternal thanks
To maintain his strictmost ranks
And bear us down to somesuch turf
As regimented serfs and heirs.

Yet the circle lies hidden
As our bidden ancestors
Call upon our Guardians…

To
Reese up, reese up, oh, MusicMen,
Heraise the black-hid earthen high
Upon the plough's swift lofting share,
And up the up-down coulter's sigh
Of oxen harness beam and shaft
And strain of jessy-jingled haft,
Of yoke-plied rope and flicking goad,
Foot upping, down, and upping rush,
To feel the push of head and load,
Keep straight that furrowed line,
Press down that rebel board,
Steady, hallowed sward,
And hold the stern wood bottom fine –
The soil is dry and the heaving's hard,

So make them work, my man, work hard,
To up-turn cast the downcast sod,
Reese up the scything mouldboard tread,
Regain the make of unmet want
And let the under breathe the sky,
Breathe the sky…

Oh Lord,
Heavenly Ruler of Thy Kingdom,
Protect Thy earthly ruling Agent
And make of us his Servants
To fulfill His fullest will!

There is no talk of freedom there,
Amongst the echelons of power,
No quarter given to the bondsman,
No open speech nor free religion,
No rights for us indentured poor,
No blossoms of the righteous new
Sprouting from some old-world view –
Only transfusions of the ancient,
Sickly, desperate for conclusion,
Bloody, leech-like on this land,
Clystered by their diamond hands
– Aie, those are the values we import
Upon our musket-barrelled whips,
Our stench of unwashed blankets
And the diseased-blue kissing
Of our deadly lips.

Crossing the ocean, crossing
The sea of last becoming,
And reticent-'spired dreams…

…letting go, letting go…

…to enter, enter in…

Church absence is punishable
By tobacco pound, or more,
Chapel wardens with legal powers bound
To cower with the strictest fines,
Sabbath journeys penalised,
No hunting, drinking, commerce
That, or any sacred day,
No card tricks, chequers fanned,
Even fishing cursed,
And blaspheming strictly banned.

…Yet we *do* play cards, gamble, bet,
And secret turn the Tarot to
The Hangman,

Grumbling for a future set...

...Since we, the craftsmen yeomen
Of England's streets and leas
Bring with us frowned tradition,
Common laws and rights
Handed down
Through centuries of peasant struggle,
Resentment to the earlman's grasp,
And know we may ne'er look to them
To grant away their powers,
Only to ourselves, the dispossessed,
To clasp the light that's ours
By unyielding fair intent
To demand our rightful share.

VIII

Hush, my sleeping lady,
Soft within your guarded camp,
This story is not for flesh decaying,
Nor minds too proud in furrowed ways;
It is for the futured clouds
Of unfettered sense and reason,
Free of prejudice and pre-concern –
For people who can learn and listen
To the truth upon the breeze
And hear the tale of WindTeller
As he whispers in the trees.

'Tis for
The inn awaking, the wenches sleepy
From last night's shrill carousing,
Drowsing coals from ash-drowned fires,
Broken bottles, plates dashed upon the floor,
Ale straw-rush spilt,
And for the man who finger drums
On an open-shuttered windowsill
And listens to the quietened hum
Of guests arising for their breakfast meal
Of ham and jam and butter dripping
– All fresh Virginia made.

'Tis for
The woman who, anxious-greyed,
To treat her husband's lethargy
And general frayed complaints,
Lanes the woods for sassafras,
Dogwood root and mint, to brew
An energizing tea, buck off

Melancholy, distemper and the flux.

...And for WindTeller, who rides the mists
Upon the mourning shrouded twists
Of his vaporous, windtone pipes,
Then trails the vales of dawnlight dales,
As he whispers into servants' ears
Sweet nothings about their empaléd fate:
"Weave your dreams, your powers,
Your hopes within my ancient bones!"

...And for the cattle who, left to roam the woods,
Move deeper into the sunlit swamps,
Where horns and wiles and wildness
Extend their bovine grasp
And they are lost to secret breed
Within the forest mast,
As a cardinal exhausted lies
Between the beans and squash,
With yet some strength within,
But knowing he has lost.

...And for the kwi-o'ko-su'k, who priestly
Enters
The high-templed ma'sha'ca-ma'k,
Ancestral abode, to flare home
The eternal fire of life that smokes
The prone, furl-curled bones
Of his hereditary chiefs,
There to pray and soak libation
For the guardians of this world.

...for the Callings...

...And for the wild-contented oaks
Who spread upon the shadowed gait
Of a rider past in hunter's garb,
Horseman, lean within the mist,
Dogs barking stern beside,
In the early dawning cast
Of overseer and field-sore hand
Picking buds and caterpillars
From surged tobacco lands.

...And for the river bubbles, sproiling
In the reflected glare of clarity,
Calm upon their woosh and lunge,
Their silted roils and rill-lisped race,
Swish-curl currents, spurling over,
Down and over, rushed and down,
Spurling over,
Jinkling between the rill-sashed rocks

In the flowing summer's breeze!

Most bondsmen and women find themselves in terrible conditions, decimated by disease, living virtually as slaves, often locked up at night, and with no hope of gaining their own land. Meanwhile, small-scale farmers (called planters) face, on the one hand, low tobacco prices controlled by monopolistic merchants, and on the other, increased burdens and laws imposed by a series of unaccountable governors who dole out huge land grants to their families, friends and cronies. As a result, anger grows to boiling point in a colony perpetually on the verge of revolt.

> Oh, as the circle breaks
> Into daggered shards of me,
> Let us become the treasured past
> Within our hidden memory,
> And distance seek from all the years
> Of legal fears and lies to come!
>
> We will not have it!
> No,
> We will not have it!
>
> And so resistance grows
> To imposéd martial law, until
> We threaten to o'erturn
> The whole old, rotten-riven crew,
> Taking strength from those proud
> Sinews of SelfSearch's hands.

To head off a threat to unseat him, Governor Yeardley agrees to set up an Assembly, though its powers are extremely limited and he will continue to rule, with the help of an unelected Council, virtually as he pleases.

> Finally!
> A petition is granted
> To spoil resistance's tide
> And provide a House of Burgesses,
> First assembly on Virginia's sweet soil,[27]
> Which meets for six hot summer days,
> Formalising our recent turn,
> In enforced gratitude,
> To mid-term servitude, close-indentured,
> Post-granting a hundred acres each
> To survivors of that early death
> And fifty to those newly come
> Who have paid their head-crowned due

---

[27] The first legislative assembly held in Virginia – and first in British North America – is held in James Towne in 1619. Indians, meanwhile, have held councils based on consensus for thousands of years, where not just a few make laws, but *all* participate in community decisions. Though seen as a definite victory by people at the time, the House of Burgesses primarily gives the largest landowners many of the powers they enjoyed back in England.

Or brought a sea-bought property
In human-voyaged 'xpectancy –
Servitude now three mere years,
Four years, seven or five,
As the Company strives to re-englow
The flow of those who thrively dread
The disease and short-termed lives
Of Virginia's brutal spread.

Thus are legal-maskéd gentlemen
Forced to grant us brighter hopes,
And those same rights, to all
Us coping servant settlers
That we would enjoy on England's shores
– Scarcity of labour mettling us the task
Of wheedling back some liberties
From the governor's tight-fisted grasp.

However, other rights are lost,
Despite our strangulated cry,
As the burgesses regulate religion,
Promulgate the Church of England,
And deny dissenting Christian belief –
In brief, they enforce the rights of property,
While dispossessing smaller men,
Impose courts and biased fines,
Penalties and martialled binds,
And plat our first four counties,
James, Charles, Henrico and Kecoughtan,
With enpooled justices, militias,
And local-stated bans and rules,
Thus sleuthing to themselves
Powers erstwhile resting in our own truths.

Though for many years it will merely be
The tool of lieutenant governors' private rule,
With this move, despite itself,
The Assembly is a small, reluctant prize
In Virginia's rise to self-dependency;
Much greater progress will come, 'tis true,
Through strife *against* its autocratic ways
And forays to unfair tease,
Through biased bills and courts,
The will of the governors' appointees.
As WindTeller will avow,
Our liberties have been seldom won
By assembly or institution,
But more usual by our direct hands,
Challenging the moral rack
Others seek to coerce, instill –
Our fists wresting forceful back
Rights taken by the powerful:

It is the *acts* of the people,
Not courts nor legislature,
That guarantees our liberties.

Oh, the call, the call
Of the swift circle
Drawn within the sand...

IX

On a lowset hill above
The tidal breezing Ok-oqu'an,[28]
Beneath the cedar bowers, cypress leaves,
Clans gather, ceremonial attire,
Tattoos and paints, feathers,
Bones and skins and ankle rattles,
To the circle of enveiléd faces,
Sacred posts where kwi-o'ko-su'k
Make u'ta-a'k'a to A'ho-ne and the mon'to-ac
In a feast of resurgence, plenty,
So that the circle be not broken;
The drums speak of eternity
And the dancers entrance the ancestors
With the gift of three young u'ero-na-us'qua
Who may ka'nti-ka'nti in a hus-pis-aan
Of curls and rattled chanting swirls
As we dancers ring the ring
In massed council of divination,
And not of secluded finery...

So come, let us sing of marriage
And play the fiddles loud,
Strum the lutes and the drums
And blow the weaving flutes,
As we round in floral dress,
Hats well-capped, to
Giddy run and place
Our hearts within the grace
Of this new-found, wondrous land...

...of new-stolen ceremony...

There were three men come out the West
Their fortunes for to try,
And these three men made solemn vow –
John Barleycorn must die!

---

[28] The Occoquan River; a kwi-o'ko-su'k is a shaman-priest; an u'ta-a'k'a is a sacrifice; A'ho-ne is a great god; the mon'to-ac are lesser gods; an u'ero-na-us'qua is a female chief or spirit herbalist; ka'nti-ka'nti and hus-pis-aan mean to dance and leap.

> *They ploughed, they sowed, they harrowed in,*
> *Throwing clods all on his head,*
> *And these three men made solemn vow –*
> *John Barleycorn was dead!*[29]

> Oh, John Barleycorn, rowing o'er the sea
> Of grain-eared mystery, just as drunk as you and me...

In late August 1619, there arrive "20 and Odd" black men and women aboard a Dutch man-o'-war.[30] These first Africans to arrive in Virginia are traded into servitude for supplies and end up on several of the largest properties in the colony, notably that of Governor Sir George Yeardley. At first, they are not strictly slaves, but exist side-by-side with white indentured servants and Indians, living and working in identical conditions.

> And so the unsettled tree of misery
> Sails from Ebony Coast and home,
> To root and wrest this spurnéd land
> And disgorge its centuries of infamy.

At the end of that year, a much happier event occurs. On December 4th 1619, Captain John Woodlief, a veteran of James Towne, leads his crew and passengers from their ship to a grassy slope along the James River at what is now Berkeley Plantation to celebrate the first official thanksgiving service in *any* British American colony. They ordain that the service shall be "yearly and perpetually kept holy as a day of Thanksgiving to Almighty God."

> At Berkeley on the James,
> In tight welcome of the resting sand,
> Captain Woodlief wades ashore,
> Bends to a knee, lowers head, and,
> As ordained by heart and Society,
> Gives thanks unto eternity
> For his safe and blesséd passage
> To this land of hope and plenty.

> ...drawn within the sand...

> ...of our sacred land...

The first substantial influx of unmarried women arrives in the spring of 1620. Ninety "tobacco brides" disembark as Virginia's population grows rapidly. Despite casualties from disease and a persistent problem with runaways, the population of the colony rises to nearly 1,400 by 1622. Local Indians watch with growing interest and anxiety.

> Oh Isabella, sweet Isabella,

---

[29] *John Barleycorn* was a popular ballad of the time, with roots in pagan English belief. It refers to the spirit of the corn as the seeds germinate, grow and are scythed, only to regrow the next year. Later, it became a term for another spirit of the corn – whisky.

[30] It may have been a British pirate ship; whichever, the Africans were probably originally taken from a captured Portuguese slave ship heading for Brazil.

Can you not redeem yourself
Within this ephemeral heat
Of humidity's swift below,
Nor grant yourself a soft reprise
From life-sere bonded hoe,
For not yourself but some profusion
Of fetter-made proprietor
Who stealthy wishes to refrain
You from your freed desire?

Or, Antonio,
Are you heathen Christian,
Black convert, mere half man,
Still with thought of Efua, Kalunga,
Nkinsi spirit,[31] medicine man,
Worthy only of unworthiness
And sullied contempt of those
Whose own contemptibility
Will be your burdened legacy?

Hoe, Isabella, saw husband Antonio,
Forget the Great Creator, Rain God,
Goddess of the Earth; mingle instead
With these white Adams, Eves,
Whose bonded servitude seems like yours,
Yet will cause *their* final freedom,
In yellow-fevered death, frontier fleeing,
Or some unhealthy acred swamp
Trapped between the grandees' wealth –
Forget your drums and spirit harps,
Your tribal dance and melodies,
Forget sharp sacrifice to river gods,
Ancestor graves and ceremonies;
Forget your rounded parent huts,
Sago, yams and fields of rice;
Forget nkinsis that jam the doors,
Unless paused by iron, skin or blue;
Forget old lifeways, nurtured belief,
If you are to find relief in this realm
Of shadows between the life you had
And the death you await in vain.

Lost within the trance of paradise,
Fingers burned as touched the sun,
Courage broken by hope nor victory,
Dreams lost as soon as dreams are won...

...While WindTeller rides the mists

---

[31] Efua and Kalunga are West African gods; Kalunga is associated with rivers, the sea and passage to the afterlife; nkinsi are spirits of the dead that pervade this world; Antonio and Isabella are 'married' Africans from that first shipment.

Upon the mourning shrouded twists
Of his vaporous, windtone pipes,
And trails the vales of dawnlight dales,
Stillborn infants within his arms,
As he whispers into servants' ears
Sweet nothings about their fates and fears
And sidles past the secret churl
Of the Sufferings at their burning burl.

Oh, the call of the swift circle
Drawn within the sand
Of the sacred ritual
Of our most sacred hand!

X

We trek the woods to find the staves,
Cut them, trim them of their leaves,
Stack and pile and carry back
To set within the new-laid ground,
Of this, our next retreat, an arbour
From disease and raped defeat,
Then bend towards and tie above
An archéd bow to overhang
And endow our sheltered cave…

…they are drowning us…

…left us in the ground…

…to dream…

The an-an-son[32] made by our ku-shen-e'po
Is from reeds new sickly sewn,
Then draped and tied upon the frame
In layers several thick to form
Our yi-hakan; and, from below,
Smoke 'scapes the narrowed top,
With door flaps, windows, shelves within
To hang our salvaged meats and gourds
And stack our remnant corn and beans,
Plus several restful pe'ta-o'ka-win,
And in the centre set around
Sacred stones of transposéd fire
Laid about the cowered hearth,
Are afearing whims of frightened ones

---

[32] An an-an-son is a mat; a ku-shen-e'po is a woman; a pe'ta-o'ka-win is a bed; a yi-hakan is a house made from mats on a frame of saplings; ria-po'ke means evil, devilish; ra-so'um is the wind, suggesting breath.

That lurk beneath ancestral pyres,
Plucked to our minds as the kwi-o'ko-su'k
Rattles his feathered skulls
And spits upon embattled forms,
With storms and shakes and hums and howls
To draw without the ria-po'ke ra-so'um,
Then drums his skins and quills of porcupine
And enters trance to divine-enhance
The kan'ti-kan'ti of angered forbears,
Yet more angered still.

...left us in the ground...

...buried for a very long time...

We are a communal people,
Decisions made mutually,
Our freedom bright in common due,
Responsibilities, not empersoned rights
Our common seasoned destiny,
As we share our lives, our hunt,
Our needs, blunt troubles,
And accept help gladly,
Settle disputes with adept grace,
Not laws imposed, nor policed at all,
But sensed by our inherent code,
Passed from mother to daughter and on to son,
As we sit in patient community,
Listen, learn and mutual care,
In tribal nights where we as one
Dance and sing and dare our story,
Seeing each as part the common glory,
Reaching out to give our all
To all who seek our care.

Yet this our ritual is replaced
By the white-eyes' reason, their
Formulaic sermonising, unbending
Authority of morals divined
By haughty priests who hold the Word
Of God the Mechanic, who implores
His followers with a despotic creed
Of unbending greed and hierarchy.

...oh, the circle...

Drowning, drowning, drowning...

They've left him in the ground
For a very long time,
Till the rains from heaven did fall,
Then little Sir John sprung up his head

And so amazed them all!
They've left him in the ground till midsummer,
Till he's grown both pale and wan,
Then little Sir John's grown a long, long beard,
And so become a man!

Then, as if to confirm our worstmost fears,
The English slaughter old Ne-ma'ta-nu,
Imbued u'ero-an'ts, highmost medium
Of our impatient confederacy,
Which provides a rapid rally cry
To a nation meek of hope and strength,
That desperate seeks a lasting revenge
In angered self-response...

With Powhatan recently buried (1618), local Indian bands, stung by the murder of their venerated medicine man Ne-ma'ta-nu, unite under O'pe-shan'ka-no to launch a bloody raid on the colony in 1622, with the intent of carrying off the women and throwing the English back into the sea. Perhaps a third of the colonists are killed, with the Indians capturing and enslaving many of the women and children. Several plantations, including Henricus, with its college and Indian school, are wiped out. The recently built iron foundry at Falling Creek is destroyed and James Towne is only saved when Shan'ko, an Indian loyal to the colonists, warns them. The assault is a huge shock for the young colony.

The Second Anglo-Powhatan 'War' consists of this single Indian raid followed by years of reprisals by the colonists; by its end, many more Indians have died than colonists, and many of the women and children have been traded back.

Feigning friendship, warming trust,
One mizzled Good Friday morn,
With sudden-frenzied hatchet flares,
The Indians massacre and scare
Three hundred, forty-seven more,
Many mutilated, tortured, burned,
Women and children kept for slaves,
Henricus wiped from this black
Day, a quarter of our gay people
Disembowelled, hewn and axed
And dragged as cowelled sacks
To villages of bloodfilled hoop –
Whooping in especial anger
At those artisans who built a college
In the hope of Christian taming
Those pre-purposed Indians
Into some game of sick-framed righteousness...

...till the rains from heaven did fall...

...to rapid swell and drown us all...

Defeated badly, mauled and angry,
The English swiftly emboat and retire

To James Towne's inmost posts,
Where they rapid reorganize and
Relaunch strong-blazed counter-blasts,
To quick regain plantations lost,
Reclaim fields, rebuild anew,
With law and power re-ensued.

And, yes, our response is rapid, swift,
Descending on those napping heathen,
Off-guard, adrift,
Who believe they have taught and won –
Ambushing without regard nor shout,
Villages burnt, crops once tended,
Now charred, gods destroyed,
Ancestors dragged from out their huts,
Their bones scattered to the fire
Of our outraged, unquenched desire,
Wile others are seduced to treaty talks,
Then poisoned with our sacramental wine,
Two hundred, shooting fifty more,
Engorging unprotected kin, no care
In an unreciprocated orgy
That sates a dozen ungrateful years
And so o'erhides the 'solidation
Of our fragile liberty by a resurgent
Feudalistic aristocracy.

And thus the Sisters wept and stood
Howling 'neath their cauldroned hoods,
As The Horseman shook forlorn his head
And timbered past on Jamesian flood
Of blood that blew from delimbed bones
And flotsam bobbed upon the glide
Of ebbing lives on a godless tide.

For, deep within the womb-welled womb,
In the caverned being of all birth,
Around the misting boil of steam
That bubbles from the watery hearth
The Sufferings three, in handheld step
Dance their drone of left-held grasps
That red and white and black grip fast
Within the candled spirit halls
Of the many ancestored, crying walls
That lichen line their dampened lair
As they chant their deadly birthing prayer;
And the women trance them to the air
With solemn tunes within their hair,
As down the canalising well they fall
To splash and under water stall,
In twists to drown, down and dark,
Down and down and down to mark

The entrance to the murky cave
Where dwell the three in fla'ed embrace
Of widowed maid and mother's weeds,
To crave the grace of ancient faiths,
Push through the gate and raise their hands
To cast their spell upon these lands
Of bearing and decaying needs...

...of us drowning, drowning, drowning...

And so we dance the circle of the well,
Drape it o'er with springtime flowers,
Bowers of green and fertile hue
To keep it pure and flowing true,
And raise the spirits to life renewed,
As we finger hold and sing about
The toss of marigolds and buttercups
Upon its new-built, shingled top.

We plunge and rise and plunge,
I-we three in hand-hold tight
Against the pain of master's light
And thought of some faint chance
To breathe, into the welling water black,
There to find and call them back
To guide us through this stricken night.

As we, Callings, pull within
The mists of enveiling discipline,
Our powers, hopes, selves inspired
To store and wait, in woven spate,
'Til time will come to more reveal
The secrets of our great ideal.

Thus we dance, in mutual harmony,
Biblical hymns to pagan steps
That lead us merry round the round
And bring us daily prayer refound,
As we attend each church,
Each ceremony,
In morning and in evening sent,
Or else we're chained by feet and neck
And forced to lie within the house
Of a plantation's angry guard,
Who makes us sweat the harshest hour
And not to leap the cowering fence,
That keeps us in, not Indian out,
And defines the limits of our realm.
If we disobey the sermon's sense,
Slander, profane or self-disgrace,
We must slave the colony for a week,
A month for an offence repeated,

A year if we repeat a third,
So round and round the risen three
Dance within dark mockery
To release to us their spirits' grace
And give place to our hoped-for suffering!

XI

But the miller, he served him worse than that...

Yeardley, miller, governor, and thus,
Richly self-appointed the best of land,
Owns several sprawled plantations –
Settlements posted to defended fields
Along rich-lain Jamesian banks –
Including Flowerdew, where he sends
Fifty bonded men to clear the woods,
Plant tobacco, tobacco everywhere,
Also grows a little corn, some wheat,
Lets cattle, hogs and chickens roam,
Builds a chapel and a public store,
A dozen houses, logged or framed,
Drying barns, two boats, and then
Orders a post mill to grist the corn,
Imports carpenters, millwrights, engineers,
Buys six of the land's first Africans,
And has his bondsmen saw the forests
For fine quarter bars, cross trees, trusses,
Then plane the wood to frame the buck,
Make whip and stock for panéd sails,
Buy light cloth from calling ships,
Import millstones, gears and wheels,
Upraise the structure onto piers,
Tailpost, chains to pull to wind,
Sacking, leather for the chutes,
Hickory for the hardwood cogs,
Bands and belts and wooden pegs,
Built by communal hands,
But for the wealth of one.

And so,
The levered burr stones, tentered,
Fed by chute and bin and hopper,
Grind the individual grains,
Fine felt by the miller's thumb,
Meal spouted into waiting sacks,
Releasing all to pent-up goodness,
Who, as individual kernels dumb,
Could not their full potential make,
But are raised within the bakehouse,

A rousing smell of mutual sight
And sharing symbol of our right.

And rolled him around the field...

I hoe, I, aye, I Isabella hoe,
As Antonio chops and saws
And the heat becomes o'er much,
So I faint and fall
And others draw to comfort me,
Molly, Peg and Mary,
And I feel the wetness 'tween my legs
And know what is become of me,
As I am womaned to the stroking shade
Of an acorn-heavy oak
And they lay a sheet and wash their hands
In sweet expectation of delivery,
As WindTeller watches sensibly,
Tick-tock,
From the shade of a mocking tree.

Oh,
Push him into my cuppéd hands
And, as you squeeze, let him come up
From his world of private being
Into the arms of our enprizéd love,
Which will shield him for eternity.

"A boy!" Mary declares, "The looks
And colour of a Tucker, without a doubt!"
– And even I adrenaline smile
As my cross-bred child is swaddled
And I hold him to my swelling breast –
Our first fruit of joint humanity.

"His name?" I am asked.
"William is his master's choice."
– And with that, silence let me rest,
Cleansed my blood and took the 'birth
To some secret hearth to divine
And bury it with due ceremony
Beneath the rooting fortune tree,
With incantation spells and mystery,
As witness to his twinéd destiny.

For you will suffer, my child,
You will suffer more than most can bear –
You will die a thousand times and resurrect
A thousand more,
You will hug the whipping post,
Hold up the hanging tree,
Weep the weight of the wheel

And feel the blacksmith's brand;
You will grow crippled, but also strong
– Broken resolutely;
You will sob, but also raise your hands
A thousand times towards the crying sky.

And the distant chopping stops a while,
As the men are told the tidings,
But then goes on, as before,
Clearing land at master's bidding,
Rolled and rolled around the field,
And we women turn again to hoe
Around the mounded 'bacco feet,
Maturing now,
In this humid-laden summer heat.

While, for a selective moment, I reflect
On whether the colony will become
A land of equal merging, free
– Of peoples in harmony and reborn,
Of races mixed, uplifted mutually –
Or if the norm will be, at best,
The few to enslave the rest,
Destroyed by an intensity
Of worn-down, working days
That none but few survive.

I dream of the first,
In some momentary delusion
That it could be other than it is,
But am sudden disabused,
As the overseer calls me back,
And,
With blood still dripping, I return
To three hundred years of bondage,
Segregation from my rights,
And the honey-sicklied loss
Of that moment's partial pride.

They hired men with their scythes so sharp
To cut him off at the knee,
They've bound him and tied him around the waist,
Serving him most barb'rously,
They hired men with their sharp pitch-forks
To prick him to the heart,
But the drover he served him worse than that,
For he bound him to his cart.

Oh Mama, things are not as they were meant to be!
Where is the freedom of our spirit,
Of our mind to believe and think,
Our bodies to farm and win

A dear life for our friends and kin?

Oh, who will reform the circle,
Return us from control,
To some sweet breath of liberty?

There is a spell descending, a mist,
A hiss of magic potions steaming drift
Upon the centuries of our veiléd eyes
That dream and, in their swift dream,
Confuse their vision with reality.

They are so strange, these mist-eyed men,
Masking the spirit of the world,
Of life in every daily task, in every breath,
Folding it within a church,
Their search for all that's love
Through a man in black and hat —
And so too, they revoke their folk's
Soft right to sit in councilled talk,
To doff to their chiefs, offer each their piece,
Until it is truly decided,
In the ring of mutual need,
And not the greed of a few.

And the cardinals weep
For the creeping pass
Of the blood-seized, weeping deep,
And seek to rest their weary eyes
Upon the sleep of the sullied prize...

...As three women, three women in one,
Spirit healers, u'ero-na-us'qua, sit about
A charcoaled fire, smokeless, dry and hot,
And strip the leaves from chamomile,
Mint and balm and silverweed,
To soak in water warmed to tease
The oils to soothe inflammation,
Reinvigorate, heal digestion,
Or poultice sores and wounds,
Then, as we relate our cultures' past,
Our histories, deepset wisdom thoughts,
We pound the rooted bark of sassafras,
Mortar mint upon a stone,
And pestle-press fresh roots
Of bayberry, burdock, golden seal,
To stop infection and quickly heal.

For, as we work, we sing a round
Of agéd fieldhand song and sound,
African, English, Indian plays
To praise the drop of summer days

And the strength of this year's crop!

They've rolled him around and around the field,
Till they came unto a barn,
And there they made a solemn vow
Of Little Sir John Barleycorn;
They've hired men with their crab tree sticks
To strip him skin from bone,
But the miller, he served him worse than that,
For he ground him between two stones.

XII

The Virginia Company loses its charter in 1624 and Virginia becomes a royal colony. Of over seven thousand who have arrived from England, barely a thousand survive; many have died, but others have returned to England or have fled to the backwoods, thus beginning a tradition of frontier independence.

The physician calls,
Striving day and night,
To treat the ague and bloody flux
That constant overwhelms,
With fever, chills and stomach cramps,
Diarrhoea, fainting, lethargy,
Demanding that the surgeon-barber
Bleed us each from out the thumb
And take a pint or more a time,
To drain corruption from our form,
Remove excess fluids and restore
Our four humours to well-normed balance,
Blood and phlegm, bile yellow, black,
Burning incense, tobacco stacks
Fumigating marsh miasma, vitiated air,
Alarmed at our corrupted water, excrement,
The influence of weather, heat and mists,
Treating our distempers with ague-root bitter,
Purging clysters, vomiting, sweating powders,
Rosin of Jalap, snakeroot, Venice treacle –
All to stall our desperate deaths,
Week on palling week.

In 1627, Governor Yeardley dies, and John Harvey, a man of little ability or character, takes his place. By 1629, tobacco wealth increases the population to 5,000. However, 1630 sees a catastrophic collapse of prices due to massive over-production, as the 'tobacco frontier' moves west. That year, the York River is officially settled, and three years later a palisade is built across the peninsular between the James and the York to keep livestock in and Indians out.

In 1632, a peace treaty officially ends the Second Anglo-Powhatan War, granting the Indians Pamunkey Neck as a reserve, protected from settlement or hunting trespass by the English. Its provisions are generally ignored. A year later, Middle

Plantation (now Williamsburg) is founded and, in 1634, a new system of local government begins with the creation of eight counties. Trial by jury is introduced.

In 1635, the House of Burgesses, fed up with Harvey's misrule, and in its first true flexing of independent thought, rebels in response to alarming discontent, and chooses John West to replace him. Two years later, Harvey is restored and packs the mutineers off to London to stand trial. But when they arrive, they persuade the king of Harvey's incompetence and his appointment is revoked.

During this period, all freemen can vote for the burgesses, but this is soon restricted to freeholders by Lt-Governor Berkeley. In 1676, Bacon's Rebellion will extend it again, but within a few years, it will once more be restricted by Berkeley to freeholders, and will stay that way until the Revolution. Who can and cannot vote proves to be a major battleground between lieutenant-governor and people during the rest of the 17th century.

> A single-masted sloop
> Crests the lapping waves
> Of the James' bravemost estuary,
> Plies the cape of comfort
> And York's tidal, sporting shores,
> Flying passengers and stores
> To settlements most cast remote,
> Cropping by the bays and creeks,
> Past sleek canoes and shallop[33] mists,
> And tacking to the landings
> Of back-black ways of summer days,
> As riders trot ill-definéd tracks
> Stride across the marshy sloughs
> And watch for fortune's bugaboos
> – For John Barleycorn gloams these parts
> And, as many times as his heart needs die,
> He's sure to resurrect and cry
> For your seed upon his scythe.

In 1638, an English minister, John Bass, marries a baptised daughter of the Nansemond tribe living near present-day Suffolk. All surviving Nansemond Indians are descended from this union. Prior to this, the English repeatedly attack the tribe and begin to settle lands along the Nansemond River.

> I am ripe and I am ready,
> My leaves are broad and brown
> With the green-gold drooping sun,
> My arms bronzed with hoe and picking
> The horn bugs and the caterpillars
> Biting my killer-blistered bones,
> Curing myself, air-flued, flowing,
> Prizing shrewd the well-toned leaves
> And receiving them on bull-pulled sled
> To lead me to the drying barn,
> Where my hands are looped and strung

---

[33] Small sailing vessels, usually with oars, used to navigate the shallow waters of the bay.

And I am draped upon a hanging stick,
Stacked within the thick of them,
Naïve kin, black-skin browned,
Our midribs crackling dry and cringing
With heat-baked singe and sawdust fumes
That brand my chest and arms and cheeks
With scars of reek tobacco time,
Plantation master, slave,
White-cured, black,
One strung up, the other looking on
With a profit's smile,
Foretelling golden-suckled fortune
Or the vile beguile
Of fragile-backed oblivion.

In 1640, slavery for life is officially instituted in Virginia. John Punch, a runaway indentured servant, is the first documented example. Two years later, the Assembly, puppet of Berkeley, enacts a law to fine those who harbour or assist runaway slaves £20 of tobacco for each night of refuge granted. Slaves will be branded after a second escape attempt. Indentured servants who run away are another problem; upon recapture, they must serve twice the length of their absence. Persistent runaways may be branded with an R on their cheek.

SelfSearch bears the scars
Of our divided hearts,
Embracing deep
Our hopes within his body, us to keep,
Memories of what it is to be
In united, caring liberty.

In 1643, a law attempts to expel a group of Puritans from Nansemond; indeed "all nonconformists upon notice of them shall be compelled to depart the collony with all conveniencie." The Puritans defy the order, strengthened by the knowledge of Cromwell's victory in England, where the Book of Common Prayer has been banned. Thus, Virginia early becomes a battle-ground for freedom of religion, as well as democracy.

Oh, the circle, the circle...

To our surprise, in this land of plenty,
Limitless soil and pious opportunity,
The strictest hold of plat control
And concentration stark of wealth,
Even now, in young colonial years,
Brings poorhouse poverty, wanderers
Destitute and more unhealthy,
To beg upon the parish doors
Of this new nation's adversity,
And wend among plantation houses,
Criers for work and hardship pity,
Defenceless, left to self-defend.

But there is no sense of wrong committed,
For rich and poor are meant to be,
The natural order and strict hierarchy
Of God's will and social harmony –
The obeyers and the to-be-obeyed,
The owners and their servants,
The masters and their slaves.
And, so too, there is no sense of union,
Of brave response enthralling all,
No guilt at the impoverished few,
Other than to grant in will or promise due
To the church or parish poor
Some deathbed salutation
In hope of gracing heaven's door.

We have no right to life,
It is only granted by our labour;
We have no right to liberty,
It is only granted by our moil;
We have no right to happiness,
It is only granted by our toil.

The circle root is broken,
The hoop droops upon the earth,
Shattered, trodden underfoot,
Left for the crows to birth…

…and for SelfSearch to hide within the earth…

With arms closed against the weeping sun
At the desperation of the day,
We creep upon the eastern shore,
As stark-setting dark wills us away,
To array the bodies severally,
– More bodies every morn –
Upon woven corn and deer skins seared,
Ornaments and tools endeared,
Beads and trinkets adorning them,
Faces painted, chests daubéd too,
With morbid hands of life,
To journey to ancestral lands
Of Mo-un-sha'qwa'tu-whe,[34]
The resting place of M'i-sha'bo,
Creator of the dawning east,
Where they will better go and be,
Free from disease and hungry need,
In the realm where all are free and freed.

The graves are dug, the women wail,

---

[34] Abode of the spirits, the otherlife; often translated by the early settlers as 'heaven'.
M'i-sha'bo is the trickster hare, a powerful spirit being from the dawn of the sea.

Their faces smeared with charcoal fat,
Sticks and grasses adhered to mats,
Bark strips for journey safely made,
The bodies careful laid within,
Covered more with grass and sticks,
The pit rebuilt with earthen fill
And fires lit four dark nights along
To guide their souls and travel on
To the realm where there is peace
And land enough for everyone.

O'pe-shan'ka-no, by now an old man, leads his loyal tribes in one final attack on the English settlers in 1644, killing five hundred, mainly west and south of the Pamunkey River. The Third Powhatan War only ends in 1646 with a treaty that limits the Indians to a small reservation, further reduced in 1677.

These events occur during a period of rapid expansion for the colony. From a population of 1,000 in 1622, it grows to 8,000 in 1644, 15,000 (plus 300 Africans) in 1650, 40,000 in 1666, and by 1681 has risen to about 80,000.

Awwaaaiiieeeee!
Awwaaaiiieeeee!
Awwaaaiiieeeee!

Burn me, Great Sun, burn me,
Shave my head in sacrifice
And reflect upon this carapace
Of my coppered heart's domain!
Cry to me the long ta-'qui'to'k [35] tobe
Of our manacled oblivion
And ring the singing, shamanic dirge
For that endless surge of massacres
And killings of our graces
On the paths and secret traces
Of our silver-passéd life!
Listen – as I stress the or-em-'ge-is
From my oil-encurléd hair,
Kiss the breath of M'i-sha'bo's veil,
Cut my pa'atch-'kis-'caw from my glare,
Throw low my sun-caught helm,
Kick to dust the m'seta-'qwa-ish of taboo
And break the apo-'kan across my knee
– For, from this mocking moment forth,
Across ten thousand ages,
We are forgotten, no longer free,
For it is our culture and society
That will be broken –
The bones of you and me.

---

[35] The fall; an or-em-'ge-is is an eagle's claw; some Indian men shaved the right side of their hair, tying the left into a knot, called a pa'atch-'kis-'caw; a m'seta-'qwa-ish is a circle; apo-'kan is a tobacco pipe.

But hush, hush…

For,
When the shrouds of mourning steal
Upon the shaded brooks and ways
Of winter's slow reprise of death,
Then will you come to waken me
With your tones of summer breath,
And will you sing to me this song
Upon the lilting autumn face
Of my even's final grace…

Awwaaaiiieeeee!
Awwaaaiiieeeee!

And in the taut-fleshed stomach pangs
Of crippled aches and bends,
A woman, two months late,
Feels blood between her legs,
Must rush to woods, there to crouch
And feel the ill-formed foetus
Rheumy to
A pool of black and grey;
And she rises, relieved and eased,
Says a prayer, kicks o'er some leaves,
And continues with her day…

Aaaiiiieeeee! I cry…!

…And sing in trancing agony,
To the dancing leaps of calabash,
Swinging tumult of red-dyed hair
Plucked from the timid deer,
Eagle feathers above in crown,
Rattle skin curling from an ear,
Raven's claw from the other pierced,
Pearls dangling from my enfierced chest,
Blue face, crimson body tight,
In sprinkle-silvered recalcitrance,
War shield draped with fur and flight,
Bow in hand and arrowed teeth,
As I ka'nti-ka'nti in swirl of breath
To angry gourd and bittered drum,
And enter dream upon upon
The circled thrum of dreadful death,
The reedy flute that drones its tune
To ruffle-shuffle, beating feet
In mourning of our natal fate
And lament of days to come,
Knowing what it is to be, fatally,
And live our dying role
In this, our dying history…

And once more the Jamesian flood
Billows the timbered blood of delimbed bones
As they bob upon the flotsam tide
Of ebbing night within the dawning flow
And birth meets death within its tides
Of watered junction between the lives
Of those who will and those who won't
See the sacrificial day...

So I cross my legs,
As I have crossed them
Ten thousand times before,
And draw ten thousand circles,
But no more upon the shore,
– Only in my memory
Of what we used to be...

And still we stand upon the western sway
You and I, my love,
But with our backs now turned away
From the gently rippled laps
That drown our sand-splashed feet,
And greet that orb of scarlet grey
That bewildered rests on our horizon
And ask, is it a sunset we observe,
Of some ancient, holy way,
Or the dawn of some new morn,
That beckons to its soft-sweet call
Beyond the moment's fall?

And thus our final hours are close
And hazard drawn in slow refrain
Upon the sinewed rose of earth
That graces not the fragile chain
That is our red inheritance...

So come, my boys, come,
Come circle round, and
Enter upon the ancestral tale,
Finally told, finally beheld,
Finally become as one
With the truth of our enquandried souls,
As, with arms
Closed and back towards the day,
The singer sings and the drummer plays
And the fiddler sparks the night,
Their spirits waft across the dales
As the dawn vies with the night,
As the dawn vies with the light...

Awwaaaiiieeeee!
Awwaaaiiieeeee!
Awwaaaiiieeeee!

Book II

The Circle Broken:
Social Division and Rebellion,
1647–1705

I

No man is an island, entire of itself,
Every man is a piece of the continent, a part of the main;
If a clod be washed away by the sea,
Europe is the less, as well as if a promontory were,
As well as if a manor of thy friend's or of thine own were.
Any man's death diminishes me,
Because I am involved in mankind,
And therefore never send to know for whom the bell tolls;
It tolls for thee.[36]

The tambourine begins to shiver
Beneath the oak's great lading bough
And the calling fiddler's moaning bow
Seeks solace below the bitternut shade,
As the MusicMen and Sufferers three
Hide their faces, hooded low, and blow
With trilling flutes a free refrain
Of willowed howl and hickoried pain,
Jingling slivers of faraway,
And memories of England's fame,
Of Hereward and Robin Hood,
Supermen of serfdom's blame,
And mockers of the blue-jayed earth.

Nu-ma'sha! Nu-ma'sha! Nu-ma'sha...[37]

I dream, I dream without form,
Swoon and swirl upon my pallet
And barely covered coarsened sack
As the devils grab me brutally,
Grasp my arms tight around,
Force me kneel upon the ground

---

[36] These lines are by John Donne, the 17th century poet. As Dean of St Paul's in London, he read departing sermons to voyagers on their way to Virginia.
[37] Go away! Go away! Go away!

Beside a darkened, shadowed pit,
Drag me to the edge, yell "Sit!"
To my ragged, bloodied back.

I hear your call! I hear your call!

Oh, Rattle Man,
Guardian of the gateways,
Delver of the hearth,
Join us in our fast
As we prepare the rite of purity,
Cleanse our bodies, out and inner,
Quick our minds for our task,
And circumscribe with sacred stick
The site of circled ceremony...

Let us take the oaken corpse
Of our passéd u'ero-an'ts,[38]
Our nights of prayer to M'i-sha'bo,
Our kan'ti-kan'ti, u'ta-a'k'a
And the vigil silent o'er the bower,
As we careful peel his skin aside,
Glide our knives within his flesh,
Leave ligaments and toughened bones,
Then leather cover, bind, restuff
Muscles to retain his form
And subtle wrap his tattooed skin,
Sewing it, disembowelled,
Brain scooped out,
Laid to smoke upon the stand
Within the templed ma'sha'ca-ma'k,
With kwi-o'ko-su'k and Kiwas guards
To transform him to the Great Abode...

...I come, I come, I come...

What is our destiny, Virginia,
You and I,
As we flicker through
That eye-flashed freedom
Enjoyed by so few,
And so soon flown?
What the choice we shall seam together
As I bide you to my hip and watch,
Slender-hearted guide,
The mourning of soft-dawned decision
And the mists of plunder sweet descend
Upon this once and verdant land?

---

[38] Tribal chief-priest; M'i-sha'bo is the great creator hare; kan'ti-kan'ti is to dance; u'ta-a'k'a is prayer; a ma'sha'ca-ma'k is a large house or temple of reed mats; a kwi-o'ko-su'k is a shaman-priest; Kiwas is a god that guards the dead in the temples.

Tell me...tell me...tell me...

I will tell you, whisperer of the wind,
Who discovers all and kines our pain,
As we watch the slaughter of another war
And the too-hasty armed reply
That hies to hew the wilderness
And spews up frontier forts anew
At Royal on Pamunkey,
James on ridge of Chickahominy,
And two upon the western falls,
Charles for the majestic river
And Henry's Appomattox banks,
Sturdy palisades, commanders sent
Each with fifty arméd men, soldiers trained,
Lent lands to till, lives to defend,
Staging posts for scouting trips
Deep to blooded backwoods dales,
Until peacesmokes rise and trading sails
Along the smalltime fringe of settlements,
With hides and pelts to James Towne's wharves,
Bartering onto swift-railed sloops
Tacking between the fall-line forts
With hatchets iron wrought,
Pots for fires, warm blankets for their homes,
And illicit powder looped for trade
With those already musket armed...

...So hush, hush,
Hush, my spooned and swaddled babe
Within the fortress of your loggened grave,
For the circle soon will be broken...
Soon...too soon...too soon...

But first, let us describe...[39]

Upon the earsound of fainted hooves
That whisper silent-springing fall,
We eight foot-shove and fleet away
From the cicada-chorused shore
In a straight-logged cypress, burned canoe,
Handshell gouged, older than the century,
And paddle the oak-creeked, steaming bays
In raccoon hats, buckskin, moccasins,
Three backwoods traders, one freed man,
Three Wicomaco paddlers and one guide,
To a taste of freedom and explore
Our deeper-spirit side.

Hugging the rushed spartina paddies,

---

[39] The rest of this section comprises *The Song of the Backwoodsman.*

We flush egrets and languorous herons
Upon their easy-beating wings
And leave the marshland booming calls
Of pond-rich frog and toad,
The rat-a-tat of pileate's call
And tremulous wave of predawn song
To gain the open-watered sway
Of a breeze-riffed, phantom estuary
That pulls our ancient, silent wash
Past burdened isle and tree-draped banks
To enter in the gloaming Chesapeake,
As the Callings call their thanks.

Laden with cornmeal, pork and salted fish,
Muskets, knives and goods to trade,
We push past smoked-wisped villages
And a shore-hauled dugout beach,
Past ill-clad fishermen, waiting spears,
Others casting widefeared nets
For silvered shad, drawn to spawn
These dawning, rivered beds.

…And as the erne calls a warning screek
To seek our aeried ancestors,
We spy them go, frequent passers-by,
Victors adapting to this, our land,
While I bend my back as I sing and dig
With grub stick into hole and drop,
Four soakéd seeds within a mound,
Hoping they will let us be,
In our shadowed, tight-bound misery,
Then repush the soil, pat down, move on,
One fat row a day,
Sister brushing weeds away,
And children playing close within
The deer-fenced garden rails
That barely veil us from that slow-lapped,
Fear-clapped, thieved and slapped
Encroachment of our lands,
Our marshes, weirs and crabbing traps…

Then we hear the ospreys call,
Circling their nesting swirl,
As we, an isle in midst of turmoil,
Make for some close-gainéd bank
And step ashore to camp and cook,
Erect our reed-mat, sheltered nooks,
And closely guard, with cautious eyes,
Our night-time safety, until arrives
The calm-dewed, ash-mist morn
And we simmer some well-brewed tea,
Cook cornpone within the subdued embers

And await the wind to change, smoking
Long pipes, reliving exaggerated lives,
Before we launch our sultry-stiffened sway
Upon the dawn-flushed, crimson waves
And paddle on the tidal high
Of mosquito marsh and black bear swamp,
To brave the freshet counterflow
Of damp, late-surging Potomac,
Our paddlers dropping up'po-woc[40]
Within the choppy confluence's fray.

Then once more we hunker lie,
Guarded during alchemied sleep,
Watchful of guide and paddlers now,
As well as forest-silent enemies,
Deep within our pent-up minds
As they try-prevent us find
That fearsome veil behind
Anger, hate and frail desire –
Until the morning mists and chills
Slip silently ariver
And we softly slide again upon
The pre-dawn rilling water,
Sometimes holding tight and close
To the slow-channeled meander banks
Of our justice guardian, dark recorder
And rememberer of a starker vengeance,
At others splashing hard beyond
Arrow-arcing range, up a rush of slow-set falls,
In swiftly paddled beat,
Watchful, joking, singing to our pull,
Then stroke awhile, until we cull and portage
The first of several monster chutes
Of crashing silten water, to meet
A longer, tranquil-muted stretch,
Two pipes before we eat…

Oh, the well that descent-dwells
Within the confines of our inner hells
And tosses unworthiness, self-reproach,
Denial, fear, distracted vice,
As we drown within our cowardice…

Once more, we gain the counter-flow,
Past islands, riffles, one-breach rocks,
Portage three more shortened times,
Until we hear the great falls' roar
And slashing heaves of bouldered call
Batter-crash their gashing chorus bore
Upon the sleepless river's dinning course

---

[40] Sacred tobacco.

And force us land and slip-up climb
The fall-line cliff and forest slime
Through sumac, briar and poison leaf,
And rattle-dance within the breeze
That trickle-flows between the trees,
As we imagine this, our ego-roar,
Beyond the gateway of compassion,
Pulling our heavy craft behind,
To return for all our pack and gear,
Then reload, refloat, reland and fear
Another impatient, gun-held night
Of watchful eye and never-sleeping ear.

Upon our next morn, fourth
From home, we await a storm to pass,
Fish awhile, then paddle on, fast
Past egret, hawk and isle
Of this majestic, wide-veined artery
Of the white-hood fishing eagle,
Talons splayed, superlative,
Rising with some twist and flash of tail
To take its food to crippled bough
And thank the mystic sirens
Of the river's ancient splendour,
As we come across some Mannahoac reach,
Palisaded, fields of tossled corn,
And coast towards the rising beach
To trade food and information,
In easy caution to outstage our tension,
Exchange hostages, keep our arms,
Slowly building trust to barter
Iron goods and copper trinkets,
Powder, shot and musket horns,
Then, when the husting deal is borne,
The whole tribe nodding satisfied,
We are offered jests, a welcome dance
And the sumptuous night-fall meal
Of happy-beckoned guests.

Oh, the drums do beat and the reeds do flute
And gourdseeds rattle their call,
As the dancers weave and dab their feet
To a bruit of rhythmic falter-stall
In the blooded scars of sunset stars
That mar the red earth's fall...

Silently, heron-eyed,
We dawn-rise once more,
Our guides praying to the gods
We will confront this day,
Fearful of the void beyond,
Where the sun sets each night away,

Then hasty feast on herb-'fused brew,
Salt pork, hot-fired ashen cakes,
And rake once more our strokes upon
The spectral fleeting flow
That currents the call of centuries
And asks us hourly for the strength
To inward go, and below –
Until we pass some higher hills, a line,
Hieing swift and powerful through
A stubborn-twisted, bouldered maze
Of swirls and rushed and whirlpooled turns,
Then push on, the counter-current
Stronger now,
Until Blue Ridge ranges either side
And we sweat our oft-sprayed brows
To groan between the soaring cliffs
Of sheer-towered, rock-cracked palisades
And boulder-brashing, spewing gate
Of vicious white and flashing hate
And hear, high beyond some
Tree-scarped promontory,
The Rattle dance his song of death,
Calabash and jawbone grate,
In swirl of leaping, trouncing fate,
And the promise of loving to abate
Our perpetual inward searching –
As we swim and curl
Upon the rim of entrance furls
That we know nothing of –
His face half black, half red,
Smeared with the blood-washed dead
And ashes of the funeral pyre,
The deamon of the gateway,
The bridge of downward go,
The inner pathway, barred and firm
– Both the fire and the terrored way –
Until we narrow course his angry force
And make a circle-eddied calm
To rest, then pull and shoulder heave
Our portaged way once more,
With slip and curse and twisted joint,
Upon the mud-soaked spuming sway
Where Potomac and the Shenando'
Merge within the cloistered gorge
Of mapled rush and splintered surge
And urge the Pillars of America
From the strife of harshest pull,
To the dream of full a spirit life.

After discussion, sleeping, a pipe or two,
We re-enter the tumbling, white-flecked froth
And stroke hard against Potomac's dream,

Then turn midriver with downstream drift,
Swift gain Shenandoah's complicit mouth
And stretch, with powered reach and arm,
Fiercesome paddles skinning through
To breach the twinning force
And make the far-bank soughted calm
Of Star Daughter's softer course.

Oh, the bluebird's windset call
Within this, our stoneset wall!

We rest again to cook and eat,
Question this new-found valley land,
Of stars that touch the waters' brows
And wrap us tight within
The mask of all their meaning,
In the bidding of our spirit quest,
And watch I dip my mind in thee
At the confluence of the flows...

Four centuries of losing lives
Forces me to compromise,
Letting the river's absorbing glow
Take my energy, return to me
The circle-cycle of eternal all,
Then re-embark and powerful pull,
Over rough-riffed, shallowed rocks,
Though now a less full-forcéd flow...

We each have barriers to face,
Fears, memories we must embrace,
If we are to delve at all, at all,
And discover who we are,
Reveal our truth and sanctify,
Uncover love and multiply
Happiness and self-content,
Dismiss the dark, unknown and feared,
And free-embrace all inner dread.

But shushhh!
There is a sudden hush from our guide
As we glide upon a slacking village
Lacking fields or plots or fixéd huts,
Of southern-ventured Iroquois,
Suspicious, warlike, canoeing fast,
With arrows cast and tomahawks,
Towards us from the mulling trees,
Gaining, gaining as we flee,
Until repulsed with musket shots
That breach their ploughing hulls
And our own fast-splash heave and heave
Takes us beyond their charge.

Within a further half-day's burst
We fall upon more serene Serendo land,
War-wary of us at the first,
But soon open to trade and offering
Our dug-out for two lighter, birch bark craft,
Won in war from the north,
Granting us another guide
By our side as we are borne
Forth within
This Valley of the Sharing Dawn.

They give us welcome feast,
The shamanic priests make their calls
To directions, moon and setting sun,
Ancestor haints upon the wing,
From spirit realm to realm,
Then inbibe soft smoke of tobacco
From a sveltestem, longstone pipe
Draped in feathers, bones and hair,
Carved with bear and moose and deer,
As we inquire of beaver pelts,
Gold and silver, the great South Sea
That lies west beyond the Appalachie –
But they merely shake their heads
And tell of rapid forest wakes,
Shawnee,
And meandering ranges endlessly.

When 'tis time,
They lead us to a wigwam barked,
Gift us maidens, bearskin rugs,
Gourds and casket meats around,
Beans and corn in woven baskets
Upon their slat-rimmed walls –
And so we keep our cat-eyed sleep,
Caution-primed by night-time whoops
And sounds of warlike preparation,
But are calmed and told it is
To alarm the 'croaching Iroquois,
Their eternal swooping enemy, as
The drum-beat whelps and ululations
Thrill the fire-blazed night
And painted dancers, feather-tainted,
Leap and shuffle-spin their spite
And swirl in anger-stirréd villainy
That launches swift departure
Through the allure of midnight trees,
To meet some blood-breezed destiny.

It is too worrisome to sleep,
So we push away when still the night
With our new Serendo guide,

Trying hard to shank canoes
Past sweatlodge set within a bank,
Then spell each other, watching,
Paddling, fretting nervous,
Wading up the shallow rills,
Dragging our sturdy, well-sown craft
Across refulgent stony riffles
That curse the dawning, seasoned flow,
Until the mountains drift away
And the meandering river slows
To fork and let us choose
The stronger, southern course
And weave the heavy forest vale
Between the mists of Massanutten
And a cloud-regaled, sunrise ridge,
Then pass another strange-born cluster
With fields of squash and calabash,
Grave mounds mustered wide and high,
With fire-set grasslands far beyond,
Where white tail and the buffalo
Wander tall-set, tended lands.

We enbank, unlade,
Discover whisky jugs
And offer them around,
For these are friendly Tutelo
And welcome our incursion
With rare and goods desired,
Exchanging meat and fish, skill-dried
And fresh-killed deer and hides,
Plus a dozen beaver pelts
That will alone most fully tip
This, our first-dealt valley trip.

But, even here,
There are poisons in the eerie mist
That steam from sbroiling raven pots
And rot upon the vultured boughs
That hold their charms within,
To spell us wandering paleface men
Against our warlike kin;
There are eyes of the future's curse
That bear with every terséd move,
That smile and prove their sicklied heads
To watch with unbeknowing
Our solemn history cold unfold –
For the MusicMen are watching,
Lifters of the veils of lies,
Playing rattle, drum and flute,
Guardians of the watching realm,
The gateway to this netherworld
Beyond the pillars of our fate –

Rattle Man, the well-held sprite
Who guards the inner heart,
Death, justice and the self;
The Hood of darker curse,
Sudden avenger of the night;
The Horseman, observer, wanderer,
Playing the pipe of herald change;
The Rabbit Saviour, trickster hare,
Caller of the Shimmerins upon
The bowstrings of our suffering;
And then Linkum, man and conjuror,
Bringer of justice to the dead,
And wanderer of the wayward night
That leaves us breathe with dread unease.

The river is slower here,
The Horseman quieter in his keep,
Wisp-treading hooves within the flow
Waving, shallow, between the bends
And steep-banked, tree-flanked hills
That quickly sweep to templed ranges
That trap the summer-seasoned wafts
Thermaling above the spiraled day
Each nimbus-cooléd evening,
And thunder-drench the speckled waters
As we carve our cleaving way
And watch the osprey, 'fisher, owl
And other birds of prey,
Red-tailed hawk and rag-winged vulture,
Following our slow-weft way.

A winsome whiff of wind
Caresses the treetop leaves
And leaves a trace of coolness
Upon the winsome breeze.

So we depart upon another day
And unshank from the zinging razored zin
Of treefrog-dusted banks
Chirping for the rain,
To wade and push our bottomed craft
Up shallow rindled sparks
Of pebble-bouncing spray,
Over riffle over riffle over rill,
Until we pass the southern river,
Leave that branch behind,
And take the Middle course,
Small, but still the stronger force,
And enter winding, thinning bends
To reach another wafting village
Of smoke and drying pemmican,
Where the Tutelo know our agéd guide,

Trade us pelts and stone-ground hominy
For beads and bells and shinning whistles
That amuse the eldest leaders there,
And let us peruse their spirit grace
Of generosity and brave embrace.

We talk a deal, in this valleyed sanctuary,
Of otter, muskrat, beaver,
Trapping mountain meals,
Weather, seasons, critter haunts,
Ripe trading ways to be,
And a tauter bond is generated
And spiritually sealed upon a pipe
That we mutually pass and imbue,
And are sworn to honour, as our due.

We see, too, some other sights,
Strange to our habit-'ccustomed eye,
Blond-haired, blue-eyed children,
Four black men, once enbonded,
A white woman wearing skins,
Phrasing rough-clipped English
From beginning childhard days.

And round and round the Rattle dances
At the entrance to the mind,
Sits and leaps and asks within
At every cavourting step and why,
What is compassion, what the way
Love is keyed to seep within
The court of whom I wish to be...?

Then off again at translucent dawn,
Upon the green, effulgent flow
That underspates and brushes slow
The tearful drooping boughs
That caress the bass-filled eddies
And the sleeping, prenoon lairs
Of the steady summer heat
That sucks humidity from the fleet
And hangs it dripping on the air.

The river never lies to us,
It has no ideology, no need,
No myth to strut our credence
With the honeyed veil of promises
And the face of squandered deed...

Then a killdeer flash-flies
From rock to upstream rock,
Heralding our course
And a smallmouth jumps as we lap

By a submergéd vee-stoned trap
Brushed with fencelike posts
The Indians boast with fish.
A green heron wraiths a willow
Then cautious-flees,
With wild-winged flaps,
To the densest, oak-lent lee…

…As the stream narrows, lessens flow
To an early summer trickle,
And we must wade our speckled craft
Past beaver dam and lodge
And final dodge and heave portage
Several miles of hike across
The grassland's lustrous spiking hills
To a fuller stream that, we're told,
Will lead us homeward to the James.

We place our packs upon our backs,
Stow paddles, pelts and goods,
Then careful lift the boats above
And begin the slogging trek
Along a thinly-crafted path still used
By bear and bison, cat and elk,
As the soft-misting, shading leaves,
Tlip in sweet-set dribble-dips
Of early flecking rain,
Half-hearted, teasing, partial drops
That sip-refresh the woodland's taste
And cool our basted journey,
But then hurry down the thunder-burst
As the thickly veiled raging pour
Drapes its twisting, misting torrents
Across our flooded way
And we must halt and muster-shelter
As the mud-scummed flashing streams,
Brown-blighted screams,
Splash and surge and scrowl
Their anger-harried reams
Down our hallowed vale.

So we camp for the night
In the cold wet comfort of our thoughts…

…But I turn, I turn, I turn,
From nightmares to less haunting themes,
Then back again,
Until, awake, I laugh and smoke,
And firelight discuss with our guide
Herbal remedies, nettle, self-heal,
The local hunting ways
Of wide-encircled game and setting fire

To the expansive shoulder grass,
Forcing smoked and panicked deer
Into small-ringed, claustrophobic fear,
Then shooting them with close-ranged bow
And making good their winter store
By stowing up the sacrificial meat
Within a cold-streamed river's flow,
To outlast the wintered months.

And too, we see within the flames
The red-black mask of other games,
Smeared with blood, ancestral ash,
From the fire of Life-in-Death, no less,
And we hear his rattle-moan,
Calabash and 'granate seeds,
Jaw and bone and tambourine
Within his six-armed grasp,
In swirl of leaping, trance-death curl,
Round and round the dim-lit coals
Of a fire that's verged on night
In the burning cave of moral flight,
And the realm of ancestral-gifted light
That gloams the depths of caverned fright,
As it linger-sifts its final turn.

This time we camp for several days,
Stealth hills and nearby streams
For signs of beaver, otter, other wealth
To relate to James Towne merchants,
Scouting trails and local tribes,
Making friends and, doubtless, foes.
We repair ripped canoes as well,
With new seams and patient gluing,
Retie the braces and recaulk
The bending floor-lined boards,
Until we rise one dawn and set upon
A late-spate gush, from e'er night's storm,
And join the speedy flow,
Downstream now, fast in time,
To a widened bank that's current-cut
And, within two days, burst sudden about
A wild-eyed river's glowing shout
Of rankled Jamesian flow.

Then simple calm
– The love of simple calm –
Unexpected, unannounced. Just there,
As a bald eagle graces the water's rise
With its bright and splendoured beak,
Black wings rising strong upon
The afternoon's shimmering heat...

A swallowtail flutters o'er the water
And two dragonflies raft and mate upon
The prow of our well-sown craft
As we drift and paddle closer to
The returning Blue Ridge Range
And enter another steep-hilled gorge
That resurrects returning pride,
From our inner, fearsome minds
– The Pillars of Virginia!
Don't leave! Don't leave! –
And takes us rushing, crashing down,
Over cascading, tumbling falls,
Then stalls us, 'til we're free
Of mountains once again
– Not free! Not free! Old habits
Mere enforced,
Turned from inner journey
To the ease of self-deceit –
And can seek the sun-tanned beach
Of a magical Monacan reach,
Where we goodbye our Tupelo guide
And trade for food and sleep,
Then wake to take two final morns
To keep the James' elfland course
Through its widened banks
And deep-spread rocks and shoals,
Gravel-rippling barrier flumes
That whoosh our way regoaling home,
To rest a day at new Fort Charles,
Then past Henricus' plantation fields,
Bermuda, Berkeley, Flowerdew,
To the eerie beat of The Horseman's feet
And the wilting winnow of his pipe,
And James Towne's welcome smile,
The circle now complete...

...The circle that once was,
But now runs counter to the sun,
Or is merely prophesised
As of itself entire,
And us but mere a part...

II

Oh! for the woodland freedom
Of careswept backwoods men,
That,
So soon as it is tasted,
So soon is lost to all except
The maudlin myther's pen...

…that calls, that calls, that calls…

…to Ergotria, three-in-one…

…As a baylined sloop swift carves
Through chipping winds of spray,
Planing her zip-blown way
Upon the rib and rise and plank
Of another re-encircled day…

And we dig an earthen well
Beyond the mountain top,
To cavern-dwell and carousel
The fountain of our breath.

Oh, hear us, hear us, hear us!

So many of us came to escape,
To restart, regale our lives anew,
For there is yet a travailed dream
Of a pristine forest glow – that
Of backwoods cabin, tobacco rows,
A cow, a horse, some chickens, eggs,
Upon a hundred well-pegged acres
Clappered from the valley plain,
A barn, fenced fields, tobacco, grain
To abundance feed a family
Year and year again!

But hush, for
A convict and a servantwoman,
Hutted harshly, fed together,
Flee tidal-farrowed shackles
And steal upon the night-time ways
Of the forest unexplored, find a holler
Below Green Mountain's narrow edge,
O'er Indian ledge and Jamesian flow,
To build a cabin caped, smoke trail,
And beget eight generations of escape
From tax and the encroaching state.

Oh, dream on, dream on…

Great Britain passes the Navigation Act of 1651, which restricts colonial compet-
ition and forces tobacco onto British ships. It is largely ignored. The next year, a
force of Puritans claims the colony for the Cromwellian Commonwealth and for
the next eight years the House of Burgesses effectively rules the colony: lieuten-
ant governors are elected by the burgesses, substantial new land grants are made,
new counties are created, and the franchise is re-extended to all freemen. How-
ever, the colony remains overwhelmingly loyal to the Crown and thousands of
expelled Cavaliers settle along the Rappahannock. When Charles II is restored,

they are rewarded with large land grants and become the basis of the northern Tidewater Aristocracy.

> Though a few bondsmen have attained
> Their freedom,
> Most are held to rich men's land
> And are indentured still,
> Working hard at another's hand,
> Or suffer acres meagre given,
> Of waste or ridge or forest land
> That they must clear 'mid Indian fears
> And plant what rows they can,
> Despite the reel of price
> And enterprised plantation man.

> Why, when the continent is free,
> Have we brought slavery to this land?
> – And not just of the blacker serving man...

> *We take no thought, we have no care,*
> *Still we spend and ne'er do spare,*
> *Till all of money our purse is bare,*
> *We ever tosse the pot.*

> *Tosse the pot, tosse the pot, let us be merrie,*
> *And drinke till our cheeks be redde as a cherry.*[41]

People in Northampton County present the first American petition of protest, demanding "free voting", relief from taxes, the annual election of magistrates, an elected colonial government and no taxation without representation in the House of Burgesses – the first expression of a sentiment made famous 120 years later.

> I hear your call! I hear your call! Resonate
> Deep the fall of inland trails...

> ...While William Byrd in hurry builds
> His trading port at new Fort Charles,
> Where Richmond now stands proud,
> And we too hear the call, and watch,
> Silent from the mists
> Of our far-seeing eyes,
> Abraham Wood set firm upon,
> With musket cocked and ears well-turned,
> The Occaneechi Trail, southwest
> From Fort Henry's Appomattox falls,
> With a hundred packed and laden horse
> To trade distant tribes
> Of the Roanoke and Dan for
> Beaver pelts, otters', hides of deer,

---

[41] *Tosse the Pot*, a popular drinking song of the time; from Thomas Ravenscroft's *A Briefe discourse*, 1614, no.11.

And, in exchange, to supply
Kettles, blankets, iron knives,
Brass rings, beads and trinkets –
Tobacco not the only stealthy way
To rapid-'cquired wealth.

Oh the call, the call
Of the ancient tree's most gnarléd boll
As it rises from heart-rot roots where
A raccoon has housed its brood
– Maybe a thousand years it's spread
Its chestnut shade upon the sward,
Borne host to bird and worm and bug,
Calmed the doe's lynx-scaréd fawn,
Seen a thousand summers gone,
And snugged the answer to a way
Of sanctity for all – and yet
We do not heed its call…

…Oh the call, the call
Of SelfTruth, guardian in her pride,
Who pokes in and out our scaried lives,
Always watching, seldom seen,
Our wisdom, truth and moral guide,
Her shimmerin form the nightly sprites
That witch the cauldrons of the rites…

And now watch, as
A hundred males, two dozen mates,
Arrive within a dawntime brigantine
With twenty cows, thirty pigs,
Three dozen sheep, a dozen horse,
And troop the plank to waiting bank
With possessions underarm, then
Walk unsteady up to dayrise stay
In the barred and anchored warehouse where
They'll be sold that very sunshine day
To five- and seven-year labour bonds
And hauled in rapid need to farms
Of a desperate-hoed tobacco crop,
And where their future will drop indeed
In Ergotria's palms…

…we call, we call, we call…

But the echoes of our voice are lost
In lingering clamour for the Grail,
Ringing her rhythms of the universe,
Across our dark-hailed fingerings…

…I hear the echoes,
Lost, lost, lost…

...As I ask Ergotria, female triad energy,
SelfTruth, Sustainer, ShelterCare,
Inner guide to deepset spirit,
Powered centre far within,
Comforter in our distress,
When will we heed *your* caress?

Oh, but Rattle Man hears, he hears,
As he dances down the plank
From England's distant-misted banks,
His face half black, half sanguine red,
Reborn, rekindled coals, an ashen face,
Tight upon the tide-swayed bourne
In skins of snake and rattle tails,
Raven winged and foetus hung,
Greasy-matted hair, black and long,
Smeared with bear to ward off fly,
As he jigs the twilight nigh beyond
Of there to here to there,
Calling to most fond despair.

A drunk hears too,
Sotted from the night before,
Glassmaker paid his weekly wage,
Without home, who curls and eats above
The glassblowing forge below,
Then snores his lay upon the porch
Of tumbled tavern steps
And dreams to purchase parcelled land
And, too, grow rich one day...

Minds, hidden, drift away,
And then the voice is strayed again...

...Since, in the back,
At an upstairs room above the stairs
Another man is snoring loud,
Having paid to spend the night
With a lady of the passage,
And of the tavern crowd...

...He merely hears the echoes
From the bedroom walls...

...For we have forgot that sanctity of all
Within the world,
Confined sacredness to a church's walls,
Ritual to a man in black,
And now lack complete connection with
The holiness of all –
And thus none of us can hear the sacred call:
Rejoin the circle! Retie the hoop!
Retie the hoop, I say!

...Too late, too late, too late,
The sunset of delay...

And WindTeller takes the reins
Of a misty mount he spurring moves
About the rims of towns and streams
And shuffles oft his unshod hooves
Within the leaves of falling dreams.

Falling dreams already!

Oh yes, oh yes!
For tight are tied the ropes about my chest,
My arms and legs wrapped firm,
As I am tossed into the sudden pitch
Of lightless trench, where I fall,
Fall and fall and fall and fall,
Until I hit the swampy clay
Half-buried, choking, vermin squeals,
And none to hear the mock 'ppeals
Of my mudded mouth's harsh cry.

Don't! I don't want to hear!
I don't want to listen to the truth
Of my ancestral hidden tears!

...the call, the call, the call...

Work, turn to work,
Blind labour, so
The rhythm of the hammer
Hides the din of worried thought...

And we hear the hooves beat still
Upon the Occaneechi Way...

...As down upon the river,
In a new-built working shed,
A carpenter dreams of backwoods schemes
As he lays the dead-eyed keel
For another baylined sloop
And watches as his 'pprentice boys,
Eight and nine and twelve,
Shape and saw the ribs and planks
That rise and curve her flanks,
As all lathe and plane and saw away
The echoing deafness of the day,
As no-one hears the curling call:
– Oh, don't break the circle's fall! –
That calls and calls and calls...

III

In 1654, Katherine Grady, a passenger on a ship crossing the Atlantic, is condemned for churning a storm and hanged from a spar as a witch.

> Ugh! Ugh! As they hurry spade
> The dark earth upon my form,
> Prone and lying, unmoving yet,
> Tied up, unable to shuffle-shift,
> Dirt dashing on my back and face,
> I shake my head and spit
> Terror from the carapace
> Of my hades funeral pit.
>
> Ugh! Ugh! Ugh! Ugh! Ugh! Ugh! Ugh! Ugh!
>
> …churning, churning, churning…
>
> Oh, I dance and rattle-prance
> The interface of life and death,
> In the mouthfuls of a hundred caves
> Where the underworld confronts the sun,
> On the banks of river glades,
> Where oaks o'erhang their silent pools,
> And on the heights of rock-strewn knolls
> Where summits touch the roiling clouds
> And where, each-on-each survives,
> Ancestors passing 'twixt our lives…
>
> I dance as another
> Sail ship drifts within
> The evenmisted banks,
> Breathing with the tropic dew
> Of heavy-humid shanks
> And heaves-to close to James Towne's shore
> As the midnight magenta slinks,
> Lays a gangway to the barrelled wharf
> Lade with ropes, molasses, trading goods
> To be planked upon the brigantine…
>
> …I hear you, I hear you…
>
> …And I dance as it darkly
> Disembarks its human wares,
> Thirty servants to be sold
> Next morn to wary-bold demand,
> Raised upon an auction block,
> Inspected, letters clocked and judged,
> Bidding to be slick, as best,
> To dispatch them smart and quick
> To new-trimmed farm or place
> Of never-setting's sunrise pace.

So we sing the song
Of the longing Rattle Man,
Peddler of dark gateways, beginnings,
Deamon prophesier of tocome
Who scratches out the round
Drawn roughly on the blessèd ground
With tobacco, feather, sacred sages,
And the wisdom of our fathered ages...

And thus we quilt the streams, my love,
Quilt with bones of joy,
The byways of our inmost thoughts,
Sew our myths, reluctant truths,
And appliqué soft demand –
To drown the screams
Of the Callers calling thee...

Oh, the circle, it is broken...!

...For, within the forest no screams are heard
Of Indian, aged or bright,
When another trap is musket laid
Against an undefended site,
And we fear our people poisoned
Upon the mat
Of naïve and bartered trade.

Bartering lives for land
– A fine tradition begun!

The Great Sun blinks His eyes,
Shades His face and sudden cries
At such sacrifice of justice
And blatant genocide!

Oh, hear us, hear us, hear us!
For the circle, it is breaking,
Our justice days dissolving,
And we can no longer practice-birth
The revolving ways of earth!

We will cry for each other, sweet Virginia,
Lean heads in mutual charms –
You for me and I for you,
In the centuries of enjointed arms,
Souls gliding,
Each...

...A bouncing tiger swallowtail
That lands flit upon a sultry pier
Where piles of deerskin hides
Are fit to be cleared...

It settle-breathes its pulsing wings,
Yellow, black, with flecks of red,
Until a passing stevedore,
Cask of shouldered wine on mind,
Disturbs and makes her flutter
About the yawl's scrub-plankéd deck,
To rest upon the tethered wheel,
Then flit again across the glow
Of the languid Chickahominy
And lay her frailty down once more
Upon the pierhead rail,
Her soul the soul of agéd men,
Her wings their dreaming flight,
Lost within the darkness calls
That dreamless men call night.

Meanwhile,
In the dawn that ope's our eyes
To the reality of our surprise
At the enterprise within this land,
We find at hand, in maid's apparel,
An indentured woman, churning,
Churning butter in a barrel:

Churn soft, churn sweet, my sweet,
Until your yearning is replete,
From dawn to dark thine up-down arms
Must round and pound the barrel mark,
Tiring thy soon-drained, waning limbs,
Enticing dreams of restful years
As the Horseman gleans your heartfelt plight
And mists his eyes within your tears.

Churn soft, churn sweet, my sweet
Beholden little one,
For your day is nowhere nearly done
Until the butter is complete;
Come, set within the frame,
Separate and globulise
And settle matters for all time,
The whither and the fro
Of hopeless blinded servitude
That vershumps a thickened cream
And leaves the weakened butterwhey.
And why must we separate?
Why must I, young bondswoman,
Indentured servant, child,
Smile at the wind-warped day
Of milking, cooking, cleaning,
Wending, weeding, hoeing,
Sweeping, chopping, tending
From pre-dawn to well-gone nigh

The lonely sigh of passéd day?

Ah, hooray, at last!
The butter 'gins to grain,
The milk to flow and drain,
The pounder stick and stay…

Oh, that I was stealth-persuaded thus,
From sisters, Hampshire farm,
Whisked from marriage prospect
By scant promises of wealth
And men, eligible and anxious,
In their drought of female company,
Only to flog a sick-starved voyage
In a reeking, hovelled hold,
'Tween decks with cattle, sheep and hogs
In our own dark-grovelled fold,
Then tossed ashore and bent
To buyer, bought and carted hence
To further starve and parted die,
With only gruel, thin beer to drink,
A little beef and stinking bread
To regale extremely sinewed muscles
Two sickly meals a day.

So I remove the batted pounder
And scrape the yellowed fat
Upon a wooden dish,
Where I paddle out the buttermilk,
Add salt to keep it fresh,
Knead and halt and knead again,
Slot within an earthen pot
And take it to the springborn shed
To slake within the cold.

Let me die!
I cannot bear this, nor escape,
For the Indians are attacking us,
And I dread the wolves and lions
That lurk beyond the gates…

Oh, what freedoms and what fears
Lie far beyond the gates…?

So I sleep inside a cabin crafted
Of rank-hewn, draughty planks,
Glassless windows, ricket door,
Straw-tick mattress on the floor,
Mouldy damp and lousy ridden
With mouse and rat and roach,
Three wretched men
And two sickly starvéd women,

One dying of the bloody flux,
The other in a childly way,
Raped by the master, but for which
Pregnant loss of laboured months
She will have to sharply pay
With extra years of bondage
To a thousand-acred family.

Thus I churn this butter,
Hour by hour by hour,
And wonder at the cream and whey,
One so fat and tender,
The other withering away,
Its juices sucked and sorely thinned
For the other's portly play.

Oh, let SelfSearch gather in the threads
Of the shrouded, drifting webs
Of women's fast-eroded say,
Their passion, intuitive desire,
Healing wisdom, nurture ways,
Knifed as they are boled around
By the silken bounds of wifely roles –
But we will mark their hidden voyage!
In the rims of distant life,
In the swamps and mountain fasts,
We will praise their lasting courage!

Jane Dickenson, a survivor of the 1622 Indian attack on Martin's Hundred, is
bought from the Indians by Dr James Pott, a famed James Towne surgeon, but is
soon petitioning for her freedom, describing his treatment of her as no better than
the bondage she had endured among the Indians.

Oh, how can this be,
This churning, churning...?

Is this a land of dreams,
Or of false promises –
A land of hope and aspiration,
Or of defeat and humble foil
To eke the soil of riders passing
In the midnight of e'erlasting toil?

And why do you keep lying to me?
Why?
Why do you still lie?

Can you not see them – can you not see?

Oh, dig the clay, my boys, dig the clay,
From hillside bank to soft-soak pit,
Then leave to overwinter, boys,

Until brickers' months and August heat,
When you can pug and paddle
The orange clayness pure, my boys,
Of wood and rock decay.

Tread the blood of whipping, boys,
Tread the flesh of weals,
Indentured necks well-collared, boys,
Ankles shackled too,
With cuff and bar and fetter, boys,
Tho' only eight years old,
And don't you spill a drop, my boys,
'Twixt stream and treading pit,
Or suffer oft the 'seer's wrath,
Or suffer oft his wrath.

Mould them fast and firm, my boys,
Pick out the sticks and stones,
Or else he'll break your bones, my boys,
Upon his cowskin welt;
Baste with sand and toss them in,
Draw them off with wiring thin,
Two thousand plus a day,
No matter age or sex, my boys,
He'll take your blood for his,
So temper well and bear them off
To sunbaked yards and boards,
And stack in dryskin house, my boys,
Until the clamp is raised.

Stack those tunnels well, my boys,
To let the draft suck in,
Set the charcoal firm, my boys,
Then place the greens above
And make sure you clamp them well, my boys,
Tilt them, dish them 'til they stand,
Then set the fire and block with clay,
Cut the wood and stoke it well,
And wait six nights without sleep,
One meal a day for keep and pay,
And for your slow-burnt change, my boys,
From hopeful beings human-dreamt,
To reluctant slaving hands.

Let them cool and let them set,
Unstack them, soft and clinkered,
Then sort the profit from the loss
And back within your draughty huts
Before the driver's whip, my boys,
Before the driver's whip...

As the butterfly flitters by,

A soul upon its wings,
And our lies hide the voices
Calling us to sanctity,
Myth denying truth,
Choices spurning e'en the call
Of our inmost stalling fears,
As poor old Grady peers
From her silent yard
Upon our churning sea.

IV

Pop! goes the weasel...

Mathews, the last Cromwellian lieutenant governor, dies in 1660 and Berkeley is reappointed – to initial acclaim, for Virginia has remained steadfastly loyal to the Crown throughout Britain's Puritan Commonwealth. However, anger at Cromwellian rule leads Berkeley into vicious reaction. He revokes all acts of the last eight years and is far harsher in his second term than his first. He even concurs when Britain passes a stricter Navigation Act, though it imposes a duty on tobacco, forbids its processing in America, and provokes the price to plummet, causing severe hardship for small planters and labourers – a hardship that will last over twenty years and be a prime cause of social unrest.

As part of Berkeley's reaction, Virginia institutes hereditary slavery in 1662. At this time, there are 300 black Africans in the colony, rising to 2,000 by 1671.

I venture to the smoky kitchen,
Kept from the house for fear of fire,
Walk in unannounced, to catch
Any slacking from the maids within,
But find none, all at work,
One scooping ashes from the fire
Into a pail for the compost pit,
Another scraping old pigs' trotters
Of their hair and blood and dirt,
Another chopping carrots, onions,
Beets and parsnips, spinach
For the well-stewed vegetables,
As the last one grates dry orange peel,
Squeezing lemons,
Adding cloves and cinnamon
For a pippin tart.[42]

Oh, the king was in his counting house,
Counting all his money...

Though two husbands are deceased

---

[42] Pippins are large, tart cooking apples; coffins are pie dishes; pipkins and sippits are serving dishes; a pottle is a pan.

Their wealth has passed to me,
So life is buzzing by honey sweet,
Replete with leisure-landed ease,
Gardens tended by my older folk
Quartered in a row at back,
Cooks and maids and footmen
As near to hand as we allow,
While field slaves plough the day-long furrows
And farrow down my gold-leafed rows.

I check the temperature of the oven,
How well-greased the coffins for the pies,
Ladle a little of the soup, stir and taste,
Then number the dishes upon the shelves,
Saucers, pipkins, sippits,
Frying pans hanging, pottles too,
Check the roasting sweetbreads,
Suggest more nutmeg, dates and mace,
Then walk to the chequered herbs to smell
The parsley, thyme and marjoram.

As I breath the morning air,
I sigh and muse, deep worries,
And am final thankful that,
With the latest Indian defeat
And regular slave arrivals,
The wealth of our tobacco surplus
Has enabled me to plan,
In brick and stone and paneled 'nut,
A house, not grand, but well constructed,
Eight rooms up and down,
With entrance hall and stairway wide,
Parlour, study, dining room,
Furnished English clocks and tables,
Sideboards, chairs and postered beds,
The many-panéd windows glazed,
Stout fireplaces well-hewn, chiseled,
Embellished all with coats-of-arms,
And lazed in satined silk brocades.

And the queen was in the parlour,
Eating bread and honey...

With Mathews gone, Cromwell dead,
The king so o'erjoyously restored,
We have a governor to our liking,
Berkeley merrily implored,
Though a little harsh on Puritans
And perhaps a little tamed of Indians,
He has named our three sons to
Multiple positions in one process,
As magistrates and burgesses,

One a monopolist of beaver furs,
Persisting to each large tracts of land
In excuse for our most loyal hands
And service to our oft-toasted Charles,
So ignobly accused and slain.

And too, my daughters have married well,
After timely English educations,
Grand European Tours, within
Our demurely set community
Of fine, transplanted aristocracy,
Cavaliers wrongly dispossessed –
Rightful heirs to English lands
Given ample 'states in recompense.

Thus, in satisfactory reverie,
I walk the bricks to my house,
Nitpick the room set fine to dine,
Greet two of my upstairing guests,
– Gentlemen who share a bed,
As I have few enough to spread
And offer them due rest –
Then tut a servant wrongly setting
Spoons and knives upon the board,
Order him to get the centerpiece,
Candlesticks and cruet sets,
Polish them and place around,
Then race him off to a doublet don,
Red-sleeved, cottoned, buttoned shirt,
Purple breeches, stockings lilac,
And buckled velvet shoes.

...As the maid was in the garden,
Hanging out the clothes...

Next, I unlock the parlour cupboard
Where the toasting wines are stored,
Choose five rhennish bottles,
Two of claret, one of sack,
Order cider from the cellar –
Bottles to replenish our splendid dinner rack.

But I have a worry lingering for,
Although my brother,
Tax collector, granter of western lands,
My uncle, cousins too,
Are ensconced most lucratively
In offices of the state
By our dear Lord Berkeley,
I fear that granting his accomplices
These prizes of well-bribed place
Will disenchant and much displease

101

Many who were once dear friends,
Including Catholics and Dissenters,
Fine men and women now expelled
To Maryland or northern parts
To practice those beliefs they hold.
Persecution is not wise, I fear –
And many of our liberties,
Once held so sacred and so dear,
Have been quashed below the heel
Of our too compliant burgesses;
But yet, perhaps, authority is needed
For heresy to be banned, and the
Eternal fortresses of property
To forcibly be manned.

... When down came a blackbird
And pecked off her nose!

And another wall is built between
Self-perception and reality,
Another fear imposed,
Another door slammed closed,
Within the centuries
Inhibiting our minds.

But hush now, WindOracle,
Do not blow your horn
Upon the mists of such vindictiveness,
For the Jack o'Lanterns glow
Within the midnight brush
Of sloe-stolen rush and whimsy
And spectral Will o'the Wisp;
A black cat crosses o'er our path
And a bat slashes the evening sky –
Oh, the witches are out tonight
To avenge you and I...

...For thus we watch,
Through portholed window pane
Upon the smoky taverned game
Of Berkeley's poodle planters,
Burgesses in nothing else than name,
Compliant to every dog-bowl wish
Of governor and collared dish
Called Council,
As they re-enforce forced marriage laws
And disgrace our free elections,
Remuzzle women, the multitude
Firmly hustled down to place,
The Church of England unreined supreme,
Rescheming orphans' indenturetude
Until they're twenty-four,

Entrammeling, in new statuted canon,
Mulatto, slave and Indian,
As kenneled servitude now is leashed
Upon *all* our racial interactions,
And it sanctions profaner masters' liens
On the tolerant and humane.

On September 13th 1663, Gloucester County, Virginia, witnesses the first serious
slave conspiracy in colonial America, when a plot involving *both* white servants
and black slaves is betrayed before it can be carried out.

Oh, SelfSearch and fine MusicMen,
Guard our spirit well!

I hear you! I hear your call...!

Dance-breath, death-breath,
Reborn;
At the verging birth of morn...

...As we sit around the council fire,
Reflections in the moon,
Passing sage-blessed water round
And drinking to our circled past,
The Rabbit Saviour slowly yawns
From centuries of his restless sleep
To dawn upon a more western land
Than the Africa he once did keep
Safe within his mystic hands –
Oh, such is the Saviour's gracing bow
To our weeping need 'midst plenty,
Hocked from us by thieving fools
In mocking castles of eternity.

Many laws repress white bonded servants. One prohibits them from traveling
without a license. Another states that, if a white servant runs away with a slave,
he or she has to serve the slave's punishment and recompense the master for the
expense of recapture; if the slave dies, he or she has to serve an additional four
years of servitude.

A few years earlier, the Planters' Assembly passed legislation to brand runaway
bondsmen and women with hot irons, shave their heads and make them serve
double their time of absence. Clearly, both interracial partnerships and escapes
are considered major problems by the wealthy white élite.

'Tis time, 'tis final time to creep
With silent sigh within the slime
Of deep-droned swamp and grass,
Until the darkness dampfire glows
Upon a smoking sultry rise, dimlit vamp
Beneath high-blown tupelos
Seep-moaning with the wind,
There to find old Linkum's mound

Where he is buried 'sleep and bound
Beneath the hillock of our contempt,
For to rise when he is called,
To gloam upon the blackened tide
And right those wrongs so deep enshrined
That we cannot in our weakness right,
Other than with the mourning song
Of a bleak and harrowed night.

Oh, let me fly south and high,
Across the tree-densed Southland swamp
Of cottonwood and maple,
Pines rich and yellow, amber-sapped,
And glide within the cedar groves,
The oaks and weed-set waters
Of Pigeon, Black and Coppahaunk,
Nottoway and Johnchecohunk,
To settle soft on the sallowed bank
Of curvaceous Blackwater's sultry shank,
Where RippleDeep, siren of the streams,
The estuaries and their meanders,
Sits with her thin-robed sisters three,
SylvanVeil, glory of our forest ridges,
SkyDawn, caller of the bright-lit morn
And beauty of the reaching sky,
And AltaMont, who raises outspread arms
To the dawning mountain heights –
The guardians of our beautied land.

About a quarter of all births to bonded white women are of black fathers, since they live side-by-side and endure virtually identical conditions. A bondswoman who loses time through pregnancy has it added to the end of her indenture.

All education for the poor, of either color, is actively discouraged. They are not taught to read nor write, nor to better themselves in any way whatsoever.

Indeed, we still must ride the sorry paths
And bridgeless slide of Virginia's roads,
Absent villages, a dearth of industry,
Most toilers' hearths scant huts,
Unglazed, unfloored, unkempt,
And people o'er a wide domain,
Bereft of simplest education,
Neither schools nor public teachers,
Since revulsion of the leechers to invest
In the welfare of our weaker folk
Means open service is not sought
– Other than courts and jails, militia –
As greed to yolk is gaining
Expectant need and desperation,
And the lords untrain a peasantry
Dependent on neglect.

In 1671, Berkeley declares, "I thank God there are no free schools nor printing, and I hope we shall not have these hundred years; for learning has brought disobedience, and heresy and sects into the world, and printing has divulged them, and libels against the best government; God keep us from both!"

Thus,
Virginians fall yet more behind
And lose more lonely freedoms –
Those slender, fraught-won victories,
In marriage laws, elections,
Liberties of faith and freedom of belief –
For now the Church of England,
Berkeley's right-handed mannequin,
Rules chief in Commonwealth and law,
If not in righteous sanctity,
And Baptists, Friends and Puritans
Are swept contemptuously aside,
Though many with pride do fight, resist,
In a spirit insistent of anti-tyranny
And a firm refusal to comply.

Meanwhile, in her kitchen
Choking smoke
A wife and mother adds a brand,
Stirs the fire with poker hand,
Lifts the lid upon the pot
And tastes the stew within.

Oh, half-a-pound of tu'penny rice,
Half-a-pound of treacle,
That's the way the money goes,
Pop! goes the weasel.

Ducking stools for gossip are now allowed,
Witches feared and vilified, hanged,
Lone women, widowed, never married,
Left-hand midwives, beauties
Resented for their pull on other's lives,
Are chivied to the whipping post,
Tried, humiliated, lost, condemned –
While others defend their beliefs
In a foremost Protestant display
Of resistance
To courts and clerks and parsons' needs
To suppress with vicious word and deeds
Dissenting factions and sedition,
Arresting preachers and meetings banned
As they instigate a "Grand Enquest" attesting
To "seditious secretaries" and transgressions
Committed to God and the Sabbath man,
Intensifying sanctions, well-repressed,
Chastising, intimidating,

And threatening with a jailhouse curse
That abominated seed, that pestilence
Of well-versed Quakerist dissent.

We must defend our freedoms and our rights!

Suffocating!

...Buried, I am being buried
By the insidious stealth of law and wealth...

The circle broken, the noose
Now closes tight...
Pop!
– No, the fight is not yet lost!

...As, in angered answer, we plan revolt,
Labourers sparked by swift collapse
Of tobacco, Dutch war, and relapsed
Impoverishment of our land;
In York County we invoke
Our English rights and our history
In petition to our distant king
To revoke bad food, our terms of service,
Slavedom's housing and such maltreatment
With, "Who would be for liberty?"
– But are discovered, secreted out,
Betrayed and tried unjustly
For "seditious words" and "mutiny".

Yet, in sixty-three we rise again,
Cromwellians, convicts, jailbirds,
Felons sent to serve our misery,
This time in Gloucester County,
As part of Birkenhead's Rebellion,
With plans to end our servitude
Or escape,
But find our heads cut from our bodies
By the courthouse butchery of the state.

Even so, resistance grows
And, the taste of freedom on our lips,
We refuse such easy-slipped oppression
From burgesses and cavaliers,
An exacting governor too,
As he grants huge tracts to salivating friends
– So we rise in opposition, with petitions,
Cries
Defying injustice, harsh and rank,
And begin the first frank clash
Of resentment that will lead, one day,
To a republican intent...

> While yet
> More spades of dirt come crashing down
> Upon my prone and squirming form,
> Crush my legs and gasping lungs,
> Face barely able to throw-worm free,
> Hands and feet in tight-gripped throng,
> As my blackness slowly drips on me.

Having secured, in 1662, a House of Burgesses that suits him, Berkeley refuses to call new elections for fourteen years – until faced with Bacon's Rebellion. The Long Assembly is merely his seal and stamp and press.

> *So, Pop! goes the weasel...*

These are years of intensifying struggle, where laws are used as the instruments of repression, often provoking riots and outbreaks of resistance, made worse by the continuing depression in tobacco prices.

In 1667, baptism no longer brings freedom for slaves (not that it had anyway – this qualm had never affected the trade). In 1669, owners are allowed to kill, maim or punish their 'property' in any way they like and not be convicted. A year later, blacks and Indians can no longer own white indentured servants, from whom voting rights are now removed. All non-Christians imported to the territory "by shipping" are to be slaves for life, whereas those who enter by land are to serve until the age of thirty.

Tobacco prices have been low for many years now, while taxes have risen to pay for coastal defences, the excesses of burgesses and lieutenant governor, land purchases for the élite, and countless other corrupt practices, all of which are causing much anger and anxiety.

In 1670, freemen are stripped of the right to vote unless they are landowners and housekeepers; and, in 1671, a law provides a bounty on the heads of "Maroons" – black fugitive slaves who have begun to form communities in the mountains, swamps and forests of several Southern states.

> *Oh, pop! goes the weasel...*

In 1671, Berkeley estimates the population of Virginia to be 48,000, including 2,000 slaves and 6,000 indentured servants.

V

> And so the MusicMen prepare
> With light of fire, naked stare
> As they dance the circled ground
> With chant and prayer that upward sounds
> And swirl their minds to free from self
> And enter the engulfing air,
> To weave our veiléd liberties
> Within their tangled hair.

We call in the energies of the directions,
The animals, plants and stars,
Earth and mountains, rivers, streams,
Then sit within the prescribed ground,
One at each corner of the world,
And drum and chant our solemn prayer
To guard the circle for its repair
One distant-century
Memoried of this day.

There was an old woman who lived in a shoe,
She had so many children she didn't know what to do;
She gave them some broth without any bread,
Whipped them all soundly and put them to bed.

She is cursing my cattle, cat catch!
They are sickly and not giving milk,
For she is riding them at night,
Sucking their teats and screaming
Banshee screeches through the starlight,
Slipping in at keyholes, blackest cat,
And whisking 'round the moonstone fields
On her broomstick, naked in the night...

...So sing a song of sixpence, Jack Horner,
Because Old Mother Hubbard
Has jumped over the moon
And the dog and the bone
Have run away with the spoon,
And Jill is sulking in a corner...

Hear us, hear us, hear us!

...As two men with saw in tow,
Prepare to down the solemn tree...

...too late, too late, too late...!

We cats, when assembl'd at midnight together
For innocent purring, purring, for innocent purring,
Purring in moonshiny weather...
But if they surprize us and put us to flight,
We fret, fret and spit, fret, spit, spit, give a squall,
Squuaaaall and Good Night.[43]

To cure the ague, go out at night
Under the fullness of the moon,
Find a crossroads guarded tight
By an oak tree, full in bloom,
Drive in a midnight nail, iron firm,

---

[43] *A Cat Catch* by Richard Brown is a popular and elaborate round of the time.

Curse three times and round the oak,
Three times three times turn,
Then with eyes shut tight, backward walk
Before the bell is done,
And let the evil do its work
Upon an innocent one.

…three-times-three-times-three…

So, with our double-handed saw in tow,
Axes, wedges, hammers held,
We stop beneath a chestnut shade
And calculate its foot-length grade,
Weight and girth and overspread,
Remove our shirts and set the mark
Where saw will cut and sweat the bark –
As Sustainer calls the Sufferers
To dance around its frightened bole,
To call upon its ancient sprites
To shimmer in the hopeless glade
And use their potion-poisoned power
To stir the stirring, misted veil, as
The Horseman rides his spurs upon
The ridgeline crest of what's-left burrs,
Turning summer seeth to hoary cold
In the orbit of his spectral passing,
Oracle eyes foretelling visions
Sword in belt, buckled fine
With glowing eyes of diamantine
And fleshing cleave of wailing bones
That howl upon the chilling wind,
And chatter of the passing time
As he watches all that spins,
Catches some, lets others go,
Holds out hope for those who know
Their dreams were sucked by others' breath
Who sleep in silver-shadowed halls
Of wealth's uneasy palaces.

But hush, let me invoke how,
Within the forested glades,
Deep upon the crossroads dark,
A father tells the ancient tales
Of Robin Hood and Friar Tuck,
Of Little John and Alan-a-Dale,
Of Norman sheriffs pursuing amok,
Oppressing Saxon peasant stock,
As they are downed a peg or two…

…While other heroes too inspire,
From the pages of the Bible's roots,
David's odds against Goliath,

Sampson's strength to temple down,
Moses' lead from Egypt's tyranny
And Christ's meek journey on a donkey
To His suffering and His destiny.

Cat catch, catch the cat
That sings the song of sixpence
And will not let us go...

VI

Lavenders blue, dilly-dilly,
Lavenders green,
When I am king, dilly-dilly,
You shall be queen.[44]

The screams of Doegs and Susquehanaugs
Echo through the running hills, mingling
With Rappahannock and Chickahominy,
Occaneechi, Nansemond,
As musket ball and typhoid maims
And Bacon massacres at Bloody Run...

Oh, the call, the call
Of the circle's broken walls...

Great Sun, who life fulfills,
Why have you forsaken us,
Your children,
With such weaving wefts of sorrow spun?

And then they come,
Ambushing with their guns,
Slaughtering our women,
The elderly and each child,
Forcing us to wild-abandon
Fields and houses, winter stores,
And watch from the imploring trees
As the deadly flaming breeze
Catches their torches when they burn
Our sacred temples, ancestors, idols,
And our past is scorched beneath
Their trivial, trampling soles...

...For the Wefts do spin their tears upon
The loom of our true history –
They alone see sparkle clear

---

[44] *The Kind Country Lovers*, anon; first published circa 1675.

Our past of well-veiled mystery,
As you and I, Virginia, stop and stare
Across the banks of Corotoman
And wonder when the dawn will dare
Return us to our old domain.

In 1673, war breaks out against the Dutch, severely hampering the tobacco trade. In addition, a disease decimates Virginia's cattle herds, which, along with a hurricane and hailstorms in earlier years, reduces many small farmers to penury.

Two years later, growing disgruntlement, especially at rising taxes and royal land grants, prompts some Virginians to petition the king in England "that there bee noe Taxe or Imposition layd on the people of Virginia, but by theire owne consent, and that Express'd by the Representatives in Assembly". Also, the petitioners want all the traditional liberties of Englishmen, so often denied within the colony.

But then comes *real* rebellion...

Lavenders blue, dilly-dilly,
You shall be king...

Nathaniel, were you,
Apart from rabid Indian hater,
The creator of our freedom's banner,
With Drummond and two Sarahs,
First against that tyranny
Of aristocratic villainy?
Or were you some drat cousin,
Rancorous, needy, jealous,
An o'er privileged cavalier brat,
Lazy, envious and impatient
In your ungracious greed?
– For you were given a Council seat
And a noble backwoods name
From nepotic uncle Berkeley,
Governor of corruption's fame.

You grew tired, didn't you, Nathaniel,
Impatient of Indian land and sanctity,
Of their recent northern 'vasion,
And were out to massacre Occaneechi
And peaceful Appomattuck
Because of the bands they placed
On haloed demands for settled space
To extend exhausted 'bacco lands.

Your chosen time was ripe, Nathaniel,
And you gelled in rousing words
Gripes at manufactured prices,
Vices of European trade, naval defeat,
Drought and hail, torrential sleets of rain,
Wars and higher taxes, a corrupt Assembly's
Monopoly of beaver pelts,

Western lands supplied to a few,
Most forbidden or denied
Backwoods claims in Piedmont hills,
Other than infilling tenants,
Temporary stayers – provided
The tilling soil was undivided
Amongst eastern-'herited heirs.

In response, Nathaniel,
Hotheaded and rebellious,
You cursed the Indians on your blade,
Drove out the north Pamunkey,
Ere you in turn were forced to flee
From an angry, turncoat governor
And recover, as a fugitive, renegade –
Your pulse-cascaded popularity
Amongst rumbling frontier farms,
Nobly enough to fiery, threat-demand
The recall of Long Assembly.

Your might proved rapier enough, Nathaniel,
To fight the first election in years
And aver Virginians' right
To representative assembly
– A step vital in our struggle
Towards elective democracy –
And, juggled into the burgesses
By your irate-tinged support,
You singed distorted moneyed minds
To swift let freemen refind their voice
And limit self-corrupted office.

Captured, apologised, pardoned, Nathaniel,
Renewed in hotfired debate,
You held a popular convention
Against tyranny of intent,
Took up arms and encamped
Around an engated royalist house,
Roused bondsmen, slaves ranked by your side,
And raved for a military commission
That was stern-blank, damnably denied.

So you rose against authority, Nathaniel,
Took full arms against your foes,
Made a declaration to the people
On corruption, favourites, selfishness,
Dished lay oaths upon supporters,
Arrayed a fleet to capture Berkeley,
That was distraught and traitor-taken,
Then besieged forsaken James Towne's fort
And strengthened its defences
Against a demented, vengeful governor,

Parading fancies on the battlements,
Until you were bent by bloody flux,
Your rebellion's head struck from its neck,
James Towne razed, supporters hanged,
Your struggle speckled to an end.

For a few brief weeks, Nathaniel,
Of soft and savoured heat,
You favoured the disenchanted poor,
But finally retreated to defeat,
Allowing the cavaliers to rescind
Their centres of recanted strength
And re-enforge their engorged will
Upon our hard-won liberties.

Your handsome struggle, Nathaniel,
Was among the first to surely prove
Virginia was not in freedom born,
But in corrupted tyranny,
And in the fight to abrupt those wrongs
Through independent arms,
To overthrow and strident fight
That land-alarmed inheritance
With musket ball and arméd right,
And say, with pride in your stance,
"Thus to all thy tyrant might!"

And your form still wanders, Nathaniel,
The dark-starred wintry nights
Of summered heat and autumn cool
That absorbs us in our plight;
You wander still, without hands,
Without heart, without head,
Without eyes in blackened orbs
That call upon our twilight dread
And will revenge us, every one,
Upon those who steal our leavened bread
And will not live in harmony.

'Tis so, 'tis so,
For thus the ancestors do call it,
And thus must we obey...

For now, I will tell you,
Tell you how...

...From the niches of the palace,
We most sneakly watch, in muted glee,
As Berkeley is recalled to England,
After heartless, shallow persecution
Of Bacon's disconcerted followers,
Hangings without hint of trial,

The stink of nepotism, shrill rapacity,
People disenfranchised, riled,
And very angry still.

Therefore be kind, dilly-dilly,
While here we lie...

Oh yes, Royal Charles removes him,
Though the king then deems it fit
To emplace rapacious Culpeper,
Cunning, vilely covetous,
Granted *all* Virginia for thirty years, plus one,
A peer of peerless villeined greed,
Accompanied in his heartless creed
By the distant Earl of Arlington,
Ruthless, blinkered, profligate,
Bloated, hated autocrat,
Unconcerned with free affection,
Liberty canceled after liberty,
Revoked,
Impoverishing and cowering folk,
Dissent outlawed,
And, by his systematic pillage,
Piling
Loquacious mounds of mislaid fortune,
Until, disgusted, salted o'er
With the curdling of their brew,
The people in renewed revolt
Are invoked to dispossess
This governor of indulgent greed,
Who is 'good riddance' push-decreed,
Once more
To live in gouted dissipation
On England's passive-prisoned shore.

Ah, victory at last!
The king hears our too much!

For you and I, dilly-dilly,
Now all are one,
And we will lie, dilly-dilly,
No more alone.

Tell me... Tell me...

What? What?

Your secrets... Your secrets...
The secrets of your spell...

Lavenders blue, dilly-dilly,
Lavender's green...

The lieutenant governor's powers temporarily limited by popular revolt, our attention is turned to securing greater wealth by exploiting our slaves, whose numbers are rapidly rising. In 1680, an act is passed to prevent insurrections among them. They are not allowed to congregate in large numbers for funerals or feasts. They cannot carry any weapons to such meets, must obtain written authorisation to leave their 'homes' and cannot remain at another plantation for longer than four hours. Any black raising a hand to a white is subject to thirty lashes. Meanwhile, Indian slaves are lumped together with African and treated no differently under the 'law'.

The House of Burgesses, more sure of itself and by now in frequent conflict with the lieutenant governor, adopts an Act of Cohabitation, requiring fifty acres of land to be set aside in each of twenty counties for a port and market town. But then we are condemned to suffer under another abysmal ruler...

> Late drifting within the sixteen-eighties,
> Once more we are a royal province,
> Now ruled by a salamander new,
> Lord Howard of Effingham,
> Who bans printing presses, books,
> Denies education to the poor,
> And controls a fawning judiciary
> That laps from his suppurating craw
> In a rapacity so shameless,
> A gratification so methodical,
> That once more insurrection
> Radicals the loudened halls
> Of popular discontent
> And calls a petition over grievances
> That once more dis-enhances
> The berated hold Old England has
> Upon this independent-minded state,
> Growing used to proud defiance,
> Growing bold in stout defence,
> Learning that the height of power
> Lies in protected self-reliance.

> *Let me be king, dilly-dilly.*
> *And you be my queen.*

VII

Tell me...Tell me...

Ssshhhhh....

Tell me, tell me,
Tell me it isn't so...

Alas, my love, you do me wrong,

115

To cast me off discourteously.
For I have loved you well and long,
Delighting in your company.

Greensleeves was all my joy
Greensleeves was my delight,
Greensleeves was my heart of gold,
And who but my Lady Greensleeves.[45]

A Nansemond village pre-dawns round,
From farms ten miles or more away,
With bread and corn pone, beer and play,
To circle-raise a timbered barn
With stalls for cows, lofted hay,
Carts and wagons, beams and dowels,
Planks and saws, adzes and awls,
Children come to watch and hinder,
Gander-dance in rings this day
Of laughter and light-hearted banter,
As holes for posts, laying sills,
And then the studs are steady raised,
The queens and kings and beams across,
Rafters, lofts and siding planks,
Threshold floor, thatch and biers,
That once are done, the communal folk
Join hands around their jointed work,
And for a brief, eternal prayer,
Rejoin the circle ever there.

And in a hugged Kilmarnock eve,
Three fiddlers tap the porchlaid floor
As men pour ale from earthen jugs,
Women lug soup and corn and beans
And a man who's field is newly scythed
Slow turns a spitted hog, the smell
Of roasting pork, basted well,
Simmering across the swell
Of a joyous summer night…

Oh, the party when the ring is held,
And welded to our friendship's hearts…

Make ye a joyful sounding noise
Unto Jehovah all the earth;
Serve ye Jehovah with gladness;
Before his presence come with mirth.[46]

Mary skips to the covered well,
To dwell within romantic lands

---

[45] *Greensleeves* was composed in the 1500s, possibly by Henry VIII.
[46] Psalm 100; arrangement by John Dowland, 1621.

Entire inside her misty veil,
Then drops her lengthy bucket rope,
Grabs the hemp and, hand-o'er-hand,
Copes the spilling pail to rim
A waiting coppered pot,
Then drops it howling down again,
And once again, to thrice top up
And raise it on her shoulder sore
To take it through the charcoaled door
Of a smoking, coughing kitchen,
There to thrill the cauldron boil
For an evening's suppered meal,
As cook prepares the sweet-oiled shad
And sturgeon braised in onion stock
For Mistress Haddock's gentlefolk.

Your vows you've broken, like my heart,
Oh, why did you so enrapture me?
Now I remain in a world apart
But my heart remains in captivity.

Another girl strides to the barn,
Grabs a goose's honking crop,
Lays its neck upon a block,
Cuts it with a well-timed chop,
And catches spurt of blooded gush
Fit for the gravy mix,
Tosses the head to a whining dog,
Scalds the flesh with kettled boil,
Then plucks the wings and breast and tail,
Feathers fit for toothpicks, quills
The maker curves and careful splits,
While the softer down is pillowed up
For ticks and full-made mattresses,
The bird then hung three days or so,
Gutted, seasoned, slowly spun
Upon a fireplace basting spit
For this year's fat Thanksgiving's gift,
The grease gone to a midwife's shelves,
To hone hard-delved deliveries.

Greensleeves was all my joy
Greensleeves was my delight,
Greensleeves was my heart of gold,
And who but my Lady Greensleeves.

And thus some sink and some do dwell,
Some lose their heads within the well,
And some delve within the sacred spell,
As, in young fields do wrestle men,
Enthusiastic revelry, boxing,
Racing, intoxicating rivalry…

117

...While The Horseman turns and reins away,
Pulls his sallow's head obey
And canters to the darkened mist
Of forgotten people's souls,
As they float the realm of in-between
Here and there and here,
And stop at the stink of tanning milk
As the skins are scraped of hair...

Oh, soft-tan, tan soft the soft-tanned skin
That is bleached within the vat
Of a dark-barked, brooding man
Who seeks to whitewash all
Yet cannot wash his sins away,
No matter call the dips and months
And deep solution strength,
Nor whiteness of the lime.

Scrub, my boy, scrub those hides
To hide their foul-griefed origin,
And let thy masters desperate try
To absolve their reeking rinds
With deep-barked cedared tea
That boils and brews the fat away
From human-rendered skin
And is treated best than you, my boys,
Is treated best than you.

Horn and soap and glue, my boys,
The pit-drenched acid stream
That slaughters hardened hope, my boys,
That slaughters hardened hope;
Lime the noxious, curléd hair
In flesh-soiled vats of sunken toil
To scrape and bleach and scour,
Until from sour-milked ferment
You come whiter than your kin.

Soak and rest, my boys, in thy weak solution,
Preserve the colour of thy hides
With oak and beech and willow bark,
And tannic rise to resolution
That alkaline and dung's reaction
In a curriered and well-dyed plan
To bleach a well-spanned generation
Of black-skinned, well-tanned men.

Oh, Greensleeves, Greensleeves...

Meanwhile,
There strolls a perfumed parasol
Twirling in the blackened berry breeze

118

Of autumn-lacéd shimmerins
That mirage England's memory;
There strolls a jasmined pathway
Of lavender and lilac trees,
Enchanted woven glimmerins
And bonnets of ribboned sanctuary…

…and who but my lady Greensleeves…

…As, stood upon a courthouse field
Within some backwoods county,
A colonel of militia, grim and gouting,
Appointed on a judge's whim,
Tries to stay mounted as the group
Of a motley dozen muskets attempts
To line and face about
Without a quarrel or a shout,
Or a long-banked inter-feud
Spouting a knock-down, messy fight
Within their sown-disrupted ranks.

Meanwhile, Episcopalian proof of sin,
Tho' it does require self-flagellating,
Still sings songs of heaven's splendour
And raises high the chapel roof…

Oh, raise the jaunty earthen jug
And hail our harvest bounty!

…For the circle will not be broken,
No matter any individual strain
That seeks in us its private gain…

It will never break!

VIII

The sawyers, blade rasping deep,
Begin the second cut, angled steep,
The old tree groaning, groaning now,
Whispering softly its creeking vow
To WindTeller, horseman-fixéd moan,
Soul-felt promise of his own to keep.

Oh, Lordy, Lordy,
My sweet Virginia,
I come, I come, I come…

To tell thee, if thou wilt listen
To my honest tale…

119

I will tell you how
You lie impoverished yet,
Your people languishing in neglect,
And are further degraded by misrule,
Immigration cooling with harsh girth
Of enslaved indentures, hangings, death,
No roads nor bridges well-maintained,
No schools nor works, your houses
Mean huts of sorry logs, best land
Stolen for plantation hogs,
A few crossroad country stores,
Your people scattered o'er wide domain,
The capital a church, few battered houses,
Lair of lawyers, judges, politicos,
And rows of mousy merchantmen.

Lost, lost, lost…

Little changes when comes from Britain
Tears of Monmouth's failed rebellion,
Raising the Welsh agin their king,
That holds so many men of culture
Sent and passage sold, themselves
Indentured servants, until paroled
By royalist brethren in Virginia.

No, nothing changes.
The poor are constant now
In angered, unconciled dispute,
Growing bitter at autocracy,
Corrupt ways, monopolies
That stifle talent and economy,
Until the eighty-eight assembly,
Turbulent, determined, in revolt,
Jolts scant heed to governor,
King or magistrate,
And avows the rights of citizens,
In an eruption of dissent that casts
A stream of pumice upon the sea
Of our hard-walked democracy.

And when the House is dissolved
By the governor's enforcing hand,
People resolve to arms and insurrection,
Until fortuitous news arrives
Of England's own Most Glorious Jewel –
The end of shameless Stuart rule.

And, in finale to this fast-usurping act,
The House asserts itself at last
And arches arms with England's march
Towards undespotic liberty.

But not for all…

In 1687-8, a widespread slave conspiracy in the Northern Neck is crushed and its leaders executed. Since the plotting was done under the cover of gatherings for slave funerals, those are now prohibited. The next year, the Northern Neck is the site of another attempted slave uprising, this one led by "Sam, a Negro Servt to Richard Metcalfe." He has to wear "a strong Iron collar affixed about his neck with four sprigs" for the rest of his life.

> …So, ssshhh, don't tell, don't tell,
> Don't break the spell
> Of our nation's brave enchantment…
>
> Instead,
> Sweep the solemn flash from starlit bones
> Of the chestnut's sultry-tinged abode
> And wrench the smart-smoked hickory root
> To fresh-fence the startled, gabled miles
> Of manacled precision
> And rows and rows of enslaved crops;
> Come, oxen, harness-yoked,
> Drag the goaded logs across
> And let us strip the bark and branch
> Then maul the ironwooded staves
> And work the wedges down –
> Drive hard upon the sundered mil,
> Take up the half and quarter well
> Then stack and stand the drying rails
> To zag and zig their snaking course
> Upon a triangulated hill
> Of line and sight and angled will
> Of rock pad, notch and lock,
> Rider, row and splintered trail
> Of red and black and white
> In cross-directioned harmony.
>
> As we split,
> So our lives are split,
> Our being split,
> Spirit and reason cast asunder
> By the stave and unopposable sledge.
>
> I work beside my fellows,
> Stripped, debarked, digressed,
> Drawn with hook and knife and blade
> To peel our dignity and our pride
> And hard drive a wedge between us,
> – Common stock and humanness
> Cleaved by racial edge and edge
> Of beams that rail against each other,
> Quartered, drawn and adzed
> With no more regard for common root

Than takes an overseer's whip
To dismember, slip and commandeer.

IX

A band of Mo-no'kan, once roamers
Of Virginia's Piedmont leas,
Copper forgers, builders of mounds,
Leave their huts, their pits of fire,
And move west once more, away
From encroaching settlers
– Tobacco in their eyes –
To the hills of Buffalo River, there to join
A few Mo-na-su'ka-pa-no, O'kan-ee'chi, Tu'te-lo,
While others of their dispersed band
Go south to Fort Christanna, to join
Depleted Tus'ka-ro-ra, decimated by their war
With too-strong English foes.

The place that we live is a wilderness wood
Where grass is much wanting that's fruitful and good,
Our mountains and hills and our valleys below
Are oftentimes covered with ice and with snow.[47]

Secretly, I dig some nails,
A horseshoe and a piece of quartz
Into the floor of our wattle hut
To protect us, keep the spirits out,
Then paint the door and window frames
The Devil's blue to stout within
From ghouls that spite the night...

...While the Rattle Man sees a throng,
Chaplin-led,
Of psalming relations solemn along
With coffin raised, then softly downed,
Between piles of new-dug soil,
Bones returned to equal flesh
Within the red-soaked, open ground;
And the new-built church,
Liming brick and whitewashed beam,
Sighs its whispered, dawndewed sigh
And wonders when this verdant land
Will quickly breathe for you and I.

Buried now, no room to move,
Dirt covering face and eyes and mouth,

---

[47] *Our Forefathers' Song* is probably British North America's first folk ballad. Composed in New England in 1643, it becomes very popular throughout the colonies.

No breath left, no choke, no squirm,
But, to my surprise, no sudden death,
As I am left to linger here,
The heavy earth piled mountain high
And nothing left but the sigh
Of darkness –
The blackness of my living grave.

And the sawmen, on the backcut now,
Push and pull the six-foot blade,
Feel the giant quiver slow,
Its heavy creaking, pleading boughs
Screaming for some last reprieve...

...As, in the hollows of the graves
That pass as quarters for the slaves,
An old man, in Yoruba tongue,
Tells of the trickster hare, how he tried
To build a ladder to the skies
And join the gods in heavenly surprise,
But fell because of arrant pride,
To the amusement of the animals,
Who laughed and laughed and split their sides.
Once finished, old uncle man
Pulls a fur foot from his shirt,
Raises the string from off his neck
And palms it to his wide-eyed son,
For him to wise remember him.

Oh, but hush,
For lo, within the nearby woods,
The fire is beginning burn,
The cauldron to weirdly bubble,
And the raven will quench her thirst
Within the potion's trouble;
The squares of quilt are being sewn,
Brer Rabbit is on the prowl,
And Linkum Tiddlum Tidy
Is howling to the growl.

...the circle, the circle...

Round and round he dances
At the entrance to the mind,
Sits and asks us deep within
What fear, what love,
What caring's softened line
Can enter whom we wish to be?

Round and round he prances
At the entrance to the mind,
Sits and asks us deep within

What fear, what love,
What way of compassion's
Mocking trance needs enter-dance
Whom we wish to be?

Tell me more! Tell me more!
Break the spell of the darkened well!

'Tis clear from our history,
If we seek to see it clearly,
That Virginians grasped most regularly
Within this past first century
Of struggle, struggle, struggle,
The hot-sparked torch of resistance
To putrefying tyranny –
Locke and Hume, Enlightenment,
Reason, rights and liberty
Now the herald bywords
Both sides of an enobled sea –
And so all Virginians do wait
The brave-fought rights and liberties
Declared by Parliament's decree
Enforcing people rule,
– At least of wealth and property –
And restricting now the privileges
Once granted king and aristocracy.

At last, at last, at last,
Some shimmerin of our futured heart!

Despite the momentary victory for the people of Virginia in 1688-9, and maybe in vindictive search for new victims, the House of Burgesses and the Council remain in aristocratic hands and set about reinforcing their rule, especially over slaves.

Fearing unity between poor whites and blacks, the wedge between them is driven deeper and deeper. Virginia prohibits interracial marriage, on pain of banishment. No black or mulatto may be set free unless the freer pays for that person's transportation out of the colony within six months. All blacks, whether freed or slave, must give up ownership of horses, cattle and hogs. Slaves charged with a capital crime are deprived of trial by jury. In addition to the usual whippings, offending slaves can now be hanged, burned at the stake, dismembered, castrated or branded.

For the first time "white" is used to distinguish the European races. Mulatto children of white women will be slaves until the age of thirty. For some time now, poor orphans and illegitimate white boys have been enslaved until the age of twenty-four; girls until eighteen.

The clothes we brought with us are apt to be thin,
And wool is much wanting to card and to spin,
If we can find garments to cover without
Our other in garments are clout upon clout.

The College of William and Mary, the second-oldest University in America, is established in Middle Plantation in 1693. Six years later, the town is renamed Williamsburg and becomes the capital of Virginia.

Along a silent tidal brook
In a Stafford County estuary,
A servant drops a pole
Within the darkset waters...

Careful take the hidden hook
And cut the gutted flesh,
Squeeze and prize the morsel on,
Then careful back draw the whip
That flicks the looping line
Under the still-black eddied pier
And dream of freedom for another hour
As The Horseman saunters by.

Cut a tobacco plug and masticate,
Scan the gum-lined river bank
And watch the sun rise its crimson arc
Of sultry-tinted enterprise,
The clouds disperse, then gather more,
The breeze to soften as tranquil hum,
And let all servile memories
Drain from my shoulder pain.

I recall my mother's words
Of shipward voyage, auction
And the day that I was born.

What am I to think, to believe,
To hold as natural me,
For,
Those that are my memories
Are not truly mine, nor my family's,
But are long imposed upon me –
A given white man's history
Of meek, self-serving Christianity,
Folk-tales, language, holidays, traditions,
To saddle us thereby.

"Don't resist – turn the other cheek."
"Oh, why look, it's branded *too!*"

So, what is *my* memory? Mine?
What is even *me*?
What my *real* thought and belief
What my *real* identity?
For if they have taken me from me,
That understanding of who I am,
The values that I abide, not they,

My Africa and my passage,
My heritage and morality,
Then I am them, shattered
Pieces they reglue, and
Have melded to their chronic mold
Empty of heart, of being and of soul.

No,
I am not mild by compliant choice,
Only by my servitude,
And I have many secret memories
Of family, resistance, hero stories,
Tribal religion and belief,
That come from strength and resolve,
Tradition and folk-told history,
Which fester behind these supine eyes
And boil my mind with hardened grief
At whippings, beatings, brandishings,
And daily humiliation handed us
By accepting deathride misery.

Oh, SelfSearch be my guide
And store the memories of my pride...!

And so I smile, lower my shaven head,
Focus my inner, dread-locked mind
On havened haunts of the hoodoo kind,
Old Woman Spell who's in the swamp,
Long 'bandoned by the paderollers,
Her charms poisoning them astray,
Her medicines healing us, her potions
Making mistress pass away,
Giving us the mental strength
To await the Judgment Day.

...Another nail. Another wall.
Another tear. Another fall...
I hear your call! I hear your call!

And the backwoodsmen now must seek
Ever distant lands to break
Their freedom's lust upon...

The clothes we brought with us are apt to be torn,
And need to be clouted soon after they're worn,
But clouting our clothing it hinders us nothing,
Clouts double are warmer than single whole clothing.

...a lilting tiger swallowtail...

Oh, hear the Rattle Man's call,
Rattling from each rock and wall,

From every tree and well and stream,
The question mark of who we seem,
Why we turn from freedom's will
To force-empress a poorness still,
So we may have labour to impress
And seek to hide from its redress
In myths of patriotic liberty!

X

Oh, tell me, speak our truth
Of how liberty is stolen from our mouths!

I am you, Virginia,
And you are me,
Eternally.

In 1700, the right to vote, already highly restricted, is subject to a religious test, bonding even stronger subservience to the pulpit and the governor. Next year, the first rewards are posted for runaway slaves.

The French in Quebec and Louisiana are trading up and down the Ohio and Mississippi, forming alliances with local Indians against the British.

West of Henricus, south along the James
Exiled Huguenots, expelled from France,
Gladly settle and sustain
Farms and crafts, weaving looms,
At Manakin Town, a fertile ground
And bastion of booming backwoods life.

I hear the echoes, echoes
Of the lost ancestral call...

...As, within the darkened ridges
Of middle Piedmont claims,
An Indian family, extended
From their Mo-no'kan core to include
A few Sen-en'do, a slave,
And a Tu'te-lo whose tribe
Has been decimated by disease,
Score a ridge of shaded pine
To gather blueberries, roots and nuts
In the chilling, autumn-falling air,
Cut to the margin of a life
By encroaching traders, miners,
Strife,
Farmers moving hasty in;
They share their famished finds,
Help the elderly wind their way,
Carry the young ones, guide the blind,

Tolerate a man of too-frayed mind,
And push the fruits of their dreams
Into their gritty bean-corn mash,
As gunfire comes from valley low
And hunters shoot with unknown glee
The last free Southwest Mountain lion.

I close my eyes and wish,
And wish and wish and wish...

In a final triumph of Virginia's aristocratic élite to impose its will upon the Commonwealth, a new, definitive code of 1705 turns slavery into a permanent condition, codifies the motley assortment of previous laws and defines slaves as real estate. They cannot own property or be party to a contract. No slave marriage has legal standing and whites may not trade directly with slaves. A mulatto is defined as "the child of an Indian, and the child, grand child, or great grand child, of a Negro."

With a final cut, the tree is done,
Wedges hammered firmly in,
The old tree swaying, tilting now,
Wind direction gauged, a final call
To clear the region of its fall;
Cracks are heard, the timber creaks,
And swaying, with one final tweak,
An era's past is toppled o'er
And the timber burnt for wood.

The code has sections regulating free blacks as well. They are subject to controls on their movements and employment and any newly manumitted slave must leave the Commonwealth upon emancipation. If a black, free or slave, resists arrest, he can be killed, and his killer won't be prosecuted. More than five slaves meeting together for insurrection are subject to death. It also defines crimes, punishments and restitutions to slave owners for loss of their property.

Slaves now make up half of Virginia's unfree, labouring population. The rest are white indentured servants, who suffer nearly as badly under their own repressive set of laws. They are whipped, shackled, beaten, starved and punished in ways similar to slaves, alongside whom they work in the fields. Under British rule, we see class exploitation much more than simple racial exploitation; always, the fate of poor whites and blacks goes hand-in-hand, though the tactic is to oppress slaves more severely and thereby give poor whites some sense of superiority.

Linkum slowly calls
The marsh oak moaning winds
And breaks free his bony arms
From the grave of his imaginings,
Watching, watching,
From those dark and hollowed orbs,
Bloodless, insubstantial,
Ephemeral chimera
Gliding upon the marsh-gas glow
Of a half-light's marshy flow

And asks, what is myth
And what our sure reality?

The circle of our life
That pulls all energy within, links
Us in our selfish plight
To all around, both day and night
In an eternal, timeless bond
That has been lost upon the tocsin sound
Of our own lost soul's most wandered flight.

…But will The Rattle release his hold
Upon this tale's old harrowed throat
And let the other Callings sway
To the music of a bolder day…?

*The echoes of our mind are lost
In the clamour for the grail;
We would rather blinded be,
Than let discovery of self prevail…*

Oh, let the tambourine man play
The sacred beats of faraway
Upon a century's hardened fame!
Let me dance my buckled feet
To the noose's swinging beat
And turn my fancy-coated frame
Within the wind's sweet folderol,
As I hear the cheering, drunken crowd
Applaud me swaying to their game
And see the shadowed Robin Hood
Upon the ephemeral drifting breeze
Of WindTeller as he coldly sighs
And gallops among the fog-dimmed trees…

…Go away! Go away! Go away…!

Let the fiddler call the Devil's sway,
Raise the roof on another day
And drag my heart, still beating pleas,
From the dungeon to the fortress wall
And leap across the moated gate
And gallop o'er the open plain
Of the 'bourine man's lasting lilt refrain
And the faint dying of the circle…

Book III

To the Mountain:
Frontier Expansion, 1706–1763

I

A three-masted schooner, hove-to,
Lies alee the Hampton Roads, flying
A smallpox flag, her crew eight dead,
The last few tossing each blistered stench
Of bloated death across and down
The gunwale of Virginia's drowning blood;
She sways in the dawning mist,
Her topsails and main unreefed,
Flapping to the echoes of a dark refrain
As the cries of the dying rise above
Our shores of servile pain.

SALE

Several **Irish Maid Servants**
time most of them **Five Years**
one **Irish Man Servant** — who is a
good Barber and Wiggmaker
also
Four or **Five** Likely **Negro** Boys.

I stand upon the mountain, dreaming of Zion,
As the feral dogs do snarl and snap...

Near two hundred coffled slaves
From the Windward Coast, Bight of Benin,
Are midnight filed from odorous bile
Of excremental death
Along a quay of Quantico Creek aways
To the quarantine of Dumfries' pens
Ring-chained to walls, blocked in dens,
Screaming swells of nightly agony.

TO BE SOLD by auction aboard the ship
Brooks on Monday 1st April next,
commencing 6 a.m. at Norfolk Wharf, a
choice cargo of 170 fine, healthy
NEGROES
Arrived after 14 days Quaranteen from the
GUINEA COAST. Utmost care has been
taken to ensure the cargoe is free of SMALL
POX and cholera, or any other infectious
diseases, no boat having been on board.

Ding-dong-dell,
Pussy's in the well...

Lord, let her be free!

Blow, wind, blow...

...The wind hath blown my plaid away.[48]

Guaranteed free from infection
Or from the bloody flux!
Buyers will have reasonable terms!
Three, six, or nine months credit!
Free victuals for all who hie
To the *Graft and Jobbery Tavern,*
Wharf Street,
Thursday view, Friday buy!

Ha, ha!
Make him dance – jump, man, jump,
Show us your teeth...
Any scars? Clip marks of insurrection?
Has she been violated recently?
Any signs of infection?

Ugh! Ugh! Ugh! Ugh! Ugh! Ugh! Ugh! Ugh! Ugh!

Oh, to hear the poor whip-poor-will sing...

Lavenders blue, dilly-dilly,
Lavenders green...[49]

---

[48] *The Elfin Knight*, a traditional Scottish ballad first printed circa 1610.
[49] *The Kind Country Lovers*, anon; first published circa 1675.

We are as free as the land will let us be,
Our seasons, and our beliefs...

For I hear Zion, Zion, calling, calling, calling...

...A gang of servantmen, slaves, who chop and axe
Girdled trees, some downed for timber, sawed,
Others ignored for beetle, fire to sunder,
And let the plough weave freely through...

...Piles of leaves and broken trash
Burning a thousand years of ash
To furnish the hungry fields withall
A season's crop or two...

...While a horse, harnessed, chained,
Drags three logs from a cypress swamp
To the new house on the hill,
To be sawn and azed, let cure, then
Hoisted to its second seemly stage,
There to form well-planked joists
And crossbeams for the ages...

As WindTeller observes from o'er the lea...

...A brace of servantmen pile up bricks
For a layer, seven indentured years, to
Mortar mix and paste and let
The great house rise betwixt
Square-set corner stones, masoned,
Foundations deep-trenched dug and cellared,
Flaggéd kitchen floor, abundant range,
Wash room, meats and cagéd store
Served by one brace more of servantmen...

...Call up your maids, dilly-dilly,
Set them to work...

...While another mason lays the markéd floor
Of an ornate piazzad parlour
With marble from northalp Italy
And gold-trimmed tiles upon the wall,
Symbols of some soft-secret masonry,
Compass, setsquare, Osiris eye,
In the ritualistic sanctity
Of a classic entrance hall.

Meanwhile, in the striving tobacco rows,
An overseer is broken-scuffle woken
To cries of "Help!" from his drivers,
Mounts and gallops too late to stop
A pair of bloody knives in slash

Of intra-slave dispute, abused
Revenge for long-sucked grievances
Tucked beneath the shadow of
A girdled chestnut tree.

The overseer curses
As a good slave's moiled blood
Washes down the dark Virginia soil
And fills it with its centuries,
As two are ordered carry back
The body to the slave-row shacks,
While two others shackle and inhibit
The avenger for the master's whip
And patriarchal fury...

...As the lines return to drooping rows,
Protesting beetles from the leaves,
Pinching suckers and the flowered buds,
While others plough and others sow,
Others mend fences, tend to trails,
Stack logs to saw, pile firewood
Onto wains for an opulent house's heat
And to beat virulent mosquitoes from
Their single, mud-floored retreats...

...and we sing of Zion...

...until midnight's weary dusk...

An enslaved Indian, shackled,
Clinks his way from hut to sty
To toss the nightsoil, kitchen rinds,
To hogs that grunt their squeals of joy,
Lost within his songless mind...

Who put her in,
Dilly-dill, dilly-dill,
Who put her in...?

Others build a newlaid wharf,
Piers pounded into suckling mud
Of a cut through harsh spartina marsh,
Planking laid, cross braces, trunnelled nails,
And an easy crane to lift and turn
Hogsheads in return
For goods of an English-costed sea...

...While the master winks his housemaid,
Pretty, young and black, baptised,
Suckling her dinky child, mulatto,
And with his master's eyes...

Oh, sing for our souls, poor whip-poor-will,
As we turn our backs on human dreams
And hoe the rows of beans...

Ugh! Ugh! Ugh! Ugh! Ugh! Ugh! Ugh! Ugh! Ugh!

...As our vengeful slave, ere
The shackles are prized upon his soul,
Breaks free and runs, is chased, but
The pace of death outlasts
Surety of life, and so
He flings himself within the swamp,
Strides within the green-weed mire,
Fly-encased, bitten, dips
Beneath the blackened flow, crawls,
And is rapid lost to pursuit
Within our cypresses of guilt...

II

In 1709, a plot involving enslaved Indians and Africans is uncovered in Surry,
James City and Isle of Wight. The two leaders are quartered and beheaded and
their heads placed on poles for all to see. Another plot is discovered the next year
in the same area.

Hush, Will-o'the-Wisp, and
Let the whip-poor-will call...

Please,
Let me have strength in my heart,
As, in fire and spit of copper lit
I broil and boil the hams,
Preheat the glaze and stir the greens
To mix with rice and beans,
Then platters embossed and clean and bold,
Of gilt and polished gold,
Venison, beef and lakeside bream
Are whistled o'er the reefing steam
From shed to shining dining room,
Where servingmen, amply wigged and dressed
In footmen's breech and coat,
Pour wine and wine and silent spoon
Wild mushroom soup and hearty cream
As silvered tunes most gentle scrape
The porcelain and painted plates,
Then remove the surfeit spate of waste,
Refill the glasses, carve the joints,
Layer yams and spinach vert,
And ladle-fork fresh salad greens,
To stand once more and wait.

This little piggy went to market,
This little piggy stayed at home,
This little piggy had roast beef,
This little piggy had none...

...But saps of our fair strength
As I scrape the gizzard scraps
Of guts and bones and wizened heads
Into a kettled boil of beans,
Corn meal, peas and chitlin rinds
To stir and spice the juba food
For hardened working fields
Who line the threshold, stand,
Wooden bowls in quivered hands,
To take their meagre soul-food soul
To downed and disappointed cabins,
There to dunk with cornbread slice
And suffice their aching joints.

And this little piggy cried wee, wee, wee,
All the way home,
Johnny Green, Johnny Green...

...dreaming of Zion...

Ugh! Ugh! Ugh! Ugh! Ugh! Ugh! Ugh! Ugh!

In a distant plantation row,
Tucked behind the great brick house,
WindTeller whispers gently so
To a dozen slaves meekly waiting
Monthly rations at the walking gate,
Sitting, women, boys and child,
One playing banjar upon a stump,
Another stalking a dolly by his side,
Others fixing hair, laughing, talking,
Talismans twisted about their necks,
Finding shade on this mud-sucked morn,
Until the overseer ope's the barn,
The men bring molasses and sacks of corn,
Salt pork, meal and unmilled grains,
Weigh them manful on the scales
And tip them into our grateful pails...

...While two slaves, him and her,
From neighbouring farms
Kiss beneath the stolen stars,
Dark within coy-copsed embrace
Beyond their masters' wills and wiles
And risk the shrill-horned lane patrols
To brisk an evening's joy...

Paying the ferryman...

He put her in, he put her in!

Our escapee slinks upon
A cold and misty riverbank,
Steals a pettiaugur, carved canoe,
And silent drifts within the slow
Of the half-tide river's flow.

Meanwhile, the great house begins
A spring clean to dust old webs
From wintered thoughts and cracks,
Servantmen brushing silver, maids
Airing bedspreads, blankets, sheets,
Dusting, smells of breakfast, eggs
And ham and bread
Wafting out to the sage and mint
Of the comfreyed kitchen squares
As a chimney sweep, indentured boy,
Orphaned, kept famine thin
By his legal master, itinerant,
Is sold up the narrow flues
With brush and trowel and scrape
To push and choke the smoke-lined
Bricks and poke his skyward head
Above his roof of chambered dreams
And slates of postponed hope...

...as the cardinal cries...

...And slaves, a few indentured men
Oar pinnaces and flats to toss upon
The tidal wave's set nets that drag-engulf
Our runs of springtime spawning shad,
To mass upon the pier, there
To gut and salt and dry
Their open-trailing carcasses,
Until they can be barrel packed
And firmly nailed
For winter plantation work,
And for the growing urban needs
Of Norfolk, Boston and New York.

But then the savior
Dusk of Sunday eve
Relieves its mercied veil,
To free us two nights, a day,
To hoe our peas and tend our beans,
Seed our pumpkin rows,
Or visit neighbouring folk.

Tommy Stout,
He pulled her out...

So tonight is a careless night
To holler-sing and banjar ring
The sacred wheels of native lore
And unstore our week's remorse
In songs of laughter and of hate,
In mockery and plaintive 'ppeal
To the gods of our revealing hand.

For tomorrow will we ascend
Ladders to amend
A winter's toll on our dear huts,
Reroof with straw and nail
Beneath the shadowed oversight
Of the great house on the hill.

And we will meet our Sunday friends,
Barbecues and juba feasts,
Dance and greet in nextdoor fields,
In those fine clothes we have hidden
Saved, and exchanged at crossroads stores
For the surplus of our gardens.

Huckstering is illegal!
Who cares? Who cares?

Meanwhile, our escapee, drifting tidal marshes
Of Middlesex and Mathews, fishing,
Clutching eggs of ducks and flighty geese,
Is spotted by the tidal patrol, called to stop,
Shots released, his pirogue hit, smashed,
And he drops o'erside to rapid swim
Within the rising tide of flit and grass,
Beyond the curse of breath and whim.

Johnny Stout, pull him out!

He never meant no harm...

In one full-moon, County Richmond night,
Another silent slave goes secret down
To the master of his smitten row
To have his face cut ceremonially
And undergo
Some ancient hidden mystery,
While yet he wears his harsher scars...

...and sing, sing of Zion, for...

...The silent screams of a pardoned man,

Escapee, tried, convicted
Of poncing from his master's barn
A horse and saddle, boots and livery,
Branded on his cheek for sake
Of taking the king's once pardon.

Oh, have strength in your heart,
And dream of freedom's day...

And watch for the ferryman,
Freedom pirated away...

For the whip-poor-will will steal our dreams,
Take our souls away, lift them clean
Upon his wings of singing sway.

The development of large plantations progresses alongside the continued arrival of free passengers, slaves and indentured servants. When their indenture is over, most servants become tenant farmers, independent craftsmen, or are allocated plots of land in the backwoods.

Immigration is rapidly expanding the population as people move up the Northern Neck, settle on the Eastern Shore, and spread beyond the fall lines of the James, Appomattox, York and Rappahannock rivers. New counties are created all the way up the Tidewater region, along with the requisite institutions of centralised power – courthouses, jails and parish churches.

I wanna kill him;
Don't you go killin' 'im;
I wanna kill 'em all;
Don't you go killin' 'em all;
For whipping my Ma,
For making her cry and bleed,
Naked, strung up, treed before us.

Leave be, son, leave be,
Pray to the Almighty
And leave be –
Have strength in your heart,
Kill mice in the farmer's barn,
And dream of freedom's day
– Of the sacred hills of Zion –
But leave the master be.

III

Ken'kut-te-ma-um!
Ken'kut-te-ma-um!
Ken'kut-te-ma-um!
Ke'show-tse!
Ke'show-tse!

Ke'show-tse!
Ken'kut-te-ma-um!
Ken'kut-te-ma-um!
Ke'show-tse!
Ke'show-tse!
Ken'kut-te-ma-um!
Ke'show-tse![50]

"Ne'pun'che... Ne'pun'che... Ne'pun'che..."[51]

In the noisome quietness
Of a somnambulant predawn bed,
WindTeller watches, lowered head,
As the Ra-pa-han-o'k are enforced
From their Portabago lands, removed
To an Indian Neck reserve, ant-acred,
Tho' yet within old-hunted grounds,
Haunted to their descendants' day,
Hidden from three-hundred years
Of winter-agéd fears,
As they are driven from centre stage
To the wings of their ancestral land.

The Tidewater and Piedmont Indians, defeated and marginalised, are in full
retreat, though they still pose an occasional danger. Some, captured, remain
enslaved, where they seem to just wither away. Others, remnants of destroyed
tribes or villages, join with other bands and head south or west towards the Blue
Ridge Mountains and beyond.

Oh, listen, spirits, to the rattle of the gourds!
Listen, ancestors, to the reeds' sharp flute!
Listen, chiefs of past-here-now,
To the weeping vow of our drums...

Within a distant rivered vale
Beneath the ridge of Ri'ko-ho'kan,[52]
We stop our gathering rites to rest
And await great grandmother to divest
Herself of this world's strainéd life,
Mother All to us, beholden band,
Healer, carer, provider, cook,
Her body crooked in morning cold,
Old and hungered past her years
Of sacrifice and burdened deeds
For her children's yearning fears.

Sing of the ancestors,

---

[50] A predawn dance chant, repeating "Greetings, Great Sun!"
[51] "I am dead... I am dead... I am dead..."
[52] The Shenandoah Mountain Range, which is the front range of the Appalachians
and now forms the border with West Virginia.

The round of circled life
As we are buried, each within
A perpetual round of strife...

So we dig beside an ancient river
A pit we line with bark and grass,
Dress her body in dark finery,
Lay her on a mat of reeds
With beads and necklace, favourite things
Adorned upon her head and neck,
Her basket, corn for travelling,
Face and shirt daubed living red,
As we younger women prevail around
An after-sunset mourning shroud
To last the night's loud-wailing tones,
Invoke ancestors from their bones,
Then in the dawnlight place her bound
Within the grave and earthen ground,
Us all behind our charcoal masks,
Four-night fires soul-lit around,
As our men do watch in subdued fast.

I cut my hair in mourning, remove
My bells and feathered mantle, my
Wings of raven, eagle's claws,
And scare my slash-scarred arms
With the blood of ancestral grief!

And what colour are our ancestors?
Red or black or white?

Oh, cradle our liberties,
SelfSearch, cradle our history,
Cradle the lessons of our past,
And hold them fast and close!

The mountains call!
The mountains call!

SelfSearch, guard our memories well...!

For I hear the Callings calling me
To be free, to be free,
Free as we were intended to be,
As the rivers and the streams,
As the bears and the breeze,
As the trees and their leaves
In the living of our dreams.

At Fort Christanna, built in 1714 by the Virginia Indian Company, Mi-i'pons'ki, O'kan-ee'chi, Mo-na-su'ka-pa-no (Saponi), Stu'k-e-no'k and Tu'te-lo Indians live in a settlement close to a backwoods trading post and a school that aims to educate and convert them to Christianity.[53] The Virginia Indian Company is dissolved in 1717 and funding for the garrison ceases the next year. By 1740, the Indians have migrated south and west to escape expanding frontier claims.

> Across the distant mountains,
> A wandering family of Mo-no'kan,
> Long dispossessed,
> Trek from a rock-lined ridge
> Down a wandering Indian path,
> There to stay and offer prayers
> To an ancestral mound, every name
> Engraved in song and mystery
> Within the minds of the elderly
> Who still, as yet, preserve the ways
> And stories of our yesterdays.

> "Oke-e'po-eshe! Oke-e'po-eshe! Oke-e'po-eshe!"[54]

> *Oh, sing of the mountains and the trees...*

> ...As a golden eagle rests within a maple tree,
> This year's fledgling, high upon a ridge
> Of the Allegheny, but is disturbed,
> Awkward flaps away, glides valley clear,
> As he hears the sound of singing near...

> ...Singing of the earth and breeze
> That brings memories of our ancestors
> And of our loss of life, lost as life
> Binds us by degrees.

> "Ken'kut-te-ma-um, Ke'show-tse!
> Ken'e-how'tos...
> Ne'pun'che... Ne'pun'che... Ne'pun'che...
> Nu-wa-ma'ta-men!
> Nu-ma'ska'ta-men!
> Nu-ma'ska'ta-men!
> Nu-ma'ska'ta-men..."[55]

> *As the red trumpets vines*
> *Crumple-dry*
> *In the falling light*
> *Of all our winter days...*

---

[53] The fort was situated on an old Indian trail near present-day Cochran, Brunswick County. Route 1 follows the old trail. It will become a post road in 1750, and in 1781 Washington will pass along its northern stretch on his march to Yorktown.

[54] "God is nigh! God is nigh! God is nigh!" A Piedmont's Indian's salutation to the mountains, as recorded by Lederer.

[55] "Welcome, Great Sun! I understand well... I am dead... I am dead... I am dead... I must keep it! I care not for it! I care not for it! I care not for it..."

And the remnant band, driven more
Into the far-sided western slopes,
Meet with salt-trading Sha-wan-wa,[56]
Smoke, barter European beads,
Talk of French trappers and To'ka-ha'ks,
Of wars and deaths and treaties long let go,
Of promises and lies, whisky decay,
Then fall asleep in fire-smoked huts,
Until near dawn they are 'waked
By gunfire, shakes and screams,
Hurry rise, stream out, see flashes,
Long Knives' coonskin hats,
Indian gashers, bounty-set
To scalp and greet for their reward
The death of every Indian met
Upon their knife and sword...

Aaaaiiieeeee............

...As we sit within the steam-rocked heat,
Steeped within of night, praying
For a path through a plight
Deep within the clay-banked sweat
Of our final-fret and crying flight.

Meanwhile, a red-tailed hawk seeks its prey
And I, last Chi'p-o'ke,
Stand upon the highest peak
Of this cloud-ridged range to seek
And spread my arms towards the sun
As I pray for our land, overrun,
For my mothers and my wives,
Brothers, fathers and the striving
Of our bleak, blank-futured prophecy:
"Oke-e'po-eshe!
An'ath, Ke'show-tse, an'ath!
Ta'na-o-wa'am?
Ne'pun'che! Ne'pun'che!
Ma'ta-kuen-a'toxo't!
Sa-sa'ko-mu-wah-kege!
No-uw'mas! Ne'pun'che!
No-uw'mas! Ne'pun'che!
No-uw'mas..."[57]

For the gourds will rattle no more,
The reeds have flute their last,

---

[56] Shawnee. To'ka-ha'ks is the Powhatan for pickaxe and probably the origin of
"Tuckahoes" (long knives), a generic Indian name for the English trappers and hunters of
the backwoods.

[57] "Hail, great mountain! Farewell, Great Sun, farewell! Where have you been? I am
dead! I am dead! I don't understand you! Be gone! I love you! I am dead! I love you! I
am dead! I love you..."

And the drums sit silent upon the floor
Of our ten thousand dreams...

...As I feel the weakness of my arms,
The faintness of my psalms
Upon the sunset-fading dawn
And all its evil charms...

...too weak; I am too weak...

And, oh, how the wind doth blow...

So I turn my back on the mountaintop
And descend to the dream
Of another's streaming prophecy.

IV

In a makeshift aleroom courthouse,
The taproom of an ordinary,
A clutch of old-indentured men,
Some time-expired women too,
Are certified their liberty,
Granted backwoods tenancies,
Corn seed for their first-year's scratch,
Barrels of meal, hocks of ham,
Muskets, cloth and kitchen tools,
To help them span their season's need.

And two, with merry-smiling cries,
Plan to marry Sunday morning next
In the new-erected church
Of this fresh-sprung, dawning town.

"...there shall be paid and allowed to every imported servant...at the time of service ended...To every male servant, ten bushels of indian corn, thirty shillings in money, or the value thereof, in goods, and one well fixed musket or fuzee, of the value of twenty shillings, at least: and to every woman servant, fifteen bushels of indian corn, and forty shillings in money, or the value thereof, in goods..."[58]

Jack and Jill went up the hill...

A working group of strong-armed men
In the Mother County of Northumberland
Raise a beam upon two posts
And ream the dovetails in,
Secure with wooden trunnels firm

---

[58] From Section XIII of *An act concerning Servants and Slaves*, October 1705.

And cross-strut post-to-post,
Then brace with shorter trusses
Of well-adzed timber oak
To must a wellset farmhouse gable
For our new-freed tenant folk,
And then enable hurdled wattle
And mud-strawed, hand-laid daub,
To absorb and dry, smoothly paste,
And make it snug and stable.

Dilly-dill, dilly- dill...

Increasingly, farmers leave the Tidewater area to seek their fortune inland,
ploughing the Piedmont valleys and hills as they begin to move towards the
distant mountain ranges.

Oh, how the mountains call,
Nearer now, nearer to Zion's sweet fall,
And sleep within the golden keep
Of Virginia's sylvan vale.

Our family seems so joyous now,
In this dreamed-of destiny,
To own and farm their given plot,
A hundred ridgetop acres,
Though barely thirty worth
The flashing, soilless plough;
Yet they are full of energy
To build a better life-with-thou
Of a 'deemed and Christian sort,
Where they can grow in childrened ease,
In wealth and plaited comfort.

And stare upon a sunset light
Across the distant ridges...

So, as The Horseman canters by,
The husband raises high his hat,
To show enchanted waves of gratitude
As the wind blows fair upon his horn
And the elfin knight sits on yon hill
Ploughing the plaid away...

...While the whip-poor-will doth sing
Upon the ringing mountain top.

Then the ploughman takes a nail
To hammer on the lintel
A shoe to guard
The new-raised building's door,
Iron wrought to ward away
Fearsome faerie spells

145

And protect those who dwell within
From a curse of witches' nights
And notions of their pixie kin.

Meanwhile, within a nearby brewhouse inn
Rise new odours of barley malted, hops,
The smell of brewing so soft serene
It drops dwelt memories of home...

...memories....

...sweet memories of home...

And, within the split-rail garden of
A tenant farm, the turkeys trail
Through a muddy 'bacco patch,
To snatch the hornworms and the grubs
From leafing curls and buds...

...and, oh, the smells of home...!

...As, without the timbered hut,
One room up, one down,
A laddered hole to the loft,
Stone-built chimney, one window sill,
Our man tends his single cow,
The woman basket weaves,
And their two young children play amidst
The greens and salad rows.

Rabbit stew, carrots, beans and chard
Wafting o'er the sleeping dog in the resting yard...

But, take care, for
Within the darkness of the barn,
The stink of mildewed hay, cow dung,
The rats and cats and hidden kittens,
Our escapee slave hunkers in
The shadows of the timbered rungs.

While our tenant chops and stacks
With split and saw and hack,
A pile beside the southern wall,
Hushed eyes peer out at him,
As he calls to clean the chicken pen.

And his wife, full pregnant, sweating,
Ker-fumps the sucking butter churn,
Up and down, up and down,
In the lowing death of day.

What is it to be?
What is it to be,

Dilly-dilly,
Climbing up the hill
To our personed Zion
Here, right here, right here ...?

There are hundreds of runaways each year; not all are slaves and not all are alone. Many are indentured servants escaping together, or whole families fleeing their imprisonment. Notices of runaways often refer to scars, limps, cut ears, missing fingers and other signs of discipline. The following notice, posted about this time, mentions five indentured servants who escaped by boat from Maryland, possibly to hide in Virginia's slashes (swampy woods), then to make their way inland to find a place of safety in the mountains and valleys of the backwoods.

---

*Maryland ff. RAN away, from the Subscribers, on Monday Night, being the 12th Instant, from the Town of **Cambridge**, on Great Choptank River, in a Long-boat belonging to **Mr. Thomas Nevett**, having a blue Vane, with T.N. on it, the following **Persons**, viz. **Thomas Ablewhite**, of a middle Stature, dark Complexion, dark Wigg, Dark-colour'd Coat turn'd; a red Duffil Great-coat, and blue Broad cloth Breeches. **Jane Shepherd**, a lusty fat **Woman**, having a Gold-lac'd Hat, a dark brown Holland Gown, and another striped ordinary One; also Cambrick Pinners and Handkerchiefs, with several Aprons and Shifts; is an **English** Woman. **Francis O'Conner**, a tall spare **Irish Man**, being thin and poorly cloath'd, wore his own short black hair, a Felt Hat, blue Stockings, a check'd Shirt, and had several other white Shirts, a Gun, a Remnant of coarse brown Holland, and several other Things. **Mary Barnes**, having a green Silk-Poplin Gown, fac'd with Yellow; a sickly Countenance, and much bloated. And **Jane Harlett**, a **Scotch Woman**, having a strip'd Calimanco Gown, a Platt Hat, and several other Things. Whoever secures the said Persons, and Boat, so that they may be had again, shall receive of the Subscribers, **Ten Pounds** current Money of this Province; or for each **Person** as followeth, if taken separate, For **Thomas Ablewhite**, the Sum of 2 l. 10 s. For **Francis O'Connor**, 5 l. For **Jane Shepherd**, 5 l. For **Jane Harlett**, 20 s. For **Mary Barnes**, 5 s. For the Boat, 2 l. As also Reasonable Charges for all or either of them, paid by **Thomas Nevett. Thomas Watkins.***

Dream of Zion, my son...!

Oh, but my belly is
Too sore to
Hide an hour more...!

So our slave, starving, risks

The smoke house, steals up the latch,
Enters, cuts some drying ham,
Until the dog hears, barks, wakes
The musket farmer, who rises, shoots,
And raises up a hue and cry to chase
The hunted to the orchard,
Then the lane, where a horseman
Gallops, fires, wounds him in the arm
And he is captured, huddled, blood
Spurting from his broken limb.

And Jack falls down and breaks his crown,
As Old Bill comes tumbling after...

Meanwhile, a horse and cart hack slowly by,
Thin and boney, stoned-out shoes,
Canvas, poles and packs of wares
Heading for the market fairs...

...Past the county gibbet, shadowed
Post and brace and arm, steps
To a wooden hell beneath,
And beyond the sleepy stocks,
A drunk snoring a second night away,
And the whipping post, silent now,
But expectant of the dawning day.

And, that night, as he breezes home,
Silent-screeching, Brer Rabbit sees
A black cat cross the dim-starred path
Before the moonlit walker – a hare
Dart o'er the farmyard breadth
And leap between a split-rail fence,
As high storm clouds gather
From a sudden black, enveiléd sky...

...As the blacksmith crosses quick
In the forge's sooted steam
With an iron-clingéd, reddened nail,
And prays him quick the Holy Grail.

For, as the rain begins to pelt
And the silent waters agitate,
Mama Earth swish-glides apart
To taste her spirit in the grey
Of Suffolk's winsome, biting swamps,
From where she slipped to market plead
Roots and pots for all her creed
Of medicine and moonmid trickery,
And now boils them up, with a curse
To reverse the calm and bring a storm
For all the rich tobacco men,

As she sings within her memory:
"And Jill came tumbling after,
Dilly-dill, dilly-dill..."

V

As more craftsmen begin to produce valued goods and farmers wives weave cloth
and make baskets, preserves and herbal medicines, there is a growing need for
markets to trade these new goods.

So,
Let us follow, let us follow our
Tenant family,
Round and round and round,
As they wander after peddlers
Muling past a brickworks,
Orphaned urchins shackle-driven,
Towards the swelling river
And the mewling county seat
No court house, log cabin for a jail,
Down the banks to a crowd
Gathered close by a ferry,
Laughing, erecting merry poles
For a maytide dance around, setting
Rings for baiting bears and dogs,
A contest of masculine strength
And a rough course for showing off
The county horses' paces.

Let us follow them down
To the market men, peddlers,
Chapmen, keepers of the boats and
Watch the wife try pickles and preserves,
Quiz for recipes, tucks and tips,
Feel and pry at wares beneath
Canvas awnings, on
Tables of temptation,
Calico, osnaburg, velveteen,
Milliners, stillators, tinkermen,
Potions, tinctures, lotions,
Remedies, medicines, a pharmacy,
A surgeon of basic surgery,
Infusions, plasters and poultices,
Potters, bakers, smiths,
Farriers, sharpeners of knives,
Quoits and apple bobbing, auction bids,
Musket practice on the ridge,
Fortunes from the gypsy teller,
Lemonade and honeyed sugar cakes,
Phaetons, gigs, carts and wains,

Puppet theatre and bowling pins.

Let us follow her as she
Buys some cloth and thread,
A thimble and a needle box,
While he drifts amongst
The thieves and cutpurses, delinquent urchins,
Signs his cross for the wrestling match,
Then hails some friends and follows them
To try the ale and cider, brandy, wine
Within the nearby tavern's arms
As they gather-sup
About a well-charmed jug or two
Of merry local ale, to laugh and try
Their farming hands
At skittles, cards or Find the Queen,
While keen upon the meadow broad
Is raised a maypole high...

To the Mountain Zion sky...!

Oh, yes! Raise the fertile maypole point
Predawned with ribbons and bouqueted air,
And set the maids a-singing round
In in-and-out, virginaled display
Of interweaving, springtime rouse
To blush the crops from winter ground
And praise the Mother of the Fields
With cavourts of springtime reverie,
Round and round and round...

He loves his maid, dilly-dilly,
She loves her man...

So go a-maying, sweet-paired child,
In dawn's dewy basket air,
Wipe grass-glass drops upon your skin
And take flowers for your fortune's kin
To drop within your good-luck well
And dream of sweetheart blesséd charms,
Tie ribbons to your lacy dress,
Add bows and bonnets and sweet caress
And take your procession's leading place
For Queen of beltane May,
Then reel and ring and rowdy sing
To the tunes of Merry England,
With fiddle, flute and drummer proud
To lead the galavanting crowd
To the open-favoured, glossy green,
Where creamy milk, still warm and thick,
And best bees' honey royally keen
Await the revelers quaff and meat

And herald summer's fecund beat,
As nurse and mother skip away
To morris race across the day,
And celebrate to Goddess Spring
Anticipation's soft harbouring...

...That you and I, dilly-dilly,
Must lie together...
Lavenders blue, dilly-dilly,
Lavenders green.

Oh, what is it to be? What is it to be?

...Upon the Eostre hill,
Dilly-dill...

For, as the singing rings its charms,
A blacksmith hammers out alarms
Upon an iron horse's shoe
And rings the ringing metaled earth
With tears of cry and hue
– Old Vulcan, in his smithy hot,
Raising the white-heat coals aloft
To temper, temper, always temper,
The seething, never-satiated pot.

Oh, blacksmith, with your tongs,
Work a horseshoe for my home
To ward the Devil, so he won't roam!

But then Old Nick appears,
Sneaks up, tapping gentle
To the blacksmith's side,
Hoping for a place to hide,
A place to reap-abide,
There to plot his crazied plans
And sow his grief among the lands.

Yet he is swiftly warded off
By the blacksmith's fiery coals,
Guardian of the gateway tight
To the descendents of our souls.

And we call the smith to kneal the rod
With the iron sword of Zion...

Oh, Zion, Zion! I hear your mountains' call!

...and we hear the singing, singing...

...That she may drink, dilly-dilly,
When she is dry...

151

A young woman, anxious for a husband,
Ties a garland of spring-rise flowers,
Wreathed from off the field-fenced rim
Of her life's ambition
To the limb of an old oak tree, prays,
Runs three times around the trunk,
Then lies and closes firm her eyes
To dream of her sweet future's ways,
As another lets her lover row
A sky-blue boat upon the flow
Of the Great Wicomico, her face full soft
And dofted by her fine lace veil.

Good morning, good morning, good morning to thee,
Now where are you going my pretty lady?
I'm going to travel to the banks of the sea
To see the waters gliding, hear the whip-poor-will sing.[59]

…While I dream of pirates, buccaneers,
Raiders of the Spanish Main,
Sailing o'er seas with seven names…

Hoe the beans, dilly-dilly,
And feed the hogs…

…And pay the ferryman well, my friend,
For he crosses the realm of souls
That plunge and leap
And will take his prey
For his nightly keep…

…As he waits, hawser tied to a tree
That overhangs the river's course,
Pet raven on his shoulder pad,
Swallowtails mad-flitting 'bout,
As Horseman steers his reluctant mount
Across the rough-laid boards
And helps recalcitrant servants hoard
Casks of cider, rum, jugs of beer,
Sacks of malt, oats and unmilled wheat,
Molasses, blocks of sea-dried salt
And claret for the tavern house,
Then unties the raft and pulls across,
Hand o'er hand o'er hand,
The rope that drapes the water close
And capes us from the downstream flow
Until, with strain and final heave,
He beaches at the leaving bow,
His raven squawks her betrayed wings,
And the swallowtails dip and sing

---

[59] Adapted from *The Nightingale*, author unknown, written in the late 17th century.

In coy joy at the ray-dripped day.

Meanwhile, within a child's imagining,
I delve deep into the Faerie Kingdom,
Land of elves and ghoulish goblins,
Friendly spirits too,
Where I don a daisy wreath,
So I may sit most dainty 'pon
A toadstool, like the harpies do,
And take the air on damsel wings,
Cast spells with wizened hazel wand
That fortunes my aspiring family,
And bring some richly handsome beau
To be my lucky paramour
And the surrogate for all those dreams
That can only through a husband's hand
Be realised in this manly land...

...of pirates, pirates everywhere...

...and of our knightly elvin lord...

But what of Balladeer,
Strumming with his lyre,
In moiety full resplendent,
Reds and greens and sunny blues,
Jingles upon his trihorned cap,
Bells upon his pointed toes,
Singing the stories of the years,
Chansons of rosy histories?
What tinted spectacles does he wear,
What glossy ibis of his recall,
What sanctimonies,
What cleansing memories,
To twist the past's dire fall
Into our gilded glories?

Oh, I heard a bird, dilly-dilly,
Sing in my ear,
Maids will be scarce, dilly-dilly,
The next New Year...

...round and round and round...

...Brer Rabbit in a spin...

...For superstition rules so many lives
At the edge of survival's door
Leads to hope in luck, that prayers work,
That misfortune is the Devil's deed,
Anyone charmed or out of turn
Is witch-bound, harmful, casting spells,

Felling children, changelings spurned
In place of healthy Christian babes
Within their sickly cots of fear –
The more extreme their seized beliefs,
The more extreme is their belief
In the extremity of enemies...

...Such as
Grace Sherwood, beauty,
Spunky, independent, unconforming,
Unmarried to the patriarchy,
Taken from the rank and musty jail
Of Princess Anne by Norfolk way,
Down Witch Duck Road to the edge
Of Lynnhaven's 'xpectant bay.
There, is she accused of shifting shape
Into a cat that's black and keyhole thin,
Of blighting crops, killing hogs,
Riding roughshod through the night
And summoning unholy storms,
So is ripped and stripped and poked
By provoked, suspicious jury women,
Who find extra teats and other marks
That prove her barking with the Devil,
Fecund to his earthly works.

So Grace is terror-braced,
Crossed thumbs to cold-numbed toes,
And rowed into the judging flow,
Thrown across the side and left to see
Whether she will drown or no,
Take the sins of lowland life
And cleanse them with her watered strife
And sacrifice – but lo,
Freeing her corpse in her passion,
She, and guilt, resurface
As the thunderous skies burst down upon
Her drenched and terrored watchers,
Who haste-enslot this harried wretch
Near eight more scapegoat years,
Until there comes forgot release
In a time less damnable in its fears.[60]

Round and round and round,
We cast the spell...

Oh Mama, things are not as they were meant to be...

Not too far away,
Down a close by dusty lane,

---

[60] Grace was known as "The Witch of Pungo"; she was 'tried' on July 10th 1706.

Two cockerels peek from out the bars
Of wooden cages, set for bill of sale
To a man who wants to train
Bloodstock for his night-time thrill...

While, at a crossroads upon the night
Of a full moon's doleful toll,
A widow woman dews some drops
Of toad's skin, nails and charms
To ward off goblins from the night
And familiars of the Devil's rings.

Oh, what elves and gnomes will spring
Succubus upon our night-time skin
Ere we sing a caring song
Of the world's fair liberty?

Oh, our eyes, our eyes,
As the wind doth blow...

Whip-poor-will, whip-poor-will –
The sound
Of wind-blowing ill...

...As, in the fields of Virginia's corn,
Women take the first scythed stalks
And make of them a dollied form
That will adorn the churches' doors,
While pumpkins, fruit and food galore
Are piled beneath the altared stores,
A harvest service of fecundity
In thanks for this year's sweet bounty –
And honey left, milk indeed,
For the harpies of our homebreed hearth.

Round and round and round,
We cast the spell,
Three-times-three-times-three,
Round and round and round...

Oh, the circle,
The circle unbound!

And nearby, a dozen freemen,
Shirtless backs to the wind,
Sweat in the mire of a ditch
To be cleared before the rains,
Knees confined by mud and leech,
Barefooted slide and grip,
As they dig the reeds and water grass
From the snake-infested slip.

I turn within the softened sounds
Of the veils, the veils as they fall...

...As
The round of hymns drift soft upon
The morning's ghost-rich haze
And our souls rise up to God Above
To raise the roof with praise,
In the hope of dusktide salutation
For their goodness, faith and trust,
In the inevitable justice of His rod
And inevitable heavenly repose.

...our bone and our switch...

Oh, raise up your eyes
To grasp once more the prize
Of your worthy dreams!

But...the softened sounds of rhythmic beat...

As a dog barks, another gnarls,
And nearby two more wildly snarl
Over a piece of rotting meat
Tossed for chainéd curs to eat.

And round and round and round
The veils of masked reality
Drift within the cask of spells
And the three wyrds raise the wind
As they dance about their well.

VI

Come, Jack and Jill, come to the well...
But don't tell the piggies
The farmer's in the dell...

In Fredericksburg, newly founded,
A courthouse, prison, scattered dwellings,
Public warehouse, wharf where sloops
Dock tobacco, corn and grain
From upper Rappahannock farms,
Mrs Livingstone, apothecary,
Sometime doctor, often gossip's friend,
Runs a coffee shop where gentlemen
Can enter, glance the latest news,
Talk all the politics they so chose,
Discuss Newton's Laws, Hume's
Latest theories of the mind,

Locke versus Hobbes, Aristotle,
Or play some game of chance,
Cards, dice, chequers, buy a bottle
Of rhennish wine, port or pottle,
In the rollicking smoke of laughter
And perfect male rapport.

"The word is young Birch, master,
Is baptising slaves again, and one
'A those darn Southside pastors
Wants to marry Negroes in his church.
Tcchh, it will not do."

"What's his thinking on't?"

"That 'tis wrong to exclude them from
The arms of the church."

"Can't the wardens hand him marching orders,
Send him packing back to England?"

"He's green. Unseasoned. Young.
More ideals in his head than reason.
Give his congregation a few months
To set him straight. Impart to him
How slaves will start to resent
Their natural station, slack, take
To reading the Bible, quoting
Psalms back to us in the field,
Treat us as equals under God,
Argue the rod,
Then expect to be addressed
As most natural Englishmen."

"'T'would be the thin end of the wedge."

"To sanctify Negro marriages in church
Would acknowledge their right to marry,
To protest unjust separation. 'T'would
Upset our whole system of trust."

"I have baptised my older house servants,
But that is all – to give them a pride,
Belonging, more resistance to flight,
Or to poison me and my tight family."

"And it does give them a certain authority,
Does it not –
Divides them from their fieldhand peers,
Makes them a lot more loyal,
Listeners to the crows,
Passing gossip on, our eyes and ears

In kitchen, garden and the rows."

"Well, there's something to be said
For marriage in that regard."

"Oh, there is? Pray, tell."

"Why sir, grant a man a family and
He will not run away, will not want
To ride the ignominy of the whip – for
Neither he nor I would wish
To break his parental pride."

"No, no, sir, for you will bring forth
The most resistant devil on this earth."

"Quite so, sirrah, quite so."

"'Tis why I let them truck
Their garden goods to market, for
The luck of favour and some reward, and
To provide
Succour to their homes,
As well as more reluctance to risk it all
On some petty misdemeanor."

"A reward that can be withdrawn."

"Quite so."

"I have a monthly market by the back gate
Where my agent sells felt hats,
Cloth, ribbons, shoes – any trinket
To tempt their simple minds,
In exchange for
The freshest eggs and chickens,
Vegetables and fish
My cook could ever find."

"Ah yes, the innocent Negro mind
Is well tasked when tending
His humble garden rows.
'Tis good to see the rascals
Mumbling happy as they sow."

"And to be so well invested by our noble gesture."

"Indeed, indeed,
Dilly-dilly, dilly-dilly…"

Willy-nilly, willy-nilly…

"Five-seventy! Five-eighty! Five-ninety!
I have five hundred and ninety
For this likely Negro fieldhand.
Who'll give me six? Six hundred?
Yes, I have six hundred.
Against you sir.
Do I hear six-ten? Six-ten? Yes, I have six-ten.
Six-twenty! Six-twenty. Against you again, sir.
No? Six-twenty then. Any more for this fine male?
Come now, a bargain at twice the price!"
He halts to glance around, make
Time for minds to volunteer...
But there are none, mere heads that shake.
"Last call at six-twenty, then. Last call."
The gavel taps the lectern with the clearest rap.
"Six-twenty to the man with a whip upon his lap."

Ugh! Ugh! Ugh! Ugh!

Little piggies sent to market
While their masters cry
Wee, wee, wee, all the way home...

...as pirates guard the seas...

In 1715, slaves can be bought, punished, sold, loaned, used as collateral, or willed
to another at an owner's whim. They now number 23,000, about 25% of the total
population of Virginia, but are not recognised as persons in the eyes of the law.
Such is the worry in some quarters at their growing numbers that more and more
regulations are passed to control their activities.

Oh, yes, little piggies...

The farmer's in the dell,
The farmer's in the dell...

...stealing all that's mine...

For my master seeks my spirit too,
Denies me writing, reading, Bible even,
Patrolling for our well-hushed arbours,
Our meetings and our praising houses,
Passes, permits, enhorsed militia,
Preachers scolding to servility,
Whipping secret opposition
From our tortured memory.

The farmer wants a dog,
The farmer wants a dog...

Yet some of us are domiciled,
Domesticated, baptised, sanitised

By the English tongue and
Three generations of breeding;
We are mulattoes, skilled oft'
In carpentry, smithing, driving
Coaches, our tiny plots thriving,
Selling to our masters' stores,
Married, earning, having children,
A fair set of coat and breeches, shoes,
And lie content
Within
The limits of our fear.

The dog wants a bone,
The dog wants a bone...

So we peer, in that self-shrugged weariness,
At The Horseman, caped in moonlit grey,
Branches wrapt about his shrouded head,
Black-masked eyes that vision leer,
Pulling heart-sinewed reins away
With a seer's numb-cast stare
Of tocome, tocome, tocome...

...As a minister of the Established faith,
Vestry appointed annually
To the county's only chapel,
Returns from stealing tithes,
Admonishing tardy wives,
And inspecting the work of his three slaves
Sowing winter wheat in his glebing field,
To pinch his servant cook, plump and young,
And fancy of the churchman's eye...

...While another's slave does wary circle
The sacred churchyard graves,
Lest the ghosts do cast him down
In his midnight soft forays.

Let's all pat the bone,
All pat the bone...

An anxious apothecary scales the stairs
Behind Mama and my sweet Eleanor,
To sit upon my sickness bed
And feel my sweat-blown brow,
Then asks my mother symptoms –
The flux, spasms, pains in my bowel,
Fits and highrise temperature.

The doctor asks some more, then reaches
Under careful covered sheet,
To rest a hand upon my stomach,

And feel-enquire what pangs,
Then unclips his bag of magic tricks,
Shelves of bottles and sulphur pastes,
Uncorks a potion, pours a spoon,
And makes me down the eeuchy brew
– A tincture of sassafras, snakeroot, rue –
Then tastes a yellowish juice to me,
Manna mixed with sennapod,
To deeply prod my bowels once more,
Nods a sedative to make me sleep,
Gentle words and a welcome smile
To relax me, mother and servant maid,
And persuade us of its gentle domicile.

Some weeks later, to reward recovery,
I enter with Papa a hardware store,
Rank with sawdust, dusty, dank,
Two men playing cards on a plank
Next the breeze-wisped window;
At the back, by the servants' door,
Two reticent women pass a boy
Their order, each item fetched by him,
Who then hands a chit for their master
And commits to serve one 'servant' more.

A low-class woman inspects calico,
A loaf of sugar, thread and needles,
So I step back as Papa checks
The shelves of tins and jars and sacks,
Then tacks further in and finds the bridles,
Inspects them, tugs, rejects,
Chooses one and sidles it to me,
– For my new piebald pony!
Next, he buys a rawhide whip,
For my mount, at first I think,
But 'tis too meaty to beat a horse,
Too many knots and twists,
And then I hear 'tis instead for use
By our overseer to impose his abuse.

Next, Papa hands a scribbled note
From Mama to the storeman
For some purple woven dimity,
Which he cuts and careful wraps;
Then Papa asks for six full rolls
Of osnaburg, fustian and duffel cloth
For our servants' winter wear,
Which they will hew and sew themselves,
Before he finger-wags Old Joseph in,
Waiting out the sunbeat door,
To bear the things upon his cart
And impart to our house by eventide.

161

In 1717, the first theatre in North America is built in Williamsburg. Elsewhere, plays are still performed in taverns, barns or the open air. A year later, the French found New Orleans.

Boys and girls come out to play,
The moon does shine as bright as day...

At the dawning day of rest,
A tiny group of household slaves,
Christianised,
Some freedmen too, amble in
Their shifty-stiffly Sunday best, to
Sit abench, or stand at back, then sup,
At last, upon the communion bread and cup.

But the masters let none others, lest
They rise to ideas above their station,
Seek to slack from out the fields
To pray, perform devotions,
Answer back with Christian wit
And refuse simple Sunday promotions...

...As, in every parish, clergymen,
Hired from Olde England's crowded borders,
Preach loyalty to their masters,
The hierarchy of Heaven, King,
And St Paul's call for them
To obey their owners' orders.

Sing, sing, sing,
Oh, sing for your sins, sing!

Come with a hoop, and come with a call,
Come with good will or not at all...

Thus those who, unbaptised,
Are left to pagan trail,
Raise up their tribal grails
To songs and dance and ribald hail
Of anti-master riffs and rhyme
Between their stiff-faced rows of shacks,
Secret rum, ill-fashioned smocks,
Bought by some
From private plots of squash and beans,
A corner crop of corn or wheat,
Ploughed and hoed and harvested
For a Sunday laboured treat, or
To sell to masters in the town.

Or come not at all, Jack and Jill,
To the call, the call, the call...

VII

Here we go round the mulberry bush,
In and out the windows,
Watching
Pirates, pirates, everywhere…

To the backwoods west and north,
A strange convergence
Of Governor Spotswood's greed,
Fake-silvered soil,
Immigrant miners and backwoods needs
See the planting of forty Germans
At Germanna on the Rapidan, beside a fort,
Soon followed by eighty more
Who found Germantown,
Clearing Spotswood's vast estates
But never finding silver,
Mining iron ore instead,
Until their indentured time is up
And they resettle Indian land,
Close-knit houses, palisaded,
Well armed, prepared and guarded,
To virtue-farm the well-leaed land.

Yet such ventures are scarce, for
It is not an equal land we find,
Nor liberty to acquire, unless
We have the pistoles[61] required to pay
Quitrent to aristocratic squires
Who corner titles to all property
And only rid of it at all, upon the highest bid.

And one of these is
'King' Carter,
Old man of Corotoman,
Sticky buyer of other's lives,
Most astute in colonial politics,
Whose English education,
Latin, theology,
Well-stocked library, position
As vestryman, church warden,
Burgess, Speaker, Treasurer,
Colonel of Militia,
Fails to prepare this immoraled man
For a healthy, caring life
– He is owner of so many slaves,
Rich beyond the graves of wealth,
Corrupt beyond the bounds of lust,
As he purchase-steals lands to the west

---

[61] A Spanish gold coin worth about 18 shillings, common in the colonies at this time.

In the thrust of law and agency,
Patents them at hugest gain, then
Retails them to backwoodsmen
Who can nary file his unfit price
For such well-thieved wonders of the wild.

Yes, Carter is one of the richest few,
With the Allens, Randolphs and Fitzhughs,
– And also Commissary Blair,
Ecclesiastic nightmare –
Who power the colonial center's pride,
Robbing by self-legaled, suckléd curse,
Flouncing a few well-favoured rides,
And amply fed from the public purse.

Oh Carter,
What have you left for your legacy,
But the shards of broken hands
That we must piece and knit together,
If we are to kneel and quiver-pray
For a society where, in mutuality,
We can gather and not fret
That common cause shivers individuality?

Or you, Fairfax, of
Absurd land grant, prosecution
Legally and forcibly
Of settlers from the Northern Neck
To the boundaries of the Alleghenies,
Pickpocket in ermine, absentee landlord
Of our suffering frontier?

Or you Edward Teach,
Bearded, woven black
With pistoled ribbons of ferocity,
Beaching the *QAR* in a Virgin sound
To rest from a Royal Navy bound
To otter out this vicious hunter
Of the Caribbean Seas…?

And then there is Spotswood,[62]
Old molehill trying to be a mountain,
Another land-grubbing thief,
With his ridiculous retinue
Of pimps and posers,
Cavaliers and drunks,
Hounds baying at the horn
Of their absurdist passing,
Confettiing golden horseshoes,
Moped in lace and servants,

---

[62] The Spotswood 'Expedition' occurred in 1716.

An orgy of champagne and claret,
Hoping to fleece the valleyed farms
That will pay and work this wealth.

And, while we dwell among the poor,
Let us not forget that scheming,
Backroom Robinson,[63] reeker of corruption,
Most powerful Virginian in the colony,
Who serves as Speaker, Treasurer,
A master of assembled process
To sumptuous feathered bellies
And silver-bribes their plied estates,
Augmenting his own politicking power
By lending others' public money
– With no intent to require repay –
To honey-licking friends,
Pigs at the trough
Of his doff-disturbing swill –
Until he final spills to disgrace
In a scandal that close unseats
The entirely riddled, wretched rot
Of Virginia's parasitic élite.

And thus does our Tidewater tyranny
Of sucking king and aristocracy
Under England's growing wealth,
More and more with stench repress,
Steal from those without,
Through tax and work and law,
And keep from us the merest smell,
Merest scent of liberty,
Lest it prove that social joining
Should grant us power to o'erturn
The rank-despiséd odours of the best.

The ranking propertied greed
Of these lapdog pets,
Is constricting what is freely given,
Controlling what is abundant
And nature-given all,
In order to impose a price
Upon the beauty of this world,
Growing at our enticed expense,
Forcing us thrice work our need,
In what has become a major theme
Of the somnambulant American Dream
– Enforced work at enforced price –
As we watch our schemes
Knocked down, knocked down, knocked down…

---

[63] Full name of this reprobate in stolen silk: John Robinson Jr.

On the vendue block or at the market stall…

Round and round the mulberry bush,
Have strength in your heart,
Dilly-dill,
To answer the call…

For there it now stands, complete,
Magnificent in
Its propositioned display,
Steeped in sanctified self-mystery
And a mystic-rounded splendour
That bounds the enfenced smell of horror
Within its sylvan-silent hills
– The terror-cotta columns
Of Tidewater's painted 'heritance,
White-hazed upon a valeside brow
And fear-drenched, juleped porch
That shimmers in the distant glow
Of shadow-hanging justice trees
And sudden-threatened punishments –
The portico of promise made
– But soon forgot –
Of Latin motto, crest and clock,
To impress with an entirety of time
And mockery of change.

The Georgian windows, shuttered from the sun,
Proportions of perfect reason
That o'erpress that more passioned plea
Of the torture-spiraled entrance steps
The chaliced hallway, polished, gleaming,
Light within such bribed magnificence
Of sideboards, mirrored sight,
The stairs of oak and hickory,
Carved to carry curving up
Ladies crinolined in dismal thoughts
Of their torpored gravity,
Splendoured majesty for all to see,
Burnished upon the knoll's caress
Of a babel built on you and me.

This is the way we wash our clothes
Wash our clothes, wash our clothes
This is the way we wash our clothes
So early Monday morning.

And in the whip-dread master's room
Libraried justice of enslavers past,
Greeks and Romans, citizened élites,
O'erhangs the arbitrariness of gloom,
And dusty tomes are visualised

To answer awkward points
On whether to beat to death or not,
How justified is hanging,
Or if 'tis best to merely maim
And let the grateful lesson sit
Within ape minds exampled
In mercy, gratitude and faith
And the Christian-palmed compassion
Of our tender-feathered hands.

Oh, how are dreams and our heart...

And yet I care nothing of this
As I sit upon my father's knee,
Tears upon my childish cheeks,
For he is to sell my Sally soon,
Maidservant whose youngest child
Has been my best companion
In plantation yard and barn,
Exploring orchard, fields and woods
Playing tag, dressing dolls,
Making house and muddy meals
From straw and stones and soil.

"Rest assured, my little one,
Though we must a dozen sell
To repay the debts of harvest,
I will keep our little Sarah
To be your endowéd maid,
Body to your female soul,
Though her mother must still depart,
And her father too, I fear –
So train her well and let her sleep
On a pallet out your room,
Teach her to dress you, keep you, clean,
Prepare your clothes and sew and darn,
Accompany you at every pose,
Iron for you, press your hair,
Tie your buttons and your bows."

And with sudden childlike delight
I thank Papa for his care bestowed
And the wonder man he brightly is
To love me and our servants so.

In 1722, two slave conspiracies are uncovered near Williamsburg. By now, its jails are full of slaves, indentured servants and manumitted blacks who have run foul of the system of propertied corruption.

...As Teach, ferocious beard of fire,
And his crew of the *Adventure*,
Is hunted up the inlets and the isles

Of Ocracoke's marsh-baited shore
Until he boards a naval sloop, enters
Into a counter-thrust of deathly cast, is
Stabbed and stabbed and stabbed again,
And his head manifest upon the mast.

This is the way we sweep the floor
Sweep the floor, sweep the floor
This is the way we sweep the floor
So early Thursday morning.

…round and round and round…

Tens of thousands slaves abound
Virginia's plantations now,
And some take swift flight to secret hollows
In Indian hills and mountains fasts,
Or the great and dismal lowland swamps,
Where they prepare a solitary lot,
From bountiers, backwoodsmen,
To village, crop and quietly trade,
For food and weapons, resentments hot,
Until one moonlit night they rise
And rouse upon a Piedmont house,
Free the slaves and kill the master's folk,
Pillage stores, steal his kitchenware,
Stoke themselves with musketry,
Then drive away the lowing cattle,
With horse-tied cart to rack-rattle the grain
Back to their harboured mountain domain
And out wait their doomed survival.

In the veil of Zion's calling…

With the failure of the Jacobin Rebellion of 1715, many Highland Scots and
Catholic Englishmen, especially Borderers, are transported to the colonies, where
they eventually settle in the backwoods. The counties of King George, Hanover,
and Spotsylvania are created as settlers move inland.

Meanwhile, slave provisions are also extended. In 1723, the Virginia Assembly
declares that "no Negro, Mulatto, or Indian shall presume to take upon him, act in
or exercise any office, ecclesiastic, civil or military." Blacks are forbidden to
serve as witnesses in court cases, to vote or carry weapons of any sort. They are
condemned to life-long servitude unless they have either been Christians in their
native land or freed men in a Christian country.

Round and round and round,
Three times three times three,
Mulberry bushes and
Pirates, pirates everywhere…

We still must bear their legacy!

VIII

Oh, how Zion calls, Mama! How Zion calls!

A family of raccoons, bark-nesting,
Rests from dunking frogs and worms
Within a hollowed swamp oak trunk
Above the black and green
Of Northwest's dark and marshy creek...

...As a family of slaves, escaped,
Flees rumours that he, father, will be
Sold upon the vendue that next day,
To pay expenses of a sickly herd
Of cripple-coughing cows...

...To hide, dilly-dill, within
The black gums, mattock sills
And maples of Landing's still
Hidden tides.

... blow, wind blow...

Meanwhile, another shoreline bandit
Gamboling close to where
Nansemond drifts into the Roads
Leaps upon a cricket frog,
Weed-covered, green rippling black,
Grips it tight within its claws,
Cracks its skull, then chews the head,
The body, arms and legs,
Licks her lips and shuffles off
Upon her head-down, snuffling way,
A ball of angry, gray-striped grit,
Scrambling through bald cypress swamp,
Then climbs a black gum to raid a nest
Of baby squirrels in their drey,
But the branch proves too weak
And shaking, shaken, nearly fallen,
She clambers chastened down,
An easier meal to find, perhaps,
At the barkened table mossed
Of the Mama of the Swamp.

We are coming, Mama, we are coming...!

Trying to find our Zion,
Hunkering within the oaks and maples
Of the Great Dismal's tannic pools...

Across a wide veil of water,
Beyond the fishing boats and sloops,

The piers and plantation fields,
And the early morning traders
Of a Williamsburg market day,
I drive with Mama and our kitchen Mary
Within the single-harness phaeton,
In new bonnet and heat-curled bangs,
To course upon the bare earth square
Of barterers, dealers, and their wares
In shiny blue and buckled shoes,
Careful not to trail my satined damask
In the waste of vegetable and horse.

We weave between the sitting women,
Crouching, weighing out with scales
That tip with stones for trailing weights,
Carrots, 'tatoes, beans and corn,
A boy with three live turtles borne
With legs tied in sturdy string,
A woman pinning chickens flustered
Upside down by naked legs,
Basket herbs pegged on her head,
A table stall along one wall,
With ash cakes, buns and dark molasses...

...As mid-morning wagons, wains
Laden with turpentine and corn
Trundle the lanes of York and Warwick...

...To Hampton, thriving shipyard port,
Exporting timber, tobacco, grain,
Foodstuffs, furs and leathered skins
For British goods and implements,
Equipping ships and fitting out
With chandlers lining piers and docks,
Ropemakers twisting long-strand hemp,
Sailors sewing canvass rings,
Slaves and servants hoisting barrels
Upon their swinging over-cranes,
Hogsheads waiting in the sun,
Imported wines and porcelain,
Trade with Afric', Carib, Englishman,
Slaves and sugar, furniture
For the houses springing up
In the profit-filling fields.

Meanwhile, the Sufferers sit and silent stare
Within the shade of the public square
Ready to repair, ready to repair –
The Sadness, weft of inner loss,
Of desperate, mindless life;
Maid Mary, weft of inward decay,
Destruction and self-born deceit;

And Fla'ed Weaver, weft of acceptance
Eternal, soft, suffering and self-sacrifice.

To take me, they their net prepared,
And had almost my soul ensnared;
But fell themselves, by just decree,
Into the pit they made for me.

But soft, for, handy upon
Norfolk's 'xpanding wealth,
Inns, hotels, warehouses by the wharves,
Tobacco, slaves and farming goods,
Down by its thriving, bustling stores
In some hidden cellar tight
With candles dimmed and watchmen set,
Is frenzied betting around a ring,
Cocks brought in, their feathers shown,
Made to peck and flare their eyes,
Glare their gaffs and glint of claw,
Then tossed upon the sawdust floor,
Roared to rooster rustle fright,
To rake and tear in blooded strike
And flash of feathered flailing lust,
A jumping, flustered jive of death,
As screaming rages urge around,
Odds and wagers constant found,
Till one sudden gives, exhausted falls,
The other stabbing cocksure down,
Upon the beaten, rigid form,
And the crowd utters no rounder sound
As bets are called, chits ripped up,
Beers and rum consumed and bought,
And all expectant bound in wait
Upon the next pair frenzy brought.

O God, my heart is fixed, 'tis bent,
Its thankful tribute to present;
And, with my heart, my voice I'll raise,
To thee, my God, in songs of praise.

In 1730, a slave conspiracy, spurred on by reports that all baptised slaves are to
be freed, is betrayed in Norfolk and five surrounding counties. After a 'trial', four

of the leaders are executed, the rest punished. In response, the lieutenant governor
demands the House pass new, stiff laws requiring all white males to join militia
patrols, especially during holidays and at other festivals and gatherings –such as
funerals – that tend to attract large numbers of slaves. The House resists, flexing
its independent muscles regularly now, but by 1737 it does pass legislation to
require, enforce and reward slave and servant patrols.

With a salt wind starch behind, I emerge
From Sheltered Onancock Creek,
Hold close to shallow spartina beds

And heron rookered marsh,
To seek a sail that gently frees
The Atlantic summer breeze,
Shimmerin the stiff Chesapeake
Towards distant Tangier Isle,
Fairie reflections dancing,
Entrancing the dawnrise leas.

In open water, the canvas billows
And my flat-lent sharpie, low of beam,
Willows to the leeward shore
As I steer and shear to Pungoteague,
Those potted, dabbing flats
Where I inspect my teeming traps.

Once upon the shallows, I reef the single sail,
Cruise-hail to my first of floats
And grasp the rope to anchor on
As I heave and pull aboat
The creel upon the culling board
With a gusty splash and scrape,
Gripe at none to pass the catch,
A latching starfish, drifting grass,
So bunk the rough intruder out,
Rebait with chunk of menhaden tail,
And trail the trap back in,
Then beckon a hundred strokes across
To a second well-yoked, tossing cage.

This time the hauling's well worth while,
Two jimmy blues[64] firmly set
Within the upper chamber net
Of the sturdy pot.
I reach in, avoid the claws,
Extract with pull and twist,
And wrist them to a wooden bucket,
Slam back the sealant top,
Rebait the hook and splash redrop
The cage cast quickly o'erside,
Then oar on to my aging third,
A peeler crawling up inside,
Move on again, and again,
Hauling on the wet-slimed ropes,
Checking traps for holes and hopes,
Mending, chucking in again,
Sorting male from smaller sook,
Softshells and the busters,
Some too small to look to keep,
Some clustered for the shedding float.

---

[64] A jimmy is a male blue crab; a sook is a female; a buster is a blue crab in an advanced stage of molting; and a peeler is a shedding crab.

Thus I spend most mornings
Upon my windswept bay,
Then turn and raise my leeward sail
And tack towards the creek,
Where I seek a lowtide hour or so
Poling through the muddened wallows,
Using dipnet scoop and drag
For those too slow to flee
My quick and flashing, stabbing eye
That has succoured life and family,
And gives me curled and hidden rest
From the traumas of a restless world...

...As, far above, the dart-halt,
Wing-fluttered start
Of a russet-gray sparrow hawk,
Predator upon the red-backed vole,
Harvest mouse and five-lined skink,
Zitter-dips, kestrel stits, zips,
And sudden shears away.

And our languorous days
Of fair and sultry weather sudden
Turn from southwestern mug
To off-ocean breeze and clarity,
Then the clouds and wind appear
And by nightfall engulf us all
In a tidal pour of such intensity
That rivers rise in muddied tumult
And boats are swiftly swept away,
The fields are drenched and overflown
And docks are burst asunder,
As the hurricane winds of wilding wrench
Crash and lash about our beds,
Trees ker-splash the lakelike ground
And we are left to cringe and flounder
In the belly of a flooded cellar...

...For the wyrd witches howl in cauldroned hate
Of Hecate's boiling, cauling spate
And the rainbird calls a hail
That threatens to tear by limb asunder
All that's wonder-known to all.

Raise up, Raise up! Is their call!

A colony of water willows,
Pink- and purple-spotted white
Flowers atop their billowed stems
Poking from the sandy banks
In low-flowed Piedmont rides
Of Pigg and Blackwater,

Peters Creek and Banister,
Suffer in the sudden spate
And mud-clogged slurries
Of topsoil washed away.

And the yellow-billed cuckoo, rain-crow,
Caller of the evening storm,
Satiated now, hunts
The dripping woodland edges
Feasting on caterpillars, grass-hidden
Beetles, 'hoppers, worms,
Then flies to her low-set nest
Within a Brunswick County vale,
To relieve the incubating male
Upon their four, fast-stirring eggs.

Then her ear is Carolina caught
By the reep-chereeps of lowly wrens,
Then by the squawking overhead
Of a passing flight of Brants, intent
On the valleyed Dan, once wild,
That is filled with plantations now,
Eastern princes grabbing tracts,
Backwoods dwellers toiling on,
Logging, stripping, cropping, on,
Elk, otters, muskrats gone,
And so o'erswells with silt-worn soil
Beneath its thunder-bursted banks
Of thick-veiled scrape and mire,
Stripping as it pulls and drapes
Its misting torrents down-swift down
Its sudden-spuméd way,
And the mud-scummed flashing stream,
Blighted brown and surging srowls
Its anger-hurried, manly spate
Hatecross the hallowed, hollowed vale
Of our growing blighted state.

Oh, Grace Sherwood, call off your spell,
Come with good will or not at all...!

Meanwhile, our family of escapees build
A crude shack of branches and ferns
Within the hidden banks
Of Elizabeth's Southern Branch,
Fish and set traps, catch
Terrapins, moccasins and ducks...

...As, in the wake of Cypress Creek
Predawn slaves make rendezvous
With a boatman, black and freed,
Who barters fabric, pipes and rum

For the produce of their tiny farms.

Come with a hoop, and come with a call...

And, at Kennons Landing on the James,
Taking advantage of the tempest swell,
Hogsheads of tobacco are unlade,
Piled, weighed and qualitied,
Warehoused and inspected,
Taxes paid,
Then reshipped for the export trade.

Meanwhile, at nearby Blanks Crossroads,
Where meet the Old Main Road
And Soanes Bridge lane,
A new tavern greets wagoners,
Drovers with beer and rum,
A licensed ordinary
With rooms and victuals,
Games of chance and merry cheer...

A halfpenny loaf will serve us all...

...As I pass a heard of cattle grazing,
Each adorned with flowered necks
About of sage and comfrey, lavender,
To ward the faeries off...

...And pass a cart of tobacco leaves,
Cured and dried,
Trundling to the barrel barn
To be coopered, prized and weighed,
Two slaves at work upon a fence,
Others mowing a late-fall field,
Scything the last of't season's hay...

...Then walk the open fields and tracks
Between tobacco barns and fences,
Across the rolling Piedmont hills
Of thrusting corn and grains,
Of wide-beamed smokers' leaves
Green and tall and spread,
To call upon the wind's sweet name
The questing game
Of our ancestors' silent-numbed refrain,
As the full moon adorns her rays
Upon the crow-boys' snoring ways
Sleeping the nights of sowing fields
To keep deer and rabbit, hare away...

...As, far distant from my view,
A King George congregation shunts

Into its class-enrankéd pews,
Wealthiest in the private front,
Always fashionably late,
Disrupting service, sermon, laity,
In cushioned gate and kneeling sacks,
Closest both to God and ceremony,
While the rest must cram into the back,
Slaves upon the upstairs balcony,
No hymns, no glory, no rousing spirit,
Only sin, morality and redemption fit
For these imposed and well-healed souls.

Church attendance is in decline,
Enthusiasm waning low,
And most enslaved refuse to go,
Flee, unless ordered so to do
By owners worried for their souls,
Tho' they keep their minds well out
The walls of such hypocrisy,
Despite their masters' preachers' pleas.

Oh, SelfSearch, where has Mama gone,
With that energy of female earth,
Proud and strong and free among
Her wisdom herbs and potions,
Her recipes of life and health –
Escaped to where she'll be alone,
Without persecuted strife and hate,
Without fear of labels, witching stools,
Deep within the dappled gums,
Where
Mere raccoons and desperate go.

Oh, they come, they come...

And, south along the new Fort Road
That pushes towards Christanna,
In Hicksford,[65] close by Meherrin,
A gang of backwoods-settled men,
Whiskeyed up and out for fun,
Take their well-trained, lathered dogs
To an amphitheatred river dell,
Mark out a makeshift battle ring,
Divide into a scratchline half
Enclosed within the roughest logs
Used to sit and shout upon,
The dogs paraded, more each time,
Then the bear chained through its nose,
The curs all rabid barking now,
Knowing what's to come,

---

[65] Now the town of Emporia.

Bets taken in the frenzied mood,
The first pair upon each other let,
Growling, ripping, snarling bites,
Wrenching, ripping flesh and ear,
Until one sudden whimpers loud,
Rolls over and pleads for its life
And the victor, bloody sered and jawed,
Is pulled rapid-ragged clear.

Ugh! Ugh! Ugh! Ugh!

Our eyes, rising to the prize – oh, Zion!

A halfpenny loaf will serve us all.
But when the loaf is gone, what will you do?
Those who would eat must work – 'tis true.

And, back in a hollow of North Landing's flow,
Mama of the Swamp still strays the lush
And cedared sides
Of a brackish stream to seek
The bulbous white of orbed doll's eyes,
Black spots, stark red stalks,
Markers of dense-coiled poison, baneberry,
To be crushed, nightshade blended, with
Jamestown weed, foxglove, boiled
Honey and crushed mint to fade the taste,
And sold to slaves who hive to her,
Desperate to avenge their lives
With the paste of vengeful murder…

IX

Oh, of foxes and of horns…

More and more settlers reach the foothills of the Blue Ridge, some erecting mills to harness the fast-flowing mountain streams, others logging timber, others clear-cutting and planting wheat and tobacco, or raising sheep and cattle.

A bearded overseer, aged and bronzed,
Knife and tobacco slab in hand,
Leans back upon the hidden porch
Of a haberdasher's cool-aired store
And laughs to a seated man within,
Then reads through a pile of posters,
Scans the *Richmond* ads, to acquaint
Himself with new slaves escaped,
Including two indentured men,
A woman and a child, fled
From Bowling Green in Caroline,

Seen headed west on stolen mares,
A mule, making camp by day,
Weaving in and out the shadowed lanes
Of the new moon's weak-bowed gaze,
Following, most like, the Anna
Or the Rapidan towards
The crest
Of the backwoods' Freedom Range.

And, with tobacco glut, fertile-gone,
O'erweening plantation power,
The seeping of our sparse-ridgéd lands,
Rising prices, illness, creeping poverty,
The family who once so proudly built
And strove to reap a harvest bounty,
Now sweep their fields and fence and barn,
Take their cattle, pigs, five children,
And drove them beyond our western counties,
Louisa, Goochland, Cumberland,
Over Appomattox, through
Prince Edward to
Bedford's mountain fringe,
Where they have distant kin,
The entire Piedmont filling now
With leap-frogging families
Or their children rebeginning,
In better shot at freedom's health
And sustenance of more normal wealth.

Oh, how the mountain calls
Our spirit to divine
The unity of all
That's worthily entwined!

…three times three times three…

Field rows labor to the songs
Of white backs bent below the sun,
Singing of Zion and Jordan's come
To their true dreams of life…

…While WindTeller explores on past, observing
How a dog slow sniffs the tether post
By a fly-troubled, kicking horse…

…And oh,
Linkum Tiddlum Tidy,
How do you go,
Prancing down the lanes
Of moonlit even glow?
How do you solemn dance,
In your avengeful, hooded mask
Of black, black hat and tails,

Black pants and bare-soiled feet
That prance to the suckly beat
Of the raven-feathered crests
Where the masters are all hidden
Deep within their nests?

Yum, yum, yummmm,
You, Linkum Tiddlum Tidy,
Will gobble all their cares.

"Hush, my baby, and don't ya tell
Dem white kids you plays wid no tale,
Less dey learns som'ting 'bout your Ma
An' she's done haul to da whippin' post
For your sweet'n tattling' mout'."

For I see the great tree spreading,
Limbs aboughed with leaf,
The darkened undershadows
Bringing into hazed relief
The form of Raven hanging,
The cauling shadows dangling
In the rite of Linkum Tidy
Rounding 'bout the solemn roots
That bubble with a troubled agony
Of tree-bound horns and flutes
That play the song of suffering
Dripping from this covert stage
And call the saints to witness
This pain-despiséd age.

Meanwhile, the two men,
One woman, child, all
Warned by Brer Rabbit's call,
Rest their horses by the edge
Of a stream, a mill's close churn,
To hide beneath a pass patrol
And eat some scraps of stealth.

But hush,
Let us silent watch, as
In the morn of mourning mists,
The tongue-tied, panting fox
Leaps and swims the fleeing creek
And hauls his wet-soaked, stinking fur
Upon the farthset bank,
To gasp and trot his breathless way
To tree or wall or hidden bolt,
As master craftsman, mason trained,
Instructs his handy laboured slaves
To haul upon the corbelled block
And raise it on a tackle rope

To set within the wooden frame
Of arched and bridging round.

Then rises the sound of baying hounds
That rapid 'pproach our ashlared work,
As men and mason make a stand
In case of snapping curs,
But then comes blare of calling horn,
As Master of the Hounds
And bounding beagles leap within
The scarce-drawn fox's flow,
Powerful paddle across the stream
And beat on with hardened hearts,
As hiding come the thund'ring riders,
Red coats, hats and whips,
To launch and splash and wade across
The peaceful misting reach.

Soon, we return to our work,
Raise high the well-sawn stone
And set it careful upon a strand
Of thinly mortared lime,
Then move with lever, rope and arm
To merge it tight between
The rising curves of well-arched lines
That measure firm the join.

We barely turn to see
A few hunting stragglers who dainty poise
The depth of water's rilting noise
The mill's new-built and tippling weir,
Then cautious peer and nip abide
The river's push and swirl,
As I square and set the stone
Within its place and pride.
Up above us, turning hard,
The creak and crindle of the wheel
Catches under-racing spurl
And turns the cranking room within,
To power half-a-dozen looms
That weave the linen-banded threads
Shuttled and combed by female hands,
Young children cleaning, tying too,
Strong men barrowing laden sacks
Of sun-bleached flaxen twine,
The beating rhythmic clanking sounds,
The wheel's ker-shum, ker-shum,
And all the while the hunter's horn
Chasing the poor fox down.

Have strength in your heart
And dream of freedom's day...

And WindOracle, teller of this tale,
Slips back upon his horse regaled,
Pulls the reins full round to watch
A servant woman, aged and black,
Washing bundle upon her back,
Shopping basket in brawny arms,
Return from riverside laundry steps
Past cattle driven through the towns...

...While nearby, on the Old Colonial Road,
At the Dumfries-Winchester crossfour,
A wagon bears fond backwoods goods
From Tacquet's Ford to beyond Red Store...[66]

...As two horsemen pass the Carolina Road,[67]
Once an Indian hunting path,
Now a well-armed road for rogues
Robbing frontier farms and
Prince William's plantation folks...

...And, close by,
Within a cramp of ghostly dust
That settles type and frame,
A printer pinches Ts and Rs,
Adds leading, tamps it down
To set each advert well-eyed straight,
Then sighs and rubs his inky orbs,
Tired of much-repeated lines,
Week by week by month by week,
That justify despairing hope
To catch the meekly banded prey
Who night abscond and fearful flee
Their cockerelled fighting pits
And seek to snake their ferret way
Down dark-lit streams and lanes
That ply the North Star's sway.[68]

Little piggies sent to market,
Jacks and Jills sent down the hill,
Dilly-dill, dilly-dill,
To their secret slaughter.

A parasitic wasp zones in upon
The rasping, zitting, zitting calls
Of a grasshopper in the even grass,

---

[66] The original name of Warrenton.

[67] Part of modern Route 15 follows the line of this ancient Indian trail, which was used extensively in the 1700s and 1800s to trade with Georgia and the Carolinas, as well as to take thousands of emigrants westwards.

[68] The *Virginia Gazette* was founded in 1736. It ran hundreds of adverts for slave sales and rewards for escapees.

Anonymous except in the need
Of wasp to plant its tiny seed
That will grow within the still-live form
And suck the juice from out the husk,
Until it bursts, full-flighted from
The theft-dry blight of carcassed dust,
While, high above a buzzard
Circle-soars, others call,
And a Swainson's hawk cuts down upon
A fall of grackle, as its talons bound
The doom-fixed bird to the ground.

The late summer harvest winds
And the ruffed grouse as it sings
Its chucking, choking call...

...oh, Zion...!

Ugh! Ugh! Ugh! Ugh! Ugh! Ugh!

Within a swampy Lancaster glade,
A cow strays, confused, alone
Lost within the forest swathe,
Slips and breaks a leg, lies prone,
And within two days, ten buzzards watch
From a nearby snag, beetle-wratched,
Squabbling, flashing black-frayed wings,
Establishing their feeding rank
As the cow's eyes starely, slowly glaze,
Upon a future hope-lit lost,
And a vagrant dog sniffs coy around
As breathing quits its harsh-boned flank.

And, not half a league away, an overseer
Clips the ear
Of a twice-escaper, soon recaught,
Whipped and with a big toe gone
From his last attempt.

Oh, Zion,
My body never mine,
My life another's bane,
My death without guilt
– No remorse at my pain,
Only anger at my spilt
And unpropertied gain.

So sing the coffin high, my friends,
Sing it high,
And run with it around the ring
Of faces from the blackened row
For Old Joseph may well let us know

If witchcraft caused his death or no
– And when the babaloawo casts him right,
Diviner, conjurer of Ifa, orishas' sprite,
With coffin laid at whip-scarred feet,
Whisking with his feathered bones,
Chanting from his lone-bleat depths,
Swinging, swaying, moaning wise,
Shrieking, bloating, groaning cries,
To spread-divine the year ahead,
Whether good crop, overseer, better bread,
Or if the year will be our last,
Bitter-fast, dropped and whipped.

And we dare not raise our eyes
Upon the distant prize...

Oh, drum to the drum-beat ring
Of the singing banjar's thrum
And wail to the fiddler's screeching cry
As we footfall dance the swirling hum
And spry our feet on hardened soil
Of our circled clap and coil,
And the dancer's twisting, rising fall
For another's dips and lifts,
As we call and clap and rift again,
And the hambone beats and tambour hits
And spoons ring bones with electric beats
In the story of our mythic hearts,
As we finally raise our eyes towards
Our dreamings of the prize!

A black-flecked whip,
Blood-dribbling ooze,
A weal-risen back
Still aching to the touch...

Ugh! Ugh! Ugh!

A branded chest,
Bubbled welt of loss of self,
Iron-scarred ankle, gash agape,
Memory of coffle chain,
Vagina tears and bruiséd thighs,
Purpled anger at white-bled rape.

Ugh! Ugh! Ugh! Ugh! Ugh! Ugh! Ugh! Ugh! Ugh! Ugh! Ugh!
Ugh! Ugh! Ugh! Ugh! Ugh! Ugh! Ugh! Ugh! Ugh! Ugh! Ugh!
Ugh! Ugh! Ugh! Ugh! Ugh! Ugh! Ugh! Ugh! Ugh! Ugh! Ugh!
Ugh! Ugh! Ugh! Ugh! Ugh! Ugh! Ugh! Ugh! Ugh! Ugh! Ugh!
Ugh! Ugh! Ugh! Ugh! Ugh! Ugh! Ugh! Ugh! Ugh! Ugh! Ugh!
Ugh! Ugh! Ugh! Ugh!

When will we be let to rest,

When will this hardship desist?
– For still
The lone dogs do snarl and snap,
The buzzards peck and stab and flap
Now 'round the well-plucked, sinewed bones
Of the ribcage, carcass-hollowed cow
Of what will be, will be.

…and of the little piggies…

Oh, let the truth of 'cestral fears
Ring down upon our opened ears
And never let them close again
Around our need for myth,
But let the mountain reign belief
Within our gleaming eye,
As symbol of our meaning
And clarity of our sigh!

X

Soft sings the whip-poor-will
Still dreaming of Zion's ancient hill,
Dilly-dill, dilly-dill…

Oh, the mountain!

Have strength in your heart,
And dream of freedom's day…

…three-times-three-times-three…

…days of preparation…

Oh! Zion's dream is calling – the mount, the mount!

With a well-trained will, I midnight rise,
Take my goodbyes of wife and son,
Forlorn backwoods farm,
For they are strong and it is
After the day and night of rapid
Reaping time, the threshing done,
Corn well-stored,
Not yet the reploughing moon,
Sowing months away,
And well before that season when
Days grow longer, stomachs shrink
And we await the meek abundance
Of newly brindled foods, born
Of splendour of the earth.

Oh, sing of the enspiralled earth,
And our eyes of ancient dawn!

I take little, a few ceremonial things,
No food, a little water, knife and flint and tin,
To stride the fields, the lanes, towards
My rise of Blue Ridge sanctity
And secret-bidden mystery,
The early autumn haze, the forming clouds
Above Old Rag Mountain speaking
To me as they welcome-peak,
Scraped bald on top, but otherwise
Draped in fall-line trees
Red and yellow, flaring bronze,
In the autumnal moonlit mist.

"Ken'kut-te-ma-um, Sah-ka-na-ga!
Oke-e'po-eshe!"[69]

I pass into
The realm of passing Indians,
Knowing this path well, for
I have a second wife within their camp,
A child,
And they always treat me mildly,
With welcome whoops and news
Of how my brothers' blood
Is faring now, backed and back
Against the mountain wall,
For I am half Powhatan, know
Their ways and ceremonies,
My wife caste quarter too,
Part mulatto,
Our scant cabin lost within
The backwoods' anonymous maze.

A marten pampers along my path
Towards me, stops,
Scents and scampers up a deadwood tree
– An omen of what is sure to be…

…For I'm marching to a Zion
That is not mine, but was
Ten thousand years another's,
And of another's God.

So I walk, I walk, I walk the paths
Of the old, old Indian ways, past
SelfSearch in her linger-stance
At the torment we impose

---

[69] A greeting to the spirit of the Blue Ridge.

185

Upon our sacred lands –
For she always marks and sees.

I pass an old mound, burial
Stones of those ancestors
Of my wife's forgotten tribe,
Long smitten by the pox,
Measles and distemper, hunted
For the bounty of their scalps,
Women, children, elderly.

I stop and pray a moonlit glade,
With unkempt grass, small trees
Now clinging to its sides,
And recall upon the biding breeze
My ancestors' fading memories.

"Oh, how the mountains call,
Great Ke'show-tse!
How the mountains call!
And how the mountains mock us,
Great Ke'show-tse,
How they mock us all!"

Then, as I rise the wooded slope,
I catch a glimpse within him passing,
A shade amongst the shadows,
Glancing to the glowing west.

'Hold to your dreams!'
He seems
To whisper on the wind.

I camp above the mound,
Beside The Callings' stream,
Sleep, and rise adawn again,
Pass SelfSearch in her tears,
Then raise my pace as near I rise,
Force-stride into the upward slant,
Push down, panting up an ancient path,
On thighs, arms to grab scant hold
And haul at saplings, branches, rocks
As the steepness heady mocks me,
To a summit false, then brief descend,
To find a winding stream,
Knowing I am dreamly watched
By those same secret-wending men
To whom this land once seemed their own,
Mother-wombed and hosted,
But now is sickly tombed and lost.

And sing, dreaming, I am tossed
Amidst the o'erwhelming cost...

I reach the summit's rise, and,
After cutting through the briared domain
Of poplars, oaks and hickories,
Some with girths of enormity,
Shading areas free to roam,
Clamber up the ragged, fallen, unsure rocks
That tumble o'er the mountain top,
Find a place that's sheltered well
From a wind that's howling now,
Lower my bundle, blanket, water cask,
And thank the spirits of the earth
For my task and my rebirth.

As sun sets and the stars appear
Within an orange-crimson-purple glow,
I trace my circle, set my pack well down,
Then stand, outstretched and pray
For my sacrifice these nights and days,
To protect two wives, my two ways –
As I reach up to my steel-edged knife,
Etch flesh away from bleeding arms,
Five, then ten, then twenty times,
And raise my pleading limbs towards
The Dog Star and dim Venus.

I sit upon the mountain top,
Seeing all,
And stare across Virginia's floral call
To breathe in, breathe in, breathe in,
Her wonder and her joy…!

…As a buzzard calls,
Glides across the closéd sky,
And a bear collisions through
The treeline underbrush, spies me,
Stops and muzzles,
Rears to scheme awhile,
Then shambles off as I, silent, still,
Return to my envisioned dream
And the buzzing of the flies.

On I sit, chanting, praying,
The moon soaked full now, white totally,
As she gives reign to ghouls and games
Of cross-barked wonder, the oaks
Laden with the faeries of her secret names.

Oh, how the mountains call,
With the mystery of the whip-poor-will…

All night,
I dance and chant and stare within

The flames of my desire;
I watch the world of cares creep close,
The world of all-is-free retreat
And, as I stand upon this top,
High above the coming storm,
The loss of way, of innocence,
Am free within the all
Of mountain, tree and sky,
And moon-blessed soft reply.

"Au-ma-umer!" I sing,
As the cerise dawn answer-rings
The peaceful mountains' call.

I have fasted three days now,
Only water let to drink,
And so my mind is feeling thin,
Warped within my body's whims
And dizzying me around, around,
Until resolution returns to me
And I stare upon the Milky Way,
The ebbing moon as she crests the east,
Pegasus, Leo, the Starry Plough,
And call upon them to help somehow
My quest for peace and tolerance.

Oh, they come, they come –
The memories of my parents' pain,
And their parents dreams and gains
Upon a century of hope's refrain.

I try to stay awake
All day, all night, all day,
Chanting, chanting,
Until the dream descends,
A vision that I follow,
Of horses, cattle, men
With spears and hunters,
Farmers with their hoes,
The lunar cusp,
People flying, up and up,
Then tumble-turning as they fall
Deep within a star-yearned well
And mingle in the liquid swell, there
As one, until
I note the conjoined flooded spell
Of water turned to blood.

Oh, who are the stealers of my dreams –
And, as they steal, revealing up to me
Their schemes as revelation's truth?

For the Sufferers are orating too,
With me around a cedar tree
High upon the mountain's pate,
Three-times-three-times-three,
Their oracle of well-cauldroned fate
Spinning deep from earth to call
The winds and tempt the spate
Of Virginia's twisted birth.

Oh, but for now
Listen to –
The Five Callers, curséd in their spell,
Tasked from bowels of stiffened myth,
Blackened rags, faces enmasked,
To ring the banshee gloaming middle
Of the banshee gloaming night,
The Brer band Tidy droning
Its mournsome groaning fright,
The Rabbit on the fence,
Ghost within the boughs,
The Horseman host, densely veiled,
In this passage rite from life,
Mama Earth within the well
That darkly spells all hope of birth,
And the Conjurer, peddler of all
That's of a forewarned worth,
Reborn, recalled, reborn, recalled, reborn…

…three-times-three-times-three…

…while oh, the prize, the prize!

…And the MindWeavers, nine Wefts all,
Dwell within a rippledeep caverned wisp
And wish upon the bondsman's wish,
As oakcrow, harbinger, windtell all
Within the mists of cavedwell fall,
Weaving ancestors' storied pleas
Across our minds for all to see.

How the Sufferers toil and how the cauldron boils!

Our eyes cannot rise to the prize!

Yet, in the cool of my third morning,
Chaliced visions coming fast
Of staff and broom and thimbled thread
Woven by a needle's dread,
I wake and take
Wooded undergrowth, scattered, dead,
And build up my fire to centre by,
Not for warmth, but ceremony

Within my circle's heart,
Then stand and begin to uparmed chant,
To lope with method 'round about
And focus on my hope of truth
Within my depth of soul.

Raise up, raise up thine eyes!

Oh, how the mountains call!

I stand and stare within the flames,
Arms outstretched again, transfixed
Upon their darting game, observe
The visions that emerge within
And dedicate my sacrifice
To the joint union that is humanity,
The visions coming rapid now,
Of soft ancestral destiny.

Oh, how rings the mountain's glee
To hear the whip-poor-will sing,
"When, oh when, will we be free?"

XI

On to Zion – The beautiful city of God!

The 1720s explosion in Virginia's population – both black and white – goes on as
the Highlands of Scotland and farms of Ireland are cleared and enclosure acts
throw thousands of English families off their land. These immigrants bring with
them a deep resentment of aristocracy and king. They come, not as individuals,
but as families, groups and clans, united in bitterness and determined hope, and
head for the backwoods…

Oh, how the mountains call,
How the blacksmith's hammer rings
And how the whip-poor-will doth sing
To catch the rising souls of all!

A group of wagoned settlers
Discovers
A narrow cut twixt stream and cliff
That winds and drifts to Massanutten's
Hidden, secret vale, pegs out
Their secret-squatted rights to land
And band to joint provide
Houses, barns, and for their prayers,
A chapel
Within the mountain's encloséd sides.

In 1727, the first official European settler, Adam Mueller, moves into the Shenandoah Valley, soon followed by others. That same year, 50,000 acres on the Cowpasture, Calfpasture and Bullpasture rivers are granted to five Scotsmen. Settlement begins there five years later.

> Jost Hite and sixteen families
> Carve and blaze
> Their pioneering way
> From York in Pennsylvania
> Over the swelling Potomac,
> As they follow the track of Indian wars,
> But find now peace and doffed acceptance
> To settle Opequon's soft shores.
>
> *We're marching to Zion!*
> *The beautiful city of God.*
>
> Then come the Irish and the Scots,
> Ulstermen and Borderers,
> People born of backwoods wars,
> Free of servility to English lords
> – Rather full of an independent state,
> Cattle stealing, drink and knives,
> And ancestral family feuds –
> Folk who loath the English fops
> As much as woodland Indians,
> Demand freedom from each pore
> And will surrender neither gun nor still,
> Nor grain of tax without due will,
> Refuse to pay Tidewater frills,
> And lay determined art and crop
> Of Zion-brewed rebellion.

There follows a flood of English, Dutch, Germans and Scots-Irish into the northern valley from Pennsylvania, Maryland and Virginia. They steadily make their way down either side of Massanutten Mountain, following the two forks of the Shenandoah River. Generally, they have to buy or rent this God-given land from rich, gentrified speculators – including George Washington and George Mason – who make a killing by interposing themselves between the settlers and the Divine through such organisations as the Ohio Land Company and the Loyal Land Company.

Lord Fairfax, huge landowner, arrives in 1738 to claim his six million acres and turn many pioneers into tenant farmers, forcing them to pay sizeable quitrents. Unfortunately, his greed inspires many to move on and stifles the development of the northern valley.

> *We're marching to Zion!*
> *The beautiful city of God,*
> *Freeing ourselves from Mammon*
> *And the culture of our greed.*[70]

---

[70] *We're Marching to Zion*, by Isaac Watts, 1707 (with some adaptation).

Across the wild state, windblown,
Brought upon a rougher tide,
Germans rapidly descend,
Hunker-fleeing war,
Taxation, persecution,
Amish, Mennonite, Pietist, Dunker,
Across the ocean, through the Quaker State,
South to seek the green-swathed vales
Of Potomac and the Shenando',
To settle Hamburg, Strasburg, Maurertown
Along the shining North Fork hills,
Bringing cattle, horses, well-honed skills,
Neat-tended farms, prosperity and will
To fight the Indian – peaceful now,
Accepting of their brethren –
And to reject
Both speculating eastern man
And strong-intentioned government.

They possess a homefire culture
Of warming stoves and ovens,
Rye bread, kraut and pfanhass,
Stoneware brightly glazed,
Woven church and family,
Frugal diet, furnishings and wear,
Tending care of animals and fences,
Diligent, sincere and pure,
A healthy despite of uncured slavery
And disgust at old-hewn aristocracy
– A separate people with separate values
Much closer to the ways of today –
A backwoods-vanguard moral pot
That brews and clots the hearty stew
Of true ideal and memory.

Shenandoah Valley settlement develops at leap-frog speed. In 1736, nearly 120,000 acres are patented on the upper South Fork of the Shenandoah. Three years later, over 90,000 acres are granted along the upper James River watershed. Winchester is founded in 1744, Staunton in 1748, Strasburg and Woodstock in 1761. By the mid-1750s, three counties have been established west of the Blue Ridge – Hampshire, Frederick and Augusta, the last of which comprises the whole southern end of the valley (and beyond!)

In 1742, a band of Indians (perhaps Iroquois) raid the valley and attack some settlers close to where the Maury joins the James River. But this is a small, isolated incident.

We're marching to Zion,
Beautiful, beautiful Zion;
We're marching upward to Zion
The beautiful city of God.

A young George Washington,

Land-grant scout and surveyor
Carves his art high upon the wall
Of Natural Bridge's arching splendour,
Installing his wonder for eternity,
And making me ponder for my straying part
What he would have done with a can to spray.

The south of the valley begins to open up now, with settlers moving in from North Carolina up the New, Clinch and Holston rivers. In 1746, Colonel James Patton is granted over 100,000 acres to settle the southern end of the valley. As a merchant, Patton brings many indentured servants on his ships to work the new settlements.

I survey my fields of wheat,
Two acres of tobacco, garden beans,
Herbs, tomatoes, peas,
Chickens, pigs at the trough,
And turn to inspect the golden grain,
Pull an ear, rub hard my palms,
Put them to my nose to smell,
And pronounce the crop well done.

So that day, with borrowed scythes,
Expectant glee, relief upon our minds,
My wife heavy with our first,
We begin to rhythmic hew
The bending stalks from dusty roots,
To bundle into sheaves, then musty stacks,
To carry back to our cattle barn,
There to thresh and sacking store,
Thirty acres, thirty days, no more,
Some delays because of rain,
Some kept for next year's feeding seed,
Half then taken to the store,
Half laden to the mill,
With bare enough for all our need
Through next year's harvest fall.

In 1749, land at Sapling Grove (Bristol) is patented. The next year, Dr. Thomas Walker patents land at Wolf's Hill (Abingdon), makes his way to and names the Cumberland Gap, and founds a settlement at Dunkard Bottom on the New River.[71] The first Virginia fort west of the New River is built there about 1756, as are the first store and first mill. That same year, lead is discovered a little to the west.

With this rising valley population,
Farming beef and pigs and sheep,
But their markets on the distant coast,
Too far for simple trade,

---

[71] Dunkard Bottom was on the old Wilderness Road (now Route 11 – Lee Highway), close to modern Radford. The New River was reached by European explorers in 1671 (possibly as early as 1654) and originally named Woods River. In 1748, Stephen Holstein gave his name to the Holston River and its valley.

Farmers take up an ancient style
Of cattle drives to market towns,
Assembling stock in thriving herds
To corral them down the valley lands
With mules and truck and ready hands,
Packhorse brandy, whisky-laden,
Corn and wares for seaboard marts,
Striding darts of mingled streams
To soft-jingled rhythms of gentle dreams
And the leather swifting drover's switch,
As the lowing lead their mowing way
Down Massanutten's high-rise sides
To cross the Shenandoah's slow-limbed bends
And on to Winchester's austere pens,
Where they are sold a foretold journey
To Baltimore and Philadelphia,
Grazing the gentle-graded pastures
Of autumned Piedmont grasses.

And two rooks dip-dive and nasal call
Across the mountain vales
Their joy at the day and each other's
Prevailing royal company…

…As our sons and daughters venture woods
To collect wild autumn berries, fruit
To mix with spring-boiled syrup
Coaxed from sugared maple trees…

…While onions, carrots, cucumbers
Are pickled up in vinegar,
Salt muled from the south and east,
Along with jars and jugs, cast iron pots
To preserve for us the cold and cropless months…

…And, upon our rivered boats,
Rough pirogues,
Sometimes doubled, boarded, we pole
The rapids of Potomac, James and Shenando'
To meet upon the Warriors' Path, now
A lively trading road,
Ferries hasty built, past ordinaries,
Store houses, barns, as small towns
Arise at Bick Lick and at Pattonsburg.[72]

Meanwhile, further south, past vale and dale,
Crisscrossed rill and hill,
New settlers court the sacred wallow
Of giant tree and deer-scared hollow
Of buffalo hoof and forest bear

---

[72] Pattonsburg became Buchanan; Big Lick became Roanoke.

That can alone be sylvan set
Within the swift-curled river's call
And the meadow grass's tall allure,
To there endeavour a frontier grow,
Flow forward, pioneer, and cure
The allure of southwest Virgin' sward,
Draper's Meadow's[73] low-set land
For other hands to careful follow
Upon the ancient Warrior Trail
And press our borders on.

We patient build our bowers
Of Presbyterian prayer, Lutheran,
Mennonite and Moravian
Within the poplars and oaks,
The stars upon our sacred galaxy…

…For *this* is our freedom, *this* our dream,
Not of escalating wealth, of opulence,
Of commercial gain, but of quiet peace,
Community and contentment, free
Of governor, soldier, tax or sheriff,
To take responsibility unto ourselves
Completely, not have others do
Our social duty and our deeds, but
Harken to belief that's free and a creed
Of mutual love, respect and caring need.

In 1738, Governor Gooch allows freedom of religious expression in the valley to encourage rapid settlement of the backwoods against increasing threats from the French in the Ohio Valley.

Oh, how the mountains call,
Zion to reborn Israelites,
Symbol of our comfort and our home.

The hill of Zion yields
A thousand sacred sweets
Before we reach the heav'nly fields,
Before we reach the heav'nly fields,
Or walk the golden streets.

There can be no talk of
Ministers, ordained or frocked
For us backwoods valley folk,
To preach to us, far-reached, disperséd flock.

And He built his sanctuary like high palaces,
Like the earth which He hath established for ever.[74]

---

[73] Draper's Meadow was just northeast of the New River, near present-day Blacksburg. An isolated settlement, it was later wiped out by an Indian attack.

As if in call to growing need,
In response to dying faith,
And disgust with preachers hocked in pay
To the sway of wealthy plantation kin,
A new movement begins within the land,
Born strong within New England's states,
That drifts upon the frontier lands,
From salvation, faith and God's intent
In how it is our fearing hands
That prove our pre-ordained selection
For a place within the Kingdom of the Lord
Through born-again conversion,
Immersion in His graceful spirit
And through His mercied merit may
Transform our lives to deeds of fame,
Exulting His name in all we say and do.

So Whitefield comes from England,
Preacher to the masses, also slaves,
Criticising established ways
That ignore our spirits' needs;
With Jonathan Edwards to the north,
Wesley sage in Georgia's parts,
Later Samuel Davies, many more,
They bring their up-revivaled message
To the backwoods door and forest poor,
To the hollered mountain glades,
A chorus of heaven-raising, enjointed praising
That all is all by God's sweet grace,
That Christ is well within us all,
A union of our souls with His,
Participation in the Soul Divine,
As God dwells in our hearts sublime
And imparts His holy, secret works
Through thy good deeds and mine.

Be Thou, O God, exalted high,
And as Thy glory fills the sky,
So let it be on earth displayed,
'Til Thou art here as there obeyed.[75]

And so, in great awakening, spiritual reburst,
Presbyterians, Baptists, Methodists
Go from farm to farm, great backwoods camps,
Proclaiming on each hillock of each county seat,
Uniting the colonies, hymning some new identity,
Raising passioned churches to the Lord,
And refinding righteousness of spirit

---

[74] Psalm 78: Verse 69

[75] *Be Thou, O God, Exalted High* was a popular hymn of the time; by Nahum Tate and Nicholas Brady.

In this time of sinking hardship
And a losing battle for the comfort life
That is heralded, but seldom seen.

We're marching to Zion,
Beautiful, beautiful Zion;
We're marching upward to Zion
The beautiful city of God.

And, for the first, most worried time,
Our rulers lose sublime control
To dictate thoughts and politics, enclosed mores
From chattelled pulpits, cattled priests,
As suddenly the poor unite
Freely from their masters' eye,
To join and secret harbour moan
In common plight, and as one plan
How spirit's freedom will surely lead
To some great liberty of needing men.

Oh, how Thy mountains call!

XII

During the 1750s, the French press their Indian allies to raid the English colonies.
The British and Americans are, meanwhile, encouraging their own Indian allies
to attack the French. Competition between the two European powers is growing
on a global scale, but its first shot is fired in North America.

The Horseman and the hare,
Piping calls to the peddling man,
Ride two abreast and gallop down the wind
Of Shenandoah's upland hills,
Its Highland dales and windblown slopes,
Across rivers Clinch and New and Holston,
To survey the undulating sundewed farms
Of Scots and Irish, unflinching Germans,
Who now flood the frontier woods...

...For a new vision is being built, surreptitiously,
Un-Virginian,
Of freedom of religion, thought, ability,
From court and jail and tax and tithe,
And from all distant government –
A brief-reigned valley Eden where
The Indian is well-treated, trade
Is honourable and peaceful,
No great owners, barely any slaves,
No courts nor army, church,
But pure equality of community,

Where each has a musket and a trade
And jointly hoes his right prosperity
Without a higher polity imposed.

Oh,
Bring the plough and carve the land
'Tween deadened, bark-ringed trees
And haul the autumn's timbered logs
To our cabins and our stout-lagged barns,
Beans and squash all gathered in,
Hogs dressed and hung and smoked,
In this the time of cloak and drawing in,
And nightly cold descent.

But, ere we can enjoy our breath,
We are seasoned down upon a war
That will yet another reason be
Why old England's throttle is belayed,
As empires toil while Europe roils
O'er Americ's eastern soil,[76]
Using hapless, angered Indians
As their carnage-arrowed foil,
The French of Canada slipping south
Through Ohio and the Mississip',
The English regrouping from the east,
Seeking Kentucky and the Tennessee,
Both reaping native 'lliances,
Arming and stress-fomenting
Seneca, Mohawk, fiercesome Shawnee,
Who, in desperate hope to return
Some of their tribal sylvan lands,
Burn our new Virginia frontier
Upon a pyre of terrored fear.

During and after the war, Shawnees repeatedly raid the Shenandoah Valley from
north of Massanutten to the New River. In 1757, they attack the Renick
settlement in the central valley.[77] In 1764, they attack a settlement west of
Staunton and, two years later, they attack settlers close to Woodstock. From
1760-1, war also breaks out with the Cherokees to the south and they raid the
valley several times.

A system of forts has been erected along the frontier, but the incompetence of the
British officers results in disaster.

The English, arrogant, haughty, effete,
In disdain send wet-eared Washington
To Fort Necessity and Duquesne defeat,
Braddock to a humbled forest squeal,
Then bumble at George and Fort Oswego,
Reeling in humiliation and retreat.

---

[76] The French and Indian War, part of a wider global conflict, lasted from 1754 to 1763.
[77] About twelve miles north of present-day Buchanan.

The grass has browned and fallen,
The buds are well sucked in,
The frosts have come to warn us
Of the winter's grim return,
And the fogs within the valley
Tell of a vindictive wind that reaps
Roar and beats upon us
In banks of langoured sweep.

Stir the kettle gentle, Mama,
Of mast and mash and river,
Stir it firm and pour the wort
Within the heavy-potted keeler,
Add hops and maple sugar, let it blend,
Then sprinkle yeast and cover well,
Stirring thrice with broomstraw wand
To quicken still a fermenting spell
That forewarns of boding hand...

For the bones have set within the brew
And hope for sunset pining,
As we reject the thin-beered air
And find the willow whining
For the swelter-smouldered days
When smoke and sweat were twining
And the breath of May was covered o'er
With the sheen of August haze
And the great tree was ever spreading,
– But keep away the white hare's gaze.

Last night I dreamt of venomed snakes,
Viperous coiled within
And this morning saw a spider black
Cast a spell upon its spin, for
There is a weirdness in the churl-turned air
That lurks upon the charméd breeze,
A wind that curls the ground-drenched leaves
Must-crumpled, grindled brown,
And ripples to the river's tide
As siren-menace to a fulsome ride
That lingers in the deep-valed fog
And it tolls its misty scarum bell
Within the veiled alarum's pride.

So brew the potion bubble folding,
Stir and sweep and pull the wold
And heat it till it's trouble boiled
Upon the thrice-burned cauldron fire,
Add poppet, peck and wiry pin,
Drape sage upon the doorways
To stop Old Nick from tumbling in,
And ward away the Shawnee dance

Now hostile war has sly begun
And French have forced retreat
To leave our mountain passes
For their unchallenged gain.

Oh, Mother of the Forest, protect us!

I halt my stirring beer to fearful glance
At trees down-dressed for winter's night,
A lay of deep-gray cloud about,
Stratus plain upon the valley's plight;
Then hear the cry of hoop and wail
And panicked eyes that see the veil
Of nothing but the rapid fall
Of tearful want-to-be,
The sound of shot, a distant call,
And terrored massacre of despair
That spells the end of innocence
And terminal digress of all.

…As the crow craaks its call
And the corn snake slips its slide away…

But then the British get their act together.

Finally, the British set a three-met attack
On Louisbourg, Carillon and Frontenac,
Win Nova Scotia and fair Ontario,
Revenge Fort Duquesne defeat
And englow new-built Pitt
As fortress guard to great Ohio,
Are victorious at Ticonderoga,
Crown Point, Niagara,
The Heights of Abraham,
Then mop up Montreal and Fort Detroit,
Suppress Pontiac in desperate stand,
To finally treat at Paris,
With Spanish now at hand,
For Florida, Canada and Kentucky,
In a pax that tucks the west
Into the British span, opens the Ohio,
Despite a cross-Allegheny ban,
And leaves a compact, well-armed force
To endorse the more resented 'pact
Of Stamp and Sugar Acts.

…round and round and round…

And then I see it, through the suffering
Of my bloodscared arms, the
Hunger of my body cramps,
The waywardness of mental eye,

The vision of tocome,
And I cry, I cry, I cry....

As...

...The waning moon crests distant pines,
Shining on the valleyed chines
Of hemlocks, maples, birch,
And a last valley beaver swits its tail
To back-feet paddle awkward down
A narrow, pre-dug channel,
Leafy branch of sapling willow
Within its growling teeth,
Submerges, and
Pushes firm within the mud
Its autumn-harvest bough
As the Four Enchanters now avow
– Ol' Hick, the Weft of Poetry,
Dylan born of prophecy,
Morgan Diviner of enchantment,
Midwife to the world,
And then the GreenWood, Weft
Of a fecundity that nature grants –
Do dance the rites of ancient times
And sing those songs of yesterday
That kept the harmony of the world.

Even with the end of the French and Indian War in 1763, the Indians are still a problem for settlers in the Shenandoah and isolated raids by small bands continue intermittently until 1781. But the Valley of Virginia is now firmly in the grip of its settlers. The mountain has been vanquished.

Now that we have conquered Zion,
Ploughed it under, made it fit
Our image of ourselves, to sit
Upon the bones of a murdered nation,
What have we left? The soil?
– Aye, for a while, ere our toil washes
Into the screams of our valley streams
And leaves us atop a ragged bald
Wondering where our hopes have gone
And gropping desperate, searching for
Another dream to scald our visions on.

Book IV

The Journey to Self:
Revolution and a New Nation, 1764–1800

I

Cotton-clinging clouds, mist drenched,
Huddle the hazéd mountainsides,
Comfort-wisping the showered trees
With such tingled touches of filigree
As makes us
Grey-clad, ghostly veils, mizzle-torn
Of vapoured convolutions, involuted,
Hang-hugging upon a fingered breeze
That lingers in a silent-tolling morn
Of bells that do not sing…

…And of a breeze, a silent-docketed breeze,
Soft-swirling
Within the sanctified motions of our breath…

To be free is to have control;
A free life is a life lived as one wants,
Not as one is told.

Ach,
Our industry is stifled, our merchantmen
Refused international trade,
And we are forced to pay high prices
For all goods English made;
Freedom, if anything, is economic,
Is the right to control our jobs,
Our pockets and our employ.

No, freedom is an illusion;
We are English-conditioned and phrased
By aristocratic society, family, mores,
To act contrary to our desire,
Derided, looked askance upon,
Forced to respect our legal rights, but
Denied the pride of this expectant land,
New-freed from the hands of French and Indian.

That may be our plight, but
We are each endowed with natural rights
To life and liberty, property,
Our king's quick jurisdiction
Granted by us in contract and consent,
Without which it becomes a tyrannic hell,
And we are, by natural justice, fit to rebel.

How can we thrive at all as men
When we are so rigourously refused
The means to mend our lives?
Surely, such relationships are not set,
But fret within a constant flux,
And we can only clasp our freedom
By grasping authority o'er our souls,
Taxed without representation
And legislated from across the sea,
Parolled in every whimper of existence:
Society, government and infant industry.

No. Freedom mellow lies
In renaissance for our lives, enjoint
In new-shared response to all,
And our single right to decisions
As we comingle with our fellows,
Are not told,
And do not have imposed
Others' self-emboldened needs
Upon our rack-fatigued, emburdened backs.

By the Proclamation of 1763, the British Government outlines a strict policy
towards the Indian lands of Kentucky, Tennessee and the Ohio, formally granting
them to Canada and forbidding settlers from the thirteen American colonies to
venture there. Also, the Indian trade is brought firmly under British control and
traders must now be licensed. This antagonises property speculators,
frontiersmen, emigrants and farmed-out families hoping to move into the newly-
won French lands, especially as the new restrictions are to be rigourously
enforced by a large body of troops permanently stationed in, and paid by, the
colonies.

Far, soft-shrouded ridges,
Wet-wisped strands
Hanging from dulcet-swifted drifts
Sink upon the mountaintops,
Wist-lifted, spowled, siffle-savoured
Swists of scurried tuft,
Sinuous drifting,
Ragged rain, half-hearted, teasing...

Within the evening mist, we turn
To watch a company of dragoons
Canter past, feathered crests, swords
And spurs jangling in the sunset lines

And rush back to our border farms,
Hide money, grain and hams,
Wait for the knocks, the orders
To billet a hundred in our sanctuaries,
Feed the oafs, listen to their coarseset banter,
Fend them off our dearest daughters,
Keep upset sons from mockery,
And watch as chickens, eggs,
Crockery, possibly our cows and sows,
Are stolen, broken and consumed
In a week or month or day
Of doomed and powerless thievery.

Then the Sugar Act is endorsed,
A tax to pay those reprobates,
A duty on molasses, rigidly enforced,
On wines and sugar, coffee and indigo,
Slowing our colonial trade, merchantmen
Already clamped by mercantile
Restrictions on our laden ships
And on our hampered industry…

So we go on hoeing, waiting
For the day...

Oh, mound and hoe, gals, mound and hoe,
Scrape 'n' high the stem-thronged soil
And toil away the suckered throng,
So the leaves droop green and long.

Pick the grubs, gals, pick the grubs,
Pluck them beetles, worms 'n bugs,
Catch for signs of curling rot,
Careful as you watch'em squirm.

Nip the buds, boys, nip the buds,
Gentle hold the jointing leaf,
Let them spread and thrive,
Broad and furred, with pointed reef.

Slash the stalks, gals, slash the stalks,
Break them over smartly now,
Drape them, keep them hale and flat,
Shape them slow upon the cart.

Bind the hands, boys, bind the hands,
Hang 'em over sawdust fumes
Into the air-blown drying loft,
And inspect the leaves, so brittle- soft.

Get the staves, gals, get the staves,
Prise the hands until they squeak,

Press and seal the barrels tight,
And blaze them with our sterile brand.

Store the hogs, boys, store the hogs,
Await the batteaux pole and dock,
Then roll 'em to the wharf-rocked side,
Hard by the river's swifting glide.

Serve ye not King nor Mammon,
But only The One True God;
Serve ye not Wealth nor Property,
Nor any Lord but He
Who Resides in His Heavenly abode;
Serve not Priest nor Pastor,
Not Judge nor Governor,
But only the Lord in His High Kingdom;
By thy own Hand and through thine own Soul
Directly as He deems, thus obey;
Serve only the Commandments
He hath set down unto Eternity.

Oh, yea, hear my Prophecy,
For we shall not rest in peace until
We hath o'erthrown all Laws and Governances
Bearing Satan's Union Flag!

I harness my old mule once more,
Sixteen pulling years, fading fast,
And lead our creaking, jointed bones
To plough the upper, barren field
Of soilless clay and sand.

I trudge the lane and linger wait
At the gate
That guards our broken railing fence,
Rake the dust between my fingers,
Roll it on my thumb, feel no fibre,
No dark and crumbling fertile matter
To toil my independent crop
Upon this rust-exhausted soil
That floods some years, and others
Dries as wrinkled as my skin.

My seed this year, as always,
Is deeded from the corner store,
Owned by a distant-bearing cousin
Who casts ten thousand acres more,
Polite, doffs his hat, rides past,
But never passes time of day,
Poor white trash, wooly hats,
Beneath disdain as relatives,
No matter blood nor class.

In 1765, the British introduce the Stamp Tax on newssheets, pamphlets and legal documents. This sparks a series of demonstrations by the newly-formed Sons of Liberty, who provoke actions against collection agents. Merchants start a boycott of British goods. There is a strong feeling that the colonies, long left to govern themselves, should control their own internal affairs and alone be able to impose taxes. Many are grateful for the protection of the British Navy and have profitted under the mercantile system; others less so.

In the transforming of the night, no moon,
Bells silent of the dawning storm,
A privateer eases up an estuary,
Oarsmen soft upon their strokes,
Until she is cloaked within a sanctuary,
And we deftly rope and slide o'erside
Barrels of molasses, coffee, tea,
To chide the cunning excise man,
And roll them up the midnight hill
To an impatient dray, covered still
With innocent-layered hay.

But then a sudden sloop appears,
Cutting the wave-crest bay, a cannon,
Shouts, the Union Jack, shots that crack,
A frigate swooping close behind,
And we are captured, handled rough,
Brigged and manacled, led tough into
A dour-faced Court of Admiralty
Where smuggling, once blind-eyed,
Is now taught Sugar Act imposed
And we, angered, resolve to fight
This new-imposed British might
And threat to long-breathed liberty.

Meanwhile, that same night,
A group of squatter families, long
Settled upon Massanutten's sides,
Are raided by a moonlit regiment
Of militia raised by some grandee
To force them from his property.

With muskets out, the Borderers reply
From their defying cabin logs,
But when their barns are torched and burnt,
Cattle turned, fields set on fire,
A truce mires into compromise
And they are permitted quick release,
With livestock and their fitful stores,
If they depart in 'mmediate peace.

Those damnable Tidewater aristocrats,
With their plantation slaves,
Their fancy lace and perfumes,

Their quitrents and their entails,
Land grubbers, speculators
Lapping at the coattails of
Their regal eastern protectors,
Legal-stealing western lands,
Revoking laws in distant Parliament!
What allegiance have we to them?
Most in this valley are Irish, German – even
Us English bear no love of homeborn privilege.
Did we escape those shores to have new debts
Imposed, new laws, restrictions,
Taxes and imprisonments?
Let's be done with them
And toss those fat and gouted idlers
Back into the sea,
Along with all their coffee, molasses
And their fancy-infernal, Chinese leaféd tea!

It's the big men who undercut us
With slaves and great production fields
Manure, rotation, fertilizers,
New-fangled gadgets we can't afford,
As we relapse to deeper debt,
Our cabins collapsing hovels,
No porches, unfloored, clay-rock stoves,
Our wives no bonnets, nor decent shoes,
Our children staring from shanty clothes,
Our boots worn out and soleless, frayed,
With no goal of prayed relief,
No jobs within the scanty towns,
Than those hired slaves will yearly take,
Driving wages down and down –
So we are left to scrape and make
The best that God may grant
In the hunt for rusting dreams
That have long ago seemed past,
And plastered us in dust…

Oh, the breeze, the breeze, the breeze…

In a Norfolk quayside house,
Beneath the crowded masts
Of brigs and schooners, British men-o'-war
Anchored in the deepset harbour,
A midwife rushes to the labour child
Of a steep-pained woman,
Terrified of bleeding, riven screams
That threaten miscarriage and her dreams,
Unless a surgeon is quickly driven
To cut her womb and pull inside
To wrest the breach-turned foetus out
And save it from its dying host…

…As the Horseman and the Hare,
Two abreast, gallop on the wind
Of the silent-chiming bells…

A growing wind, groping,
Blowing o'er our stale and slowing hopes…

…While a merchantman, twin-masted, rigged square,
Part-filled with Carolina indigo,
Bears tobacco, molasses, turpentine
And select naval repairs
From Hampton up to Boston, where
She will take on manufactures,
Furniture, spices, linen cloth,
Imported on pricy British ships,
Higher than by foreign craft,
Banned from our will,
Denying us the right
To fulfill our industry
And our mighty skill…

Meanwhile, not far away,
Within the call
Of the bricked and stuccoed hall
Of a Charles City plantation,
A well-bestowed and lordly mistress,
Desirous of a dress
– Blue-refashioned bows,
Ribbons, wide-bloomed satin,
With matching shawl and hat
To wow the season's balls –
Calls the overseer to her study
And informs him of the need to sell
Jacob,
A goodly Negro for the price
– Though he has a so-called wife and child –
To the vendue block,
Where he will be locked to the south,
Immediately,
Not given a chance to hold,
To sigh, nor say goodbye
To friend nor crying family…

Sally, help me, would you,
Get this corset on, breath in,
Pull it tight and heave those laces firm,
Then pass my hoop and bow it on,
Drop the satin o'er my head,
Slip my arms within its sleeves,
Pull out the cuffs at wrist and neck,
Then button up the back,
Slip emerald velvet o'er my feet,

Jade cabochon about my neck,
Gloves upon my speckled hands
And pass me up my woollen shawl –
It's cold this fall morning and the fire's not lit,
So I might catch a chill,
Unless you wrap me warm, my dear,
Against the world's persistent ill.

Oh, really, man, not so tight,
Let out the sleeves a little,
And the back. By the way,
I recall distinctly, boldly
Ordering silver thread, not gold,
On the borders' red lapels –
And are not the buttons ivory,
When I requested pearl?
Tisk, my man, such surly work
Will not adorn the wedding of
My eldest daughter into such
A well-born, debted family.

The veils, the mists that swirl and curl
In the silent-docketed breeze, soft-swirling,
Swirling soft and curling amid the trees...

II

It's not the swift-corsaired brigantine
Splicing the Windward Coast
For the roast of human-bonded blood,
Nor its reefed endeavor to lee
Between the fortress isle and baracoon;
Nor the soon-bribed chiefs
With bars and beads and brassy trinkets;
Nor the coffle lines of Muslim traders
Leaving the sick and fading to hyenas;
Nor the forest-terrored orphans,
Ash-cast village huts and smoking crops
Left to the breath of machetéd bones
And those too dead to march
This voyage of lonely death.

It's not the last-night feasting in the smallpox cells,
The crowded canoes and on-deck stripping,
Nor the rash-lashed-happy mate,
The fettered twos and fours,
The tight-spooned bodies in three-foot cramps,
The children groping at fetid planks,
The women pleasured on the sailors,
In the racial rape of a continent;

It's not the twenty inches to each man
To breath the choke-ensuckled air,
Nor the copper-kettled yams,
Plucked beans and rice
That I and many will not eat
In passive, self-starved device.

It's not our necks chained to the floor,
The vile reeking of decaying flesh,
The frenzied thresh of braying women,
The foaming mouths of those gone mad,
That make us want to roam-avenge
Every twinge of every seaboard day;
Nor the floggings, hands chopped off,
In manic-whipped deterrence;
It's not the sudden storms of passage
That cleave us to the timbered sides,
Crushing us upon ourselves
In putrid, devil-yelping helplessness;
Nor the child level with me lain,
Flies floating eggs upon her eyes.

It's not the hour-tossed bodies
Plunged to frenzied sharks,
Nor the lunging scars of anklets
Cripple-ironed,
The rusting neckties, heavy-hearted chains,
Bolts and bars and broken bones,
The gasp at grated hatchways,
Prayers for latch-free exercise
And the chance to flee the gunwales
With the grace of our despair;
Nor the humiliating nakedness,
The fury and the unrelief,
The angered conjury of disbelief
At such sour-fetid, putrid injury.

It's the damasked philosophies
On rights and liberties of man,
The manicured discussions
On the nature of our condition,
And the sanctified and nice
Prayers in the churches of the Christ
Whose oppressed, deplored compassion
We so sweetly ignore.

Oh Mama, myth of Zion's call...

The hazy-laden horizon and hazen-laded sky,
Smoke-leavened shroud of white translucence,
Melts upon wisps of mountain air,
Cirrus-streaks, banks of close-riséd clouds,

Spurling heads in distant-patchéd sun,
That undermerge within
A glaze of speckled rain…

…the breeze, the breeze…

…And sparkle-searing glare
Of a sudden-flashing sun…

…As WindTeller reins his pale steed tight,
His cape and hat pulled frightly 'round,
And hypes a tune upon his pipe,
As Rabbit pounds his griping fiddle,
And the boxed grave lain within the mist
Of a river mound's translucent dawn
Mocks the ceremonies of gods and gifts
That hanker-meek our servile guise
And acceptance of such abject wrong
As will a raven's heart despise.

And I pass a spreading chestnut tree
Close-sheltering the crossing frame
Of a new-laid Baptist church, self-proclaimed
By independent ministry, statement
Of humble-woken whites and slaves,
Builders of this mission, whose admission
Will be a slinky balcony, behind and out of sight,
And tiptoed outside sills where
They can whisper-watch and receive
Christ's separate lesson in respect
For their fated grief and neglect.

A mile beyond, in another sphere,
Once forested, but now well-cleared,
A landed gent has set aback
A large-penned oval track,
At Fredericksburg's woodland fringe
For this year's binging jockey races,
Market stalls and lacy fair,
Mint juleps, whisky, finest claret
To amuse the country-wedded set
In felt-tinged hats and mid-length coats,
To gloat their dainty-fingered luck
And melt their timed subversive groans,
Condemning George the Third,
The indolence of Negro slaves,
As they bravely bemoan *en masse*,
Squander-bet and crassly yell,
Before retiring to a dwelling tavern
For a dose of ham and grits,
Buttered yams and collard greens,
Pork, peach cobbler, seasoned fruit,

Washed down with sumptuous local ale
Served by some still-indentured,
Tired, master-impregnated, yokel female.

Oh, but we will not tolerate secret-hollowed dissent
That preaches down Christ's sweet tone
And locks our liberty in how to treat
Our servants as our blocks and stones,
That subverts our instigated laws,
Fairly stated and for us conformed,
Or demands more rights and manly votes
To those who would so rude revoke
Our natural right to rule, and defend
Our privilege in bonded men.

You know, sir, despite
Appearances,
I treat my slaves tolerably well;
They have wooden shoes,
My overseer goes easy on the whip
And I forbid my drivers to
Dock them *too* aggressively,
Other than with stocks or chains,
On occasion,
Though it pains me,
And bless them with an hour of rest
During the sour winter dark;
They have their own gardens,
Can share their surplus at the fair,
And so too, their food is fairly-tokened,
A pound of pork defrayed a week,
With extra every festive day.

Oh, I *do* so agree –
You know, the better ones
On my estate are granted passes more than most
To visit monthly wives and family.

Really?

Oh indeed, sirrah,
I let them gather for their meets
And even provide a preacher,
Tho' I swear I cannot abide
Them learning to scribe or read
An aside, even of the Bible.

What, even though it raise their minds
From childish lies and soft pretence?

Oh, most definitely, dear sir,
For, I'm afraid the Negro is endowed

213

With a will so weak,
Passions so subdued,
A disposition so gentle and affectionate
That he will instinctively obey,
As a child his father,
The white man's stronger-potioned say,
His superior mind and culture,
And I will not disabuse him
With mere ruse of independent notion.

Oh, I *so* agree,
But feel, don't you, that,
Though naturally good-tempered,
Unambitious, non-intellectual,
Quite unreachable of civilization
And unfit for mere amalgamation,
We must seek, endeavour to teach
Their submissive, obsequious nature
Our most simple moral code,
Or else bold, natural tendencies
Will condemn the Negro forever
To that indolence and degradation
To which he now – seduced
Through no fault but his own –
Finds himself reduced.

You know, dear sir,
It is my firm consideration that
The slave and the inferior white
Have one blight at least in common –
Their mutual inability, it would seem,
Through some deem of generationed history,
To comprehend the plainest law,
The simplest flaw or responsibility –
And thus their inheritance is inevitably
An incapacity to understand
The most basic, most noted
Principle of evenhanded governance,
Such as the notion of assembly,
Majority,
Or even what it is to vote.

Oh, sir, I do *so, so* agree most heartily…

And with the debate concluded,
Argument most clearly won,
Let us now repose to
A well-lit summer room,
Full open to the morning air,
Where Paul stands and clips the hair
Of Mister Madison, master,
Contemplating the hoped-for arrival

Of guests for that evening's ball
To mark the birthday of his wife.

Son of an English trader
Who raped his enslaved mother,
Part, in turn, enslaved Indian,
Paul snips and thinks
Of a friend's wife too, long past due,
Pregnant by the master's overseer,
Straining in the rat-filled barn
At that same disjointed time.[78]

And the Horseman rides his spurs upon
The ridgeline crest of trees
That grace Catawba Mountain,
Poor and Pilot, Paris,
Turning heat to hoary cold
In the orbit of his passing,
Oracle eyes foretelling visions
Of death and grievous suffering,
Sword in belt, buckled fine
With glowing eyes of diamantine...

...Oh, the tremulous breeze
Within the anxious trees,
As the bells begin to waken...

A goldfinch,
Free-flash melody of
Startling black and yellow
Linger-darts within the springtime fingers
Of a Back Creek walnut tree...

Oh, the veils that shelter and sustain...

...When will they chime the end of our night
And the rise of our forestalled morn?

I sit upon the shadowed porch
Of our Essex County farm
And cut a chew of tobacco plug,
Watch Pa scorch his corn husk pipe,
Jeremiah itch the strings of his violin,
And Mary hum and sew with running stitch
Upon her quilting frame;
The cows are tucked within the barn,
Evening milking folded, done,
As the sun withcasts its chuckled vow

---

[78] Paul Jennings, James Madison's 'body servant', was never freed, but was sold and eventually earned his freedom from another master. Later, he helped a group of slaves escape on a schooner, the *Pearl*; he also wrote recollections of his time with Madison.

Upon our private soul…

…While a washerwoman rises from the boil,
Hands to her back in steamy toil,
Stretches, groans, waits awhile,
Then rumbles in another pile…

III

I see the great tree spreading,
Limbs aboughed with leaf,
The darkened undershadows
Bringing into hazed relief
The form of a raven hanging,
The cauling shadows dangling
In the rite of Linkum Tidy
Rounding 'bout the solemn roots
That bubble troubled agony
Of tree-bound horns and flutes,
Playing the song of suffering
Dripping from his covert stage,
And call the saints to witness-rage
This pain-despiséd age…

…As, from an evening brigantine,
We are shuffled midnight off,
Coffled to a basement stock,
Uncoupled from each other, locked
To rings upon the walls, chained
To the solid oaken floors,
One pot to piss in, passed around,
Thirty, forty to a danklit room,
For three gloomy days until, by-one,
We are dressed in dandy rags,
Pressed to brush our teeth, stand handy straight,
Smile, greased to hide our scars,
Released into a bar-crowd room,
With booming cheers and laughter howls,
Are cowled upon a block to turn and smile,
Run up and down, jump, churn our arms,
Prodded, inspected, pants pulled down,
Grin teeth to agitated frowns,
Called rapid sums, hammered, murmurs, nods,
And are firmly tripped away,
Stripped, returned to coarser clothes,
Shipped upon a cart, where we are gripped
Up, retied, manacles reapplied, and,
Two men, a woman and a child, are
Cobble-slipped away.

We rattle past tobacco, wheat and acres
Of grazing cattle, sheep,
All new, all new, without the words,
As our driver tells us this is where
We will work, a huge plantation phased
Into several sprawling farms,
Are amazed through a daunting iron gate,
Down to a row of rough-hewn huts
Close by a haunted woodland copse,
Some gardens roughly fenced
In silence, tense, deserted,
An old woman keeping guard,
Some children tending boiling pots,
Watching us unload and each
Be marched to our sharded ticks,
No words to speak of this
Horse straw and pallet on the floor,
Rough-sewn osnaburg to wear,
Hats and shirts, one pair of pantaloons,
A bowl and spoon of rough-hewn wood,
Then told to sleep, our chains still on,
For come the yielding pre-dawn horn,
We will keep
Harsh company with the fields of new-born corn...

...As no-one speaks my words,
Knows my gods, my tribal king,
My sacred scars, nor my suffering.

That night, late, I meet
Strange other tongues, a ladder
To a lofty ten-by-ten,
Three men, a boy,
A family of five above,
The chimney coughing warm,
Choking on my lungs,
Slapping a mosquito swarm,
Singing silent delta songs,
Hymns to my memory, as I
Am taught the whip-poor-will words
Of my new-bound misery...

...While the Horseman stealthy views
The lights within the big house rooms,
And counts the years upon the bones
Of his chest
Before our strength may lead us home
To peace within exhausted breasts.

So we, in a dungeoned cabin, gather tight
Against the windblown agues of the night,
A glinting firebrand hidden by the coals
That huddle-force our huddled souls,

Bundled in our night-crouch ring,
Listening to our leader sing
Work tasks for the followed day –
Who will crop the lower field,
Who hoe the peas and garden greens,
Who dig the ditches, repair the roads,
Or goad the South Field oxen teams.

Some anger, hushed, then whispering again,
As we discuss the newest driver,
His keenness to improve his worth
With easy-clicking whip and stick,
And whether 'tis worth a risky lip
To spill him to the master yet,
Or direct the man a trick or two
Behind his unsuspecting back.

Some laughter, hushed, then whispering again,
As we doff our talk to Jacob, Sally,
Their desire to slave-way marry,
And how to best impress the mistress
With permission to carry off their plans,
Maybe tote and man a barbecue
With scraps of pork from weekend roasts,
Though that was thought at most, remote.

Some arguing, hushed, then whispers waft
Of permission soft for married men
To visit again their monthly wives
On neighboring plantation rows,
Forbidden since old Josh was caught
Stealing a hock from the smokehouse rack,
And was suspended back a month,
His carcass crisply meat and dried
And whisped away for stray dogs to eat.

Some tears, hushed, then whispering again
About that Saturday's secret meet
By the graveyard on Sweetmorn Hill,
Amidst the dense of oaks and pines,
There to flood a midnight shrine
In heated praise to ancestral souls
With sacrificial chicken's blood
And the rhythm of our juba beat.

Some praises, hushed, then whispering again,
Consensual agreement to let old Samuel
Lead the service, read the rites,
For he alone could tell the signs
Written in the Gospel lines
Of meek inheritance of this earth,
Nature-given by the Lord

To every human birth…

…And can commune with our ancestors
To divine their needs and why.

Oh, give me strength
To toll the bells of our eternity.

No, son, let it be, let it be,
Think of tomorrow,
The meeting by the river,
And this shouting Sunday's ring;
Think of freedom in your heart,
Hold to that firm and pure,
Let your manhood's pride abide
In the patience of your mind;
Hold down that head in feigned respect
And keep your heart firmly pure,
In hope of that sun-blown morn
That will surely herald our final dawn.

Oh, I have not strength to feel the breeze…

…Give me the strength!

As we return from noon-day fields,
I am told to venture with Ol' David,
Household spooning man – don't call him slave,
For, though a past like us, he has his pride,
A lighter hue, can read and write,
Knows a thing about the world or two,
Gaits with Mas'er to the city – and even,
Hands say, out of state,
As butler and his personed man.
So, as we rise the bootworn steps,
A century of its hardened heels,
He guards a reminiscent breath,
And proudly feels the columns' depth,
Whitewashed,
Yarning how his gran'pap helped
Erect that symbol to our deep respect
For the owners of our life and debt.

Oh, the veils, the mists that swirl
And spread confusion with each curl
Of might and right and slinking night,
As Virginia seeks its own sweet light.

But she will reside in darkness yet…

Oh, the veils that hush
Noises from the distant hill

Where the great house stands poised, shaded still,
As the horn blows, signal to us men
To bring our scythes and metal tools
And have them sharpened by a peddling man
Who comes each month to blade and spark,
Aid our blacksmith with his mark,
And secret pass to us the news
Of lightning views and revolution…

…While here I lie, in the jail I built,
For running from the driver's whip,
Hiding in a neighbor's barn,
Drunk and angry, fighting back,
And getting for ingratitude, caught,
The padderollers dragging back, until
My master wills to pay the fine
And shackle me return again…

…As The Horseman,
Crowned in thorns, dead fronds,
With face of gnarled, bark-linéd grin,
Stops his trot to peer within
The huts of our continued plight,
Of freeish blacks and poorest whites,
Peddle-begging town to town,
With no land to call our own,
And welcomes Rabbit to his saddle,
There to leg towards the mists
That wisp this stormy dawn.

I see them pass
As I drop my pole and trailing line
Over the rim of bridge and rail,
Baited sit and wait
For the catfish bite that shows my dreams
Of Africa not faded
Completely from my trace,
Knowing this will be my life,
My hope no more than daily strife
To fulfill my master's graces
And listen to the lisping toll
Of the tongue on lip.

Oh, how
I cry in their denial of me,
My hands strumming in the silence,
My eyes bearing down in anger
Disguised as searing fear,
As the veil descends
Once more,
Between thee and me and thee,
And I flash-recall the stalling

Shackles of the brigantine
As Linkum Tiddlum Tidy cauls
His ancient rite and bells
Silent hang, foretelling crowns
And our drowning cries.

IV

I ride upon my well-groomed bay[79]
Through the gated, well-fenced day
And o'er the bridge of near-new stone,
Past a hand who's dropline casting
For our evening catfish stew,
Then cross within the cool-breezed dawn
Of meditative, wood-dewed ways,
Of cart and mule and temperate walk,
Of well-met gents who also stalk
Their expectant, jaunty gait towards
The county-havened tavern where
We'll be entertained this ringing morn.

The lane-stoned track of solitary sway
Passes Colonel Gray's
Manicured eternity,
Burgess, warden, justice too,
His Georgian house a colonnade
Bathed in sultry oaken shade
Across a private fence of classed domain,
Offset by glowing corralled frames
Of merry servants' backyard rows,
Carpenter, smithy, houseboy, maid,
To serve the ladies on the porch
And the man within his library,
Sipping porter, Plato, Cato,
Plutarch too, all very
Advocates of merit votes
Kept to property, fine order,
And the rightful place of citizenry.

I and my stout fellows,
All anxious for the show,
Stride from fence to fence and stream,
Discussing as we lusty wend
Past tended fields and coppiced woods
And sylvan parkland mowed by cows,
Which all combine to quaint present
A painted pastoral symphony,
A minuet of pitched precision,

---

[79] This section comprises *The Song of the County Courthouse*.

Cultured ditches, willow-draped,
And freedmen excavating where
We riders saunter through
The liberal-dappled, mellowed light
And smile across the garden ploughed
At merry-distant hovels, slave-endowed
And playful urchin children stanced
In bare-foot, ragged innocence.

…as patient flows the James…

And the ravens do call and bells
Do raise their silent lips to tell
Of murders, rapes and violence…

…While we ride in educated leisure
Past a well-trained, split-rail snake
And civil cornfield's 'crow,
To pleasure listen, as we go,
To a team of willing women sing
As they serenely pea-crop hoe
Against the sipping green
Of tended tendril rows,
And I hat-tip to a well-eased man
Upon his arboured horse
Draped within a hickor'ed lee,
Whip harboured upon his kindly knee,
Dog at his chiding roan's feet
In a pastoral eden idyll scene
And peaceful meadowed charm –
An ambrosia-tinted fantasy
Of dream-entended phantom fields,
Tilled and weeded, grown content.

And, as if to confirm this
Well-husbanded and mellow mien,
A coffle of new-sold men, belled
In jingle chain and doubled line,
Carouse their hymnal praising stride
To their new land of cottoned pride,
While still others join our sunny way,
Many on expectant foot,
And we banter about the day's fair play
And anticipated encouragement,
Until the tavern comes within our view,
A many-roomed establishment
Crowded yet with vending peddlers,
Card-sharps, gamblers, traders,
Paw-paw, dice and huzzle-cap,
To loudly tap this happy crowd.

I dismount and tie my horse,

Push through the hustled throng
And call a wench to bring a jug
Into a well-packed alehouse room
That is the tempered chamber of
This justice-tensioned fair,
Then squeeze upon a heavy bench,
Quench a full and lusty throat,
And banter with old neighbours
In unsobered, coarse sobriety
About their estates and mine
And the notoriety, betting odds,
Of each slated trial this time.

There is a partial hush
As the magistrates appear,
Swear each other in and begin
Their deliberation upon suppression
And drunken verdicts on a race
In white-skinned, hasty guilt's
Inverted justice of the blind's
Impassioned 'ssuaging of its fear.

The first defendants to the dock
Of public-chastened vengeance
Are three slaves accused of poisoning
Their well-proportioned master,
A violent blackguard, so I hear,
But dour justice must be done,
Its fist the glove to our power.

Throughout the witness testimonies,
There is a rising roar
Of tipsied anger and demands
For blood to even up the score, or more –
To instill relief in us
And fear for our most paupered law.

There are cries to hush as the victim's wife
Describes her husband's throes of death
And how she found some magic breath
Of powder in the unwashed crease
Of her maid's faint-aproned smock,
A trace of which she gave a dog,
Who foamed around its mongrel mouth
And creased upon the ground, deceased.

As she spoke, the tension rose
And, upon her teary-eyed conclusion,
Fierce cries for hardy retribution
Broached the liquored air.

Next, the accused each testified,

223

One deferential in denial,
One pathetically admitting,
The other defiant still,
As I slugged another earthen jug
And sprang five-to-four on all three
The next day being hanged.

And thus this tavern-sitting court,
Which knells for short and rapid transit
From cell to Virginia's dropping tree,
Works within the beersop eye
Of a bespectacled and bemuséd crowd
Rowdy spitting on its misery,
Bustling, betting, cheering boos,
Jeers and murmured disagrees
With testimony and solemnity
And intoxicated verdicts upon a race,
The sour emotion of a fragile power
That gives bastard masters the semblant mask
Of humane-'spired legality.

Amid the mercury-tainted spittle
And tavern-rowdied, hanging victuals
Of ale and argument, ruby-throat revenge,
The justices sit with statute smiles
And bloodied gloves set tight beneath
Their silvered-suckered, frightened chins
To deliberate upon such soft-thieved sins
And stolen wisps of aspiration
Long since denied to those whose skin
Is where we carve our legal lies.

I await the penny-pitching verdict,
Glib-certain of its course,
And when Jacob's to the gibbet sent,
There are expectant, cheering yelps,
Tho' when Sally's spared her life
For her abject-whelping plea,
Assuaging e'en the court
That her cowering is enough
To guarantee her loyalty,
There erupts a round of legless boos
That makes the justices repent
And bow to the crazied will
Of their self-corrupted crowd.

Then the final judgment comes,
And to the defendant's horror,
He is terrored to the burning stake
For his unrequited misery;
The bawdy-rousing room erupts
Into super-passioned delight,

And the ordinary is quick booked
For bawdy night-time nuptials, and
The knelling-ruptured spectacle
Of gibbet, fire and flames to the sound
Of resounding Christian bells.

V

And thus it begins...

In 1763, Patrick Henry, lawyer,
Declares, in Parson's Cause,
With the resonance of revolution,
That a king who disavows a people's laws
Degenerates to tyrant and,
In consequence,
Foregoes all right to moral obsequience.

Two years evolve and, bare elected,
He decrees, in *Stamp Act Resolves*,
That pernicious tax beyond the law,
Subverting liberty, flawed, resistible,
And so inflames us to a passion
That will not be assuaged,
But frames Fauquier, agéd governor, snob,
To snub an upraucous Assembly,
Proud and angry chorus,
And rescue his curséd collector
From a rioting Williamsburg mob...

...As the breeze, the silent-docketed breeze,
Soft-swirls
Within the sanctified motion of our breath
And the bells do lip their silent tongues...

Tho' the Stamp Tax is repealed,
New duties are with zeal imposed,
Townshend's,
On tea and glass and paper, lead and paint,
So tensions rise to digressed passion
And frownéd brows seek swift redress
In independence from Old George's crown.

Tidewater aristocrats,
Long shuffle-snuffling on the arm
Of that mad dodderer for their power,
Grow sour at sad Britain's inability
To quell the undermining of their rule
And set Virginia against *them* as well –
For this is to be a revolution *within* the states,

225

As much as contra imperial power –
An upswelling revolt against
The ossified class and hardened privilege
Of a miniscule élite that has striven
To keep state and land, belief
Firmly beneath its oppressing thumb,
Denying most of us our spiritual relief,
And clasping each well-fed, ripened plum
Tightly in its high-ranked grasp,

Distant thunder rolls,
Heavy-shadowed shrouds,
Grey-scratched, slashing flashes
Of cut-lipped light, zip-clipped,
Clapped, roaring,
Heavy-stoned and growling,
Templed cumuli,
Columned omens of tumult turning,
Up-surging, mushroomed from the haze
Of our determined passing...

...that beckon to us liberty.

Meanwhile,
Virginia's arteries lack improvement,
Her bridges, buildings in decline
For want of governance or prosperity,
As the British, rather than invest,
Incline to further repress,
And decide to transport and to try
Americans condemned of treason
On England's confinéd shores,
Far from justice, piercing eyes,
While insistently dumping every
Pimp and spoiling prostitute,
Felon, thief and murderer
Upon our reluctant soil,
Until yet more of our declaim
Forces a renewed and doddering recoil,
And a Boston riot, massacre
Incites victory and Townshend repeal,
Except, perchance, on tea.

I am the journey,
I am the quest,
And I am the prophecy...

In 1771, a disastrous flood devastates Virginia as it rains for ten days in a row,
sending a twenty-five-foot wall of water across parts of the lowlands. Meanwhile,
the eastern counties of Virginia suffer from over-farming, loss of topsoil and a
rapid decline in production. Small farmers, especially, are suffering, many

looking to the west to start anew. But the British government refuses to let them go, for fear that it will provoke more wars with the Indians.

I hate spiders weaving webs
Of silent-soft deceit…

…the veils, the mists that swirl…

The riverways of the state are aboil,
Tea Act o'erboarded, Coercives resisted
As intolerable, dismissed and defied
By fasting, humbleness and prayer,
As the old Virginia naysayer guard,
Political cabal, intermarried friends,
Toils to resist the regard of force
By Piedmont youth of more divergent course,
Who parlay the tumultuous spoil
They plan for our deranged soil with
Committees of Correspondence and Inquiry.

Oh, hear
The distant thunder rolls…

Jefferson writes his *Summary View*,
Outlining his countrymen's definéd rights –
Conclusions that would upset and challenge
His own well-planned inheritance
Of Britain's dwindle-doffed respect.

And then congregates a seaboard continent,
Peyton Randolph its soon-sworn chair,
Rebating o'erbearing England's trade,
And blading to our own Convention
That explicates an exhorted plea of Enough!,
Thwarting a ship and troughing in the York
Two half-chests of imported tea.

…A breeze, a wind, a thunder-cloud
And sudden clap of strident bells…

Once more dissolved by sternish governor,
Our burgesses bode to Raleigh's Tavern,
Defiant on their seditious road,
More hostile, open in contempt,
Attempting a ban on British goods
And a Continental Congress renewed,
Evolving, in hue-brewed Alexandria,
Mason's solemn *Fairfax Resolves*
On the necessity of freedom…

…of the veils, the mists that swirl
And spread confusion with each curl

Of might and right and slinking night,
As Virginia seeks its own sweet light
Within a rousing dawn…

…dong, dong, dong…

…I hate spiders weaving webs
Of silent-soft deceit…

And I recall, as I hack the stalks of corn,
Turn them back, for a bended woman,
New-forced wife, though she speaks
Not a word of mine,
To twist the husks, then toss high upon
The piling wagon mound,
With nightmare dread, that passage trial
Upon a terrored brigantine,
Those last words shouted
In my lost Yoruba tongue,
My faith and land and family
Long gone, long gone, long gone.

…there can be no words…

Oh, hear
The distant thunder rolls…!

…No words for
Spiders weaving webs
Of silent-soft deceit…

"Knives to sharpen! Scissors too!"

I sing my wares and push my cart
From harried house to house,
Crying "Knives to sharpen! Scissors too!"
For bonneted ladies, houseboys to view,
And let my ragged freedman looks,
My conjure ways and well-masked face,
Win sympathy and well-graced work
From the mansions on the hills
Of this fenced and driven rural life;
The children come to watch the sparks,
Elder aunts and uncles too,
And sometimes several fieldhands stop
To let me shine their scythes anew…

"Knives to sharpen! Scissors too!"

…For I peddle news, secret plans,
Rhymes and rhythms, songs and tunes,
Tales of 'scapes and burnings, poisons too,

Peddle potions, drugs and secret blades
That them's as wants 'em buys;
Peddle techniques, trades, routes and roads,
Safe houses, swampland news,
And mental maps of landscapes
From The Gap into Philadelphia,
Then to Canada's teared embrace;
I peddle trends in hiring freedoms,
Ways to beat the 'rollers' traps,
Things I've seen and heard and guessed
From boatmen, sailors too,
Tradesmen from the north and wars,
And countries where all men are free…

"Minds to sharpen! Willpower too!"

…Oh, but let not the mistress catch us,
For her time, and ours, is not yet due…

Cirrus-streaks,
Distant thunder rolls…

…the bells of our eternity…

Liberty for you is liberty for me!

And SelfSearch guards the night
Within her sleepless fright,
Calling out to passing whispers
That what is right, is right.

The first battles of the American Revolution take place at Lexington and
Concord. The Americans are defeated at Bunker Hill. At the outbreak of war,
Virginia has a population of 550,000, residing in sixty-one counties.

Unsaddled, watered, being fed,
I hate fat spiders, loathe them,
Love squishing them with my thumb
And watching
Their juices splat.

Called back from memory,
I take the reins of an old man's horse,
Lead his mare to the rear,
Many others waiting there,
Unsaddled, watered, being fed
As burgesses enter expectant upon
The sacred shrine of St Johns
On Richmond's Church Hill side,
To plan their next rebellious step
From old England's hopeless pride.

As more curious come, dismount,
Their coats and tricorns, dusted boots,
I brush the horse's foaming flanks
And strongly feel an urge within,
Wondering what will freedom bring
Me, a coachman, from Albion's defeat –
Will it grant me liberty,
End my servitude, enable me
To set up business, buy
New brushes, land, a place to crop?
And will my voice be louder then,
My taxes lower, prices flop a bit,
Or will they all remain the same,
No-one care if I die somehow,
The way I have died till now?

The grooming done, the speeches loud,
I am told to enter in, carry water
For the assembled gentlemen,
So wander over to the pump,
Fill an urn, lump it on my arm
To the church, a crowd already there,
Squeeze by, push in, listen
As one sits down to moderate 'plause,
Another rises, a walking cane,
Goes to the pulpit front,
Coughs,
Plays the buttons on his coat,
Looks out of place, remote,
A little anxious, but then begins,
In compelling, quietened, reasoned tone,
To tell a case that none dare jeer,
Or cheer,
Just nod in mutual introspect.

I stand at the back, my urn delivered,
Next a marble bust of some old man,
Whom, I am told, is George the Third,
The old crackpot king himself,
And notice set within the eye
A black, fat spider weave,
From cheek to brow,
Nose to temple, legs flicked so,
A web of delicate deceit,
As the orator regales the crowd
With such impassioned conceit
That 'tis natural for us to rise, indulge
Illusions of bright-blinded hope,
To refrain our eyes against the truth
And anger at entrenchéd Britain,
Now the struggle has begun,
Whether we want it to or no.

"We must fight!" ring the eaves and the pews,
"We must fight" echoes the nave, the pulpit too,
And I wonder, when he talks of liberty,
When he appeals to the "people",
Whom he means by that:
Me, servant, landless, reading not a word,
Or just *his* powdered type – males,
Landed, white,
Of sustained property,
Presiding o'er lands and libraries,
No dirt to smear upon their civil hands?

"Give me liberty or give me death!"
Is the man's ultimate refrain,
Met in a trance of subdued awe, silence
As the reason of his frank-clawed words
Sinks deep within awareness
That time has slipped us by
– The choice no longer ours,
Either revolution or suppression –
And so is met with a sudden call,
"To arms!" "To arms!" "To arms!"
Re-echoed, shout and shout about,
Above the strident 'cophony
Of a people new decided, newly risen,
Newly found in voice and passion,
In philosophy and righteousness,
And abrupt impatient of delay.

And I wait for the spider to come to rest
On the marbled nose of its guest,
Jab it, hold it, rub and turn
And watch its ooze suppurate upon
That old and dusty form,
Roughly brush all web away,
And push through the wigs and silken vests
Into another grey, ephemeral Virginia day.

Lieutenant Governor Dunmore orders British marines to remove gunpowder from the magazine in Williamsburg. He is stopped when Patrick Henry rouses the Virginia militia and chases after the stores to win them back. This is the first armed revolutionary action in Virginia.

The second Continental Congress meets in Philadelphia. Peyton Randolph is elected president. George Washington is made commander-in-chief. George III declares the American colonies to be in rebellion.

Dunmore, now aboard a British warship in the York River, orders a raid on Norfolk and razes Hampton to the ground. He issues an emancipation proclamation that imposes martial law on Virginia and offers freedom to indentured servants and slaves willing to fight for the king.

There is a slave insurrection in western Virginia.

Swirl-hugging,
Thunderclaps that riot, clamp
The peaks with powered roil's revenge,
Ker-rashing boo-rooming growls
In whorls of vapoured toil,
Fume-rising credescence,
Voluminous, riled and cankered,
Swirling, blackened dark, foreboding chill
Upon the evening's unforgiving will.

There are no words
For the veils, the unplanned veils,
Of thund'rous misunderstanding.

VI

It is hard to imagine, master,
As you stalk these box-trimmed lines
And well-laid garden plans of
Orchards, walks and summer houses,
That in your mind has congregated
Thoughts that will transform
A world from kingly hierarchy
To public rights and democracy.

I watch you amble gravelled paths,
Mumbling to your focussed self,
Secretary fussing quick behind,
Taking notes as you dictate, desist,
Observe the lately morning mist
Rise from the marshy-lying shore
Of sleepy-snoring Chesapeake
As it washes your plantation fields,
And see you note, with hurrumphing smile,
The brave-hoed, drove-ganged labouring
Of your doted, yielding slaves.

I pull around my rough-loomed slip,
Bend,
And clip some deadhead blooms,
Add turned manure, dehip,
Tug persistent weeds and grasses
Parasitic passing through
The strangle-flowered roots,
Black soil feeding your white shoots,
As you, my master, nod and recognise,
Ask how well the blossoms do,
Then meander down a nearby avenue

To dictate the state of human rights,[80]
Declaring that by nature born,
All men are equal free,
Have inherent rights to property,
Life and liberty, happiness, safety –
That all power lies within the people,
No mere monarch-ruling denizen,
And that government is for its citizens
– Tho' not the mass, but some gentry norm
Based on Greek and Roman forms
Of civilised enslavery –
And thus it is our right to transform,
Abolish or reform, as we care to be.

I rise from my task, dawn-to-dusk,
Knees brown with muck and soil,
Back coarse from prenoon sun,
Sweat dripping down my hidden chest
Beneath my os'burg roughened blouse
As you frown, pause, wait a while,
Move on,
Mumble something – freeing slaves? –
Halt, then shake your head, tell your man
To delete that phrase, too dangerous yet,
And I wonder at *your* inheritance,
Your lordly rule, *your* tyranny over me
And hundreds of the other graves
Your drivers work so mercilessly,
None of whom you will *ever* free.

Then I hear you pronounce
Upon elections,
Suffrage for men of property
And freedom of religion,
Though what that can relieve for me
I do not know,
As I am denied all spirit thought,
No church, no Bible, no reading let
For my private-set advance,
No enhancement, thought to disagree
Tolerated by this man, whom,
Like those other notables who hie and call,
Washington, Jefferson, and journeying more,
Have no intent of ever ending
Their unbending tyranny of me.
Ah, you are busy, your mind elsewhere,
On separation of judicial powers,

---

[80] George Mason, author of Virginia's *Declaration of Rights* and a main influence on both the first Constitution of Virginia and the US Bill of Rights, is the largest slave owner in Virginia. Not only does he never manumit a single slave, but he refuses them education or the chance to read and write. Human rights only extend to citizens; slaves, by definition, are not citizens, and thus have no such rights.

Whate'er that might subtle be,
For there is no justice here, no judge,
Other than a master's stern decree
And the transitioned whim of your strict fantasy.

But I can wait, I can wait;
The principles you have laid,
My sweet, defiant master,
Will found the Modern Age
And will, one day, be taken up
By all who deem it human right
To oppose o'erbearing mastery.

In 1776, Thomas Paine publishes *Common Sense*, which has a huge influence on revolutionary thought.
Governor Dunmore sails for England, thus ending British authority in Virginia. On May 15th, the Virginia Convention declares the state's independence. On 12th June, George Mason's *Declaration of Rights* is unanimously accepted, and on 29th June, Virginia adopts its first constitution. Its introduction is written by Jefferson, but it is mostly the work of Mason. Patrick Henry is chosen first governor of the newly independent Commonwealth. Slaves currently form 40% of her population.

I am no hypocrite,
So will openly admit
I am a revolutionary only so far
As the boundaries of my property,
And do not seek to plunge
Further than my independency,
Dependent, as it may be, as much upon
Others' labour and their slavery
As freedom from British suzerainty –
I will deftly argue with all monied will
For a constitution bereft of democracy,
Responsibility or community,
That mere instills freedom for a class,
A way of life
That relies as much upon others' lack
Of rights unto themselves,
As it does upon fine phrases
To sustain our mouthed philosophy.

Following other states' declarations of independence, a Second Continental Congress is held in Philadelphia. Delegates propose independence from Great Britain and announce the *Declaration of Independence* on 4th July – and with that single action – a culmination of many previous thoughts and actions – begins the Age of Human Rights, which has brought representative democracy to the world and rendered liberty upon its lips.

This year is another drought-poor crop,
Tobacco grubs and other pests that
Terror-take our wheat and corn,

Peas and squash and beans,
And force us hock our cow and mule,
Harness and outworn plough,
Then rent them back and hope
We may cope on extra pennies
Digging ditches, mending fences
For our grander neighbours,
Though now they do suffer too.

Hey-yup, ye-oddle-ey!
Knives to sharpen!
Scythes and shears, scissors too!

Let us now retire to Weedon's,
Tavern and seditious meeting room,
Where billiards are bandied in the back
Patriotic vitriol in the front,
Over jugs of earthen ale,
Bread and ham and cheese,
While private clubs in secret meet
To discuss Freemasonry or revolt,
Take up copies of the *Gazette*
Read articles to each other's ire
And proffer laughter-heated debate,
Oft with Weedon at the head.

Here, in seventy-seven,
Between billiard bet and payment
Of Jockey Club and racing odds,
Jefferson, Mason, Wythe and more
Meet across their pewtered plates,
In tap room or reclusion,
The fireplace stoked with burning brands,
To draft Virginia's education laws
And *Statute for Religious Freedom*,
Imbibing beer and toddied rum
In the heady days of revolution,
No mention here of Christ alone,
Refusing limit to one set form
Of our spirit or its godly norm;
Thus, these men, open-armed to all,
Refuse to rule-define
America as the Bible's soil,
The Testament as its final word –
And most specifically to deny
Restrictive powers to seek control
And force such re-conformity,
In denial of our diversity,
As the British had required.

And thus the snake doth slough its skin,
Renewed in timbered heat of sun,

235

Brighter, newer, seemingly reborn,
But yet bearing colors of yestermorn...

...And thus do the bells now toll
For you, but not for me...

VII

Closer thunder rolls,
Heavy-shadowed shrouds
Loud within our stalling hearts,
While history and our destiny call...

In 1778, the new Commonwealth of Virginia becomes the first government in the
world to ban the African slave trade, but it is more from fear of being outnumbered
by slaves than from any concern at the inhumanity of the trade – and certainly not
because it opposes slavery. Two years later, the legislature votes to reward each
Revolutionary War veteran with 300 acres and a slave.

In 1780, the British start major military operations in Virginia. Many slaves flee
to them, including seventeen belonging to George Washington. On the other
hand, a few join the American militia, hoping to win freedom for their efforts, or
are impressed into the effort involuntarily. The capital of Virginia is moved to
Richmond, for fear of British attack.

In 1781, the British *do* attack, burning Richmond and forcing Governor Thomas
Jefferson to flee to Charlottesville, where he and several assemblymen narrowly
escape capture and flee to Staunton. In October, the Assembly moves back to
Richmond.

With Virginia sadly divided,
Tidal Tories staying loyal,
The estuaries of the Chesapeake
Are a haven for those without parole,
Aiding British ships to navigate
The well-spied, silent channels,
Tangier Island privateers,
Picaroons to the English royal,
Raiding Somerset, Frederick,
Holland Straights and Pocomoke
To seize anything or one who floats
And aspires to patriotic hopes –
Joseph Wheland most notorious
In his fiercemost disruption, looting
The unloyal coastal population.

And, in the secret starlit
Seconds of the night,
Seven slaves slip to marshland flight,
There to hide and await the day
The British win and free them all
From the master's whip and dawnhorn call;

But they find no redcoats, pestilence alone,
Of mosquitoes, biting bugs,
And the watchful eyes of Mama Swamp,
Who discovers, rescues, feeds their needs,
Until the day that other freedom frees
And flees them from their waiting grief.

...as the bell cries out for victory...

Meanwhile, another life goes on
This a cold Twelfth Night in Williamsburg,
Amidst the cressets, lanterns, fire logs lit,
And slaves joyous in their merry grog,
Carousing loud their carol-deemed content,
The mumming boys in rags with sticks
And veiled in dim-lit masks,
Dancing jigs and drumming tasks
To well-sequestered homes,
As we roam and stroll to be seen
At the season-tinted ball,
Masked in turn, with glittered stones,
Velvet feathers, painted plumes,
Holly green and ivy hunched
On bay-lined window ledges,
With bowls of rosy, steaming punch,
Chestnuts, pies and ginger boys
To thrill our hearts against the chill
And let our reels and gay-pranced trots
Relieve our freezing, icy thoughts
From Virginia's war-gripped grief,
And hurry to the balcon's ear
For rousing songs of nationhood
That blaze the torch of hopeful tears.

...As the thunder rolls above
Our fearful flight
To some vale of hopeful plight...

Oh, how we drill, we drill!

...Drill barefoot, hungry, starving,
Starch-marched to keep us warm,
Instill some martial pride,
Uniforms unfit, derided,
Shouldered muskets born,
Wheeling left and wheeling right,
Eight thousand to uphold the fight
Of a once-proud army's slight command,
Now logged in dank-smogged, smoky cabins,
Waiting for some wagon food
To trudge our narrow-mudded valley
From Susquehanna's thankless banks

And Hessians warmly lodged…

…Until, as we rapid fire in ranks,
No ammunition to tamp nor waste,
Washington saunters on his horse,
And we attention, stand, salute,
While he inspects us, commands
With brotherly encouragement
And reminds us of our sternest duty
To the freedom we demand.

And I think of my overburdened mother,
Father killed at Brandy Hill,
Brother lain in Lancaster
With frostbitten feet and hands,
Too sick to stand or soldier on;
I dream of lower taxes,
A nation to be proud, relaxed,
Better farmyard prices,
Westward liberty as we wish
To revival our pure religion,
Now a forbidden vice,
And permit, God-willing,
A farmhouse sure in its location
Fit to sit in porchside thrill, next
Our general's old plantation.

During the Revolutionary War, Virginia sees thirty-one separate engagements. In 1781, the British send Brigadier General Benedict Arnold into the Chesapeake Bay to raid the James River and Richmond. He severely damages supply lines and war industries before returning to Portsmouth.

With the arrival of further forces under General Phillips, the British begin a major campaign up the James River, striking at Yorktown, Williamsburg and the Virginia State Naval Docks, then move their fleet and army to City Point to attack Petersburg, defended at the time by the Virginia militia under Major General von Steuben.

The British march north, burn the barracks at Chesterfield Court House, destroy several ships at Osborne's Landing and burn the foundry and warehouses at West Ham, just up the James from Richmond. However, American regulars under Major General Lafayette prevent the British taking the new capital. Later, in Petersburg, Lafayette's army briefly bombards the British encamped there.

When the British, under Cornwallis, attack to the south, Nathaniel Greene retreats over the Dan, then stops the British at Guilford Courthouse, and eventually forces them into defensive positions at Yorktown.

During the war, food grows short, rampant inflation sets in and the countryside and industry are ravaged by the marauding British. However, once forced back to Yorktown, the arrival of Washington's army and French reinforcements on land and sea puts them into a hopeless position and forces their final surrender.

Oh, how the bells do ring!

Virginia,
The alpha and omega of British rule,
An empire's hope and confoundation,
Its hesitant beginning and more strident end,
In the culmination of seven years
Of bloodshed, maneuver, fear,
Meets in victorious Yorktown siege,
Washington's patient liege authority,
Rochambeau's seasoned, French-led aid,
De Grasse's encircling, defending fleet
That off-greets the British at The Capes,
And the night-time charge of Thomas Nelson,
Who, with Lafayette, leads on the final rout
Towards the trouble-twined redoubts
Of despotic foreign rule
And terminal bastions of our tyranny
– And thus we force that old monarchy
To capitulate to a new-born destiny,
A victory heralded by the oppressed
And lovers of their freedom,
In France and Spain, England too,
Such as Pitt and Fox and Wilkes,
Who yet endure that infamy
Of a rapacious idiot king
Americans have just shot-rescinded
On this most glorious October day
Of human-struggled history!

VIII

And then 'tis past,
As sudden calmed as angered come,
Left about the dazing mountains
A fraying fringe of Allegheny rain,
Distant-washéd rocks a-glisten
And a wind-shimmerin heaven grass
That's flashing flecks
In a gathered pool of scattered sun.

Oh, but the veils, the veils
That have descended between us today
And the truth of our Great Fathers...

In 1786, the Virginia Assembly finally passes the *Statute For Religious Freedom*, drafted by Thomas Jefferson in 1777. It resists any attempt to define religion as Christianity, partly because it sees Virginia as embracing *all* spiritual beliefs, and partly because many of Virginia's Founding Fathers, including Jefferson and George Washington, are not Christians at all, but deists, who have themselves suffered under the hegemony of intolerant Christian belief.

It is precisely to *prevent* Christianity controlling our lives that they pass the statute – not to promote it as 'America's religion.'

> *Swing within the fall of fall*
> *And let the soft-sweet bluebird call,*
> *Twitter, twitter, twitter. That is all.*

> Beside Richmond's bumbling falls,
> A hundred slaves begin to blow
> Two trouble-briefed canals
> To navigate the tumbling force,
> Feed new flour and foundry mills,
> And spill batteaux from nearby mines,
> Upper farmlands, West Ham forge,
> To Richmond's engorged basin,
> There to dock and cart their stock
> Into resurged, swiftwind ships
> Departing from the lower wharves.

> So here is our answer – no change,
> No change at all
> To our enslaved condition,
> Still indentured – secret slave trade still,
> Poverty and starvation, no change
> In our plight or reality of our will.

> Once more, the bells chime silently...

> They still take our names, our words and wealth,
> Our thoughts and symbols, private mystery,
> To fill us with their ways and schemes,
> Prejudices, and replace our dreams
> With subtle-tended stealth...

> ...still...

> There are no words...

> ...can be no words...

Prompted by Madison and Hamilton, a Convention meets in Philadelphia in 1787 to draw up a constitution for the thirteen states.

> Soft, often silent, Washington,
> The Convention's stately president,
> Is authorative and thoughtful,
> Never one to fleece in speech,
> Its Solomon and its Noah,[81]

---

[81] George Washington was a lifelong Freemason and incorporated many of its esoteric principles into his life; Freemasonry strongly influenced the design of Mount Vernon, the Capitol and the Mall in Washington. The first Freemasonry Grand Lodge in America was

A royal master selected
By our dear and fractious founders,
Who are too often self-enwrapped
To cleave to our central cause
Of a strong and powerful union;
A great attentive listener,
He compares the working group,
In part,
To a net of starry fixtures
Who are by their light connected,
Wide-meshed, but letting nothing fall
In their search for ordered justice,
And the human soul of all.

But one great question they must decide
Is how to define the slaving class,
Whether they be citizens or no,
Rightful numbers up to vote, decide,
Or not men at all, rights denied,
And to be discounted when it comes
To distributing seats for Congress –
Until they agree a blackman bonded
Is three-fifths of a white with land.

Twitter, twitter, twitter,
That is all…

…As the bells do silent call
And the storms clouds give away
To the graying skies of giveaway.

James, oh James –
Are you merely three-fifths a man,
Like those slaves you sternly control
On your expansive Orange 'state,
Or are you Father of the Constitution,
Organizer of Convention,
Defender of religious freedom,
And proposer of the Bill of Rights?

Like most contemporaries
Of your class and fit,
You were, I surmise, a bit of both,
Republican and anti-financier,
Yet advocate of stronger government,
Secret-working with firebrand Hamilton
To impose underhand and in seclusion,

---

formed in Virginia in 1778, with Washington, and possibly Benjamin Franklin, among the members. Their influence and power continued in Virginia throughout segregation, when some prominent members bore responsibility for the state's most undemocratic, repressive practices.

241

The Constitutional Convention,
Desirous, too, of firmer presidential rule
Upon dueling, fractious states,
To prosper trade and industry,
Protect slavery and its fate,
And better repress rebellion;
But, in later years you grew more anxious
At bank and debt and speculation,
And joined with Jefferson, friend and mentor,
To oppose enhanced central power
And support revolutionary France.

Yes, James, your timely contribution
To the Constitution was prime,
The *Virginia Plan* its herald point,
Its three branches clearly mapped,
Senate and House there prescribed,
Your memoirs of its debates,
Your secret stratagems, compromises,
Determination, dedication,
Reasoned arguments
Essential to cement its success
In Philadelphia and, on your return,
Its relentless battle through Virginia.

Yet there are questions to raise with you,
About your vision's democratic lack,
Your backing of an unelected Senate,
A president chosen by cabal,
Not mere slaves and blacks denied the vote,
But most demoted whites as well,
A judiciary appointed, not elected,
And thus beyond our meek control,
And protecting the antique slavers' trade,
Despite Virginia's earlier vote charade.

And there are other questions I must ask,
About deceivings with your 'property' –
Like most fellow founders, you mouthed distaste
From the pasty comfort of your study,
But did nothing to manumit or alleve
– Even Paul, your faithful man,
Was not freed by your hand –
And were for displacement of that race
To malarial Liberia, and thus to
Purify America and finally be rid
Of conscience and forbidden burden.
Oh, how your tender liberty
Rested on the enslaved community
Of your tended slaves.

But hush, WindTeller, horseman of the night,

Don't criticize, lest you be scorned,
In your cape and hat and ready whip,
As you ride the freeze of Tidewater creeks,
And note the empty, bereft barns,
The toried houses ruined, left,
To be claimed by loyal hands,
Dividing old, abandoned lands.

In 1788, delegates meet in Richmond to debate the new Federal Constitution.
Patrick Henry, James Monroe and George Mason oppose it, but Washington,
Jefferson and Madison (despite reservations) support it. Debate is, at times,
heated and intense, the outcome never certain, as they discuss the role of central
government, individual rights, the limits on government, their concern that no
standing army ever resides in Virginia, the rights of freemen to bear arms and
form militias, trade, taxes, issuing money, a federal bank, whether the federal
government would ever abolish slavery, opening up the new territories, especially
Kentucky, road-building, education and religious freedom.
On June 25th, 1788, Virginia narrowly ratifies the Constitution and becomes the
10th member of the United States. The new Capitol, designed with Jefferson's
help, is built in Richmond.

The veils, the mists that swirl…

'Tis well, George,
Architect of the nation, its mason,
Symbol, and its columned apogee,
Its compass, set square of liberty,
Blessed with wisdom of great Abraham,
Life crafted by careful, reasoned degree,
The iota, alpha, omega of nascent hope,
And its sure-measured mastery.

In your eight-year presidency,
You rose to the foundling height
Of wisdom, grace and empathy,
Sought a stronger federation
– Though doubtful of its efficacy –
A central bank, financial loans,
A federal-bonded currency,
With turnpikes and canals to link
The country geographically.

Lover of order, proportion,
Mathematic symmetry,
You sought to turn America
Into a cornucopia
Of reasoned, structured beauty,
Yet never loved democracy
Nor the common crowd,
Fearful of Illuminati, Shay and Jacobin,
Surrounded, as you were, by calls
For universal suffrage, an outrage

You vigorously opposed,
Seeking close-handed neutrality
In the French-led European war,
And cautioned those who were
Freedom-raging Republicans,
Francophiles, haters
Of increased, baphomet centrality,
Not to pursue demands too literally.

Nary a sanctioned Christian, deist rather,
Worshipping the Almighty
In His many natural forms,
Endurer, steady, unemoting,
Harborer of mysteries, true to your word,
No great philosopher, nor great thinker,
But focused leader of the talent
That shaped us so remarkably –
The needed anchor, rudder,
Affirming hand upon the wheel,
And freer, finally, of your slaves,
As the last sweet grains of well-lived sand
Dropped within
The hourglass of your life.

IX

And thus it begins, of necessity,
The myths already,
Stories to fit some scheme
Of whom we wish to be;
But there are many stories,
Many versions…
Yours, mine,
And ours…

…As we at last walk free,
And finally face our search for self,
For the journey and the quest is me.

But who am I and what is this new nation?
What identity will it cleave unto itself,
What new meaning and delved philosophy
Will emerge from its prophesy and its will?
And who will I become, now
I am free to wander with my own name?

I am dreaming – am I dreaming?
Forgetting, recasting an illusion
Of self and my country…?

Or is this the beginning of our greatness?

And what is the meaning of our new freedom
– *Am* I free?
What of I the slave and I the pauper,
I the bondsman, tenant farmer,
I the orphan, beggar or the peddler,
Who are not free even in our sacking cloth,
But only in our final breath of death?

What is the meaning and intent of this new land?
What its beliefs and where its journey?
And, now that we are faced with just ourselves,
Where will we voyage in our need –
Towards ingrate greed, or great deeds
Of selfless compassion, love and community?
Upon which stream will our prospered élite
Deem to lead us?

For I am the journey and I am the quest
Of this land, where even churches
Dwell in the loneliness
Of their silent bells and impel
That westwards move
To populate a continent.

So, inspired in thought,[82]
But willing to let all depart,
I circle the Callings to my side,
Bound to Tsena'ko-ma'ka's soil,
Its red my blood, my spirit, and my soul.

But why this terror that I feel?
Why this reticence, this undesire,
This unwillingness to rest, be still,
Let thoughts fire, face the pallid
Lips and sagging lids
Of my age come full 'round
To circle me within the ground
Of my trepidatious struggle-mind?
And who *are* these Callings,
Twenty-seven, one for each for all
Stations of Virginia's bloodrich soil?
I, SelfSearch, am the first, then
The Five MusicMen
– RattleMan, The Hood, and Horseman,
Also known as WindTeller, Whisperer of the Wind,
Then Linkum Tiddlum Tidy and the Rabbit Savior –

---

[82] The rest of this section comprises *The Song of SelfSearch*. Tsena'ko-ma'ka was the Powhatan word for the land occupied by them and their neighbors – in effect, the Tidewater region of Virginia and northern North Carolina.

Each left-handed, bearing of the raven's wing,
Coming and going with imagining;
Then the Nine Wefts, or MindWeavers,
Who loom the mists and fogs,
And draw the strands as sunlight warms
Their hollowed mountain lair;
Then the Four Abundances, guardians of our beautied land,
The drappered sky, tenacious waves, sylvan forests glades
And storm-calmed mountains of ambition,
Deepest fear and intuition;
Then the Four Enchanters, eternal in their dance and song,
Interweaving with the Wefts, a constant presence
At every sacred place and dwelling throng;
Then the Sufferers Three, Fla'ed Weaver, Maid Mary,
And The Sadness, shuffling around their well
Of infinite pity, stubborn depth,
Of self in sacrifice and 'ternal-suffered acceptance,
Of inward decay, destruction and deceit,
Inner loss and desperation;
And finally, Ergotria, Three-in-One,
SelfTruth, ShelterCare and Mother of the Earth,
Guardian of our inner birth,
Our spirit guide, who cares, protects,
Comforts pain and forgives,
Shelters and sustains…

…shelters and sustains…

Oh, let me draw the circle round,
High above the swirling ground
And the Great Falls curling roar!

As the soaring dawn begins to rise,
Let me descend to the crashing force,
Fill my libation pot, dip it thrice,
And thrice times thrice times thrice
Thrill and drip its flow
Upon my upturned brow,
Thrice times thrice times thrice,
As the sun recalls its pleaing glow
Within the heart of prophecy.

Oh, the circle will be reformed,
Community will be triumphant
And the Daughter of Care
Will at last defeat Despair!

But first let me call my question to the wind,
Seeking who I am and whom I feel
I need to be, now that I am
– Supposedly –
Free…

…searching for who I am…

…As the Callings, mute in 'baccoed repose,
Drift upon the herald mist,
To appear within the veiléd dawn,
And sit on mats above the swelling pool
Of rush-sprung water, there to watch
The gush and flashing overflow
Of vibrancy and life
And lift their music to the wind,
Sing the songs of yesteryear
And call the ancestors in to hear
This, my quest to self-aver
My search for life and meaning.

Let go, let go, I must at first
Let go…
…of all my life before…

As the daylight turns to dusk,
The Callings call to me,
In search of our sweet prophecy,
To light the glory of discovery, burn
Torches to illume our souls,
Implore the drums of Great Falls' roar,
Twist and turn in gorgetop blaze
And braze the circlings' sour delay,
Rhythmic round and rhythmic sound
Of seducing visions, hazened way,
While the evening day re-returns
To rhythmic, cleared emotions,
And settles soft the breezéd night
For another starry-fled display.

Give up, go down, clean away,
Open your spirit for a better way…

…As the dawn is raised once more
By prayers and scented sacrifice,
The Callings quietly drum and watch
Me leave, our staff in hand,
To stride the fall-line river path
And sing the tidal fasts,
Soft and strong,
Mind cleared, direction my only song,
O'er ridges low of oaks and tupelo,
That follow old Pot'au-ma'k's banks,
Round marsh and stream and flat,
South and east about the bay,
Prevailing ancient Indian trails,
Humming the songs of Po'hik's loss,
Of Ok-oqu'an and Ne-abs'ko, the Quan'ti'ko's

Harsh echoes of our history,
The Shopa-wam-si'k, A'kwe-a,
Pot'au-ma'k's saline marsh,
The Masha'do'k and lost Ma'tox, to heed the sound
Of Ra-pa-han-o'k's ghostly reeds,
A ridge stride furl between the curls
Of winsome trading paths and swirling shafts
Of my phantom Indian past,
Bear tooth necklace, deerhide bag,
Staff carved with mystic scenes
That grace me in solipsist dreams,
Moccasins gaiting strong along
Strides of hunters, migrating families,
The Pan'ti'ko, Me-no'kin and Ye-o'ko-mi'ko,
Names that haunt my centuries,
The To-tus'kee, Mis'ki-mon, Wi'ko-mi'ko,
Who haunt the paths and ways
To that windswept point where meet
The river and the A'ko-ma'k Sea,
My spirit engulfed by a breezing bay.

And I must give up my self, toss it far away,
Turn my back on my past, open
Both mind and soul
To all, to all, to all...

Where the river prides the Ches-a'pe'k
In great, soft-tided interflow
And the morn-grained dark of brittle stars
Caresses the flesh-stained sands,
I approach with reverential care,
Lay down my staff upon the beach,
Feathers of the erne, a fox's claw,
A raven's wing from out my hair,
Bear paw, skin from off my breast,
And tear of my ceremonial attire
To stand
Naked as the dawnrise day
That overspurts the eastern bay,
Before Great Ke'show-tse[83] glowing, glaring at
The ringing songs of prophecy,
Blessing our journey, so my way
Will come full circle in its mystery.

...all is all is all am I am all...

I enter in and we are blessed,
Heads under as we stand reborn,
Returned and re-addressed...

---

[83] The Powhatan sun god.

...As I settle for the springtime night,
Fire-bright,
Constellations of light
To question doubts by, imaginings,
Prying down, within
The convoluted caverns where
Right and wrong and strident lies
Quilt my sleepless synergy.

Awake all night, I pray and pray,
Letting my past drift away, away,
To no belief, no prejudged sway,
And the relief of an open day...

It is only then that we,
SelfSearchers all,
May assume the symbols of our call
And rise from off our doubting knees
To push within the Sea of Searching,
And paddle-flume the dug-out spray
East across a spuming bay,
Chanting with each pull and dip,
– Wanting, seeking, bold –
To the isle we hold so sacred,
Wishing on the cold-cued waves,
Questing our song of tasking spray,
Until the gray and asking architraves
Of tree-breezed, ancient boughs
Droop across spartina beds,
And we may hush-beach and push
Onto a smallset reach,
To head within the marshside grass,
Light a fire and circle pass
To hopeful pray
For the dawning of a different day:
"Oh, Father Care,
Your circle will not be broken,
E'en tho' you were taken,
Slaughtered by Despair,
To whom I am now token
Gifted, step-aware
Of my mistaken identity!"

And the night drifts in and on,
Within the heart of prophecy...

After another sleepless stay,
I paddle the dawn towards
A shimmerin eastern shore-lined bay,
Where, with staff in hand, striding strong,
We sing soft and south along
The low-lain ridge betwixt the farms

249

Of eastern sandy shore, of long-ago
O-nan'ko'k, Nasa-wa'dox, Mashi-pon'go,
And the lost Kip'to-pe-ki, on the galing tip where
Ches-a'pe'k and Eastern Water meet,
And stand upon the greeting roar, pelicans
Guiding overhead, a sleeking pod
Of raylined dolphins riding in the bay,
And horseshoe crabs dash-rolled ashore,
To stroll the soaring swash of wind
Of those two bold and tidal sprays,
That mark I'a-pam's[84] hold,
To stare once more, and pray,
Arms raised, staff to the dawn,
To the wonder of this wondrous bay.

Dip-beat, dip-beat, dip
Across the sand-spite waves,
To the point they were first sighted.

And I sing of the Ches-a'pe'k
And the Nan-se-mond
As I stride south and,
Within the gloaming, post-rain mists
Of the gray and owl-black lake
That haunts our heart's most dismal swamp,
Where the daunting Wefts obey,
I pretend my hands to the sky, and cry:
"Oh, Great Ke'show-tse, deliver me!
Give me proud sanctuary within the mounds
Of our sacred ancestors' memories,
And let our shamanic voice impel
The telling of such ensoured stories
Of this place of death and mystic healing,
Where we seek our visions and our meaning,
And commune with messengers of the past,
To learn what is to our become,
Our oracled and hidden being!"

Oh, let my song recall
The spirit of how we were!

...and rise to how we wish to be...!

...Watching, watching
From those hollowed orbs,
Bloodless, insubstantial,
Ephemeral chimera, Wefts
Gliding upon the marsh-gas glow
Of a half-light's marshy flow,
To ask of them, what is myth

---

[84] I-a'pam is the name the Powhatans gave to the sea.

And what is sure reality?

Is it flag, song and anthem,
The patriotism of mystery,
In stars and stripes and the brave and bold,
In the blazes of mythic history?

I wonder, as
The Wefts hear my call, drifting,
Floating upon the mizzled steam
That drizzles between the cedar glow,
Dancing arcs of slow encircled lights,
That waft the spirits from their hands –
Bondsman, controller of our inner bans,
Weft of laws and rules and strict obeying;
OakCrow, breaker, social outcast,
Our dark and dangerous, hidden side;
Will o'the Wisp, the Weft of deep
Desires and wanton selfishness;
The Harbinger of ominous fate,
Of justice reaped and foreboding;
GlimmerGleam, Weft of hopes kept past
That call upon the present;
Lady of the Dales, lent
Of memory and forgetfulness;
UnderFrenzy, of uncontrolled emotion;
MeAsGod, of notioned self-deceit;
And CaveDwell, contrary Weft
Of plunging to the depths
And intensemost self-discovery –
Each weaving the threads of wonder from
Their palms and fingertips
Into a sundered tapestry of calm-ripped
Description of our future gripped
Within a rangle-tangled moss
Of twigs and trees and swampish dross
That dangle from their hair and rags
Of black and silvered filigree.

And I sing of the bear and the fox,
The lynx and swamp raccoon,
As I wander, myth-as-truth,
And swim within illusion
Up the black-streak streams,
Green-scummed,
Of cypress-casting sentinels,
Humming oaks and spanning maples
Of the soft-draped Ki-ko'tan,[85]

---

[85] The area around the river now known as the Elizabeth; the James River was originally called the Powhatan by the English, while the York was originally the Pamunkey; it is reasonable to assume they may have been the original Indian names.

To emerge into the wistful Pow'ha-'tan
And the reach of the Po'quo-son,
As the stars emerge from sunset's veil
And I worship at their clear-blown grail,
To sit upon an all-night vigil,
Self-starved, still,
My mind a chanting blank filled
With little but compassion, so
I may beguile the marsh-backed wind,
And flit among the fragile stars
For whom we really are,
Spy our realms of loneliness,
Within the overwhelming sky
Of constellations, galaxies,
Each star a trick of liberty,
An illusion of you and me,
A shivering of our history,
A lie, and yet
A giving spark by which to live.

...all in all in all...

After my night-scaped wait,
A meditation on inward flight
That draped across the ocean
In the embers of my dying sight,
I drift awave and tidal soar,
Hugging old Pa-mun'ki's shore,
Picking up the songs of Ka-pa'ho-si'k,
Poro'po-tan'k, Tas'kin-as and S'ki-mi-no,
To and fro its holy plying
With a muggy Ma'ta-po-ni
And the water-laden airs
Of sticky, late spring heat,
To stand within the meeted streams,
Palms outspread,
And dream the earth's calm mystery.

It is not for us to unravel,
But to revel in the joy!

Then I leave again, singing up the eastern reach,
With staff in hand, striding strong,
To a promontory and a beach
That silent-bears
The grassy mound of Pow'ha-'tan,
There to drum the ancient rounds
Of our ancestral wish tocome.

"Oh, Pow'ha-'tan, dispel
Guilt and sin and misery,
As illusions we seek to live by,

To self-oppress through voluntary
Choice of leaders and philosophy
That pander to our despondency!

"Our nation, like me,
Must rediscover truth,
Remove the veils of lies
And myths of superiority."

After a brief prayer, I turn
And wade within spartina marsh
To stride, with staff in hand,
Soft and tall and strong,
Raven in my hair,
South and west to
The Falls of Pow'ha-'tan,
Dogging the trees and paths and streams
Of Ku-ri'tu'k and Chi-'ka-hom-ini,
Crying the ridge and mucky bogs
Of our ancestral anonymity,
Until I rest upon a rock's swift rush
And contemplate the sweet soft hush
Of interplay of all – How
My mind reflects that wider world,
Its notions mine unveiled –
For here Abundances were born,
Their resting place upon the rocks,
Singing songs of dawn and morn,
Of river, stream and estuary,
Chants of mountains and the plants
That gleam Virginia's destiny,
Tremulous and rushing praise,
Past emotion and intent,
To lure thoughts gushing in
Then let depart, soft silent-spent.

Humility! Humility! Humility!

Then I rest awhile upon Belle Isle
To dream the questing pain of man,
The sacrifice and loss, and the gain,
Then traverse the falls and stride

South,
Singing soft and strong,
To where A'po-ma'tu'k grows
The tidal flows and tranquil-turning air,
To offer up more churning spells
That foretell our glee and our despair,
Before we turn towards the Dan
And the flooded slick of Ro-an-o'k,
To sing of Chi'p-o'ke, As-a-mu-si'k,

253

Me-har-in-e'k, Se'kok and Chero-en'ha'ka,[86]
The Mo-na-su'ka-pa-no and the Tu'te-lo,
To wander-gyre 'tween mire and grave,
Marsh and black-root cypress tree,
Splashing paths of stray raccoons,
Of weed-scummed, fly-hummed ways,
To the lowset O'kan-ee'chi isle,
There to sit and watch the pointless rush
Of thoughts and thoughts and thoughts,
Images, reactions, unhushed passions,
Until, exhausted, I soft turn towards
The calm and ease of mountains where
The breeze will psalm my frowns of care.

Oh, let my harmony recall
The spirit fall of how we were,
And rise up to how we wish to be!

From the confluence of flooded Dan
And overflowing Roanoke,
I stride past farm and stream,
With staff in hand, soft and strong,
O'er the ridgeline raiséd road
Of railing ups and valeline cuts,
The spurs of highridge, treeline juts
Of a people's past quick-thieved away,
Tricked before their fame was named
By encroach of English identity,
Through Halifax and Brookneal, Campbell,
Bare-broached Lynchburg
– Home of Friends –
As I lend-call the hollow sadness
Of tobacco, wheat and corn,
The forlorn generations gone,
And the land, stripped of tree and soil,
Burning in the tumbreled broil
Of tempestuous roar and spoil,
To reach the thankful shore, once more,
Of Pow'ha-'tan's shady banks.

Oh, where are the trees? There are no trees!
The trees have left, to drift upon the breeze!

I waft upon a present without passion,
Without regret nor retrospect, yet
Sing the slaves and tobacco rows,
The railing fences and the crows,
The centuries of the cemeteries
And craven lines of forgotten brows

---

[86] The Chero-en'ha'ka are the Nottoway; "Nottoway" was a derogatory term used by their enemies. The Mo-na-su'ka-pa-no are better known as the Saponi.

Sweating in their raven nights,
With a smile that will *ne'er* forget.

So, on I stride,
Singing soft and strong,
With memories of Tu'k-a-ho,
Mish-aw'k, Mo-aw'k and Mo-no'kan
Northwest to the Sah-ka-na-ga,[87]
Weaving creeks and crests,
Double-sided views,
Visions of who I am and whom I wish to be,
Simultaneously, flashing from
One side to the other
In a hopelessness, an anxiety
Of indecision, shifting dreams,
And drifting complexes of reality.

Past and on, we stride,
To the close-tight rising sides
Of the Pillars of Virginia,
Striding through with staff and soft-soled shoes,
To the rapid falls that trap canoes,
Where I hear the whispered wind
Repeat the Callings' prophecy –
Liberty in Community! –
Upon the Four Enchanters' song
And riffs of pious MusicMen.

I bless the sweet Maury
Where it grows within another's flow,
Bow and walk head-bent below
The Great and Natural Arch,
Doorway to all valley visions,
And pray beneath the haughty reach,
Open, sacred, silent,
Then briskly stride up to the slope,
Singing soft and strong,
Of Sah-ka-na-ga as it trails
To an escarpment that o'erhopes
Our Piedmont rivered vales,
There to stride with staff in hand
Until the wayward wending path
Seeks out the cloudbound, bouldered gray
Of Otter's windcrest-shrouded peaks
And hail with hands held open wide
The pride and glory of this land!

Then on!

I stride our Sah-ka-na-ga way,

---

[87] The Blue Ridge Mountains.

With staff in hand, soft and strong,
To Big Lick pass, where again
I hear the sultry 'Chanters' Song,
This time soft, demure, luring in
With their enduring, wafting call,
Descending fast the limestone gorge,
To where they dwell beneath the wall,
Casting their ephemeral spell,
Within a hollow-chambered echo
That reverberates a-thru the state
And keeps the myth from slowing –
Dylan, Weft of vision, prophecy,
And fearful, haunting inspiration;
Ol' Hick, Weft of poetry and the daunt
Of its companion, philosophy;
GreenWood, Weft of growth and fecundity,
Verdure, rebirth, hidden sanctity;
And Morgan Diviner, enchanter,
Midwife to the world –
Dancing the Trance of Illusion,
Entrapping me within their mystery,
Unable to focus, stand nor see,
But floating above the discing flow,
Risking destruction on rocks below –
And ask of me, SelfSearch, striven mist,
What it is I must persist away
If I am to be given all:
What is more lost the more it seeks,
More trapped the more it ekes to be,
More lonely when it stresses company,
In more distress when more in happiness,
Is you, yet is refused by you?

And I answer with a smile,
For, without knowing,
I know, I know, I know…

…and so they let me wander free…

…To stride on,
Singing soft and strong,
To rise upon the crest of ridge,
Unto the lofty moors of Dan,
Lea-clipped on their sunset ledge,
Stopping there to pray and bless
The power of this Blessing Way,
As the MusicMen in circle round
Smoke to this profound journey,
Beneath an ancient oak, still there,
Bearing leaves above a silent pool,
Reprieving the lives of all Virginia…

…my mind, I know, aglow…

…Then I stride
South and west to swift caress
The vales of endless streams,
And humbly kneel at Mon-don-ga-cha-te,[88]
Curvaceous, tumbling gorge,
As it seeks its bumbling course
Past surging Balsam peak.

Then up I stride, in the night,
To use the moon's translucent light
To guide my pace between the trees
And rise the rise of sultry breezes
That caress its rhododendron sides,
To a fir-lain, berried peak,
There to adorn the airy stars
And open arm the welcome dawn,
In prophecy of a newsworn morn…

From the purple-flowered slopes
Of our triple-sacred mounts,
Whitetop, Balsam, Pine, through
Firs and tree-sprung ridges, to stir
The tight and forest-gripping coves
Of thicket rip and catbriar,
I stride my frail-songed way along
An ancient Ani-Ki'tu-hwa-gi trail,[89]
Until I greet a chambered hall,
A tunnel, water carved,
And a marveled, deepset pool,
Where the ancestors crown all our calls
With oracles of their own.

There, I hush, as
The Callings sit with me around
The night-time fire of fantasy,
And sing their prophecy once more
To the core of our journey bound.
Upon the morning's dawn,
I follow the hollowed way
Through that hallowed shaft, into
Briared shades of tall-brave trees
That mark the ways of ancient elk,
Bison and the white-tailed deer,
Up steep streams, bulk-feared bluffs,
To welcome-find
The SelfSearch trail of warrior days,

---

[88] The New River. This is the gorge that flows through Grayson and Carroll counties. Balsam Mountain is the original English name for Mount Rogers.

[89] The Cherokee, who hunted in south western Virginia at one time.

And yaw upon the mountain scene
At Cumberland, there to foreswear
The seductive Vale of Tennessee.

Turning east and north, I stride
And sing of cuspéd ridge and rise
Across the high-bridge, soaring glide
To rise and hide the deep-gorged trail
To where the rivers far below
Join and turn and rock and swirl
In near-isle close about
A towering rock of moaning trees,
That is the birthstone and the rite
Of Ergotria, urging birth,
Three-in-One, our energy
Of SelfTruth, ShelterCare
And Mother of the Earth,
Nurturing all who curl to her,
Seek her and beseech her,
And where she weeps for the world...

...three-times-three-times-three...

...And, after standing upon
The Tower of the Earth,
Arms raised in mornrise prayer
Three sunsets and three dawns,
We turn to stride, singing soft and strong,
The rocky forest waters' spate
And lusty throng of the great
Mountains of our state,
To follow back an old Sha-wan-wa[90] track,
Winding up and down and through
Tight-shadowed, cold-creek valleys
Of dense-alleyed trees and spurs,
To the curling Clinch, there to sing south-east
Of the Stony and the Rich,
Heaven's feasting bowl,
Past verdant herds of fleeing deer,
Lone and herding buffalo,
To the source of the Ho-go-hee-gee,
Lurking on a valleyed side,
To raise up'po-woc to our rivered pride
And settle deep within our mind,
Letting go, letting go, letting go...

Then from that tender-springing cove,
I stride with my staff,

---

[90] The Shawnee; Ho-go-hee-gee is an Indian name for the Holston – the source of its North Fork is also the source of the Tennessee; up'po-woc is sacred tobacco; the Wa-la-tu-la is the Cowpasture – its source is also the source of the James.

Singing soft and strong along
The Buckhorn and the Rich,
Wolfcreek, Brushy, Walker
– All names that will later ring
These steep-sward glens
With the axes of another time –
To wend up the swelling New, now forded,
As I climb to find the heights of home,
Where the waves do roam the sky
In the secret station of The MusicMen
As they espy, within the mountain's well,
The tears of generations' fears,
As they weep and sigh
In empathy and in dread,
For Virginia's sons and daughters,
Lives o'erspanned, choppy, rain-dimpled,
Eddies and reflections, simple
Hopes, spiritual dimensions
Of our need to understand…

…That all is all is all…

…And let us call
All is all is all,
For I am all am I am all…

And the ancestors are here too,
Upon the amphitheater's hills,
Observing our lives, their tears
Filling the lake's soft sides
As they dance-explore their sunset cries
Around its tree-lapped shores
Every full-moon rise,
Trapping tight the circle,
Blessing all who fight
To return our dimming sight
As the waters surge and brim
To the Callings' urgent tears…

And for twenty-seven days I stay,
Twenty-seven nights, one for each
Station of Virginia' reach, as they
Encircle our bounded state, to pray
For the round to be rejoined
One single-minded day…

Then one morn,
With the blessings of the MusicMen,
I stray-stride along, soft and strong,
To sing the Salt Pond, swift Johns Creek,
The sinking mountains, peaking to the rise
Of Brush to linger for the source

Of the Roanoke, tree-covet
Within the let of a sharp hill,
Where I pray for my harpish thoughts
To drift upon the loving clouds,
Then lift on, singing proud and strong,
Following the valley of the stars,
Catching the scarp of North and Patch,
To sip of the confluencing Jackson
And the rock and ripple Wa-la-tu-la,
Pray, take stock and eat,
Thrice dipping and thrice praising up the dawn,
Then beating up the forceful course,
Meandering to its eventual source,
A tree-tucked hillside spring
That wells the side of Buck Mountain,
There to lay a sage-spelled gift
And drink of our pure energies,
Praying for our prophecy,
Searching for our trace of self,
Letting go of thought and place,
Any notioned grace
Of memory, possessions,
Brief within the lithium springs
Of the Callings veiled imaginings,
Ere passing o'er some blue-ranged peaks
To seek the sweet-sourced Pot'au-ma'k,
Set within a remorseful bank,
There to drink of its pure swell,
And raise my arms to call in to dwell
The energy of all to help us find
Our prophecy of compassioned mind,
Then venture south to sate and kneel
At the fourth of our great healing flows,
This time the graceful Shen-an'do,
There to dip and dip and dip again
Within the pureset, earthy source
Of our universal coursing energy…

…All is all is all…

And then, once more,
I stride along,
With our stiff staff in hand,
Singing soft and strong,
As I prevail the mountainsides
And cantankerous, steepened vales,
To follow true the Warrior Path
To the overmath of Cen-an'tua,[91] there
To raise my arms in hailing praise
As I feel care regale me 'round

---

[91] An old Shawnee name for Massanutten Mountain.

And am engulfed in love, to watch
The mountains sound
My eternity –
And am so o'erspanned by wonder at
This great encircled land...

...All am I am All...

...I *am* the land; and the land is me!

As darkness descends, I hie east
Of Cen-an'tua's enbowléd dale
To rehail the ancient entrancéd way
To a sacred undercaverned world
Where the MusicMen unwombed ago
And the Sufferers slowly sing and dwell,
Peering into an infinite well
Of lightless limestone pit and fear,
Around, around as they delve and leer,
The Sadness, Maid Mary, Weaver Fla'ed,
Of inner loss, deceit, self-sacrifice,
Calling on them to uncross this strife,
And bless our journey to a deeper life...

And let us tell you, circling three,
Of the Sufferers' guardian hold,
Within the myth of complexity,
As they dance the mirror of their birth,
To see all suffering's horrored worth,
Translucent depths, its plunging sound,
Piling each upon the most profound,
Around, around eternal fate,
That is their oracle-cauldroned gate
Of hope retasked in hate,
Each beyond their painted mask,
Red and black and white, ragged rags,
That tag upon the fullmoon night
To fright the spirits of their plight.

Then I stride on,
Bearing high our staff along,
Singing soft and strong,
The Shen-an'do-a's wander-sides,
Until it roars into the roiling Pot'au-ma'k,
Rising to the mountains' call,
Where I enter in the fall
And final place of journeying,
To stand within the melding waters
And stare at the uphallowed heights,
– The glowing, glaring, shadowed lights –
To know we are the water, that all belief
Is relief within the breath of these mountains

261

And the sighing of these streams
That give wonder to our fearless dreams...

...All memory gone, all desires,
All attachments, needs, and all fires...

...gone...

So we stride on,
Through the Pillars of America,
Singing of our song,
Close along Pot'au-ma'k's side,
Through the highside valley walls,
Until we sigh from rapid hills
And stride the southern shore,
All mind of self now drained away
Within the joy and love of all
And the lamp of simple journeying,
To arrive once more at the falls,
Replete within the Callings camp,
Me entwined in We,
Liberty within community,
The source of our new identity,
And true calling of the self,
Our pilgrimage complete,
The circle celebrated and rejoined,
The pipe handed round, sage water too,
Smudged and greeted,
The aging journey passing through,
And the prophecy now firmly planned
Within the power and support
Of Ergotria's ancestral thought...

The first *will be* the last,
The circle *will not* stay broken,
But will rejoin triumphantly –
That is the prophecy.

X

Oh, how the tom-toms drum...

...drive in the nails of our tocome...

And how the silent bells do hum...

...As, deep within The Virgin's heart,
Beneath her swelling surface soil,
Lurks the darkened, secret dream
Of a deep and richly coal-filled seam,

From Chesterfield, Midlothian
Inclining under James' flow,
To Henrico's Chickahominy,
Deep pits beam, pumps put in
To drain the logged and water-gleams
Of slaves' and freedmen's hacking strain
Of pick and shoveled demean,
To whack the face and crack the fall,
Grip and gouge and letdown smack,
As shadows flicker-stark extreme
And there is no sound but smack and grunt
Of cracking pick and troweling ton,
And odored dust within the eyes
Of sweat's intense and seeping ardor,
In glim respite of coal-black hope
And death from fire-damp keeping...

...of the veils...

...the mists that swirl and curl...

...Within,
...Within,
The solace of the dawn's sweet call...

...Of secret strums and totem drums
Hanging from the juba trees,
Remembering of our ancestors, as
They toll the bell soft-silently.

...The veils, the mists that swirl
And spread confusion with each curl
Of might and right and slinking night
As Virginia seeks its own sweet light.

...A breeze, a silent-docketed breeze,
Soft-swirling
Within the sanctified motions of our breath.

And, with the winter season on us once again,
We are hired to a county town,
Bricklayers, carpenters, strong
Laboring men, to construct
A new courthouse, colonnade,
Grand steps up, Revival façade,
Fine windows, doorways, archéd rooms,
Paneled, architraved and pilastered,
With all the benches, tables, necessary rails
For this place of truth and tales.

I bow my head in the gentle-seeming breeze
That hides the trees within the mists...

…of aahhhhhhh….

For, as I was saying,
Before interruption by the war,
We treat our property so very well,
Providing those ungrateful wretches,
Too childlike innocent and naïve
To cook or market for themselves,
With a paternal guiding hand
To direct and discipline, where proper,
And teach them each their special place
Within this, our well-placated world
Of God and king and autocrat,
Then planter, yeoman, servantman,
Each in his well-respected sphere
Of pleasant-geared society.
They are but infants in our care,
Sly devils who must be taught
To respect property and life,
But once are tender bought,
Seem blithe and let content
To know they are provided well
From our most undivided pocket.

And it is upon this rock of certitude
That we may rise to the noblest heights
Of classic-reasoned philosophy,
Of Plato, Cicero and Ptolemy,
Literature, politics and enquiry,
Fine china, inlaid marquetry,
And, one must suppose,
The greatest libraries in the country
For our uplifting, calmed repose.

Oh Moses, can you hear the dawn…?

For, at that very time,
A little further down the track,
Some slaves assemble-stack
The skeleton of a rib-built jail,
Skull-stoned steps and sheriff's carapace,
Gates and bars and grinning chains,
Honing its flesh-encloistered frame
And new-erected, gibbet bones…

…Just in time, for that night
The paderollers[92] stagger-fight
From their evening alehouse merriry
To clumsy-clamber up aboard

---

[92] These vicious night-time patrollers, often brutalized poor whites, took a delight in catching runaways and teaching them a 'lesson.'

Their mounts for nightly slave patrol,
With dogs and whips and pistols out
On dirk-fled lanes, carved woodland edges,
Ditches, swamps and sabered ways,
A bounty for each seasoned runaway
Without pass or valid reason.

Well-lit moonlight is the best,
That's when they like to bolt
– When the corn is high
Or at Christmas time,
During a trackless tempest,
Or over their weekends free,
For but a day or two.

Such are the cares of our lives.

The 1792 slave code contains fifty-three acts that cover the importation of blacks,
freedom of movement among those enslaved, prohibitions against bearing arms,
punishments for rebellious behavior, unlawful assembly, trading with blacks,
attacks on whites by a black, punishment for attempted rape of a white woman
(castration), procedures for capturing runaways, prohibiting slaves from
administering medicines, setting the punishment for perjury (cutting off the
offender's ears, plus thirty-nine lashes), and prohibiting ships' masters from
transporting slaves out of state without their owners' consent. The code also
defines a mulatto as a person with one-quarter black blood.

And so, in softer spoken words,
Less obvious, more circumspect,
Virginia passes liberties for its élite
While insidious new controls
Are passed, year after year after year,
For those sold least fortunate.

No free black or mulatto may migrate into Virginia; heavy fines are set for
forging documents that allow a slave to pass as free; a person convicted of
inciting slaves to insurrection or murder will be executed; if convicted of
harboring slaves, he or she must pay a fine of $10 or receive thirty-nine lashes.
And on and on and on...

Also this year, the Nansemond Indian Reservation on the Nottoway River, long
abandoned by tribal members, is sold. Remaining Nansemonds, Christianized and
living as whites in Suffolk County and nearby towns, continue with their lives,
largely in anonymity.

Old WindTeller sits among the ashes
Of a homesteader's abandoned hut,
Brer Rabbit whining by his side,
Linkum Tiddlum Tidy running wild
Within the wintered staves of trees
That vine-clad drape the willowed breeze
Of the new-cleared hills of Abingdon,
As the Sufferers, three in kind,

Pause to rest and weary-sigh
Upon their memoried knees
For the wolves that old Boone destroyed
In their hidden cavern home,
And pray one day that wildness will again
In Virginia's mountain wilderness,
Hunt and mate and roam.

Meanwhile, with sartorial unconcern,
Washington lilts his eyes of enterprise
To the nation's largest distillery,
Canals and swamps and drainage,
And rapid assuages new bridges, roads,
Old Cape Henry Lighthouse
In fine octagonal form,
Ashlared, of thick-set stone,
Hammer-hewn and dressed,
Seventy-two from base to crest,
To shine upon old Chesapeake
And guide stormed and harried sailing ships
To Hampton Roads' calm safety
And the mouth of broad-banked James.

And guide old Jefferson too…

For, hush,
Sweet nailer's smithy,
Forge of ark and trough,
Don't stir
As we enter-peer the dim-lit hell
Of ten-year devils, boys and girls,
In ragged stands around
Central rings of burning fire,
Six to a brazen-smeltered share,
In the smoky, dirty, damping filth
Of black-coked floor and charcoaled roof
And tiny slits and door,
Of smoke and ashes, steaming water
And clouds of dreadful dust,
And watch their little muscled fists
Pince within the white-hot hearth
Of bellowed, tuyered forge,
Pick and hammer, whip them out,
Smash-lash the nail rod cleaved,
Cut them sharp and hit them firm
And bend them to the nailer's block.
It's your duty to impose your will
And make the unwilled mend
Their ungrateful, disobedient ways
To the stiddying anvil
Where the hammer blows
And throws sparks upon the nightly air

Of some reluctant servitude.

Oh yes, let's hush, as
They sit upon their crampéd stools
Midst balance and the weights,
And cut brief lengths identical
Against the hardy truth of race,
Six-penny brads them all,
Dip the nails within the trough,
And drop within the bore,
To bash the countersunken head,
Spring the whimsey sudden loose,
And let the nail tink-link within
The bag upon the floor –
Four a minute,
No time for cough or wheeze
Within the stall-burnt air,
Their black rags and blacker skin
Merging with the floor within,
Bashing till the late night hours,
Then dropping close next door
In the clay-floor, boarded cabins,
To rise once more at four...

And begin, begin, begin...

XI

For most, the storm still rages
And the silent bell still tolls...

...While we wait,
Our sweet dawn forestalled...

Oh, hear
The heavy-shadowed shrouds
That cloud with veils our memory!

Grey-scratched, slashing flashes
Of cut-lipped light, zap-clapped,
Roaring, heavy-stoned and growling,
Thunderclaps that riot, clamp
The peaks with powered revenge's roil,
Ker-rashing boorooming growls
In whorls of vapored misery,
Swirling, blackened dark, foreboding chill
Upon this land's unforgiving will,
Bong, bong, bong...

I stare up at the smoke-wisped ceiling
Of half-board beams and joists

And from my baby's screaming face
Flick a racing cockroach
As the storm billows stern outside,
Its fingers scratching in at us
Through cramping gaps and holes,
My yester husband's pillow moist,
Clothes, damp straw tick
Still warm from his onetime repose –
For today he's gone, sold south to buy
My mistress's season dress –
And so our children, reason-pressed,
Must suffer on with me
In this brief respite we call our home,
But which we requite with other selves,
Eight within our ten-by-twelve,
Six more within the loft,
Lice-laden straw on mud-high pallets
Scattered on the crud-soaked floor
As the tempest blows and wicked sends
Its bitter-goring winds
Through every shingle, every wall
And stuffles out the single fire
Where our pots are simmer-stalling,
Stealing heat
To make our cornpoke meal.

I remember Moses leading his people
To the Promised Land
And how the waters steeple-parted
For the faith of that one man
And the belief of the Israelites,
Frighted and oppressed like us,
Their masters mazed Egyptians
Who, like ours, never let them free;
But there our hope does end,
For our Moses was recaptured,
Whipped near death,
And now is breathed away.

...and I recall how sweet the bells did ring...

So I pat my crying baby
Who cannot understand
Why Papa had to go and we
Can't follow on his journeyed way.

Sleep, my baby, sleep,
For one day you will wake
And tremble the world
With your anger and your skill.

In 1795, a devastating flood inundates Virginia. The over-farmed land, stripped of trees, is unable to absorb the days of rainfall, so thousands of tons of topsoil are lost to the choking Chesapeake. However, with the British off their backs, enterprising businessmen begin projects to improve trade and transport. Roads are resurfaced, rivers dammed and widened, canals and locks completed, mills erected, manufactories built, and an air of enterprise imbues the state.

Ah! Court days again!

Called by bells of churchtide ringing,
I ride to town once more,
Past Colonel Gray's plantation,
Tobacco 'placed by grain,
Beans and peas in fields this year,
With fertilizer and rotation
To nitrate his austere yields.

Tho' the ditch is gravely overgrown
And the fence line in decay,
The road is just the same,
With ruts and roils, tricky fords,
Fields of hapless toiling slaves.

But there is a new courthouse now,
The tavern long disused for trials,
Tho' still a house for whiling folk,
Gentlemen who share the rooms,
Sip and eat bespoke victuals
And attend the market stalls to gossip
And belittle the time of day.

There are new churches also now,
Their congregations milling,
Whites in finery still attended
By well-groomed blacks,
Coats as shiny as the mares
Who pull the chaises and the traps.

The English Church is well-maintained,
But few remain in attendance,
Most hoving to the Baptist hall,
Rough planked, pews unsteady,
A preacher who's a fiery man,
And draws them in their droves.

There is too a blacksmith's now,
A livery stable where I dehorse,
Lead her to be fed and watered,
Lathered down, then saunter over
To goodday the gathered crowd,
Pass stocks and gibbet, dowdy used,
A hardware store retailing tack,

Clothing, nails and sacks of peas,
A barrel-maker, warehouses
For tobacco crops and grain,
A smudge of lawyers for the court,
Bailiff, sheriff, clerk and judge.

Next, I pass a row of stalls,
Fruits and vegetables, 'mongers, bread,
Three Negroes, one poor white,
A woman cooling pies and cakes,
Another ribbons, threads and wool,
As a twitching, rakish boy
Switches a herd of sheep and cows
Through the browed and bleating street.

The road is wide between the houses,
Men on horseback, carts and mules,
A returning wagon loading timber,
A Negress passing, two churns of milk
Limbering from a chestnut yoke,
Her shoulders choked in strain,
As a slave girl squats forlorn,
Selling butter grained that early dawn.

I note a peddler with a chestheld tray
Of bows and trinkets, an array of brasses,
And two men who remould
Bricks upon a garden wall,
A Negress who tends the grass within,
A boot shine boy who helps appareled trade
And another who shoulders a sack of oats,
White dust upon his weathered coat,
While a final boy hustle-routes a barrel
That leaks brown molasses out.

I climb onto a raised boardwalk,
Doff my hat in passing praise,
At crinoline and bonnets, parasols
Set for a hazy morning stroll
To haberdash and milliner,
As the ladies of the county
Renew and relate
Opinions on the prisoners' fate
Within the stewing jail.

And our bells toll the morning heat
As the sun stops to beat upon the day
And riffles down to speckle drops
Of gnats upon the river's spray,
Sighing for the checkered sky...

In 1798, President John Adams passes the *Alien & Sedition Acts*. In protest,
James Madison writes the *Virginia Resolutions* and Jefferson writes the *Kentucky
Resolutions*. Two years later, in the final triumph of the revolution, Jefferson is
elected President of the United States. But the country is already moving on...

A pair of white peacocks,
Wings clipped and tamed,
Call their melancholy chill
Amid the boxwood geometry
Of a dawning moonlight hill...

Sleep well, my love,
Let your ardor rest within my arms
And let me hold you tight against
The cold of night and revolution
While you take your consolation, poured
Within my awe and love for you.

I love you, my love,
Soft-tongued lip of propertied rebellion,
For your devotion to freedom,
Whose pealing calls more true this day,
E'en though that throng of liberty
Tolls for you and not for me;
I love, my love,
That great man in whose words
Reverberates the world
And rings unwilling freedom
Upon a doubting crowd –
And I sense you will forever be
The resounding bellwether
By which we judge true
Ourselves and our country,
And that your chiming melodies
Will inspire
My sons and servant daughters
In their centuries of crusade
Against your slaughter
And your tyranny.

I love you, my love,
Steeled forge of Louisiana,
Foundry of Lewis, Clarke and Pike,
Educator, caster of men,
Optimist, humanist, philosopher,
Who has wrought for us the chance,
Perchance,
Black and red and white,
To furnace a harmony of future
Without repeal of consequence.

I love you, my love,

Though your community includes not me,
But a prosperous Piedmont heredity
That views paternalistic wisdom
As the guarantor of property,
Status and continued slavery,
And whose politics are consensus of élite,
Not democracy, nor equality;
I love you, my villainous hero,
For your innocence and staple carillon
Of all that's sound within humanity,
The embodiment of a dream,
Its definition and its apogee
– But also the portent of a naïveté
Abused by crowning wiser men
To give them rhythms for their need
And skirts for their mistruck envy,
And for their greed.

I love you, Tom,
As I stare with bowed and soulful eyes
Upon this isolated mountain in the sky,
For your true-honed honesty,
Without Savior nor tolling God,
A self-willed deism, not untuned
By the clang and curved hypocrisy
Of sanctimonious Christian tones
That gild us to our slavery;
I love you, despite
Your buried call
For westward expulsion
Of black and red, to leave mere white,
In your quest for some solution
To the gloom of our impending plight;
And for the simple, frightful deed
Of suckling from the bosom of my need
As you feed of passioned liberty.

And yet I wonder, can there ever be
Any tempest-tendered restitution
To cast the dreadful thunder of the night
From that denied and deadly-toned delight
Which no sanctity can respect,
Of letting others' sweet-toiled labors
Rhyme to thy personed wit and charm,
Pour your daily wine to ease ferment,
Horses, carriages calmed, stables too,
A daughter's Paris education
Fine cuisine, guests, a library or two,
All so you may recline
Your sore bones upon
A slave-made rocking chair
While my brother gently fans

272

And I tipple you yet more Madeira
Than I will ever sip, nor scent,
Your secret Sally, and,
Since Martha's flight,
Your only heaven-sent delight?

Oh, sweet love,
Take your respite in me,
Merge within my mulatto arms
Roll your sweat with mine
And let those neat dreams curl unfurl
Of your extolled liberty, if not mine –
Hush, my darling, do not wake,
But let me caress those light-red locks
And ease the troubles of your country;
Let me soothe your conflicts
And remove your pains
With the true ring of love for all;
Let me pull the sheets to cover you
Against the midnight cold
And wait with open eyes, my love,
For the palling pre-dawn horn
That calls our hands to your fields
And marks my hurried pitch and rise
To dress and strike your morning meal
Before you broach your eyes
And forestall our night of mutual love,
My dear, in the solemnity of
Formalized appeal.

...We sleep, we sleep, we sleep,
As the distant thunder rolls
Slowly fold within
Our years of veiléd mist...

And a breeze, a silent-docketed breeze,
Soft-swirling
Within the sanctified motion of my breath,
Takes the moments of my being
And lifts them up upon the clouds
To offer dreams of newborn care
And calms with sweet soliloquies
Of hope, compassioned justice,
And the eternal promise of the trees...

...For we are the journey,
We are the quest,
And we are the test of our own prophecy.

Book V

Dancing on the Bones:
Virginia's Harsh Decline, 1801–1860

I

Amazing grace! How sweet the sound
That saved a wretch like me!
I once was lost, but now am found;
Was blind, but now I see.[93]

Oh, his call, his magic, mystic call
– And how the raven knocks…!

…At the dance,
The turning, turning swing
Of the dark and swirling dance
As we descend within…

…VisionMind,
To live the life Life planned…

Sing, Moses, sing!

Lord, let me see the dawn!
Let me live to be free
And walk among those counted souls,
Ancestors of ancient wisdom's ways
Who can whisper who I am…
Who I am…

…Ask who I am, blue-eye-veiled,
Walking down the aisle, to
The cheering march of hymns
And faint, white-laced smiles
That call, that call, that call…

Why am I so masked from myself?
Why so hidden from my soul
Within the trace of wedding dance
– The marching death of life's entranced embrace?

_____

[93] *Amazing Grace* was written in 1779 by John Newton, a slave ship captain, in response to the horrors he had experienced on his voyages.

And why do you lie to me?
Why?
Why do you lie?

And why lie to yourself?

I do not; I do not lie!

Then why pretend in progress when
The land is dying before our eyes?

Because in my dance to confettied bells
I can only hear my songs of youth
And the sweet sounds of harmony…

…of the Callings and the MusicMen…

Oh! Let me wander with your hands in mine
Along the once-green flows of forest pine
And falls of barren vale, exhausted, stripped,
And ripped of all but blood-sapped dust
That mocks our crying memories…

…oh, sing…!

…For there is no need to stroke
The earth's sweet gentleness,
Since the secret is to melt
The soil's frail crust
Within a season's turn and turn,
And turn and turn and turn,
To slash and burn, exhaust,
Slash and burn, exhaust,
Until the land is mocking gauged
In the vision of a miraged age.

And so the dawning century
Wipes its eyes on barren rocks
And the fields and hills of our dreams,
The horizons of our sparkled hopes,
Are become
A mortuary of generations,
As the scheme is lived, whate'er the cost
To earth or fellow man…

The dust, the dust,
The calling of the dust…

…Oh sing,
Sing Moses, sing down da hoe an' plow,
Sing Moses, sing down da hoe an' plow,
Sing Moses, take me to da Promise' Lan'.

Hallelujah! Hallelujah!
Hear ol' Moses' call!

I pray, how I pray
For that hallelujah time!

And I, WindTeller,
Whisperer of all hearts,
Thy heart in mine,
Veiled sufferer of the centuries,
Rise upon a thermal shout
To the heated heavens' clouds,
To where I vista swerve and swing about
A once-green land that's overworked,
Treeless, soilless, harrowed sick,
Unable to repay the plow
Whose farrow lingers silent now
Within our barns of wintered hopes,
As a raven swings upon a rail,
Wings sputtering, cawling, frail,
Waiting for the dead to fall,
While a caterpillar feasts upon a leaf
In this Lent of dreamtide ringing,
Of fasting harvest and starved belief,
That forces Virginia's poor to run
To Kentucky's sunned relief.

We work so hard for nothing,
For dust...

...as we call, we call, we call...

Call upon the magic, mystic mind...

...As if to discover our secrets
On the soft-tuned Whisperer's breath
Vapored, gray-frosted, surreal death,
And as we descend to peer within
Pinion gear and worn-out ring,
Pulley belt and ricket shaft,
Where we grind the grain of history,
Flume the chute of our tocome
And overrace the gushing rack
Of ever-splashing destiny
– To work with another on our back.

So grind the corn most carefully,
Poor within the hopper's throat
And sprinkle to the wooded shoe,
There to agitate the damsel shake
Upon the making mace head held
And dribble through the boot and eye,

Betwixt the sighing runnerstone
And let it masticate the coarseset grain
Upon the bedstone's granite base,
To trace it through the trough and chute
Into the smoking sack of flour, to
Feel the fineset velvet thumb
And powder-silkened skin,
To slack the skim of millstone wheel,
Trim the closeness damask tight,
And gauge our fine-ground, rounding plight,
As we enter in, enter near into
The darkness of internal fear.

Oh, WindTeller, caster of the siren's joy,
Where is the lantern we hand by our side,
To tell us who we are and why,
Where Moses is, and the Promised Land?

...I must descend-escape, to resurrect
In energetic pride...

...As you linger, linger,
At the Rabbit's call,
Horseborne by my side, Virginia,
To stop where once
The waters melted easy through
Their yearlong wooded glades,
Past beaver lodge and deer-path drink,
Beneath the shaded evergroves
Of sycamore, cottonwood and birches' boughs
– For now they are stark and naked lurk,
Sharp-gashed gullies, bleeding rushes
That rootless swirl the eddied gushes
And steal the gasping, toppled roots
Of felled and girdled, treeless fields
Where cattle drown the treaded banks
And topsoil drains and floods away,
Carving creases on a land
That once was calm and gay.

On we ride, on, galloping the hills
To the Savior's call.
As I descend into the lair,
The labyrinth of styxian sea
And my cerberian dream to be
– My destiny!

But hush, lo!
For there I see the Rabbit in his hat,
Bobbing close upon his head,
Black as riddle cloak and veil,
Bearing fine his wail-fired fiddle,

Ears pricked for the Devil's notes
And wandering where he wanders most,
From nowhere come, to nowhere go,
To magic-make and stare confound
With tragic peg and bow-bound woe,
The witch-briared spirits bold
That in the trancing mists abound
To the mystic wedding jingle sound
Of the aisle of a thousand mingled parts,
And promises of our veiléd hearts...

Oh, his call, his mystic fluting call!

II

I trip the stairs to polished boards,
All in my dancing finery,
And am greeted by my caller's words,
Hooded, masked, announced,
Pronounced within the gentle scuff
Of a falling dancer's ruff,
As I tap with foot the blinded trap
Of oaken floor, expectant crowd
That rims the gathered stage about
And hangs upon the caller's prayer
As I sudden feel the Virgin reel
And skip the convulsating trip
Of the hushed and collared dance
And memories flash askance my mind
Of Jefferson's disabled promise
And Monroe's confined reprieve,

Twist and turn, I twist and turn,
To spin within the startled stare,
Called surprise,
And the raven knocking in the gloom
As I blaze the pluming charcoal stench
Of shoe and wire and brazier,
The clang and ting and burgeoning
Of scythes to pikes and swords,
Waiting for our justice time...
...Oh, Solomon!...
Twist and turn, twist and turn,
Kick and kick and kick...
...Twenty-seven dancers...
Eternal hate in angered state...
Twenty-seven – twenty-seven!
The caller's trace...Turning, turning...
Dancing
Forger of my race,

Eyes blinded from the fleeing dawn
I was not graced to see.
Turning, turning,
Turning,
Dancing to the threads
Life has handed me.[94]

And even on that seasoned dawn,
Upon the graves of nameless slaves
A new plantation house is raised,
Hall erected, ballroom, stairs,
Cornice, frieze and architrave,
Their bones rescattered, re-interred
Beneath its fineset ashlared walls
Where dance the gray-eyed wedding veils
That march the tune of vivid death
And mock the bones of church and man
To moan the breath of *Auld Lang Syne*.

Oh, we'll take a cup of kindness yet...

...And lets us quilt of ailing parables,
Sew the seams of Jonah and the whale,
Patch a work, a frieze of Jacob's ladder,
The northern stars and Pleiades,
Then guides the stitch of path and ride,
Fence line, mount and town,
And hangs them on the railings for
The secret-shadowed farer's gown
To pass and frown and understand,
For, from this day, my soul,
The lie regales new piebald clothes
And reaction re-enjolts itself,
Exposed by Stono's Caroline revolt,
To enclose our suffrage more and more
And explore new slave controls,
Fearing now what we might lose,
Rather than what we might gain
From freedom's boldest stance –
Liberty no longer to our advance,
But glancing of our power's hold.

Honor that is barbarity,
Duty that is brutality,
Honesty that is mendacity,
Respect that is rapacity,

---

[94] In 1801, Gabriel, his brother Solomon, and twenty-five other slaves are hanged after an abortive uprising to march on Richmond, secure the arsenal and Capitol, burn Rockett's warehouse, and wave the white flags of rebellion. They believed that Monroe, Governor of Virginia, would free all the slaves. However, on that August night, a thunderous downpour destroyed bridges and made the roads impassable, forcing the conspirators to flee.

Generosity that is paucity,
Hospitality that is slavery:
To be a Virginia gentleman is
To dance upon the bones...

And the Rabbit, savior, judge,
Parades in red coattails, top hat,
Golden breeches of brocade,
Herald and confuser, adjudicator,
Trickster, conjurer, veiler,
Foreteller of tocome, then
Stands me on the ancestral rail
And listens as they all inhale
The breath of my exhaling guilt, as...

...down, I am sent down...

...Into a labyrinth of self-imposed despair,
Dark passageway
Of tricks and turns and passions
Without care for others or for self,
Swayed in ruins of unreasoned breath –
Path to my rebirthing death.

Stripping off the layers,
The layers of mental lies
And centuries of self-deception...

I have followed this path so many times before...

Two men spade a ditch and turn their heads to me,
As I watch from my mounted view
And silent curse them hurl the clay
Upon reedy banks of rise of day,
Then watch a potter redig, impart
The earth into his tumbled tumbrel cart.

Digging deeper the ditches, when we
Should be building bridges...

...As, in the corner of a cabin's night,
In the flickercasting light
Of oil-lamp fear,
A master beds his new-bought slave,
His wife in burrowed bedroom near...

Oh, Amazing Grace, how sweet the sound,
That saved a wretch like me...

...While, on some softly-dawning porch,
I, wet nurse, let the baby suck,
This turn a boy as black as I,
Nat, growing, but his master's still,

Who some say shows already fine
Possession of some higher will...

I once was lost but now am found,
Was blind, but now I see...

Despite the poverty of Virginia's soil, new farming techniques increase the
exploitation of labor and the rich get richer. The women of these wealthy men are
raised onto a pedestal of effete moral purity and are eased from any political role.

At that break of day, many miles away,
A mother-daughter pair
Slip across the dusty, street-blown air
Of Chatham's olden-laden street
To clip an apothecary's talking boards
For leeches, Epsom salts and laudanum,
And watch him grinding up his chalk
Within a powdered pestle cup
For Papa's suppurating heart;
We ask of quinine, calamine,
Carbolic and cinchona bark
For his dark, arthritic pain,
And vinegar of roses for
Mama's nausea and
The screaming of her aching brain.

Next door, a shoemaker sits
At bench and wooden last,
Measuring, pinching, cutting,
Stretching fast the oil-soaked leather,
Nailing firm and letting dry,
Then turning to a newer shoe,
Prizing the upper from a shelf,
Sizing it against the sole,
Clamping, skewered with an awl,
The needle threading through.

Meanwhile, a child strokes her pet,
A rabbit, taupe, named Hope,
Feeds her a carrot stalk, then returns
Her to her hutch and lonely wires
Of platted cage, before she is recalled,
Engaged by her governess to come,
Fetch her chalk and slate,
And hornbook[95] for her alphabet...

Sing Moses, sing me down and down and down...

"A woman's spiritual beliefs are her soul,
Her very being; she is less

---

[95] A hornbook was a handheld paddle pasted with the alphabet and covered with a thin
layer of cow horn, on which to trace the letters.

Her deeds and more
Her thoughts and motivation,
The *impulses* she has to act,
Not the outward form
Of dress, position, power."

Sing Moses, sing me down da hill an' row,
Sing Moses, sing me down da hill an' row,
Sing Moses, take me cross da Jordan now.
Hallelujah! Hallelujah!
Hear ol' Moses' call!

I turn, unable to wander-sleep,
My night pursued by dreams,
Tunnels and pathways, gateways
Closed, walls to deeper thought,
Emotions ruling, uncontrolled,
Within my deep asylum sways,
Push off the quilt my mother sewed,
Until I'm total naked there,
My husband snoring loud beside,
In rhythmic, singing agony,
Deploring every move I make,
As I fly-imagine from his symphony,
Some knight to shimmer me to love
And value what I do and wear,
How I act and think and bear myself,
And not dictate, shrill forbid
Me life or choice or freedom's will,
Nor chain and force my daughter,
As I glimmer rise to pour some water
And sit upon the chirping porch
To try-escape the palpitating beat
Of my heart and yet another
Night's oppressive heat.

Sing to the turning of our souls...

...falling, falling... I am falling...

...Reading:
The wingéd seeds, where they lie cold and low,
Each like a corpse within its grave, until
Thine azure sister of the Spring shall blow...
From Shelley's *West Wind* ode.

"Religion precisely suits a woman's temperament,
For it donates to her a dignity best suited
To her dependence on Husband,
Father, Son –
Without it, she is restless and unhappy –
It belongs to her by Divine right,
A gift of God and Nature,

The virginal Flame of Piety,
Lighted by Heaven in her breast
To throw its beams upon
The shameful World of Men,
Its Greed and commercial Sin..."

To fulfill this regard, as women,
We must represent to men
Those four great virtues
– Pious, domestic, submissive, pure –
We were raised upon,
Be paragons of womanhood defined,
Retired from any indulgence of the mind,
Or mere household chores,
To deplore-refine
Children, servants and décor,
While our errand women,
Still indentured yet,
Must stay their freedom or be sold,
Find new ventures in the cotton mills,
And drill the drill of colder hours and
Longer working days...

...As women are reduced from active thought
To hang in docile finery upon
The smiling arms of gentlemen...

Meanwhile, from the court of fencing rail,
Where Brer Rabbit convicts my heart,
RattleMan, the gateway guard, takes
Me to the towering door,
Of a shaft within the ground,
His turtleshell and tambourine
Shaking rhythmic-memoried schemes
Within the temples of my mind...

...Stripping at our memories,
At those images of ourselves
That have comforted and betrayed
Us to the enemy of our praise.

But then WindTeller whisks me far
Upon the night-time mountain air,
Sharp within Virginia's mind,
Where a frustrated frontier lurks,
Unwinding fear by embracing fears,
Plowing scarps of worked-torn land,
Unleavened, low-traced poverty,
But where arise upburst showers
Of revivaled calls to heaven's door,
With simple reborn heart and song
That Christ, Our Savior, walks among

Our campéd meets and Sunday throng…

…As, far from this unhoneyed land,
Driven westward by our need,
We mark the Corps of Discovery
Meriwether Lewis, William Clark,
Pole St Louis, the strong Missouri,
And cross the winter Bitterroots
To Columbia's tidal-suited mouth,
There to affirm a continent,
Upon our own inspiréd terms,
Lay oath to our destiny
And forge a hundred years of dreams –
Until dustbowl and our reckless slaughter
– Westwards' wild daughters –
Denude the plains of teeming life
And leave us with but shards of memory,
As we, Midas cursed, touch-devour
Our dreams, our loves, our naïve sanctity,
Expecting always, always more,
Always too much more.

Oh,
Dreams can be our enemies,
Lies we try to live by, shriveled
In denial of what appall becomes
Crabbing hypocrisy as we swivel
In the empty carapace of our imagining
That we are perfect, sanctified and blessed –
When we are sometimes worse than evil.

On Jordan's stormy banks I stand
And cast a wishful eye
To Canaan's fair and happy land,
Where my possessions lie.[96]

Oh joy! Oh joy! Oh deathly joy,
Suck me in and down and in!

…the bones, the bones, the bones…

I am bound for the promised land,
I am bound for the promised land
Oh, who will come and go with me?
I am bound for the promised land.

Hallelujah sing and cry it out!
For we no longer need be bossed about
By haughty missionaries from the east,

---

[96] *Bound for the Promised Land* was written by Samuel Stennett in 1787, at the start of the Second Great Awakening; on the frontier, the revival persisted well into the 19th century. Shelley's poem *Ode to the West Wind* was published in 1820.

Well-bred, educated, doctrinaire,
Minds manicured and arrogant,
Their moralizing contemptuousness
And their condescending smiles
That seek to tame a mountain land
They deem ignorant, backward and unkind,
Devious, drunken, devilish proud,
But that secret-sighs a heart more devout
Than all their sugar-fined and citied ways,
Of praising hallelujah and tempest shout
That marks us for sweet paradise
From life's exhausting, beaten doubt,
And promises us sweet heaven's bliss
In honeyed Canaan's land.

Oh, for that hallelujah time
When Thee and I are one,
With none to beetle in-between,
No laws, no sin, no angry doctrine
Of preachers and their catechisms
– Just Thee and I enjoined
In the unity of all!

III

Hush now, hush within the arbor
Of our crush and prayer, and whisper
To the orishas' dance…[97]

I hear them, I hear them all…!

See the poppets in the branch and totems
Nailed to the bark and roots?
The horseshoes?

…I do, I do,
By the dawn's early light…

…Ghede, Legba, to the spirit sphere…to the egungun…

…Rock, won't you hide me…

…Down by the secret marshtide mists
With the humming cauldrons overturned,
Where we are taken secret to
The lip of homes where ancestors roam…

---

[97] Orishas are the lesser spirits and deities of the Yoruba, from Nigeria and Ghana. Ghede and Legba are two of their major gods and the egungun are ancestral spirits.

And in a soft-set arbor by the swampland mists,
Others steal to insistent meeting, prayers shushed
To the Lord's deliverance one soon hour –
Turn pots upon the ironed door,
Festoon blankets, window slats,
To keep the hallelujah shout
From weeping, seeping out
And invocations of our Conjure Man,
Whip-scarred, paddyrolled of course,
For provoking the spirits of our sorcery.

Oh, carry me over, Lord, carry me over!
I can't take one more day o' this!

Where's our Moses? Where?
I hear his call…

Turning, turning, turning…
The bones are slowly turning…

…In this land of proudly free,
Where Irish navvies,
Famined out by English lords,
Bound from New York, come to work,
But refuse indentured wages,
Slave conditions, strike,
Abandon ramparts and canals to return
To fight for Northern rates of pay
And the gleaming of conditions
Braver, more humane,
While in the flagging fields nearby
I hear the poor white screaming cries
As they suffer yet the red-glared lash
Of the 'seer's proudly hailing slash –
As bonded to their labored lives
As slaves across the twilit way.

"It be terr'ble bad luck to turn back after you done start a journey. If you wanta make it better, draw a big white cross on de groun' and spit on it three time."

"Allus take a rabbit's foot wid you to ward off devils lurkin' by de crossroad. Hold it tight and pray to de Lord Almighty as you go. But never run, lest dem devils sees you'se afraid."

"If'n a black cat cross your pat' to de right it be good; to de left it be real bad."

Don't try to understand…

Just dust the books most careful now,
Refill the inkpot, cut the quills,
Change the blotter, recap the wax,
Tidy the stacks of papers on the chairs,
Empty the basket of its cares,
Reset the books upon the shelves,

> But always let the desk alone,
> Tho' sometimes quick a delving look
> At tomes with pretty colored prints,
> Etchings of strange-glint beliefs
> Within slick-worn pages leafed,
> As dreams and images of distant reefs
> Reem through our gay imaginings
> And allow such soft-empassioned lies
> At freedom's wander-spelling hand,
> To write and sail and travel well,
> And live the life Life planned.

In 1807, Jefferson imposes the Embargo Act forbidding all foreign trade; however, this severely harms Southern agriculture. In 1808, the external slave trade is officially abolished in the US, but it goes on surreptitiously until the Civil War. To feed the growing demand for slaves, northern Virginia becomes the main reproduction factory for a rising domestic breeding industry, with Richmond as its major commercial hub.

> We held a fear, a silent depth of dread,
> That we would clearly be o'erblown
> By such a flowing import
> Of unhappy Guinea slaves,
> But now can nap more handily
> In our harm-contented beds,
> That we are a majority – yet,
> On our Piedmont farms and
> Empires of strident Tidewater arms,
> And that the thread of Afric' spent
> Will slack as growing generations, inbred,
> Create compliant, well-bent blacks
> Untainted by their tribal strife, or memories of
> An independent life.

Meanwhile, the British abolish the slave trade in their dominions. There were 493 documented slave revolts on British ships during that trade.

> Sheep, sheep, breed them unto sheep…

> Let all reason go…

> Oh, sinner man, where you gonna run?

> Let yourself descend…
> …without self…

> *Run to the rock. Rock, won't you hide me?*
> *Run to the rock. Rock, won't you hide me?*
> *Run to the rock. Rock, won't you hide me?*
> *All on that day.*[98]

---

[98] *Sinner Man* is a popular hymn of this period.

...yet within
  ...the illusion of
    ...caring reason,
As you dance upon the bones...

Lord said, "The rock, rock will be crumbling."
Lord said, "The rock, rock will be crumbling."
Lord said, "The rock, rock will be crumbling."
All on that day.

Oh, Moses, Moses, Moses...

So many daemons...
So many bones...

...As we pause, digress,
Stop awhile
At a Richmond County house,
A plantation's colonnaded steps,
Where a gentlemen turns to impress his host,
Hat handed him by mute valet,
And commends that Southern hospitality
Renowned of Virginia's western shore,
As a butler stands by the double door,
House servants hand him cape and cane,
Two maids accompany his lady wife,
Proud in pelisse, empire waist and gown,
As two more platter travel sweets
And a footman bears his large valise
Past doormen downing marble steps
To a coachman at the carriage door,
Horseboy holding tight the reins,
Blacksmith, wainwright gazed amazed,
Cook and dishwasher, scullery maid,
And distant gardeners who briefly stop
From raking leaves to look across and up
At the couple's well-served leaving.

Oh, Moses...!

I so abhor this evil institution, fear
It will destroy us finally, yet
Am unwilling to manumit or educate,
Relieve either hours nor the whip, ease
On bartering and selling, splitting
So-called marriages, families, and
Will never let them read nor write
Nor self-improve, lest
It leads them to unnecessary thoughts
Above their station and disrupts
Our most delicate order of society.

Though I fear what slavery may bring us
I will not give up one spoon of claret
Nor relieve them one minute of the day,
Lest it bring forth that day one minute sooner.

So many philosophies,
So much to defend...

But let us turn from pointless rhetoric,
Close our minds and soft observe
Our ladies belvedered upon the hill,
Laughing, running in their overgowns,
Parasols and ruffled, ribboned hair,
Freed from whalebone stays and normity,
Reading *Sarah, Or the Exemplary Wife*,
Gothic tales,
And morals of female piety.

Observe and pass,
In temperamental tranquility...

Oh,
Lead me down, SelfTruth,
Past that female statuary,
And be a guide to my being
As I lose all being, stripped
Of will and reason, sanity,
And myth's midwife to the world...

...As curricles and clarences,
Horse-shafted,
Driver-drawn and whipped,
Wait to gait the marshaled arch
Of the justiced entrance steps...

Until we, with a "Whoa!"
The folded steps unfold low,
And in our gowns and stockings enter there,
And are good-dayed before the stairs
By a spider man, John Marshall,
Exempt from fear, ingratiated,
"Tall, meagre and emaciated,"
Awkward, absent-minded, that's clear,
Even, I'd say, unkempt.

I do admire the man, lover
Of poetry, philosophy, prose,
These 'lawyer dinners' rightly renowned,
In Richmond's engorged society,
For he is patriotic to an extreme
And was among those stoic few
Who knew tormented Valley Forge,

Devoted husband, honest to a hue,
Though lately some would argue
Less so in defense of Aaron Burr,
Or when, as Secretary of State,
He nicely concurred to be
Appointed our Supreme Justice
At that midnight hour.

A Moselle comes, with bass par-steamed
And filleted in sauce béarnaise,
Then a prideful Bordeaux
At glazéd venison's panting side,
A wine reduction, carrots, yams,
Lamb and Chianti hams,
A cream bread pudding,
Claret well-examined,
And retirement to
The wood-fired smoking room,
A cognac, first-grade cigar,
And his light and breezy views
On the promulgated federal right
To regulate commerce between the states
And tightly coerce the Cherokee.

**ACT IV, SCENE I. A swamp clearing. In the middle, a boiling cauldron.
Thunder. Mist. Enter the three Healers.**

First Healer
Thrice the brinded cat hath mew'd,
Thrice the marshland slaves eschewed.

Second Healer
Thrice and once the hedge-pig whined,
Thrice the bell of freedom chimed.

Third Healer
Harpier cries, 'tis time, 'tis time,
As Justice wrings her name and thine.

First Healer
Round about the cauldron go,
In the poison'd entrails throw;
Toad, that under harsh cold stone
Days and nights has thirty-one
Swelter'd venom sleeping got,
Boil thou first i'the charméd pot,
Watch the souls as they arise
Black and red and whitesome wise,
In this misted cauldron grave,
Where acts of vile remembered are,
And none are mortal saved.

All
Double, double, toil and trouble;
Fire burn, and cauldron bubble…

In 1811, the Richmond Theater burns to the ground, killing seventy people. Many wonder if it's an act of God directed at the evils of slavery. But we know it was Linkum Tidy dancing on the bones…

…for I am taken down…

…As a family heaves a harvest barn,
Cattle bier to one main side,
A threshing floor, undereaves for straw,
And sacks of corn and grain,
Hoes and scythes and harness hanging
From the arms of wooden dowels
Spangling on their Fluvanna farm.

…As, in thriving Portsmouth town,
I sit upon a hard school bench
In cotton pouch and apron,
Hair pinned down, ribboned well,
And prick my finger with an ouch!
As I strive, like all us girls,
To needle "Home Sweet Home"
And point some sugar-bandied rhyme
Above a sylvan kitchen scene,
A serene Easter sport for mothers' time,
While, down upon the fetid wharves
Of Norfolk's teeming port,
Batteaux men, sailors from the ships,
Dip into taverns, bordellos, backstreet dives
To swap stories, women and quick-flash knives.

Turning, reeling,
Deep within the entered mind
Of leaving this and this and that behind…

Twisting, turning,
Down and round and round and round,
That maze of jilting labyrus,
Forks that mental muse
And talk within my thoughts
And will not let me sense nor be,
Other than infallibly…

…As, from our hilltop sanctuary,
WindWhisperer, Linkum Tidy, I
Watch red-faced Madison,
In a fit of patriotic pique,
Seek stolen frontier gains
In the quietude of Canada

From French-distracted Britain,
Declare us in a jingo war
Amidst rank unwise demands,
And devise for us humiliation
As a sudden seabrave British squadron
Attacks Hampton, Norfolk,
Havre de Grace,
Facing ill-trained, badly backed,
Courageous, anxious minutemen
To Blandensburg defeat,
Then takes DC, marshed and heated,
Madison and Dolly forced to flee,
The White House burnt amid dismay,
Until defiant Henry restakes hopes,
Our resplendent banner unfurled free
Over bombarded, battered battlements,
From where a nation's anthem rays
Came from her spangled, starry cries:
Oh, say, can you see, by the dawn's early light,
What so proudly we hail'd at the twilight's last gleaming?
Whose broad stripes and bright stars, thro' the perilous fight,
O'er the ramparts we watch'd, were so gallantly streaming?
And the rockets' red glare, the bombs bursting in air,
Gave proof thro' the night that our flag was still there.
O say, does that star-spangled banner yet wave
O'er the land of the free and the home of the brave?

IV

Digging deeper ditches
For our deeper hopes...
Trying to find a way...

...As I spin a spin of mindless sense
Deeper, deeper in a gnostic maze
Of circles, spirals, convolutions
That wrap around my endless thoughts...

...While the rivers of Virginia slow-sweep
Their sleepy-shallowed way...

...As, with chained refrain, a gang
Of slaves upon a Blue Ridge crest
Dresses walls of stone for winter fall
And splits chestnut logs to stall-retain
The wild and rambling hogs that stir
These slopes of freedom's graves.

In 1814, the worst flood since 1795 devastates Virginia, caused by over-farming
and logging. Floods are an annual problem now, often with several disastrous

293

inundations a year. In fact, Virginia has steadily fallen from pre-eminence to impoverishment as its land is laid to waste and its communities fail, as a result of overfarming and poverty. In 1790, Virginia had twice the population of New York, but by 1840 this statistic is reversed, as hundreds of thousands of Virginians quit the state for the West and immigrants prefer the free North to a South of impoverished land, indentured servitude, slavery and pitiful wages. As one observer noted, "sad spectacles do her lowlands present; wasted and deserted fields! of dwellings abandoned by their proprietors! of Churches in ruins!" [99]

In 1815, financial opportunity improves a little in the state with the founding of the Federal Bank, the Bank of Virginia and the Farmers' Bank of Virginia. But they each print their own banknotes, rapidly provoking a devastating financial disaster. During the brief boom, the first regular steamboat service begins on the James River (1815) and City Hall is built in Richmond (1816).

>
> Oh, how I hear the Enchanters call…!

>
> Load, boys, load!
> Load and let us descend, and
> Eye-catch the freshet waves of storm
> That raise our muddy upthrust flow
> To lust us on to Richmond's wharves
> Before tomorrow's moon is carved –
> Pull the king-plank free,
> Rudder-heave and haul the ropes
> And cleave the *Lotus* clear,
> Then swift-jump, haul aboard,
> Pole and pole to stall and tweeze
> From rapid-rising, clay-leaed bank
> Of Buchanan's fleeting mental surge
> And picket *chevaux de fries*.

>
> 'Tis now current-speeding calm,
> Until the river plunges us
> Swift down and bounced upon
> Its woosh and sudden lunge,
> And I steer the slower glow
> Of river veer and inner bend,
> To a whisper of enchantment's song,
> Silver-singing of my river
> And the chaos of desire,
> Wending harsh-cut bank and snag,
> And overhanging branch enshank
> That tangle-tags our canvas top,
> Direction kept with curve of sweeps
> That carve their hardheld, raresome beat,
> Wrestling with the busting drive,
> Holding, trenching, hard-borne sway,
> To lust my current's wrenching flow,
> Its beckoned swift and sultry force,

---

[99] Report of the Committee of Roads and Internal Navigation, 1815.

Its troubled roils and rill-lisped race
And soft-slept, meandered afterglow.

We bank to moor and rest,
A swig of cider, fiddle jest,
Flames in the embered night,
As mountain music drifts the smoke
Of boiling beans and night-fall fires,
Ham and bread and dripping jars,
Then blanket sleep and veil-fog curl
Upon our sacking, token beds,
In some stilled and listing grove
Against the star-draped cooling mists
Of the midnight heron's call.

...As midnight brings me waking peace,
While the undercurrent water rages
Within the cages of my darkest depths...

Waking to returned awareness
Upon the morning's dismal light,
The calm-cloud river echoes bright
To the mournful cockerel's cry,
And soft drone of my enchantment song
Heralds me be gone,
As the mistled misting dawning shroud
Damps and freezes stony bones,
Ere a dew-sunned warming breeze
And the scwaaks of cutting geese
Provoke the squeaks and chips,
The songed meow
Of the catbird's secret grovéd call,
And a 'piper head-bobs, scurrying through
Low-braced rocks and darting wing,
Its skimming flutter swift towards
Its far-shored, waiting mate.

We pack our things, kick at our fire,
Footset onboard the boards again,
The brindling river low once more,
Calmed with loss of memory,
Actions thwarting its charade,
Bearing any chance of trade,
Tobacco, whisky, brandy, grain,
Pigs, and sometimes turkeys too,
Apples, lumber, sacks of corn,
To Richmond's market falls,
Where the Enchanters softly call
Us to our riffling miseries,
There to side the river's dock,
Break her for her timber's worth
Or recaulk, relimber and return,

With cottons, pans and household wares,
Furnishings, implements, tools and guns,
Frontier men and women too,
And many times a cargo linked
In drovered anklet chains.

And I stride upon the fall-line rocks
To enter in the 'Chanters' call
And sleep within their memory
Of myth and veiled reality,
Tranquil in their aid, to reguide
Me to the mountain of my calm,
Until...

...'Tis time for us to re-ascend,
Forge yonder Lynchburg's wharves,
Swerve the draw-tweaked Blue Ridge Gorge
And verdant valley there beyond,
So we uncast our frontmost sweep
And re-employ two crew anew
To fast the rocky surge
And trick the streams that imp-glint glow
And weave their tumble-rumble through
Those water swirls and graylined curls
That make our tempers fray,
With sweated, muscled, bended arms
And torsoed, rip-jerked wills
That thrill upon some liquored fate
Of a brother's distant still...

...distant still...

So pole, pole, my boys,
Pole against the flow,
Walk the gunwaled length and push
Hard against the graveled floor
And keep our teamed integrity
When the current is so strongly firm!
Push-pole through the eddied swirls
Of granite-rapid pools
That swish-swish-curl the mental swirl
Boiling up and over,
Down and over,
To fall to rise, fall to rise,
Rush and rush and down and splash
And rush and gush and over,
To another calm of push-pole strain
That lets me rest awhile, before
New push-pole heave, push-pole rend
Against the bank-trend thrusting force
That threatens to impale my course
Upon the snags and sunken sycamores

That lurk within my tempest graves,
O'er splash my low-set gunwale waves
And crack my battered nosecone down
The shallow-riffled, gravel-rushing,
Tossing-tumbled, rackled
Fleck-whipped spash of sudden surge,
Of dip and sweep and tumble-throw...

Oh, how the Enchanters call...!

Then sudden flatness, calm,
Currents cleared by balming pools,
And swift-soft deepset flow
As I sweep the sudden-basined swirl
Of eddied rock-fled twist and twirl
And sideways edge a ledge of riffle-fall,
Of the swift-swiped swallow's shadowed grief
That flit-flies, zip-soars, dips and dives,
Skimming the skin of watered past
And warns me of my destiny.

In 1819, a financial panic caused by profligate printing of banknotes hits the country, resulting in widespread depression and the failure of both banks and businesses. Inflation, debts, corruption and speculation rocket.

As WindOracle rides the state,
I stop my lilting, piping plea
And watch with eyes of enormity,
For greed dominates the business halls
And speculators plunder, take with ease,
Refuse to invest and strip all care
From canal and turnpike, forge and mine,
In a scramble for each desperate dime...

...While departs,
In distant-valleyed Flint,
A Conestoga for Tennessee
With iron stove, bedstead,
Rocking chairs,
As one more family declares apart
Its desire to final flee.

Also in 1819, the Passenger Act finally ends the importation of indentured labor. For over 200 hundred years, many white workers have lived as virtual slaves, especially 'orphaned' children; only now does that practice slowly disappear.

Hallelujah!
Hallelujah!
Hear ol' Moses' call!

...I fall, I fall, I fall...

Under the terms of the Missouri Compromise of 1820, Maine enters the Union as a free state and Missouri as a slave state. Two years later, Jacob Mordecai and Richmond's growing Hebrew community dedicate Beth Shalome in Shockoe Bottom as the state's first synagogue.

Oh, the bones,
Turning, turning,
Twisting in the burning air
Of silent-suffered care…

I peer from my ditch of dreams,
White man forced to be a slave,
Rich-stenched,
Leeches quivering on my skin,
Ragged linen on my back, trenching
Beneath the bridge as my master pauses,
As Monroe in his chariot pair,
Once a breezy rebel, fiery
Youth of revolutionary causes,
Seizer of the governor's arsenal
And wounded under Washington,
Then personally governor in his right,
Entrusted US senator,
Ambassador to France,
Secretary of State, then War
During Madison's brief furor with
The British over White House décor.

There was a time when I hailed you,
And my father too – a Revolutionary soldier,
But wounded, forgotten, unsoundly
Left fifty tawdry acres, later sold,
As now my sisters deal in laundry
And I work your old ditches
For my pennied meal.

Though without a vote, Mr President,
You were cemented in my mind,
But then you dallied cravenly
To a Missouri Compromise
And dillied through the banking crisis
As my mother lost her certain savings,
Paper-tossed to loss of home and pauperdom,
While you yawned behind your carriage curtain.

Why should I favor Florida,
Or your doctrine for a continent, other than
It distracts me from my indignation
And riles my patriotic fervor
That foreign powers must stay away
From our continental gain?

Oh no, sir,
My ditch gets deeper,
Your bridge grows taller,
As my life is leeched away...

...turning, turning, Moses, turning...

...As we whirl, Linkum Tiddlum,
Whistler of the Wind, and I,
To merge with the Sufferings by their well,
There to circle rail and cry,
And beat the drums and pipe the flutes
Of the ancestors' questions why.

While I fall, I fall, I fall,
To the call, the call, the call
Of my inner VisionMind...

Then imp I tense away,
Past night patroller, fence and dog,
To wade among the rotting boles
And fly-fed, black-slimed holes
Of briar-thatched isle and moccasin,
Haloed midnight's lumen gray
And foxfire spurts within the flames
Of hope's moonlit-bugged delay,
To lie opossum in the swamp
And dig myself a darkened sty
Enclumped with leaves and somber lie,
Then thieve at night to steal a hog,
Snare a scornful squirrel,
Check my springs for snarl raccoons,
Swing a sack of near-ripe corn,
Or catch a catfish on my line,
Then shiver through the winter months
In mildewed damp and smokeless fire,
My attire of quilted rabbit skins,
Bitten, badgered, but not out-foxed
In my deep-hid den of a dozen years.

Sing Moses, sing down da pea an' corn,
Sing Moses, sing down da pea an' corn,
Sing Moses, take me on dat chariot to Heben...

If I wanted to cry for my life, could I cry
In your arms, could you be the cradle
To rock my memories to tearful sleep
And be there to hold my hand,
Even when I am crying not for you?

A woman sits upon her porch,
O'erlooking the Harrisonburg Pike,
In bonnet, apron and coarse cloth dress,

Holding a heated stomach stone
To ease her monthly cramps,
As the sun beats mercy from the sky
And even the shadows have no shade
To soft her seasoned comfort by.

The mail coach passes, a team of four
Walking up the short incline
As the driver waves hello
And a well-dressed woman
Pokes her bonnet head, coughs,
Then lowers down her window screen,
In the dust and humid heat
Of the oppressive August beat.

A Front Royal potter slabs some earth
Taken from his timbrel cart
And parched beneath a drenched sack cloth,
Wets the wheel and throws it down,
Then sits upon his arching bench,
Dips fingers to the splashing pan
And fans his feet upon the tread
To band the wheeling humbrel turn,
Then firms his pointed, pressured hands
In tight-fist push and ease
To open up the jug and raise
With thumbs its slippering glissade
And smoothly arc and softly bow
Its gently arching shoulder flow,
Shape its narrow, tightfit neck,
Then check the wheel and stop
To careful cut and add the lip,
Roll and crop the looping hold,
Join both with scalpeled slip,
Then cut it from the grayclad deck
With drawn wire taut and tight,
To push upon a rightful board,
Cramp upon a cautious shelf,
And damply overnight.

Meanwhile, from buffalo lick and Shawnee kettle
To furnace and deep-drilled mine,
The Kanawha Salines burst on tap
With the richest source of curing salt
The States have yet to meet,
Raised and dried to coal-fired heat,
Then shipped on rafts to western farms
Or muled across the Alleghenies
To grateful Southern arms...

...As, on Warren County's Blue Ridge,
Above the coves and forest ridges
Used to furnish charcoal stacks

For valleyed iron forges,
I see cattle gorge in summer groves
And mountain blue grass dreams,
Or sheep flocks graze, in springtime clip,
Their wool trans-shipped to lazy mills
That weir our mountain streams.

Meanwhile, within the hills of new Giles County,
A fox scents some ragged bee balm,
Red under the calm-bespeckled trees
That line the hidden highland veins
Of Wolf Creek Mountain's
Steep and sleek-rise slopes, hidden
From the hopes and silent vagaries
Of our uncertain centuries.

It is first harvest day and the fields are fresh
In the lea of Great North Mountain,
The men are ready with their scythes,
The women behind in line assembled,
To bundle-sheave the oats and rye
And bring the trembling harvest in;
But first a prayer, a giving thanks,
A cider jug lugged around the ranks,
A song, a cheer, the men aligned,
To see who will fastest be this year –
And as they start, I stop to catch
The prime of that first snatching scythe,
Take up the stalks and plait them tight
Into a dolly for the threshold door
To sate the pixies of the moors
For guiding us this autumntide.

Meanwhile, a cooper
Gauges tannin and the texture of some rings,
Length of trunk, merrain and grain,
To log to bolts, stave them well,
Split, then age in open tiers,
Lengthed and planed and careful grooved,
Tapered, beveled, hollowed fine,
To set upon the 'ssembly jig,
Hammer hoops to hold them firm,
And rapid raise the barrel rose
Within South Boston's prizery,
Then heat and steam upon a fire,
Windlass into bended shape,
Trussed and hooped and toasted sure,
Headers pushed with crozered care,
Doweled and plugged and liquid sealed
With one last mallet, planed once more,
Sanded, solemn signatured,
To proud assert my finished work,

Cooper to this nation
Of many stavéd shapes and hoops,
Bounded by gradation.

I am the wheel of the nation,
Coping barrel of the generations,
Bridging ditches for our hopes.

In 1819, Virginia passes a new slave code, which forbids teaching slaves.
Ironically, it's the same year as the University of Virginia is founded.

"It is a favor we do unto them,
For Africa is barbaric, backward, godless,
A pagan sway of witchcraft, ignorance,
Bestial striving for the day,
Bristled war, slavery self-imposed
Upon their brutish, sacrificial lives
Of mutilation, magic, masks,
And the frightful drums of night."

"Aie, 'tis not wrong, but a benevolence we do,
For these Negroes would be lost, children
Without our guidance, gainful employ,
Protection from the vice and strain
They must induce if they were free
To enjoy
The unrestricted pleasures of unjust use."

"The Bible itself is on our side
Re separation of the races,
Natural, Cain and Abel,
One to grace, one to guide,
Condemning mixture or conjoining
Of our bloods or livelihoods."

Two girls, far-flung
In Tidewater County Caroline,
Glowing in their bows and frills,
Toss ribboned rings upon two sticks,
From each to each to fill the day,
A game of graces, fitly called
For young ladies to display…

…As thus we dream our lives away
Imagined childlike, but strictly wary,
And keep our memory within our souls
To germinate some treasured story
That will, through myth and reformed image,
Create in us a sense of worth
And give us all some well-staged birth,
Through made-up, comic play
That has redealt the sermons of dismay
With moral right renewly felt –

As meanwhile, cursed within their dread,
Are un'venged corpses of the mocking dead,
Ancestors who cramp and tremble-pray,
Upon the swamp-fed wander limbs
Of cypress, bay and tupelo
And call us, dare us to respond
To the divining of a future bonded
Without reprieve from our despair.

For the graves are dreaming,
Dreaming still, bodies turning,
Sockets open-eyed,
Whispering to those who know
The secrets of beyond,
What's to come,
And wail their memories,
Lost to us,
But harbored in their bones.

Oh, how the raven sneers!
Moses, won't you come!
Oh Moses, hear the call
Of our field-burnt tears!

You are within the vortex of my mind...

V

Swing low, sweet chariot
– Swing high!
Turn and turn and turn
Sweet home, sweet home,
Pie in the sky...

I wander to the quarters where,
By the hutted row a ring is set,
Stumps circled round the hardened ground,
And we sit and sing as Joseph drums,
Michael plays his balafo
And John his banza strings,
To fret with sorrowed, squeaking bow,
As we with bones upon a jaw,
Slap and clap and stomp our limbs
And flail our blindness round and round,
Jiggle bodies to the ground,
Twist and yield and moan and shout:
Run, nigger, run, the patrol'll get you,
Run, nigger, run, it's almost break of day!

Meeting in Richmond from 1829-30, a constitutional convention extends the
suffrage to leaseholders and householders, but does not grant full male suffrage

nor change the unfair distribution of seats against the growing population west of
the Blue Ridge. The governor is still selected by the Assembly and his Privy
Council still selects all judges and sheriffs, retaining two of the most élitist
aspects of state government.

But hush, for this is a pleasant summer night
In Charlottesville, close by the river,
And I hear the gentle sounds of clinks
And merry jangles of a coming band
Within this scene of rural harmony.
I watch
From the shade of a hanging tree,
As by me wander the jingled rhyme
Of a soft-harmonious coffle-line,
Singing sweet its way to Mississip',
Sons of sons of sons of sons of sons
Shackled in mutual resplendency
As they gospel biblical modesty
And savor the gentle Virginia caress
Of the buyer's cattlehide affray as
He merrily leads them on their way.

Revenge, Gabriel!

Hush, hush, hush,
Accept and be – loyally…

'Mid pleasures and palaces
Though we may roam…

It's the damasked philosophies
And the sanctified prayers…

A child, dressed in adult crinoline,
Tempts a cat with a ball of cotton,
Makes her play, picks up and scolds,
Then pets and purrs and swaddle-hugs.

We keep our pets in childish state,
Cats kept kittens, dogs kept puppies,
Slaves kept slaves,
Denying them their full-wild station,
Their maturity and skill kept safe
For our purrs and hugged elation.

Oh, Linkum Tiddlum Tidy,
Dance and prance with me tonight,
Take me on your hauntings
Of ballroom, hall and flight…!

…And hear the voices of the others,
Of the ancestors calling!

…Calling out our names
On the bones of their pain,
And demanding we acknowledge
The truth of our shame.

*"…while laboring in the field, I discovered drops of blood on the corn, as though
it were dew from heaven, and I communicated it to many, both white and black,
in the neighborhood; and then I found on the leaves in the woods hieroglyphic
characters and numbers, with the forms of men in different attitudes, portrayed in
blood, and representing the figures I had seen before in the heavens."* [100]

Herise, herise, herise,
Vision master of intense descent,
Chosen spirit of the Spirit,
Prophet of thy people's doom
And seer of the boon and flood
Within the speckled fields of blood,
The Serpent fled upon the Sun,
The Great Tree clasping out its limbs
To grasp injustice to its boughs,
The river come to endow those born,
In eclipse and night-time blaze of star,
So that the last will arc the first,
At last,
And by those heavenly signs ye see
Know 'tis time to march
The bloodcast road of liberty!

*"…about this time I had a vision – and I saw white spirits and black spirits
engaged in battle, and the sun was darkened – the thunder rolled in the heavens
and blood flowed in streams…"*

From my cell I see
My brothers dancing on the tree
Of Virginia's harsh humanity…

*"…and I heard a voice saying, 'Such is your luck, such you are called to see; and
let it come rough or smooth, you must surely bear it'."*

Oh, Gabriel, Gabriel,
Angel of our deliverance…!

I, raised prophetic from my infancy
To the wealth of African desire,
In its mythic heart and ancestry,
Of prayer and fasting fire,
Have been sold, resold, resold again,
Yet have kept pure my timeless faith,

---

[100] Taken from the visions of Nat Turner, as recorded in his death cell confession. With
about forty other slaves from Southampton County, Nat heroically rose in rebellion in
August 1831.

Never drinking, swearing nor resenting,
But fasting, Bibling, surely prophesying,
Reading scriptures, omenizing,
Going to the mire to pray
– And say, "The Holy Ghost is I!"

"...there were lights in the sky, to which the children of darkness gave other names what they really were; for they were the lights of the Saviour's hands, stretched forth from east to west, even as they were extended on the Cross on Calvary for the redemption of sinners."

I turn, I turn on,
As the elemental tides
And revolution of the planets
Confess predestined season
And the Sun burns aquamarine
With the translucence of the sea
And the night of mounted death,
Unbridled in its breadth
In blood of man and woman, child,
Runs in a flood of wild expectancy
That the Final Day is here,
At last,
Turning, turning...

...And enchurning pain
Is reaped
And lifted final from
The shoulders of my people...

"...the leaves on the trees bore the impression of the figures I had seen in the heavens..."

Then the orgy of retribution,
Four times slaughtered as from black hands
By a rampant, zioned mob of whites
Bonded, in our terrored misery,
To avenge ourselves upon ourselves
By quartering the heart of law
In such blood-fanged brutality
As would defy the jaws of lions.

"Death or Liberty!"
– Here are Patrick Henry's words
Stripped of all hypocrisy
And woven within our people
With a total hope and vibrancy –
No slavewhipper merely preaching
To those he refused to reach,
Nor mewling pastor sermonizing
On servants serving masters,
But the harmony of 'passioned justice
Verving from o'erreached disaster

To beat the tocsin of rebellion
And the Christian solemn Gospels
As they were meant to be
– In full view of bloodied war,
The saber sward of justice,
And the freedom field of a people to
Whom justice lies long o'erdue.

– Aie, a disaster for us all.

As The Horseman rides among the ruins,
Bodies burnt, decapitated, limbs hanging
From the nearest timber-shrouded tree,
I bow my hat and bear countless tears
For such pointless deaths in savagery
That have been and will yet be,
Till we jointly breathe our joint humanity.

And, as if defiantly,
I turn to watch the Rabbit lean
Upon a picket fence before
A home where singing rings
The rafters and the beams,
His fiddle in his paws:
'Mid pleasures and palaces
Though we may roam,
Be it ever so humble,
There's no place like home.[101]
A charm from the skies
Seems to hallow us there,
Which seek thro' the world,
Is ne'er met with elsewhere.

Oh Moses, Moses,
Have thee forsaken me,
Turning, turning, turning,
Down
Into the mazes of my mind,
To amaze and defy the daze
Of veiled and saddened misery
With the clarity of kind
That lets go, lets go, lets go…?

…to dance upon the bones…

Home, sweet home, nigger,
There's no place like home,
Dancing on the tree, nigger,
There's no place like home.

---

[101] *Home Sweet Home* was composed in the 1820s: words by John Payne; music by
Henry Bishop; with some changes…

Oh,
Sing Moses, sing down da strap an' lash,
Sing Moses, sing down da strap an' lash,
Sing Moses, take me now, don't you take me back.

A planter saying he treats
His slaves as well as kin
Is akin
To a thief telling his victims
He never really stole,
And that his theft was really
No swift theft at all,
But merely relieving them of the worry
Of life and living property.

Bury him deep, mistress,
Under heavy earth and slab,
With Bible, cross and ring, mistress,
To keep old Tidy off,
For Linkum Tiddlum is watching you,
Perched in the ritual boughs of fall,
And he will be out charnel roaming
With claw and tooth and gall
To root old master and gnaw his bones
In the darkest veils of hell.

Oh, I dream of a time when I
Can call you brother, brother,
And not be hacked for my humanity,
Nor beaten black for my audacity!

VI

In the Shenandoah Valley in 1831, Cyrus McCormick invents the first
commercially successful horse-drawn reaper. Many are bought by Virginian
planters, who are increasingly turning to grains.

Also this year, William Johns, a Monacan Indian, purchases fifty-two acres on
Bear Mountain, near Amherst; two years later, he buys another 400 acres and this
land becomes a settlement for Indian families and a center where members of the
tribe can maintain their identity and community.

In 1833, Great Britain bans slavery throughout her colonies.

In new-found County Page,
Hard by Massanutten mount,
A man invests in wood and straw,
In harness, smith and tack,
To build a livery stable at the back
Of an oldtime country store...

...While a cart, doled with sacks of corn,
Trundles the old Winchester Pike
To Highland Corner, pays the toll,
And heads south on Newtown Pike
To the Shenandoah, one of several roads
That croak cross the state, rippled planks
Or corduroy of pine and oak,
That crank our hubs from the ruts
Of whine and soaking mud...

...As still the caterpillar munches on the leaf,
Growing fat in lazed belief
And the seasoning of hunch and truth.

Richmond's population grows from 5,700 in 1800 to 20,100 in 1840. Nearly half are slaves or freed blacks, as tobacco processing, coal mines, flour mills, iron works, railroads and textile mills move to a city that is finally gaining in prosperity. Its first steam railroad begins service in 1836, running to Weldon in North Carolina. Soon, trains connect Norfolk, Portsmouth, Petersburg and Fredericksburg, as each city builds itself a railroad.

So let's now go to Petersburg's booming streets,
Where new railroads trundle-meet,
One to Norfolk, another steaming south
From Richmond to the Carolinas,
Sporting hogsheads of tobacco
To be processed, sent to port,
And where an auctioneer is knocking down
Slaves at Sycamore and Bank,
And the city's rising mills
Are filled with timber, cotton, grain,
Swank new wharves and bridges built,
A courthouse and a trade exchange...

Then to teams of Irish,
As they slave the haze
Of the Muddy-raving James,
Navvying from Richmond's dock
Past Lynchburg's flocking wharves
And the call of Blue Ridge falls
To Buchanan's hooded port,
Where they greet the road that sorts
Salt and mountain goods
Past Clifton Forge and Covington
To Kanawha's keeping channel
And the deeper grand Ohio,
Where they vow to dour try
The railroad gorging, rushing o'er
The southern brush of Allegheny's power.

Meanwhile,
Others, cheap and easy-housed,

Join Crozet at the Rockfish Gap
To sap and blast a tunnel's path
Through the ridge's rouséd overmath.

And in a thousand farmhouse rooms,
Lit by sun-slit window gaps, loom
Ten thousand women, wool or flax,
Treadling warp and taxing weft,
Shooting shuttles swiftly whinning,
To deftly spin their jinning clouts
And tout a bundle to the store.

In 1839, the Virginia Military Institute is founded in Lexington.

A man, not rich, nor over poor,
With three slaves, no less, no more,
Sleeps upon a brace of pistols
Loaded, cached beneath
His pillow,
Doors well-latched,
And wakes a dozen times each night
As the swirling Linkum Tidy wind
Rattle-shakes the furl-sinned light.

Oh, the loneliness!

And I see him, hooded there,
Dark justice, revenger, avenger
Of the hidden night, who
Comes as demon to our terrored mind
When it shirks from gnostic might
To surrender to the gleam of day
When all our knowing drifts away
Upon the shine of forgotten self.

…pass through, pass through…

John Tyler is elected Vice-President in 1841. After Henry Harrison dies in office, he serves as President, then retires to his plantation in Charles City County. Both men are Tidewater Virginians.

In 1841, a revolt occurs on the *Creole*, a slaver *en route* from Hampton, Virginia, to New Orleans. The slaves overpower the crew and sail to the Bahamas, where they are granted their freedom.

Packet boats now ply the James,
Batteaux slowly on the wane,
As passengers prefer the decks,
Horse-drawn pace and canal course,
High seats, meals and bedtime rests
Endorsed by those most stately voyages;
Indeed, a woman sits upon one roof
The humid breeze amid her hair,

Ruffling her parasol, back to the smoking stack,
Turning pages of *The Deerslayer*, Cooper's
Latest attempt to righteous
Soup up a frontier sense of self –
A mythic past of Christian piety
That masks a surety far from pure.

For where lurks our truth,
As we reveal away our layers,
Steal deeper in,
Through fears and denial's memories,
To the encircled gateways
Of our secret mind?

Oh, the hidden lies of mystery...

...As softly we stroll, arm-in-arm,
Through Richmond's fine crafts district,
Past cabinetmakers, chairmakers,
Silversmiths vying with tinsmiths,
Watchmakers, saddlers,
Harness makers, gunsmiths
Carving works of still-great beauty
That will linger in our memory,
To witness a pair of men at dawn,
Vapored editors of turbid papers
Born and bled in Richmond,
Stand and start a few yards apart
Their sideways pistol aim,
One never to stride the earth again.

– Thus the intensity of our decline,
Our anger at the pressured sin
Of the boiling, roiling world
We are plunged within.

Yet the markets of the Commonwealth
Are buzzing with their fussing prosperity...

For,
Lurking by the slow-cascaded river,
Between ironworks and warehouse,
The docks bustle with the jostle
Of brave-slaved women's feet,
Bartering from bay-lined boats
That fish and trawl the reaches
Of Chesapeake and inlet beaches
For shad and mussel, oyster shells,
Quick-stepping to their market stalls
Where domestics gossip dwell,
Buy catches for their mistresses
And stop to spend a few earned cents

Upon ribbon, lace and calico,
To make themselves a choker, skirt,
Or go with other dutied folk,
Alert for vegetables and fruit
Brought from brute-flailed farms
By surefoot cart and packhorse trail,
Or maybe buy some cherry tarts,
Proven cakes or berry pies
Baked in pre-dawn ovens...

...As a merchant couple,
Two velvet-hatted gentlemen,
Sample breasts of chickens
Frying on the grills, barbecued,
Then wander with their stickied hands
Across the James,
Mute and mirror-hued,
To old Manchester's smoky side,
Where most weekdays they invoke,
Along the rambling cobbled streets,
Those flying flags red without,
For a market stock
Of blacks and mulattoes, hobbled,
At auction room and vendue block,
Softer chained, better fed and frocked,
Lined and seated, swirling for their part,
"Fifteen likely Negroes to be sold
'Twixt half-past eight and ten
– Two girls, six women, two boys, five men."

We settle, notice
A quaint lithograph, a list of dos and don'ts,
Buyers masticating tobacco,
Milling about, grumbles, shrill cheers,
Inspecting teeth and eyes and ears,
Penises, labias, rumps,
Asking illnesses, tribes and reputations,
Breeding age and previous hire,
Checking lash marks, missing toes,
Clipped ears, other disobeyment scars,
Until the auctioneer approaches
And indicates his men unlatch
The first of this day's four-limbed catch,
Makes her run and jump a bit,
Plumps her high upon the steps,
Turns her, lies about her cooking skills –
No scars of whip, missing fingers, toes,
Or other nips of discipline –
Then raises up her skirt to view
Her undiseased and sturdy thighs.

Five hundred, six hundred,

Seven hundred, eight,
Eight-fifty, nine, nine-fifty…pause,
Repeat the bid, hammer, down
– For a five-and-twenty breeder,
Seamstress, housemaid, cook,
A bargain for a hungered man,
Whose eyetold glint and stifled smirk
Reveal a more penetrating plan at work.

And, when night falls o'er the sold,
Owners send their old overmen
To shackle-walk their property,
Leased or partial paid,
Through midnight streets of scuffing carts,
To make them shuffle-stalk behind
Their new masters' bridled mounts,
Lost of hats and coats and pants,
The women now in coarse-lined frocks,
Scant handkerchiefs to hide their heads
In some renewed pride of servitude…

…As the fisherwomen still call their wares,
And still the domestics trail the squares
Of Richmond's daily dreams,
Nothing out of seems, it seems.

Later, we drift to Snyder's gables
After work that night,
To meal and laugh at sturdy tables
And steal our bread of secrecy,
Then sneak into her darker bar
To tweak rum and jugs of ale,
Forswear formal brothered oaths,
Play hands of cards or five swift corns,
And gift the masters with our fitful scorn…

While Brer Rabbit sits within
The roots of darkened heavening,
The croft of burrowed den,
And undermines and promises
To unleash a swift revenge…

…Deep, deep within
The labyrinthine tunnels,
Dancing in our minds…

Turning, turning, turning…

Oh, Moses, hear our call!
It has been so long,
So long between
The bones and the dance.

"You ain't got time to serve The Lord. You barely got time to serve me!"

Free blacks pose a constant danger to the slaveowners. They often travel between plantations as itinerant craftsmen, consort with sailors from the North and with foreigners, can often read, and always spread news and sedition. Various methods are tried to control them or be rid of them. Some are hanged or beaten; others driven out of the state, especially to the West; and those newly manumitted have to leave the state within days or face re-enslavement. Perhaps worst of all – yet supported by leading slaveowners such as Madison – are plans to repatriate them to Africa – whether they want to go or not.

> I hammer swift and muscle steady
> Down and down and down and down,
> Drown the hoe within the trough,
> Then throw it back into the coals,
> Heave the bellows down and up,
> Spit upon the black dust floor,
> And am about to hammer more
> When three men sudden swift appear
> At my devil-darkened door,
> Demand my exit, show vague remit,
> Then tackle-chain me, manumitted,
> Into the rear of some dung cart,
> And dance me, shackled under hay,
> To a warehouse entrance, some
> Norfolk bayside shanty,
> And that night shut me, a hundred more,
> Next butts of whisky and molasses,
> To toss on bitter 'Lantic waves
> In some reverse of ancient trade,
> Then row us to a malarial grave,
> Sherbro, off Liberia's coast,
> Toasted, I learn, by wealthy holders
> Of societies that intend
> To cleanse Virginia's seditious knaves
> And more deeply sheepish pen
> Their weeping plantation slaves...

...dance...

...to live the life Life planned...

> Standing ready, partner watching,
> Mr Jack Kent opposite me,
> A fine man, but without a cent,
> Though that glint will get him far.
> So, fiddler ready, and off we spar...

> *"Honor your partner, forward and back,*
> *Honor your partner, forward and back,*
> *Now swing your partner's right elbow,*
> *Two-hand swing and around you go..."*

He's a pleasant dancer, light of step,
Yet a strong and forceful, charming man,
Not like Tobias, the Colonel's son,
Who, though rich, is really drab,
A hopeless specimen, all fits and flab,
– Yet those acres and slaves do allure.

"Two-hand swing and around you go,
Now swing your partner's left elbow,
Two-hand swing and around you go,
Once around with the doh-se-doh,
Two-hand swing and around you go..."

Then there's cousin Franklin, but he's too close
And our families have intermarried
Five times yet, so he won't do –
Oops, here, we're off! Don't slow!

"Head couple reel down the track,
Meet in the middle and sashay back.
Heads cast off and down you go..."

Now Jonathan Stuart, he has wealth,
Father a magistrate, burgess too, promised
Ten thousand acres on his marriage,
Eldest son of the estate,
But too underage for me – I need a man
I can respect and will keep me tight
Upon a righteous household rein.

"Now raise that arch and raise it high,
Others duck and away you fly.
Raise that arch and raise it high,
Others duck and away you fly.
Side-step down and take your place
Newest couple heads the race..."

My word, tiring, exhilarating, swirling,
And so real to feel those fine arms
And strong bodies pressed to mine.
Now comes Richard Brierley, with his betrothed,
But I still hope he looks at me,
Lawyer son of parson, planter too,
But really three hundred acres will not do.

And off again...

"Honor your partner, forward and back,
Honor your partner, forward and back,
Now swing your partner's right elbow,
Two-hand swing and around you go,
Now swing your partner's left elbow,

Two-hand swing and around you go,
Once around with the doh-se-doh,
Two-hand swing and around you go..."

...Though Brierley's a militia ensign now,
Parish officer, and they say, will soon
Replace old Stuart as the new burgess,
So maybe he *is* a prospective catch...

...While two-hand swing and down we skip,
As yours and mine do jointly trip,
The caller heeding as around we go
In incestuous steps of doh-se-doh
That breed within our blue-blood halls
While fields of pale-white skin enthrall
And distinguish gentile pallid skin
From our lowbred, well-tanned, planter kin.

Two-hand swing and around we go...

"Now raise that arch and raise it high,
Others duck and away you fly.
Raise that arch and raise it high,
Others duck and away you fly.
Side-step down and take your place
Newest couple heads the race..."

Turning, turning...
Dancing on the bones, within
The swings and turns
Of all direction lost...

VII

Oh, how the raven knocks,
And how the bones do turn!

Come, Moses, come!
Join our merry dance!

Read the fortune cards, Mama,
Old and worn and torn,
Shuffle-feel them well,
Greasy, eared and bent,
Cut them, deal and place
And mental lay them, Mama,
In their patterned space,
At death's aloof despair.

Read the swamp-aired leaves, Mama,

The bark and crawling of the crabs,
The fall of sudden sticks –
What do they portend?
Will our flight grab quick success,
Or end in some slighted trick?

Take my palms, Mama,
Hold them tight and up,
Trace my lines with dry-skinned hands
And peer your solitary eye
Close to mount and line and crease
And tell me,
Can we win this time?
Will insanity cease…?

Oh, how the raven knocks…

…As, upon the windswept Eastern Shore,
Close within Broadwater's reach,
Beach grass tries to dig and keep
Its seeking roots within the sand,
But hurricane and well-farmed sheep
Make too good grazing for it to expand
Higher than an inch or so.

We must enter in to understand,
Attain the center, depth of truth,
Then in equanimity open up
Our hearts to the world –
And dance…

…For my loss is necessary
To spiritual rebirth,
So don't be sad, be glad for me
As I writhe and squirm
Towards my newfirmed destiny,
E'en tho' I myself
Will battle it most bitterly.

So swing low, sweet Moses, swing low…

…And char the coal, boys, char the coal,
Pit the hearth of cone and pole
To collier pile and cut-down dry,
To rise the corded stack so high
It will flare-ignite the fire alight –
Then drape soil and clay to cover toast
The smoldered smoke and caséd ghosts
That choke and suck the lifeness out
And leave dry and brittle-blackened snaps
In charréd synapse of one-now life,
To crack and brickle back the stack

317

And process our fickled impurities,
Raked in cool, respiring course
For the waggoners to shovel-haul
From the wild-rife forest, dousle-tamed,
To metaled furnace bank
And strong-shanked charcoal house.

From there, barrow, fillers, barrow,
To opened top of grueling blast
And layer limestone, ore and fuel,
In constant relay, night and day,
While below, in
Furnace-fumed and tuyere-tongued array,
The bellows' fershump, fershump, fershump,
Pumping brick-lined, clay-glazed
To the blaze of new demand,
Bosh-blast, bellowed molten rasps
Of ripple-crusted lava flows,
Rife-hagged, slag-hot cindered,
In a tindered crucible of
New-wrought life…

…While, back from the forge, in even light,
I sit upon my half-wide porch
As the eldest helps my wife,
Cook and children breeder,
After a day upon a logging gang,
And my next, aged eight, brackets his bucket
For tomorrow's slog,
Stacking water for the men
And their midday meals.

We are owned of the master forgeman,
But in the cabin next to us
Are several men waged out
Each first of January,
By endebted farmers, hired and loaned
Until the year is replete,
For clothes and keep,
Plus quarter rent to masters' homes,
Some hard-wrought overwork
And the fruit of tiny garden plots.

Oh, how the raven knocks…!

Down tools, come on, let's out,[102]
Strike, puddlers, Welshmen all,
Show Joseph Anderson his iron plan

---

[102] In the 1847 Tredegar Ironworks strike, skilled white workers protest the hiring of slave labor. However, the slaves are more than able to replace them and the strike fails. Tredegar uses slaves until the end of the Civil War.

To roll and strip skilled artisans
From the dinning roar of Tredegar
Will not work one day more –
Don't let him enjoy his cheaper slaves,
Blacks hired each January year
To profit-edge those Northern mills
And hedge their acquiescence and success
In this shrill-blazed, hammered stress.

...oh, hear us...!

...As Brer Rabbit plays his fiddle,
Linkum Tiddlum bangs his drum,
And The Horseman pipes on past,
His hat across his wizened stare
That sees all, but does not dare the prize
Of its glowing, sultry glare.

Swing low, sweet chariot,
Coming for to carry me home...[103]

Oh,
The raven knocks not gentle now,
Unheeded, threatening our gory fall,
While devouring the blood-galled heart
Of a house ushering its last-ditch reverie,
Hidden from the suppurating light
In some Plutonian refusal to comply
With the dawn of compassion's fledgling call
Of "Let's pretend!" – a once-grasped hope
That has been clasped so long within
The black-corpsed prophet's curse,
That even the poet cannot regain
From its mythset, guilted hearse.

Oh, lets forget! – Before it's too late!

It knocks, oh, it knocks,
But we will not let it in,
Yet it will enter, willing or no,
To impose its sanguined truth upon
Our night-eyed Southern glow.

Oh, Moses, hear our plaintive call!

...I am lost, I am lost, I am lost...

Turning, turning to the dance...

---

[103] *Swing Low, Sweet Chariot* was composed in 1840 by Wallis Willis, a slave of the Choctaw Indians. The next stanza is a requiem for Edgar Allan Poe, who died in 1849.

Oh, the raven knocks…
And we dance
The dance of inner mind entranced
In the loss of memories and soul,
As we refuse to unpeel, reveal,
The hidden dragons of our mind.

There is a balm in Gilead
To make the wounded whole.
There is a balm in Gilead
To heal our sin-sick soul.[104]

Oh, Moses, I is afeared
You will come to us too late!

In 1850, as part of a compromise over Texas, California and the slave trade in
Washington D.C., the Fugitive Slave Act requires citizens of free states to help
recover fugitive slaves. It denies a fugitive the right to a jury trial and recruits
more federal officials to enforce the law. For ex-slaves in the North, the new law
is a disaster – the beginning of a reign of terror. Zachary Taylor, president of just
sixteen months, and a Virginian, dies during this crisis.

That same year, Virginia holds a constitutional convention that is bitter and
acrimonious, but at which the western part of the state finally wins fair
representation, white taxpaying males finally win the suffrage, the governor and
other officials are finally elected, and multiple votes are finally abolished.

An eastern pipistrelle flashes-glides
Across a mosquitoed glade,
Its leather-flitting flatter wings
And echo-blipping ears
Pipping as its flips and whips
And turns in flight-repeated flight,
Acrossing and across, recrossing,
Taking moth and beetle, twilight fly,
In the sunburnt dying of the sky.

I watch it flitter-turn above the moonlit banks
As, smokestack rumbling, paddles cranking,
I lean upon this arcane-crafted rail,
Listen to the dinner laughter,
Waiters popping champagne corks,
Then drop another soft-worn tear
At *The House of Seven Gables*, romance
To escape a generation by,
And trance from fears of war,
Insurrection,
Losing all we own and grow,
As I pull my shawl about my blouse,
Calico,
And retie my bonnet close

---

[104] Based on *There Is a Balm In Gilead* – a traditional African American spiritual.

Against the chilling evening blow.

Ugh! Tumble-bump, tumble-bump,
When will they e'er repair this road,
Tumble-bump,
Atrocious at the best of times?

'Tis no wonder emigrants are deserting
For Kentucky, Texas, Tennessee,
Leaving only the stain of anger to remain,
Frustration at our education,
Broken bridges, transportation,
The collapse of our yeoman class
And our retreat towards the past,
Anti-town, anti-abolition,
Anti-every new-threat thing,
In a faint-traced strangulation
Of our culture and democracy,
Our arts and well-laced imagining
– Why, have we not now banned
Freedom's abolition speech, refused
The importation of Northern news,
Attacked Methodists and Baptists for their views,
And has not pernicious Thomas Drew
Evolved of desperation
And such total moral approbation
A philosophy where
There is no room for aught but fear
In this terror-seized and morbid land,
Paralyzed by a cancerous demise,
Yet unable to self-medicate, turn its head,
Waiting for its death, surmised
At the hands of some external-hated,
Much resented,
But understandable compromise?

Deny! Deny! Deny!

Ugh! Ugh! Ugh!

Oh, how the raven knocks…

…And a Surry County fly,
Attracted by a pitcher plant,
Tries to crawl upon the hairs,
Fails, falls plop
Into the bulbous brewing soup
Of its water crop, struggles
For a generation, until, gives up,
And resigns itself to slow consumption…

…As o'erhanging a nearby garden pool
Of some Henry County farm

321

A drooping willow waits to weep
And deceive our eyes with deceptive sleep.

Joshua fit the battle of Jericho,
Jericho, Jericho,
Joshua fit the battle of Jericho
And the walls came tumbling down!

Oh, the echoes of your call!

"If your dog lay on its back an' howl, it be a ter'ble sign o' death."
"If you done drop a dish rag on the floor an' it spread out, a 'ungry woman's
gwana visit you house; if it don't spread out, it gwana be a 'ungry man."
"If a hawk done flied over you house, 'tis a sure sign o' death, 'cause de hawk
come take away de corpse."

A lot of hawks and hungry men are gathering.
Ravens too.

Light on my feet, heavy fisted,
I hold tight my ticket bet, cram forward
To glimpse the knuckled sparers,
Blood splashing o'er my face, my hero's teeth
Knocked from out his puffing jaw, the crowd
Swaying, giving, pushing back and back
As my man's blood face is beaten raw
By jab and hook and uppercut,
And his legs finally withdraw the fight.

Up to the walls of Jericho
He marched with spear in hand,
Go blow them ram horns, Joshua cried,
'Cause the battle's in my hands.

…Into the darkness,
But not to discover,
Rather to dissemble and to cover…

Oh, for the air of fresh honesty!

The singer sings…

Swing low, sweet chariot,
Moses is coming for to carry us home…

Mama, things are not as they were meant to be!

No, no, not as they were meant to be,
But hush, for some are rushing
To escape the condemned walls,
Forestalled, and yet foretold
By our sweet-dreamed mythology…

...As
A candle shines within the night,
Finally! and
Faintly swung by Linkum Tidy
To receive us in our flight,
While others haint the 'rollers on,
To taint the swamp-lit fiery glow
That heralds brisk the moonlit night
When risking fleers descend to wait
Lest angels lead them quietly on,
Then point them down the darkened track
And watch for dimlit lantern light
Or quilt across the split-rail fence,
Marks upon the barnside door,
Or other sparks of welcome stored,
There to hide until the dawn,
Bread and corn and sleep to take,
Until we are on our dread once more,
Through field and wood and marsh,
From stationmaster's hideyhole,
Recasting clothes, feeding quite well,
Along the moonbeaming river's bead,
Following the shine of Old North Star
And Linkum's steady streaming light
In visions of some predawn glow
That rests upon the anxious night,
Flows the fleeing wanderer
Fast upon her meanful track,
And provides her all her succor needs
As she watches for the howling pack
Of bloodhound-mounted riders
Hacking at the fretful countryside
In frustration at their flaunted pride.

So, stay safe within the briar thicket
Or lie beneath the bridgeway arch,
Sure to set the bear's pure path
Upon the weaving mountainside,
Then march the ridge and vale again,
Wade the shallow river's bed,
And sail its northing, western flow,
Remembering all the secret things
Brer Rabbit said and did,
Nor' by north by north to head
Until the house of lantern light
Beckons you enter in once more –
And now we're with an expert band,
Guards with Sharps are trained to watch
Hay carts, horses, boats at hand,
Patrollers of our own batched out,
Catching roads and riverways
To ensure the crossing's clear

And Jordan safely gained.

Then on again, hailing freedom now,
But still with bounty hunters down
Upon our frantic freshet trail,
Deft from barn to mine to bed,
Left in bales, in coal and shed,
Until we reach the Great Lake towns
Of Erie, Huron and Detroit,
There to disembroil, get clothes, uncoil,
Buy a ticket to a dream and steam across
And there embrace the seldom soil
Of Canada's engraced freedom.

…Pick your card, Mama, pick your card
And let the hauntings in the night
Grow more intense each passing slight…

Oh, how the raven knocks!

The singer sings and the drummer plays
And the fiddler sparks the night,
Their spirits waft across the notes
As darkness seeks the light,
And the raven knocks upon our plight
To the turning dance of flight.

VIII

Oh Moses, I hear you coming!
I hear your clarion clear!

Anger at slavery and the Fugitive Act is mounting in the North, especially as
Southern bounty hunters drag escaped slaves back (and often free blacks as well).
Several runaways are forcibly freed from Northern courtrooms during their trials.
In 1854, such is the anger in Boston that it requires two thousand federal troops
to return Anthony Burns to Virginia. The case of Sara Lucy Bagby, who fled
Wheeling, Virginia, for Cleveland, Ohio, also produces a storm of controversy.

Two slaves, resold once more,
Woman and older man, escapees,
Branded by a master tired of whipping,
Are taken from their Richmond bond
In shackles through the night-time streets
And loaded to a boxcar made
For cattle and for hogs,
With half-a-dozen terrored more,
Chained to the slats, one tub of water
And another to squat upon the floor –
Corpses sent to cotton graves.

But there are new forces stirring, surges
Of some subtle energy seeping from the ground...

...For Richmond's coalfield now gains its peak,
Moling shafts steep down and deep,
Pumping up to waiting rails
For Manchester's docks and windblown sails,
Or straight to Tredegar's ready works,
To fuel a new industrial breeze,
Forges, mills and factories,
New turnpikes built, and bridges too,
As a brewed revival ridges anew
Virginia's quilted edge.

Go down, enter in!
Find truth in our confines,
Honesty in the barriers
To our delving thoughts...

...VisionMind...

Anti-slavery anger continues to mount in the North, especially around the case of Dred Scott, who claims his freedom because his master has taken him to free soil. In 1857, the Supreme Court denies that such movement makes Scott free. It rules that he is neither a citizen nor has any right to sue, and it holds that Congress has no right to ban slavery in the Western territories, striking down the Missouri Compromise. This causes virtual warfare between pro- and anti-slavery factions in 'Bleeding Kansas.'

The eyes, the eyes of the world
Glare from their sockets
As they reel above the heat
Of self-justifying cartwheels...

...As a raven pecks a dying carcass
Of a rabbit that was petted once, taupe
And fluffy, children-kept and wept,
Whose name was Hope.

I am digging still this ditch
A thousand times a day,
A millennium for a lifetime
Amongst the slime and squirming leeches
That suck my blood away, just
As they suck old Ginnie's soul
And bleed her of morality...

For then I see a black rat snake,
A shaft of shadow through the corn,
Who darts from out the waving wheat
While we, white family and two owned slaves,
Scythe it from the rising dawn
Unto the dusky fall of night,

325

Oil lamps lit to guide our path
And harvest crop before the rain
Is brought upon a threatened wind
And we lose another year's hard yield
To the vagaries of nature's whim.

Hold on. Hold on.
Keep your hand on that plow, hold on.

Five minutes late from the field!
Rip the rags from off her back,
Let breasts and buttocks spill at will,
Tight-tie those deep-scarred wrists
And grip with such an energy of man
As will lash her independent mind
And teach those thin-starved bones
Tossed across a high-roped beam
And hauled until those tiptoes twirl
Shadows upon the sun-swirled dirt
Of our muted whipping barn –
Then force a rail between her legs
To stop her cunning twists
Of slash-lash wists upon her back
And gashing, unfed ribs.

A dozen men tighten round,
Their laughs like rhythmic chants,
Pounding, pounding barnstall walls
With open thumping, drumming hands,
Lashing to the left, in fright
As they spin and dance to the right,
Widdershins,
Sight of the southern sun…

…and of the Kalunga Line[105]… passing through and through… the realms of night and day… to Oldumare[106] and Orun, the spirit sphere… to the egungun… the egungun… down… alone, in my despair…

Oh, Moses, take me there!

We rip her to her tears of bone
And sanguine splattered sacrifice,
Thumping on the well-palmed boards,

---

[105] A Congolese term for the watery threshold between this world and the next. When crossing the Atlantic Ocean, slaves believed they were being taken to the land of the dead, never to return. The Kalunga Line is an imaginary line in the ocean; once crossed, you become one of the dead; the only way back is to recross the line and return to Africa, where you re-enter the world of the spirits, even though your body has passed on.

[106] The Yoruba know their supreme god and creator as Oldumare; Orun is the world in which the gods and the egungun (ancestral spirits) abide; it is also home to the orisha, which are lesser spirits and deities. Anansi is the trickster spider god of the Ashanti.

Psalming to the solo rant
Of cowhide wrench and burn,
Then abide our rhythmic chant and ring
As the paroling moon defies the stars
And jars our midnight's silent toll...
Our midnight's silent toll...

We stop,
Exhausted by our sport,
Yet have more cruelty to impart
In this assuaging of our guilt,
Wiping clean our hands of blood with blood,
To smart her suppurating wounds with brine
And harsh-ground pepper dust,
Then leave her swinging all that night,
Next day and next dawn-light too,
Until we final hew her bands,
Refuse her food or helping hand,
And mock her as she crawls to lie
Upon her clay-packed sacking bed,
To die before the sun is dead.

Oh, Moses, sing
To the turning, turning,
Turning of our burning,
Never-learning soul...

We take up Mary's bonethin rack
And clean her blood-caked, blackened back,
Tie her jaw with maudlin cloth,
Groom her best we can in white,
And make a crude box coffin tight
To lay upon some sturdy stools
Within her bare-earthed cabin room.
We while with her all day and night, telling
Bright-fool tales to make her smile,
Of Anansi and the trickster hare,
Of Oldumare, Creator care,
And joke about ancestral throngs,
What fun she'll stoke,
Praying, chanting, ringing songs
That start off sad, but end in cheer,
For she has drifted final clear
Of this weird and shapeless world
And is traveling 'neath the sparkling waves
To the chuckle with our homegay gods
And brave eternal guardians,
Whose totems we have secret carved
And drum in new and stern display.

Oh, Mary,
We have cooked you opossum, okra,

327

Corn and fish for Eshu-Elegba,[107]
Goddess who will chronicle you,
Be your guide,
Now you're striding full the circle,
From Aye to Orun's side; so be joyful,
Be happy for your new-found peace,
Your release of tearful reckoning,
And leave us each to our dear beckoning
Night of rivened fears...

...our bleeding night of rivened fears...

...As the pounding dawn appears
And the field horn first-time sounds,
And we lay our hands upon your temples
And bid you final, swift goodbye,
Tho' one old one stays to watch you ever,
Till we drift at night's revere,
To boil and sere tomorrow's corn
And eat what toil we can,
Then bear your box up shoulder high
And three times bold and sigh around,
To bind crying ancestors to your side
As we loudly sing our journey down
To the mist-morned, marshy ground
Where you will find your final form.

Swing low, sweet Mary, for you're
Joining Moses now...
Oh, take us, take us too!

With the full moon risen,
Abounding night with glow,
Let the drums beat mournfully slow
The stop-go Death March sound,
And let us dance our dirges
Of spirit wants and urges,
Until the crate's laid snug beside
The seep-dug, bog-tied tomb,
Preset with blood of rooster, white,
Broken pots to wind-define
And colored bottles on the trees,
– Souls to jingle in the breeze –
While we let our preacher moan
Of Jordan and the Israelites
Suffering under Roman might,
As he raises up his circled cross
Of Sun and Water mighty fording
To the four most sacred points

---

[107] The trickster god of the Yoruba; a protector and messenger for Ifa, their supreme deity. While Orun is the abode of the gods, Aye is the earthly abode of humans.

We all one time shall grace,
Lacing through Kalunga's Line
To face Oldumare's grin,
Deathly Lord of our Creation,
As we chant our massing voices
In chorusing recant,
To rouse rejoice and visualize
Our own sweet passing want.

So, lay the coffin gentle, Mose,
Within that soggy ground
So she may final enter in
With no more earthly sound,
That underwater beckoning
Where spirit rivers 'bound
And orisha take her merit hand
To shiver her to glory,
Show her to The Promised Land
And stop our goried turning, turning,
In our VisionMind…

…sweet Mary, sweet Mary…

Then we reshuffle hymn in rhyming file,
Widdershins around,
Those piling high the sodden soil,
Boiling up our hallelujahs
From the trodden ground,
Letting go those solo singers, entranced
To dancing drums and mojo flutes,
As bembe[108] fall possessed upon
The grave mound's tossed pursuits,
Arms outcrossed and wailing full,
As we chorus out a dull response,
Until mornlight turns and mourns towards
The flight of aweful dawn.

Oh, Moses, Moses, Moses!

Mary wore three links of chain,
Every link was Jesus' name;
Keep your hand on that plow, hold on.
Hold on. Hold on.
Keep your hand on that plow, hold on.[109]

The Hare smiles as he watches
Us filing in the glow
Of the moon's full light slowing,
Fiddle in his paw,

---

[108] Bembe comprises a number of exhilarating drum rhythms of the Yoruba that can be played at several different tempos to invoke the orishas.
[109] *Oh, Mary Don't You Weep* – a traditional spiritual.

And walks upon the rows of graves,
Leaping mound to mound,
Then craves 'pon a fallen marker
And proceeds to phrase the tune
That will raise the ghosts of all
In final, spectral reckoning
One bright and soon-come fall.

And the raven sharps his bloodied bill
Upon the splitrail cut and drilled
That long ago by slaving men,
As a scarecrow parenthetically
Weeps his cross-winged sleep
O'er Gabriel's mostly secret grave,
And I bring up my ill-got view
O'er the nibbled, caterpillar-chewed
Vegetables of a widow's plot,
Set behind her cabined logs,
Next the wind to slow latrine
Down by the hid-cough bog
Of a putrid stream,
Watching WindTeller approach the pane
Of the windowed cabin's frame,
Peer at the lonely form within,
Hunched across a ragged mat
Woven for a market sale, then
Watch him remount, rattle by,
Wondering how many now must die
In the scouring battle lines
Drawn across our crying sky.

"...what's to be paid out for this business? How much are you going to cheat me, now? Out with it!"

"Wal," said Haley, "if I should say thirteen hundred dollars for that ar fellow, I shouldn't but just save myself; I shouldn't, now, re'ly."

"Poor fellow!" said the young man, fixing his keen, mocking blue eye on him; "but I suppose you'd let me have him for that, out of a particular regard for me."

"Well, the young lady here seems to be sot on him, and nat'lly enough."

"O! certainly, there's a call on your benevolence, my friend. Now, as a matter of Christian charity, how cheap could you afford to let him go, to oblige a young lady that's particular sot on him?"

"Wal, now, just think on 't," said the trader; "just look at them limbs – broad-chested, strong as a horse. Look at his head; them high forrads allays shows calculatin niggers, that'll do any kind o' thing. I've, marked that ar. Now, a nigger of that ar heft and build is worth considerable, just as you may say, for his body, supposin he's stupid; but come to put in his calculatin faculties, and them which I can show he has uncommon, why, of course, it makes him come higher. Why, that ar fellow managed his master's whole farm. He has a strornary talent for business."

"Bad, bad, very bad; knows altogether too much!" said the young man, with the same mocking smile playing about his mouth. "Never will do, in the world. Your

smart fellows are always running off, stealing horses, and raising the devil
generally. I think you'll have to take off a couple of hundred for his smartness."[110]

The ravens are gathering...

...As, in the ballroom of bones
We dance upon the blistered blood
Of flesh-seared hands and backs,
On the drive of whip and lash of fear
That wrench mere minds from thought
And tear the soul from race of men,
Give them lie-ripped glares of hate
And call them innocents doped upon
No self-life, learning, grateful hope.

We reel upon the bone-blind boards
Of oak-hewn hearts and branded arms
That were sent to ditch-spurned death
And raped and raped and raped
To the breath of fiddlers three,
And Nat King Cole's sweet jigged refrain
That taught our children honeyed lies
Of birth and rightly ordered place
And placed our generations in despair,
In the name of prospered liberty.

We trip upon the tongue-tied lie
Of happy-realized hypocrisy,
Aware of wrong, no excuse required
For the righteous screams we now deny,
Screams we drown with click of heel
And skip of spiteful melody,
As we parody the cellared bones
And manacled eyes that sugar call
With marrow-dripping moans
From beyond the ballroom walls.

We skip upon the branded souls
Of blinded, shadowed specters
Who drag between our tripping toes
And touch our eyes with ghostly tips
That finger length across our years
And suckle flickered-scarring orbs
Of the chandelier's black-flashing grace,
Splashed with eyes of spacéd skulls,
Each glazed reflection a sparkled glare
Of slave-skinned tears and muted stares
That dazzle with the tortured smiles
Of a people lost to wiles of saccharin.

---

[110] From *Uncle Tom's Cabin or Life Among the Lowly* by Harriet Beecher Stowe, 1852.

We pant and pause our pent-up grief
To sup from guilty-silvered bowls
Of field-burnt rum and sanguined blood,
Of defleshed grapes, cauter hung
From Piedmont voices and the vines
Of red-specked switch and pole,
And caress the punch-spoon, drenchéd tears
That dole within the clotted glass
And melt the heart-burnt, groaning bones
Of the silent-suffered fields,
Where fences, tight-lipped bray
At ditches hurried with hidden graves
Of humans tossed away.

And I want to call the reelers' call,
Back to all sense and decency,
To acknowledgement, apology,
To redress-admit upon our knees,
Beg and press those afflicted up
To some historic equity,
To ask forgiveness for our theft,
For all our plund'rous greed,
And for the onward deft succor
Of all our past's misdeeds.

Oh, to envision love, compassion,
Rescheme, rewrite, redraw
The traumas of our past, give
Them new endings, new hope,
And recast them in a happier mien –
And finally be free to open
Our dark and closéd minds
To the universe of liberty!

In 1857, a catastrophic flood devastates large parts of Virginia.

And Linkum sighs, holding low his head,
Draped with raven's feathers, cauls,
Skulls of squirrels, and other garbaged things,
Fingering the dried umbical that holds
His handless watch, time-stopped sins
Whose reward we soon must all behold.

In October 1857, John Brown seizes the federal armory at Harpers Ferry, intent
on rallying and arming a vast slave rebellion. Nothing of the kind happens.
Federal troops kill some of his followers and Brown himself is hanged. But, to
Southern horror, many Northerners consider him a martyr.

Meanwhile, in defiance of law and morality, and with war pending, the Atlantic
slave trade has begun again to Virginia, with ships from Africa, the Caribbean
and South America openly calling at her ports.

All reason lost,

All hope of truth dissolved,
All righteous pretence
Abandoned –
Let fate take its course
And consume us at its will!

"The North has no stomach for a fight,
They will let us go in peace, or else
Sight a mere slight resistance that will
Be resolved by Christmas…"

Sing, Moses, sing down da hill an' row,
Our time is coming, coming slow,
But it is coming sure eno'.

A thrice escaper, Matthew,
Captured, whipped and starved,
Is taken to the blacksmith
To have a face mask carved
And bolted tight about his head,
Grill set across his mouth,
Spikes around his straining neck
Iron horns upon his head,
Shackles bolted to his ankles,
– And dangling between the clasps,
A chain with jingle rope to lift
And bind
His gasps of clanging, drifted mind.

I turn, I turn, I turn,
Dancing on the threads
Life has handed me.

Oh, come, Linkum Tiddlum Tidy,
Symptom of such poverty,
Dancing within your bones,
High black hat and tails of night,
Visions sparkling in your eyes,
Hollowed orbs that sear a glow
Enticing all who dare.

Moses,
Let the trumpets play the minor key,
The drums roll sharp and solemnly,
The bearers carry the coffin down
Between the ranks of family,
WindTeller, Linkum, Brer and me,
As we doff our hats to unreality
And walk the silent mill, no flour
Left to grist the harvest year,
Its wheels and chutes in silent wait
For our horizon's fearful fate.

Hallelujah! Hallelujah!
Hear ol' Moses' call!
Oh, come let me see the dawn,
Let me escape to honesty
And finally be free!

Book VI

Into the Cave:
Release, Redemption
and Retribution, 1861–1901

I

Hush, little fellow, hush!
The song is nearly over
And the moon has come to rush
Into the soul of the night,
When unclear minds descend
To our cave of dreadmost plight...

The Parable of the Crippled Man and His Blind Dog

Once upon a time a poor man with a hunched back, deformed arm and clubbed foot lived in a little hut, alone apart from his sole companion, an aged, blind dog. He loved that dog and believed he treated her very well. However, the reality was very different. He would get angry at times and beat that poor cur ruthlessly if she did anything to displease him, and that could be at any time and on any whim.

Every day, the man would hobble down to the store at the bottom of the hill, pulling his dog along with him. There, he would meet the conjure man and gamble away a few games of cards. On his walk, he passed the large mansion of his neighbor, who was rich, with many new-fangled machines to save labor on his fields of tobacco, cotton and grain. And every day, as the poor, crippled man walked past the house, his dog would do something that annoyed him and he would start hitting the animal with his cane, kicking it and beating it mercilessly, dragging it down the hill with him, then dragging it back up again on his return.

This went on week after week, year after year, until one day the rich man became so angry at this ill-treatment that he stormed out of his house and complained loudly at the cripple's inhumane treatment of the animal, threatening to call his sons and forcibly take it away from him. The poor man was indignant at this interference with his property and angrily pulled the cowering dog away with him, protesting that it was for the dog's own good, and that he should mind his own business and look to his own house first.

The next night, the mansion caught fire and flames blazed high from every window, until a lucky rainstorm doused the inferno. In the morning, the rich man was found dead amongst the charred remains of his study with a bullet hole in his head and it was clear, even amid all the burnt timbers and still-smoking ruins, that some of his things had been stolen. Investigators, learning of the argument the day before, went to the cripple's house and there they found the stolen things. The

335

poor man was jailed and brought to trial, while his blind dog was left to helplessly roam the countryside.

The man was clearly guilty, though he denied it throughout the trial. However, when the judge, who was about to sentence him, asked him why he had done such a terrible thing, he finally broke down and confessed. "I was forced to," he gasped, in anger and tears. "My neighbor threatened to stop me kicking and beating my dog. So I had to do it, your honor, I had to. He forced me."

The first part of the Great Lie
Is to deny
That slavery was savage, barbaric –
Instead, bleating and placating
With soft metaphor and subtle explication
That *so* many owners were good and kind,
And *most* slaves redeemably well-treated,
Never whipped, never maimed,
Never shipped into coffle lines,
Iron masks or necklaces of horns,
But lofted with warm clothes, adorned quarters,
And a living comfortable and soft.

The second part of the Great Lie
Is to deny
The evil of the system, comparing it
To northern industry, wage labor,
Whining that New England factories
Had slaves engaged for sorry pay
In conditions just as forced, or worse,
And to ignore the curse of servitude,
Of rapes and killings, broken families,
Branded hands and faces, clipped ears,
And the right for us to choose
Our lives and our fears.

The third part of the Great Lie
Is to imply
That most enjoyed their bondage,
Paternal-dwelt, indentured,
Childlike, unprepared,
Household servants cared for well,
Enjoying beds and meals and comfort,
Too simple or unstressed to venture
Into a savage, killing world
Where their lack of skills and laziness
Would squeeze them into destitution,
Rather than soft plantation ease.

The fourth part of the Great Lie
Is to deny
That the war concerned slavery at all,
To quote Lincoln, extend excuses

That states' rights, homestead
Protection were the real concerns
For Davis and his plantation friends,
And to ignore why so many poor
Refused to fight, fled, deserted,
Or were enthused by the Union side
– Half of white Virginia seceding from
The enslaved creed of the state.

The fifth part of the Great Lie
Is to deny
Slave wisdom, endeavor and capacity,
As competent as whites,
As brave, hardworking and as fit
– Or that they craved their freedom
Desperate with each flighted hour,
Stating that most plantations snoozed
Unperturbed by warred dispute
– Loyal in repute, trusted, free –
A whitewash that bruises to today,
In unabashed denial of equality.

The sixth and final part of the Great Lie
Is to deny
Even the *existence* of wartime slaves,
Their flight and engraved resistance,
Their willingness to ambush,
Burn barns and houses, poison,
Refuse to work, sabotage, go slow about,
Flow freedom into their own firm hands,
Fight for Union forces and to scout,
Despite the frenzy-butchered slaughter
Of Confederate soldiers' assault
On a race's quiet-enobled valor.

Let us no more apologize nor lie,
Let us no more glissade nor simplify,
Let us no more squirm nor ignore,
But let us straight and truthful say,
With courage in our humbled hearts,
That we were terribly, terribly wrong,
And slip upon our bended knees
To beg forgiveness for inhumanities,
Seek ways to give in recompense,
Build memorials to their memory,
And take their peaceful offered hands
In final joint identity.

I do,
I bow my head
And beg forgiveness
On behalf of all

Who have defended slavery
And defend it still…

…As I go,
Gathering in the sheaves…

And silent I abide,
Within the swallow of the ground,
To sit-round well and spell
The deep-cleared pool of
Callings calling to their past,
In waif-thin veils of drum and mask,
Our selfdom's heartsick weeping,
For it is not until we are entirely
Stripped of our lies that we can
Heal and seek relief once more
In insight, love and self-belief.

…as patient flows the James…

Meanwhile, in the twilight of this time,
Between the death of day and birth of night,
We gather round, boys and men,
Light the fire and dance the round,
Chant to the heavens' power
And enter in the lodge to sweat,
Stones brought with, a drumming sound,
Sage fumes and tobacco-scented air,
Pithing impurities from our skin
And from our worldly cares.

Waiting for the harvest…
The harvest of even-handed justice… [111]

…As we watch from distant trees
Across the lemon-tingéd rows of leaves
To hear the distant drum-beat fire
Deep within black freedom's mire
And wonder,
Why must there be so many tears
Between now and the to-come?
Why so much to cry about,
When all is done, is done?
Why must my upraised hands
Unfold with pleading destiny,
And why must we suffer such remorse
On our most needed journey?
Why, oh why, oh why?

---

[111] This, and several other lines, are adapted from *Bringing in the Sheaves* by Knowles
Shaw and George A. Minor, 1874/1880.

Hush, hush!

There is a sudden storm, rain rages down,
And two men, one white, one black,
Shelter 'neath the bending shade
Of a draughty-shacked tobacco barn
That has longtime sheltered both.
They stand silent until the pour is past,
The old blind dog has whimpered by
And they can resume their roles again.

Waiting for the harvest,
And the time of reaping...

Hush, little fellow, hush!
For patient flows the James,
That shallow-riffled crease
Between suffering and release,
And the Conjure Man is sighted
In the fated swamp of night.

Come under, come under, come under,
And let the quiltwoman wonder tell
Of directions, paths and midnight ways
O'er rivers, streams and stalking fogs
To mountains where the bear claw walks
And mnemonic symbols trigger memory,
Symmetry of stars, plantation houses,
Roads and rivers, bridges, tradesman shops,
Anvil, Saw, Wheel and Square,
The first to gather tools, prepare,
The next to provision a wagon trip,
The third to slip directions near,
The fourth to signal all is clear.

As she sews she sews of Jordan,
Of Exodus and Moses, Abraham,
Of God's chosen people, looking o'er,
Searching most the Promised Land –
And she warns of the night-time Sand Man,
Come to fright the youngest child,
Brer Rabbit, Fox and Bear,
Their tricks to 'scape the paderollers,
To glide and hide and climb and watch,
Catch food and slide in secret bogs,
Elude through swamps and defeat the dogs,
Shake off trackers, beguiléd chasers,
Use the stars and wind-cast clouds,
Proud finds for a vastness wild
And lost within our quilted mind.

But more this time, as they gather round,
For she speaks of Lincoln and John Brown,

Of secession, anger, war preplanned,
Of fiery speeches, Calhoun, Henry Clay,
Of Fort Sumter and lines drawn in the sand,
Of volunteers and halcyon Southern pride
To whip Yankee hides, naïve, proud,
And sip that julep of bucolic life
That grips most in strife and poverty.

Oh yes,
We know,
As the masters know,
The gladness that is their despair,
And we excited grow in the scheming
Of escape, resistance, preparation,
That quilt and story, arbor preacher too,
Have long prepared us now to do.

Oh yeah! Hallelujah!
Finally, finally!
We be crossin' dat ol' River Jordan!

And so they come, and so they come,
WindWhisperer and the MusicMen,
Callings, Callings, draped within the day
Of Mama Swamp's laid broken promise
And the crippled dog's last hooray,
As they pipe the smoke of dispelled illusion
And the self struggles mighty hard
To resist its falling calling
To enter-plunge the well-spelled waters
That will engulf and take me down
To the depths of self-surround –
For this is the myth of falling light
And the sound of marsh decay,
When the crows will hound and the foxes bray
Upon the morning of our reaping day.

Hush within the misting shush
Of melancholy songs that drone
In the arbors of this burning night –
What drums may call,
What bones and banjos wail,
And what signs may rise
Upon this haloed vale?

For we must descend, enter dark,
Dwell within the cave's surround,
Plunge within the drowning black,
The decayed lives of countless limbs
That await our spirits' floundered ease
Within the descending of our souls,
And hope of reborn midnight light.

Hush. It has begun.
I love you, and it has begun…

We must descend to be reborn…

II

[112]Crow fox, upon the tempered lea
Of girl with lover clasped to form,
Delving within the meadowed swarm
Of dandelion and buttercup, flowers born
To bank and stream and shroud
An arbor
Of rose-cheeked boy and lilied girl,
Flattering with a sweat-kissed ardor –
For it is spring and the hare is roused
Upon his watchful, sullen mound,
Whistling to the unlistened sound
That peddles news of Sumter foes,
And burning breeze as it blows
Its secret need to flare engorge,
With sword and flashing Minnie ball,
This havened hall of Southern world
And loose the claws of 'necine strife
On the harbingers of blood-soaked grief.

So take your place upon the rails,
Fox-lipped vixen lady, crowing
To the great tree's veiling boughs –
Craft your chain of life-plucked daisies,
Dying as you wrap them 'round, tie
Them to your pride-flushed love,
And lead his well-sunned, anxious glove
To the sound of courthouse band
As we descend, descend, descend
To tocsin-cheering volunteers, and
Rowding speeches all for those
Who cannot read, but
Are roiled to self-defense
Of homesteads, big-house slavery,
A way of life, and
Freedom from invasive reason –
And to heady praise our history
Of states' rights, valor and conviction
That it will end by Christmas time
In prime and total victory!

Thus our lover signs his cross,

---

[112] This whole section comprises *The Song of the Confederacy.*

Snugs the ranks of baited men,
Some boys and some too old,
Bed rolls, letters, mugs and forks,
A kiss upon the north-blown wind,
A promise to return, keep his troth,
Then is dragoon-marched by boots
And rattle-hooves of cavalry,
As the cardinal pips a warning chip
And the nubile wanders mindless back
To her lover-lonely farm, dismayed,
Her father, brother grayed and gone,
Two women now to tend the crops
And harness their three slaves alone…

…While Brer Rabbit pipes gentility
Of underburrowed, sad-cast hostility,
And strokes soft the blooded cardinal's back
As he hacks off western counties in debate
Of loyalty to the nation, not atonal state,
And side with many less than eager
For a big plantations' cotton war,
As they hunker in forgotten valleys
Of mountainous determination
To never buy Confederate bond,
But look beyond, to reintegration…

Oh, but the fox of war is circumspect
And so, not far away,
Within rife and early summer stench
Of cockroach drill and heat,
Of typhoid-fevered tent and trench,
The ranks of ill-equipped
File and beat and shoddy turn
To rhythmic rag of drum and fife,
Haste-sewn Southern flags,
Old muskets and a few scarce rounds,
Then are hurried sent, break camp,
To northward threat of blued advance,
Meet at Manassas' bridge and hill,
And are repulsed, 'til Stonewall instills
Courage in troops upon the ridge
To hurl the Yankees in confusion
Back upon the bloodied run
That fox and crow now feast upon.

And my sultry love, crying within
The meadowed grass of winter feed,
Lays her head upon a stack
And plucks a bearded dandelion
That she blows soft twice upon
– He loves me, loves me not –
And tears come to her russet eyes

As the sounds of harness trot below,
Slow upon the rivered road,
And a dozen wagons rumble crawl
Medicines and munitions hauled,
Rustling into the sunset eve,
As girl and seeds fly aimlessly
Across the fox-grayed leaves...

...For the river bubbles broiling by
In the glare of blood-silt gravity,
Intense upon its woosh and lunge,
Its fearing roils and thrill-lisped plunge,
Wish-curled currents, praying over,
Kneeling rush and down and over,
And finger-link the altared rocks
In the gentle mourning's breeze.

Then, six months late of anxious wait,
A flare of crimson peaks beyond
A lilting melody of clouds,
November rinds and harsh descends
O'er fall's sweet autumn call
And her lover finally a letter sends,
Dictated to lieutenant,
That tells of love and battles fought,
With fear of death and missing her,
Of boredom, drills, dissent,
In a cold-creased Highland winter.

Barely a fortnight later, soft one night,
An owl hoots and glares within the barn
As the cattle low and fidget-hoof,
Sensing some come stranger,
Who gentle lifts the stiff barn latch
And scratches up a ladder
To hide among the loft-lined hay
And await his love's sweet scent of day
Upon the predawned air.

She hasty comes to milk the cows,
Businesslike, now no time to mess,
Heaves Old Daisy's bilking tail,
Stresses her into a bier-fed stall,
Wipes her udders, sits upon a stool,
Headrests sideways against a flank,
Pull-presses in thumb and finger squeeze
Warm swishes zipped into a pail,
Then startle-stops, head thrust around,
As swift he calls, soft, not to assail,
Jumps down and they embrace,
Climb back to kiss within the hay
And grace the new-warmed morn away.

Once satiated, hunger calls
And they careful cross towards the house,
Lest militia searching for deserters
Are skirting in suspicious stealth,
Then feed the man with starving health
A desperate soup, smoked ham and jam,
And impart to him untethered fears
Of guards, inflation, stubborn slaves,
With none to steer unkempt farms
Or restive human property.

Then, as the screech owl call-implores,
He's ghost-gone, bold once more,
Reveiled as soon as revealed,
To depleted regiment, cold,
Dispirited,
Officers furlough flown, until
Jackson cyclones stern command,
Wins rapid at McDowell
And launches an audacious, swift campaign
In vicious-valleyed counter-moves
That outmaneuver Federal troops
At Front Royal and far Winchester,
Then recoups Massanutten's engroovéd flank
To Cross Keys and Republic's port,
Wins, repulses, victories,
And climbs the Blue Ridge to support
Old Lee rebuffing
Huffing McClellan, fool,
At Gaines Mill, Glendale, Malvern Hill,
On the bloody-cast peninsular,
As the *Virginia* and *Monitor* blast
To spurned inconclusion
And the Union blockade, ever mightier,
Norfolk taken, Hampton burned,
Tightens even tighter…

Soon, for our lover,
Manassas looms once more,
With encored Confederate result,
The Union suppurating in its rout,
Clara Barton ministering to the spoiled
As Lee scouts onto Northern soil,
But is in turn repulsed, rammed back,
Upon the war's most blood-ridged day,
Twenty thousand bloated dead
Crammed within the flood-fled swerves,
The shaded banks and arching bridge
Of undeserving Antietam.

And whose side is God upon,
Whose blood does He bear,

And whose innocence of despair?

I love you so much, my love…

A fox hunts the graves,
Shallow dug in stunted haste,
Paws and snouts and savage pulls
A hand, a wrist, an average arm,
Then drags the running, rheumy limb
Back to her dim and hidden den…

…As Linkum Tiddlum Tidy
Is riding through the stars
In hat and tails and misty trail
To the dancing of the scars –
And, oh, you watchful answer many cries
With swift and angry death,
And blow upon their sudden graves
Your stenching, vapid breath;
You rip and wrench their monuments
To grandized columned tones,
As you jingle on the moonlit trails
Tunes upon their bones…

…While the raven sicklies with the gore,
The poppies hang their sanguined heads,
And forget-me-nots do oft implore
To droop their sunken, soaken roots
Within the ichor-glutted streams
That slowly suck the warming blood
From great Virginia's dreams.

Meanwhile,
Politicos ramp their distant laws,
Turning the South to prison camp,
As the carts of cadaver collectors,
Slaves or low-paid blacks, never yield,
But clatter-clink from scene to scene
Of youth-sown, congealed fields,
Racking corpses upon their backs,
Coldly naming those they can,
Flinging trinkets into regimental bins,
Then hurry-digging massive graves
With lime and stamped-down sod,
As letters are by commanders sent
To wet the gently sighing eyes
Of maiden girls as they await
Details of the last-thrilled days,
Of battles fought and brave last lies,
While others sob and brittle yearn
With womb-grown graying pains,
And pray that, one day,

Their sweets will gain return.

And the crippled dog follows the fields
As our young girl, eyes hollowed now,
Her frame swayed violent thin,
Despite her subtle pregnant ways,
Raises her tired and bruiséd hands,
Pulls the daisies from her neck
And heeds her mother's nagging call
To sweep the house and stir the meal
While she beckons the slaves to hoe and weed.
Then, as she wanders up the hill
Through slants of slack tobacco plants,
She sees upon the road below
Coffled children in chingle pass –
A hundred on their cottoned way,
Toys and dolls in frightened hands,
From threatened northern fields
To safer 'bama bolls...

...While Brer Rabbit sits upon a broken fence
Beneath the dangling, hang-turned feet
Of a neck-braced, captured servant man,
Militia caught and quickly raised
To stench the bowel-dripped, sweating twist
Of flesh-rot gust and fisting blow,
As cawing crows pluck head and eyes
And a fox jumps at his bloodied toes.

But then the battles ease and armies rest
To replenish cannon, guns and fodder,
Each side of Rappahannock's running flow,
Until boredom slows the posted watch
'Mid months of wintered lingering,
And our lover signals fellow foes
To drift across the shallow stream
And trade tobacco for coffee beans
– But not for long, as they swift return
To scanning sharpshoot murder,
As Lincoln, avoider no more,
Cautiously, hardly brave, proclaims
Part-time emancipation of the slaves,
The slow-bright light of spring invades,
And a fugitive loops old Hooker's troops
Across a pontoon bridge, to enter unopposed
Chancellorsville's woods and ridgelined banks,
Until the indecisive Union man
Surrenders his ranking within the day
To old gray Lee and flanking Jackson,
The XI surprised, pushed back,
Dealt death with impunity,
Until Jackson's jumpy pickets,

In the twilight gloom,
Panic, shoot in tragic 'bush,
And the general loses, first an arm,
Then fights to dodge the draining life
Of the greatest Virginian soldier
Of all our blood-soaked strife.

Then, after a hasty Federal retreat, once more
A quiet river marks the bound
Of North and South, but not for long,
As Brandy Station heralds a Southern push
Into a nervous Quaker State,
Wheeling 'til the armies frigid face
In fated ill-embrace,
At Gettyburg's calm-endooméd ridge...

So for a day and startled night
The blue and gray maneuver
To dire rhythm of last-dawn fires,
Regiments crisscross the pre-death gloom
And generals rage point and spite intent,
Enduring angered disagreement,
Until sharp orders are sternly sent
And the highest sink into sleepless rest,
A bed bug biting General Lee
As he bivouacs in his audacious tent,
Servants caring to Traveller's needs
In deathdawn's dewdamped hours
Of veiled and destined tragedy,
Waiting for the hubris hand
To chilling wipe the fox-red world
With the sanguined, draping cloth
Of fifty thousand men
Who charge and yell the broadax fields
Of orchard, corn and wheat,
Raked by ball and canister,
Or pinned within the Devil's Den,
Bottle-stopped at Little Round Top,
Custer's stand at Hanover,
Culp's Hill barrage, Cemetery Ridge,
And Picketts' hopeless, desperate charge –
Until the loss of grayclad life
Is too great to more sustain
And, once again in sad retreat,
A mere interlude at Mine Run's banks,
The armies fall to an old refrain
On Rapidan's winding ranks,
South and North again to trade
In tobacco, news and fading strength.

So Linkum Tiddlum scans and grins,
Thrumming upon his rollcall skins,

347

As the Rabbit ghosts his violin
And they jump from corpse to twisted corpse,
Gallivanting barefoot round,
Never touching the muddied ground,
As men lie in their festered heaps,
Brains spewed across the fetid grass
And the crows and rooks howl their glee
As they circle high and ravenously
Upon this stench of muscles ripped,
Of bowels and limbs and eyes
That drip no more upon their loves,
Who fall upon their broken knees
In desperate tearflown agonies,
As the news of loss and loss and loss arrives,
And the phantoms of our spirit's gloss
Dance across the spattered forms,
Contorted, ripped and ragged torn,
Of cadavers that gasp in shreds
– Among them two the girl has known,
Brother and father, side by side,
In the pride of their pointless suicide.

Fields of battle are no place
For intrusive monuments that sanctify
Meaningless death and anguished pain
– They are the place to silent swear
That it shall happen ne'er again.

Then, upon this silent-battled grave,
Lincoln stands and bows his head,
Addressing those who suffered there,
To promise a country that, in liberty,
Is preserved of all, by all, for all,
And shall not perish from this earth,
But be spread to Southern states,
So long outside of freedom's gates.

And our lover, scarred veteran now,
Steals again to winter barn and love,
To find her softly born a son,
Three months and suckling hard,
So careful hides within the loft
As guards patrol the knavish night,
Their slaves still loyal yet, it seems,
Close-lipped within their pride,
And remains to ingest his weakened frame
With a side of last year's harvest
– Much reduced by requisition's strife
That has provoked the farmers' ire
And despondency at corruption rife
In Richmond's stuccoed halls –
And which soon provokes that city's belly,

Swollen by soldiers, casualties and whores,
Slaves forging Tredegar's munition guns,
To riot – three thousand women in revolt,
Enraged by suppressive martial laws,
For bread and meat and something more –
Until they are dispersed and promise-kissed,
Only to starve once more, the poor
Heroines of our desperation,
Inheritors of our justice struggle,
Condemned as traitors to a cause
That never served them well at all,
But bruised them even lower down
Than ante-bellum wealth had done –
And to my mind, are the bravest
To stand so well against
That violent, selfish tyranny
Of Virginia's Confederate hell –
And I dream one day to see and read
An epitaph to those women indeed
Who struggled so for their children's bread,
For, as Richmond starves,
Lynchburg, Petersburg, Danville too,
Speculators hoard-abound,
Carvers of ground corn and grain,
Money worthless, a zero
Of useless bonds, fortunes flown,
Habeas corpus swiftly gone,
Deserters, looters, vigilantes on their trail,
Plantations prevailing less their share
Of a deepened Southern burden,
As slaves seek out the bluecoat fires
And mountain sympathizers ride
To raid unprotected, crying farms
And roam the Allegheny crests
Until the crippled dog is laid to rest...

Then,
In a sudden-sharp surprise of snap,
As the soft-hushed springtime air
Drifts across the green-tinged land,
Brer Rabbit is sudden gin-tooth trapped,
His leg gouged ugly within the jaw,
To wrest and scream in anguished pain,
Until late that evening comes a boy,
Who brains him swift and cleanly outs
His limpness,
Throws him shoulder over,
Whistles proud and jaunts well clear
As the trickster dances joyous near...

...To a sudden crash and bugle call
That heralds Yankee charge and carnage fall,

Met by a gray-sharp volleyed wall
Of counter charge, repulse,
Retreat, attack, reply, retreat,
Within four hundred murdered feet
Of Wilderness, confusion stumbling,
Densely groping, bumbling,
Shooting fear and rustled flashes,
Until both sides gash-gasp and final lie
Exhausted,
The boy's sweet carcass bullet-holed,
The rabbit stiff within his grasp.

The presumptuous race then quick resumes
To outflank Spotsylvania's Plank,
There to slaughter more in gore,
In days to gain the Bloody Angle,
Killing near two thousand score,
Until insanity once more reprieves
And Grant slips clever east, deceives,
And pushes on to his Richmond goal,
Is nearly yorked at North Anna's fork,
And badly mauled at taut Cold Harbor,
As fifteen thousand more are called
To perish with their heads asunder...

And her lover, hungered, barefoot now,
Most companions harried, dead,
Sits within the drizzled rain
And carves a love's twin heart refrain
With his upon the log that heads
His trench and breastwork line,
Until the shower turns to storm
And he must shiver-hunker down
In freezing drench and mud-soaked lie,
In case of sudden Union reply...

...While bare ten crow-crazed miles away,
Across the creek and zaggéd line,
Federal soldiers carve *their* names
Upon another soaking trunk,
This time a once-enobled oak
That guarded some old plantation home,
Its stores all plundered, livestock gone,
Slaves long fled and flown away,
The house a flaming fury,
Unabated by this thunderous day.

And, in a further valley field,
The girl, her baby dead
Of typhoid weakness, dysentery,
And bleakness of her mother's food,
Stands within the lonesome gloom

Of a hot-shelled farmer's house,
Eyes bleeding deep and ashen shed
As Union soldiers line a ridge,
The family cellar-cowed, frigid-feared,
As starched cadets from Lexington
March in thankless ranks towards the guns,
Through orchard fields and mud that sucks
The boots from off their teenaged feet,
Down and up the ravined banks,
And storm unflattered odds believed,
Until their heroism is relieved
By a charge upon the battery,
Forcing back the bluecoat lines
Until the day is won and lost, and
Brer Rabbit comes to hold the hand
Of the faintly haloed girl, who weaves
Her faintly whispered way
Across the mud-drenched, faintly field
Of faintly-swirled and pointless gain
And calls the faintly of the world
To bind a tight-linked bobbing round
And faintly sing of rings and roses,
Of sneezes, pockets and sudden posies
In which faintly we *all* fall down.

And the ghosts of the bootless boys,
Honor ringing in their lifeless ears,
Valor on their white-veiled lips,
Rag-clad ghouls of fathers lost,
Walk the red-clayed, furrowed fields
And haunt the cratered, sloping brows,
To mark the death of simple reason
And demand their vows' reprieve...

As, in the slaughterhouse of the ages
They hang each famished carcass
Heel by heel by heel,
Slit their throats, one by one,
Let gush the spurting blood reel down
Face and hair and dangling arms,
Then split their bellies side to side
And charm their stomachs' fall,
Cut livers, lungs, kidneys, breasts,
And slit apart the heart-filled chests,
Sever heads and suck the brains,
Of one, then two, then five, then ten
Hundred thousand nameless men.

By now, famine scours the land,
And countless deserters fan and hide
In secret caves and valleys wide,
As fox-eyed ravens greedy peer

Upon a clear-leafed mocker' tree
To black-eyed watch so close below
Militia drag a questioned fellow
With answers hollowed lies,
Loose a rope about a bough
Then droop the noose across,
Pull it firm, switch harsh his horse,
And let his twitching body jerk,
Feet kicking, stinking, working down,
Hands clutching as his tongue burns blue
And duly chokes this lost man's life,
As the raven blinks her winking eye
And Linkum Tiddlum stalks the limbs,
In grim and desiccated leper's cry
To Virginia's bent and sighing trees.

While, not yet fifty miles away,
A blue detachment scours a ridge
For house and mill and field
To burn, 'quisition for its need,
As Richmond slow is slow interred,
Steady flanked to embanked east,
Cavalry rankling to the west,
James River crossed audaciously,
Petersburg circled and contained,
As lines of fortress trenches,
Gambions and staked fascines,
Snaking zigzag entry lines,
Revetments, breastworks, drowning ditches,
Salients, redoubts and prickled forts
Exhort chaotic overflow
Of subversive growing earthenworks
Southwest in sinued, lengthened curve
To threaten 'Federate railway lines.

And among Richmond's trenchant maze
A slave unpacks his captain's case
Within his board-plinthed, well-spaced tent,
Polishes buttons, shines his boots,
Lays out all neat to stand at rest,
Then shuffles off to cook a meal
As hookworm men have never seen
In a dozen lean and hungered months…

…While lingering on small Belle Isle,
Dank within the fall James' banks,
Captured troops in fetid camps
Of ratted, elemental, typhoid tents,
Stench latrines, bare hospital care,
With less food than vermin dare
Sniff their cold-stiff noses at,
Are starved and left to dachau die

In summer heat and dysentery,
As, despite winter's starving freeze,
Flies and roaches multiply
In the worst of bestial inhumanity –
And Union officers fall the same
Behind squalid Libby's warehouse walls.

Yet, not ten miles from this sour scene
Federal soldiers dig their latrines
While others secret mine beneath
Pegram's haughty salient,
Then charge and blow and charge again,
Into a crater's mud-filled shoot,
A massacre of suicidal, maddened rout,
Especially delirious because, in fact,
So many troops are black.

Then, in some distant, last-tossed attempt,
Jeb Early raids on Washington
But is rebuffed, must defend,
With exhausted, starving men,
No grain, no horse, no powder,
As Sheridan pursues him louder, louder,
Burning Shenandoah farms and barns
In a ruthless valley rush and push,
Until they meet at Fisher's Mill,
– Defleshed bones of blacksilled chimneys
Standing stark in carrioned memory
Of smoke-burnt homesteads, cadavers
Blowing upon the blood-soaked wind,
In this Valley of the Ravens, aflame,
Where even buzzards find no name
For their rude repast,
And the clouds are crying tears of jet
At this hushed-besetted land of waste,
As resistance is most final crushed
At gory Cedar Creek, our bones basted,
Twisted, bent
In rabid, flesh-torn sacrament.

Then, as the final spring days dawn
The girl now lazy lies,
Her eyes but hollow frozen orbs
In sunken, drifting, hazy form,
Prone within a fishing punt, blue,
Her face hidden by a taut lace veil
Upon the musing Fluvanna's flow,
As Custer's raping, raged command
Fresh from chilling Waynesboro feat,
Thunders 'cross the old bridge road
And gallops down a narrow trail
To Batesville, Scottsville and the James,

Burning bravely in his knife-splayed swathe
All deathly discoveries of Virginia life.

Meanwhile, Sheridan and Grant's last surge
Outflanks the Rebels' western edge
At Dinwiddie and Fork Union,
Cuts the sustaining railing ways,
Then bursts through Southern lines
And hurry turns on Petersburg
As, finally, the siege destroyed,
Richmond is mistaken set ablaze
As the invading Union forces
Are hurrahed by all the joy-freed slaves.

As I stand upon this cross of blood
The raven gloats the haemy ground
And the bloated, headless corpse
Of the girl's most sacred love,
Her notes still bedded deep
Within his clotted heart,
As ex-slaves still perform the task
Of throwing bodies upon the carts,
Liming more and hurry-burying
The never-ending, lifeless parts...

For now the armies race to
Amelia Springs,
As a caterpillar hungry begins
To gnaw upon a new-sprung leaf
Of this year's raw tobacco crop,
The girl and mother dropping there,
Dead between the battled rows,
Sabers carved on silent brows,
Their slaves all final fled.

So, in our story's final throes,
After Saylor's Creek's crowing call,
Lee's force, disintegrating fast,
Meets its last retaining wall,
As it is denied its re-supply
At Appomattox Station,
So reins upon its futile cause,
Surrenders to a foe's respect
And files before the blue-ranked men,
Heads proud but thinly domed,
And, crying at its hopeless end,
Trudges a tearful journey home...

...As the ghoulish girlish face
Rises slow upon the misty morn,
Her heart a sickened morbid mess
That vomits at the wreckage done

To the life that once was hers
– And the hollow-shadowed orbits
Of her lover's hand-held form
Now sing of sparkle-ravened wings
And search their graveyard's 'maginings,
Hand-in-hand to a Rabbit's prowl
And Linkum Tidy's wierdsome howl,
To haunt the wistful wanderways
And wonder where the beauty went
That turned this proudly bounteous land
Into an empty ghostyard hell
Of walking dead and crippled nights
In which ne'er heart nor love could dwell.

And the Horseman hangs his head
In silent-sifted memory
Of all that's lost, the futility,
Turns his shift-shimmered steed away
And searches somewhere dark to pray,
As the singer sings and the drummer plays
And the fiddler sparks the night,
Their spirits wafting across the notes
As death becomes their light...

And even now we stand,
You and I, mousy real,
At that brickframe Appomattox house
Where the fence is white and sparkled paint,
The garden blossoms pinking out,
The grass well-trimmed and cut,
And stutter-tack from plaque to plaque,
Grim arms *in* our *memoriam*
To an unhealed world of broken zeal...

...Oh, let us quilt the frame of memory,
Of cheating life and sad defeat,
Of wishes and half-splendored hopes
That vanquish-soak that windy porch
And grope the sultry torch of misery –
That wear our tears and bear our woes
And weave such stitch of sowing blows
That herald thoughts of salt-bled eyes
– Of man or son, sweet victory –
And veil our smiles within such wiles
As work our wraithful fears away
And absorb our troubled mystery
Deep as drops that will remain,
But will never rest nor stay.

III

Oh, the time of reaping...

On April 14th, 1865, President Abraham Lincoln is shot; he dies early the next day. Congress, lead by Thaddeus Stevens, is determined to abolish slavery and ensure civil rights for all citizens. Later that year, the 13th Amendment, abolishing slavery, is ratified. In 1866, Congress passes the Civil Rights Act. That same year, the Ku Klux Klan is founded.

...going forth with weeping...

Blood on the rose,
Blood on the rose...

The Negroes are resisting! Save us!
They will no longer plow, nor pray
With us,
But insist on their own way
And will devour us any night now!

...As I see where stands
A landscape of charcoaled chimneys
Where once great houses stood,
Fences broken, fields sumac turned,
Catbriar, grasses, invading oak,
The soaring croak of bullfrogs
Or moonlight whoops and wails
Of whip-poor-wills sailing o'er
The calm of pale whip-poor-will farms.

But not for us! No!
Within *our* liberated breasts
Swells the spreading fever
Of free at last! Free at last!
As we bound a summer hallelujah
Of dancing joy and unexpressed relief
That it is finally over, finally no more,
That we can now walk freely down
To the lounging hardware store,
Perch our limbs, talk with belief,
Read, buy a Bible, go to church,
Build ourselves a school or a chapel
And impel our divorced soul its confessions
For newssheets and reading lessons,
To re-avow enforced marriage,
Or dizzy seek long-sent family,
Singing the creeks and boisterous streets
Of towns in undisparaged revelry.

Oh Daniel! Going forth...
Rejoicing, rejoicing, rejoicing!

So much elation in such simple matters!
Taking two names, neither one our master's,
Buying new clothes, furniture, shoes, a bed,
Threading abandoned plantation rows
For *our* sole gain, no longer theirs,
Sassing proudly into town,
Downing cornpone, devilled shrimp,
Owning tools, a horse, a shed,
And the promise of Thaddeus Stevens,
Saint and haven, our forgiven friend,
For forty acres and a mule
This riven first of January.

Sowing in the sunshine...
Fearing neither clouds nor winter breeze...

And so begins our chanting dance around
To find deep within what cannot yet be found
By outward sight nor reason...

...As a man, black, poor, recent freed,
Enter-fears a postmaster's store,
Asks to send a telegram, but cannot read,
Cannot write, so hesitates in effacery,
His simple message to a previous town
Where he once lived,
And family still roams,
In his lingering, new-pulsed memory...

...While two whites stare him down hatefully,
Unready yet to concede...

...And others, finally freed from Slave Row slums,
Cockroach-'fested ticks and earth-packed floors,
From one-roomed families, a single pot,
Beans and corn and mush,
Pack their rags and join the rush
To Richmond, Washington, Northern
Ports and towns, Norfolk, Hampton-bound.

Let them try to reap, but we
Are not yet ready to surrender
The glory of our past. No,
We shall yet be victorious
And shall overcome!
Come, thick night,
And pall thee in the dunnest smoke of hell,
That my keen knife see not the wound it makes,
Nor heaven peep through the blanket of the dark.

For this is *my* myth, as I descend,
Losing limbs and hackered flesh,

Deep within the dark recess
Of self and mind and selfishness,
As rejoicing is soon torn and pressed
By vicious-'stored Assembly,
Intent on myopic self-destruction,
Unable to grasp
The totality of its defeat,
Cheating public education, new works,
Resmirking slave conditions
Upon the backs of freed blacks,
Now vagrant named, whipped and chained,
Strict-ingrained labor contracts, tenant laws,
Enforcing vigilante patrols, clawed
With drunken, angry CSAs
Roaming, lynching, maiming,
Blacks to tame their work,
Killing Union veterans, black and blue,
Raping, beating, shrewd intimidation
With the legal blesséd sanction
Of plantation courts and legislation,
In conditions as deplorable as before.

The old Confederate Assembly refuses to accept the end of slavery, so *de facto* reintroduces it through a Vagrancy Act; it also refuses to endorse the 14th and 15th Amendments.

Bind them to the land,
Keep them tied to our fields,
Don't let them wander –
Legislate and whip their hides
If they try to sidle gander
To some Promised Land…

Get from the sidewalk, cur!

And, nigger-minded, I concur,
Hat lowered, eyes averted,
Thank him for his mercy
And my blesséd misery…

…Among the milling streets, prostitutes,
Paupers, war-torn cripples, wandering
The burnt-down stores of Richmond's
Dead and deadly wharves.

…*sowing in the shadows*…

Daniel, Daniel, Daniel in the la-la- lion's…
Daniel in the lion's den.[113]

---

[113] *Peter on the Sea* is a fieldhand spiritual from antebellum days.

Vindictiveness gone too far,
New repressive Southern laws
So incense the Northern Radicals
They overrule complicit Johnson's
Unlicensed cruelty and impose
Military rule, reconstruction,
And disband the Slave Assembly –
Virginia now Military District
Number One –
Insist on taut oaths of loyalty,
Forbid pardons to those who fought,
Deem those traitors who swore "Confederacy!"
And hold Jefferson Davis two more years
In stinking Monroe Fort, manacled in fear,
Ill-fed, distraught by jailers, enraged,
And left to rot in forgotten age and infamy.

A black family, newly free,
Move onto a tenancy, pay rent
Of half their annual crop, but
Must clear the wooded swamp
With their borrowed saw and chain,
Push their borrowed mule and plow,
Sow their borrowed seed,
And build a one-room cabin bones
From mud and rubbled stones...

...As, with the help of secret Union League,
Intimidation, organized control,
And carpetbaggers salivating at the spoils,
Scalawags flap their enthralled tails,
Call conventions to caucus and select
New legislators in their salivating pay
– Underwood, Hunnicutt, Bayne –
As poor whites and blacks, many swayed,
Elect them by o'erwhelming voice,
Since most who had upridden arms
Against the Union are now forbidden
To exercise their voting choice.

And so our chanting dance goes around...

...As freed slaves plant their yams and corn,
A few beans, salad greens, just like before,
In their same plots, same huts,
Masters gone, houses burned down,
Orchards left to drop
Their forgotten fruit upon an earth
That The Horseman, too, has let slow rot.

Peter, Peter, Peter, Peter on the sea, sea, sea
Peter, Peter, Peter, Peter on the sea, sea, sea...

Peter walking on the sea...

Now is the time of reaping...
Sowing for the master...

...As, throughout the South,
Black judges sit upon the benches,
Black lawyers argue before the bar,
Black sheriffs hire black deputies,
Black postmasters handle mail
And black legislators go to capitols
To pass education, public works,
14th and 15th Amendments,
And orate on fundamental rights
And states' equity.

I cry, I cry, unwilling to surrender,
Unwilling to accept
The horror of my eyes.

And, as the blood is washed from the rose
Within the florist's window gaze,
I wonder if it is the case
The blood will e'er return once more,
More bloodier yet than e'er before.

IV

Throughout Tidewater and Piedmont acres
Old plantations lie abandoned, forgot,
Except for ex-slaves who occupy and farm
Their small plots to survive and remain
Within their Slave Row huts,
Avoid the white house, shut,
Or long burned down,
Ransacked, plundered, lost and bled,
Where yet old widows of the war,
Their sons and daughters fled
To Brazil or Honduras, Caribbean isles,
Rock their somnambulant, dreamy way
Upon porches of sorrows and regrets
And recall with ante-bellum smiles
Those balls and beaus of their youth,
When all seemed such simple truth.

As a copperhead slips within the grass...

...And other poormen drift to new-swelled towns,
Richmond, Alexandria, Petersburg,
Where riots uplift the slim-drowned yells

Of beggar wages, scanty jobs
And re-ranting slavedom's mobs...

...And where a woman quietly calls
From a warehouse wall
To a man in shoes and hat, passing her,
Winks and asks him follow
Her down an alley's burnt-out bricks,
Rats and fallen chimney stacks,
Agrees the price, lifts her skirts,
And closes her eyes as her body jerks
And the man withdraws without a glance,
Hands her his coins, rebuttons his pants,
And turns back to the life-packed streets...

...Where the blind dog passes,
Observing all...

...While a father sits his daughter on a knee,
To tell her the plea of Moses, basket-found,
Who fought up from his bound poverty
To lead the proud Egyptian court;
He snuggles her to take up heart
In her new-plagued, exile struggle,
Drapes a cross about her neck,
A sun fleck on its brazen breast,
Plus a talisman of the Rabbit's hair,
A paw forged in the Savior's silver,
To forever hang upon her chest.

Roll, Jordan, roll,
Roll, Jordan, roll,
I want to go heaven when I die,
To hear Jordan roll.[114]

Descending, descending, thin and down,
We are descending, descending, thin and down...

...So much so, the Callings sit and wail
For the failure of their prayers,
Rhythmic drumming to the skies
That offer neither cloud nor breeze,
As crops fail, rains fail too,
And severe drought hits the land,
Infertile, exhausted, drained away,
Into the streams that veined its life
And to the mud-choked, leaching bay,
As new floods silt and breach canals,
Destroying locks bare half-rebuilt
From Sheridan's destructive guilt,

---

[114] *Roll, Jordan, Roll*, an established fieldhand song.

Virginia unable, it now seems somehow
– Psychically unwilling –
To dream itself from sprawled reclusion
Within the slough of desperation,
Kneeling, sobbing before the cloth
Of someone else's candled table,
As still her arms
Are severed by her sufferings,
Her flesh wrenched off, despite her will,
Which still descends despondently.

Going forth with weeping,
Sowing for the master…

With the interest paid on seed tripled, more,
With store-bought mule and cart and cow
Indebted now beyond what he has in store,
The poor white tenant plows his furrow
For his cheating landlord's day
– One man earning from another's brow.

On many farms, the ex-slaves
Linger from their lingered fear,
Near-despair, as near-deprived
As ever they were in years before.

And what seem'd corporal melted
As breath into the wind…[115]

…When it rains, down pours,
And, in sixty-five and sixty-six,
The harvest grains fail badly,
In sixty-seven mere moderate well,
Plunging sharecroppers, tenants, farmers
High in hock for seeds and tools,
Foods loaned to see them through,
Into sudden-deepened debts
They will never see repaid;
Tobacco is barely plucked,
For no hands are there to stay,
To pick and hoe, unstem the flowers,
The animals slaughtered long ago,
With scant mules to pull the plow,
And so starvation races on apace
And recovery seems so far disgraced,
It were a dream, some cruel illusion
Sent to perforate our confusion
And spin-twist our inability
To comprehend or understand
The awfulness of our complete defeat

---

[115] From Act I of *Macbeth*.

And loss of so much property.

Impoverished now, money burnt to the wind,
North Virginia is laid to waste,
The Ravened Valley no better place,
Wytheville, Bristol also razed,
Our state some hell-born desolation
Of somnambulant and blinded fear...

...While, agéd, gray, deteriorating,
Beaten, saddened, dying,
Wealth gone – walking free
Or lying fallow among the weeds –
White-haired beard, thinning hair,
Heart failing like the wheat
Blighted in the pare-plowed fields,
Old Man Lee,
Black-cloth buttons upon his chest,
Medals to a culture lost, and pockets
Stuffed with Confederate bonds
Not worth a match's cost,
Strains weary Traveller through
A biting Lexington rain,
Unrepentant of his shattered cause,
Stunned, in shock, unable to be
In this horrored vision turned reality,
Occupied, powerless, friends all flown,
Lost amidst the crying lost,
Calm amidst the unbecalmed,
Steady amidst the Apocalypse...

...with no way to recall-return...

...For I sit alone, the cold, the fear
Of cramping limestone walls
And crushing rocks above me, so
Begin to chant, to memorize
All my father impressed on me
To be, visualizing
My eternity.

And the crippled man, his eyeless dog
Sidling by his side, directionless,
Snuffling from the past to present,
With no hope of future yet aroused,
Searches the lair of the Conjurer...

...As, a gentleman,
Attorney by his trade,
Specializing in tort and family law,
Goes to an apothecary on Hillsville's ridge
To purchase a pair of spectacles,

His eyes grown tired with late night oil
And from some niggling, ringing ache
Tingling in his head since war forays
With A P Hill's artillery,
His vision confused, blurred these days,
In need of readjustment to new ways
And to stare through some rose-cut prism
At a reinvented life's belief
That can redefine despair...

And a train, rebuilt, boiler fixed,
Gathers up the steam
To press its way o'er restored tracks
To carry scant tobacco stacks
On to Richmond's prizeries.

I raise my arms to the unknown,
As I tumble, tumble, tumble down...

...And lose all sense of being,
All body, arms and legs,
All reason as I jumble down
And cannot save myself, nor try
To control my mind as I die
Within the head-first crevice of my tomb.

Meanwhile,
Within a Mecklenburg parish
Black Baptists break away
From racist whites, who once
Controlled their prayers
And now have raised enough,
In cash and promised farmyard kind,
To cut the timber, saw it clean,
Raise the posts and roofing beams
And frame that tiny, hidden haven,
Cover-shingle, add a tower,
And commingle benches, rough, but firm,
That can be pushed swift awall
When the spirit moves them all
To raise the roof and shout their ring
Of joyous song to Son and King...

...As, under the gaze of Union troops,
Uniforms swarming o'er the state,
A line of berated whites and blacks
Await the door with hats held lax,
To receive from Freedmen's Bureau
A dole of grain, some corn, a ham or two,
Maybe a pair of donated shoes,
A coat to guard the autumn rain,
Medical regard for pains and wounds,

Complaints around ill-treatment, or
To question the captain once again
About free land and a mule,
If not this year,
Perhaps before next season's due.

Then, a few miles away,
A white woman, teacher from New York,
Enters a new-built schoolroom framed
Upon a low-lying hill, no higher than
The Greensville mire,
Of wood that's from a plantation barn,
And, with fireplace, hired help,
Tells the children all to rise, adults too,
Then begs them sit and begins,
Without a board or chalk or slate, to relate
ABCs and Bible tales, to add a sum,
Count from one to ten,
Spin of Jonah and the whale,
Regale from her favorite book,
Uncle Tom's Cabin, a revelation
To these people culture-forgot,
Then hangs a map of reunited States,
Talks of Lincoln, Jefferson and their rights,
And ends the lesson with sweet rendition,
Rousing, a little uncertain,
Of that spangled banner bright
That drapes once more across the plight
Of this great and suffered state…

And not far away, in Boykins town,
A man proposes to his brother's wife,
Widowed by the war, mother of four,
To merge hers with his, his wife deceased
At gangrene's vicious door
After a terror-dwelling, still-born birth
That took her life in lingered hell.

Oh, the pain, the total pain
Of the desperate loss of self, of all,
Of my entire being, hope, until
I am left with nothing but
The solitariness of being –
And nothing's left but death
Or, in dying, some humble, earthly born rebirth.

I lie exhausted, no thought…

And, as the beggar slips and falls
In drunken, hungered stupor,
The eyeless dog lost by his side,
The copperhead still slips within the grass,

Slides into a sleeping pile of wood,
Attracted by the scented trail
Of rats within the log-framed shed,
Their squeaks and feces easy signs
For the crevice hunter's poisoned fangs.

V

Enough of this! There is no more
To cleanse and pare away;
Let me reattach my arms, reform my legs,
Regather wits, reascend
And fight my way to break of day!
– But the cave will not let me,
I am not yet ready, not self-humbled yet,
Not ego-lost, dismembered
From my past's dark infamy.

Soon, soon they will come...

...For the old soldier, limping, one arm gone,
Who stands before a simple stone
In the rows of countless simple stones
That mock this simple graveyard fenced
With memories most now forgot
Of sacrifice and values lost,
As he is lost, a beggar now,
Forced to sit on Lynchburg's streets
– Or those of any Virginia town –
Pan in hand, dust, uniform stained,
Complete humiliation finally attained.

Enough! I must fight; I cannot any longer descend!

But they are yet to come...

...Even for the Concord man,
Standing by the latticed window
Of his upstairs hotel room,
Who wets his strap and whips his blade
Of cutthroat too and back,
Slippity-slap, slippity-slap,
Then raises up his chin and careful shaves
Stubble from his reddened neck,
Awaiting a chance to change the tide,
Scanning, preparing, planning,
As a cart piled high with hay goes by,
The blind dog sniffing by its side...

...And even for the laborer,

Beaten white, fingers burnt,
For smiling at a Negro woman,
Talking, joking, flirting, as she brought
Lunch to his hoeing gang,
Lesson hasty learnt.

Oh, hear the weeping
Of enough! Enough...!

...As we hobble to the Freedmen's Bureau,
Where humbleness helps a while,
But free food and free sympathy
Is never long for you nor me;
As we crawl to the hospital,
Where prosthetics give us hope,
But soon blister, sore and braze,
Till we can bear their graze no more;
As we drag ourselves from an institute,
To a home of doleful widows,
Overfull with orphans, the happily insane,
Who cannot recall our yesterdays;
As we pull our bodies to the grave
To beg release and demand
What it was we did so wrong,
What the crime for which we pay,
Other than to fight for daily bread,
Our homesteads and our families?

Were we wrong, Lord, that you treat us so,
Half a nation crippled, nowhere left to go,
No one to blame, no reasons why,
Other than torn memories
To help us cry –
And unbearingly deny?

There is nothing as indecent
As this Negro government,
Nothing as profligate, nor absurd,
As illiterate blacks ruling their betters
While the fair women of this state
Are fettered by such dreadful villains,
Omened at each corner of each street
By mean scalawags unabashed
And shameless roving nigger blacks,
While 'our' legislature slacks its money
To honey-educate an inferior race,
Food and clothing spent with no trace,
Hob-nobs jobs on roads and bridge and rail
At our expense, set upon our knees
In a disease of spendthrift debt.

Coming, we are coming,
On the night's dark wings.

It is time, gentlemen of this Commonwealth,
Those of you with self-respect,
To unearth and re-oil those pistols
So careful hidden, counted away,
Remount your roans and surefoot steeds
And redeed this state for decency –
No matter the cost in Negro blood,
Nor in the strains our ropes apply
To the trees of this unhappy land.

Enough! Enough! Enough!

Then, barely a few hours later,
Upon a lonely, night-blacked lane
A Republican is taken-slain
Before his house and wife and child,
Dragged out and tied up to a fence,
His tongue cut out, then his eyes,
KKK carved on his flesh,
Drenched in kerosene, set alight,
And burned for each resistor
To view the rabid scene
And rapid take swift flight.

Meanwhile,
In not-so-far-off Tennessee,
The old guard frown-collect,
Colonels, judges, owners of plantation,
The rich intent to raise a rabble
Of vicious, bloodied riders,
And elect that murdering, baseless cur
Nathan Bedford Forrest secret head
Of hooded knights, Inquisition white,
Gliders of moonshine epiphany,
Burning crosses throughout the night
To impose a Nigger Judgment Day,
Cast fear upon the Southern plight
And regain their powerful sway…

And so they come, and so they come!

…As we glance back
Upon our porch of dreams,
To old idyllic schemes, calm and free
– Deny the screams, deny! –
When all was in its place and meant to be,
Before the Yankees destroyed our liberty,
Before the Irish, Jew and foreigner
Taught crime, disease and false ideas,
Betrayed us, stabbed us in the back,
And brought us to our cracking knees –
And rejoice instead in refound cause

Of righteous supremacy and ease!

Enough!
Enough!
We are come to fight and
Regain our mortal soul!

And thus Northern visions of abolitionist peace,
Harmony of races, human decency,
Released to each his education,
Jointly striving towards proficiency,
Sharing trains, streetcars, hotel rooms,
Marching towards unity, equality,
Meet the reality of Southern Codes,
Vagrancy laws, apprenticeships,
Church burnings, Red Shirts[116] and infamy
Of intimidation and assassination,
Racist press and lynching trees
That seek-restore white liberty.

Oh, but hush, little fellow, hush
For what fiddles are playing
Down in the arbor tonight?
What drums may rush,
What bones and banjos wail,
And what signs may rise
Upon the shallowed vale?

Enough! Enough!

Give in, let go, let go the past, surrender…

Never!

Yes! Oh, Dixie, Dixie,
We shall restore your ringing pride
Upon our riders' night-time wings!

And yet this *is* democracy, for the first time,
Imposed by Union troops and welcomed by
The poor, who vote with intention,
Dedication and conviction, despite
The machinations of the old élite
To restore their controlling seats of wealth –
And there are mixed race meetings, factories too,
Parks and coaches, streets and neighborhoods,
Without the segregated halo of our later years.

Twenty-seven state legislators are black,

---

[116] The Red Shirts were a violent, reactionary vigilante force in North Carolina, but similar forces were at work in Virginia.

> Blacks run Petersburg and Danville,
> Have militia units, posts in government
> And as postal clerks, Federal appointed,
> Are present on many city councils,
> Yet face constant harassment, rows,
> Intimidation that grows with gray threats,
> Burnings, killings and the KKK.

In the state election of 1868, the 'Conservatives' (Whigs and Democrats) win control of the General Assembly. Realizing that they need to get rid of the Union soldiers and regain control of state affairs, they reluctantly pass the 14th and 15th Amendments – requirements to end the military occupation. They have every intention of undermining the Constitution once the Union soldiers have gone.

> And thus is Virginia redeemed,
> Elections won, Assembly reaffirmed,
> White Apocalypse foresworn,
> And, in its place,
> Black Apocalypse reborn.

A referendum overwhelmingly passes the Underwood Constitution. It is inspired by the Union Army's desire for some degree of fairness and democracy in state elections, but is seen as unfair because it would keep many ex-Confederates from voting; however both the 'iron oath' and the disenfranchisement of CSA soldiers are defeated. That year, the National Woman Suffrage Association is founded.

> *Oh, I wish I was in Dixie!*[117]

> And so I shall be,
> As enough-is-enough is turned
> Into triumphal ecstasy!

> I sigh. In my love for you, I sigh…

> *…reaping, reaping, bringing in the sheaves…*

> Old grievances redeemed,
> Revenge for justice stalks
> The haunted fields of screams…

> *Hooray! Hooray!*

> Round the back, nigger,
> Don't soil my porch with your shade,
> And serve your turn, nigger,
> For what your grade deserves.

> Back down, nigger, back into the gutter…

> *Hooray! Hooray!*

---

[117] *Dixie* echoed around the state in celebration when Virginia was 'redeemed.'

A jeweler sits beneath a lamp,
Next a window veiled with lace
And the dusty trace of wagons
Passing, carving an opal cabochon
Into the profile of a lady
Who wishes to parade it to her beau
As sweet memory of how prime things
Flowed
In more pleasant times…

…While, in Leesburg's clopping streets,
A photographer from the neighbored North
Daguerreotypes all willing soldiers
To send to Yankee homes, prints
For loved ones anxious for some sight
Of their sons and too-late husbands.

Oh, I wish I was in Dixie!
Hooray! Hooray!
In Dixie Land I'll take my stand
To live and die in Dixie,
Away, away,
Away down south in Dixie!

You will pay a thousand times,
Nigger, for your audacity,
A thousand times in the years
Of our new-swift prophecy.

A crippled man,
A crippled boy
A crippled you and I,
Left to wander, left to cry,
Left to reflect, left to die,
An old blind dog by our side.

Outside the Capitol, on the steps,
For daring to creep upon the hill
Of the white élite's preserve,
A carpetbagger is stabbed to death,
His assassin shrouded into the crowd,
No police nor judge nor soldier grim
Bold enough to search for him.

The singer sings and the drummer plays
And the fiddler sparks the night,
Their spirits waft across the notes
As dawn, once more, becomes the night,
As dawn, once more, becomes the night…

And enough! becomes revenge,
Checkered and unchecked…

Also in 1868, Judge John F. Dillon fundamentally alters the nature of state and
local relations by limiting the power of municipalities to those "expressly
granted, necessarily or fairly implied, or absolutely indispencible [*sic*]" to local
governments, thereby straight-jacketing Virginian towns and counties, and
denying them the right to run many of their own affairs. The rule is aimed at
stopping local resistance to state-imposed segregation.

Oh, Dixie, Dixie, Dixie…

VI

And, oh, the chilling breeze!

So on it goes, as those
Who would drag us back
Refuse to accept new ways,
Revolt at taints of democracy,
And are determined to regain their sway
From poor whites and black Republicans,
As night-clad vigilantes patrol,
Storekeepers rudely deny us food,
Factories sack us from our jobs,
And thugs intimidate us at the polls,
With guns and whips and artillery rolls,
Drilling openly, the old militia gone,
A new one avowed in its place,
Poor whites insulted, humiliated, cowed
For alliance with barely poorer blacks,
Carpetbaggers, Northern greed –
Slogans promising to emancipate
And return the state to its rightful seed…

…As Swamp Mama, with bright Hecate,
Suffices from the shimmerin marsh,
With Fla'ed Weaver, Weft of self-in-sacrifice,
Acceptance of eternal sufferance,
Trances lonely round a pot, a pail
Upside turned to reduce
The knotted sound
Of her far and distant wail…

…While WindTeller and the Rabbit
Reap their tears upon their shoulders
And jointly weep for a hundred years…

Oh, Brother, you oughta bin there,
Yes, my Lord,
A-sitting in the kingdom,
To hear Jordan roll.

But is it, after all, Jordan's shore we seek?
And who will be our guide?

A tall, enshadowed musicman,
Sweat-black, ritual scarred,
Thin, barred hat upon his head,
Banded tight with rattler skin,
Jabbed with feathers of the crow,
Ambles down the back-dust lane,
A gnarled stick with wolfhead knob
Clicking to his jobbing pace
In the blackness of his servile grace,
As he watches, listens, stops apace,
Shadow-moves to let The Horseman pass,
Then finds a track across the grass
To a creek, past sleek tupelos,
Sweet gum trees, to a hut
Where his customers will cut that day,
Lays out his neckerchief, spreads his things,
Crows' feet, hardening fat of bears, jangling
Possum bones, skulls of cockerels,
Rags and mojo bags,
And sits upon an old trunk log,
Takes out his pipe and jerks a tune
That lurks the wanting to his den
And welcomes soon his old blind dog.

In 1870, Virginia is readmitted to the Union. Its new constitution sets up a public education system, but the races are to be taught separately and the Assembly illegally uses the money set aside to pay off its banker friends.

From 1870-71, the US Congress passes the Enforcement Acts – criminal codes that protect blacks' right to vote, hold office, serve on juries, and receive equal protection of the law. They are widely ignored.

Meanwhile, a catastrophe strikes the Capitol in Richmond when sixty-two people die after an upstairs floor collapses; in 1871, a disastrous flood hits Virginia, the James rising forty feet above normal at Richmond. There are also floods in 1870 and 1877, which devastate industry, as well as canals and river traffic, as dams silt up and burst.

The typewriter is invented in 1868, effective barbed wire in 1874, and in 1876 the telephone is created by Bell. The next year sees the phonograph and, in 1879, Edison invents a bulb that heralds a new era of lighted streets, factories and homes. Also invented around this time are the flush toilet, tin can, Kellogg's cereal, the refrigerated railroad car, cigarette roller (1880) and Singer sewing machine. Telegraph poles – the telegraph was invented before the war – now stretch across the state.

In 1873, penalties are placed on interracial marriages of one year in jail or $100 fine; to perform such a ceremony incurs a $200 fine; and, if a mixed race couple who married in another state enter Virginia, they face 2-5 years in jail for their audacity. In 1874, Mayo begins the manufacture of cigarettes in Richmond.

And so life and strife go on

– Though most
Care more to repair their lives,
Strive for prosperity, and raise
Themselves from struggle,
Merely to survive…

…While Alexandria repairs its docks,
New warehouses, factories and shops
On busy King Street, businesses
Finally popping up above
Pre-war tip and tuck…

…And Bristol, ravaged of the Union,
Razed,
Warehouses, shops set ablaze,
Sees upward lagging railroad trade,
Slipped revival, factory upgrades,
As Virginia slowly drags her hips
From the mire of despond…

For even WindTeller ambles by,
Tips his hat,
Cape of gray, charcoaled eyes,
And plays his fife to the tune
Of the denying dream of you and I,
The denying dream of you and I.

In 1875, Congress passes a Civil Rights Act, which states that "all persons within
the jurisdiction of the United States shall be entitled to the full and equal
enjoyment of the accommodations, advantages, facilities, and privileges of inns,
public conveyances on land or water, theatres, and other places of public
amusement…and applicable alike to citizens of every race and color, regardless
of any previous condition of servitude." But it is just as useless as previous
attempts. The South will not comply, and soon Northern radicals give up trying.

How to describe it?
The corruption beyond words,
Bribery rampant, vote-rigging,
Buying crosses with railway stocks,
Jigging favorites to run the booths,
Manipulation of registers and polls,
And constant moves to undermine
The role of poor whites and of blacks,
Overwhelmingly Republican.

And The Horseman watches a loaded stage
Clatter upon old Hampton's roads,
Taking the mail from steamboat sacks,
Packing passengers, valises upon its racks,
The driver whipping, guard urging high
As they cobble through the tree-veiled byways
And wobble west to Williamsburg.

Depression sweeps the South during the mid-seventies. A panic in 1873 sends farm prices tumbling and throws many farmers off their land. Others are heavily in debt and cannot get credit. Many walk to town barefoot and in rags, and suffer from a string of diseases. Hired hands earn less than $10 a month (35 cents a day).

...sowing in the shadows...

In 1877, Rutherford Hayes becomes president after a seedy compromise with Southern Democrats to remove Federal troops, who are rapidly withdrawn, finally leaving blacks and poor whites to their fate.

> Public education's due,
> Despite state promise,
> Is siphoned of to repay
> Outrageous antebellum debt
> To those outrageously wealthy yet,
> Leaving Virginia's impoverished mass –
> The richly empowered excused
> Their rightful share –
> To barely amass, but who cares,
> As the governor[118] declares,
> "Our fathers
> Did not need free schools,"
> Which are but "a luxury"
> – For, to educate is to empower,
> The very least desired
> By those who guide the strings
> Of their mere underlings.
>
> So the Callings raise their musicked tune
> With drum and flute and tambourine,
> As deep below the well-streamed pool,
> My spirit is cast yet soon before
> The altar of eternal care,
> Languished bare in fleshless plight,
> As the moon and stars defeat the night...
>
> ...While, in white chapels congregations sing
> Of deliverance at God's blessèd hand,
> Even as their ministry brings
> A knife darkly dressed with night,
> Sanctioned, but totally ignored
> In their sanctimonious prayers,
> As Baptists, in segregated choirs,
> Condemn blacks as "naturally indolent,
> Extravagant and careless," savored only
> For slavery or manual labor.

---

[118] Quoted from that *non sequitur* Governor Holliday, in 1877. Another legislator of the time regarded public schools as "essentially communistic," while another said they would "relax individual energy and debauch public morality."

All hail the power of Jesus' Name! Let angels prostrate fall;
Bring forth the royal diadem and crown Him Lord of all...[119]

But watch, for Linkum Tiddlum Tidy
Still wheels upon this ferris land,
Hungered, starved, emaciated,
Gated eyes staring black,
Searching out the lack of justice,
Revenge upon his memory,
As he prowls the courts and alleyways,
Gnarled staff paced within his grasp,
Caul and skull around his neck,
Snakeskin beckoning from his hasp,
Yowling bound,
Grinding flesh and blood
To the howling of the crippled hound.

...waiting for the reaping...

No! I cry!

I cry upon the centuries
That have suffered in the past,
And cry for all those centuries
With suffering yet to pass!

Hush, little fellow, hush!
For patient flows the James,
That passaged dream that yearns
And calls us to its realms...

Ye seed of Israel's chosen race, ye ransomed from the fall,
Hail Him Who saves you by His grace and crown Him Lord
of all...

Finally, in tiredness, I seek to rest
Upon the altar of compassion's breast,
Surrender up my fighting chest
With calm and sleep and disasunder
Of my weak and trembling flesh.

I am no more...

...As reaction,
Instead of rebuilding in some
Semblance of social harmony,
Lets terrored infamy stalk
Our lynch-white plantation fields
And dispossesses its savagery
On the unarmed and undefended,

---

[119] *Coronation* by Edward Perronet, 1779.

While the politicians of slavery,
Propertied and revengeful
Enforcers of human misery,
Rabble-rouse poor whites
In dreadful anger, fearful antipathy,
Towards those who parade their say
In genuine-mouthed democracy.

Grrrufff!
Grrrufff!
Grrrufff!

Hark! I hear the blind dog bark
Its anger and remorse, stark
In naked impotence to deny,
Forced to comply, comply, comply…

Aie, so, whipped and kicked from above,
We snarl our vicious, salivating bite
Upon Virginia's lust-freed neck,
Gnawing for a rabid Black Code just,
If not more, disgraceful than
The slavery it replaced.

…gnashing in our blinded savagery…

In reply, a desperate family,
Tenants mired in debt,
Slip out one night,
Head north, but are met
By a set of dawntime padderollers,
Beaten, whipped, cart rolled over,
And shackled back to repay
What debts they may or may not owe –
As close to the curse of slavery
As in their father's day.

Meanwhile, in a nearby city,
Women hurry drone their
Full-day shift at some dim factory,
Making fancy, well-bowed hats
For ladies to at-church display
On fancy, well-bowed Sundays
As they slate money on a plate
For silvered missionaries to ascend
And bend Virginia's mountain folks
From ignorance of backward ways
And the power of woodland crones.

What are these,
So wither'd and so wild in their attire,

That look not like the inhabitants o' the earth,
And yet are on't?[120]

They are you and I, staring aimlessly,
As patient flows the James,
Yearning, yearning, fearing
Both clouds and chilling breeze.

VII

The graves are still dreaming,
Dreaming still,
As they ever deepen...

Now, even greater than before,
Poor whites and blacks,
Are divided socially once more
And lost within their shattered union,
As they are tied again,
Like the days of antebellum greed,
To the rhythmic needs of plantations,
As vagrant laws recorral and reinvent
A renewed slavery of sunburnt fields
And reinforce unfreedom in those factories
We so recently sought to flee –
An apprenticeship and labor code
Forbidding quitting, unions, wanting what is owed,
And tie us servants to our masters' heels
In the starkest ideals of Virginia's reign –
And prove that terror was not slain in sixty-four,
But for us, is gaining even more
Terrible than was thought could be –
Making many hark back to the
Comparative joy of slavery.

As they ever deepen...

In response, an exodus begins
As blacks flee Klan and lynchings,
Barbaric massacres of human life,
To rebuild from strife in Northern cities
And reclaim what little peace they can
In those conurbations of segregation;
Others migrate to mountain towns,
Work down the railroads, quarries, mines,
Norfolk docks and Hampton wharfs,
Or settle in dwarf secludities

---

[120] Act I of *Macbeth*.

Around new-sprung mills and factories,
Build bridges, tracks, new town streets,
Settle discreetly near old freed blacks
At City Point, Pocahontas,
Downtown Norfolk, Alexandria,
Jackson Ward in Richmond,
Lynchburg, Danville's northside, Bristol,
Or across the tracks in Roanoke,
Where they still tread the mills,
The factories and the warehouses,
Load schooners, work the yards,
Repair the lines and harbor hards,
And, in a silent guard of suspicion,
Build their own communities
At the hidden margins of permission.

For the graves are still dreaming,
Dreaming still...

...As the Sufferers round the altar place,
Heads bowed in solemn solemnity,
The sun still locked within its box,
And await the time of desprized life
That dreaming will one day see; for
Where is the American Dream for me,
Cropped from my calloused hands,
Turned within this raisined land
Of empty-farrowed, dust-blown pity
That I've just cleared of rocks and stumps,
For my owner to then restake
And make me move to another site,
There to break for him again,
While wife and daughters till his crop,
Pick worms from his tobacco leaves,
As I must scythe and bundle-sheaf,
Winnow and bag and cart mine own
To that owner's streamside mill,
For mere two-fifths of paltry share
Of wretched, sun-backed will?

Descending still, rill after rill after rill...

For even weather and the soil
Conspire to oppose us, wither crops,
Destroy fertility, reduce our yields
And rile the very fields against
Our struggle to arise.

Can it be that our dream is based
Upon us building others' dreams
– Those who have the destiny we desire,
And dangle it before our eyes,

To let us rub our sockets dry
With hopes despaired in cry-rent
Debts to the magpie store
For seed and tools and year-long wares?
Perhaps such dreams are not to be,
Ever wracked on dry reality,
And on the ruthless driven pride
Of a few who grasp the streaming tide
And beat the rest upon our heads
With a lying, dead mythology.

Oh, the graves are still dreaming,
Dreaming still...

Yet still, still they deepen...

...As I push the worm-sucked moldboard down,
And old Betsy pulls the harness worn
And heaves the red-clayed soil around,
Long topless now, and starved,
And my eldest totes a few frail eggs
To the paupered market town,
Where ailing tenants, artisans
Of a serving new-defined,
Share in a mutual minded poverty
That pulls the whole South down
– For freedom for the lowest means
Freedom for us all,
And when we're placed in tyranny,
Our chains embrace enjointed fall.

So, is this the American Dream?
When we, those yeoman farmers
Once engraced by Old Tom Jefferson,
Are steadily displaced
Of land and livestock, savings,
By lines of credit, imposéd taxes,
Foreclosures caused by waving prices,
Bankers strict to intervene, evict,
Auction lives to bigtime growers
And the shackles of a commerce
Free only in its deceit imaginings
Imposed at every cultured step.

Unless we *all* can live the dream,
No-one lives the dream;
As long as there are rich and poor,
Where wealth denies so many more
Even the semblance of humanity,
Poverty will hold us in its thrall;
And, as long as the poorest share
Of the poorest crop is none,

Then we are all the slaves
Of our own, self-imposed,
Self-bred, and self-led misery.

Going forth with weeping,
Sowing for the master...

A deer nibbles a low-crept teaberry,
Its fragrance mildly soothing, wintergreen,
Balming to its parasites, among
Rue anemones, pink-stained stars of white
Bobbing the bright woodland banks
Of April's budding mountainsides...

...While, in the darkened woods above
WindTeller casts his rare phantom mare
Amongst
A translucent choir of ghostly hoods,
Gossiping Indian pipes, whispering
Silent between their drooping heads
Within the fallen woodland mast.

Meanwhile,
In a spirit quite contrary,
William Mahone,
Slippery, skinny squeak of a man,
General in the Confederates
And 'hero' of that remorseless slaughter
They called the 'battle' of The Crater,
Is now a railroad president, builder of
The Petersburg to Norfolk line,
Who unites the Atlantic, Mississippi and Ohio,
And pays himself an annual fortune
As he founds the Readjusters,
Which he hocks with backhand bribes
And well subscribéd railroad stocks.

In seventy-nine, mining votes of blacks,
To readjust antebellum debt,
He captures the Assembly and
Sets a tight-noosed, trussed machine
Of bribery and corruption,
Political appointees at every post,
Until he is hoisted to the federal Senate,
But divulges not a *sou* of power
To those blacks who first indulged him,
Other than as flower-dressaged doormen,
Sweepers, clerks, and message boys...
Yet he *does* readjust the debt,
Finances public education,
Musters black colleges and an asylum,
Funds an agricultural institute, purges

Virginia's judges, boards and charities,
And abolishes the poll tax, whipping post –
But so too, he roasts the state
Upon the backs of big coal, logging,
Bankers, railroads, mining co.s
As he toasts *nouveau* industrialists
Against the high and cankered Bourbons.

However,
Once he's lost most Democratic support,
Resurgent now, with irate whites
Embittered at the tyrannic toil of this hack
Riding Virginia's enbroiléd back,
He folds to manic pipsqueak
As reaction wreaks its hold.

Hooray! Hooray!

A drifter, white man, gambler,
Leans back in his porchside chair,
Chews his quid of blackened juice,
Squirts a splurt towards the road
As a blackman happens past,
Grins at his fellows' guffaws
And scares another swig of rum
From its earthen jug.

Hooray! Hooray!

The graves are still dreaming,
Dreaming still...
And still they deepen...

Oh, Mama, oh Mama!
Play the tune of the Conjure Man...

...Calling, calling, calling
From the depths of cavern grim
Up to him who will hear
Our falling, falling, falling hymn...

...As I stroll quietly along
The shaded Kanawha Canal,
Long my favorite haunt
On days away from orchard picking
Or pruning apple trees,
But notice that the flow's well down,
Fish flapping desperately
In the muddy waterway.

Then, as I further walk, I hear
The clamor of shovels, picks and shouts,

As I soft approach a working gang
That interns the watered banks
With heavy spill and reddish soil,
Another toiling near behind,
Laying piles of casket stones
For a new-born railroad track
Upon the course's dying way
That packets once choked up and back,
And with a memory-lingered eye,
In memoriam I cry for the sacred loss
Of old ways, once so plainly engraved,
But now encased in requiem
And tossed within our angered grave.

And the Callings call me up
From the altar of the sunken sun,
To rise, in rewholed and armed intent,
And rebuild a life still unbegun.

...I hear their call, deep within
The voided cavern walls...!

But it is too soon...I am still falling,
And will fall forever yet...

Am I a soldier of the cross,
A follower of the Lamb,
And shall I fear to own His cause,
Or blush to speak His name?

In zealous-rationed coffee rooms,
White ribboned marches of passion,
Bands of Hope, crusading saints
Are rallying Christ to the dens
Of inebriated citizens,
To save those lust-lost souls
Drowned in liquored incapacity
As they instigate
Reading rooms, church societies,
Pamphlets, picnic lunches,
Bunches raised of gold and meetings,
Ten Nights in a Bar Room hotly sold,
At rallies to denounce
The foul vapors of an intoxicated world,
Rum's powerful and covetous hold
Upon wives and undefended children,
And to lecture, morally cajole
Us about the devils in our pursuits
And the watchful vengeance waiting...

...Blaming poverty's moral flight
On symptoms, not disease...

Are there no foes for me to face?
Must I not stem the flood?
Is this vile world a friend to grace,
To help me on to God?

Virginia State College is established in 1882.

The graves are still dreaming,
Dreaming still...

...As several men hurry from
Their Church of God in Christ,
Their hallelujahing,
Their praises and their gospelling,
Their swaying and the losing of their minds
In the careless freedom of dispelled worrying
About the Kingdom of the Lord,
To hurry-sneak The Horseman's trail,
Past black gums, oaks and cypresses,
Into the swamp where'n old hut lies
And the Conjure Man strays his flute,
Sitting in his vest and suit, red necktie
Loose around his throat,
Hares' feet hanging from his belt,
Old-worn, dusty boots upon his feet
Blind dog sleeping by his side;
And they root around in congregation
As he closes eyes and chants
To the spirits of the underworld,
John the Conqueror and nkinsi
To give up all their ancient rites
And their ephemeral spirit power,
Casting dust and powders over them,
Making all in circle secret-swear,
Then uncovers his ancient potions,
Lets them look, inspect his wares,
Asking what they need to prepare
For a lover's quick reply,
To fly off hoodoo, magic spells,
Make someone's life a hell,
Or bring good luck in games of chance,
Where fingers play and money is advanced.

Oh yes, the quickened graves are
Still dreaming,
Dreaming, turning still,
In their endless, churning dreaming...

VIII

Crack!

There's one! There's one!

Oh, to be a true Virginian!

...weeping and a-moaning...

In 1883, the US Supreme Court strikes down the Civil Rights Act of 1875,
allowing states to overturn most of the progressive laws of the last eighteen years.

A-sowing in the noontide
And the dewy eve...

...soon be over with...

The same year, a tobacco workers' strike hits Lynchburg.

Oh, let us stop a while,
Virginians,
Cease our stressful journey,
Remove our hats and lower heads
In solemn shedding for those six souls
Murdered in premeditated blood
By Democratic thugs, blackguard cowards,
Pre-armed, primed by convention,
Who provoked a conflict, shot without reply,
One, two hundred sighing times,
Then haunted hunted streets
In half-an-hour's blood-tainted gore
– There's one! There's one! –
That flared the state with a furor of
"Negro Rule!"
Intimidating Republicans, blacks
Who held the fleece of Danville's Council seats,
Judges, officers and police,
Rabble-rushing o'er the state,
Flushing out Readjusters
– There's one! There's one! –
In a spinning spate of racist fears
That will now begin for us
Ninety – yes ninety –
Dreadful, absolutist,
Dixiecratic years.

Don't let the sickness spread...!

I cry, my darling, how I cry,
And the Sufferers wonder, wonder why,
Mirages floating within the seem

Of calling, calling midnight dreams
To see a monument to Danville's forgotten pride –
For *those* victims are much more heroes
Than the Marshalls and the Madisons –
They are good women and the men
Who have stained with their blood
Our fields and our neighborhoods
Time and time and time again.

A-weeping and a-moaning will soon be over with,
Soon be over with, soon be over with... [121]

Until we destroy all memorials to enslavement,
Eradicate their names from our memory,
And raise instead true monuments
To the struggle for our liberty,
We will never, ever be completely free.

Oh Mama, things are not as they were meant to be...

...one day, one day, one day...

The Democrats, salivating victors, now devour,
Determinedly entrench and strip
The opposition governor of so much power
And build a machine statewide to deflate
The election process, and thus the state –
County officials berated, fired
– There's one! There's one! –
Sympathetic ones rehired,
Then enact Anderson-McCormick to flout
Elective rule, reduce black turnout
– An invitation wide and broad-wracked
To more corruption, intimidation, fraud,
As that party buffs and pure perfects
The mechanics of skullduggery,
Of jerrymandered ballot stuffing,
'Losing' voters from the registers
– There's another one! –
Creating bogus names, blank-filled ballots,
Letting friends vote ten times or twice,
While mugging and assassinating
Blacks who yet aspire to some choice share
Of Virginia's faint and flagging voice.

Meanwhile,
On the economic plane
We too lose many of our gains
As, the South defeated,
Northeastern entrepreneurs,

---

[121] *All Over This World,* a fieldhand spiritual of the time.

Bright Yankees,
Swoop with vulturous rapacity
To hanky-panky all our mineral rights,
Our forests – from mountains to the sea –
To strip the wilderness, swindle settlers,
Bribe-claim an appalachian's coal
From what once were quiet, strolling havens,
And drive down many southwestern lives
With theft of life and common lands,
Rights scratched away by legalese,
Unfair squeeze, or intimidated fray.

So too do the railroads, merged,
Tentacle their sucking way
Over Jamesian canal, infilled,
And struggling highland valleys,
Tucking coves and hollowed vales
To Tazewell, Wise and Clifton Forge,
Engorging all their myriad hills,
Scattered coal pits, mines and rills,
Grinning speculators intent on gain,
Lawyers, realtors, official men
Disrupting traditional mountain life
That they label backward, ignorant and rife
With feuding, drunkenness and poverty,
But which is really firmset, proud,
Happy in its isolation, content to be
Free from tax or debt or rent
And outside the moneyed market's claim
Upon spent labor and its gain.

Meanwhile,
In Highland County, new revived,
Invalids and men of substance
Come to take the healing waters,
Sulfur-fed and mineral-rich,
As they bathe, the healthy and the sick,
In dinners, balls, picnics on the lawn,
Teas and splendid evening toasts
While boasting fortunes, prosperity won
Upon segregated backs, as they relax
Their wearied, anxious bones
And linger-laze in lithium daze
Within the fuming water baths
That Jefferson once extolled
Across a hundred years.

And two women, parasols
Twisting, lace collars and cabochons,
Stroll the hilled main street
Of Wytheville, in the hollered heat,
Straying stores and houses postwar built,

To find a restaurant fit to sit and eat,
On this quiet and most replete of April days…

…While, not too far away,
At the county's poor-housed farm retreat,
Three hundred, plus forty middlin' acres,
High-valed, hidden, crept alone,
Sixteen destitute sharpen scythes
– The unemployed, insane, and old –
Feed chickens and the bleating hogs,
Scold laundry in the stone-flow stream
Of a darkened washhouse's shaded gleam
And dream of thankful one-room nights
Under the severe, forbearing brow
Of the overseer's endowed stare,
Set just above their one-roomed rows.

…a-sowing in the noontide…

Closer to the bay I steal a glance,
Across the deck of a paddlewheeler
Steaming up the wind-flecked James
Linking Chesapeake to Norfolk, Hampton,
Richmond and plantations in-between,
The *Pocahontas*, *Ariel*, or *Middlesex*
Plying the smoky rivers of our dreams,
You leaning on my arm in seaborne breeze,
Laden with passengers, cows and mail,
Hogs and grain and tobacco for the mills,
Timber, paper, cotton packed in bales,
Card sharks, tables, music-musing gentry,
State rooms, bridal chambers and romance
For those dancers of Virginia's estuaries…

…As, with winter snows now gone,
Storms and sudden warming heat,
The dogwoods and the serviceberries
Mingle with the redbuds and the scarlet
Of early leafing maples, waking
To another hopeful starlight year.

Then I watch a mother bear,
Having birthed her cubs,
Lead them up a springtime hill
Through flowering bloodroot, mayapple buds,
To scavenge carrion, honey, herbal shoots,
And maybe steal an egg or two…

…As a large male fisher, fox-sized,
Scents a porcupine within a tree,
Scampers up, pursues to outmost branch,
Forces it to fall, leaps down

And harasses, nips and bites
Repeated at its head,
As the quills attempt
To rapid swerve
In hopeless self-defense.

And upon the call of summer showers
That sudden storm from mountains' drift,
The latest butterflies emerge, silver blues,
Orange sulfurs, fritillaries, to flit the Maury's flow,
As great herons, belted kingfishers, mallards
Feed their nestling hoards or decree them follow
On the eddies of the river's southern furrow...

...While Thomas Nelson Page's novels paint
A rainbowed portrait of an antebellum South
Where owners all had dainty hearts, never whips
Nor coffle chains, auction blocks, nor switching sticks,
And slaves were smiling "Mamas," "Uncles,"
Devoted to an idyllic sylvan land...

Romance of a bygone time to hide
The evil in which we now reside...

For, in a Danville warehouse,
Women sit in silent rows,
Picking piles of paper,
Pads and trimmings,
Licking, filling, rolling, twisting,
Stacking little boxes, packed
For the growing fad for cigarettes...

...Smoked by men in a Suffolk field
Where they jest and work and rest
From hoeing peanut vines,
Turning up the shells
To dry awhile before being piled by
All three nations of Virginia,
Clad in bewitched and oaken wiles,
Aged and darkly shrined in hoods
About their wierdsome, dreaded locks
That tangle round their furrowed brows
In black and red and white, as they
Weft their fieldside ceremony
To call the pipers, phantoms three,
Horseman, Linkum, Rabbit Brer,
To mock their solemn revelry
As laborers rise to bend and heave
Tangled nuts into a steamed machine,
To be removed and sacked and cleaned...

...As three women, children in cahoots,

Bring lunch in tins and cornbread pots,
Brunswick stew, strips of pork,
A skillet full of scrambled eggs,
And compassion in their patient gait...

...While high upon the Blue Ridge Range
Mountain laurel is well in bud,
The azaleas now are past their peak,
But flowering raspberries' sticky buds
Are just showing signs of pink.

And, at Bear Mountain,
A cabin twelve feet square
Built as a mission room, is now a school
For childrened Monacans,
Segregated, defiled as black, mulatto,
Are not permitted public schools,
But served by church-fund teachers
In isolated, poor-soiled rooms.

Oh, I feel those adzed log walls,
Touch their laughter and their memory...

...As, far above deforest sills
And silent-quested groves
He has minted with his coin,
An owner joins with his four guests,
Legislator, doctor, judge and manufactory man,
Amidst half-paneled oak, Venetian glass,
Gilded silver serving ware, Limoges,
Leaded crystal chandeliers, to relaxéd stare
Upon an expansive marbled view
Of ten-thousand-acred calm that hides
The wanderings of the WhisperMan
As he cigar-describes his vision of
A newly unencumbered South, free
Of notions of democracy:

"The great thing about America, my friends,
Is that it doesn't penalize the rich, but celebrates
Our unending accumulation
– As individuals, mind you –
And protects us from such over-zealous
Communities that would restrict our rights
Through taxes, laws and other bars
On doing what we feel we might,
While punishing those abhorrent 'deals
Of *social* accumulation and *sharing* wealth.

"Culture is no right, my friend,
But must be bought, like all else,
And only be available to those

With the class and mannered finesse
To appreciate its subtleties
And the delicate, uplifting nuances
That would, quite frankly, be absurd
To waste upon the poor;
Culture is the key to confidence, to rule,
To superior control –
To waste it on the lower classes
Would simply inspire unwise ideals
And succor usurpation
Of the noble by their inferiors.

"Let's take Darwin, for example,
Currently sweeping o'er the North,
But rightly opposed
– In more cultured Southern society –
As contrary to God and Bible,
Natural order and moral hierarchy;
Why, it preaches *inevitability*
Of change to those who would use it
To upset conforming society, and thus
Is a crime to our perceived need
For everything in its place,
Set and settled for all time…"

"But sir, is it not the truer case that
Darwin is far more our guide,
The eternal prophet by our side,
Herald of our American Way of Life
More than ever Jesus Christ? Why,
The survival of the fittest,
With the weakest to the wall,
Should be our psalm for a thousand years,
If we can survive that long.
The teachings of The Christ are naïve –
Fine enough to deceive our paupered folk,
And give them some forelorn hope –
But irrelevant to our laws and moral gropes,
Being nothing more than rivaled gloss
Upon the struggle for survival…"

"Certainly, I will give grace and attraction
To a certain *social* Darwinism,
Survival of those who in action are the fittest
– With us at their virtued head –
The poor to wither naturally, and thus
Confirming laws of competition,
Selectivity of the best,
To be rooted in our very history,
A survival of the rest that is natural,
With the meekest to the wall
– And thus no need for charity, false compassion

To maintain the weak through artifice –
For we are justly at the royaled helm,
Our servants by nature loyal lessers,
In this, God's best and blessèd realm."

Meanwhile, his daughter
Sits upon a window seat with
Huckleberry Finn, root beer
And a purring cat
As she listens to the phonograph
And dreams of riding to the fair
Upon a Richmond streetcar, dwells
On knights and ladies of the castle,
Or relives some antebellum belle
Who treats her 'servants' oh, so well,
Her colonel husband noble-clothed,
Without flaws, as he defends
The tragic South's Lost Cause.

John Mercer Langston was born into slavery in Virginia. He left to become a lawyer and was the first black president of a college. After the Civil War, he became an official for the Freedmen's Bureau, then Ambassador to Haiti.

In the 1888 Congressional campaign, Langston loses to corruption so malignant and outrageous that many ballots are disqualified and, eventually, he is declared the winner – the first black man to be elected to the House of Delegates from Virginia. However, angry and embittered, he is not re-nominated, partly because blacks have been fumigated from the political process and from jobs as postmen, police and officers of the court, in a remorseless racist witch-hunt aimed at regaining political power for the white male élite. Memories of the Civil War are used to more than merely commemorate. They also reinforce the permanence of oppression. For example, in 1887, Monument Avenue is laid out in Richmond as a setting for overbearing statues commemorating prominent Confederate heroes.

Hooray! Hooray!

Meanwhile,
Hookworm, diphtheria, polio,
Pellagra, measles, dysentery,
Mumps, malaria, yellow fever,
Bubonic plague, typhoid, TB,
Rickets, pneumonia, influenza,
Meningitis, smallpox and cataracts
Remain the facts
Of the poor's o'erdue domain.

Oh, how we destroy this sylvan land
With a-weeping and a-moaning...

To be a true Virginian
Is to wander down our lanes
A-weeping and a-moaning,
Sowing sorrows with a dewy eye.

Oh, when the weeping's over...

The driver of a train slows, blows his whistle
To warn the gang working on a trestle
As he passes an old station
Of a once-great Nelson County plantation
That has just been auctioned off
In fifty, hundred acre lots somehow,
Fences stolen, outbuildings gone, laid low,
The mansion fallen, a merely ruin now...

There's one! There's one!
– A true Virginian hiding
In the shadow of the hanging tree...

Hooray! Hooray!

Get him! Get him quick,
Before his sickness spreads!

All over this world, all over this world,
Weeping and a-moaning will soon be over,
Soon be over with, soon be over...

In 1890, the 'Force Bill' is defeated in Congress. It is the last real attempt to protect Southern blacks at the polls.

So are we finally
Left to ourselves, defenseless,
Abandoned, resigned, waiting out
Our inevitable decline.

I hear the clinks of the coffle chains
And slam of the jailhouse door...

Oh, our weeping and a-moaning will soon be over...
Yes, soon be all over,
All over this land, all over this land.

Is a true Virginian one
Who refuses to adapt, forgive, forget,
But still lingers in antebellum regret,
Indignant gray-clad anger, uncivil pride
In defense of a mendacious, vicious lie?
Or is the true civilian of this Commonwealth
One who accepts, forgives,
Asks us to move on in jointed liberty,
Futured tolerance and democracy,
Who recognizes problems,
Does not hide nor justify,
But rides along with love and charity,
To make this once-great, noble state

Great and noble once again?

There's one! There's one!
– There's someone willing to stand
Against oppression.

Yes, watch him swing in the wind
Of the hopelessness of this land.

Oh, sowing in the evening,
Stripping the sickness,
Stopping life and all vitality...

IX

Oh, we shall come rejoicing...[122]

As sunset burns its magenta frown,
We gather down the golden sheaves,
Cart them to our simple barn
And toss them on the threshing floor
To store and let them dry and turn...

...as patient flows the James...

...And rich springs growth of autumned lives
That linger-dwell in smoke-mist dells
Of secret-ridgéd hollows,
Coves that brook no sudden twist
Else doctor, midwife, neighbor,
Over-scarpéd visitors
To this careful-knit and tight commune
Of family, tersely married bonds,
Strong for all their hidden ways,
With chickens pucking through the house,
Cats curled within the starlit barn,
Unfurled cattle on the hillclined fields,
And hogs snuffling thru' the highland mast.

Here, in the shadowed vixen veils grow
Corn and squash and beans 'tween-mixed,
A field of grain that's wheat this year,
Garden roses, herbs and vegetables,
As men, some women, steer their mules
Along furrowed ruts for next spring's sow,
As others sit on needled porches
Of ancient 'nut and weathered shingles,

---

[122] This section comprises *The Song of the Mountains.*

Patching quilts of dress and sack
To varied spreads for well-loved brats
That share their tight-squeezed beds.

And down within an up-flat bottom,
A farmer grows his rich forth corn,
Young beefs are fatted for their sale
To whipgripped drovers headed north,
While a field of flax is cut to bleach,
Then pulled and leached and weaved upon
The women's treadled shuttle looms,
To groom enchanted moonlit eves
Of spirits in this melded air.

This rivered level's fine-framed house
O'erlooks a ribbled, brockling stream
That breams and drips the mountain dale
Past tracts of sparsely sharecropped land,
Ex-slaves and still-poor tenant whites
Whose race flows next the ford-borne trace
And stores that lane the valleyed road,
Past the chapel to which we each aspire
For weddings, baptisms, funeral byres,
And the barn we sometimes hasty clear,
Hay heaved heavy, walled aside,
To glance a moonshine dance or two,
With fiddle, washboard, 'ccordion play,
Harsh clogs and feet upon the boards,
In reels of barntrance-led display
As winter seeps the haloed cove,
Misty-wove, gladed by the shade of trees
Oaken in majestic breeze, shrouded,
O'erhanging the secret delled divine
Between this celled world and soft-winged pride,
Where encaved Sufferers weave soft aside
The weft of calling MusicMen
To come and dance the cauldron 'round
And spell awhile the sacred ground.

Sharp upon a James incline,
Narrowed on the Blue Ridge scarp,
A farmer seeks some winter cash
By sawing boles from his stash of trees,
Dragging branches for the New Year's freeze,
Hauling down the stern-lain slope
Trunks to float the upsprung surge,
Bound and steered to Buchanan's mills,
Rafted, poled and thrilled upon,
Until they meet their annual friends,
Spend a drink, get drunk once more,
Then rewend with stories new related,
Kerosene, bait, some nails,

Sugar, salt, an iron pail or two,
Bathtub, kettle, new pairs of shoes
– Enough of what they spartan need
To last another yeartime through.

...oh, bringing in the sheaves...

Elsewhere, each fall, the sheep are driven down
From their rillside clearings on
The hidden, buzzard-soaring hills
To brown, winter-sheltered folds,
There to dip and shear, then sell along
To passing eastward drovers,
Or slaughtered quick for coldtide meat,
Some kept to overlinger, then lamb and rest
In springtime barn and field
For early summer upland fleece,
To let the gyre re'gin apace,
Of peace content in unrefinéd space,
Where money does not measure grace,
But self-contentment and sufficiency
Unbraided by the unrelenting suck
Of high commercial muck,
Merchantized and mechanized,
Of our traditional hub of life.

Oh, we shall come rejoicing,
Bringing in the sheaves...

For the widow-healer, midwife, crone
Of lone spirit worlds, animals and lore,
Upland shadowed, deep-bored within
Her moss-turned, lichen lair
Of harbored rooks and caverned hold
And secret-dallied stare,
Sees all evil, hears all sin,
And forgives all who come within
Her damp-walled, ridge-cleft hide
Where, never married, without child,
The old shy learnt her woodland craft
Of herbs and healing, wards and warts,
Spells and potions, salves and worts,
That keep the hollow-valleyed folk
In scared and hallowed, 'specting fear,
To blame her all and yet to trek
Upwards for their wants unmet
And give in kind for moss-grown seed
Concocted under dark-delled boughs,
Spells beneath the ravened sky
That harbors grief and searches why.

...bringing in the sheaves...

And thus the Enchanters four,
Wefts of philosophy and mystery,
Poetry and prophecy,
Vision and enchanted soliloquy,
Midwives to this world,
Its verdure and fecundity,
Rise from their rivered gorge to ascend
These mountain rifts and sills,
To ring the round, foretell the sound
Of the history of our ancestry,
From winter unto the spring...

...As, once a month, we descend
Those rag-rut roads and lanes
Past new-sown corn and lowland grains,
The valleyed store and rich man's house,
Two-storied, barns, and porch around,
New plowshares shining on the ground,
To the county crossroads, courthouse,
There to find
A month of gossip, trade and smiles
Beyond our years of farming wiles,
And welcome tavern-candled, addled bars,
To settle upland family brawls
Or some internecine feud,
To drink, play cards and gamble hard,
Then wander down the mud-stained streets
To bargain out the courtroom steps
O'er broad-chested 'braska mules,
While nearby, within a high-walled shade,
Linger an itinerant barber, doctor, quack,
A peddler of needles, pins and tacks,
A stand with skittles, hoops and sticks,
A gardener selling seeds, molasses, jugs
Of brandy, whiskey, apple wine,
Salt blocks for our cattle licks,
Wagon parts, farm implements,
A hatmaker vending felts and brims,
All melding stalls meandering down
A Main Street broad with profit hems,
And a fair
Of jugglers, acrobats, children's rides
And the latest well-gamed gadgetry.

Here, we buy some coffee, read
A paper two weeks old,
Purchase a saw, some galvined tin,
A reading book for the little'uns,
To take back and teach to them
What we know of lore and pride
– For we are their sole and moral guide
To the world's invasive, swelling tide.

...bringing in the sheaves...

And, once a while, we dress and wander
On carts and horses, maybe afeet,
To the monthly congregation meet
Led by our Baptist preacher, greet
A distant cousin, upbred relation,
Who serves a round of highland chapels
Where, like us,
They raucous rap the haloed hymns
In four-tone *a capella* shout.

Oh! Let the sacred harp ring out
That resonates the vibrant hills
With shape-note hallelujahs!
Air and counter, tenor, bass
Resound in four-part harmonies
Beaten out with indexed grace
In such a vibrant voiced tradition
Secret-kept in oral heart
Of this sacred, non-conforming region.

Oh, we shall come rejoicing,
Bringing in the sheaves...

So, let the bans be read, the couple wed,
Confetti grains on borrowed dress,
A banquet of autumn hues upon the grass,
The chapel emptied in joyful glee,
And a garland wagon in bright solemnity
To bear the pair, giggling cousins too,
Pressed in careful Sunday best,
Up the boulder-shouldered lane
To a new-cleared glade and field,
With near-dug well and rustic room,
Kitchen, loom and loft, a stove,
Back shed and a porch in front,
Where she is borne across the 'hold
To a mattressed, new-roped bed
Of tick and sheet and banded fold,
And the young bride, blushing led,
Inspects her new life's abode, while
A youngster couple, fresh to the game,
Kiss and fondle, explore, explain
Differences, interests, hopes and pains,
Carve initials, touch and quiz caress,
Then embrace beneath that tulip tree
Where Grandpa stole his virgin kiss
Thirty years or more before.

Oh, we shall come rejoicing,
But how shall we depart

When there are no more trees
And no more sheaves, and we are left
With memories of a broken heart?

…As Dylan prophesies a primeval song
And wefts inspiring vision along,
As, within a secret still and sylvan dell,
The Enchanters trill their suitored song
Wailing for the soon-to-pass
Of this great and free-thronged mass
– So rapid Yankee stolen –
For such is the strife of deathless life,
Such the struggle and relief,
Where all we desire from our sweet land
Is freedom, bare enough to eat,
No taxes, outsiders, nor intrusion,
No interests ordering what to do,
Stealing minerals from beneath our souls,
No logging of our common goals,
No state police, bribe-enforced,
Left to imbibe our disbanded escape
In this forgotten Appalachian land.

Oh,
Bringing in the sheaves,
Bringing in the sheaves,
We shall come rejoicing,
Bringing in the sheaves…

X

Jim Crow came not dancing…[123]

Hooray! Hooray!

Descending,
We meet the breeze, the cold heat of
A stub of bouldered stalagmite,
The mud-slide slip beneath our feet,
The smell of smoke and sweat,
Until we breach a caverned room,
Open, huge and high, enthralled
Images of life derived upon
Its limestone-carvéd walls,
Still dank within the cloven halls,
Unable to leach nor rise
To the ranks of human decency.

---

[123] The expression "Jim Crow" arose in the 1830s when Thomas "Daddy" Rice, a white who danced a comic representation of blacks, introduced the character.

For, angered at beset despair, poverty,
Falling prices, rank and rising debts,
Tenant farmers, sharecrop families
Are trussed from their inheritance by
Absent bankers, lawyers,
Railroads thrusting mindless through,
And so, desperate for some binding hope,
They try an alliance of farmers,
Then turn to a People's Party, offering
Leaflets, meetings, understanding,
Platforms, local cells,
Speakers with a fluent, well-laid plan
To reform rural credit and the currency,
Debit income tax's unfair burden,
And are for an eight-hour day,
To shank in corporations, biglie business,
Monopolies, banks and transport trusts,
To restore a caring silver coinage,
And elect unelected senators.
They flare up a million votes,
But too soon fall in disarray,
As Democrats restoke racist scares
– Violence, white fears, solidarity –
And corruption soon assays the day,
As hopes descend once more to poverty.

Meanwhile, in hypocritical piety,
The misnomered, godless
Charity Organization Society,
With one paw dogs out countless sums
To veterans of The Cause Not Lost,
While it condemns from dewlap craw
Public welfare law as quite contrary
To hard work, sobriety, responsibility,
And waddle-schemes Virginia towards
A model industrialist's lordly dream.

And I wonder why, in my unfolding trance
Of compassion for this world,
It is we yet allow,
With all our frail impunity,
The 'ccumulation of one man's wealth,
While we so scorn and rail against
The 'ccumulation of social health?

My hands I join, my breath I form,
My mind I seek to 'dentify,
Understand, accept, no more deny
But refind truth and life and honesty…

…As Jim Crow slinks into the caboose
Of Virginia's shrinking business noose.

Hooray! Hooray!

In 1896, the US Supreme Court, in perhaps its worst-ever judgment (there have been so many!), *Plessy vs Ferguson*, rules that racial segregation and "separate but equal" are legal, opening the floodgates to Jim Crow. That same year, the Confederate Museum opens in Richmond and the first of five National Confederate Reunions is held. One year later, the Richmond Chapter of the United Daughters of the Confederacy is established.

Two years earlier, in 1894, the Virginia Assembly passed the Watton Law, introducing a literacy test for voters. As there are 150,000 illiterate adult blacks and 80,000 illiterate adult whites in Virginia at this time, nearly all of them Republicans living in the mountains of the west and southwest, this effectively disenfranchises over two hundred thousand radical voters.

Meanwhile, northern industrialists are massively investing in Virginia's coalfields, railways and related industries. Norfolk, Hampton, Newport News and Roanoke are booming. In Richmond, cigarettes, warehouses, the Tredegar Ironworks and woodworking at the Richmond Cedar Works contribute to new jobs, which is just as well because farming is in a desperate situation, with many farmers raising stakes and heading for Kansas.

Hooray! Hooray!

So much of America is conflict,
People tearing at each other
With a Dark Aged vindictiveness
That is tribal at times
– And often at its weeping heart
Is a struggle for some total power,
Or one to challenge that totality;
Both are born of raw survival,
The backwoodsmen,
Immigrants with nothing,
Clawing bloody dripping
From the bottom of their lives
– It was thus for Jamestown, Bacon,
The army at brave Valley Forge,
The Suffragettes, trade unionists,
And those who battled slavery.

And often, in the midst of these struggles,
As interwoven on our psyche
As the emotions in our hearts,
Some men seek compromise, to reach out,
To mollify, ease the pain, convince
Both sides there is another way,
Not violent, not hopeless, not to tear
At the deepest fabric of our lives,
But to teach by example, fairness, calm,
Education, reasoned argument,
And to show we mean no harm,
Are not ogres out to fright,
But rational, patient men and kind –

Such a man was Booker T Washington,
Not long a slave, who wished
To replace white fear and strife
With the subdued crafts of Tuskegee,
And raise his folk to respectability
Within the confines given them
By a white and scared society,
Who strove for answers that were his,
And yes, a compromise,
But one he felt was dignified and right...

Hooray! Hooray!

And I hear the jangle
Of the chaingang lines,
Momentarily recalling
The coffles, pens and starving times...

...As Jim Crow comes thru' swinging
On the back of Jack
The Conqueror,
Singing in his misery...

...While yet another young black man,
Resented for his upright gait,
Answering back, is accused of rape
And taken from an unopposéd jail,
The sheriff on his 'break,'
Militia refusing to attend the scare,
And wrangled to the courthouse square,
Strung up and left to bob and jangle
From that stark Virginia tree
That has mobbed so many during
This dark and dangling century.

Can anyone be free when
So many are enslaved,
And when the nature of that slavery
Is no longer written in the books,
But hooked in our mentality,
When it is a psychic thing, a mood, a look,
A tendency, a sense of good that
Knows no right,
Yet insists upon morality?

And what of the imposters, of their thoughts,
Their honest and internal being,
When with impunity they repress,
Maim and hang and kill,
And still ride to church each singing week
To ring out their righteous pride?
How can it feel to feel so wrong,

To lurk conflicted deep inside,
Belong to anger, suspicion's high,
Yet fret in timid-calm regret,
At the less-tanned, gold-palmed hand
Holding down its fellow man?

If you wonder about your role
In this unequal, unfree society,
Look not up, but down,
At the man and woman *you* oppress,
For there is the heart of your suffering
And there the soul of your redemption.

– And, if you feel you don't oppress,
Even by disregard,
You need look twice as hard, I guess.

Oh, no, Jim Crow came not dancing...

Hooray! Hooray!

XI

In a local synagogue, a rabbi
Reads a passage from the Bible
At the bar mitzvah of a teenage boy
While his family gathers round,
Always careful not to make
Too much noise in this intolerant state
Where they are tolerated only so long
As they outwardly conform.

...still descending, descending still...

...Waiting for the harvest,
And the time of reaping...

...For the weeping Horseman, blackened face,
Masked within the green-sprayed vines
That wrinkle about his agéd crown
Observes from orbs of poisoned veil
Tomtrickery that rails against us all,
As, above an eddied shoreline deep,
Upon sleepy Rush River's creep,
Beneath steep Massies' mountain height,
Two white kids swing a rope,
Laugh and shout and gaily splash
While, a hundred bashful yards below,
Two black kids silent watch and stray
To await their turn to scream and game

Once the two have lamely tired
Of their oblique and solitary play.

It will be a long, long wait...

A scarlet tanager nests,
Chik-brrr, chik-brrr, chik-brrr,
Within a densely foxgrape vine,
Wild honeysuckle,
Overpowering a young beech tree,
Struggling for its patch of light
Beneath the red oaks and hickories
Of Craig County's Sinking Creek...

...As a downy woodpecker dek-deks
Above a bobcat's silent prowl
For fledgling doves fallen from
A gray-patched molting sycamore...

...While a deadrise, built by rack of eye,
Slips from the morning hug of mist
To bob upon a listing Chesapeake
And drift the soft-dawn breeze
To a private-harbored oyster reef,
There to anchor, lower sail,
Shank the heavy-weighted tongs,
Slide overside and let the rake
Scrape the mud and ride and churn
Empty shells where dredgers scoured,
And dourly clamp what clumps return
Of once-great humps of oyster banks,
Grab them up, and lift and stack
Upon the wracking culling board,
Hammer, hoard and roughhusk gauge,
Toss back and sift the underaged,
And many empty, sickly shells
Swelled up with every lick.

...Descending, descending still,
To find the depths of my despair,
Before I can hope to rise again...

In 1898, the US Supreme Court, in *Williams vs Mississippi*, identifies entirely with segregation when it okays a new Mississippi constitution that uses literacy tests and a poll tax to openly disenfranchise blacks.

Virginians are now involved in the Spanish-American War. Several black units volunteer, but refuse to serve when a white colonel is imposed on them.

In 1900, by one vote, the Assembly decides to segregate street cars. This year marks the beginning of the 'lily white' movement, in which Republicans seek to become the 'white man's party' and exclude blacks from their political process.

But the Callings are still awaiting,

Sitting yet in circled round,
Knowing, but not staring
At what is found, is found.

"Wheel about and turn about
And do just so,
Every time I wheel about,
I jump Jim Crow."

Waiting for the harvest
And the reaping of our kind...

Oh, the cavern of our minds,
Riven with such doubts, such hate,
Unable to find too late escape
In the compassion of our fate.

For Jim Crow came not dancing,
Oh, no –
Rather, he came stealthy, creeping on all fours,
A cur in the night, reluctant even,
Weaving blacks from their railcars,
Restaurants, hotels, soda bars,
As if it were some natural thing,
A progression from the wrongs incurred
– Revenge for... –
Union occupation and control,
Wherein society must restore
Such rightful place and justice
To the Southern-fancied game
Of slavery in all but name –
Theaters with black entrances,
Back balcony rows,
Separated waiting rooms, bus stops too,
Parks, water spouts, swimming pools,
Movies, drive-ins, and telephone booths
– Technology's latest finds and challenges
Unfurled with an invention and conviction
That seemed to correct the world,
Restore each to his rightful godly space,
Deny the black all grace or station,
Displace him from his job, his education,
In an imposition of oppression
As unrepentant as two hundred years
Of the step-by-step enslavement laws
That silent sloughed the pre-war South.

Hooray! Hooray!

Fed up with the corruption necessary to ensure that blacks and poor whites were totally excluded from the political process, a Constitutional Convention is called from 1901–2 to officially disenfranchise the mass of Virginia voters. In the words of Carter Glass, a leading segregationist of the time, "We are here to discriminate to the very extremity of permissible action under the limitation of the Federal Constitution, with a view to the eliminating of every negro voter who can be gotten rid of, legally, without materially impairing the numerical strength of the white electorate."

However, many poor whites *are* affected by the new constitution because, in addition to a literacy test, it requires that voters prove they understand it by answering questions about it. It also requires registration six months prior to an election and imposes a poll tax of $1.50 per year on each voter. New voters have to pay $4.50 to register – a large sum of money at the time.

The new constitution is not put to a referendum, so sure are these cowards that Virginia's people would reject their proposals. Instead, it is 'proclaimed' and we are disenfranchised by stealth – a thievery upheld by the fawning, duplicitous court system of the time. Within ninety days, more than 125,000 of the 147,000 black voters in the state are stricken from the rolls and the overall effect is to cut the electorate by half. After 1902, barely 100,000 people bother to vote – less than 15% of the adult male population – and 10,000 of those are state appointees in the pay of the Democratic Party![124]

Now the Assembly can really get down to business. It passes legislation segregating railroad cars, street-cars and steamboats and clearly defines a change of atmosphere that will rapidly exclude blacks from white society and from many public amenities and services.

> A racerunner darts from its sandy hole
> As a cricket dandy scampers by,
> And in a flicker mouths its kicking prey,
> Black legs sticking from its jaws,
> Gulps and gulps and sucks with zeal,
> Then seems to almost lick its lips
> In satisfaction at a docile meal.
>
> Denied all culture, education, care,
> Left to struggle mouth-to-hand, there
> Just to be a paupered serving man...
>
> Oh, no, Jim Crow came not dancing,
> But darting furtively, as, even yet...
>
> ...The calling Conjure Man,
> Dispensing magick root,
> Medicines for our mojo bags,
> Black cat bones, bear fat, skins of snake,
> Rakes up his roots and totem stones,
> Amulets and lucky potions,
> Rises high and smiles a dark goodbye,
> Tilting once his old top hat,

---

[124] The convention also finally begins to control those robber barons and huge out-of-state corporations that are leaching Virginia dry when it establishes the State Corporation Commission. It also replaces the corrupt monthly 'court days' with a system of circuit courts and makes several state offices elected.

Dusty, battered, raven-feathered,
With havens for his long-hared ears,
Twilight nose, Brer Rabbit style,
Playing pipes and sashaying sway
Down The Horseman's death of day,
Followed by his near-blind hound
And the cripple's doleful, mooning sound,
As he traces to the river's call.

Hush, little fellow, hush!
For patient flows the James,
That mirth-rushed gleam
Between suffering and the dream
Of that passaged glow that yearns
And shrills us to its unceased realm
To find relief and seldom re-rebirth
Within its soft-winged rills
That angel-frill upon the cusp
Of this world and the next
And whisper easing sufferings,
Gurgle discontent,
As Kalunga sits upon the rocks
Of Richmond's cascaded dole regret
And calls all pained and crippled souls
To brief, but welcome-sunned refrain
And grief-compassioned, rippled flows
That mark the furrow of fated peace
Upon our great disserving brows...

Oh, Awake, Ke'show-tse! Great Sun! Awake!
Rejoin the circle, keep its hold
For a bolder-peopled time.

...As I sit amidst the twisted sheaves
Of my eternal wait,
While Jim Crow grieves without the gate
Of my misty mind...

...That dances, dances, dances,
Within the ancestral breath
Of our joint-entranced eternity...

...As a Racial Curtain draws across the South...

And will not let its deformed ego flee
Upon the breath of caverned misery...

Hooray... Hooray... Hooray...

Book VII

In the Shadow of the Dance:
Virginia's Darkest Years, 1902–1940

I

Zee-zhiff, zee-zhiff, zee-zhiff...

How does our twentieth century dawn?
With glory days and hopeful rays?
Magic songs?
Midnight's moonshine praise?
Or with darkness, poverty, strife,
And a recklessness rife
Within a call of saw
And blackened hammer strike
That cracks the heads of all?

The year 1902 epitomizes Virginia's suffering. Jim Crow laws are entering into everyday life with a vengeance and soon most blacks and poor whites are disenfranchised. The state is in the midst of an acute depression, with many small, unproductive tenant farms and sharecroppers unable to provide even the basics of food, shelter and clothing for their families. Diseases, such as TB, smallpox, diphtheria, measles, polio, hookworm and pellagra[125] are endemic, yet Virginia still has no health commissioner. There is no compulsory school attendance and are very few high schools. While *all* public schools are ruled unsanitary, many rural schools consist of one teacher in one poorly heated room crowded with up to sixty or seventy pupils of all ages sharing a single outhouse.

People are undernourished and illiterate. Large parts of the state are a wasteland of abandoned fields. Our highways "are appallingly inadequate"[126] and most rural houses are hovels of rough planks and ramshackle roofs with dirt floors and no electricity or running water; they are cold and draughty in the winter and unbearably hot in the summer.

We must descend within the worst
Of Virginia's striven years to steer
Our stiff climb to some worth of heaven's tears...

...Plunge until we understand,
With all our being, that it seems

---

[125] Pellagra is a potentially lethal lack of niacin caused by a heavily corn-based diet. It causes skin lesions, diarrhea, sickness and lethargy and is symptomatic of rural poverty.

[126] Dabney, *Virginia: The New Dominion*, p 451.

The only alternative is oblivion...

...If we are to save those two
Nocturnal flying squirrels,
Their nest within an attic, who
Scurry beyond the hidden walls, emerge,
Then leap towards a darkened oak,
Limbs stretched out in gliding, hopeful skin,
Tails splayed wide in trusting grope,
And black eyes bulged for inward need
Of chestnut, pine and acorn seed...

...Just as we leap across
Virginia's darkest night...

Yet we are determined still
To merely spill our tears within
A veil of honeyed years
And not to face our understanding,
As we
Dream dance, dream trance,
Down and down and down...

Oh, grace my eyes with viole and lace
And spite my visioned soul to veil
The sighing of ancestored rights
In the vying trails of night.

Disease, ignorance, poverty...

...wealth, carriages, European holidays...

It's only a dream...

"We have to keep them poor to make them stay."

...a naysaying dream of caverned night...

Oh, how I love this dream and this country...!

...but not yet; we are not havened yet...

...For, can't you hear the echoed spin
Of darting steps within
The rich and gloried canopy
As it dims and fades to the beat
Of our echoed hearts
That chime within some silent misery
And still refuse to be...?

Come! – Watch with me two ladies driven
In their sightly surried pair

To the daring August races, taking
Of the highnoon air, twirling
Parasols, feathered hats, suffering
Tightly in high-necked bodices,
Corset stays, hooks and laces,
Gloves with buttons at the cuffs…

…Then from the track, let's follow back
With WindTeller o'er the dales
Of old Indian trails by Allegheny's side,
To those forest-gladed mounts
Of Virginia's less than gracious fame,
And see how we are faring
In today's commercial game
Up once-silent-sided hollows
Of our striven ridgeline quest,
Where speculators roam-connive
Mineral rights and timber stands,
Whole mountains for a broken song,
As band saws are dogged along
Rivers deep into the Appalachian chain,
And Shays engines cog and climb
Steep slopes, lugging blades and frames
To logging camps set high upon
Clearcut ridges once the shadowed home
Of deer and bear, cow and pig,
But now cleansed of trill and call,
Of shrub and once-rich humused soil,
Bared to rock and tindered flame
Set by slash piles, sawdust waste
And trees stripped without their branching leaf,
Then flumed down stream-lined, muddied slopes
To crash and stack and wailing wait
For spoke of dam-dashed spuming spate
That hurtle-floods away in
Clip-stripping banks of all that were,
Of tree and bush and woodland flower,
To logjam rivers lumber-choked,
Bound to cabined rafts that slowly float
Down timber-rivered highways
To mills and engines, billowed steam,
Smoke and honeydreamed scent of dust
That strips the coats of varnished vales
To bareset, debored, heartreft rock
Lain within its stock-veined core.

And hard upon the logger's heels,
Carving upland, sharp-cut spurs
The railroads blast and tunnel fast
O'er heavy furl and funneled bridge,
Kneeling creosote ties upon a bed
Of endless headed, chaingang spikes,

Their chuffing, smoking, sooted stacks
Pervading trees and ballast sky
With dust and smoke and cleated roar
As they whistle down the melted way
Of mountains' lean and lingered life,
To mill and valley floor.

So band the saw and rasp the flesh
Of ten million million trees,
Skid and roll the chainéd marriage,
Peavey prize upon the carriage,
Rind and rade the zinning blade
And zip the rings to one-inch board,
Clat and brag and wagon drag,
Dry and shrink and warp the planks,
Cant the dogs of debarked claw
And weep the swell of razéd flanks,
As 'Teller's silent tears observe,
Cape pulled 'round his glowing orbs,
Mute amongst his sighing pain,
Asking why and why and why again…

The dance, the dance,
The shadow of the dance…

But hush,
For I still hear…

…zee-zhiff, zee-zhiff, zee-zhiff…

…and the crying of the squirrels' fear…

In 1902, Richmond City Council threatens a white contractor who employs black mechanics. The city refuses to hire *any* blacks, even as janitors or street cleaners, as do several other Virginia cities.

Oh the dance, the dance,
Mere echoes now of our chance
To prideful step and reel,
As another shadowed trance
Descends
To whiten-steal our thoughts
And turn us from our fancy fright…

…As a woman, actress, performer, singer,
Sits before her mirror, lights around,
And applies a foundation thick of cream,
Pallid, translucent, smeared to hide
The deep-torn scars that have died inside…

…stare deep, Virginia, deep inside
The mirror of your soul…

…And see a girl, seven, barefoot,
Sackcloth torn, with
Worn holes for arms and head,
A string belt, stare at Momma
Boiling pork fat, collards, corn,
As she gnaws a token husk among
The chickens and the rats…

Oh, the stupor of the dance,
Of our own sweet immolation…

…For the axes are still ringing,
And the saws are still singing,
Zee-zhiff, zee-zhiff, zee-zhiff…

Blues on my mind, blues all around my head,
Blues on my mind, and blues all around my head,
I dreamed last night that the man I love was dead.[127]

We sing, we sing, as we dance
To keep the earth's soul turning,
As we are taken down and must
Snail-horn furl into our shell
To survive this segregated hell…

…Still singing,
And denying, pretending
A reprise to some ante-bellum life
– To old warts and sins –
Will allow us resting peace…

II

What do you see?

Nothing!

What do you see?

Only smoke and ashes!

What do you see?

The lost souls of our ancestors,
Veiled calls to the Teller of the Wind
Mirrored in our hearts…

I went to the graveyard, fell down on my knees,

---

[127] *Graveyard Dream Blues,* by Bessie Smith; credited to Ida Cox.

413

I went to the graveyard, fell down on my knees,
And I asked the gravedigger to give me back
    my real good man, please.

Come, Callings, come!
Hear the axes ring!

…zee-zhiff, zee-zhiff, zee-zhiff…

I wrung my hands and I wanted to scream,
I wrung my hands and I wanted to scream,
But when I woke up, I found it was only a dream…

We dance within the scream,
Axes ringing in the forest of my dreams…

…While a potter turns a wheel, spins clay in
A Shenandoah pottery, kilns
Of folk ware, red ware glazed,
Storage jars, whisky jugs
For the mountains' secret trade…

…As the woman careful sponges,
Then takes a dusting brush, briskly flashes
To merge her mask and colored skin
Within the collars of her hair and chin,
And the MusicMen mirror round
To grind the growing disaffection
Within our self-made, haughty horror.

We dance within the scream…

Two men stop digging a latrine
To sit on the seed store stoop
And swap trade cards awhile, as
Next door in a tea shop, a woman
Whiles away a *Literary Digest* and
Another reads a romance defined
By medieval, knightly times and
Through the haberdasher's door,
Two others search *Sears Roebuck* for
Seersucker in navy blue.

We dance within the screaming dream…

…As we go down, down, to
Dance-plunge within the madness,
The trancing depths of our souls,
To save ourselves from what's to come,
For it *is* to come,
Though desperate in its sadness.

We are still descending!

It seems, reluctantly,
That we must find
Our deepest ignominy,
The depths of our own selfish lies,
If we are
To discover
Some shade of honesty
And emerge
From the shadows of our desire.

Meanwhile, the girl, seven,
Rises from that straw bed
She shares with three sisters,
Washes in an icy bowl, combs down her hair,
And splices 'midst the pre-dawn spilling
Of children to the mills.

Oh,
Rattle Man, Horseman, Hood,
Brer Rabbit and little understood Linkum Tidy,
Guardians and the MusicMen,
Watch the creeping timber rattle
That lurks within the grass,
His alternating blacks and browns
Hiding hidden-eyed intention
Behind "This is all," "This is all,"
Of hypnotic self-illusion.

I will search for you.
Let me come down, descend
Into the bowels of Virginia's night.
Let me descend!

In 1903, the US Supreme Court upholds constitutional clauses that disenfranchise
blacks. Out of 8,000 adult black males in Richmond, only 760 can vote. In Norfolk,
the figure is 509 out of 6,000. One white voting registrar proudly boasts that,
"We have... paralyzed the negroes..."

The recent law that segregates all transport in Virginia, such as steamboats,
railroad cars, street-cars and coaches, really begins to bite, with signs erected,
separate facilities built and objectors beaten or arrested.

A woman calls upon her hostess friend
For cake and coffee, gossip,
Dressed in a moiré suit engraced
With velvet, braid, padded hips,
Bustle, goréd skirt and flounces,
A cameo at her neck, and denounces
The growing influence of drink upon
The desperate working poor...

…As eight men, cold, two blacks aways,
Stray over to the day-hire line
Where local farmers, businessmen
Offer picking, digging, hoeing,
Laying down a road
For thirty cents a day.

Why open our wings when
There is no air on which to fly?

…zee-zhiff, zee-zhiff, zee-zhiff…

Meanwhile,
In a surreptitious grasping
Of uncompromising power clasped
To his white and racist bosom,
John Barbour builds remorselessly,
In latter-century years,
A political grooming, milling machine
For Thomas Martin to inherit –
A senator with a railroad spine,
Who handle-loads a combine
Undemocratic in all but name,
Nefarious, corrupt, renowned,
Drowning debate and intimidating
With lucrative place, threat of disgrace,
Slimy manipulation and conniving
– A wheedler of conventions,
White élitist, schemer, thief,
Who cajoles upon Virginia's soul
An era of impoverished grief,
A hardship suckered by that greed
Upon which he erects his mansioned need –
No prowler of the night, not he,
Stealing green and greasy notes,
A candelabra or a midnight jewel,
But a robber of the bloated light,
Who filches oft our votes, our daylight hopes,
Gripping the throat of our state,
Till Byrd inherits the gullet-gilded plate…

…A mud turtle, deep within the reeds
Decaying at a tidal edge,
Mouth open wide, calm, still within the sun,
Who deceives to entice small creatures in,
Hiding its voracity
Under the mendacity of a civilized skin…

…As, yet,
Brer Rabbit lopes the lanes
Of compassion's forgotten smirk
And four drunks, a sheriff, ride-harass,

Begin to lash and spit,
Dislike his nose and ears,
The color of his fur,
And some perceived insolence,
So dismount and whip and beat,
Then string him by his kicking feet
Across a wide catawba tree,
Pull him through and high and easy laugh
At his struggled plea.

In 1904, Newport News segregates its tram cars. There is a protest and attempted boycott, but they both fail.

A black fireman works a tender
Upon a gleaming plate,
Shirtless stance before the grate,
Plunging coals within the dance
Of flames and boilered steam...

Dance, dance the rhythmic steps
That lead to meditative trance
And let us delve the world
Of the spirits and the oracles.

All I want is to escape, to find
Some inner sanctum, peace of mind,
Where I can dwell in innocence
With my sweet Lord, who maketh all...

...maketh all alright,
In the myth of darkened day...

...While a typist, Pitman dictatee,
Beneath a scene of Christ
Praying in Gethsemane,
Repeats with flying fingers
The tickety-tack, clickety-clack
Of new laws segregating
White and black, white and black
Prejudices, opinions, rants,
As you, Swanson, governor in oh-five,
Wheel of oily Martin Machine,
Scan with horror the Virginia scene
And pledge to invest in public schools,
Health, sanitariums, highway repair,
To root our state from sidewater despair,
Eradicate hookworm, urge mosquito control,
Give vitamins for the pellagra scourge,
A hospital for the deaf, the blind and mute,
A commission for our fisheries, expand
The Department of Agriculture
And pay for a geological survey

– The first of Virginia's backward land.
But when you grow to senator,
Junior Byrd grabs control,
And you are, without ceremony,
Dumped from your prestigious seat,
In a transference within the state élite
That plunges Virginia's need once more
From paternalized compassion
To openly oppressive greed...

...While the Sufferers dance their desire
About the midnight moonshine fire
Reflected in the rushéd lake
Of the mountain's fool-fired wake
As we watch and watch and watch...

...the century that has failed to dawn...

...And the squirrels try
To regain within their nest
But find their flyway burned,
Logged with all the rest...

Oh, WindTeller, WindTeller...

...We dance for you –
Guardians of ancestral souls,
The rites and potions, magic songs
And harbingers of tocome,
As yet the axes hum,
Zee-zhiff, zee-zhiff, zee-zhiff...

III

Oh, ladies at your tea and calico,
In your laces, boots and waists
Tightened against compassion so,
Dueling the depravity of liquor,
Resisting sisters who want to vote
And venting off your latest fears
Of Negro blood and rule...

"We *must* protect our womenfolk
From the sinfulness of politics, of
The dusty road of business concerns,
And from the leers and lusts of Negro men
Who seek to flood our empured blood
With the defiled disgust of corruption."

Aye, of corruption, of working for your life...

...So clang the iron spikes and clamp
The hammer-levered rail
In the travail of midday sweat
That beats upon our chanting song
As we heave from horse-hailed car
Irons in place with cant along...

Move along, move on down the line now...

Gaugers measure rail to rail, re-alie,
Then spikers sledge more riven heads
Into the dusty, black-tarred ties...

Move on down the line now...

Then follow close as bolter teams
Plate the rails, giving some,
Trending forward endlessly
To grade the gorge-enforded trail,
Gouged and shimmed and level-rimmed
O'er trestle bridges wrestle-built,
Or tunnels blasted recklessly,
Until the limits of Virginia's span
Are a joinéd, many-fingered hand
That grasps all coal and farmland goods
Tight within its smoking clasp
And invests this new-industried land
With neither sleep nor restful brood.

Move along, move along
And whisper, Sufferers,
Whisper dear our song,
So that WindTeller may hear
And whisper it along...

Move along, miner,
Move along alone,
And sing your tired old song
As you
Hack the face and smack,
Grip and gouge and let it fall,
Crack and crash upon the floor;
Rack and grapp and crack the call,
Where white is black and black is all
Within this musk of blackened dust
That lines the throats and lungs
Of shadows
Flickering in enstalled extremity
Of no souls, nor poker faces,
Other than the jokes and raged refrains
Of solitary images that maintain the void,
And are no sounds but the crick and crack

And shovel load of cars,
Their squealing wheels upon the tracks,
As laughing banter hides your cries
And trickles darkness in your eyes
While you fail to find
Some meaning to it all...

Move along, move along alone,
Be the Conjure Man
And magic up some fair employ...

...Unwilling to accept compassion,
For others or for ourselves...

...As, in some down Tidewater town,
A drunk whip-wanders home,
Falls sotted to the ground
And snores away an entire day,
Until, at the renewal of the night,
He demands more money from his wife,
Curses life and guilt and shame,
And stutter-zips to barward blame again...

And while he sleeps his wages off,
Two children keep to Quaker Oats
As their father foams and careful scrapes
His new-honed safety razor,
A Marlboro dangling from his lips,
And mother slips soft Ivory Soap
Upon her speckless neck and face
Before she begins her seamstress day,
Home bobbing with a loft-leased,
Owing Singer sewing machine...

Move on, move on alone...

...And a lady and a gent enjoy
Advertising hoardings, lean
Bicycles by the music store
To explore new recordings,
Cylinders for
Their hand-turned phonograph,
Home delivered by an adult boy...

...a black, nigger, adult boy...

Alone in your world...

...For our two ladies are now dressed
In challie kimonos, to express
The height of *art nouveau,*
Escape in séance, eastern rites,

And esoteric denial of the world
That they are steady bleeding white…

"We *must* stop the ignorant poor,
The half-breed and the macaroon,
Who stubbornly spoon-inbreed
As they explore their desprized floor
Of sub-humanized existence –
Oh, please, sterilize them before
Their Negroid blood mocks a-more our
Pure-bled Caucasian stock, for…

"…Niggers are sly, lazy, full of spite
Against the simplest task, stubborn,
Unwilling to learn, shiftless, ignorant,
Ham-fisted, obstinate and must
Be watched at all times
Against subterfuge and trustless crimes."

"Ah, but ol' Joseph, he's not the rule,
A white man's nigger he,
Good and cool and proud
To listen, learn and show respect,
And praise his master true and loud…"

Move on nigger, move on alone…

A nightwatchman with a spark upon a pole
Lights gas flames in the streets
As winter evening swift descends…

…And the hurdy-gurdy turns and turns,
A monkey dancing to the drone,
Red hat, hand held hanging
To the passing workers' filing
From Petersburg's mills and factories,
The jangling, rolling melodies
Sparkling a few cents of sympathy…

…As a preening lady tuts
A spot of butter on her skirt,
Wipes it clean,
And passes on her muttered way…

…For the MusicMen are all afright
With starkened eyes that darkly haunt
Gaunt days and rake the crying skies
As Virginia walks in blinded spite.

I see the ancestors on their knees,
Their tears the leaves of countless trees,
Their sighs the sighs of centuries.

But it is not over yet, no, not over,
For, in the spinning room
Of a Roanoke cotton mill,
Girls tie threads to empty spools
As an eight-year veteran doffer boy
Removes them full and stacks them high,
And racks empty bobbins in their place
Upon the endless spinning frame
That takes their lives and twists them tight
And loses light of day,
Loses childhood, loses health,
And spins their dreams away.

One girl climbs a shaking frame
To retie some rapid-broken threads,
Her bare feet on the frictioned iron,
Then walks the aisles from dawn to dark
For fifty cents a day,
Threading warp through tiny holes
To loom the weave-worn, clanking cloth,
Hot, vibrating spindles whirring,
Girring, kerzooming canvass belts
Driving, pounding, motored wheels
That crank and whiz and toss
Cotton dust on lint-blown loss.

And oil drips upon a mechanic leaning in
With monkey gun and faceless grin,
Nifty-nimbled fingers, exhausted eyes,
Face masked with grime and surprise,
Head so heavy it could fall
Through every millhouse floor
And happy bury its lifelost self
Within the welcome spore,
While, barefoot, wearing dust and rags
In the damp-whirled, cotton-tufted air,
Bobbins stacked across the top,
A seven-year sweeper, brooming straw,
Reaches under the kerlanklank whirls
To pull the bronchial, greasy lint
Within his full-breathed lungs.

There are no age-limits nor
Inspections here,
Amid the nightly twelve-hour days,
No health provision, no insurance,
For the injured, debilitated, maimed,
Burned to death in factory fires,
Escape routes padlocked shut
And windows barred against fresh air,
To rebound the deafening sound
Of cannibal cer-rank, cer-zvilt and whim

Within the burial-shrouding din.

And, at the final end of shift,
In a headbowed, sunless dusk,
Crossing rail tracks too tired for fun,
We drift to our hovelled shacks
Of mud and rot and tar-lined damp,
One room to grace a wood-fire furnace,
Bare ticks upon the floor,
Strewn where even loyal vermin,
Cockroach, mouse and louse,
Huddle in the windy cracks
Of pain-drenched piney backs,
Paltry-fed and blinded meanness,
That all but e'en the brightest bloom
And most glorious heat of summer
Can raise from its pernicious gloom…

…For we can only dream in strife,
Moving along, alone,
On, alone, alone,
Bleeding, bleeding us of life…

And The Horseman reins his passion in,
To stare within the window frame
And plays the tune of destiny
Upon his droneful pipe,
As he wonders how this differs from
The endless years of slavery;
Then, pulling round his horse's mouth,
Wrapping gown about his uncouth crown,
He flies upon the midnight wind
To halt outside the alleyed door
Of a music hall, dim and bored,
Where the woman will perform that night,
As she lines her brows, applies some gel,
Then highlights, gently rubbing in,
Faint her blended hues of skin…

And I go down to face my fears,
In the barrio of some downtown years,
Alone, to where the ghouls do play
Upon the harmonies of my mind,
Stepping cautious between the piles
Of rat-strewn kind and liquored souls
Shimmerin their wiles away –
Past fire escapes and shadowed alleys,
Smoke drifting over veiléd stares
Peering from the dusky windows
Of backlit lamps and musty cares –
Watching, watching, as I search
Down steps of Bristol honkytonks,

A basement by a railroad stair,
Where dare a black and blind guitarist,
Crippled player on the harp,
And skinny, balding bassman to
Tap a hurtful heart in blue
About some woman who
Rapped them late,
Done took their mojo thru' an' thru'…

…While the prostitutes and pimps,
Clients and the drunkards sway
And nod in limpset empathy,
Knowing just the way it is,
And the way it will always be…

…For now it is Brer Bear plucking
On the deathly double bass,
Brer Turtle on the sharp-state guitar,
Brer Raven deadly on the harp,
As they observe and note and patient wait
To give their watchers moment's pride
And record their sacrificial date
In the mosaic of a doleful ride…

…as I go down, go down, anxious of my fate…

…And two men in ribboned derbies
Lean upon their dusty bikes,
Glide a break from weekend ride
To pull a pair of Lucky Strikes
And take of the morning mountain air…

…While, happy, laughing, a family
Kick-splash the edges of the waves
Of the Beach's brave, eternal strand,
As Daddy clicks his brand-new Brownie
And we sip our soda Pepsis,
Then push our brothers in.

Meanwhile, a black man,
Family, preacher,
Wife, two teenage kids,
Walks a platform to a sign –
"Coloreds Only,"
Pauses briefly at the fountain,
Dirt-cracked, next the gleaming "Whites,"
And pushes at the creaking door
Into a steaming waiting room,
Cramped, deserted, wooden, bare,
And hears the nextdoor air fan hum,
Knowing they are cool, relaxed,
With new benches, papers, coffee bar

Amidst the sanctimonious pride
Of Virginia's deepening apartheid…

…that's bleeding us all a moonlight white…

…As still the hammers crack the heads
Of those whose spikes are dared in dread
To rise above the general ground
In anger at profound despair.

IV

Down I drift, down –
Spin, MusicMen,
Round and round and round…

We dance to one day raise the sun,
We dance to help us through this time,
We dance the dance of everyone
To keep our circled hopes in rhyme…

An elder shows her granddaughter
How to cut
Squares and pentagons, triangles,
To hem and appliqué stitch upon
A fill of cotton batting, backing
Salvaged from a nearby mill.

…oh, how the spider spins her lies!

In 1909, 'Mother' Maybelle Carter, part of the 'first family' of country music, is
born Maybelle Addington in Nickelsville, Scott County. Meanwhile, Ford starts
production of the Model T.

A scattering of Chickahominies,
Living their introspective myth
Within a quilt of alien farms
– Legally, they don't exist –
Walk from their disparate shacks and homes
Each side of their ancestral flow
To a school erected so
They needn't quite endure
A total loss of native soul;
Some pass the Baptist church where,
Every Sunday, they meekly pray,
Even as a teenage boy
Ponders how they wonder-lost
So much pride and heritage
To the white man's weakling ways.

Meanwhile,
In another church-whelped prayer,
Quietly working, with regarded help,
Dr Dillard and Virginia Randolph
Strive to give rural black kids
Au unward hook in tiny schools,
One room, a hut, no pencils, books nor desks,
And only the skimpiest, illset meals,
As Linkum coldly folds his hands,
Wearied, bowed, but ever proud,
As he bears his arms about the world...

Down I drift, down, within
The honkytonk of my dumb mind,
The drowning dance of trance,
The humming drum of hearts
That beat without a reasoned beat...

...Upon a myth of ante-bellum guise,
Rememorizing the pre-war South
From fabricated lies...

...Mythology as truth, the truth of myth,
Myth as belief no longer held,
System, ideology no longer told,
But that once formed an in-core span
Of every antiquated past, Roman,
Celtic, Egyptian, Greek and Incan...

...Myths we hold to hide our pain
And reject ungainly truths
That are too hard to e'er accept...

...and yet I pray still for a better day...

...As, beneath the shade
Of Natural Chimneys' lime-stained towers,
Knights do joust for fair maids' hands,
Lance the quoits and merry band
In a medieval dream display
That bans the night with e'erlasting day
And permits self-suck historians,
Preachers, scientists, newspaper men,
Page and Harris, Gilmore Simms,
Novelists, poets, apologists all,
To redefine and reforget,
And gore their moral gall once more...

Those who know the truth,
See it plain, leave the South,
Never to return again...

Yet still some literary circle

426

Talks of ante-bellum days,
Slaves as unfettered family,
Conditions never brash nor harsh,
Life happy, better then,
Contented, each in their place,
The children and the elderly
Well cared-for in an ageless grace,
The men chivalric Arthurs,
Doting Cavaliers
Pleasing to their sightly maids,
Who never dreamed to work nor vote,
And ordered house with gracious ease...

...As ghosts of our Confederates stand,
Heads bowed upon the glint-veiled plinths
Of every square of Virginia's towns
– An army buried, but ne'er laid to rest,
Asleep, but ne'er forgot...

...As our veterans march
Through well-starched step and medals
Honoring selfless, godly sacrifice,
While Daughters of the Confederacy
Save regimental colors, poems written,
Generals' uniforms, lives and letters
Preserved in monuments and museums,
Monies raised, battles lauded,
Parades and homes and eulogies
Once more risen for those people
Whom the South should e'er recall
– Tho' their sons are landless now,
'Croppers, tenant farmers, laborers whose
Slim grip on rural life is daily chopped
By steam plows, harvesters and sackers,
Packers, threshers and steaming tractors
Reaping of our fractured Commonweal'.

It is not just them we must resurrect;
We must aspire to corrct
All our valiant men,
Our poor and women too
– Of every race and hue –
From their dire internment 'neath
The time-expired, unjustified,
Myth-stored, aching victory
Of the undeserving rich
Who have filched our hard-won story
And embossed their lives
With sacred gilded stitch.

It is time for us to reply, instead,
To all dread romantic spider lies

That throng about our laureled heads
With a new-spun, nobler song
– To rescind, not glorify,
The wrongs of our long-lived history,
And in our heightened, courageous hearts
Build a vision that's honest, forgiving,
And takes us forward, hand in hand,
Man and woman,
In sickness and in health,
White and black and banded red,
To stride once more as one upon
The pride of our joint Commonwealth.

Oh, how then will we rejoice!

Starting in the 1910s, a fungus decimates Virginia's chestnut trees. Industrial
pollution rises as cars, especially Fords, become mass transit across the country.
But roads in Virginia are deplorable. Several cities start bus companies; new
movie theatres draw in millions of customers; advertising takes hold; and mass
production spreads from cars to clothes, houses and countless useful gadgets.
Republicans continue their 'lily white' policy of excluding blacks from the
political process, as parks and other public places are segregated across the state.
In 1910, the Assembly redefines a "Negro" as anyone with at least a sixteenth of
black blood. The next year, it segregates house-building in the state; although this
is overturned by the US Supreme Court, segregated housing is now the norm.

The darkset woman, costume on,
Sparkling leotard, headdress,
Silk and silver stockings drawn,
Straightens her hair with heated tongs
And careful paints her lashes black,
Thick and heavy, liner beneath
And rich bronze shadow bright above
To make her eyes look thrice the size
And transform her age to newborn mask
Of performance gaiety, troubles past.

Meanwhile, a lady in a blouse and moiré skirt,
Boots muddied by her Winchester street,
Is confronted by a drunk, rooted for a dime,
But in revulsion turns, is pursued
Until a passing gentleman dismounts,
Recounts away the man, whips him to the grime,
And bids the lady proud *adieu!*

And, with a final powder dust
To remove the shine from nose and chin,
Our lady of the dancing line
Readjusts her feathered bustle,
Muzzles a tiara in her hair,
Drags a pull upon a cigarette,
Takes a swig of water down,

And, last call bellowed loud,
Joins the chorus-pushing crowd
Up the stairs to backstage wing,
Waiting for the grand finale to begin…

Oh, take me with you to the edge of sun,
Where only drums can be heard
Within the surrender of my tocome,
And I can wake to liberty and peace,
And to the quilt of great democracy…

Aye, let's to the quilt makers hurry-go,
As they restitch our memories,
Taking comfort from our worn-out history,
Rainbow-cycled squares and strips
That sew our blinkered counterpanes
In nine-patched window grains
And show us sorrowed mysteries
Lost to reason's mere domains…

For quilters are visionaries;
They hold a firm idea of what they want
And determine to create it;
They are poets of the needle,
Threading images, ideals, visions
Into missioned patterns that comfort us
During the chill nights of our regret,
When all will has deserted us
And we need guidance from their skirts.

Thus the soft-pieced quilter's art,
Brown and black and red and white,
Appliqués piece by penciled piece
In blocks of patterned human toil
And designs harsh-trimmed emotions
In seams that dye in thumb and nail
And let us weave imaginings
Upon colored patchwork symmetry
Of hand-stitched cultured lines,
And bring our human entity
Within its self-sewn, crafted times.

There is a cathedral window here,
Green and blue and bay,
That speaks of dainty plantation days
On porches sipping the heat away,
Of moonlit walks and reeling balls
And dressing for some spring foray
Of well-craped hair, gowns in crinoline,
And a soft-laid napkin on display
That would entice a lover's eyes
And tempt his catch that summered day.

There is a cross of kings sewn here,
Tan and black and gray,
That resonates a mother's calls
Upon the barren quartered hill
For children to tiredly run in haste
Their tiny-hurried heels
From the distant reaping fields
And rest their weary souls awhile
With cabbage soup and black-eyed beans,
Jowl of hog and collard greens,
Then sleep on tick and pallet floor
To gain short rest before
The morning horn once more appeals
And the overseer's whip and frown
Make them scamper frightened down
To the reeling fields.

Oh, history, do not let me
Patch my tumbling blocks
And make of vile abomination
Some candy-dewed and minted melody
Of barn-side song and moonlit walks,
Of fieldhand glee and chanted ecstasy
In solemn-sight eternity;
Do not let me resew, repattern,
Repatch our ancient ancestry, nor rehang
Maple-sugared mythology
Of some sweet-quillowed memory,
To trim and thimble-shear the guilt of our paternity!

How can we, as a nation, hope to fight
The new challenges we face,
When we still live rose-tingéd battles
Of our failed imaginings?
Give us a new vision, quilters,
For Virginia has such wonder
And there is such hope we can imbue
Once we recognize our faults,
Exalt our heads in honest pride
And lay firm upon the foundation piece
An unbiased, well-seamed bindery
Of a new-patterned, vibrant symmetry –
Oh, how I long for that ringing day!

V

I wrung my hands and I wanted to scream…

A zebra swallowtail flits in front of me,
As I dance the dance of mystery,

Soul of souls, glitting my misty way
Through the dews and shrouding fogs
Of this low-lain, dawnburst day,
Through a realm of forest fire,
Dead snags raising broken limbs
In silhouetted funery –
Fire-poisoned, burnéd-blazed,
Bleach-black, death-ringed trunks,
Woodpecker holes and broken plates
Of carboned, half-lopped bark,
Beetle-drilled and naked poised,
Shade choked, caterpillar-filled,
Gray-boned, crippled at the knees,
Cascading onto still-green sprees
Of pregnant budding spring
That call the song of yesterday
To drape her words in moss upon
Their scared and scar-flaked arms.

And there, as the butterfly visits
Upon a welcome crack,
In the misting dawnfall's whim
Of gently powdered rain,
I see the lichen, woven coils
Of hessian rope around a trunk,
Sliméd skulls set on two spikes,
Carved images of Ghede, Legba, Loa,
Who beckon me along the path
To Swamp Mama's hidden domain.

And there, as the butterfly flits yet still,
The lynched remains of bones and rags,
Buzzard-beaked and pecked and crowed,
Flesh rot, maggot-chewed, stinking,
Dropping, foxed and gnawed,
Eyeless sockets, rips of skin,
Blood-white bones drooping thin,
As, upon the infected ether's wing,
Come haunts of secret-trailered laughs,
Echoes to guffing, bottled tales
Of teaching niggers lessons
That will hold a race enthralled.

And there the butterfly flits, bouncing on,
Its soul enraptured by the rain, and
Is taken deep within the marsh
To Ghede's welcoming domain,
Where spells and potions talk of wait,
Of patience and revenge to come,
Of a day when there'll no more be
Flitting swallowtails that need to steal
Lost souls from Virginia's hanging tree.

I wrung my hands and I wanted to scream,
I wrung my hands and I wanted to scream,
But when I woke up, I found it was only a dream.

Dream-dance, dream-trance,
Trance-dance, trance-dance, trance,
Spin and spin and spin and spin
To the world within...

Tho' our dance is no longer part
Of our connection to the land, to
Its soul and our animistic heart...

Twenty-nine links of chain around my leg,
Twenty-nine links of chain around my leg,
And on each link is an initial of my name.
It takes a worried man to sing a worried song,
It takes a worried man to sing a worried song,
I'm worried now, but I won't be worried long.[128]

A hotel porter, feet carbuncled,
Nipped by too-tight shoes,
Rests his soles in a bowl of steam
Boiled by his daughter
Upon the corner stove
Of their one-roomed cove;
A dog barks in next door's yard
And the dim light of dawn flicks through
The smoke-laden haze of Nigger Town
As he gazes back in his broken chair
And the salts begin to ease
His drowning bones
From
Their bland night of patient standing.

His wife pours more water into the bowl
And their baby lolls on the linen bed,
The mill girls rub their tired eyes
And the miner howls his coughing dread...

...if you fall, I will catch you...

A domestic stows her Hoover,
Dusts the Victrola phonograph,
The glass and bottled whisky cabinet,
Tidies master's paper and his crossword puzzle,
Madame's *Cosmopolitan* and *Vogue*,
Plugs in the iron, lets it heat
As she fetches washing baskets, blankets, sheets,
And starts to careful push and crease

---

[128] *Worried Man Blues*, performed by The Carter Family in 1930.

Her master's cottoned shirts and suit,
While the AC whirr-zins its steady beat,
Then stops, as the phone begins to ring...

And I spin down, down the shadowed streets,
Alley-dark eyes, windowed retreats,
Anger-scared, fearful proud, denied
Hope within my downward plight,
Forever lost within the night...

...I plunge, I plunge, I plunge...

– Oh, will you catch me?
Will you? –

...To downtown Jackson Ward,
Between the cemeteries on the hill,
Shockoe Creek and the broad main street,
Where a troupe of minstrels backroom in
A hotel for unsightly blacks,
Then shake the stage a Second Street night,
White-faced, flailed in evening togs,
Mr Tambo, Bones at his side,
Black-faced, gaudy evening tails,
Trousers striped, big-bowed ties,
Bright-lied silks, flashing socks,
To joke and sing and ballad ring
To plinging banjo, Nat King's violin,
Then next act in jest some medley prance
Of elegant dance and tapping acrobats,
Jugglers, crooners, magic men,
Building to a hoedown, cakewalk crest,
As watchers hail and raucous rail,
And crescendo with the mounting farce
Of burlesque melodies in bright-lit hues
Imbued with all the saddened hearts
Of voluptuous, 'raptured reverie,
That eventual' slows to memory...

I will shout, (I will shout),
And I'll dance, (And I'll dance),
And I'll wake up early in de morn;
And I will arise, and rub my sleepy eyes,
When old Gabriel am blowing his horn.[129]

Meanwhile, as industry begins to bite
In Virginia's slowly resurrected night,
At Newport News, newly risen
On the marshes of the lower James,

---

[129] *Angel Gabriel* by Frank Dumont and James E. Stewart, 1875; printed in *Minstrel Songs, Old and New*, 1883. It was a popular 'end song' at minstrel shows.

Huntington spikes a line of ties
And buys beachfront acres, there to build
Shipyard repairs a mile in length,
With wharves and drydocks, warehouses,
Piers and yards and o'erspilling shops,
Foundries and engineering mills
New-laid grided roads, hotels
And houses in neatened rows...

...but not for all...

...For, from eighteenth to twenty-third,
Shanties vomit up, no water or power,
A ramshackle slum for blacks and whites
Who work the yards and planks, taking
Low-ranked jobs, sometimes skilled,
Forced to live thigh-by-thigh
With bordellos, honkytonks,
Illicit stills and whisky joints,
Cycling past early morning whores,
Seamen weaving in and out red-light stores,
Longshoremen gambling, all-night bars,
Drunks and dogs on the cobbled floors,
Murders every rabid day,
In Hell's Half Acre, tossed away,
Until the twenties, when it's razed
For railyards, shacks torn down,
To tar and pitch its sharded soul
For a more respected, sanitary town.

Meanwhile, not too far away,
A chain gang works upon some
Anonymous Campbell County road,
Improving rutted tracks of mud
With rankled grit and rock,
Striped in grey and sweating black,
Some with hobbled ankles grabbed,
Leg-irons chained to cuff their wrists,
Most crippled with venereal disease,
Suppurating lack of medicine,
Shacked in crowded, stuffy hovels
Huts with full-fleaed bunks of ticks,
Stinking garbage for their meals,
Their rate of death a crime itself,
With their shovels, bending low,
Picks or scythes, hammers, drills,
Faces tired, breathless, black,
Skin their solitary, shackled crime,
All with lashes, scars of sticks,
Or thumps of guarded rifle butts;
All who bounce in fetid cans
With tiny grilles for sucking air;

434

All who lapse in fenced-in life
Of rotted meat, old beans and corn,
Of vermined mattresses, crowded dorm,
Violence, anger, rife and petty filth;
All incarcerated for some mundane crime,
Leased to neo-slavery's private frown,
To coal mine, railroad, textile mill,
And some reaping boss whose paltry pay
Is a sin far bigger, worse –
Yet who is rewarded soundly well
For keeping curséd niggers down.

Twenty-nine links of chain...
And on each link an initial of my name...

...of my name...

It takes a worried man to sing a worried song,
I'm worried now, but I won't be worried long...

...Though, in Mathews County now,
An old threshing barn houses
A new machine, steam-driven,
That does the work of forty men,
So they must learn new farming skills,
Or wander down the lanes around
As nomad packers, season pickers,
Menders of fences, hoers, sprayers
– Any work to allay
The hunger in their eyes...

...While still we flit, souls in swallow tails,
Whit-whit-whit, along our country way.

VI

"Awake, Ke'show-tse, Great Sun! Awake!
Call unto our savior's dawn!"

But there is no reply, for
We have forgotten why,
Forgotten how to sing and sigh,
How to dance the grass and stream,
Buffalo, elk and beaver's dream
Within the common vision of our eye...

Birth of a Nation is made in 1915. It leads to the resurrection of the Ku Klux
Klan, the membership of which soars, along with other hate organizations. The
Klan is vehemently anti-union, anti-Semitic, anti-Catholic, anti-smoking, anti-

'petting', anti-dancing and anti-liquor. It seeks to keep women in their place as much as those who are non-Protestant or not Anglo-Saxons.

> Bigotry using the robes of
> A whitewashed Christian hope
> To justify lawless extremism.

The red-baiting, anti-Irish and anti-immigrant scares promulgated by that scoundrel Woodrow Wilson add to this new climate of fear. As a result, many minority groups are forced to join together to protect themselves. But for Southern blacks, especially rural, the only answer is escape. Exhausted by segregationist violence and hatred, during the Great Migration of the 1920s and '30s, two million (about 40%) of Southern blacks leave for Northern cities.

> *Oh, when the hunter comes to call...*

> Oh yes, Woodrow Wilson, of
> League of Nations fame,
> Wears two masks to foreigners,
> Pretending anti-colonialism
> And so-called work for peace,
> While he expands the US army to impose
> His will on Nicaragua, Cuba, Panama,
> And implore unwilling Haiti to accept
> Demands to repress its anxious poor.

> At home, he sports two masks too,
> Anti-tariff, anti-trust, for a taut banking law
> And other New Freedom legislation, as
> Farmers get well-planned loans,
> There's workmen's comp,
> Better lives for railroad workers,
> And child labor is by the letter banned
> – For the worst of the worst of the worst
> Is not tolerated by this man,
> Lest he up and lose the rest, as
> Donning his other putrid mask,
> That of tyranny, our hero suppresses
> Opposite opinions, cultivates hate,
> Red scares, German-baits, Irish scapegoats,
> And, racist to the core,
> Segregates the federal government,
> Demands employees' photographs
> To prove the color of their skin,
> And refuses to flinch a muscle to fight
> For the desperate churning plight
> Of drowning black America.

Ella Fitzgerald, one of the leading female vocalists of all time, is born in Newport News in 1917. The next year, Pearl Bailey is born in the same city.

Now, if you're so foxy and old Chief is so dumb,
Then why does that hound get the fox on the run?
'Cause he's got the hunter –
And the hunter's got the gun –
Ka-blam, elimination!
Lack of education![130]

In a downtown Norfolk store,
Hardware run by a sour old man,
A customer sits and sips a soda
Checking numbers in her almanac,
Births and marriages, other dates,
Movement signs of the stars,
To rate the likeliest, luckiest set
Combining for her fortune's fate…

…While a family rides a taxicab
From north DC to Arlington,
And stops at a Piggly Wiggly,
New concept aisles, prices marked,
Baskets, checkouts, clerks
Perking choice and service,
Then are off again, past
Enticing gas stations, motels,
Charlie Chaplin in *The Tramp*,
Billboards, trolleys, Model Ts,
Their daughter fanned out on the seat,
Next to her Raggedy Ann…

…And at a dancehall bandstand night,
Musicians play a break-away,
The couples prancing, holding, turn,
Then splitting, grasping fingers firm,
To remerge and keep the beat
Of impromptu sashays of their feet,
Natty suits and flashy dresses,
Slicked back hair and ironed tresses,
Away, together, round and through,
To the intoxicating syncopation
Of the alleyed morning few.

They dance to forget
There is a tension growing
As news filters slowly through
Of Germany's invasion, the French reply,
England, Austria, Russia, more –
Even Italy, Africa, the Turks at war…

…As Europe's heart is from its body torn,
To purge a sad age through mindless death

---

[130] *Elimination – Lack of Education!* by "Big Mama" Pearl Bailey.

And assuage the guilt of those gone mad…

Don't ask,
Don't ask me why…
Only the ancestors hold the keys,
Only they see it all
Down the tumbled centuries…

Just watch as,
Desperate war in mud-drenched France
Welcome-spurs production's gain,
Coal and weapons, iron and grain
Shipped to trenches of the Somme and Marne,
Until in seventeen, the Devil knocks
And thousands flock to khaki up,
Join the eightieth and twenty-ninth,
Or expanded national guard, then
Are monthly trained in hasty Lee,
Or fresh-faced Norfolk Naval Base,
Spree new money in old-bleak cities
Of Richmond, Hampton, Petersburg,
Regurgitating a stagnant economy,
Until they are ripped from Jamesian Roads
And shipped with coal and cans of food,
Horses, mines and aero parts
To the flood-soaked, shell-shocked sea
Of bloody, pointless zees
On the Meuse-Argonne line.

…oh, when the hunter comes to call…

The Germans claim twelve hundred,
But at home we lose twelve thousand
To our worst attack of 'flu –
If we had diverted more
To health and less to war,
The *real* tragedy might have been subdued.

And when our soldiers finally return,
Blacks are softly, firmly told
To re-adopt old Southern ways,
But have seen how others fare,
Tasted the world's equality,
So decide to quit old hatred's den,
Drive to northern cities, and then
No more abide
Virginia's prejudicial fratricide…

…As humble farms, prosperous while the war,
Sudden-languish in o'er supply
And prices tumbling, tumbling…

438

...I dance, I dance, I dance,
To the MusicMen in my trance,
Grace the ancestors, impart their fears,
And cascade into the rhythm of my heart
With the mercy of their tears...

...While the Chickahominy boy, sixteen,
Enquires about his past,
What being an Indian does require,
What the inspiration of the dance,
And is told in heated native truth
Of the animals as one, the spirits
Of the creatures and the trees,
Of the Sun and Wind and Earth,
Who guide all things, are intercomplete,
We mere guardians of this trodden land,
Branders of a future's flame,
– Of community, sharing, family –
And of how his tribe – every band –
Has striven to survive,
Driven west, as the English swift arrived,
Then slowly drifted back
To old ancestral lands, revived
In numbers and slowly refound
Identity in this, their native ground...

...Oh, Great Ke'show-tse!
Sufferers, ancestors, WindTeller, All,
Listen to our forgotten history
Of when the Callings came to call!
Help us restore the memory of dance,
Of the rites and ancient ceremony,
And of how we circle to regain
The harmony again of All!

VII

In this time of struggle to regain rights
Once held, but long forgot,
One dormant fight now strong emerges –
Campaigning for the women's vote, as,
In heated street and parlor debate,
Woman's League and Suffragettes
Provoke relentlessly to persuade
Would-be protectors, self-made guides,
That they are themselves intent
On deciding equal-statused lives.

But enfranchisement is opposed
By many propertied, coiffured women

In the UDC and DAR,[131]
By church leaders, ever prejudicial,
Who fear giving females blacks the vote
In a time of segregation and supremacy,
Worried they will impose their place
And demand unpleasant change to displace
The status quo of a ruling race –
For a woman's place is at the hearth
Giving birth,
Rocking with her suckling child, and her
Maternal instincts must be conserved,
As men protect and preserve
Their interests quite adequately.

Even when the Constitution is amended,
For years Virginia refuses to conform
And allow her women votes,
Until forced to by Supreme Court law,
And even then, poll tax, tests for literacy,
Other stratagems and trickery,
Keep most of this new electorate,
White and black, their men also,
From partaking of their rightful role
– Just one more sign of Virginia's decline
From first in democracy to the last,
From spirited liberty and élan,
From prosperity and rural health,
To the mire of rich white male hypocrisy.

...oh, when the hunter comes to call...

But not all well-off women are lost within denial,
For some stand high upon the plinth
Of the struggle for democracy,
Such as that Corinthian,
Lila Meade Valentine,
Who helps, with Anne Clay Crenshaw,
To found the Equal Suffrage League,
And though she dies within a year
Of the ratification of her hopes,
Lives to cast that oh, so golden vote.

So too, Sarah Lee Fain, borne aloft
To the heady House of Delegates,
And, later, Helen Timmons Henderson,
Sent to Virginia's lilywhite Assembly,
To be followed in her victory
By Sallie Cooke Booker and, later still,
Helen Ruth Henderson, pioneers all

---

[131] United Daughters of the Confederacy and Daughters of the American Revolution, which both opposed women's suffrage, for fear of giving black women the vote.

Against risen male ascendancy…

…yet are still of that elitist class…

…And, unfortunately,
As if to balance victory
With the face of sad defeat,
We have Bishop Cannon, schemer,
Political intriguer,
Gambler, speculator, hoarder,
Protestant bigot, Catholic hater
To the point of spitting virulence,
Who yet presumes to campaign
For prohibition, moral rectitude,
Crusading with an intolerance league
Of Anti-Saloon, Women's Temperance,
Methodists and Baptists –
Continuing an ignominious craze
That has inherited the crying ages
Of moral tyranny in the name of Christ,
By preachers immoral to the core,
And sees all divergence as Satanic plot
And tolerance as unworthy of respect…

But, so too, this is the age of prosperity,
Throwing off our wartime cares
And letting us turn, as the hunter,
To more surer fare…

So I pull off my hood and gallop free
Within the energy of the dance
That serves alone to distance me
From the myopic zealots' trance
As, in post-war ecstasy and glee
Of new-wealth wages, returning men,
Industries and spurred economy,
Money burns our pockets,
Cars beep and swerve the new-paved streets,
Shops stock goods tinned or frozen,
Records are made, sheet music played,
Big bands, singers, dancing's craze,
As ragtime gives to swinging jazz,
Arbuckle, Keaton, Valentino,
The Texas Tommy, Turkey Trot,
Stockings, cigarettes and flimsy dresses,
Flappers, bobs, lipstick, rouge,
Cocktails, sex and petting parties,
Skyscrapers, radios, *art deco*,
As we are raised to new heights
Of confidence and light…

…for, one day, I will be the hunter.

VIII

Blue, blue, I got a tale to tell you, I'm blue
Something comes over me, daddy, and I'm blue about you
Listen to my story, and ev'rything'll come out true...[132]

Oh, for a new Jerusalem!

At rural Tappahannock's pier
Two boys kick their toes, chew gum,
Joke as their fishing poles
Lazy hum of sunset linger, and
Mosey as their lines to-and-fro
In the falling river's falltime glow.

Meanwhile, further south, summer crabbers,
Springtide snatchers of shad,
Drift the estuaries and the Chesapeake
To net their catch, dwindling now,
As the old Surry railway line
Drops huge loads of yellow pine
From fast-stripped Southside land
To logging mills and paper manufactories.

...And a barn swallow,
Russet, white, and black,
Flickers too and back
In tacks of zipping glided ease
Above a water-gilded pond
Of frogs and ducks and cows
Fondly cooling in the shallows...

...As our cotton fails again,
When the boll weevil devastates, attacks
And forces many tillers to back
The humble peanut in its stead,
Provoking a rolling growth, need-led,
For Planters, Suffolk-based, home
Of Mr Peanut and the Nickel Lunch
– So welcome in Depression's years,
Healthy, protein, fun –
Assuring a wealthy farmers' hunch
For Southside's lagging farmery,
As Gwaltney, others bag and cure
Smithfield's Virgin' ham, then
Load windblown steamers plying
Pagan's wharf to Norfolk's sultry town.

Hey, bo'weevil don't bring them blues no more,
Hey, bo'weevil don't bring them blues no more,

---

[132] *Blue Blues*, by Bessie Smith, 1923.

Bo'weevil's here, bo'weevil's everywhere you go... [133]

Sing, mockingbird, sing and cry
For the passing of the sun,
Sing, mockingbird, sing and ask me why...

...I dance and dance and dance,
As I in my silence cry
For a new Jerusalem...

...When I see
A Henry County family,
Sharecrop tilling,
Still in glooming penury – tho'
They have at least a floor to their house,
An extra bedroom, lean-to shed –
But no inside toilet yet,
No running water, electricity,
And are neck-high tied in debt...

Oh, them blue, blue, blues,
Them bo-weevil dancing blues...

Then I see,
In nearby Patrick's dales,
Ol' Tom Wyre, tenant, wise
Set his 'bakker barning fire
Of oak and hickory, a little pine,
And stay awake those curing nights
To stoke the smoke and watch
The drooping leaves turn golden brown
And scoop his scented hopes...

...While a Franklin 'cropper,
Cashing in his stock of leaves,
Is told his tally for the year,
That he owes more than he receives
And, despite the crop, is more in hock,
And suspects the bully storeman
Has deceiving book accounts –
But what can he do, illiterate as he is,
But curse and oath and sell his mule,
Then rent it brusquely back again,
Agin next year's risky growth...

Blow your trumpet, Gabriel,
Blow louder, louder,
And I hope dat trumpet might blow me home
To the new Jerusalem... [134]

---

[133] *Bo'weevil Blues*, as sung by Bessie Smith, 1924; first performed by Ma Rainey in 1923.

Meanwhile,
An old Rockingham livery stable
That ably cares for horses, mules,
Farm machines and plows,
Invests in hand-pumped gasoline
And builds a garage to repair
The flaring trade in passing cars,
Its aging store a truckstop now, though still
It offers finger-lickin' chicken,
Barbecue on buns,
Fountain orders and a view,
With ice and malt or soda...

...As an expanding Cape Charles cannery,
Shovels oysters from the docks
Into baskets, laden, prized and steamed,
Sealed and labeled, boxed and stored
For trains that stop, unload gay passengers
Who wish-explore the bay-mouth ferry trip
From this new-laid, burgeoned town
Of crabber, farmer, businessman.

The infrastructure of the state remains a disgrace. Roads are so bad that, in 1921,
a national automobile association advises motorists to detour the state entirely.
As late as 1926, the only long-distance, hard-surfaced road is the antebellum
Staunton-Winchester Turnpike.

WindTeller rides across the state,
As prohibition, malignant fear
Grows below police and agent brows
Into a chaotic sot menagerie
Of honkytonks and secret bars,
Hip flasks, hidden bottles,
Bootleggers, bosses on the run,
Protection rackets and bathtub gin,
Women drinking more and more,
Smoking chic now, risky, fun,
Moonshine valleys, 'grape juice' sales,
Blindness, death and poisonings,
While yet the secret home abuse,
The prostitution and the crime,
Are both left to fester and explore
New spores of slimy growth.

1920 sees the start of nation-wide prohibition, though Virginia had instituted its
own, less harsh version four years earlier. This new and total ban on alcohol
results in a rash of speakeasies, secret fireside drinking, crime syndicates and an
explosion in moonshine, bootlegging, 'bathtub gin' and illicit stills.

I grate the gears and grimace

---

[134] *Blow Your Trumpet, Gabriel*, an old Negro spiritual.

As my new-loaned Chevy flatbed
Full of Madison County apples
Picked by ill-fed migrant labor,
Once black and white, now dusty red,
Strains up a new-laid hill
Past a road crew tarring, rolling,
Flagman waving lazy through,
All on Virginia state relief,
Finally regrading sedate roads
After centuries of neglect.

I am careful not to speed too hard
Less the secret casks of bootleg gin
And whisky hauled beneath the crates
Tip off the vigilante motor cop
Watching for my unpaid taxes, tires bald,
And overladen load – yet can't resist
A perverse verse or two
Of *I Married a Bootlegger's Daughter*:

I know that the stuff's full of poison,
But me and my sweetie won't die,
When we want a drink, we go out to the sink,
The bootlegger's daughter and I... [135]

My co-driver's riding shotgun,
Thompson below his knees,
As we hive for Roanoke's speakeasies,
Then breeze to Franklin County, capital
Of the moonshine world, to pack a load
Along the road of dank Danville honkytonks...

Oh, the bootlegger's daughter and I...

In 1924, Virginia adopts the Racial Integrity Act, which reiterates the illegality of interracial marriages and classifies Indians as colored, thus expunging them from the record books. It is based on the theory of eugenics and is so racist it will serve as a model for Hitler's Nuremberg Laws. It is enthusiastically enforced and becomes the basis of sterilization programs for people of mixed race, criminals, the poor, and the mentally and physically disadvantaged.

"This is a white man's country
And it is our Christian duty
To keep it from such racial impurity,
Degeneration and corruption
As mixing the races will bring down
Upon *all* the ethnic groups."

"Almighty God created the races
White, black, yellow, Malay and red,

---

[135] *The Bootlegger's Daughter* by Frank Crumit, 1925.

Placed them each on separate continents,
And but for interference with His arrangement
There would be no cause for inter-marriage;
Rather, the fact that God separated the races
Proves He did not intend them to mix."

"The Negro is a system in which one traffics."

"It is only right that, given the white child's
Naturally superior intellect and brain,
He should receive a better education
Than the mentally inferior Negro child."

"The Negro is incapable of understanding
Concepts such as justice, truth and fairness,
So how can we expect him to bear witness,
Or serve upon a jury, much less act as a judge
Upon his moral teachers and superiors?"

"The Negro is naturally lazy and incapable
Of will or independent thought,
So must be led, shown right and wrong,
And is in constant need of supervision,
So should not expect wages of a similar kind,
Nor the same conditions as those given
To civilized men and women –
And nor does he *need* them,
For his expectations and needs in life
Are less than for our more cultured race."

"Never let a nigger hold a tool."

"The Negro as a laborer is most valuable,
And if it were possible to preserve
The race in all its purity in our midst,
He would indeed be a most great asset;
Yet, because this cannot be done,
And because the mixing of breeds
Is a menace and not an asset,
The results linger as the most destructive force
That confronts the white race
And our American civilization."

"Negroes are quitting the countryside!
We are losing our farming workforce!
Give them at least a rudimentary schooling,
Elementary wages and respect,
To encourage them to stay!"

In 1925, all public events are segregated in Virginia. In the elections of the previous year, only 18% of potential voters actually voted, as most were debarred. Blacks are totally excluded from voting in primaries, which are all-white and, given the virulence of the Democratic chokehold on the state, effectively determine who wins elections.

In 1926, Carter G. Woodson founds Negro History Week, which will evolve into Afro-American History Month. He was born in Buckingham County and earned degrees at Berea College and the University of Chicago, as well as a doctorate at Harvard. He organized the Association of the Study of Negro Life and History and established the *Journal of Negro History*. He knew the meaning of justice.

> "With their lack of morals,
> Criminality and licentiousness,
> Negroes constitute a racial peril
> And it is with disgust I note
> That the white Virginia male,
> In his lecherous abandonment,
> Is far too casual in sexual liaisons
> With the inferior Negro woman;
> He betrays a lack of self-respect
> And moral duty to his race,
> Viewing mulatto children as a joke,
> No less lamentable a sight
> Than the sickening, saddest plight
> Of degenerate, white-skinned women
> Giving birth to unsightly mulattoes."

> "Let us abolish once and for all
> That shiftless, ignorant, and worthless class
> Of anti-social whites in the South,
> Sometimes called 'poor white trash,'
> But to my thought, not white at all,
> And certainly not deserving to reproduce."

> *...oh, them bo'weevil blues...*

In 1927, the US Supreme Court upholds the concept of eugenic sterilization for people considered genetically 'unfit', stating that, "Three generations of imbeciles are enough." In the next forty-three years, 8,000 forced sterilizations will be carried out in Virginia.

> John Powell, Earnest Cox, Walter Plecker,
> Madison Grant, Harry Laughlin Powell,
> You were perhaps the worst prancers of
> Our periodic racist dance, cavourting
> In the name of science and religion,
> Investing in a drooled intolerance
> That dribbles from each generation
> To flood the pools of America's fear –
> May the future forgive you,
> For the outcast past most surely can't.

"I Will Rise" clubs prove popular meeting places for blacks to share their troubles and try to improve themselves. Others attend night classes to gain new skills. Many thousands more are fleeing to the North to escape the worst of segregation.

By the sultry summer Dan,
A white smock gathering sways its way,
Flocking to the water's edge,
Led by the sun upon a Cross, a staff
Held hallelujah high
As a pastor paddles in and calls the first
To be rebaptized and reborn
In a mass rejoicing of the Holy Ghost...

Listen to my story, and ev'rything'll come out true...

...As The Horseman gallops o'er the hills
To the Pa-mun'ki, tight pulsed
Along a bank of their river's name,
Trawl gill nets from old john-boats,
Setting floats to surround and catch
Migrating roes and bucks of shad,
To gently squeeze their mass of eggs,
Add smelt, harbor and preserve the fry,
To fill Old Virginia's rivers
And keep true the tradition and skill
Of this once-great Indian nation.

If I should take a notion
To jump into the ocean,
'T ain't nobody's bizness if I do, do, do, do.

If I go to church on Sunday,
Sing the shimmy down on Monday,
'T ain't nobody's bizness if I do, if I do.[136]

Oh swing me, swing me down,
Roun' an' roun',
And raise me from this shadowed ground...

Charleston flappers sweep the state,
Jazz-free babies, misses
Light of stockings, heavy cottons,
Ankle dresses, conformity,
Running onto dancefloor rings in
Calf-length skirts, slender, gay,
Tasseled to the swinging wind
Of leg-kick prancing, headhung steps,
Short hair, lipstick, gaudy beads,
Held and swung, out and in,
Jigging kicks of laméd heels,
Rouge and hair bob, bracelet flight,
Cigarettes in holders, glossy kisses,

---

[136] *'T Ain't Nobody's Bizness If I Do*, by Bessie Smith; Grainger and Robbins, 1923.

And light release from tight-fit corsets
Grown tighter through the centuries…

Grab your partner, one an' all,
Keep on dancing round the hall,
Then there's no one to fall,
Don't you dare to strut
If your partner don't act fair,
Don't worry there's some more over there,
Seeking a chance everywhere,
At the Christmas Ball… [137]

Stomping to the offbeat jazz,
Each dancer slapping hard their butt,
Hopping forward, leaping back,
Stamping left, then stamping right,
Stomping quick, then back again,
A heel-toe scoop, shimmy whoop,
Fingers pointing to the air,
Eyes rolled up in frenzied stare,
As we repeat around around,
That unforgotten,
Black Bottom sound…

Do not fear –
Fall, fall, fall within
The eternity of my waiting arms,
For I am waiting for you
And will hold you,
Time after time…

Meanwhile,
At rural Tappahannock's pier,
The boys long gone to supper,
A floating showboat moors, as twin tugs
Haul Adams' clapboard theater
From the touring Chesapeake, where
It lugs from week-to-week, town
To sultry town, playing riverside
Melodramas and romance, with orchestra,
Vaudeville and minstrel hype,
To gay and glowing farming types,
Summer crabbers, labor hands,
Who cheer the band most gratefully
And forget their darn boll weevil woes
For one more evening show…

Hey, bo'weevil don't bring them blues no more,
Hey, bo'weevil don't bring them blues no more,
Bo'weevil's here, bo'weevil's everywhere you go…

---

[137] *At the Christmas Ball*, by Bessie Smith, 1925.

449

IX

A boy on a bike throws morning papers
Onto the dawning lawns of suburbia...

If my friend ain't got no money,
And I say, "Take all mine, honey!"
'T ain't nobody's bizness if I do, do, do, do.

And 't ain't nobody's business neither
When, in unruled and cynical denial
Of Virginia's founding principles,
Sleazy deals and clubroom scams
Slink within the leathered smoke
Of the Democratic machine élite,
A cabal controlling all
In narrow-havened backroom halls,
Deals and careers, bargains struck,
Promises ducked and values that veer
With the blustery weather vane –
As all with a voice are kept away
From a hint of either freedom's fame
Or the hypocrisy of choice.

In 1927, the US Supreme Court declares that election primaries, which have long been exclusively white affairs in the South, must be open to all races. Virginia reluctantly obeys, after trying to wheedle out of it.

By now, separate entrances have been built to movie houses, theaters, racetracks, museums and other places of public entertainment. Facilities in factories, such as washrooms, pay counters and dining rooms, are segregated. Sports facilities and taxicabs are segregated, as are phone booths and drinking fountains. With buses now plying the streets, they too are segregated, as are park entrances, boats, pools, beaches and playground facilities. Meanwhile, black business districts develop in most towns to provide basic services for their people, such as barbers, finance companies, lawyers, funeral parlors, churches, plumbers and electricians.

An electric streetcar stops and squeals
Atop Richmond Hill to let on board
Morning-collared laces, whitecollars too,
As Chevies, Buicks, Oldsmobiles,
Rewards for monthly finance deals,
Steal past Model As, taking
Clerks to shops, department stores,
Managers to topmost office floors,
Salesmen, service personnel
At Philip Morris and city colleges,
Builders pledging theaters, hotels,
Houses in the Fan,
Public parks and spanning billboards,
Or lines of tangled telephone poles,
Piping water, gas and power
To new ex-urban settlements

Meant for managers and their families
As the economy booms and we
Zoom around in new suits, new gadgets,
Make out low-interest loans,
Take vacations to the sea
And escape the time-clock drudgery
Of typing pools, deadline desks
And late, late hours with pesky forms
That fill office-filed bureaucracy,
As the marketers stress cool comfort, ease,
And nice middle-class conformity.

And all the while, the boy throws papers
Onto the seried suburban lawns, as
Mechanics repair, reoil the line
Of Chesterfield's new brand cigarettes,
A telephonist pulls the plugs
To connect Phenix to DC,
And salesmen knock door-to-door
Selling appliances and home décor,
While managers of our banks rain loans
As they consume the rising credit boom,
And speculators wryly gape
At a gushing tickertape of unsustained prosperity...

Meanwhile, a family, husband a Fairfax clerk,
Drive their Dodge Tourer to the drifting banks
Of Pohick Bay, there to picnic, as
The children play and Dad sifts through
A copy of the *Evening Post*,
Sharing cans of tuna, salmon, ham,
With sliced white bread and margarine,
Playing with a baseball mitt...

...As, In the Crispus Attucks theater,
Down Church Street, Norfolk way,
Brer Rabbit strolls the fiddle as
Linkum dances a fol-de-rol
And the pair, in veiled and mystic stare,
Prance the trance of Virginia's past
And share the gifts our future casts,
Once the shrouds are from our eyes,
For they have vowed to be aware
Of the terror that this new greed
Is soon to bleed upon our lives...

For then, in nineteen-twenty-nine,
With a frail, o'ernighting fright,
The stock crash hews Virginia down,
Pursued by a devastating drought,
As textile workers are Danvilled out,
Coal mines sudden closed,

Shops and traders boarded up,
Tobacco prices tumble, wheat as well,
While banks crumble in South Boston,
Richmond too,
And unemployment arrives in thirty-two
At a hundred and forty-five thousand;
Breadlines form in every town and
Thousands tramp head-cupped back
To abandoned farms, mountain shacks,
There to cower the Depression out
As they repair to towns each hopeless day
To hawk and plead for misered pay.

Why us? – 'Tis not our fault
That we were sudden vaulted
Into starving penury…

Rather than be state protected,
Our distraught folk are abandoned
By Virginia's callous-mooded élite,
More concerned with finances than with food,
For a while supporting Hoover's
Paternalized approach,
Then Byrd opposing, after some rapport,
All of FDR's New Deal,
Repealing relief for Virginia's poor,
Other than a few brave roads,
Leaving families to starve and lurk
Within the hooded, craven shadow
Of his fat-carcassed, backhand smirk
While a quarter million are remanded on relief
And the federal government stands alone
To save us from despair,
Electrifying our fields, in some attempt,
With fertilizers, seeds and subsidies,
Roads and bridges, planting trees,
To ameliorate the arrogant neglect
Of our self-selected Assembly.

"The character of the poor, their pride,
Must be preserved at every cost,
They must not lose their dignity,
Nor their sense of manly worth,
Which soup kitchen and bread line
Is bound to compromise and undermine."[138]

Meanwhile,
A hotel porter, feet carbuncled,
Nipped by too-tight shoes,

---

[138] Based on a quote from a Virginia legislator of the time to justify *not* supplying free food to starving Virginia families.

Is called into a hotel office,
Paid off, let go without a word,
And, as he is escorted, led to the rear,
Stares at a white man trying on
A porter's uniform in his stead...

...As, on railway lines across the state
Black firemen are replaced,
Dockworkers, railyard men,
Even waiters, barbers, shoeshine boys
By whites in need of *any* work,
Shunting poverty down the restitution line...

...shunting down the line...

Housing starts collapse,
Mortgages relapse,
None can finance, buy,
So many try to rent,
Or collapse into
The growing homeless lines...

...While, in the lee of a Salvation home,
Two score resist the winter cold,
Bedraggled men, women too old
To care, barely able to persist,
Children barefoot,
Rags and empty stares...

Hoovervilles form outside our towns,
Jungles of hobos, tramps and bums,
Cardboard cities, sewerless slums,
Women taking washing in, picking fruit,
As their men suit up and hope for work,
Or thread in glum, dispirited lines
For soup and daily bread...

Have you ever seen the day...?

...dancing down the veils...

Nobody knows you when you down and out,
In my pocket not one penny,
And my friends I haven't any,
But If I ever get on my feet again,
Then I'll meet my long-lost friend. [139]

...shunted down the line...

---

[139] *Nobody Knows You When You're Down and Out*, recorded in 1929 by Bessie Smith; credited to Ida Cox and B. Feldman.

It's mighty strange, without a doubt,
Nobody knows you when you down and out –
I mean when you down and out...

Then the vet visits to treat our mule,
Aged and lame, in some miracled hope
That we can cope, but are
Denied and can merely give
To his always kindness with
A chicken and a dozen eggs,
Then, shyly wonder-beg
If he would diagnose my children,
Thin, pot-bellied, with cataracts,
Diarrhea, cramps
And itching rashes on their soles,
Which we know is hookworm
Eating through their damp and naked feet
From the wood-dark excreta we leave
Each day within the border trees
Of our twenty-acred tenancy.

...lying down...

So he bills us some pills, bartering
Two more chickens in return,
Then turns to my tired woman's skin,
Aged and browned and deeply thin,
Crowned with peeling, scaly sores,
Crazy fits, blacked-out memory,
Lethargy and lack of will,
And he knows she has pellagra,
Vitamin deficiency of too much corn,
Warns us, imparts niacin for our meals,
And with a secret shake of heart,
Smiles and bids us surely well,
More doctor than a vet,
More coping than a cure,
More prayer than a hope...

However, this is not a depression for all –
Some grow rich, avoid those stalling
Companies, invest wisely, profits up,
Make a killing and seek new ways
To defray their millions, rub dollars
With ease at cocktail bars and night-time clubs...

It is these winners who,
In a stylish merging, dance affray
Of break-away and Charleston,
Drunken jock the Lindy Hop
To a slick epiphany of trance
Buried in gin and jazz and midnight swing...

…As we amble arm-in-arm
Down Wytheville's main street slope,
Past Ol' Mayfleet, smiling, coping,
No legs, playing his harmonica
Beneath the barber's squeaking sign;
We greet Mrs Martin, daughters,
On their weaving a.m. stroll
To purchase satin for a dress
At a fashion sale, next the butcher's,
Then hurry past workmen paving tar
Outside our only cinema,
Stop to see what may be playing,
Arbuckle, Gish or Keystone Cops,
And rest our feet at an old teashop
For coffee and a fancy bun,
To defeat the midday heat
And gossip – just to pass the time.

And who is Ol' Mayfleet,
Passed with mere a smile?
Where does he crawl to,
Upon his wooden-wheeléd seat?

Why, to sleep beneath the deck
Behind the hardware store,
Among the rats and cockroaches,
Fighting raccoons for the scraps
Chucked out by that same house
In which the ladies sit and sip
And fuss at napkins on their laps.

I wonder, as he leans and stares
Through his drifting dragging roll,
Within the shadow of the sidewalk glare,
At the constant life-long lowering
Of his hopes and naïve dreams,
Until reality became unlivable
In its desperate, dreamless means.

In 1932, Patsy Cline, perhaps the greatest female Country and Western singer of all time, is born Virginia Patterson Hensley in Winchester. Meanwhile, the great migration of blacks from the South continues.

Have you ever kissed your dreams,
Have you ever touched the rain…?

Well, the young Chickahominy has –
For, now a man, he has grown aware,
Learned to observe nature's cycles,
The signs upon the season's air,
And the power of the sacred dance,
So he asks his uncle to relate the rites, tell

Him all the secrets of his tribe, try
To relearn the ancient ways and restore
Some of his traditional earthlore pride.

Soon, he is taken to an Amherst meet
With updated Monacans,
Rappahannocks and Mattaponi
To rebestow the ancient ways,
Of mask and paint and skin,
The dances of the bear and buffalo,
And so meets an elder medicine man,
Who lets him greet his youngtime help,
Herbal Woman, of the Pamunkey clan
– About his age –
For she has learned this fifteen years
The sacred art of blending mixtures,
Tinctures, lotions, potioned pitchers,
And how to search the woods and streams
For the freshest gleams of nature's tears.

So they sit, hidden in
The shadow-bidden dell
Of some dimlit, secret woodland cloak,
Where their rites, o'erlooked by the oaken smile
Of WindOracle's all-seeing, fiery eyes,
Can be practiced, handed mystic down,
In bath and sweat, a smoke of pipe,
And the darkness of the lodge where dwell
The ripe spells of our universal heart.

Oh, heed and free the ancestors,
Guardians,
In our veiléd future's plea!

…anything to escape…

So WindTeller watches from afar,
The green-leafed shoots of his crown
Hanging down as he pipes his tune,
Reining high from a balding hill
Under the shade of a hanging tree…

…As a union organizer who comes to town
To work within the textile mills,
And merge the workers into one,
Rural immigrant, woman, child,
Divided in a hundred ways
To make them easier-morseled prey,
Thankful for their poverty.

He careful suits an office, recruits a staff,
Hands out leaflets, calls a meeting,

Bands some disparate souls
Determined to draw a line and fight,
And calls a hopeful, hopeless strike
That is greeted with mere fake response,
As company spies and foremen take
Names and faces, intimidate
With communistic scare,
Soviet threat,
And the bosses, in a secret union
To set their wages, prices and conditions,
Truck in blackleg scabs,
Dragoon those who stiff resist,
Recruit goons and sheriff, governor,
Search for workers deputized
To march aside the National Guard,
Who terrorize the pickets, crazy shoot,
Smash the organizing room, set it ablaze,
Club the leaders close to death,
Blacklisted, driven down
From this proud, non-union town.

Oh, those are our unnamed heroes,
To whom
We should bestow our banners high,
To their forelorn struggle for
Our communities and our liberty!

Prohibition is repealed in 1933, representing a total failure of this most obvious, but not most extreme, attempt at moralistic social engineering.

Also this year, just south of Dillwyn in Buckingham County, CCC Camp P-56, Company 1367, opens. 192 men live in 52 small barracks and a dining hall while they build bridges, lookout towers and 275 miles of forest roads, as well as a number of recreational buildings. Other camps across Virginia help young men gain similar work experience and education.

In 1935, the National Labor Relations Act for the first time protects the right of workers to organize and elect representatives for collective bargaining. It has taken over 100 years since the union movement was born, and lasts just twelve.

During the late '20s and throughout the '30s, Virginia experiences a huge boom in road building. From 4,000 miles of paved roads in 1918, it has 47,000 miles by 1940. This fosters trade, suburbanization and tourism.

As the singer sings and the drummer plays
And the fiddler sparks the night,
Their spirits waft across the notes,
And dawn now cracks with light,
Yet every morsel of our rights
Are still hatefully denied
By the runners of this state...

From 1935-8, Governor Peary continues with the attitude that the poor are undeserving of help and that relief programs only make them worse off. 250,000 are on relief in Virginia in 1935, yet a mere $1 million a year is spent on them.

36% of those are black. In fact, Virginia's response is to *reduce* state spending, thereby exacerbating the tragedy. Old age assistance is put off until Virginia is the last state to adopt it and unemployment insurance is rejected until the Assembly is forced to institute it by the courts.

Oh, still so far to go until the day
When the veils of our misery
Are rapid torn away,
So that we may see, most clearly,
Who wilt among the innocent
And who are truly guilty.

X

Can you see the dawn, can you?
Can you see the dawn?

The faint trance of premorned glow
Glances o'er the stream's soft flow as,
In these kettle-liquored hills,
Far from flashlit revenue eyes,
Under the shine of a full-graced moon
Malten mash of sugared wheat
Ferments,
And ash is set to slowly burn
Beneath a stone and copper cauldron;
The flume is swung and water bubbles
To ice the coiled distilling worm,
The stovepipe bourne to understream
And the distillate careful leaned
Through gooseneck and condenser barrel,
To drip within an earthen jug,
Stoppered, buried, left to age,
As the shadows merge and surge once more
With trees and rocks and stony soil,
And the hillmen traipse upon their beds,
Their lives once more in harmony…

Oh, let us dance-entrance the morn
To flood our lives within gay rays
Of another glorious, joyous day!

…As I, Indian, well-elder trained,
Despite inherited Christian ways,
Find a new philosophy of right
Within the soil's fecund plight,
And take my hand of herbalist,
Who re-awakes in mutual tryst
As jointly we recite a sunrise rite
To celebrate our commitment day:

"I will learn to find a way
To praise the earth and stars
And those who grace,
With an empathy of place,
A land of love that's yet confused
With fear and sunless pain;
I will learn to gain compassion's smile,
Rather than to judge, dismiss or blame
The world as evil Satan's realm,
And us as sinful, godless folk;
I will learn to see the world as all,
Us as part, an integrated whole,
No longer seeking some hereafter,
As we embrace the Now and enter in,
My morality swinging far from hate
To inter-understanding,
Granting, not to take, but to share and care
And no longer of the earth forecall
That which she cannot give to all."

And we then jointly pronounce
The *Diamond Rule*, superior far
To its self-defined and 'golden' cousin:
To treat all as best we know
They wish to be treated
– To listen humbly,
Understand, and let them behold
The agile life Life planned.

When we are taken from the earth,
Separated from its subtle ways,
Removed from interaction, empathy
With its minute moods,
We are torn from ourselves,
From our rooted mystery,
From our wholeness, from our life,
From our beating soul…

…Oh, hear our beating soul,
Dear ancestors,
Hear our beating soul!

And I dance that beating soul,
Butterfly-entranced,
The earth my womb,
Her fleeting streams
My birth-sustaining caul.

Can you see it, can you?

Oh. how I love the smell
Of early autumn dawn,

The ripened apples in the gloam,
The bubbling coffee's call to warm
My cornpoke kin and I before
One more picking day begins;
And how we wave
As The Horseman, smiling,
Gathers pace
Through the morn, frosty-veiled
To trace the shaded vale
Where apple trees align the dale,
And pears and other autumn fruit
Await
The ladders and our curlblade knives
To pare their stalks from withered lives
And gentle drop the unbruiséd orbs
Into wickerworking baskets, to be rushed
By bigger children unto caskets
Waiting on the wagon carts
That Papa loads on rutted roads,
Wet from harsh October soaks,
To Arlington's old rail depot, or Crozet,
Madison and Orange, to be huffed
And chuffed to haling
Richmond's hungry mouths,
Or along the patient James
To Norfolk, then the inner coast
To seaboard targets that return
Cured tobacco for the mills
And Virginia's golden cigarettes…

Oh, round and round the reel,
Go round and round the reel,
And celebrate the falltime meal
Of apple butter's steaming pots,
The honey and the cider tots,
The fiddler and the double-bass,
Who entertain the fair-bright guests
As we wander 'twixt the stalls…

But the dawn, the dawn,
Where is the dawn you promised?

I dance,
Dance, to emerge from shadow,
And merge within the light…

I step from a Greyhound bus, bored,
Drop a nickel into a vending machine,
Open a carton of week-old milk,
Buy some gum, a fashion magazine,
And reboard as the driver calls…

…As a young man breaks out a loan,
Pays down upon a taxicab
And rents a room near Hot Springs,
Bath County town,
Where the wealthy come to play…

…While those of us who care, gather round
A Roosevelt fireside chat that instills
Reassurance, willing us to re-attain
Hope, a plan, and handing us a future
Back again…

…at the sight of starlit dawn…

Oh, the dawn, the dawn!
The dance has called the dawn!

It is not until the defeat of the Byrd Machine by Price in 1938 that any more assistance is given to the elderly, unemployed or disadvantaged. It is only then that more federal money is used for housing, as longer-term and less risky mortgages cause a huge increase in house starts from 1937 onwards. Furthermore, it is only under Price that PWA[140] public building projects take off, teachers' salaries are greatly raised, and the nepotic appointment of friends to lucrative posts is curbed.

Price also wants to modernize an inhumane penal system by introducing probation and parole. Byrd resists, but the next governor, Darden, is able to push those reforms through, along with compulsory school attendance, more money for black schools, higher standards for teachers, new school buildings, and more resources for higher education, especially UVa.

The country is beginning to emerge from the Depression, but the stimulus comes from the federal government, not the state. The policies of Virginia's leaders actually slow this development, rather than help it. Despite this, Roosevelt's electrification program reaches many areas, new roads are built, and the Tennessee Valley Authority provides jobs, fertilizers and other help for southwestern Virginia.

XI

I, washerwoman, rise at the call of crow[141]
From a distant neighbor's yard,
Stare up a moment from my straw-filled tick,
Then pick myself from off the floor
And shake my eldest daughter 'wake,
No need to dress, no shoes to wear,
And scrape the stove with a poker iron,
Pan out the ash, roll in coarse paper,

---

[140] Public Works Administration.

[141] This section comprises *The Song of the Washerwoman.*

Then shove on two logs, for it to lick
The day's first steaming kettle boil,
As round I step and gently roil
It with a stir of my laundry stick.

I've got the blues, I feel so lonely
I'll give the world if I could only
Make you understand –
It surely would be grand... [142]

I push the hanging, screen-ripped door,
Ginger down the sagging porch,
Avoid the lurching, crazy stoop,
Then tread in bare a dawnrise daze
Past our chicken choir, caged in wire,
To the endyard privy, stinking,
And an overbrimming stench of flies,
Then am back again, daughter risen, standing
At the alley pump, handcrank gushing
Splashes into a sudding bucket, bearing it
To the kettle, returning twice again,
Till 'tis filled and heat let build
And we can scurry down the unlit entry
To a street of gentile shops, neat hotel,
A night-time sot and midnight woman
Keeping restless sleep upon a bench,
As a copper, young, strides fast past,
And a wagon of grunting, rural pigs
Trundles down the abattoir path
To the river's tanyard knell.

A record unwinds its mellow song,
Drifting from a broken window:
I'm gonna telephone my baby,
Ask him won't you please come home,
'Cause when you're gone,
I'm worried all day long...

Soon, I and daughter hurry over
To the Grand Hotel, where
The night-tired janitor lets us in,
And we can haul the waiting laundry,
Shoulder, bend and take its weight,
Kate lifting up the smaller load,
Then shuffle back to grave-sick home
That scanty sheds my five brave kids,
Father three years gone, since he,
Hired by a local firm, was fired
When Negroes were forbidden
To build in downtown housing sites –

---

[142] *Baby Won't You Please Come Home*, by Bessie Smith, 1923. (Williams/Warfield)

And so, one drunken, saneless night
He killed a man who pulled a knife,
And within the hour was lynched and hanged,
His putrid form abandoned there,
Left to dangle-turn and warn,
'Til the well-masked funeral men
Cut the rope and took him down.

Baby won't you please come home...
Baby won't you please come home...

My eldest knows how to raise the boil,
Fill the tub, add suds and let the linens rub
In the hurly-burly of their spell
With a stirring stick, as the others rise
To breakfast on the least I have,
Feed the chickens, collect the eggs,
And beg them to the hardware store,
New opened past the county court.

Baby won't you please come home...
Baby won't you please come home...

I wash, do my hair, tidy up,
Then rewalk the halflit alley past
The returning night-time working shift
Of women from the mill,
Children, men a few, most
With delicate fingers made to blend
Cigarettes, roll and pack them tight,
Seal and sort and box and send.

I stride across the electric street,
A truck gearing as it rides,
Full of nearby whites from paupered farms,
Day labor charmed to town-apply
To work the sewer by the bridge,
Old black jobs white-taken now,
As pride and vision go to hell
In this penniless, desperate Southside shell
Of a once-bright tobacco town.

I have tried in vain
Ever more to call your name,
When you left you broke my heart
That will never make us part,
Every hour in the day
You will hear me say...

Up the alley 'tween seedysided rooms,
I'm catcalled from the door
Of the whorehouse neatly tucked

Within the backcat shanty walls,
But smile as I pass, know them well,
Pray I never see my daughters there,
And hie the hill towards the homes
Lined in pretty-tended, ridgeline rows,
Pillared porches, screens, imposing
Glass within their doors, roses,
'Susans, chrysanthemums,
Gravel paths, well-tended lawns,
And quietly enter the unlocked back,
Don my apron from the larder rack,
Wash my hands and turn on the gas
To cook the family's full repast,
Allowed an egg and slice myself,
And serve the husband, Mr Gray,
Doctor, fine, of good intent,
But soon to leave the town's decline,
His patients leaving anyway.

Mrs Gray is a homekeeper, and
They have two young boys, twins,
Whom she brings downstairs to me;
I help them to their chairs, give them
Cornflakes, milk, a hardboiled egg,
Then help them wash and dress
And press them off to kindergarten,
Other domestics milling there,
Briefly chatting, chewing news
That Mr Grade, barber, black,
Has lost his business trade
To whites who have impressed
Others of their race to fly distressed
To their own businesses,
For fear of black shirts in the day
And white sheets in the night.

Baby won't you please come home, I mean
Baby won't you please come home...

Next, I hasten down the road
To explore
The new market store where madam
Prefers to grocer now,
Rather than the downtown shop,
Which she says is dirty, old, hopping
With roaches, rodents, flies,
But I know where her reason really lies –
The old 'keeper insists he serves
Blacks with a nerve to come
The front way in
And not steal behind the back,
As she feels they ought to do.

Baby won't you please come home
Cause your mama's all alone...

I buy them bread, milk, vegetables,
Some sirloin for their evening meal,
Return, refridge it, then switch on
That darn-fangled vacuum cleaner,
Do the carpets, dust the ledges,
Make the beds, fold the children's clothes,
Clean the inside toilet bowl,
Then truss the dirty cotton sheets
Into the basket set upon
An electric wringer he has bought
To make washing days a little less fraught,
While madam has her coffee guests
To laugh and play some whist,
Then takes her car to pick the twins
From their half-morning, two-hour school,
And carpools them home with friends to play
As I finish housework for the day,
Take my week's six dollar pay
And traipse to that selfsame store
That madam sadly frequents no more,
Meekly purchase for our scrape-by week
And lower my eyes to avoid the stare
Of Mr Roy, always quick
To find offence in nigger guile
And presume too much of overjoy
In an uppity-seeming smile.

I have tried in vain
Never more to call your name,
When you left you broke my heart,
That will never make us part,
Landlord gettin' worse,
I've got to move May the first...

Back across the cobbled street,
I pass the man who leaves the mail,
Cars parked beneath new-leafing trees,
A sidewalk dug by white road gangs
That a year ago were black;
A telephone rings in the realtor's shop
And starlings rest upon the line,
As a salesman goes from store to store,
Hawking galvanized pans that shiny-shine,
Utensils to hard-pressed hardware doors
Where unsold goods sprawl far across
Sidewalk-weary plots
And hang from dreary, flaking walls.

Baby won't you please come home, I need money
Baby won't you please come home...

I walk back down the stale
And muddy, shadowed vale
That crawls between the shanty huts
Of renter land, the sprawling roofs
And decrepit, sagging walls
Of unkempt landlord slums,
No running water, showers, no heat,
Except woodlog stoves, brown paper stalls,
No carpets on our bareboard floors,
No beds, nor wardrobes for our clothes,
Just the sound of chickens in the yard,
Open doors with tattered screens,
Noxious flies slide-buzzing in
And infesting our forgotten lives,
As the cock crows upon our eventide...

Have you ever kissed your dreams...?

Oh Mama, things are not as they were meant to be.

XII

Am I ever gonna dance?
Never gonna dance...

...Unless I dance the haunting shadows
Across my screaming hands...

Or accept this way is wrong,
That the new will make me strong...

...waiting, waiting...

...Waiting at the railway station,
Trains shunting once a day,
Buses lining the street,
While I pick my teeth, disgruntled,
Watching vaguely for a fare,
As, behind me, second-in-line reads a paper
He will pass along, crossword done,
Blondie read, Popeye too,
To the third, who takes a nap,
Arms folded, hat prized flat
To shade his flick-dreamed eyes
From the intensely noontide sun,
Waiting, waiting,
In the mountain ease that tourists come
To breeze
From the dusty August broil
Of a humid-riven tidal rim

To Appalachian spas and pools,
Sulfur waters whose bubbles spool
From lithium springs and coiling moil
In round-built bathroom globes,
As attendants with their towels and robes,
Massage parlors, restaurants
Of high-priced, flighty names,
Spoil and pamper lofty tenants
Here to take of air that's fresh
Descended from the mountain heights;
And so we wait for hand-me-downs and table tips,
A fare or two, to share Virginia's wealth –
So less to spare these days, it seems,
Other than in stealth of lazy dreams...

...waiting, waiting, waiting...

Meanwhile, the Indian boy
Daubs his face the sacred way,
Black as the great humped buffalo, ties
Walnut rattles on his elbows,
And his ankles too...

On June 15, 1936, Virginia opens its first six state parks: Seashore,
Westmoreland, Staunton River, Douthat, Fairy Stone and Hungry Mother.

To alleviate the pain, Porterfield,
In distant Abingdon,
Maintains a theatre of paupered actors
Who win well-bartered meals
Brought by impoverished, grateful patrons,
Until, in better-martyred times,
It climbs to statewide pride...

...And there are food banks too,
Donated shoes, coats, rooms,
Free schooling given to our children,
Not by the ignorant, miscreant state,
But by volunteers and helpers,
Donating dimes and fated tears
In these desperate trying years.

Oh, can I at last partake of the dawn,
Have I descended enough,
Found the depth of my plunging well,
Been stripped of all I wear,
Taken all I can ever bear,
And may I cry, in finality,
"Awake, Great Ke'show-tse! Sun, Awake!"?

Only when I slip within the skin
And mask of horns and trance

To stamp and glance the Buffalo Dance...!

And all I have is you...

...Stripped of me, 'til
All I have is you...

Meanwhile,
Jim Crow laughs,
But does not share the joke
And Brer Rabbit pokes fun at my palm,
Sprinkles goofer dust upon my sagging head,
Some mojo for my necktied bag,
And a slice of John de Conqueror
To tag my luck in times to come...

...Dancing in the trance of
Drum and flute and rhythmic chant,
Being and becoming one
With the panting buffalo...

Am I ever gonna dance?
Never gonna dance...

During the 1930s, Shenandoah National Park is established and CCC workers dig out a ridgeline road from Front Royal to Rockfish Gap, planting trees and offering employment to the mountain people, many of whom are forcibly removed from their peaceful, isolated lives to the lowland valleys of Rockingham and Madison.

Taxes hate a vacuum,
Government hates a man alone,
Law hates the sight of liberty,
And so when the Hags of the Apocalypse
Ride into town, up state and down,
They turn independent communities
Into dependencies on distant clowns
Who steady burn away our pride,
Self-respect and power, upon a tide
Of bureaucratic corruption and control.

The park, like all others in the South, is segregated, and while its creation relieves harsh poverty for many young men, it pulls numerous old, independent mountain communities out of their traditional way of life.

The union organizer,
Beaten up again, broken jaw,
Can do no more, no more, no more...

...So he jumps an empty boxcar
Beneath the shadowed scar
Of the old Great House,
Where it stands amid

468

The timbered stumps of oaks, magnolias,
Rotting steps, porch rail spokes,
Peeling pillars, broken stairs and base,
Old couch and rusted iron tools
Where once boxwoods and azaleas stood,
And a plundered auto, weed-unruled,
Under the blasted beetle branches
Of wizened, dying apple trees,
Mostly hacked for winter fuel.

The driveway, tulip lined, once-proud,
Is now two rows of stumps, deeply gullied,
Barbed with wire to keep the neighbor's cows
From scattered fields of corn, melons and
An acre of tobacco, non-descript kitchen garden
Unfenced beside the hand-pump, trough,
Next a barn still lined with scythes,
Old rakes and harness plows,
Its roof caved in, a rattlers' nest,
Feral cats and rats and clucking fowl,
A flail upon the threshing floor
And dog biting at its testing mange
In a landscape of the picturesque
That once leached life from a toiling land
Whose blood is clotted yet
Within Virginia's once-rich soil.

Two families live here now,
One upstairs, one below,
The windows paneless,
Chimneys long condemned,
The once-proud cellared brickwork
Cracking, its mortar dusty-drained,
Shutters unpainted, hanging loose,
No screens to taint an outer door,
And the upward balcony framed
With dry rot, beetles, funguses
Where once proud ladies fanned, observed,
Has collapsed, its planking used
To fuel the fires that bind and keep
The spanking winter winds
From mattresses lain on the floor
And children running barefoot down
The cramped and sharded corridors
Where sworded gents once stood
Hand in glove with adoring loves,
Offering punch and julep, lemonade
To belles in crinoline, fine arrayed,
But whose fading pictures are timeless frayed
And cobwebbed in the attic sky,
While all the glory of their past
Is forgot amongst the junkyard plot

And empty-haunted rooms where lie
Old sacks, rusty chairs and pots of paint,
Half-used and dried, but never tossed away.

Only gonna love you,
Never gonna dance...[143]

Did you ever kiss your dreams
And watch them dry away?
Did you ever cry and cry
For your soul to light the day?
I did, once, once...

...but now I'm waiting, waiting...

...As Fred Astaire and Ginger tap and dance,
Swing Time numbers, Bojangle swirl,
Leap and step and elegantly twirl
Our lives from reality to a girl
Who meets a handsome man
And all her troubles smile upon
A world of grace and elegance...

Nothing's impossible, I have found,
For when my chin is on the ground,
I pick myself up,
Dust myself off,
Start all over again.[144]

Waiting for the possible
To return...

...As I scrape and bellow, fume,
Charge my horns and graze, striding
The ways of the buffalo, being
One with his nature, one with all...

...And WindTeller,
Insubstantial horseman of the night,
Moonshine phantom, breath of dewy mist,
Crow's wing upon his hood,
Gallops across the dusty fields
And fades his pallid, bloodless form
Within the wisps of a wind's delay,
As our somber president,
Calling all to fireside chat,
Warns of the worsing, freezing threat
Of the Nazis and the Japanese...

---

[143] *Never Gonna Dance* by Jerome Kern, from the musical *Swing Time*, 1936.
[144] *Pick Myself Up* by Jerome Kern, ditto.

...pick yourself up...

...And dance, dance, until the dawn arises,
Faster now, faster, don't relax, don't stop,
Spin and spin and round and spin
In hypnotic, conjoined trance, until...

...I'm never gonna dance...

A daughter, actress, singer,
Sits before a mirror, lights around,
To apply her thick-laid cream,
Pallid, shiny, smeared to hide
The scars that linger deep inside...

...as we wait and wait and wait...

Is there yet glory and most hopeful rays?

...still no way to dance...

No, not yet, not yet, oracle of the wind,
Not yet.

The trees sigh and autumn colors fall...

Never gonna dance,
Pick yourself up,
Never gonna dance,
Dust yourself off,
Only gonna love you,
Never gonna dance,
Start all over again...

Oh, the dance, oh, the shadow of the dance...
Am I ever gonna dance...?

The poll tax, corruption and intimidation are so effective at keeping black voters
from the election booths that, in the Deep South, only 2.5% of them vote in the
1940 presidential election.

Never gonna dance...

I wrung my hands and I wanted to scream,
I wrung my hands and I wanted to scream,
But when I woke up, I found it was only a dream.

...waiting, waiting, waiting...

...zee-zhiff, zee-zhiff, zee-zhiff.

Book VIII

Up From the Dark:
Whirlwinds of Revolt, 1941-1971

I

I'm dreaming of a white Christmas,
Just like the ones I used to know,
Where the treetops glisten
And children listen
To hear sleigh bells in the snow...

...May your days be merry and bright,
And may all your Christmases be white.[145]

I know not...
Know not whom to blame...

...As I listen to the screaming of the rain,
To the silence of the dream
And to the humming of the trees...

...it begins, it begins...

...When Pearl Harbor explodes
Upon our thrown and reeling heads
Into a raging fire of angered zeal,
And I sign my shaking name,
Mobilized to Pickett, bustling
Brothers scant game for Quantico,
Our wives mustering packers' jobs,
Drillers, inspectors, sweepers
In Radford's powder plant...

...While WindTeller watches from afar
Many thousands more, friends,
Uncles, workmates, cousins,
Sent to Lee and Peary, Hill,
Eustis, Pendleton,
Patrick Henry, still more, even
Bellford's quartermaster store,

---

[145] *I'm Dreaming of a White Christmas*, by Bing Crosby; written by Irving Berlin, a Jew, in 1942.

Training sailors, officers, marines,
Restocking ships at Newport News,
In Hampton Roads, Portsmouth's docks,
And Norfolk's Naval Yards...

...Where a chorus of war sings
In Virginia's ringing ears,
Unfurling this once-coy state
Onto the buoying oceans of the world...

For the times, they are a-changin'...

But not for my lover and I –
Home-front workers
In a Piedmont factory
That weaves nylon parachutes,
She so light, she passes Anglo,
Sewing handles onto ripcords,
While I scrub the toilets, sweep
The factory floor, and peep past
Her swinging entrance doors,
Close enough for entranced glances,
But must endure more racist wiles,
Keep my distance, never talk,
Tho' once a while I sneak a smile,
Mouth a phrase or two, and together
We creep-sneak to enjoy
A guilish, girlish, hidden kiss,
She a harness maker, girl élite
Who sews the risers to the furling lines
Or needles nylon domes,
Triple sewn in homing lines,
And team-explores the seams
Of fabric rips and hemming flaws
Over boxes' beaming lights
– For ours is a secret love,
Dangerous and condemned,
Struck out three times when we were born –
Women, black, and butch and femme...

We are watched and coached
Comfort to our ears, patience, hope,
Allays to our fears, and blows
Of compassion o'er our tears...

Rosie-cheeked riveters all...

...stirring, stirring, stirring...

Dig for Victory! Walls Have Ears!
Your Country Needs You! Save
Gas and rubber, metal, guard

For saboteurs of the arsenal
Of liberty's e'erlasting stand!

Dances at the USO,[146]
Bing Crosby, Cagney, Kay,
Swing bands to trance
Our lonesome nights away…

DiMaggio's fifty-six game hitting streak,
Dumbo, Abbott and Costello,
Gary Cooper's Sergeant York,
Patriotism, and love and valor
In our trepidatious hearts…

Faster, faster than a speeding bullet!
More powerful than a locomotive!
Leaping tall buildings in a single bound!

Though nearly twelve
And able bare to read a word,
I skip school to venture up
The wilds of Cemetery Hill, where,
Amidst the tumbled gravestone guards
Of that lost and lingered war
Fought on Lynchburg's rampart walls,
I shoo away a crippled dog
And lean against a tilted stone
To read *Superman* sixty-one,
Ogling as my hero zooms
Faster than the speed of light
Through barriers of space and might
To trace in looming Krypton's haze
His amazing origins,
Explore his birthing kryptonite,
And defend himself from Lux Luthor,
Schmuck,
Who synthesizes crystals that are green
To painful scream our Man of Steel
In a reeling battle for The American Dream,
Invented in these media years
Of posters, broadcasts for more tearful
Sacrifice for freedom and democracy,
As the overgrown, neglected stones
Stare up from their prone display,
Forgotten memories of another war,
And another curséd day.

Our dreams are stirring,
Courage rising, to fright
The real demons of the night…

---

[146] United Service Organization, which brought performers to entertain the troops.

…For WindTeller watches patiently
As he feels the pulse of beset delay,
While more coal is cut for
Railroads, power stations, factories,
Women pulled to production rows,
Modernizing tractors, plows,
Prices on the rise,
Markets guaranteed, tobacco in demand,
Unemployment halved,
As we are banded up to breeze
The fields and trees of England's south,
To wait and train and wait and train,
Then bob the June-strained Channel seas
And land
'Mid chaos-slaughtered Omaha,
Caught in savage-banked bocage,
To finally uncage with Patton's flank,
Rally at the Bulge,
And tank to final victory
In a thankful, liberated Germany…

…While my brothers atoll battle
The tenacious Japanese,
Suicidal foxholes, tunnel-warrens,
And foreign kamikaze charges
Reaping their crazy toll
At Guadalcanal, Leyte, Iwo Jima,
Okinawa and scores of islands more…

The atomic womb of death…
…can we be forgiven?

…As a riven world goes wild, with
VE Day, then victory o'er Japan,
Ecstatic cheering, trumpet parties,
Snows of bumper ticker-tape,
Singing bells and beliefs, merry
That griefs and stresses are, at last, escaped…

Over 300,000 Virginians join the armed forces in World War II; about 9,000 die.
May they rest in peace and their sacrifice be remembered forever.

II

"Hey boy! What you doin' here?
Get your sorry nigger ass out where
You belong…"

So the black man shuffles off,
Quits the warm, abandoned house

To sneak a bridge to sleep beneath,
A month ago employed, wanted, fit,
But fired so some returning GI Joe,
White, could stow his job away...

Still hounded by the blind dog...

And by the
Four Noes of Backwardness:
No votes, no education,
No towns, no economy...

Deliberately kept that way...

...As over the bridge a family walks,
Three generations, two suitcases,
One place in mind – the bus station
And tickets north to escape
Southern rulers, white, cultured,
Polite in the day, but in the night
Rabid dogs of a racist war that
Salivate at their jaws
The spittle-dribble of spited hate...

How to tell our children,
How to explain?

...striving, striving, we are striving...

...Each alone – I, father, with
My trusting daughter as we sit,
Legs crossed at a bench in the park,
– The only one we are permitted,
Far from the climbing frame,
The "Colored" fountain,
And swings my girl cannot claim.

"Why not, Daddy?" the shiny shoes remark,
"Why can't I glide upon the see-saw,
The slide, or the paddling pool?
Why can't I play over there?"
Her shoes kick against our pew,
In need of care and rusting,
While others in the lunchtime park
Are repainted, slick and new.

I, father, tow her to my knee
To explain the mores of a world
That no young girl could understand,
But that, as she grows, she will need to know:
Waiting rooms roach-infested,
Unfit seats on coach and train,

Alleys where she must remain,
Dark and dowdy, tucked away,
How to wait while whites are served,
Though she deserves the first in line,
How to creep to some rear door
For a dour white boy to seek her order
And return with somewhat she desired
– More often wrong than right,
In some strange, elusive spite –
How not to deplore the shoddy goods,
But learn to smile, accept, curtsy
"Thank'ee sir,"
Lest you be ignored next time,
And labeled "Uppity Nigger"
In unjust reward.

"What does 'nigger' mean, Daddy?"
The shiny shoes kick back.

"That you aren't free,
My daughter dear,
To use those lunch counters,
Restaurants or soda fountains
Allocated to the whites;
That you aren't fit to drink
From their clinking cups or glasses,
To share a source of cooling water,
Aren't fit to pause your weary limbs
Upon their chairs of castlery,
Aren't fit to touch their cutlery
Or presumptive plates and wares,
Aren't fit to walk the shadows
Of the valleys of their cares.

"It means, my daughter dear,
Where you can, you must repair
Up black-shadowed backstairs
Into movie theaters, libraries and clubs
– Those that don't snub you from
A hint of culture that will guide you
To equality with their pride –
Art galleries and theaters,
Museums, zoos, car rallies,
Sports clubs and swimming pools,
Athletics fields and bowling alleys.

"It means, daughter dear,
Giving way on sidewalks,
Tipping your hat, averting eyes,
Talking demurely,
Surely tripping "Massa," "Yessir,"
Answering to "Boy" or "Nigger girl,"

478

Crumbling to the gutter, numbly waiting
For an ambulance that never comes,
Or dying on some distant road
To a hospital that will curse you in,
Vying for a Negro doctor, dentist, nurse,
Your own barber, banker, hearse,
Crying at your select church,
Singing in your select choir,
And lying in your select funeral parlor,
Learning the unspoken laws of the color bar.

"It means, daughter dear,
Playing in this corner of the park
That has no sandpit, no paddling pool,
And that you may only fool around
At baseball games of your race,
Watch football teams tied to their place,
Use tenth-rate, black-shack huts
Or change in bushes way out back;
It means you won't get that job,
Robbed, though you're most qualified,
And even if you do, your wage
Will cage your family
In a penury that's vilified.

"It means, daughter dear,
Sitting in a school that's barely fit
To be a bare broom cupboard,
Let alone a room to learn,
Where the teacher's scarcely paid
And the class is thrice as full
As the white school down the road,
With its library, gym and dining hall;
It means, daughter dear,
You must eat your sandwich
At your twitching, broken bench,
Scratch with chalk upon a slate
And quench your skyward looked desire
With a single subject book,
Greased, dog-eared, torn,
In a forlorn hovel without heat,
Or broil in a beating summer sun;
It means, daughter dear,
Beds you're not fit to snooze in,
Ticket windows you're not fit to cruise,
Colleges you're not fit choose,
Clubs you're not fit to be amused by,
Restrooms you're not fit to use."

"But, Daddy, can't we *just do* those things?
Can't we all share? What have *I* done wrong?
Can't we say that way's no good?

Won't they listen if we explain,
I don't mean no harm, but
Just want a share in their game?"

"My child, it's not that easy;
We strive to fight, to keep our pride,
But get so run down by it all,
By battle after battle,
Scar after scar,
Derided, jarred and hassled,
Until it's not worth it any more
– Best let dogs lie,
Keep to ourselves and let life flee
Free before our captive eyes
– Let things dwell and live our lives
As we were meant to be."

"But Daddy, I don't care,
I don't want to wait,
I want to play on the swing
Straight away –
If you won't take me over there,
I'll take myself – I don't care."

Meanwhile,
The family at the station,
Three generations, brave
The angered glares and taunts
Of "Nigger traitors!" and
"Don't come back!" as
They climb aboard
A Greyhound facing North...

... Where the treetops glisten
And the children listen...

...just like the ones I used to know...

We are stirring, stirring,
Stirring, stirring yet,
From our three centuries of neglect...

...Stirring within the flames of war
– The final cause of our rising
At last within the temporal rays,
As the fleet clock sure begins
Its tick-tock-ticks to that sweet day...

For, though the war is won
And we return from a grace of years
Exposed to near-equality of race,
Liberal England, its democracy

So advanced from seventeen eighty-three,
We are ashamed by our parochial plight,
And that white poverty of soul and charity;
No! We want equal pay,
Education, respect and pride
This day
And are not prepared to reside
In the still-embittered ways of those who,
Even while we fought and died,
Raised the specter of their racial pride,
That black domestics would revolt,
Laborers slack, refuse to work,
In some sick incitement to preserve
Their cranking, crumbling, racist world.

...kicking against the bench...

Although there is now emerging
A questioning of old values, doubt,
This is yet a time of celebration
For those with money, once tied up
In wartime austerity and the need
To reduce affluence to a respectable creed...

...Of Dior's New Look, pageboy hair,
Mid-calf dresses, waistline femininity,
Proud nylons, ballroom gowns, bars and drinking,
Fun down, laughter, music loud,
Jitterbug and big band sounds,
Silks and sequins, wide-brimmed hats,
Buicks, Plymouths, Cadillacs,
Gas cheap again, new highways,
High heels, make-up, sweater girls,
Hayworth, Crawford, Tierney,
And the huge boom in front room radios,
To listen to Milton Berle and Sullivan,
Comedies, contests, cornball series,
The *Abbott and Costello Show*,
Baseball, football, basketball
Back with big names and salaries,
As production booms, new home appliances,
Kitchens, vacuums, 'fridges,
Toasters, blenders, washing machines
Bridging ends to drudgery...

And an organ grinder keeps his song,
Tinkling the wheel of a fateful throng,
His monkey spinning in well-learned leaps
As the handle grinds and the music flocks
To the sound of whirring, whirring clocks...

...tick-tock, tick-tock, tick-tock...

...While a white taxi driver in Arlington,
Outside DC, refuses a ride
To a black doctor, anxious to attend
A premature birth, and breached...

...And a black GI, returning from Japan,
Coaching quietly through Virginia,
Uses a restroom for just too long,
Is shut out by the driver, flips him off,
As he rings the police to kick him hard
And let their batons sing, "Black bastard!"
Again and again and again,
Until he is so grimly beaten, an eye is lost,
And he is permanently blind.

"We gotta keep them uppity niggers down!
Jus' 'cause they been to war
Don't give them no right
To thoughts above their station –
Keep 'em down, I say,
Afore they get used to new
And fancy-pantsy ways!"

Hitler's eugenics laws have been disgraced,
But Virginia's, upon which they were based,
Still remain firmly in place.

– And we'll kill and kill and kill to
Keep it that way!

...kicking, stirring, ticking...

And thus an ancient bigotry
That's abused Virginia's veins
For three hundred ill-gained years
Re-begins, stirred to resist,
Under the wing of Senator Byrd's
Insidious machine,
Willing inheritor of segregation,
An élite's firm grip on social pride,
Through corruption, bribery,
Intense intrigues that most deride, condemn,
And will not partake within –
Elections a mockery, tiny turnouts,
Six percent enough to win
Elections in a sewn-up state,
Where even minor change is viewed
As intensely grim, communist-inspired,
And resistance efforts are stiffly made
To restore the old, pre-war life,
Blacks burnt alive, shot, families
Striven out, diehards of the Klan,

Nazi supporters, now in secret gowns,
Reinvigorating their plans
To incite racial hatred
And drive back the black man down.

At least 4,743 people are lynched in the United States between 1882 and 1968.
Many Southern politicians defend the practice and repeatedly filibuster to prevent
any anti-lynching law from passing Congress. The last attempt occurs in 1949,
and it too is defeated – by, among others, Virginia senators and representatives.

Sometimes it takes a new generation,
Or frustrated outsiders,
Horrified, finally belligerent,
To open the eyes of those
Who refuse to see,
Who accept their suffering
And view it as inevitability.

In 1946, the US Supreme Court overturns a 1930 Virginia law requiring segrega-
tion by rows on bus travel between states, effectively outlawing that practice on
interstate transport; it is still legal *within* states, which causes conflicts and
absurd situations on buses from Virginia to DC.

Finally,
The Federal Government, once consort,
And the Supreme Court, once chief culprit,
Are weighing in,
Less willing to take or tolerate
The South's outrageous ways…

…singing, stirring, ringing, whirring…

…Though yet still
A barbarism haunts this land,
It is at least now seen by more
As a barbarism to deplore…

…As a white reporter from the North,
A television crew, cover
A murder and a rape, racial hatred,
The parrot-mocking trial, endure
Death threats, car windows smashed,
Tires slashed, "Commie nigger lovers!"
As the country hovers in shock
At the cancerous clots it has let
Rot in its Southern heart…

Education in Virginia is the worst in the country; the state has the second-lowest
overall attendance rate, near-highest dropout rate, lowest high-school attendance
rate, near-lowest college attendance rate, and appalling facilities and standards of
teaching. That's for everyone – black and white.

'No education' is deliberate,
A policy to keep us ignorant,
Free of news and views and unions,
To rest instead
Compliant tenants, workers,
Laborers by the low-paid hour...

...But no education means no economy,
As the brightest flee and companies choose
More enlightened destinies...

Within the context of these figures, Southern states spend twice as much on white children as black, four times as much on white school facilities, white teachers receive higher salaries, and virtually no black children get transportation to school.

Yet there is strenuous opposition to improving education, since the backwardness and prejudice it generates are vital to the Byrd Machine's hold on power, even though it means our economy falls further and further behind the rest of the US. A repressed people, as Stalin discovered, cannot compete economically and is bound to fail. But that is precisely the condition of Virginia under the chokehold of the Democratic Party – dramatic failure caused by intense racist oppression. In 1946, yet another of Byrd's protégés, Bill Tuck, is elected governor.

Demagogues and despotic charlatans
Use the methods of communism – its
Repression, racism, show trials,
Controlled media, fixed elections,
Intimidation, rabble-rousing murder,
Inciting fears of alien invasion,
Foreign wars, to keep our people
In a similar-soviet check.

Commissar Byrd...

Then we get old Tuck – Oh Tuck,
Is there enough farmyard muck
To hide the horror of your views?
Integrated star of a Byrd Machine
That rules Virginia's feudal scene,
Commanding votes by commandeering jobs
In statewide courts and county towns,
For the boys to grin and muster results
Precisely how the senator demands.

Some things you do quite well, Tuck –
You raise income tax and gas
To pay at least a little more
For school buses, education, health;
You rein in prison flogging, long o'erdue,
De-phase chains on enprisoned gangs,
– A reform passed elsewhere long before –
And try to cut bureaucracy,

Though Anti-Byrd soon stymies that;
But when it comes to us, the people,
Sick of prejudice, still more ignored,
Of poverty wages, dispossession
Of our most basic civil rights,
You *de facto* ban state workers' strikes,
Recruit us to the state militia,
Force through an act called "Right to Work"
That denies decent wages and conditions,
Seize state utilities to break our protests,
Freeze closed shops and take our union's role,
And, with Byrd to thwart democracy,
Demand that Virginia no more elects
The nation's president, but instead
Holds a Democratic caucus to select him
– An outrage so outrageous it provokes
Statewide horror, fistfights, protests,
And forces you to scurrying, styward flight.

Virginia politics continue as before, despite hopes of change inspired by victory in the war. The fraudulent use of absentee ballots stuffed into infamous 'black satchels' is so prevalent that a judge declares one election to have "the purpose of seeing that no election vices be left undone." In 1945, after one 'stolen' primary in south-west Virginia, where 24 ballot lists go 'missing,' another judge overturns the result, stating that the offending county is "impregnated with political crooks and ballot thieves" – which just about sums up the entire Democratic Party during this period.

Under the sweeping vagrancy law,
A tenant family, homeless, thrown
Upon the lanes of Pittsylvania
By tractors and automated harvesters,
Is harassed, arrested, jailed, moved on,
Mother, father, daughters, son…

…While The Horseman, caped in gray,
Branches wrapped upon his head,
Black-masked vision eyes that peer,
Strives his sinewed reins away
And gallops towards old Harrisonburg,
Where a line outside a movie theater
Sees *The Best Years of Our Lives*,
An inspiring, tear-jerk, post-war look
At soldiers returned from years of fear,
Enduring haunted, sacrificial minds
– Nobodies who come from glory's fields
To nothing – no wife, no home,
Nor prospect of a decent life…

…And something resonates deep within,
Some desire to force a thorough change,
To no longer deny our blighted truth,

But face up to segregation's lies
So we may defend, next time, with honest breath,
The democracy we have so long been told
Is the sacred possession of our brave land.

…Kicking, kicking, yes –
We are learning to kick against
The stench of our segregated bench…

A train rumbles the Clinchfield line
Through Freemont, Stratton, Nora, down
The valley of McLure, sounding slow
Through Dante, center of aspiring company,
Of coal and track and engine fire,
Its tiny, valleyed renter town,
Lines of cramped and smoky homes,
Damp lines in strong community,
With schools, post office gossip-filled,
Theater, hospital, a commissary
That fear less production now
The war is won and demand has slowed
For its coal-producing sanctuary…

…While ex-GIs, in education,
Go back to school to learn new skills,
Raise qualifications and buy new homes
In the all-white suburbs poking up
In Richmond, DC, Norfolk,
Bristol, Arlington and Roanoke...

As a tulip trees springs its cups,
Yellow, green, tinged in fragrancy,
To the glory of the sun…

And a swallowtail, chrysalis
Dead-twig furled, curled within
A twisted soul, black-brown, crusty-frayed,
Breaks free, emerges, wet-singed,
To shiver-stand on bended threads,
New vigor pumping embedded wings,
As it prepares to flutter up and merge
With the tens and hundred thousand souls
Of butterflies surging to the chiming,
Winging beats of a bolder time…

Is you is, or is you ain't ma' baby?
The way you're acting lately makes me doubt,
You'se…is still my baby, baby,
Seems my flame in your heart's done gone out.[147]

---

[147] *Is You Is, Or Is You Ain't (Ma' Baby)*, by Billy Austin and Louis Jordan, 1944.

And I feel like walkin' – yes I do!
I feel like walkin' – yes!
I feel like lyin'
I feel like lyin' down... [148]

The Byrd Machine is so outrageously undemocratic and bears such animosity
towards the liberal wing of the national Democratic Party that in 1948 it tries to
keep Truman's name off the presidential ballot in the state, until a storm of
protest forces it to retreat. Four years later, its delegation is nearly barred from
the Democratic Convention for refusing to promise that its presidential candidate
would appear on the ballot in Virginia.

"Hey, boy, here's a nickel,
Take these bags up to my suite,
Turn down the sheets,
Air the rooms,
And give a once-over with the broom..."

I feel like lyin'
I feel like lyin' down...

Oh, but keep us blinded with the myth of ease,
Of The American Way –
And sing us all White Christmases,
As our dreams are missing
Every other beat...

III

Oh blues, I wanna have a little talk with you
Yeah now blues, I wanna have a little talk with you... [149]

With bended backs we grab
Armfuls from the Brunswick sand,
And bundle vines of tumbreled shells,
Dug, inverted by the tractor
That leaves them lying in their rows
For us to stack and pole,
Push down, wrap around,
Eight-feet high,
And let them black and wither-rot,
Under besotted days of August heat,
Then hitch the harvest sled to mules,
Load the vines and poles
And drag them back, pitchfork on,
Shake upon the belt, then break within
An ancient, groaning harvester,

---

[148] *Flyin' Airplane Blues* recorded by Blind Man Fuller, 1938; author unknown.
[149] *Conversation with the Blues* recorded by Big Bill Broonzy, 1941.

To wrack the nuts from tendril tails,
Stack the waste into bales,
As fresh-shelled nuts are spittled down
Into large-packed hessian sacks,
Tops sewn, ladened and tractor-towed
To the drying sheds, great billows
Of blowing, warming air, drying,
Shelling out the crop...

...While, in a distant field, beyond
The racket reel of belts and wheels,
The stink of diesel, gasoline,
And smoke winnowing in the dust,
A new Benthall-Windrow combine
Marches up and down the peanut rows,
Bulktank on its top, no need to pole
Or sled-board mule, no need to shake
Or bale or careful watch, four men
Where we use ten,
Turning over long-grown nuts,
Exposing
An underworld to dewy light
Of a morning sun that makes
Us wonder what new dawning is
About to shake us in its throw.

Yeah now blues, why don't you give poor Bill a break?
Yeah now blues, why don't you give poor Bill a break?

And I feel like walkin' – yes I do!
I feel like walkin' – yes!

Then WindTeller watches as
A recruiter
For a Detroit auto firm, quietly
Linger-saunters sidewalk planks
Of a black community, whispering
– Lest the sheriff overhears and
Arrests him, beats him, packs him home –
To all he passes on the street
Where to meet, the time and place,
Transportation paid, job guaranteed,
And, next morn, the place is gone,
– Grandpaws, Mommas, kids an' all –
Northward, saved from Southern greed...

...As nearby, in a Boydton hall,
Between cues and black-filled laughter,
Lights shining down on baize and balls,
We slip secret sips of rye and gin
And side bet on the slide and win
Of pool and cards and other fruit

Strange to our sight and taste...

...For the sun shines, too,
Its honesty on
Those
Who replace our need with theirs...

...our dreams postponed...

...tick-tock, tick-tock, tick-tock...

Are we there yet, Daddy? Are we there?

1947 marks the start of the Cold War. Truman creates the Federal Employees
Loyalty Program, the CIA, the Department of Defense, Joint Chiefs of Staff and
National Security Council. A year later, he brings back the draft. In the first
major UFO scare, newspapers report over 1,500 sightings of 'flying discs.'

And so another process of reaction starts,
Corking up our bottled anger
And our work for change...

...As the UN Security Council ascends,
Iron Curtain descends,
And East Germany, Albania, Poland accede
To terrored communist control
And the Reds in broken China
Increase their choking hold...

...To provide renewed excuse
To abuse a domestic fear
And preside
Over severe laws and regulations
To stop our slide to liberal views...

...And so do the
Impossible
Optimism and silliness
Of movies on defense against
Nuclear war, such as the hack
Survival Under Atomic Attack
Advising we store water, cans and batteries,
Throw mattresses over windows,
Hide under cardboard, stairs,
Fallout shelters made of tin,
Blast assessment, ducking drills
Misleading terrored children
About medicines and our chance
To survive a human holocaust
That would reap the winter of our lives.

...tick, tick, tick...

Rising credit, debt and spending...

Are we there yet, Daddy? Are we there?

And Linkum holds a stopwatch in his hands,
Dancing down the lanes, laughing
As he juggles feathered hat and cane,
Brer Rabbit fiddling by his side
As they snicker at our hubris and our pride...

...For there is a crisis in our psyche – old
Puritanical values, of thrift and careful spending,
Cracking under the sizzle of the new
Hot commercial buzz of marketing...

...Of *It's a Wonderful Life*, of hostile
Red Scare, trials at Nuremberg,
How Much is that Doggie in the Window?,
Communist insurgency, infiltrators,
Bing Crosby glowing, Bob Hope flowing,
Kerouac spinning down his road
Of Beats and counter-culture Zen,
HUAC and the Hollywood Ten,
Hank Williams, Sinatra, bebop, jive,
Nuclear bombs and o'erreaching speeches,
FBI and other leeches,
An austere abyss of Chinese war,
Jerry Lewis, Martin, Marilyn,
John Wayne braving it on the chin,
Accentuating the positive,
As fear screams in our ears...

...for we are a cowered society...

...Just like the Jewish boy,
Walking home from school,
Who is confronted by four Anglo youths,
Taunted for his darkish skin,
Firm nose, accented lips and reluctance
To join with them in tormenting others,
As leering turns to anger, then to fear,
And he is pushed, then pushed again,
And, in his passivity, they push him more,
Grab his books, pull off his bag,
Dash him to the ragged ground,
Where they kick and kick and kick,
Until vomiting blood turns them sick
And they flee their scene of courage
Back to their parents' sanctuary
Of bigoted remarks and memory,
And next day leave their cage again,
This time to let
Some nigger slake their rage.

Yeah now blues, why don't you give poor Bill a break?

   ...tick, tick, tick...

People begin to hoard supplies in case of war, rationing and shortages. Fallout shelters are included as part of home construction and schools conduct regular duck and cover drills against nuclear attack.

> The aliens are coming! Men from Mars!
> War of the Worlds! Two worlds collide!
> – But only whites are deemed fit to fly
> To the planet of our dreams...

From 1948-50, most of Truman's Fair Deal is obstructed by Congress; the Chinese Communists take power and invade Tibet; NATO is set up; and Fuchs is caught sending nuclear secrets to the Soviet Union, which tests its first atom bomb.

   ...tick, tick, tick...

In 1950, The Korean War takes more Virginians to distant shores, most of whom cannot vote before they go, nor when they return.

   ...tick, tick, tick...

Meanwhile, Truman orders the development of the hydrogen bomb; Senator Joseph McCarthy insists that the Department of State is filled with communists; Orwell writes *Nineteen Eighty-Four*; Dorothy Parker, Danny Kaye, and Edward G. Robinson are named in an FBI report; Pete Seeger is indicted and folk guitars become a sign of un-American activities.

   ...tick, tick, tick...

Virginia is gradually dragged out of its isolation. Unable to change itself, external forces start to change her from outside when, in 1950, the Supreme Court undermines segregation in college education and train dining cars, especially the notion of "separate but equal." It does this in three landmark cases: *Sweatt vs Painter*, *McLaurin vs Oklahoma State Regents* and *Henderson vs United States*.

   ...tick, tick, tick...

In 1951, the US government begins nuclear testing and military exercises for nuclear war in the Nevada desert and greatly expands its nuclear arsenal; a year later, it detonates "Mike," the first hydrogen bomb. Meanwhile, the nation follows the trial of Ethel and Julius Rosenberg.

   ...tick, tick, tick...

In 1952, Virginia finally ratifies the 14th Amendment, giving women the vote (women have voted in the state, but it's taken until now for a very reluctant white male élite to formally stomach this aspect of the 20th century).

   ...tick, tick, tick...

And Linkum tries to rewind
Our clock of a thousand years,
To smash it, drown it, jump upon
Its everlasting glass,
For he fears
Those who wish to turn it back,
And will maim and bomb and kill
To impose their terrifying will
To do just that…

I hear the rain,
Ticking, dripping…

…tick, tick, tick…

…As fears of communist infiltration
And un-American activities
Grips hysterical heights, attacking
Government employees, film stars, writers
In a scare of red-baiting intensity,
With memos and confessions, witnesses
And anonymous investigations,
Vetting people with no right
To testify nor clear their names,
Innuendo, supposition, subversion
Of civil rights insane decried by
That false mask of democracy –
A ranting McCarthy waving lists,
Shouting down witnesses, shaking fists,
In scenes as defiled as Nazi trials –
All to repress that leftward swing
The War To End All Wars has helped to bring
Upon us and our country…

Oh, superstition rules so many lives,
Within the sickly cots of fear –
The more extreme our dear beliefs,
The more extreme our dear belief
In goblin-potioned enemies…

There is a wall across America,
An arbored veil of silence,
A curtain of conspiracy, tracing
Mason-Dixon, south of which
Lurks a single-party state, police
Expressed through bullwhips, jails and dogs,
From where escape is only possible
In the slink of moonless night,
Along hidden paths and subterfuges,
News controlled, media throttled,
Opposition beaten, maimed and murdered,
No freedom tolerated, no votes,

No unions, marches, speech
Free enough to condemn
This
Swamp of a thousand lies....

...While Brer Savior and Our Linkum
Dance along the lane,
Tripping to the dripping sounds of
Our softly-teared refrain...

Meanwhile, the Byrd Gyration,
Through its many slimy machinations,
Carves up spending on our schools,
Unions and electoral reform,
Counting pennies as Virginia starves,
Conspiring uninspiring ballots,
Turnouts kept deliberate low,
Strident, arrogant, self-contained,
Republicans ordained nationally
– Never liberal northern Democrats –
And setting the scene most shamedly
For vicious McCarthy lies,
– For which he is much to blame.

And yes, Byrd, you *are* to blame,
For, from such rabid hatred as you provoke
Is born, and close akin,
The constant-bullied intimidating
Of segregation, KKK and lynching,
Oppressing thought and resistance
To outright wrong, constantly
Disempowering, holding down,
Instituting a moral fear
That has toiled three hundred years
On Virginia's executed soil...

...I hear the rain dripping on the bones...

...And I hear the Callings sing
Around the fire, glistening
The surface of the lake, stars
And moon reflecting hopes
Of our ancestral souls, as they pray
For us
In the dark before the light...

In 1953, the communists in East German suppress an abortive workers' uprising, the Korean War ends in stalemate and the CIA overthrows Mossadegh in Iran. A year later, it overthrows the popular government of Guatemala, which is handing vast United Fruit plantations to its impoverished peasantry. That year, Nautilus, the first nuclear submarine, is commissioned, a hydrogen bomb is tested on Bikini Atoll, and the 'domino theory' is expounded.

I hear the rain dripping on the bones
Of my solitary heart...

...tick, tick, tick...

And I feel like walkin' – yes I do!
I feel like walkin' – yes!

May your days be merry and bright,
And may all your Christmases be white...

IV

Tick, tick, tick...

Are we there yet, Daddy? Are we there?

Who am I? Who am I? Who am I?

Am I still dreaming? Am I? Am I?

Who cares who I am, for
America's now atop the world –
Its hope and its savior!

I am Momma,
Pregnant for the third time,
GI husband home and set,
Cheap mortgage, easy debt,
Who polishes her electric range, entranced
By Perry Como on the radio
As a salesman drops by happenstance,
Escapes her from her gloomy props
And sells her dusters, brushes and a broom...

As the organ grinder's winding on his solitary tune...

I am that salesman too,
Selling house-to-house
Toasters, washers, refrigerators,
Fitted kitchens, mowers,
New hopes and desires, as
Adverts, sales and marketing
Manufacture dreams, conform
Us to a new reality, defined
By jingles, tunes and puffs of smoke
From the magician's sleight of hand...

I am democracy, I am
Liberty, I am honeyed Christianity,

And I am a dream of money – lots of it!

Yet the price of my dream
Is the reality that
I strive six days for another,
Spend mere one for myself,
And have thirty minutes just to spend
Each tender nightly life
With my trusted kids and wife…

…tick, tick, tick…

Get me out of here! Get me out of here!

Oh, cast the bones of present follies
To faith's ancestored realm,
And sing the song of severed praises
To the man who names the man I am.

For, I ask again: Who am I?

Am I just American?
Or also Irish, Swedish, Arabian?
White, Black, Native American?
Italian, Hispanic, Cuban?
Christian, Buddhist, Muslim,
Baptist, Catholic, Jew?

So many races, religions, beliefs –
A rainbow of hopes and doubts,
Lives left behind and uplifted griefs…

What does it even mean to be American?
Do I look to the whole for my safety,
For my comfort and my culture?
For my partner and my family?
Or do I fear the whole,
Fear the streets I do not know,
Neighborhoods to never venture,
Cultures that do not greet me,
Some faith I cannot live by, nor respect
– Ideologies that terrify?
And what will it take to break me free
From the myopia of my individuality
And feel at one with every distant chord –
Flag and anthem?
Lord and country?
"In God We Trust"?
White House? Presidency?
Or something else,
Closer to the reality
Of freedom's harsh complexity –

Something bearing more
Than scant-veiled testimony
To inner-city life, the strife
Of unemployment, racism's
Relentless droning song,
Worthless wages, hours long,
Exhaustion, poverty,
Or desperate, single-parent prophecy
That drags us *all* below the line?

...oh, the bones, the bones...

The bones echo to the cauls
Of our ancestors' weeping walls
And at the Four Enchanters on their rock
Beneath the towering gorge
Of the rushing Roanoke, there to sing
The songs of joys and sufferings,
Ol' Hick, Dylan, Greenwood
And Morgan Diviner of the world...

...oh, the bones, the bones, the bones...

I believe one America will emerge
From community and family,
A joint merging of responsibility –
Not individual screams of property,
Nor the constant stress of work and work,
Destroying self and spouse and child,
Plunging to horrendous debt
The more we strive and more we get –
No, I believe it will arise
From sharing, caring, interbeing,
And mutual-powered dependency.

Give us control upon our lives,
Our work, our cities and our state,
For only when they're our true fate,
Not the myopic domain of a few
– When the weak are well-protected,
Schooling more than prison life,
Old age more than poverty,
Skin more than prejudice,
Potential more than inheritance,
And those who do *not* succeed
Are cared for as much as those who do,
Will we have that caring heart
To give soul to this great nation
And knell the bells of victory
In this great historic commonweal.

A polio vaccine is discovered in 1953 and vaccinations begin in 1954, the year of
Brown vs Board of Education, in which the Supreme Court declares segregation

496

in schools to be unconstitutional. While this is *not* the end of segregation, by far, it does mark the strongest victory yet in a war that will take another twenty years to win. Virginia politicians rapidly denounce the decision, vow to resist it, and start to see the 'Earl Warren' Supreme Court, finally free of the shackles of Southern segregationists, as a profound enemy.

    Suddenly we see
    An explosion in schoolage culture,
    Money in our pockets, *Seventeen*,
    Bebop, rhythm and the blues,
    Records, dances, jukebox bars,
    Soda fountains, cigarettes, cars and stars
    For those most willing to rebel.

*   The things I see about me, the big things and the small,*
*   The little corner newsstand and the house a mile tall,*
*   The wedding in the churchyard, the laughter and the tears,*
*   The dream that's been a-growin' for a hundred and fifty*
*   years.*[150]

    …And the beginnings of a counter-culture too,
    Of *Glass Menageries* and streetcars
    Named *Desire*, Brando *On The Waterfront*,
    And the silent death of a salesman
    In his tragic loss of soul…

Them, a movie starring terrifying mutant ants, scares the pants off America and Brando scares them even more in *The Wild One*. The next year, James Dean hits the screens in *Rebel Without a Cause* and *East of Eden*, while Glenn Ford and Sidney Poitier star in *Blackboard Jungle*.

    Oh, you are my desire…

    …For a tract home, free
    From inner-city poverty,
    And for an office job,
    White collar, suit and tie,
    Driveway, lawn, bar within the lounge,
    Swimming pool and barbecue,
    Martinis, a carafe of friends,
    Where all is the same, regulated, safe,
    Ozzie and Harriet,
    Conforming in our mutual rise
    To a uniformity that is comforting,
    Eases the worry of depression, war
    And threats from overseas
    In the tranquility of knowing
    This day will be just like the last,
    Tomorrow a replica of the past,
    And we need not be aware, nor care

[150] *The House I Live In*, by Frank Sinatra, written by Robinson and Allen, 1945.

About any but our family.

However, our children,
In fledgling beats of rebellion,
Are letting down their hair,
Greasing it, coiffing it,
In a growing air of prosperity;
They want more, are guiltless
About the desire to spend,
No memories of war nor want,
And reject
Conformity, as they seek
Life and fun and rebellious truth
With fresh heroes for fresh youth.

"Children should be seen and not heard."
"This is my house, so you'll do as I say."
"If you don't like it, you know what you can do."
"If you don't like my rules, then go live somewhere you can make your own."
"It's my way or the highway."
"I'm not keeping you here. The door's open. You can leave whenever you want."
"Is this how you repay our sacrifice?"

Subservience as respect,
Silence as good manners,
Lust between the sheets called love,
As we tremble in mismanaged fear,
Or rebel in anger and disgust.

Oh, is you is, or is you ain't my baby?
Is you is, or is you ain't
America to me?

We *will not* obey…

There has been throughout our history
A deep struggle for tolerance,
Acceptance, inclusion,
That we are *all* beliefs, *all* communities,
That everyone's ideals are equal
And we have no right to impose
One morality upon another…

…And those who oppose such views
Are little less
Than KKK without the robes…

I slip quietly, nightly upon the landing…

…And hear laughter between twin beds,
The end applause of

498

The Ed Sullivan Show
Masking the willful stairs,
Aware they will soon say
Their goodnights and roll
Their separate ways,
As I cajole the silent kitchen door,
Careful close the screen,
Ease along the porch and race
Across the lawn to Freddie's Chevy,
Heavy kiss and slide off merrily,
To accelerate away, revving, radio blazed,
Bill Haley, Jerry Lee,
To a dazéd party at a friend's
Of rum and cokes and daiquiris,
Barbiturates, amphetamines.

Why Johnny Can't Read, The Family of Man
Or *The Power of Positive Thinking?*
Sexual Behavior in the Human Female,
This I Believe or *The Holy Bible (Revised Version)?*

New insight into our lives, desires,
Children, partners, families,
New impetus to succeed, or
Reflections on why we don't –
A time of search and doubt,
Not mere prosperity and fun,
But questioning of our lives and those
We weary left behind…

A time of new mythologizing,
Redefining America in brash fresh terms
Of dreams
And righteous proclamation…

Oh, the calling of the bones!

Call us! Call us! Call us!

I see a funeral file of limousines,
Manufactured wreaths, designer suits,
Dresses from Chanel, a polished box,
Gilted handles, bouquets
Not self-made with purpose or with
Memoried pain, but cold
Ordered from the florist's,
Sandblasted tombstones
Made from stencils by machine,
Plastic churches, tannoyed hymns
Production lines of ceremony
– Where once we buried our own
In simple, sistered harmony.

Don't give up on us!

Each age, it seems,
Is faced with some particular morality
It must piece into design,
And is defined by its success –
So what is ours?
And will the oracle of our futured lives
Downdress us too harshly?

Ancestors! We will follow you –
One day, we will listen!

Oh, the destiny of our dreams!
– For once upon a time they
Flew with us
Beyond
The horizons of success, but
They have failed to adapt
To the high-pitched desecration
Of our slow-paced paradise.

And who will cry "Enough!"?

Not I, not I, not I…

Then we must listen to the Callers' cry:
"Let us care, let us care!
Let us live together,
And let us care!"

The singer sings and the drummer plays
And the fiddler sparks the night,
Their spirits waft across the notes
And ask, for a hundredth time,
When will darkness become the light?
When will it become the light?

I am still dreaming,
Dreaming still…

…of voices, voices of the veils…

And the callings of all suffering
From the whispers of the vales…

…tick, tick, tick…

Oh, is you is or is you ain't
America to me?
Is you is or is you ain't
My faint dream's soft memory?

V

On a hot July the Fourth
The skies are star-ripped alive
With brocaded bombs and jiving rockets,
Ferris turns, sugar candy smiles,
Coconut shies, darts and hoops and BB guns,
In the loud wheeze and scream and dashing styles
Of a fairground's pleasing crowds...

Ah, life is good – and always will be,
As we get richer, richer
Year after year after year...

...and this year's model is nineteen-fifty-zee...

At a damp and starry drive-in,
Moonlite Theatre, Abingdon,
A boy slots his father's Cadillac
Onto the rearmost ramp, and his girl
Chucks off her hidden blanket,
Climbs to the seat in front
As he unlocks the surprised trunk
To let his best friend out.
Then the three press on a button
For the intercom, order burgers,
Popcorn, dogs and fries,
The car hop roller skating over
To hang a speaker on the door
As smells of griddle, concession stands
Rise through the loud-pitched evening air,
And they swoon below a towering screen
To the thrills and terrors of
The Creature From the Black Lagoon...

...Marilyn in *The Seven Year Itch...*

...Marlboro Country...

...Playboy...

...Peyton Place...

Oh, is you is or is you ain't America to me?

...While,
Within a West Point barber's,
Away from prosperous mansions
At the sacred-stanchioned confluence
Of Pamunkey and Mattaponi,
On the shrill and dusty highway
Linking Richmond to Saluda,

Loaded trucks of shot-gun trees,
The drifting aroma of a paper mill,
'Mid cars and wheezing traffic,
Men congregate to talk and wait
Their chance to diss the government
And conditioned segregation,
Wondering if there still ain't time
To stop the huge explosion coming,
If whites don't change their line…

…As SelfSearch wanders high the mountain
To find a hollow glade,
There to sit beneath the sun
And grade a circle with a bone,
Light a fire and circle round,
Chanting to the lonely skies
About that loss of soul behind
Those fleeting, crying eyes
Of a generation escaped
From not enough to eat…

To meet where gypsies play down in that dim café
And dance till break of day – that's my desire.[151]

A peanut farmer
With a booming crop
Buys twenty acres from his neighbor,
Who is selling up to journey north,
And has just enough to buy a mule
From the fuel and general store,
Rents new tools, a second plow,
And will let his youngest,
Sixteen now,
Rein it by himself next spring.
For life is good!
My eldest home from Germany,
He has been to college, bought a house,
And works for a mid-west company
Selling vacuums door-to-door,
With enough to give my wife
One for our brand-new carpet floors.

Oh yes, life is good!
At our suburban home
In burgeoning Virginia Beach,
For my peach of a man,
Gunner on a Norfolk cruiser
Sends me enough each month
To buy more gadgets,
Linoleum for the kitchen floor,

---

[151] *That's My Desire*, by Frankie Laine, 1947; written by Loveday/Kresa, 1931.

Better Homes and Gardens,
A coffee maker, gramophone
To sing along with Bing
And Armed Forces Radio;
I even have new bouffant hair
And a pert new gingham skirt
To flirt with Sis and her old man,
Who earns for Hoover in Ohio,
Toiling vacuums door-to-door,
While we burn the midnight oil
On some Friday bandstand floor.

The house I live in, a plot of earth, a street,
The grocer and the butcher, and the people that I meet...

Oh yes, life has turned indeed!

Hey there cats, don't be square!

From a southwestern factory shop
That manufactures furniture,
I truck a load of tables, cupboards, chairs
In my new cab, heater, radio,
A pulldown bed behind my head,
To stop upon my Shenandoah way
To see my family and
Our newly settled singlewide
Within a well-abided trailer park
'Neath Paris Mount, Montgomery,
Get on my powered Harley,
Slide down a glass, listen to the game,
Return to burn a barbecue,
Thick slabs of steak, coleslaw, creamed
Potatoes, chilied beans,
Buy my kids a trampoline,
New Kodak for my wife, with film
To capture every scene,
And call my father on the phone
Shouted in from tractor-spraying
His new-sown peanut rows.

Meanwhile, families drift to a potluck
In the heat of a Salem sun,
Pork, spare ribs and sucking sauce,
Macaroni, yams, popcorn of course,
Our church a thoughtful sanctity
Within this anxious world...

As, in some southwestern Pulaski place,
Workers saw and mill, cut and drill,
Measure, glue and trace around
Beams and joists and wooden sills

To preform, ready softwood make
The panels, floors and timbered walls,
The roofs and doors and window frames
For ten thousand hopeful bursting homes
Erected on a myriad plains
Thirsting o'er Virginia's towns.

Aloft across the state's wide wings,
An electrician inspects the props
Of a Cessna, runway bound,
While the radio plays and in he drops
A gasket, belt and six new plugs,
Then hears the siren blast for lunch,
Lugs down his ricket ladder,
Wipes hands and fast rejoins
His fellows in the slight canteen
As low-skilled workers all,
Sweepers, cleaners, gather-stall
And linger by a hanger door
Listening to *their* radio,
Separate tuned,
Laughing at a DJ's jokes,
Calling boogie-woogie blues,
And visioning a Friday night
At their billiard hall.

You know, my temperature's risin'... [152]

Are we there yet, Daddy? Are we there?

The jukebox's blowin' a fuse...

Daaadddddyyyyyyy....!

Saturday night and I just got paid,
I'm a fool about my money, don't try to save,
My heart says, "Go, go, have a time,"
Saturday night and I'm feelin' fine.

I'm gonna rock it up, who-oo-ee
Rip it up,
I'm gonna shake it up,
Gonna ball it up,
I'm gonna rock it
And ball tonight. [153]

A teamster, hauling four-by-fours
From Buchanan mill to a Loudon 'burb,
Tunes his radio too, also taps his feet,

---

[152] *Roll Over Beethoven*, by Chuck Berry, 1956.
[153] *Rip It Up* by Little Richard; lyrics and music by Blackwell and Marascaico, 1956.

Then slows to the flagman flagging
At an intersection near-complete
For a new, four-lanéd interstate,
The bulldozers, earth movers
Covering, leveling, filling firm,
As a drill of trucks await, crawling
Towards the rising berm.

And in the distance blows a whistle,
Warning traffic at the railroad crossings
To hurry-hustle quick across,
As twin engines grind a line
Of coal from western mines
For lowland power stations
Refueling Virginia's boom.

I'm gonna rip it up, who-oo-ee...

One who waits is a truck that idles
Proudly lettered siding signs,
A carpenter, fulltime employed
On new townhouses, framed, pre-designed,
And assembled at the building site
On brick pillars, standard set
With steel sinks, bathrooms, kitchens fixed,
Electric lights and socket walls,
Three bedrooms and a porch installed,
Screen doors, boilers, oilcloth floors,
Driveways, gardens front and back,
Fenced, with seeded lawn and garage too,
Indeed –
All the conveniences of suburban need.

In one house, recently complete,
Its drive fresh laid, flowers not yet displayed,
A hairdresser rinses the dripping curls
Of a wife and mother,
Husband on some business trip,
Elastic kids screaming on the lawn
In a blown-up paddling pool, half-filled,
With hose and plastic guns,
Hoola hoops, bikinis, coonskin caps,
The dog barking, TV on,
Watching soaps without attention,
Reading *Redbook* and *McCall's*,
As the woman towels her new-dyed hair,
Then props her up and begins to snip
At the bleached peroxide locks,
Roots, once brown, now blonde;
Bored, she reports her dreamed-of house,
The leisured life, but
Is clearly sad she's left her friends,

Her shopping trips, the kids' old school,
Forty phonecall miles away,
And is glad to clip a foolish day
By nodding to the stylist's gossip…

I'm gonna rip it up, who-oo-ee…

You know, my temperature's risin'…

Next door, another wife, also ignored,
Drops her *Life*, melancholy, bored
Of Cold War and red-scare hype,
Sputnik and Explorer 1,
You Can Survive shelter plans,
Trouble fussing on Montgomery bussing,
A-bomb, H-bomb, China and Korea,
And ponders a book she has just bought,
Look Younger, Live Longer,
Thinks of coffee, but instead,
Wanders behind the household bar,
Slink-clinks a gin, one rock of ice,
And resits to file her fingernails,
Then rifles through a fashion mag
At Dior and Givenchy,
To sigh away another dragging day…

My heart says, "Go, go, have a time,"
And my soul keeps singing the blues…

One of her daughters, a teenager now,
Works at the Woolworth's counter
Plating breakfasts, lunches – just to whites,
While the rest of the knick-knack store
Keenly accepts *all* greenbacks,
No matter origin or color,
Though one clerk always wipes her hands
After a Negro tends her cash,
And gripes she doesn't wish be seen
Dealing with the common unclean…

The jukebox's blowin' a fuse…

The other daughter, Elena, is at school,
In her senior year, and she
Gleefully scats from class to grass,
Squats excited with the other cats,
Discusses what to wear, where to go,
Which hip drive-in flick to miss
As she back-row hugs and roughly kisses,
Then agrees to meet at Joe's on Main
And rushes off to make the bus
That will drive them swiftly cussing past

Black kids from the county school,
Who must walk or carpool home.
Once back, she raids the fridge,
Digs at ice-cream, home-made,
Runs to her private room upstairs
And blasts her radio way up loud,
As Bill Haley crowds the house,
Jerry Lee strolls a spell,
Little Richard ramps it up,
And Chuck Berry lets it roll…

You know, my temperature's risin'
The jukebox's blowin' a fuse…

Homework skipped,
Friends phoned, confirmed,
Mom grinning, sipping gin,
Red Skelton on the box,
A packet of pills by her side
To keep her smile from suicide,
She reheats a meal, takes a coke,
Sits and silent broods, then
Stokes her dishes in the washer,
Dashes up to change her clothes,
Bobby socks and nylon mesh,
Cinch belt, scarf and petticoats,
Blouse and polkadotted skirt,
Saddle shoes to varnish her effect,
Then hies across to Emilie's,
Her father home, always slack
To drive into town and back again.

My heart's beatin' rhythm
And my soul keeps singing the blues;
Roll over Beethoven
And tell Tchaikovsky the news…

From the Main Street soda fountain,
Floats and malts and lemonade,
A jaded jukebox in the corner,
The guys arrive, joking, equal smart,
Flat top hairstyles, dancing shoes,
Kieran in his parents' Zodiac,
And cackle off to evening view
From Here to Eternity in a drive-in row,
Close the windows, park at back,
Order root beers, then smooch and fondle,
Near-to-sex in back seat dark, lipstick locking,
Windows steaming, chassis rocking,
Girls as anxious as the boys
For new sensations, be with it, hip,
Not be square, but flip the risk,

Be moody, brusque, make James Dean,
Reject their elders' Fifties' ways
Of straight-laced jobs, respectable days,
And hidden, in-house hypocrisy
Of drinking, fights and infidelity...

Oh, beat, beat, beathovin'
To the beat of segregated feet
As our temperature's rising...

On the way from segregated movie
To segregated dance, they stop for gas;
An old black man walks slow across,
Is nasty told to fill her up, ordered,
Obeys without a word,
Wipes the hazy windshield and the lights,
Two packs of Camels from the store,
Is tip ignored, then lets them rip,
Laughing, radio blasting loud,
To the Friday hop in a downtown hall,
One line for whites and one for blacks,
Five toilets clean, one of tacky grime,
One full counter, one tiny hatch,
As the band, all black,
Trumpets, drums and tenor sax,
Guitars and singer, chorus girls,
Latch onto that rockabilly sound
As colors, roped apart, joined in soul,
Jive the midnight chimes
And, hot and sweaty, hive into a night
Of fathers waiting to take some home,
While others have to walk their way
To a distant side beyond the tracks,
With no lights to guide them back,
No pavéd roads, no garbage canned,
No bus stops, restaurants or stores maintained,
And where no taxis ever stray...

...As a brown myotis bat
Zips and flits in moths,
Mosquito clicks and clips
'Tween myrtles and magnolias
Of the richer tended gardens of
The wealthy white élite.

Oh, roll over Beethoven
And tell Tchaikovsky the news,
'Cause I'm gonna rock it up,
Rip it up,
Shake it up,
Ball it up good tonight.

Meanwhile,
Across the Chesapeake's sweaty mouth,
On the salty eastern shore,
Log canoes and deadrises explore
Oyster beds for Cape Charles factories
That steam and can the flourishing trade,
Though catches are diminished now,
While nearby, in the wind-broad mist,
Dawning hands pick tomato dew,
To hurry crate and heave and load
For Washington's dear-stalled market booths,
As, in adjacent, dieseled fields,
Harvesters crop the o'er-ripe corn
For chicken feed and cramming hogs
At Smithfield's pens of Virgin' ham.

And in a nearby dawnlit bed
A girl sits and barely reads
Dr Seuss, makes up words,
As mother girds her eldest,
Sends Chiara out to wait the bus,
Then grandma comes to mind them in
As she hastens off to cuss and work
At a launderette on old Fairview street,
While her husband, long departed
To some upstart Southside town,
Steals a day from *Jack in the Box*
And sneaks upon a river bank
To cast-away for catfish
And smoke half the day at play.

Nearby, two kids swing on a rope
And thank the river's cool,
Since long ago the swimming pool
Became Whites Only and was to them denied
– Their teachers never note their absence,
Nor care,
And their sotted mother lies in bed,
An invalid since her 'operation,' when,
Scared of yet another babe to feed,
An unsterilized scraper made her bleed
And she lost both womb and cervix,
Her ability to sit or walk,
And lies in a poisoned stupor
Upon the blood-stained, gangrene sheets
Of her abhorred abortion.

And so her husband loops
An extra shift
At the Pulaski sawmill, lifting
Beams for pre-seamed, cooped suburbia,
To raise the doctor's bills incurred,

Tears drooping from his eyes…

Oh, let us return
To the sacredness of all…

And let me cry the sacredness
Of our years of tears,
This hot Fourth of July.

VI

Southern trees bear strange fruit,
Blood on the leaves and blood at the root,
Black bodies swinging in the Southern breeze,
Strange fruit hanging from the poplar trees.[154]

Oh, how they jip me
With obedience and meek modesty,
With "Hard work, my boy,"
And their secret family,
With "One day you'll be free,"
And the black skin that betrays me,
With "individual liberty"
And the enslaved reality
Of an inhumanity imposed
By searing hypocrisy –
Of freedom for them
But not for me…

…As a black family, husband, wife,
Five children, are burnt
From their ricket-walled shack,
All possessions lost,
In the costly anonymity of a night
Stormed with vindicated revenge
For arguing about their rent
And protesting random charges
At the crossroads store
Owned by their tenant lord.

This is a form of feudalism,
Tying us to the land,
With no rights in thought nor hand…

…echoes…echoes of the days…

…Heard across the bays and estuaries

---

[154] *Strange Fruit* by Billie Holiday, 1939; lyrics by Lewis Allan (Abel Meeropol).

And caught across the centuries
Of people long forgot…

"I truly believe the state's legitimate purpose
Is to preserve the racial integrity of its citizens
And prevent the corruption of their blood
By interbreeding, and thus causing
A mongrel mix of citizens
And the obliteration of racial pride.
Thus sterilizations must, I fear, go on,
Until we have removed all epileptics,
Psychotics, the inherently poor and insane,
All mental retards and schizophrenics
From our genetically gentile strain."

Strange fruit hang from the trees…

I load my dogs into the truck,
Check my rifle and my pellet shots,
Then explore an Appomattox tract
To splat squirrels, but mostly hazy drink
A lazy Bud or four – or maybe even more…

For, in Southampton County's moonlit lanes,
Tools and talents honed by war
Prove catalysts for an economic surge
Of urgent paper mills, cellulose and chemicals,
Logging, peanuts, soybeans, hams
To replace agéd plows, country stores,
Tobacco, corn, subsistence farms,
Abetted out by encaged debt
And the lure of factory wages.

And, not far away, garbage trucks
Stop-start hydraulic dawns
With wheezing breaks, bang-clangs of cans,
Vrooms and screeching stalls,
Then push on to landfill sites
To dump with dust and stench and flies,
As the waste of our consumption
Trails behind our lifestyles where
Waste is a virtue of our affluence.

…I swing, I swing, I swing…

…buy, consume and toss away…

…tick, tick, tick…

…the sands are running dry…

…As a drop of rain, poisoned by

511

Acidic paroxysms
Of suffocating factory fumes,
Reluctant falls upon a pine
Whose needles are now deadened brown,
Then drips down some soft shaggéd bark
To sink within a topless ground
Of a thousand cloying rills
Of hard-baked, naked clay
Forsaken-stripped of nutrients,
Other than the tears
Of SylvanVeil and RiverMere,
Abundances of our rivers and the forest,
As it joins a billion others gleaming
In their silt-lade rush to riffs and streams,
Cut banks of horse and plow and cow
And mud-hoofed mush of pat and slush
That suffocates the pesticidal run
Of nitrogen enriched, o'er-grazed,
Treeless, shrubless, over-warmed,
Outdone death of caddis, fish and fly,
Starved of oxygen within
The shameless, shadeless sun.

Harsh it spills and rills in o'erranked rush
Of silt-soiled rocks, choking life
Of crawdad and invertebrate,
Root-tumbled banks, flesh-sided,
Red and raw and bloody,
Bereft of 'fisher, osprey, heron,
Willow, arrowhead and sedge,
As spates of unimpeded gush
Rip the cattle-mangled sides
In rudderless roar of mud-filled tides
That wrench plant and rock and spawn
And drain the land of year-round life
In sudden flash, then drought,
To leave but signs of morbid breath,
Leech and worm and algaic slime,
Giardia, feces, silt and grime
As our solemn-felt inheritance.

And a shad, unable to climb a dam,
Turns belly up, spawning full,
And floats its silvered stomach down
Past doleful fisherman, catchless, dull,
A cattle farmer's discharged sludge,
Sewer pipe and spewing factory,
As the churning flood of sud-spate rain
Churns the rheumy banks again
And roils the rankle-tumbriled water
With the flush of choking death
When it turns its lethal sway

Into a larger gashing fray
And boils its trash-gathered, tortured draw
Past sand-washed bank and spray
Into the widemouthed Smith's dashed craw,
The Sandy or the Mayo's yawn-free surge,
Their once-treed banks now half-submerged,
Dead cats, car parts, plastic toys,
Junk-tossed sofas, mattresses and clothes,
And hurl into the angry-risen Dan,
To unfurl upon the bespoilt bayous
And the harsh-ran hush of Albemarle.

Other streams surge into the Chesapeake,
Over-fished and oystered out,
Chemicals and effluents,
A drought of crabs to sift the silt,
Algae blooming, grasses in decay,
Zebra mussels, Asiatic clams, alien whelks,
Phragmites, nutria, mute swans honking,
Unwebbing an ecosystem once OK,
With its over-nitrate tidal ebb
Of ship bilge, trash and station glow,
Air-borne pollution settling low
Its fine net of suffocation
Upon the oily-surfaced brine.

And in the fields, slow-abandoned,
Untended saplings springing up
Where once corn and tobacco grew,
Kudzu roots the clay-clad soil,
Springs its coils and tendril wends
And overbends the new-topped trees,
While loosestrife, floribunda rose,
Tree of heaven, chicory,
Fescue, Bermuda, timothy,
Clover, honeysuckle, wine raspberry
And virulent English ivy
Claw and push our natives out,
Smother o'er their natural light,
And out-compete in force-fed spate,
As ragged-sinewed vine and shoot
Choke our sadly-bred nativity.

For those forests, once chestnut domed,
Now fester parasite and blight,
Elms diseased and fast-gone past
In the eye-click of a funeral breeze,
Hemlock trees in constant stress
Of woolly adelgid, white spot, filament,
Loss of needles, withered shoots,
Cherries covered with caterpillar tents,
Or gypsy moths, burnt by fires

513

Raging fierce in underbrush left
As our forests cannot hush-define
The ridges, slopes and past declines
Of unrecovered hopes,
While the present bears a lonesome cast
And the land falls failing to its knees,
Praying for last-hope reprieves
That never seem to relieve
This moping, stricken land.

With you I swing me down,
With you I drink and drown...

Oh! When will the sun cry, "'Tis time
To stop our shadowed lives,
Raise unshaded eyes upon the skies,
And ask for our forgiveness?"
For we have grabbed and selfish snarled
And hacked and gnarled our misered way
At each others' souls for too long;
We have forgotten what it's like
To live in caring harmony,
Where the sun can shine and spread its rays
Upon one contented family.

I rise, I stir, I pluck
The cobwebs from my eyes,
Brush dust and soot and grime
And slowly step one step a time
To leave that judger of mankind
Deep within the drumming bones...

...And from the twisting cross recrossing
Of the turning and returning
Forks within my fractured mind,
Defying reason, will and kindly loss
Of hope upon a futured dream,
I seem
To linger for eternity
As WindTeller whispers through the trees
And SelfSearch, sitting at her circle,
Calls the spirits of her past
To enter in upon the breeze...

Pastoral scene of the gallant South,
The bulging eyes and the twisted mouth,
Scent of magnolias, sweet and fresh,
Then the sudden smell of burning flesh.

With you I stand...

Oh, cast the bones upon the sea,
Yes, cast them, one by lonely one,

For you and you and you and me...

Daddy, are we there yet?

With you I stand,
For I hear the rain,
Pitter-patter,
Seeping to the bones...

...For the graves are still dreaming,
Dreaming still,
Whispering to those who know
The secrets of tocome,
Singing of the future
As they wail to anguished memories
Still lost upon this world,
But harbored in their trailing bones...

This rusting, wind-cold, log-cut room
Has been our school for many years,
My Mom was taught here, father also,
Perhaps, someday, my daughters too,
Monacans alone, with
One underfunded teacher
In a chapel passed for cabin room,
Last lingerers of the Mountain Bear,
Forgotten in our homeland,
Passed by, uncles gone, left to fear,
Mere a few to hold the light
Of our bare-remembered plight;
For we are taught no history
Of our culture or our pride,
But only white men's values,
Their words and their songs,
Strong imposed upon us,
While our own identity is
As wrongly most denied...

And why is it that, in this land,
It is not just Indian culture that is lost,
But the culture of *all* our pasts?
Our previous heritages, always richer,
Whether European, Jewish, Asian,
African, Latin or Hispanic,
Abandoned within the lowered mix
Of eyes fixed upon a moneyed prize?

Traditions,
Once bound to earth and season,
Dresses, customs, dances, songs,
Are surrendered by some generation
Within a melting pot that gray-veils all

515

And loses soul to the strict impose
Of commercial Christian white control,
Or television and mock tradition,
Of plastic Disney and shopping malls.

And I ask, is this obliteration,
This deliberate wrenching of our pasts
To mutual identity and loyalty,
Primed to keep our spirits confused,
In backwardness and credulity,
And deny the culprits of their crime?

Others ask this too, others who,
In their anger and their pride,
Reject their parents' fear, their
Unwillingness to question, acceptance
Of government lies, brutality,
Spies and lies, corruption,
As they tear away, expelled,
Reviled, pushed to the margins
Of society's intolerant lies,
To discover their passion, truth
And their praise
In New Age communes, colonies
Of Hippies, flowers, naked drugs,
Within the secret valleys
Of Virginia's sluggish vales.

We must release ourselves from deep within!

Here is fruit for the crows to pluck,
For the rain to gather, for the wind to suck,
For the sun to rot, for the trees to drop,
Here is a strange and bitter crop.

I search for my life.
I search for it
Within the widows of my years…

…For, as I stand and stare,
There is no crying to the sun,
No one to hear when my day is done,
So I settle within the setting glow
Of what I thought was life, but now do know
Was the passing shadow of another's eye,
Within the blink of birth to graveside cry
For all of us who cannot forget
Those childish hopes we were never yet
Allowed to touch, except in that
Quick blink of another's eye.

I can only listen and be that eternal lover

That says it's never too late to rediscover
The path of our self-baring truth –
That is your greatest sacrifice to me,
Your noblest offering, and the hardest,
To surrender your present for the all,
To leave solitary strife and pain behind
In the glory of the universal mind.

With you I stand and stare
Beneath your swinging feet,
Your dripping lips and fears,
Your deep and singing tears...

We know, we know!
We know your call!
Yet we still renege and simper-stall,
Build walls, build walls, build walls...

Echoes...echoes of the days
Caught across the centuries...

Hey now, if your baby leaves you,
And you got a tale to tell,
Just take a walk down Lonely Street
To Heartbreak Hotel.[155]

In Montgomery, Alabama, Rosa Parks refuses to move to the rear of a bus and provokes a boycott led by Martin Luther King. That same year, 1956, ninety-six Southern Congressmen, including the entire Virginia Congressional delegation, sign the "Southern Manifesto," which denounces desegregation in public places and schools, rails against the Supreme Court, and promises to stridently oppose its decisions.

Are we there yet, Daddy? Are we there?

I get so lonely,
I get so lonely I could die...

...Oh, I stand and stare as blood
Drips onto the leaves and barks at the root...

VII

The seed of Esau swells within Isaac,
The heart of Cain beats within Abel,
I am my brother's sweet being
And his soul dwells within me.

---

[155] *Heartbreak Hotel* on the Elvis56 album; by Axton, Durden and Presley.

...as the joint begins to swing...

In 1956, Israel, France and Britain invade Egypt to suppress Nasser's plan to
nationalize the Suez Canal; meanwhile, the Soviet Union invades Hungary to
suppress its revolution and declares that it, too, has developed a hydrogen bomb.
Long-range missiles are being developed and, once again, the world seems to be
perched on the edge of nuclear war.

An engineer at Langley Research Center
Jet tests a slim-shelled Scout,
Aluminum flares,
In a sound-scared tunnel, as NASA's Glenn,
One of its first eight pilot men,
Gains initiation, space mission help,
In F-106s, intense G-force,
Coursing his responses,
Diagramming routes,
Satellites and suits,
High-sky probes, altitudes,
Attitudes, arranged pursuits,
And manned reentry programs
From the Wallops Island range...

...While on the nearby Eastern Shore,
Beneath a solid-fuelled rocket's roar,
I harness my old mule once more,
Rake the dust between my fingers,
Roll it on my thumb, no dark fiber
To grow my independent crop upon...

...as distant thunder rocks and rolls...

...And in the ghettoes of Richmond,
Petersburg, Norfolk, Hampton Roads,
Blacks simmer in the summer heat,
Fed-up, angry, beat,
And ready to explode...

Please, let's forget the past,
The future looks bright ahead,
Don't be cruel to a heart that's true,
Don't be cruel to a heart that's true.[156]

Meanwhile,
In a Norfolk hospital
A woman gets an epidural,
Air and gas, is shaved,
Catheter and drip,
A screen put up as doctors carve
A crescent moon upon her womb

---

[156] *Don't Be Cruel* on the Elvis56 album; by Blackwell and Presley.

And pull her babe reluctant out,
Names it "Freedom",
Secret fetus, clandestine impetus,
Shame-saddled, brindled by her fear of birth
And journey to an earthen tomb...

...As a Coeburn coalman, early retired,
On social benefits, sickness pay,
A meager pension dole-defrayed,
Years of seeping pain,
Coughs one last time, then slumps
In his silhouetted home,
Twenty by twelve,
One bed, a chair, a TV set,
Of creeping miner's lung...

...And I hack and stack the rotting rails,
Vine-covered now, but that once
Zagged and zigged their snaking course
Upon a triangulated hill
Of line and sight and angulated will...

...While the Horseman rides stiffly by,
Linkum heaves a heaving sigh,
And the Sufferings do dance around
The boiling cauldron of American Pie.

Still the night, still the night,
But just a glimmer of the light,
And a smile upon ancestral lips....

We impose the American Dream
Upon ourselves,
Like some compelling straightjacket
That must be worn,
Else we are traitors to our country,
Unworthy, held in scorn
– So, in fear, we let it eat away
At our sultry unbecoming
From dream to teardown reality
Within a realm that's self-imposed
– Flunkers of a mythic strain
We can never hope to e'er attain.

I sense my senses stirring,
Intuition returning...
A mighty, rushing wind...

...As The Horseman, spurring on his
Spectral mount, playing
His pipe of final justice,
Gallops about an interstate,

Next black musicians bussing deep
Into the South, reluctant players
In segregated halls,
But needing any money from
The watermelon route…

It's closer now than it's ever been –
I can almost hear the trumpet
And Gabriel sound the chord,
At the midnight cry, we'll be going home… [157]

…While the peddler,
Suitcase next him on the seat
Of his old jalopy, a thirties Ford,
Pulls into Emporia, stops for gas,
Then asks for the black neighborhood,
Is directed south and west,
Turns down Dry Bread Road
Onto Easter Street, pulls at the store,
Gets out, takes his case,
Straightens his tie and greased-back hair
And begins to peddle round
The gardened houses, one by one,
Brooms and brushes, table polish,
Bath scrubs, soaps and pads for floors,
But also news of growing strife,
Of anger in the cities now,
Riots that threaten summer long
Mississipp' and Alabam',
Bus boycotts, coming plans
To final resist the terrored lives
At the begging margins of our rights.
Then news of new wave movies,
Breathless, 400 Blows,
Kerouac, Ginsberg,
Pete Seeger and resurrected folk,
Help shake the yoke
Of Father Fear's oppression,
At the margin of our minds…

…And I walk unsteady through
The countless gyrations of the wind
As it bustles thru' enmazed walls
Of this Land of Seedy Hustle…

…As I wheel and wheel
And spin and wheel
In the vortexed chakras of my heart
And see mandalas on the walls
Of my often chambered sight…

---

[157] *Midnight Cry* is a traditional gospel song.

...Where a person's value, his esteem,
Is measured in a dollar's gleam...

Echoes...echoes of the days
Caught across the centuries...

...Get rich, get rich, no matter
The cost to others, as fatter
And fatter we grow, and lower
And lower they go...

...one winner requires a thousand losers...

We must, I feel, insist upon control,
Through wealth and influence,
The law's illegal means,
Of the entire culture of this country,
Its history and biography,
Its papers, radio, TV too,
Its education, what is taught
From kindergarten to college,
The whole montage of politics,
Two parties in superficial dispute,
All religion, thought and literature,
Ideas, values, myths, until
All blink as we wish them blink,
And do as we will.

...oh, our cultural web of hyper-lies...

And I, Whisperer of the Wind,
HorseTeller, satyr,
Sagittarius of the wishing veil,
Observe in silent mystery
That image of my mind to be,
SelfTruth, soothsayer, goddess,
Shimmerin through the guided light
Weft by Sufferers, Callings too,
Enchanters of the midnight light
Where all is true and none are right...

...As thirty beauties, bouffant hair,
Curled and manicured, permed,
Lipsticked, heels set proud,
Parade their fronts and fannies
In bathing suits, bikinis,
For judges at Virginia Beach
And drooling, reaching crowds...

Sinners! Thou Shall Not
Blaspheme or profane our
Commandments in this land
Of Satan's skillful hand!

521

...But I ignore, buy
A crystal, then, to divine
My futured astrology, an almanac,
A Tarot deck, prayer wheel,
Books on Buddhism, yoga, Torah,
And rainbow-colored sacred stones,
Not knowing,
No firm connection, as I seek
Something spiritual and meeker to
The pain of animal and earth...

...For I am consumer-consumed,
Myself a consumable, commercial soul,
Sold for a whisper of possibility
That it could be otherwise...

...That I could be Esau as well as Isaac,
Abel dwelled in Cain's soft heart...

...Rights, but no responsibility,
Individuals, but no society,
Laws, but no liberty,
Government, but no community...

Freedom is not of the ego
To scamper at its will,
But of the I to lose itself
In one with all eternity.

VIII

A mockingbird sits in an ivy bush
That parasites a hackberry tree,
Popping berries into its craw,
Watching passers-by in finery
Attend a pre-election barbecue,
Pork spare ribs, coleslaw tucked away,
Confident whites, blacks in serving bibs,
Never speaking nor passing time of day;
And, in its trill and vibrant stall,
It mocks the voice of liberty's call,
Mocks democracy, the sloganed speech
Of dreams that are so out of reach,
And fills its white-tint throat full shrill
With berries black and juicy plucked
Never mentioned, invisible still.

...dilly-dill, dilly-dill...

The owner of a Marion motel,

Rural Virginia,
Registers a traveling salesman,
And casts a glimpse of TV news,
Teargas flares, jogging cameras,
Reporters stumbling as they watch
Shields and guns and helmets,
Police dogs, water cannon, billy clubs…

"Just the two of you?"
"Yep. Them niggers riotin' agin?"
"Uh-huh."

Batons beating to the song of marching bands…

"Name and address, right there…"

Silent lines, placards, chanting,
Hoses battering panting skulls
Of children across brick walls…

"Car and registration…"
"Getting too darn big for their nigger boots."
"Uh-huh."

Students, preachers, girls,
Thrashed, threatened, hurled away…

"Hit 'em hard, hit 'em hard, I say."
"ID?"

Alsatians savagely barking, ravaging
At marchers hemmed in, terrified,
Clothes ripped, cuffed and gripped…

"Why don't they let their darn dogs go?
Niggers can't take dogs."
"Nope. Guess not."

Sirens, firemen, a smoking church,
Flames from its choking windows;
A police chief denies brutality.

"Always got to blame the cops, ain't they.
You know, those reporters, they're just
A bunch a liberals,
Always inciting trouble. Shouldn't let
Those darn red reporters near.
I wouldn't. Always causes trouble."
"Uh-huh."

One journalist, bloodstained, complains
The police restrained him, beat him up.

"He's upset? Why's he there in the first place, huh?
Serves him right. Commie ass-hole."
"Uh-huh."

The owner rolls a cigarette,
Checks the book, and deposits the deposit
In his stash of cash.

"How many nights?"
"One. Send 'em back
To Africa, where they belong."
"Number 9, ground floor, but watch
The hose and stash of nets; we've been
Meaning for some time
To clean the pool of trash."

Lowest, fewest, least,
Thus sounds the bell –
The Virginia bell that knells
The lowest, fewest, least…

…As the Byrd Organization,
That museum of democracy,
Where liberty is on display
As an antiquated fossil that bears
No resemblance to today,
And where the principles of Jefferson
Are safely locked away
In the catacombs of vampired vaults,
Rants to resist Supreme Court rulings
With massive legislative display
Of unwilling steadfastness, to firmly squeal
Its encoffined lie, "Separate but equal,"
With the full intent of bloody battle
To defend its segregated ways…

…tick, tick, tick…

For now it is *our* blood that's dripping…

*"I shall use every legal means at my command
To continue segregated schools in Virginia."*

*"We will resist this illegal encroachment
Upon our sovereign powers."*

"There is no middle ground, no compromise…"

*"If you ever let them integrate anywhere,
The whole state will be integrated in a short time."*

*"Unyielding opposition to integration
In any form whatsoever, so help us God!"*

"We have just begun to fight!"

"Hold the line!"

"Massive resistance!"

Oh, Byrd, with your dictatorship
Of segregated racism, your grip
Upon the throat of Virginia's slipping life,
Choking her, refusing her relief,
Holding us within your medieval fief,
Your time is dripping out...

...As the mockingbird calls from the street,
Tweet-tweet, tweet-tweet, tweet-tweet...

Oh, the rain, the rain, the rain,
Dripping on the sacred bones!

Oh, why
Am I told to humbly pray,
When my prayers are not answered;
Why am I told to beg forgiveness,
When it is I who must forgive;
Why am I foretold of justice,
When justice serves me cold today?
I am warned to meek abide,
While others sidle-stealth
The wealth
From my hungry-praying mouth
And the blindness of forgiving eyes.

I see no justice, no waiting,
No meek turning of the cheek;
I see no compassion, no love, no relief
Upon the smirk of that thief;
Oh, no, the rain won't stop until
The crows, in their black display,
Gather in the baretop trees
And caw their pleasure to the world –
And how I live for that day!

For, as the Sufferers cower in dread
At a world that's torn, being born,
Fla'ed Weaver sits in silent hope,
Acceptance as her sacrifice,
While Maid Mary weaves her heart's decay
In destructive self-deceit,
And The Sadness lingers inner loss
Of desperation at this mindless way
Of lifelessness in unkind life.

But I am leaving them...

In 1958, Governor J. Lindsay Almond closes schools in Charlottesville, Norfolk and Warren County rather than integrate them; however, these districts are soon forced to comply and reopen. When 'massive resistance' ends in 1959, 'passive resistance' begins, including white flight to private schools and the suburbs. Prince Edward County decides to close its public schools permanently, rather than obey.

Daddy, are we there yet?

The John Birch Society is founded and a resurgent KKK launches acts of intimid-ation, bombings and murder across the South.

> Why do we allow ourselves to be cowed
> As a state, a nation, by such
> Racists, bigots, charlatans?

In Cuba, Bautista is overthrown by Fidel Castro and Che Guevara. In China, Mao has inaugurated the Great Leap Forward, a purge of ideas and intellectuals in the name of progress.

> I am leaving the sufferings of my mind
> Behind, behind, behind!

The Civil Rights Act of 1957 establishes a Civil Rights Commission and gives the Justice Department the power to serve injunctions against voting rights infractions. In 1960, Congress passes another Civil Rights Act, further extending federal powers to protect human rights. Meanwhile, the Soviet Union launches Sputnik, sending alarm bells around the country. A war in space now seems likely.

> Inspired by Kennedy's victory,
> Rosa Parks, TV screens of baton charges,
> Water cannon, salivating dogs,
> CORE[158] students, black and white together,
> Ride from North to South,
> Passing through Virginia's towns,
> Where blacks are asked to leave white stands,
> Go to tumbled sheds instead,
> And on their journey deeper south
> Are beaten, victimized, abused,
> Punched and kicked and bruised
> By Ku Klux Klan, tear gas rounds,
> Motor chains and hardwood axes,
> Fists and feet and mobbing spit,
> Until photographs of enraged hicks
> Wrack the world to the pit
> Of its churning stomach.

> And then CORE sends a thousand more,

---

[158] Congress On Racial Equality.

Taking the fight to movies, restaurants,
Lunch counters, restrooms, stores,
And plunges Virginia , sister states,
Into the bowels of sick remorse,
To force decency and justice on
Reluctance and recalcitrance,
And bring right to a fearing that,
For three-hundred-and-fifty years,
Has doused the fire of liberty
From the light
Of our great Commonwealth.

Let us fall to our knees and thank
Those who fought for our freedom,
Not two hundred years ago, but fifty –
Who finished the task that Bacon sought,
The battles of Jefferson and Patrick Henry
Of great Nat Turner, Gabriel –
Thank the fighters and the strugglers,
Those who refused to fold their knees,
But rose to claim humanity
And raised us all upon the breeze
Of their firm and fair-seized shoulders!

Oh, America,
Since James Towne, the land
Of bartered lives, we have been
Entombed, enwombed, dug out,
Foxhole-style,
From the red-feared darkness awe
Of a starving, staring world
That has grown adult while we
Have hidden in the womb
Of our blinded misery.

Sounds like I'm hearing moaning,
Death bell ringing all in my head... [159]

Oh yes, the Virginia bell is tolling
As our blood still drips,
Drips still, tlip, tlip, tlip,
Upon *all* our suffered bones...

...As the office of Dr King sends
Phonecalls, messages out to
The parishes of the South,
To pastors and committees, lending
Instructions for the week ahead...

While, at some downtown counter,

---

[159] *Death Bells*, by Lightnin' Hopkins, 1961.

We stride into a store,
Minds made up, resolved,
Our patience finally dissolved,
Sit at seats reserved for whites
And are implored to quit
By waitresses who refuse to serve.

The police come, but can do nothing,
Some whites support us morally,
Whispering, "It's about time," – not too loud –
While others hurl at us sugar,
Ketchup, mustard, coffee, milk,
And bilk us to the ground
With rant and frenzied kick.

But we, bloodied, calmly resit,
Don't resist,
And next day there are a hundred more,
The next day two hundred in addition,
Until the chain of stores decides
The adverse publicity, boycott threats,
And hostility in the North
Cannot be beaten, and desegregates.
So the fight is won, but only there,
And must be fought a thousand times
In railroad rooms and public squares,
In stores and bars and theaters,
In restaurants and in bowling alleys,
In hospitals and dental chairs,
In clinics and in pharmacies,
In schools and café stalls,
On the sidewalks and the buses,
In the pools and sporting halls,
The diamonds and the changing rooms –
In a struggle that will decades take,
And is not won, e'en now,
So long as black slums linger
And the rural poor are let decay
In trailers, junk and poverty.

In 1961, the Soviet Union launches Yuri Gagarin into space. Then, in late 1962, the Cuban Missile Crisis threatens to develop into all-out nuclear war. Fallout shelters are restocked and school drills take on a new intensity as the country plunges into fear. Virginia, home to the CIA, numerous military bases, and major space and rocket technology, is pulled relentlessly onto the world stage, its backwardness and isolation, its segregation and undemocratic political system, increasingly at odds with the needs of the US economy and world strategy.

Virginia bluebells break
Through the darkened soil,
Marking an end of winter
Starker than

Our memory can take.

Meanwhile,
In a Carroll County family,
The son finds work at a store,
The daughter marries, leaves,
And the father's logging employ
Slowly grows and grows until,
One day,
They have saved enough, borrow more,
And can visit Danville's outskirts,
There to buy
A trailer with an inside toilet seat,
Running water, hot and cold,
Even butane gas to cook and heat,
The winter hours much shorter now.

...leaving my sufferings behind...

Oh, that Promised Land...!

SelfSearch sings within her circle,
Eyes closed, her mind ringing to
The sounds of argumentative rounds
Of enemies, those she's failed
To love, care for, or respect,
And brings them in, by-one, by-one,
To listen to those tales and woes
She deepdown knows as well
As anxieties of her own, then
Enters into dialogue, explains,
Listens, relogs again and again, until
She reconciles and envisions
Them reconciled with her too,
And can reach out, embrace,
Cry upon a forgiving grace
That's mutual, intense and so deep
That she and they might final sleep
And dream of dancing in the mass
Of their circle-passing years.

Are we there yet, Daddy, are we there?

In 1963, Kennedy's Civil Rights Bill is brought before Congress. CORE and the Southern Christian Leadership Conference (SCLC) organize a march to the Lincoln Memorial in Washington to demand equal justice for all citizens under the law. And it is here that The Reverend Martin Luther King makes a speech:

"Now is the time to make real the promises of democracy. Now is the time to rise from the dark and desolate valley of segregation to the sunlit path of racial justice. Now is the time to open the doors of opportunity to all of God's children. Now is the time to lift our nation from the quicksands of racial injustice to the solid rock of brotherhood.

"...The whirlwinds of revolt will continue to shake the foundation of our nation until the bright day of justice emerges.

"...I have a dream today. I have a dream that, one day, every valley shall be exalted, every hill and mountain shall be made low, and rough places will be made plains, and the crooked places will be made straight, and the glory of the Lord shall be revealed, and all flesh shall see it together.

"...So let freedom ring from the prodigious hilltops of New Hampshire. Let freedom ring from the mighty mountains of New York... Let freedom ring from Lookout Mountain of Tennessee. Let freedom ring from every hill and molehill of Mississippi. From every mountainside, let freedom ring.

"When we let freedom ring, when we let it ring from every village and every hamlet, from every state and every city, we will be able to speed up that day when all of God's children, black men and white men, Jews and Gentiles, Protestants and Catholics, will be able to join hands and sing in the words of the old Negro spiritual, "Free at last! Free at last! Thank God Almighty, we are free at last!"

Are we there, Daddy? Is this it? Are we there?

The 1964 Civil Rights Act makes racial discrimination in public places, such as theaters, restaurants and hotels, illegal. It also requires employers to provide equal employment opportunities. Projects involving federal funds can be cut off if there is evidence of discrimination based on color, race or national origin.

There are still too many
Gyrations of my pain
As I strive to gain
The convolutions of the light
Within the lateness of my night
And drive towards the gate...

...Let freedom ring!

In the forgotten dells of our cities,
Where the poor are forced to live,
The Horseman roams observing eyes,
Playing on his flute
Mournful tunes,
As his gray-veiled spectral mount
Paces Manchester in Richmond,
St Peter and St Paul, North First,
Petersburg's West End, Kennelworth,
Danville's north and failing streets,
Roanoke's Across the Tracks,
Newport News by the backs
Of Eighteenth and Twenty-Third,
Lynchburg's Twelfth, and Madison and Clay,
Charlottesville's Vinegar Hill, where display
The problems of our lives a-fester,
Abandoned, lawless, housing so bad
It's well beyond a madness of
Thieving landlords, no repairs,

Unclean walks, trash dumped on sites,
Vandals, unemployed and hopelessness –
The legacy of segregation, white flight
And centuries of neglect that blights
Our urban memory and denies the name
Of civilized society – until they are made
Wholesome, clean and one again.

Strive...

...towards the gate...

...As the Virginia bell still knells
For the lowest, fewest and the least...

...For still, despite all change,
Less than a quarter of our people vote,
Because of poll tax, literacy tests,
Gerrymandered boundaries,
And other techniques of exclusion –
Indeed,
The South wallows in a poverty so stark
That it harkens everybody down:
Lowest spending in her shops,
Lowest capital for her projects,
Lowest incomes for her workers,
Lowest wages for her farmers,
Lowest investment in her infrastructure,
Poorest roads and services,
Lowest value of her goods,
Lowest deposits in her banks,
Lowest savings by investors,
Lowest births in her hospitals,
Fewest pupils in her schools,
Fewest books in her libraries,
Fewest farms with running water,
Electricity, radios or even phones –
And add to that the potent mix
Of every disease released to poverty,
Of rickets, cataracts, pellagra, TB,
Cholera, typhoid and dysentery,
And you have the potent mix
That is the South of Dixie.

Dong!
Dong!
Dong!
Dong!

So there it is,
The gateway to our soul,
Through the pain of others coming in,

Entering it upon our breath
And merging in our mutual death,
To be reborn in re-union's maze
And the convoluted gaze
Of an immutable union of all life...

Oh, let the bell now toll
For tolerance, acceptance and democracy –
The keys to health and economy,
To enterprise and endeavor,
And to the raising of us all!

IX

Are we there yet, Daddy?

Not yet, not yet. But we've
Not many miles to go.

I am up at six to make deliveries,
Return to feed the plants, drift on
The sprayers, open up
The garden shop, where I work
Till eight, or later,
My wife a cardiac nurse on shifts,
Intensive care to pay
Our son's fine education,
Send him to the Ivy League,
Tho' now we watch in disarray
As he drops out, dismayed, rejecting
Us without a damn,
Our values, hopes and plans,
As he gropes his hallucinogenic way
Through drug-induced psychosis
And the addling of his mind...

Oh, where have you been, my blue-eyed son?
Oh, where have you been, my darling young one?[160]

I have no idea...

But, at least I'm happy now –
You brought me up to live my life
As I saw fit,
Not vegetate in a cubicle or factory
Twelve hours a day – like you,
To work my life away, eroded,

---

[160] *A Hard Rain's Gonna Fall*, by Bob Dylan, 1963.

And die with all my dreams
Buried, unrealized and unforeseen...

I've stumbled on the side of twelve misty mountains,
I've walked and I've crawled on six crooked highways...

If I had a hammer,
I'd hammer in the morning
I'd hammer in the evening,
All over this land.

I'd hammer out danger,
I'd hammer out a warning,
I'd hammer out love between my brothers and my sisters,
All over this land.[161]

So I buy a Bug,
Painted it orange, blue and pink
With flowers, rainbows, "Peace Now" signs,
And hew due east on Fifty-One
To an Appalachian commune
Of tents and tipis, hogans, yurts,
Children naked, running free,
Parented lax communally,
Between
Peyote, trances, shamanic dirges,
Sweat lodges and ceremonial dances
About a fecund maypole tree,
Organic gardens, free love, nudity,
And marijuana in the woods –
Where all is shared till all runs out
And we will one-by-one drift off
To bum our dreams elsewhere.

I've stepped in the middle of seven sad forests,
I've been out in front of a dozen dead oceans...

If I had a song,
I'd sing it in the morning,
I'd sing it in the evening,
All over this land...

...No rules, no laws, no tyranny
Of parents, police or society...
Free love, man!

Well I got a hammer,
And I got a bell,
And I got a song to sing, all over this land.

---

[161] *If I Had a Hammer* by Peter, Paul and Mary, 1963; written by Seeger and Hayes.

It's the hammer of justice,
It's the bell of freedom,
It's the song about love between my brothers and my sisters,
All over this land...

...and it's a hard rain's a-gonna fall...

...As a father sits his daughter on his knee
To tell her tales of Uncle Remus,
Brer Rabbit, Tiddlum Tidy,
And how Old Linkum freed the slaves...

I am the Whisperer, the teller of the wind,
Who sways within the branches of the breeze
And glides the misting waters
Of this gladed land, calling, calling
To the lives of our ancestors,
Lost, lost, within the mixing tides
Of the suffering of a fateful demise
That we could not control, but
Could only final watch in our years
When poverty descended,
Called its mortgage upon our souls
And meant we could fight no more,
Struggle no more for the light,
Give no more, hope no more,
Deceive ourselves with humored lies,
Missed imaginings, memories denied
In the whirl of what we dreamed
And what we were deemed to endure.

In 1964, the 24th Amendment finally makes the use of poll tax requirements in federal elections illegal. The next year, the Voting Rights Act is signed into effect, banning literacy tests and sending federal examiners to the South to stop persistent and insidious – indeed, *endemic* – corruption at the ballot box.

Then, in 1966, the Supreme Court strikes down the Virginia poll tax, which has been used since 1902 to disenfranchise blacks and poor whites, making it illegal in statewide and local elections as well. This finally sounds the death knell of the Byrd Machine and his utterly corrupt and nepotic Democratic Party. At last, all men and women in the state can vote – full democracy reaches our statute book after 358 years. Meanwhile, the battle goes on for *social* justice, as the tenements and slums of the US are torn apart by riots from Michigan to Florida, LA to Boston. And there is still plenty of intimidation at the polls.

Daddy, are we there? Are we there?

Sixteen-seventy-six,
Seventeen-seventy-six,
Eighteen-sixty-six,
Nineteen-sixty-six –
Every hundred years or so
We are dragged from our night

By enlightened leaders,
Only to descend at their passing,
And have to spend
A lifetime learning
How to rise
To their vision and their prophecy...

There have been two great generations in our history,
That of Jefferson, Washington and Henry,
Mason, Madison and Monroe,
And two hundred years in arrears,
That of Kennedy, Johnson, Jackson, King,
Of Dylan, Milk, Friedan, Dean
– Ten million more anonymously –
Who brought to Virginia and America
A revolution in thought and society
That comprised a massive strive of will,
A mobilization of the country,
A democratization of us all,
And laid the temple plinth of today
On which the Virginia bell now tolls
To our joy and liberty –
Finally, oh, finally!

...nearly there, nearly there...

I've been living a dream,
A roving fantasy
That has drifted into gleaming light,
Now the mask on our reality
Has finally been removed...

I'll let you be in my dreams if I can be in yours... [162]

Finally, I am rising through the passageways,
No string for my guide,
But faith and intuition by my side,
SelfTruth leading on and on,
As I discover wrong and right,
Dancing around the circle
Of our mutual delight...

...As, at last, in sixty-six, Byrd dies,
And I say, shaking my head,
Good riddance to his trash...

...But two years later,
In much deeper grief,
Dr King,
Returning to his Memphis room

---

[162] *Talkin' World War III Blues*, by Bob Dylan, 1963.

Is shot,
And a shocked nation
Grieves the sudden passing
Of the greatest orator
And the noblest martyr
Of its great and noble history…

…Are we there yet, Daddy?

No my daughter, I'm afraid
We still have a ways to go…

X

Two boys, expectant, prepare to watch
Another challenge for the Green Hornet,
And his kung-fu Kato, as they protect
"The rights and lives of decent citizens,"
And proudly don Roy Rogers suits,
Ray guns ready to tame all foes,
Zapping Operation, Spirograph,
Twister and the Memory Game,
Barbie and gruff GI Joe…

…the light, the light, call me to the light…

…As Madam Tarot,
Pagan for the day,
Ventures to a New Age love-in,
Undresses, dances, takes free sex, LSD,
Smokes marijuana, forsakes spinning-sick,
And misses a week of consciousness,
Drug-transfixed.

Meanwhile,
Our TV sets still beam
Vile segregation on our screens,
Beatings, water cannon, snarling dogs,
Missing persons, lynching mobs,
Boycotts, spitting, hurled abuse
As unfurling from a bus, come
Children, mothers, peaceful men
Marching for their omened rights…

…For our horror damns no bounds,
As Vietnam pans the newsreel with
Scenes of naval shelling, bombing runs,
Napalm, a village burned to hell,
Orphaned children, foxholes blowing,
Shocked GIs and bloody suffering

– And then a cut to campus riots,
Inner city barricades, lootings, fires,
Then to Gay Pride marches, California,
Workers striking, reaching for rights,
Factory closures, a presidential speech,
Denial, lies, and counter-blasts...

I found an island in your arms,
Country in your eyes,
Arms that chain,
Eyes that lie –
Break on through to the other side,
Break on through to the other side... [163]

And we contrast encapsuled towns
Held in some locked-past frowns,
With a crime-filled world that's fast outside,
Russia, China, the Cold War threat,
And turn inwards, dread the day
That anger bursts upon the lives
Of our remote and rural hideaway.

...eyes that lie...

...break on through to the other side...

And the only sound that's left
After the ambulances go
Is Cinderella sweeping up
On Desolation Row... [164]

I am the Wanderer of my pain,
The undenier who won't play the game,
The fool who curses away the wise,
The seer who sees all their lies
And will not die for another's wiles,
Nor the charms of a nation's guile,
But will call all who walk before us
For the suffering of the poor,
And for those who suffer still...

For they are my fate, my prison bonds,
The history of my wanderings,
My impatience for salvation,
My unwillingness to compromise,
My journey upon the countless lanes,
Searching for the remains of love that
Will not abandon, but sings low
The song of the earth, the mother's cry,

---

[163] *Break on Through (To the Other Side)* by *The Doors*, 1965.
[164] *Desolation Row*, by Bob Dylan, 1965.

And raises me from my own sweet death
And the fate of dying powerlessness
– That inevitability which descends
With inability to control
My life, to change a thing,
To remake the past or recast my psyche,
To restart again, better born this time,
To have a say, to influence
The future of my ordained path
From the wrath it has seen to this day...

...Oh, cast the bones
And call me to the light...

The gateway is most feared,
But it is the fear most endeared
That we must plunge within,
To discover there
Our inmost being, deepest care
And our secret heart...

As the echo of the wedding bells before the blowin' rain
Dissolved into the bells of the lightning
Tolling for the rebel, tolling for the rake,
Tolling for the luckless, the abandoned an' forsaked
Tolling for the outcast, burnin' constantly at stake,
An' we gazed upon the chimes of freedom flashing.[165]

The key is letting go;
The key is to never search;
The key is entering in
With nothing but surrender
Of self and will to All.

Daddy, Daddy, are we there?

Listen, child, to my story,
And see if you can tell...

...As, low upon some observation hill,
Stripped of trees, mud-trod filled,
Trenches, lines of wire, sandbags placed
To offer some defensive ridge
Of hunkered bunkers for the men,
We radio for more treetop bombs,
Napalm to intern Them, flares
Spent high into the night, blaring
With M-29s, distant pumps of hand-grenades,
As They come again, in suicidal flows,
Lines of helmets, crouching low,

---

[165] *Chimes of Freedom Flashing,* by Bob Dylan, 1964.

From treeline through the grass,
Elephantine, man-height tall, to stall
At the base of our positions,
Machineguns ripping, falling across
The coils of ragged wire, cutbarbed,
Blown with bangalores, satchels,
Then are through, despite the cost,
Heavy bombards now
Hitting our exposéd hill,
Forcing us to foxhole flee,
As shells pummel and the radio calls
For helo support, evacuation,
Dozens killed, and the shrieking wounded
Seem never to be heard,
But by the cawing of the crows,
And I glance up, see the enemy
Through a screen of smoke, screams and flashes,
Leaping the line of trenches, yelping, bayonets,
To the second line of wire, soon exploded,
And I rise, lob an M-26, fire in fear
At anything,
Abuse my squad to firmly stand, return their fire,
As two scramble-raise a mortar
And begin to slaughter 4.2s, as they fade
Into the mazing smoke of blazing AKs,
Antitanks, ChiCom grenades,
Forcing us to hunker back,
Terrored hands above our heads
At artillery shreds and smacking crashes
– And then the rent of slashing rotors,
H-34s across the net,
Rocketing the NVA, pounding,
Rounding back with sickened crumps,
As mortars thump their scaring ranks,
And artillery yet in anger flares
As a shell thuds close and glares the mud,
Rocks drowning 'round, lumps of flesh,
And my head is threshing, I cannot hear,
Nor sense my legs, my searing groin,
Dregs of rushing, pulsing loin,
Thigh unjoined, no medic care,
And fall back to let the night
Fly from my staring eyes…

…As I hear Quantico sigh
Across the bow of ages,
Its *semper progredi* vow…

"What do we want?"
"Peace!"
"When do we want it?"
"Now!"

How can they so betray our soldiers?
Long-haired hippies!
Peaceniks!
Go back to Russia now!

All we are saying is, "Give peace a chance..."

...and call me to the light...

...For I am forgetting who I am,
What I'm for,
And all my purpose to the world...

Then there's yet another newsreel,
This time a rain of flesh,
A screaming girl, her skin
Napalm-burnt and peeling,
Wounded soldiers, heads and eyes
Bound with saline drips and rushing stretchers,
Body bags and flags
Draped over coffins lined
In silent rows, sentinels –
For what? A nowhere piece
Of goddamned country
On the stranded edge
Of despair?

"Power to the people!"
"Resist police brutality!"
"Give peace a chance!"

In 1967, the Supreme Court strikes down Virginia's eugenic Racial Integrity Act, which has branded all citizens as either Negroes or Caucasians, banned interracial marriages and allowed sterilization of "the feeble-minded." Only now can different races legally marry in Virginia.

In 1968, in *Green v. New Kent County*, the Supreme Court places an affirmative duty on school boards to integrate schools, abandoning the principle of "all deliberate speed," and demands desegregation of schools "at once," thus ending ten years of token integration and strenuous resistance. Within the next year, more schools are desegregated than in the previous fifteen. Two years later, the Court rules that bussing is constitutional, further helping the process – but anger persists and riots continue in the cities and on the campuses.

Come senators, congressmen
Please heed the call,
Don't stand in the doorway,
Don't block up the hall,
For he that gets hurt
Will be he who has stalled –
There's a battle outside
And it is ragin',
It'll soon shake your windows

And rattle your walls –
For the times they are a-changin'.[166]

With Vietnam still ringing,
The campuses and slums still burning,
Gays still marching, anger still mounting,
Now women enhance their struggle too,
Demand equality in employment,
Sit-ins for equal pay, protections from
Discrimination, sexual advance,
Harassment, unequal benefits,
Lighting another front in the fight
To gain rights promised so long ago,
Yet so diligently denied...

...And, as if nature wanted to add her throw,
Hurricane Camille, worst of the century,
Devastates western Virginia, dumping
Twenty-seven inches on Nelson County,
Raging its rivers, crashing
Houses through valleys, smashing
Bridges with a drift of uprooted water
That slaughters a hundred and fifty.

Are we there yet, Daddy?

Nearly, nearly...

...the light, the light is calling...

I can see the light!

In 1969, a commission revises the Constitution of Virginia, which is adopted by referendum in 1971. It removes most racist and undemocratic clauses from the Segregationist Constitution of 1901 and makes issuing bonds much easier; removes Section 129, which allowed the state to close any integrated school; allows US army and navy personnel stationed in Virginia to vote; abolishes grandfather voting clauses; abolishes literacy, handwriting, and other registration tests; abolishes the property qualification for local elections; ensures fair and contiguous voting districts, that will be reviewed every ten years; and requires fair registration and recording of all eligible voters.

It is time to reclaim the banner
Of this eagle-staffed Republic,
To reclaim liberty and brotherhood
In the name of tolerance and acceptance,
Of inclusivity and sharing
For all our common wealth of people,
If this once-great state is yet to be
Once more great again!

---

[166] *The Times They Are a'Changing*, by Bob Dylan, 1964.

The segregationist Dillon Law remains, petty felons still cannot vote, Assembly members are still not paid, many statewide posts are unelected, and 'right to work' is still used to undermine trade unions. There is still a durational residency requirement (removed in 1977); a voter's registration is canceled if he or she doesn't vote for four years (scrapped in 1995); all petty felons still lose the right to vote (a racist law still on our books); a man and woman living together, but unmarried, are still breaking the law (and can only make love in one position!); and Virginians living overseas still cannot vote (changed in 1999).

On balance, after 364 years, and long, long after most other states and countries, Virginia has a constitution it can, with some certainty, call democratic. The final defeat of segregation and of the nepotic grip of a white male élite at last brings some economic stimulus, confidence and social pride, while it also rapidly implodes the Democratic Party machine.

Oh, yes, now I see the light!

And so I sit, in this pew of dreams
That lives a past of seems,
Veils of future to my front,
Face-lift scars behind,
As a caller praises out her heart,
The choir in clapping, swayed reply,
The voices of 'once was' all in shout,
Taking sup of the communion cup,
Joining hands across the rows,
Rising, walking through the doors
Of an inclusive spirit way,
Standing in the grassy yard
Among the markers of our ancestry,
Calling passers-by to come and join,
Their lives in bold, untold story,
As our circle opens to include
All our griefs of mutual death,
All our births of mutual dawn,
And the forgiveness of our single heart...

...While our two lovers,
Butch and femme,
Forty years enjoined, as
Friends divorced, had affairs,
Still remained, and
Can walk in public now,
Work together, avoid the stares,
Dine together, vote in sync,
Swim together, skate upon a rink,
Share a hotel, even join in bed,
Though our state still somewhat lags
In its intrusion into privacy,
And the prejudicial carcass stinks still
– A little now –
As they await equality

And that sweet-won confirmation
Of loving civil vows...

...but it will come, one day...

...For the crows are cawing,
Finally cawing,
In mutual pleasure and relief
At the ending of the rain,
As we cast bones upon their refrain,
Sing of grief and hope,
And let SelfSearch rest at last
From the arching, coping memories
Of our faded nightmare centuries –
For we are reborn, finally,
Upon that strange and hidden infinity
Of our ancestor's buried history
And the dawning of the sun.

Finally, daughter, finally,
We have arrived.

Book IX

Circle, Dream and Prophecy:
Democracy and Prosperity, 1972–2007

I

Click, click, click, click –
A child, afraid of the dark,
Clicks her nightlight off then on,
Off then on,
From the white of night
To the black of light,
The faint red filament near-lost between,
In her ghostly fear of men…

…as the cardinal sings…

…And WindWhisperer glides once more
To observe a woman, Isabella,
Farming wife and mother,
Caring daughter, feeder
Of horses, pigs and chickens,
Even cows come winter time,
Rushed to a maternal ward,
Her waters broken, contractions
Every minute now,
Coming fast, cervix dilating, pain
Knifing in, wishing never to see again
Any man in her life;
Sirens stare and a stretcher is rushed
To the hushed emergency ward,
For they are twins and one is breach
– So a quick injection's given,
Incision made, hands pushed in
And out the two new girls are laid,
One white, one black,
Bloodied, greased and wet, gasping air,
Their throats blown clear, wrapped
And set beside their well-numbed mom
As her husband rushes to her side –
For this time she is alive.

And I sing of the woman and the births,
Of the doctors, hospitals and nurses,

Of the sirens and the wails, the cries
And the hails
That bring renewal to this unavailing earth...

I sing of Isabella and that first child...

...And I sing of two other girls,
A few years older, sitting
On the stoop of their dreams
In a rotting tenancy, two-storied house
Amongst South Manchester's lousy pride...

...I sing of their old world, as it comes
Full circle round, slowly back
To our profound humanity...

...finally...

...As a hummingbird catches the dawn
And an indigo bunting ranges,
First-time flick of wings,
From a fence post, back again,
Upon a field of daisies, ox-eyes,
Echinacea, susans, black-eyes,
Parsnips and mothly mullein,
Sipping at the promised day...

...Of the summer shine, as
I spill emotion to the sun...

...Hidden yet, as a scrub fire fitful burns
Among the remnants of
A timber stand, smoking, barely
Drifting old the wood away.

How infallibly it burns...!

Finally, finally...

Meanwhile, on the glade's turned edge, next
A logged and churned terrain,
A cardinal flower pushes up,
Emerges from beneath a stone
Into the choke-hazed morn.

Finally, finally – free to vote...!

...As one man sighs for clientele,
White flight, prejudice,
While another researchs
New markets and new prospects
Now that segregation is
Slowly scorched away...

...Tho' our cities are still wracked
With the tension-time of change,
And of the pent-up centuries.

And I ask, to vote for whom?
Those despicable Dixiecrats –
No! I will turn Republican just
To get them out – though
It thrusts my craw
To do e'en that.

But I *may not* do e'en that,
Oh no, for look, outside the booth –
A zoo of angered men with
Dogs and pick-ax handles, hurling
Abuse, threatening death or tarring
To those who do dare enter in
With a different color skin.

In 1970, Linwood Holton becomes the first 20th century Republican governor of
Virginia, an immediate result of the abolition of the poll tax and literacy require-
ments to vote. He has fought the Byrd Machine for decades and resists those
segregationist Democrat rats who, upset with the national party's stance on
desegregation, are jumping ship to the Republicans.

And the rats *are* jumping ship,
In their tens of thousands,
Moving out of inner cities,
Away from rural towns,
From anywhere
Their kids might have to school
With black children, fleeing
To barricaded suburbs,
Laagers of last-ditch opposition,
As the social curb of slavery
Finally arrives –
A hundred years too late...

Holton immediately employs more blacks and women in the state government,
funds Virginia's first-ever community mental health centers and supports efforts
to protect the environment. In 1973, he founds the Virginia Governor's Schools
Program for gifted children.

I hear the shrill rasp of a wren
In a pile of shattered branches,
Her nest and eggs devoured,
Calling out her joy and her pain...

...Trill, wren, aye, as you eye
In stop-start passes, worms and beetles
Beneath the grasses of your sigh...

...For this is still a fight for civil rights,
Gained on paper, but barely yet in sight
For women, blacks or gays
Within the workroom and the cubicle,
The school and bank and office,
Housing, sports and army ranks,
As the ailing male élite
Drags its tired, resentful feet
In spited anger and the incitement of defeat.

If an addict's to start healing
She must first declare her habit
Of lying about the past, of denial,
Of cloaking her history in some myth
And vicarious symbol of success,
Of everything is "OK," fine,
Absolute the perfect best,
And that her life's been some great plan
She's stuck too through and through –
An anthem of emotive highs
That lets her forget her troubles – and their sighs,
The pain inflicted on her family –
And denies the teared reality
That she's another lost unfound,
Whose constitution, once so profound,
Is now a drug and mystery
She clings to for lack of lies
– Another paradigm to template need,
As she wastes her ringing talent
In growing debt and growing greed
For a constant rush, patriotic feed,
Drip, drip, drip, drip,
To forget her final fall from grace,
Her slip to lowly cultural place,
And a contempt of self she so despises,
Rejects along with inner loathing,
And the passing of her glory days.

So bye, bye, Miss American Pie,
Click, click, click...

As racist ex-Democrats flood the Republican Party, which is actively seeking
disgruntled white voters as part of its 'Southern Strategy,' the national
Democratic stance is beginning to attract more liberal Virginia voters. This
Virginia Reel, whereby both partners dizzily swing across to the other side of the
dance floor, is forcing the parties to realign along national lines.

As part of this resistance to our truth,
Falwell,
Long-time segregationist, racist, bigot,
Hijacks our Christian message and
Turns frustrated insolence upon
Women, gays and liberals who

Call for social change and challenge
To those embossed in rural fields,
As he guerillas still Confederate loss
And harkens to those knights of slavery...

...Turning Our Lord's sweet message
Into anger, hate, and vindictive futility...

...For now there are new demands,
– Constant threats to
A husband's rule of wife and family,
And to out-of-hand police
Whose racism and displaced abuse
Has long been a
Statewide, nationwide, disgrace –
To resurrect our roads and schools,
Our abilities and our human tools,
And self-build from centuries of neglect...

...White power, misspent, looking for
New ways to vent...

"The moral degeneracy of our society is due to
Women out at work, leaving home,
Turning harlot backs on family,
Children without fathers, left alone,
Liberal teachers, evolution, history,
Big-nose government's poking snout
In our lives and self-sustaining misery
– For there lurks within us
A Hollywood-preached conspiracy
Of indecency, corrupting values,
Abortions, gays in the military,
And a global warming doomsday
That is nothing but a lie..."

"Birth control is the enemy – the pill! –
For we must aspire to abstinence,
'Sex' – that dirty word – purely to
Procreate, with God's mercy, and never
To instill pleasure nor desire..."

"We, as Christians, must preserve
The American Way of Life, whose enemies
Are perceived right upon our borders – so
Must fight the immigrants, cheap-labor thieves
Who steal social security and hospital beds,
A zealous police for radicals and addicts,
And jealous guard against dread
Communist insurgency,
An army, navy, missile defense,
Huge arsenal of warheads, strong CIA
To topple reds like Castro and Allende..."

549

– All in the name of Christ,
Dressed as Ronald Reagan…

…or as Mickey Mouse…

…Buying and selling our souls
As spirit and religion
Become commodities for evangelists
To cry and fawn and conjure spells
That mime and veil and lie…

They preach a new bigotry,
But that same old tyranny of mind,
Teach us not to think, but cower in
Blind absurdity of belief.

It is even called "The Gospel of Prosperity,"
Reaching out to preach to donors who
Give generously
– Pentecostalists plus new technology –
TVs, satellites, piers of phones,
A-moaning and a-crying televangelist tears.

"Give to us and God will shower you
With riches and with health,
With inner-seeking happiness,
Success in all relationships
– Spiritual life for a dime –
Get in line! Get in line!
Pledge your support,
Donate!
Donate!
To God's Pearly Gates and
Earn rewards here on earth,
As well as more heavenly swards,
Showered-be with blessings!
Sob, sob…
Halleluiah!
Sob-sob, sob-sob…"

I watch as The Horseman
Leads Jefferson from his grave
– Father of religious freedom –
And shows him the slim bravery
That has inherited him.

And I knew if I had my chance
That I could make those people dance
And, maybe, they'd be happy for a while…[167]

---

[167] *Miss American Pie*, by Don McLean, 1971.

Oh, Miss American Pie....

Click-click, click-click...

As a result of mass political and social migration, in 1974 Holton is succeeded by Mills Godwin, a Republican who was previously a Democratic governor, a leader of 'massive resistance,' and an organizer of Democrats for Nixon.

In 1982, Charles "Chuck" Dobb becomes the first elected Democratic governor in twelve years, as both parties continue the Virginia Reel. A fiscal conservative, but socially progressive, he pumps a billion dollars into state education and appoints the first black justice to the Virginia Supreme Court. He will later be elected as a senator from Virginia.

Click-click, click-click, click-click...

II

In 1972, the Surry nuclear power station on the lower James goes online. Within five years, a second station, at North Anna, begins production. They seem to mark a new beginning for the state, based on modern technology and fresh ideas.

> Slowly are we distracted from
> Our more ethereal concerns
> By an unrefracted boom that looms
> In our ears, despite inflationary oil
> Toiling our hopes to our knees
> – And closer to our senses –
> As people buy more tapes, TVs,
> Cassette players, calculators,
> Microwaves, skateboards, Rubik cubes,
> As satellites are launched, Voyagers
> To Mars, Venus, stars beyond
> The solemn solar system,
> Even though prices rise and production
> Soon begins to freeze...

> *Bvvvvverrr–daaaa–derrrrrrrrrrrrrrr,*
> *Bvvvvverrr–daaaa–darrrrrrrrrrrrrrr...*

> In Richmond, a small retail chain
> Expands appliance sales and repairs,
> Invests all in a superstore
> – Wards Loading Dock –
> Forty thousand feet
> Of sweet warehouse-showroom,
> Displaying an array of audio,
> Video, TVs, home appliances,
> And is so successful it expands,
> Acquiring, chasing, to become
> The Circuit City brand,

That's still, today, centrally
Richmond planned…

…While, at West Point,
The founding of the York, where
Pamunkey and Mattaponi
Merge, just downstream
From Powhatan's ancient mound,
Chesapeake's great paper mill
Thrives its production
With Number 2 Machine,
And trucks arriving five-minutely
From timber stands throughout
Central lowmarshed lands,
Stacked high, craned into the mill,
Bleached pulp broken down,
Squeezed and dried and rolled,
Then transported abroad or shipped along
Our Eastern Seaboard ports.

Bvvvvverrr–daaaa–derrrrrrrrrrrrr,
Bvvvvverrr–daaaa–darrrrrrrrrrrrr…

For timber now constructs
Nimble suburb projects,
Filigrees of softwood webs,
As carpenters cut studs to size,
Build unit frames, cross-braced,
Cut doorways, windows, headers
Made,
Strengthened upon great kings,
Double top plates, cripple studs,
Fire blocks, spacers, trimmers,
Sheathing, girders,
Joists laid span across
To floor the upper rooms,
Spliced and solid blocked,
The subfloor nailed onto the top,
Double trimmed and double-headed
Around the stairwell gap,
Then roof joists strapped up higher still,
Rafted, ridged and valley sheathed,
Raked or gable-ended,
With hip and jack and rafter tail,
Chord and web and gusset set,
Then met with paper, tar and tile,
House after house after house,
For mile after mile after mile.

And a siskin, searching for her seeds
From the pines and firs she needs
To harvest for her fledgling nest, rests

And hears a nearby saw chain down
Another Southland yellow crown...

...As a nuthatch stops, a flicker flies to roost,
And overhead the last red crossbill
Flees is timbered host.

Bye, bye, Miss American Pie,
I drove my Chevy to the levee
But the levee was dry,
And them good ol' boys were drinking whisky and rye,
Singing, "This'll be the day that I die,
This'll be the day that I die..."

Meanwhile, The Horseman,
Clothed in rags of spectral black, veiled
Against the winter of our centuries,
Leads Jefferson to Father Washington,
To hock him from his ghostly chamber,
Then inspect those 'burban tresses
That mock Mount Vernon's modern view...

And, they wonder, as they watch,
If the fire can really douse the night,
The cauldron cease its bubble,
And the raven quench her final thirst
Within the potion's cravened trouble
– If the squares are sewn at last,
And Brer Rabbit needs no longer fast
For all past rumbles of his discontent.

Oh, pie, pie, pie, die,
Dream-die, Miss American Pie...

And can the Muse of Hindsight
Finally take her troubled rest,
Shut her eyes upon the lies
And reinvest her recast dreams
With no-longer-lingered myths
To sanctify our mingled past,
But, with the sword of vibrant truth,
Reglorify our lives?

Let us see – for that is the struggle
We have faced – and still do face –
To attain the reality of democracy,
Empowerment, life and grace,
And lift the gray veil from off
Our self-effacéd imagery.

Bvvvvverrr–daaaa–derrrrrrrrrrrrrrr,
Bvvvvverrr–daaaa–darrrrrrrrrrrrrrr...

Meanwhile, SelfSearch walks
The silent sides
Of Alberta, Windsor, Hickory,
Holland, Nurney, Ford,
Stony Creek, Boykins, McKenney,
Petersburg, Suffolk, Hopewell,
Keysville, Chase City, South Hill,
Norton, Wise and Appalachia,
Grundy, Bland and Marion,
Tazewell, Haysi and Vansant,
Coeburn, Emory and Glade Spring,
In a roll call of deserted towns,
Stores abandoned, shoppers flown,
That raps into the twilight sound of Taps:
Bvvvvverrr–daaaa–derrrrrrrrrrrrrr,
Bvvvvverrr–daaaa–darrrrrrrrrrrrrr,
Bvvvvaa-daaa-daaaa,
Bvvvvaa-daaa-daaaa...

...As now our mounted leaders
Visit with counted hats in hands
Old Hollywood Cemetery,
Richmond's rows, past Jefferson Davis
Reflected in J.E.B. Stuart's heart,
Presidents Tyler and Monroe,
As The Horseman tells of centuries
Of wars, neglect, misspent blood
That drown our graveyard hills,
And to extol e'erlasting respects,
Winding within the paths and trees
To those eighteen thousand souls
Who float upon the Confederate breeze...

Bvvvvverrr–daaaa–darrrrrrrrrrrrrr,
Bvvvvaa-daaa-daaaa...

Then we, forefathers of Virginia,
Visit the Kennedys in Arlington,
The miles of engraved crosses,
To praise the dead from out their graves,
Then wander to those brave memorials
For Vietnam, Korea, the Civil War,
Raising each stored body there,
Their spectral forms to march with us,
Restored to fill their parchéd lives,
And read Old Lincoln's reasoned words,
Then take his hand and lead him by,
As he sings so fine of democracy,
– And wonder, will
Virginia one day be known
For peace, and yet no more
For glorifying the tragedy of war?

Bvvvvverrr–daaaa–darrrrrrrrrrrrrr,
Bvvvvaa-daaa-daaaa…

Next, we fly the vales and dales
Southwards and west, to high-raise
Patrick Henry from his vestibule
Of agéd sanctity, then to silent stroll
Upon another funery – a cemetery
Of farming hopes, the slow death of
Hardship's vanity and final-setting sun,
Hiding a yet stranger rebirth…

For, with the righthand hardship
Of declining wheat and cattle,
Migration,
Urban factory jobs,
Rural decline,
Farms are abandoned to prairie wealth,
And our trees lefthand forgotten grow,
Allowing
The land to breathe a respiting sigh,
Of, "At last! At last! At last!"

Thus, the grateful stream, reshaded now,
Sheltered banks once more,
Can again slowly flow,
Grass over, flower, root its mat
To hold the soil, retain the good
And clear the meandering, sultry ease,
Slower now, calmer winding,
And year-round renewed, reprised,
Flushed of silt and trash and cattle shit,
And friendly home to growing life,
Deer and mink, raccoon and skunk,
As Virginia regreens anew,
Through the beneficence of abandonment,
The wooding of our leas and parks,
Washington and Jefferson,
And the hope that paupered indifference
Of defeated dreams directs,
And now inures our lungs and heart
To begin their o'erdue cure.

So bye-bye, Miss American Pie…

Meanwhile,
In a scrappy Floyd County forge
An ironworker crafts an archéd gate,
With wrenches, hammers, scrolling tools,
Curving, angular, wrapping round,
Bow pliers on a well-gripped collar,
Grooving with a one-inched fuller,

Welding hummingbirds and flowers,
Great sun in sunlit display,
Caring not to gall a wingéd ray,
Then turning to a new-made shoulder
With monkey, butcher, set aside,
Squaring tenons, bolder beveling,
Welding sections, eyeing straight
And raising up the wroughted gate
Of radiating candles, snicker-smiles
To ward Old Nick from off some vile
Handled enterprise...

...As Henry, Jefferson,
Our Father Washington
Ride the miles of Shenandoah vales
To sidle Old Man Lee from out
His veils of cobwebbed mystery,
And venture once again upon
Traveller's reins of silent gallop,
Then to beg the sun regain
Hope across our shadowed land...

...And I still switch off and on,
My nightlight off and on,
Clicking to the music of a
Long-forestalléd dawn.

III

Come, oracle, come, prophesy
Within the temple of the circle
That spirals up and down,
To the center of the earth
And to the heavens' crown...

...Let the Callings dance around
The multi-colored ground...

...Then return, circle, return,
Back, around to our more simple selves
And the simple life we had once found...

...As the ghosts of wolves now howl the wind...

...As the veils of Frasers wilt-skin expire...

...As the bark of elms thinsheer diseased...

...As the gypsy moths enmock our trees...

...As the adelgids crack our hemlocks' vow...

…As the shad and blue crab, oyster now
Are long declined and deceased…

…And as,
In seventy-four and seventy-five,
In Hopewell, on the lower James,
Long used as toxic sewer dump,
Proud "Chemical Capital of the World,"
Life Science Products – Allied Chemical –
Decants kepone into the river's stream,
A pesticide that burns beetles, ants,
And cripples workers' nervous systems,
Destroying them for life,
In million-dollared human strife,
Contamination and compensation,
That final-forces restoration
Of the corrupt and rank-dark James
From dank and vile pollution…

…Even as, not far below that flow,
A lay-barge captain careful steers
His craft upto its secured piers,
Three-hundred foot of tunneled section
Suspended, hanging in the humid mist,
To enlist the eastbound funnel of
The Hampton bridge and tunnel,
As longshoremen, welders,
Spectators on the portals cheer,
And weary tugs slide free their ropes
As an aircraft carrier slopes out to sea
In distant hazy rays of mist
Silhouetted against a bay
Of destroyers, cruisers and tankers in array.

In 1977, the Federal Government passes the Clean Water Act; seven years earlier, it enacted important amendments to the Clean Air Act; both significantly restrict pollution of the environment. Finally.

An FDA inspector, veterinarian,
Trained in animal welfare,
Splices thru' the stench of hog manure,
Parks before a manager's office
And is taken to the donor boars,
Each deviced in separate pens, then meets
A batch of sows, some in heat,
Others yet too young, Yorkshires,
Bred for white meat, docility,
Survival indoors under lights
In the perpetual day of commuted lives.
Next, he visits the farrow pens,
Inspects the pregnant sows,
Enough room to stand or lie down hard,
Their litters with a little more

557

To squeal and tumble round,
Until at twenty days they're hauled
To a mousing maze of pens, still small,
Then later to the finish house,
Hemmed tight to muffle-muddle legs,
Or scuffles that might mean tougher meat,
Delay their weight, give some delight,
As they are penicillined, ironed, vitamined,
And straddled over slatted boards
To hose the slurry slime and slick,
Till 'tis time for hurry trucks
To slaughterhouse them quick away.

He nods and finds nothing wrong,
Clean bill of health, commends
The manager for his artful display
Of efficient skill and training...

...While the slurry slowly flows downhill
Into the rill of a Shenandoah stream,
Killing bass and spot and trout and bream...

...As, in a north Virginia office,
Secretaries, clerks, support and sales,
Marketing and personnel
Are hemmed in rows, penned cubicles,
In perpetual day of commuted lives,
Underneath a manager who displays
An artful array of certificates
To his efficient skill and training.

...the oracle and the prophecy...

And The Horseman, leading slow
The heroes of our past,
Sad and gray and veiled,
Glows in upon their canned travail
And asks of their workday lives,
Is this the paradise we planned?

Meanwhile, a woman, black
And over-qualified, to
Compensate for sex and color,
Is the first non-Anglo in Personnel,
Solely employed, she suspects,
For federal contracts and appearances...

...And, boy, don't we resent it,
Joke, rebuke, hurl sexist attacks,
Mime apes behind her back...

...click, click, click...

But let us now return awhile
Unto another sanctuary,
An old-time bastion –
The mansion that was once resplendent
With magnolias on the crest,
But now rests in roofless sacrament,
Windowless, porch collapsed,
Termites, rats and feral cats,
Vineclad, overgrown and rotting,
Until begotten by a consortium,
Reroofed, rewired, replumbed,
Treated, sealed, repainted,
Exterminated and fumigated,
Hacked and scraped and sprayed,
Stairs rebuilt, floors relaid,
Offices and conference rooms,
Gardens rebloomed, paths retiled,
Library, kitchen, dining hall,
Two new wings, a pool and spa,
Nurses, masseuse, therapist,
Sheltered porches for the elderly,
Buzzers, frames and meals well-served,
Woodland walks and tennis courts,
A doctor's visit once a day,
As our history is regleamed, reglossed,
Our wrinkles creamed away
In the loss of memory and tint of eyes
That see greatness, never pain,
Yet somehow let the truth remain
Hidden in the creviced walls
And sealed-off loft above,
For us to rediscover them one day
– The masters of our ancient truth
Softly secreted away…

…beneath the bluebird's call…

…As The Horsemen and his ancient guests
Raise James Madison from his chest
Of restless-waking peace
To watch…

…Two elderly women, Baptists
In both love and fear, adhere to
Cheery Old Time Gospel Hour
On the radio, fine chiming choirs
And tears of organs hymning…

…While, on another talk-show band
A shock-jock, deliberately out-of-hand,
Replies to listeners' burnt concerns
With bigotry of his own to burn…

...And, in the secret-shadowed beds
Of self-denial, immune disgrace,
AIDS spreads its selected, silent way,
First through the community of the gays,
Then to straights, blood banks infected,
Wives and babies, transfusions too,
In an epidemic that tanks allthrough
This fast-imploding world.

"AIDS is the wrath of a just God against homosexuals."
"AIDS is not only God's punishment for homosexuals; it's God's punishment for
the society that tolerates homosexuals."

As if AIDS was not too deep
A vigil now to keep,
Famine blacks o'er Ethiop',
Gripping our uncoping screens
With faces wracked and griefed,
With bulging eyes, infested flies,
Bulbous bodies, skin-thin limbs
In the genocide of a harvest hunger
That generates a compassioned surge
And reminds us of Atlantic crossings,
As we urge in million sums
To alleviate their starving plight
And prove we yet have hearts and will
To save the world from man-made killing,
And, as individuals, care for life
Across the strife-filled continents...

The price of one missile silo would be enough...

In 1987, Jim and Tammy Faye Bakker's Praise the Lord empire collapses amid
allegations of financial and sexual corruption. The huge televangelist bubble
bursts overnight as the Moral Majority and Old Time Gospel Hour collapse into
huge financial debt. Two years later, the Moral Majority is disbanded.

What ails us, what ails us,
In this land of the free...?

...our dreams, our dreams...

We should be happy, rich, full of flair
– After all, the Dream is here –
Yet there lingers still an inability
To be aware of liberty.

"You are not free!" the horsemen cry
In anguished unison and dismay...

...at our too many commercial lies...

...At adverts, billboards everywhere,
Sales promotions, special offers,
Deals and dealers sharply aware of
Christmas, Easter, Thanksgiving Day,
Mother's, Father's, Valentine's,
Harried, impulsed to overspend,
Cheap credit, telemarket calls,
Slopping debt to the tops of souls,
As all-compelling noise destroys
Our peace and our relaxéd joy,
Bodies stressed, worn out, tired,
Instead of lives mindful and inspired,
Without demand, rich
And content, spent indeed
With the little each we truly need.

Oh, is this the prophecy at last
Cast close upon our futured eyes?

...I ask, as I sit
In a cubicle,
Somewhere...

Somewhere
In north Virginia,
– Somewhere,
In an eight-by-eight-by-tunneled-air,
For a publisher of books –
Or do we make drugs for infirmaries,
Work for the Pentagon...
...The NSA?
Perhaps we are a pressure group
For paper mills or cotton power,
Or maybe we provide
Clean laundry to DC hotels?

I know this much,
As here I sit,
Reflecting on my present,
Desirous of my past,
That I am the daughter
Of that sheller
In a Cape Charles packing plant,
Born in Parksley, who moved back
To work at her husband's factory;
I am the daughter
Of that secretary at Fort Lee,
Born in Cheriton, who fled to Parksley,
Married in twenty-one
And died in seventy-three;
I am the daughter
Of that concierge in Poquoson,
Who was urged to Cheriton in oh-six

To buy a house for her young family;
I am the daughter
Of that hairdresser at Gloucester Point,
Who did permanents and dyes
During a lifetime of cuts and dries
And drove to Poquoson for a lover there;
I am the daughter
Of that dancer in a minstrel show,
Born in Marion,
Trailing graveyard nights across the South,
Until her body gave at Gloucester Point;
I am the daughter
Of that teacher who reached
From St Paul to rural Smyth, near Marion,
To work a school post-Civil War;
I am the daughter
Of that nurse, born in Christiansburg, who
Was versed in wartime hospitals
At Charlottesville and Lynchburg,
Before she retired to St Paul;
I am the daughter
Of that mother, wife of a haberdasher,
Who worked in a Dinwiddie ribbon shop
Then moved on to Christiansburg;
I am the daughter
Of that pianist, wife of a dentist,
Who was born of landed gentry
On a plantation in Lunenburg;
I am the daughter
Of that mistress of a house,
Controller of domestic servants
On a plantation by Kenbridge town;
I am the daughter
Of that wife of a wealthy Sussex man,
Widowed, remarried to a colonel
Who fought in Washington's campaigns;
I am the daughter
Of that Lancaster sea captain,
Who did better, made his fortune,
Mother, home worker, mistress
Of two Norfolk servant girls;
I am the daughter
Of that King and Queen lawyer
Of moderate success, who progressed
To Isle of Wight and raised a family;
I am the wife of that Surry farmer
Who hurried up a logging company,
Did well, sold it for a sum,
And rumbled on to Nottoway;
I am the wife of that farmer who raised
Family and garden plot
In a Spring Grove tenancy;

I am the wife of that farmer who plowed
And hoed tobacco fields, owned a cow,
Raised his Surry children,
Swept and sewed and sowed;
I am that indentured servant, cook,
Later wife of that indentured man,
Who raised tobacco and did quite well,
Before rainstorms, drought, and prices fell
– I am all those daughters and all those wives;
I am the generations of my past
And I sing down those patient stations
Every dawn of every day.

Then I walked across the street
And caught the Sunday smell of someone frying chicken.
And Lord, it took me back to something that I'd lost
Somewhere, somehow along the way...[168]

Oh, descend to the Oracle,
To its candled cave,
And cast the sultry bones
Within the dark pool's waves...

...of missing Miss American Pie...

IV

Who are we?
We ask as we gather
'Round our fire of fathered ancestry,
And who were we meant to be...?

...click, click, click...

Madame Tarot, born again,
This time a Native American,
Sits by us,
Straining with an unborn child,
And calls upon her spirit guide,
On this her latest vision quest –
Which can only last but half-an-hour
Because she's got eight special guests
Coming for her baby shower.

One cries "Abortion!"
While another cries,
"Let it be free...!"

---

[168] *Sunday Morning Coming Down*, by Johnny Cash, 1970.

...As The Horseman leads our
Mounted specters, eyes afire,
To raise George Mason crying from
His ancient funeral pyre...

And, on our screens,
Sean Connery swings
From one hero to another,
James Bond, Zardoz, then
Robin Hood to Hepburn's Marian,
Fighting evil baddie old King John,
To right the pangs of oppression
And rescue us from cozy wrong.

But why is it we *still* need rescuing...?
Eh, George?

So we listen to Queen, The Eagles, Manilow,
Searching for some echo of
Our lost egos and our heroes, as
They vie with Bee Gees, disco, rock 'n' roll
To win playtime on the airwaves
Of music centers and car radios,
As we stall-sweat in commuting jams,
Frequent our air-conditioned malls,
Or jest our nights in heady bars
Staring into beer and gin and ecstasy.

Oh, the bluebird's call!

Crying a freeway,
Crying a cliff,
Crying a plunge to our devotion
Of slough-slipped waves
And echoed lost emotion...

As we, at last, turn
To sing of the quilt makers
And ask of them our mystery:
"Who are we and who were we meant to be?"

Myth and Truth, mother-daughter,[169]
Sit and sew upon a single frame
Within the caverned glow
The Great Virginia Quilt,
A backing verdant in its green,
Patterned wild with nature's flowers,
Streams and unkempt mountainsides,
With the center an appliquéd globe
Of Golden Ke'show-tse's sunrise glow,
James Towne fort and settled ships

---

[169] This stanza comprises *The Song of the Quilt Makers.*

Silhouettes on tumbling slips
And radiated threads projecting
Their needwork's hand-stitchéd seams
Up river, road and lowland trail,
Past Henricus, Suffolk, Westmoreland,
To fill the valleys and the hills
With towns and city settlements;
And, around the motif bossed and central,
Four panels tell of storied souls
And histories of ancestral roles:
One panel writhes within the deeds
Of battles 'tween the states,
Of Lee and Jackson, Stuart, Hill,
Chancellorsville and Sailor's Creek,
Of heads in cold and proud defeat;
One marches to the fife and drum
Of blue-coats lead by Washington,
Of fleets and French and Yorktown scenes,
And joyous hurrahs for liberty;
A third blazes Patrick Henry's speech
Rousing our nation to its feet,
Madison, Jefferson's free religion,
Conventions, Mason's human rights;
And the fourth consoles remembrance
Of slavery, segregation, all those unfree,
Native American, the working poor,
And their struggle for their dignity;
Then the whole is bordered round
With circles of a pleasured kind,
Of unity, voting, jobs held firm,
New houses, wages and serenity,
As the land, once barren red of clay,
Regains its primal verdancy
And we, its people proudly claim
Our future's matchless history.

Is this who we are, or who we were meant to be?

Oh, how the bluebird calls to our mystery…!

…As high upon old Harvey's Knob, birders
Zoom up and in on autumn's wheels
Of ospreys, red-tails, sharp-shinned hawks,
Broad-wings, Cooper's, harriers,
Mawking kestrels, golden eagles and
Red shoulders who fly upon the dawn…

…And I stare high
At the cloud-bearded sky
Dream-drifting o'er our land,
As a late-spring mist
Rapid rings the hickories,
Chestnut oaks and tulip trees…

...And a bluebird sings the sun's soft setting,
As she asks,
Is *that* who we're meant to be? Singing
Our soft soliloquy to the mystery
Of this ringing land of ours?

Then I ask,
"Is this a gleaming dawn, or yet another sunset
Upon the history of our dreams?"
I raise up'po-woc to the rising sun
And my soft soul begins to stir
In the wisping furls of summer swirls
And calls the energies of east and south,
West and north, the sky above
And ground beneath my feet,
To thank the earth for all her care.

"Are we truly the seeds of the new,
Fed by a world's awareness
Of our human destiny
And eternal unity
Within the crying earth?"
– This, I ask as I sing-turn,
Questing of the trees,
Blesséd be the breeze that wafts
Between my leaves, and song-start
A blaze to brew some tea,
A plastic bag of chili,
Open-rip a power bar,
Apply new Band-Aids, Vaseline,
Thick socks, battered boots,
Tidy, say goodbye and wave
To later-rising guests striding
The Appalachian Way.
Oh, I sing and I sing and I sing,
Ringing out the names
Of the generations and the centuries,
As I hike with rousing steps the slopes
Of Lost Mountain, Whitetop, Buzzard Rock,
Heels well-weathered, soles bending to the rock,
Backpack lighter now,
Three weeks peeling in,
As I clamber-slide, and slide and clamber
From ridge to gap to ridge
Of Pine and Rogers' highest peaks,
Ascending from the cauldron vales
To the zenith of Virginia's range,
The land reclaimed by oak and cedar,
Ash and maple, tulip tree and hickory,
Where I can comb among the deer and bear,
Watch the fox and possum roam,
And WindTeller can smile at last

With the resurrection of the sun
Upon the vibrant forest canopy
And feel the rising spark within
The drying boughs about his head,
That sped a surged rebud display
Upon the greenery of his thought,
As he spirals joyous between
The clouds
Of drifting drapery…

And I sing of WindTeller, horseman,
Of my ancestraled soul,
As it wanders
The history of this rolling land…

…I sing, I sing, I sing,
From the Tennessee Valley Divide,
Ringing through Little Wolf Creek,
Lickskillet Hollow, Big Horse Gap,
Sugar Run and Sinking Creek,
To Catawba's high-peaked side,
Where Indians roamed and died,
And yet is home to dogwood bracts,
Red clustered berries in the fall,
Buzzard-soaring ridges, thermal deemed,
Dawn-dared azaleas, flaming flared,
And amethyst balls of violet petals
Set upon a swathe of green
That climbs the rock-leafed rhododendrons
Under oak and pine and leaning fir.

And of what do I sing?

Why,
I sing of those dogwood bracts,
Azaleas,
Buzzards, hawks and crows,
Hickories, pines and oaks,
Roots and stones and narrowed rocks.

I sing of the corn snake, red and tan and gray,
Who uncoils upon a sunbeat rock,
Then quickly slips away.

…I sing of friends lost upon the way…

And I chant the chant of ancient times,
Of the ancestors of these paths,
Their stories and their memories
Carved in every step
Upon the calling earth, until,
At last, I skelter-reach

Another wooden shelter,
A spring to wash and water boil –
Campers laughing, blister tending,
Hanging soiled socks and underwear
Across soft maple branches, there
To dry and mend,
Coaling franks and tins of corn,
Spreading jelly on week-old rolls
Toasted carbon in the flames,
Then sinking to an evening read,
Flashlights held for sleeping heads,
As we let the night soft nod to ease
And midnight steep our snoring zzzzs.

And again I thank the beneficent sun,
Let him rest as well awhile,
The moon well roused, her face
Welcoming my safe domain
And my nightly prayer of thanks.

In the morn, once more I call
The energies of all come in,
Join our journey
To meaning in our lives,
The bliss, the inner joy
That comes from opening out to all
In care and love and empathy.

And I sing the chanting of the names
Across our highland meadows, draped in sun,
Of black-eyed susans, ox-eye daisies,
Chicory, soapwort, Queen Anne's lace,
Sorrel, late-graced buttercups,
Dandelions and enspired mullein,
Fritillaries and wiry swallowtails,
Sulfurs, blues, coppers, whites,
Monarchs on migration routes,
Flycatchers clinging to the grass,
Swifts clipdarting sparse and close.

…And I sing those meadowed vales,
Sing the dales and the words,
Sing the souls of the butterflies,
Sing the flowers and the birds…

…As a harrier hovers in the stillness,
Sudden plunging, veering, flapping
And flies low across the fields
That drape this range of Virgin west,
From blaze to white-trimmed blaze,
Across this crest of continent,
Singing as she goes.

Is that me? Am I the harrier,
Or the butterfly? The question or
The mystery?

Oh, sing with me,
Sing with me forever...

Join with us in prophecy
Of our future's verdant majesty...

...And demand, who are we and
Whom were we meant to be...?

...As Madame Tarot, palmist now,
Reader of horoscopes, diviner,
Practitioner of eastern yoga, meditation,
Holds her weekly stretching class
Next to the insistent music beat
Of a Jane Fonda workout meet,
While Tae Kwon Do martial artists
Mat each other across the corridor
Of a squat, converted hardware store...

...While religion loses further truth and
Is left within community, but
A community agin the world,
Insularity and fear unfurled,
And can no longer answer
To reason nor humane belief,
Who we are,
Nor whom we were meant to be.

And then our ancestral guides call upon
Nat Turner's grave, our nation's slave, but
For us today, with Gabriel, hero to
An empaupered population.

Jefferson takes his hand,
Raises him to a stand, then lets
Old Man Lee hug his shaking frame
In a brotherhood of centuries
And mutually forgiving shame.

Hear us, hear us, hear us –
VisionMind, will you listen now?

Tread soft, Virginia, as you do,
Lest you step on our faint voices,
For within the warmth of dawnlight reverie,
I hear the fiddler and the banjoer play
Far up the lost-called hollows
Of our ancient memory.

"For who are we, who are we?"
We still ask as we gather round
The fire of ancient ancestry,
And sit in companioned co'ka-ro's
Upon the sacred shore of yesterday,
George Wythe and Nathaniel amid us now,
Settled within the flicker flames
Of our futured visionry.

So, MusicMen come and join,
Gather with us 'round
Our reflected lake of dreams,
As we seek to answer who we are,
Highland proud, still beneath
The night-time glow of a moon full bound,
With SelfSearch taking up the hands
Of The Horseman of the woods,
WindTeller of the breeze,
RattleMan, The distant Hood,
Linkum Tiddlum Tidy, our Savior Hare,
And with the Sufferings, Enchanters,
Abundances and Weavers of our Minds,
Bare within the twelve directions
To find the hands of delved humanity,
Our ancestors all...

...Drumming, calling in ceremony
To re-enstall all memory
Of what we'd hoped would be
And dance-fall within the trance
Of soft-encircled prophecy
And the ancient mountain's call...

We sit, ancestors in our round,
Forefathers, Callings, crouching,
Puffing the pipe of intensity and truth
As, one-next-one-next-one, we center-walk,
To spin-talk that ancestral mystery
The voices sing to us
– The voices, oh, the voices –
The wefting Sufferers of their way,
Telling us their stories, over, over,
One-by-one-by-one,
In some joint history of our tocome
Compiled from each one's sanctity...

...Stories of the nine-book path
– One of many –
To understand, within
The depths of our soul,
That James Towne's ways are erroneous, dead,
And we must break the circle of before,

Then begin a search, in mind
And thought and action, to
Redescribe the circle and then
Seek new possibilities, to
Dissolve into the search for self
Within the unity of all, to
Surrender to the mountain,
Sacrifice being and begin
A pilgrimage within the world, to
Discover reconnections,
Intimate within that love of
New songs and ceremonies,
Accoutrements and chants,
Mantras of our new belief,
Then dive into the caverned well, to
Plunge, stripped, finally bare, only to
Re-emerge, cleansed and whole
Within a celebrated ecstasy of
Truth,
Of love of all in all, within
The deepest
Meaning of our soul.

So, come, enter,
Enter in with me
If we are to discover who we are
– Our sweet mystery –
The circle of a tocome that's past,
– The returning of our ancestry –
And cast the bones upon
The mountain's heights, the fire,
The breathing cavern's deep,
The spiral of weeping direction's wind,
And the templed heart we keep
In the circled dancing of our mind.

Come, oracle, come,
Give us your prophecy,
As you cast the bones
In the hope that what is done
Is done – finally...

"Please, Great Ke'show-tse,
Before it is too late,
Awake! Awake! Awake!"

Come, come, come,
MindWeavers in your imagery,
Sufferers, three-by-three-by-three,
And join us in the prophecy of
Tocome!

For our freedom and our dream
Was not of escalating wealth, of opulence,
Of commercial gain, but of quiet peace,
Community and contentment, free
Of governor, soldier, tax or sheriff,
To take responsibility unto ourselves
Completely, not have others do
Our social duty and our deeds, but
Harken to free belief and a creed
Of mutual love, respect and caring need.

So once again we ask,
WindTeller and the Callings,
Who are we? What does it mean to be?

Rights and individual liberty?

Sure, but more, much more:
It began on that first beach,
On that first shore,
When those in fear met those in fear,
Cultures clashed and peoples fought,
With something lost as well as gained,
An innocence and a purity,
A belief in an edenic phase,
An honesty in our hearts,
And a love of our fellow man.

Virginia was not born in nicety,
Liberty and sweet democracy;
It was born of anger, strife,
In bloodshed, hate and terror,
Oppression and conformity,
And survival-sundered destiny.

Yet the servant bonds we all once wore
Are now the millions who have since explored
Confusion's sharp, confused discord
Between the myth and patriotic chords,
And our harsh-tuned reality.

The truth of Virginia, my friends,
Is the difficulty of our lives,
Yet the richness of this land,
Which, if we can take it to ourselves,
To have and hold and safe preserve,
If we can learn to comfort and to share,
If we can build on that fine trend
Of family, society and mutual care,
If we can learn to salute-forgive,
To live a past devoid of shame
And stand as proud instead,

As adults come full round,
Who have faced our ghosts,
Our vampired, mental games,
And risen before the world full height
In the pride of our righteous might,
Then the last four hundred years
Will live as thronging glory within our soul
And will lead, with salvation's final song,
To the greatness we have dreamt upon.

Dream with me.
Enter the circle of the oracle,
Enter the prophecy,
And dream with me
The *true* dream of our ancestors
And dream that to reality…

Not this hell of debt and greed…

"Awake, Ke'show-tse, Great Sun! Awake!
Call unto the dawn!"

In 1983, the Assembly formally recognizes six surviving Indian tribes in Virginia: the Chickahominy, Eastern Chickahominy, Mattaponi, Upper Mattaponi, Rappahannock and Pamunkey; two years later, it recognizes the Nansemond; and in 1989, it recognizes the Monacan. Only two tribes have reservations, the Pamunkey and Mattaponi. None are federally recognized.

V

I sing again of the prophecy
As Southside slowly populates
With centers of correction,
Prisons and reformatories
At Sussex, Nottoway, Lunenburg,
Southampton, Mecklenburg,
Brunswick, Lawrenceville,
Jarratt, meek Dillwyn,
Baskerville, Halifax, Indian Creek…

…And I sing of the inmates, lost
To uncompassioned souls,
And call for some new answer
To the hatred, revenge and pain
That worthless prison gains…

…As Dale Earnhardt,
Spinning through the spring,
Thrills the 1987 NASCAR tour,
Winning the Sovran 500 at Martinsville,

The world's richest short-track prize,
In a Wrangler Jeans Chevrolet,
His third victory at the oval
In the thrilling heart adored
Of Virginia's raceway country...

...While, in Wythe County this ill-spent year
The marijuana crop is excellent,
The summer hot and moist,
And the Feds not too near...

...For such new crops, new enterprise
Are fast replacing old skills, as,
In the southwest, once coal-rich, booming,
Mining is in long decline,
New machinery, competition, strip technology
Replacing jobs, degrading soil and forestry,
People unemployed and leaving,
Kids to find a better life
As the old centers of Appalachia,
Norton, Wise and Big Stone Gap
Are abandoned, stripped by outside malls,
Their populations steeped in decline,
And only Blacksburg's Virginia Tech,
Some industry in Christiansburg,
Radford college, Lebanon,
Give hope of futured renaissance.

Other towns suffer a similar grilling,
Wakefield, Kenbridge, Victoria,
Brookneal, Farmville, Lawrenceville,
Once thriving centers of tobacco, milling,
Cotton farming, forestry,
Now suffering consolidation, cancer fears,
Overproduction, quotas, inconsistent soil,
Third-world competitors, Taiwan,
Mexico, China, India and Brazil,
People leaving, their skills and money too,
As these cities retreat, their shops gaunt close,
And dereliction haunts their shadowed streets...

...and I sing of those vales, where...

...A turkey gobble-gobbles to her progeny
Jumping branch to branch within
Their night-time roosting tree
As a sapsucker drills precise rows
Of holes in the bark of a walnut lee,
And in the evening vale below
Canada geese tuck nightly necks
In a rivered verge of winery...

…As a Guatemalan with no English
But hardwork ethic, strong hands,
Is taught how to prune the canes
Of this year's harvest vines,
To remove old wood, leave last year's,
Fine-tune with saw and knife and shears,
Then weigh the cuts and twine the buds
That will sun the next crop's bundled fruit.

And late he works, kerosene lights,
To tie tight the thirsting branches to
A wide-gapped trellis, wrapping tops,
Netting from the summer birds,
As along the Piedmont counties
Of Madison, Albemarle and Nelson
Vineyards burst on sunny slopes.

And I sing of those slopes…

…As an augur-haunted tractor stops,
Positions, twist-drills, roils and
Coils out the tumbrel soil, rises,
Drives on, as we follow, drop
In square-sawn, leaning stakes,
Back-fill with earth and level,
Upright perfect, beveled, lined by eye,
Stamped in, moved on, taking from the pile
One
Every three yards or so,
Straining posts tamed at the turns,
Notched and tension strutted,
Butted with tenth-inch tensile steel
Conducting wire, uncoiled, pried
Through insulators, hammered on,
Dispensed and terminated at
An insulation tube, metal strip
Gapped 'tween wire and corner post,
Earthing our perimeter, self-enhosted,
Battery and cold charger poled,
Tested for resistance, what ohms lost,
In-line ratchet winder fixed,
And double crimp sleeve joiner used
To bound
Lengths that surround
Our naïve field,
One red man, one a white,
The third of us full black,
Kept well still and wandering from
Too greatly deep creatively,
From any nobility of choice and will,
And learning too skilled or radical
– Still tightly fence enbound.

...And I sing of those fences
As the bluebird calls...

For there is change in the air –

...Even as I sing of Southside still,
Of its history,
With The Horseman as my guide,
Chant the rivers and the lakes,
The hills and well-cut banks,
The forests and tobacco squares,
Corn and cattle, trailer parks,
And new-laid avenues of hope –
As the oracle sings its prophecy
Of community, care and sanctity,
Of us as one upon the earth
And its hidden, sweet abundancy...

...And as I sing within unmanufactured vales
Where mid-century farms have left
Their cattle and their standing corn,
Victims of lost competition
And where fields now costless lie
Under scrub and oak and pine...

...And as I sing of those vales,
The cattle and the corn,
And dance with you until the dawn
Of our lost, regretted morn.

In 1986, Gerald Baliles is elected governor. He increases spending on roads and prisons and appoints Elizabeth Lacy the first woman to Virginia's Supreme Court.

Meanwhile, a single mom
Hurries from a Magnum rerun
To climb aboard a yellow bus
Sunning in her trailer yard,
Clicks her belt, turns the key,
Grinds the gears, frees the brake,
And eases onto the shaky highway
Towards a nearby Franklin school,
Thankful for her part-time job,
Even with its part-time pay.
Her daughter, sixteen, works a shift
At Burger King, mopping floors,
Cleaning restrooms, drifting tabletops,
Seats and isles of messy condiments,
Pressing buttons on a register,
Cutting bills, counting change,
Headphone orders, drive-thru dudes,
Kids fooling, parents getting mad,
Praying that a treat will becalm tears,

Regulars for burgers, colas, fries,
Whoppers and our Value Meals
Sealed and stacked and handed out
With ketchup, mayo, sweet sugar packs
In a serene and mindless part-time drudge
Of "Have a nice day!" greet and fudge.

In a rural trailer, deep down
Some dead-end, creek-swamp road
Of plastic deer and rusting wrecks,
Her estranged father, invalid,
On benefit, in denial, overweight,
Diabetes, swollen legs, inveterate smoker,
Watches that same senile rerun,
A couch-choked mile away...

...As, at nearby Emporia,
In a Lions Foods superstore,
Another mom rings a register,
Price after price after price,
While, in the next row a man
Installs a barcode scanner
To amend the process, speed it up,
Record for inventory, weed out robbery,
And, in the process, steal her job.

Her family, who proudly built up,
Then down, and strove to keep
Their final, low-paid work,
Now leave their rental house and shed,
Take their truck bed, motley things,
Six children murkly educated,
To rebegin in a more western state,
California, where they can relate
Their sad story to some distant kin,
In better hope of freedom's health
And the sustenance of barest wealth...

...While, close by, two farm kids
Make way beside the road,
The end of their driveway in the cold,
As a yellow bus appears, slows and halts,
Flashes all its lights, its stopsign arm
Restraining a line of cars behind;
They enter, hi the driver,
And run to the farthest back
As the bus revs and tracks towards
Their school, integrated, mainly black,
Though once it was not nearly so,
As most whites have fled or now send
Their kids to private, non-black schools
As segregation dances in the shadows,

Silent, hidden in the glances
And other subtle prisms on the face
Of ever-present, demeaned disgrace.

They pass a billboard that
Advertises Marlboros,
A cowboy leaning on a fence,
The image of the open West,
Of freedom, independence
Tied to a smoker's breath.

...click-click, click-click...

In Madison Heights, close by
Lynchburg's James, a brickworks
Takes crushed clay and shale
From an open pit, huge excavators,
Crushers, powered belts shuttled
To storage banks, blended clays,
Then vibrates it thru' desizing screens,
Lumps and stones removed,
Tempered to a plastic mass,
Pugged and milled and mixed
Between revolving shafts and blades,
Textures added, special coats,
Cutler-sliced, cored and dried,
Then fired for thirty hours or more
Within a moving tunnel kiln,
To build a hundred thousand homes
In Virginia's vintage brick –
And not an indentured boy in sight,
Not a chain nor whip nor
Mighty overseer
With us within his grip.

I am still dreaming,
Dreaming still,
Of the casting of the bones...

...And of my share of American pie,
As we, forefathers all, meander
The cupboard stalls
Of a Greenville antique mall,
Converted garage, service station,
Where we find an
Old butter churn, handle missing,
A moldboard for a plow, rusting iron,
A dusty mount of careful pinned
Swallowtails caught in 'ternal flight,
A hornbook for an alphabet,
Worn, torn and faded, rent,
An old bent saw, double-handed,

For cutting ancient chestnut trees,
– And with each they feel the breeze,
As they wander under-sufficed,
Clutching Virginia's memories
Of her ancestors' mournful touch
And of their soft-couched sacrifice…

While Gabriel walks into the sun,
A washboard underneath his arm…

Then we see an old man
Hunched against the wind,
Limp-shuffling in
His Salvation Army shoes,
Jacket, cap against the chill,
And, knowing he is us and we are him,
Slip a bill into his tin…

…And fly to Danville, where
We spectral pass another bank
Opening yet another ATM
And drive-by window,
As Business 29 sees new showrooms,
Chain restaurants, hardware stores,
Chain supermarkets, beauty parlors,
Chain pet food and chain malls
That draw the one-time trade
From a downtown stuttering yet
To revamp its decayed façade
And replace its urban flight
With new-prospered city life,
And make us wonder, is this our dream…?

Meanwhile, at an Augusta interchange,
A giant Exxon station, food store,
Trawls people from the interstate,
A Denny's, MacDonald's, Quality Inn,
So the nearby county garage store
Cannot compete many months more,
Expires its pumps and shelves,
Home cooking that doesn't sell
These days –
And you can see it still, a boarded shell,
Bat-haven, vandalized, overgrown –
A forgotten day in our history.

Am I still dreaming,
Dreaming still, of my slice of pie…?

Why, oh, why, oh why?

VI

Click, click...

A horned owl waits within a tree.

In 1989, Douglas Wilder is elected governor. The first black governor of this, or any other state, he is socially and fiscally a conservative, fights on an anti-crime platform, and when he's confronted with a revenue shortfall and economic downturn, guts Virginia's arts programs and slashes education spending.

Also in 1989, the US Supreme Court rules that a Richmond scheme of positive discrimination in public works projects is unconstitutional. In September, a riot breaks out in Virginia Beach between police and black students.

Meanwhile, Eastern Europe throws off the shackles of the Soviet Union and the Berlin Wall comes tumbling down. Within a few years, the Cold War is over.

Oh yes,
There is change in the air...
American Pie...
Bye-bye, bye-bye, bye-bye...

For, with several years of steady boom,
Fuelled by federal debt and wargame growth,
North Virginia shoots an economic rush,
High-tech jobs in armaments, the Pentagon,
Health and medicines, software, education,
Lobbyists, corporate headquarters,
New Dulles Airport, AOL,
Interstates sixty-six and ninety-five,
Suburbia engulfing Fairfax, Loudon,
Prince William, Fauquier, Clarke,
Expanding Fredericksburg, Warrenton,
Culpepper and Front Royal,
With gated lives and outlet malls,
Green space and our heritage
Rapid-sucked and drained,
Plus encroachments on Manassas,
Spotsylvania, historic Chancellorsville,
In a fundamental clash of values
– To build and build in the name
Of a cancerous growth that kills
Trees and culture and our fine health,
Or to try to plan, preserve the wealth
Of our past for our children's lungs –
To renovate Mount Vernon, Monticello,
Protect the rest, build museums,
Cultural centers, refind our history
And give future generations understanding
Of how we came to be – for that is the heart
Of retaining our democracy.

It is left to retirees and the self-employed

– Potters, turners, quilters, artisans
Of baskets, woodwork, photography –
To create new beauty from ways of old
For the shops and tourist malls that foretold
Our stops and slotted byways...

...As WindTeller rides
With our proud ancestors
Down Monument Avenue,
Past statues to their memory,
Into the gardens of the Capitol,
Jefferson's ideal and
Washington's memorial,
As banks, financial institutions
Rejuvenate centertown Richmond,
Wachovia, BB&T, SunTrust,
The University of Richmond,
Virginia Union, VCU,
Colleges and seminaries,
Dominion Power, hospitals and health,
Communications, tobacco,
New roads, suburban growth,
Malls and hotels, as tourists come to see
Battle lines and battle scars and
Lee lowers his hat as they pass
The White House of the Confederacy...

From January to March, 1991, US troops invade Iraq in The First Bush's War.
Many Virginians are involved. At home, the conflict is used to attack our
democratic rights and maintain a huge military, which has searched for and
gleefully found a new enemy now communism has collapsed and the US is the
sole superpower.

Then I learn that
Father Washington wishes
To return to his tomb, tears of wrath
Singeing his pallid eyes
At the abuse our military takes
Of Old Dominion's cries...

And all the ethereal ancestors,
Upon their spectral mounts,
Weep at the federal spending,
Military encampments,
Religious bigotry, still entrenched
Tidewater aristocratic lies
And developers desecrating what little
Pure land still resides within us...

...They sit in circled mount, hold hands,
Close eyes and memorize
Their lurch against old state control,
The British and their Church,

Public intrusion into our lives,
Taxation beyond our control,
And power in the hands of a few...

...For it is our poor education,
Our ignorance and disempowerment,
Our sense of frustrated anger
At the powerlessness in our lives
And politicians who always lie
That allows such foreign escapades
For arms and monopolistic oil...

...click-click, click-click...

I am All am I...

Here is my dream – it is forestalled,
For a last-gasp pall is yet to come...

VII

In 1992, Republicans sweep to victory in Congress behind Newt Gingrich and the
Contract With America: a combination of conservative moral values, Christian
activism, enormous military spending, anger at big government and high taxes,
and an uncompromising 'reverse the tide' social attitude.

Suddenly, to most's surprise,
A Christian McCarthyism haunts the land
To revoke recent gains,
Segregation lost, women free, so
Angry thoughts turn to misery,
Preying upon our thoughts and deeds,
Thinly-veiled, throwback agitprop
To rabble rouse and push us in reverse
To some pre-Darwinian cursèd land
Of an intolerance that, 'tis true,
Has not evolved one moral hue,
Incanting,
Through fear and ranting radio,
Television evangelizing that barely hides
Pedophilia, adultery, moral hypocrisy,
Invading the privacy of our lives,
Preaching abstinence and childhood purity
While filming pornography, hiring rooms
In seedy downtown motels, luxury hotels,
Bakker, Swaggart, Haggard,
Catholic choir boys,
Cadillacs, binge parties, expense accounts,
Huge mansions, swimming pools, golden watches,

> Distorting opponents' views, video tapes,
> Supporting dictators' diamond mines,
> Covert arms deals, spying, nuclear war,
> The murder of opposing news,
> In a total perversion of Christ's soft message
> Of love, compassion and surrender
> To the humanity of all.

"Nothing short of a great Civil War of Values rages today throughout North America. Two sides with vastly differing and incompatible world-views are locked in a bitter conflict that permeates every level of society…

"The struggle now is for the hearts and minds of the people. It is a war over ideas. And someday soon, I believe, a winner will emerge and the loser will fade from memory."[170]

In 1994, Senator Chuck Dobbs narrowly defeats Oliver North, of Iran-Contra infamy, to retain his Senate seat. North's near-victory, despite his alleged conspiracies and illegal activities, shows a swing towards moral conservatism in Virginia at this time. In the Senate, Robb is barely distinguishable from the Republicans. He is the only Democrat to vote for all the Contract With America, and is in favor of high military spending and an aggressive foreign policy.

> …click-click, click-click…

> Yet this proves a final gasp, a
> Last-ditch stand and most
> Soon realize that
> It is time we stopped
> Virginia being abused
> As the boxing ring
> For racists, bigots, liars…

On January 28, 1997, the Virginia Senate finally 'retired' *Carry Me Back to Old Virginny* as the state song, and initiated a contest for a new one. No substitute has been found. Maybe one that isn't racist…?

> For there is a new spirit brewing,
> Simmering at the edges of
> A refound humanity, a call
> To our natural-pledgéd past…

> …a turning turning…

> *We are all, are all, are all…*

> …Since, despite the rantings of
> The rabid Christian right,
> Who see their world in rapid
> Flight from nonconformity,
> Even the Gospel itself is changing,

---

[170] *Children at Risk*, by James Dobson, 1994, pages 19–20. Dobson is founder of Focus on the Family Ministries.

Our concept of God, once united,
Whole, firm and sure, the Bible
Taken word-for-word as pure, heaven
A place of angels, God elderly, supreme
Upon his throne, o'erwatching all, Hell
A realm of fire and bile, lurking miles
Beneath the earth – Now
We are less sure, more thoughtful,
Questioning,
Differing in our thoughts, realms
Symbolic somehow to many,
God a form of consciousness,
Necessary cause, no more – Cain and Abel,
Adam, Eve, the Garden and the Flood
Metaphors for our relation to the world,
As Eastern views mingle in our thoughts,
Yoga, acupuncture, chakras, yin and yang,
Opposites interacting,
Compassion for our fellow man,
Enlightenment, awareness, meditation,
Mysticism revived and sought
As we, self-taught, find new beliefs
That will better serve our Christian Lord.

...While the horned owl watches,
Twilight-skilled,
Hunches down, rests
Upon a branch above me –
As I lie silent, hidden, still,
In the glint of the moon's slim crest...

...And we mourn the passing of Arthur Ashe,[171]
Born upon a segregated Richmond day,
Who had to travel north to play
And fight with courage in his strokes,
Serving well his folks and cause
By winning three grand Opens,
Davis Cups and other titles,
– Fifty tokens to his name –
Devoting life between his matches
To stripping from South Africa
Apartheid's segregated bones,
Meeting Mandela in his home,
Speaking to a UN assembled
And arrested twice to raise
Funds for AIDS and city teams –
Fighting every day of his life
For justice, fairness, caring, calm,
Until he finally lies in state,
His coffin passed by thousands –

---

[171] His funeral takes place in 1993.

A hero to all who desire to fire
American aspirations, empathy,
Quench manipulating need
And the ignorance of hateful greed...

...As a sudden storm drench down-pours
Across a humid lowland scene
Of basswoods, alders, hornbeam trees,
Elms and certain mulberries,
Pelting them with half-an-inch, until
We see the sparkle-sear, the glare
Of the proudly flaring sun,
Wrapped upon within
The light-embrazoned clouds...

We had dreams, Virginia...

...both undaunted in our hope...

In 1998, Republican Jim Gilmore is elected governor. He abolishes property taxes on vehicles, the largest tax cut in Virginia's history, but throws the state's budget into chaos. He also creates a statewide technology commission.

In 2000, the Republican Party takes control of the House of Delegates for the first time since Reconstruction. But it is a very different party than then.

So how does it set,
Racism's century of fear and prosperity,
The white élite's rearguard action,
The height of its vindictiveness,
Repression on a world-wide scale,
Born in segregation's greatest victory,
Languishing through prohibition,
McCarthyism, two world wars,
Cold War, Cuba, CIA and NSA,
Korea, Vietnam, Panama and Chile,
Depression, starvation, soup lines,
Eugenics, sterilization, civil rights,
Poll tax, burnings, lynchings,
Christian dictatorships of the mind,
White flight, inner city blight,
And the desperation of the poor?

Well, it sets well, for
It has also seen our greatest upward climb
To health and jobs and wealth
– Tho' built on borrowing and debt –
With cars, computers, astronauts and planes,
Radios, TVs, mass communications,
Electronics, telecoms,
Roads and rails and phones,
Schools rebuilt, college education,
Liberation on a colonial scale
Of blacks and women, gays

With new-given rights,
Empires defeated o'er the globe,
Urban renewal and democracy
Bringing humans towards each other
For the first time in our history – after
Four million years of journeying –
America probing into the world...

And Virginia is part of that globe, at last...

So yes,
It sets well – remarkably –
With hopefilled rays,
After decades willed of darkness,
Disease and trying stress...

...But don't forget our state's
South and west,
Lingering yet,
In Lee and Scott and Wise,
Dickenson and Washington,
Russell, Smyth, Buchanan,
Or the social battles still to come,
To make this state for everyone...

So – yes...

...Though I sing the centuries of our pain,
I also sing of our hope and gain,
Our dreams,
Our courage and our prophecy –
I sing the glory of our days
To come, to come, to come...

...And I hear them singing too,
The forefathers, ancestors,
Callings around the fireside pool,
The Sufferers and the MusicMen,
The Wefts and Four Abundances,
Fooling with the Four Enchanters,
Ringing woods and Piedmont slopes,
Mountains and the tidal swamps
With the power of our revamped hopes...

Brer Rabbit and Linkum too,
Whistling of the prophecy...

For, can you not see the smile
Upon our parents' lips
As they slip between the leaves
Of the leafing springtime trees?

Hope is finally blooming on the wind
And in the oracle of the air
– Is, at last,
Giving us, the proud, a glimpse
– A glimpse –
Of the promised pie,
As the slackened hoop rejoins
And clouds circle back complete...

But we cannot lade our pudding plates
With promises alone...

Come, oracle, come,
Attain for us your prophecy,
And break the spell at last!

For even in the rain,
We had dreams, Virginia,
Didn't we...

VIII

Governor Warner, Democrat,
Oaths in oh-one to redirect
State tax to Southside growth,
Main Street revitalization,
Restoration of old shops,
Art centers, roads and colleges,
Government jobs and Ethernet,
Resetting both our memories
And the future of our hopes.

For example,
In downtown inner Charlottesville's
Old runs of encagéd blacks,
Belmont, Fifeville, Tenth and Page,
Vinegar Hill and McIntyre,
That were once the scenes of negligence
Both blind and deliberate, where
Black businesses slowly starved
And city fathers, white, forgot
Their pledge to reinvigorate, are now,
In a head-to-toe reflation,
Desirable, near-town chic,
Prices up as whites move back
To mingle in the rich-stacked streets
Where cultures new-fleet bloom
And leave suburban dullness, gloom,
To enjoy the other side
Of renewed and urban-centered pride...

...For now the bluebird sings:
"All are We are All...!"

...As I recall, appalled,
At my Nelson County desk,
Within the Rockfish River vale
And Jefferson's fall-breezed ridge,
Blue risen in the mourning trees,
Staring at the flame-'gulfed horror
And the ashen streets of screams,
At the standing, mouth-hand crowds,
Figures jumping, falling, twisting,
On and on the voice of dreams,
In newscast shock and terror seems,
And then another ear-crash boom,
Inferno, cold-blood, streaming plays
Of a faint jet circle-targeting,
And another huge crashing splay,
Then a blazing tower implodes,
Cameras spilling, pointing to the ground,
Feet jerking, fleeing sounds, explosions,
Ash and dust and pleas, "Get out!
Get out! She's going! She's going to go!"
Another blaze, news of more,
Tossing plumes of smoke and a choking
Witness lost in paralyzing shock,
Stunned and stammering,
Mock hands pushed through hair,
Gawping, staring, mesmerized,
As another tower crashes down,
News flashes of the Pentagon,
Slain, smashed,
Rumors of a Pennsylvania plane,
Battered, turning, shattering
Illusions in our isolated lives,
Beyond Kyoto, international law,
Or the desperate excuse of those
Across the poor and lonely world
We have scorned, abused
And turned our backs upon.

It was our sense of destiny, of right,
Of justice and supremacy,
As Americans,
That was infernoed that brutal day –
Our arrogance, our naïveté,
Our unfaltering belief in righteousness
Shattered on the altar
Of the crying world's despair.

Oh, hear the crying of our pain,
And don't ever turn your back

Again on the strain
Of humanity's stifled sigh!

"The abortionists have got to bear some burden for this because God will not be mocked. And when we destroy 40 million little innocent babies, we make God mad. I really believe that the pagans, and the abortionists, and the feminists, and the gays and the lesbians who are actively trying to make that an alternative lifestyle, the ACLU, People for the American Way – all of them who have tried to secularize America – I point the finger in their face and say, 'You helped this happen.'"[172]

...click-click, click-click...

"If you're not a born-again Christian, you're a failure as a human being."

"We're fighting against humanism, we're fighting against liberalism ... we are fighting against all the systems of Satan that are destroying our nation today ... our battle is with Satan himself."

"The primary cause of this national crisis is the feminization of men."

"I hope I live to see the day when, as in the early days of our country, we won't have any public schools. The churches will have taken them over again and Christians will be running them. What a happy day that will be!"

A few weeks later, at
Love Gap you and I stop and park,
Clamber-walk our favorite stroll
Up, through the gate and scramble-loll
The ridge's forest crown
Of Virgin' pines, mountain laurel,
Mosses, oak trees, bear-dragged snags,
The Horseman riding soft beside
Sad memories of the breeze...

...And there we meet those aging men
Of Virginia's 'chanted past,
Cast beneath old oaken trees,
Singing of their omens,
And the cycles of the centuries.

Once back,
We halt to watch a cardinal,
Red reflections
In the mirror of my truck,
Fighting all the world's chimeras
As he flails in feathered rage
Against and again against
The unremitting glass,
And I speculate upon those reflections
At which we tilt ourselves,
Sad memories of our warlike soul,
And wonder, can

---

[172] The Reverend Jerry Falwell, referring to the attacks of 9/11. The ACLU is the American Civil Liberties Union. The next quotes are also by Falwell.

The dunderheaded cardinals
Ever learn to share
The re-emergent forest glades,
Our new aware of human care,
And forge in joint, untaloned beak
A meek-grown grieving surge
Of hopeful, peace-dewed leaves
That can cry to us of common belief
And self-harbored, sighing sanctity?

Oh, when will you come,
And join me in the prophecy...?

You and I are one, Virginia,
I am you and you are me,
And there is no I between us
Anymore, anymore, anymore...

We are of the earth, of its fertility
And of its strength and power,
As we redraw the circle,
The sand about the fire,
The universal energy
Called to come and enter in,
To protect and sun its strength
Upon our ritual soliloquy...

...As we call a lover's call
To enter us as we enter All...

Oh, the bluebird's call...!

Remember how sweet the bluebird's call!

The singer sings and the drummer plays
And the fiddler sparks the night,
Their spirits waft across the notes
In darkness and in light,
In darkness and in light...

IX

I hope you still feel small
When you stand by the ocean...
...
I hope you dance... [173]

---

[173] *I Hope You Dance*, by Lee Ann Womack, 2000.

And, yes we do, we dance,
Entranced, as we fare
A muddle-headed fifty-eight
From shielding beach to Cumberland,
Past cotton, timber, tobacco yields,
Franklin, Emporia and John Kerr,
Crossing through a Southside land,
Danville, Stuart, Galax,
Easing Rogers' crazy bends
That relax the forest breeze
With simple banjos plucking,
Violins and mandolins,
Grailing on a crooked road
Of ancestral hymnal blues,
Abandoned rails, new biking trails,
Damascus sporting wares,
And such closely zedded skews
As wend and bend and stop and stare,
On descending into Abingdon, then on into
The coaling railroad fields
Of St Paul and Norton, Pennington,
To gleeful hitch the shunning swales
Of Walker's prevailing pass and pitch
Into Kentucky and rich-valed Tennessee.

On our planned way back,
Between Bland and Rocky Gap,
We slog into a country store
That retails coffee iced, turning dogs,
Breakfast sandwiches, spicy barbecue
Warming on the tillside ledge,
Tobacco, jerky, cigarettes,
Its owner in the neon dim
Of dusty shelves, a few scant tins
Of corn and milk, pork'n beans,
NASCAR models in tight jeans,
The toilet bowl too well used,
An old food counter, soda light display,
Lays chips and too-frail taco shells,
Twinkies, bread and processed cheese,
The owner hunting, cleaning deer
For friendship's freezers, cans of beer.

Meanwhile, in Sperryville,
At a spanking antiques mall,
Coffee shop and fairy stores,
Tourists rank to claim the night,
Restore high street named delights,
And bring a town back from the brink
To sightly famed and joint prosperity.

I pick up an earthen jug, feel

591

Its cool age in my palm
As I smell the peace of centuries
In its reflected calm.

A few days later, years beyond,
You and I, arm-in-arm,
Walk Albemarle's old courthouse square
In Charlottesville's uptown heart
Where Madison and Monroe stood,
To admire a good pavement laid,
Jackson inspired upon his horse,
As the Revolution cannons in our ears,
Pass a plaque that marks the spot
Of the slave-raised auction block
Lost across the years,
And meander to the Paramount,
Its black entrance demolished, gone,
Tho' still the memoried balconed cries
Linger on, in
The mist of our mutual eyes.

Then we wander, you and I,
WindWhisper by our side,
One hot and steamy after-morn
To stroll-adorn the pocket homes
Of Pocahontas, free black town
That has survived, commonly intact,
On the centuried margin of neglect,
Close by the hip of Petersburg,
Its resurrected port and slip and dock,
Where once great ships unlocked
Their lades for sweet-morned piedmont folk
Their barrels stoked of tobacco, timber, corn...

...And we hold each other tight
Against the journey of our lives,
Within this living memory,
Still several years away...

...For, further on, across a railway line,
Under the overpassing road,
We enter-stride upon a site
Of foretold and passéd memories,
A new visitor center, brochures
Glossy, new, computer-aged,
And the silent railroad wharves
Of River Street,
A market farmers-bought,
To the drafty antique stores and crafts
Of Second, furniture, plastic bric-a-brac
Sprinkled up and down North Adams,
Abandoned, forgot, aback

Between the coffee shops, re-adorned
Buildings hidden-past from change,
State-sponsored preservation,
Revitalizing, reguessing and
Re-engaging stressed tobacco jobs
That will presage new myths
And new memories – once
History and our culture gain
Their worthy place
O'er the pace of commercial pain.

Oh, such a dream…

And maybe one day, the Tiffany windows
Of Blandford church, memories too close
Of segregation and Confederacy,
Will be seen in their rightful space
– As myth and hope and vexed despondency…

…As WindTeller lowers soft his head
For the victims of those Southern years,
Removes his tattered tricorn hat
And creeps upon the fearful breasts
Of our ancestors' weeping, weeping,
Weeping, weeping chests…

…While yet we dance a new dance
And search a homespun truth
To hang our dreams upon…

Continuing our tour of the state,
One spring afternoon we stroll
From an oversated parking lot
To slot between the well-trimmed bays
Of Norfolk's botanic gardens,
Its arboretum and lakeside ways,
And avoid those children running wild
Through tranquil maples, willows,
Pines and snowbells, cherries mild in flower,
Ponds and streams and lanterns set
Amid paths of hope and gravel.

I look around me,
Slowly, slowly, slowly…

…slowly inspired, slowly fainting…

…As, in a mileless thought
You and I downstroll the wharf
Next Norfolk's tall *Wisconsin*,
Lower our heads to blown-bronze leaves
Of soldiers' last-wept words
And grieve deep within an Elizabethan view

Of modern ships and dry-dock yards,
Dreaming regard of James Towne's years,
The terrors and effulgent shards
Of our memories' softly witnessed tears,
Calling, calling, calling trails
Through four hundred wall-cracked veils
And the loss of our heart's ambition,
As wailing eyes sail swift upon
The rending of our fears...

...As we witness Washington with
His head still lowered there,
Between his powered knees...

...The past is slowly fainting,
Fainting before
The inspiration of humanity...

Soon thereafter,
Within the springtime maples
Cypresses and Great Dismal oaks,
We laugh our darkened, swamp-soaked way,
Scented, smeared to off the bugs
That manage to persist and sting
Around the faint-ringed wooden walk
That shrugs assured and towering trees,
And wonder how old slaves endured
This plague of biting flies.

After a short drive, we
Stroll the loblollies and the cedars,
Maples, swamp oaks, gums and tupelos
Slapping at old Pungo's ferry beach,
Kicking through the sand,
Watching the black waves lap
And inhale the moistened air,
Flies still nipping at our eyes,
As we breathe this happy day...

...While still I look around,
Slowly, slowly, slowly...

...And see the prophecies fulfilling
And signs of the times...

...they're inspiring everywhere...

...in respringing freedom's breeze...

...the Callings and the swaying trees...

The circle rejoined in every way...!

…As you and I embark
Within a fiberglass canoe
Upon that languorous flow,
Summer shallowed, pebbled,
And lie within its hollowed shape
To soak the sun's high glow
With a bottle of Virginia wine,
Goat cheese, apples, local bread,
And a basket sweetly o'er-full
To reflect upon the stream's reflections,
The progress made and progress yet to go
Towards self-honesty, acceptance,
Replacing myth and want-to-be
With remorse at our reality,
And entering fully, finally, the journey
Towards a deeper flow of truth…

…and I *do* feel small…

We are the crazies, Mama,
But one day soon, we will
Be the rays of summer dawn…

…slowly, slowly, slowly…

…click, click, click

…reborn, reborn, reborn…

We watch a green heron,
Bent eye-crept low,
Beak out, still, harpoon ready,
Drop a junebug, wriggling,
Struggling, rippling,
And wait for a sunfish, crawdad,
Immature perch or minnow,
Pondside roamer to investigate,
Then pounce with darting flash
Of speckled neck, rufous, arrowed back,
And whisk the splashing silvered form,
Bill it down, repeat swallow,
Shake the dew from a feathered crown,
And preen its throat and green-backed wing,
Then launch into ungainly flight
To another favorite screen within
The marsh's spartina light.

Meanwhile, in
The twilight of the saline marsh,
John-boats beached for the day,
The rhythmic rips of pooling bass
Echo in the darkened cool,

An angry heron raucous clacks
It rights and its territory, mosquitoes
Jitter on some slackened water, mayflies,
A chickadee, two tufted tits, a wren
And a sudden owl, barred, talons splashing,
Missing, flashing grit
In her heavy treeward flight
To her watchful perch again,
Eyes blinking, swiveling
In her gilded grain of mystery.

Then a rifle crisp-cracks the evening air...

...And I recall that late spring noon
We parked beneath the blowing dunes,
Stroked on sunscreen and repellent,
Took our water and,
Bent by a ranger station, hot and spent,
Meandered o'er the board-clacked walk,
Mind-in-mind, relaxed,
Through reeds to Back Bay's cormorants,
Warblers, red-winged blackbirds,
Distant egrets,
And a glossy ibis not twenty feet away,
Then hiked the highrise sandy banks
Of False Cape beach, Atlantic breakers
And a distant herd of pinto horses
That grazed the seaworn grass;
We breathed in this wonder,
A cornerscape escaped,
Heeled off our shoes and ran stoked to
The warm and sundowned ocean waves,
Then broke to watch, eyes wide,
A thousand surging horseshoe crabs
Merge and mêlée spawn,
Laying sacs of eggs within the tide...

...Only to turn on a promise
And see a craven hunter pouch
Eggs from an endangered nest,
Rifle crouched about his chest,
And shoot my heart upon his glance
Of careless chance and enterprise.

Then, later that year,
In a rising Accomack noon, we watch
The Horseman gallop yearlings, foals
Cowboy hemmed to a leeward sea, there
To swim to Chincoteague, the penning isle,
Rounded, caught and ridden,
Auctioned for the highest bid,
Remaindered, loosened, sparse returned

To their saltmarsh pastures, cordgrass,
And wildness cures and spurns.

We watch them corralled, interned,
Individuals confused, yearned expressions
On their manéd brows, eyes flared,
Snorting to the mists of fearful dread,
And wonder how we too are corraled,
Liberty taken swift from us,
And must submit to periodic indignity,
Our wildness, freedom's spirit,
And our bold intensity
Controlled for none to see.

For no,
We cannot lade our pudding plates
With promises alone,
Especially with new terror laws,
Alerts of orange, yellow, red,
Prying on our phonecalls,
E-mails, huge computer lists,
Massive deficits and tragic spending
On arms and arms and arms
That are driving us to witless end
With the nonsense of their charms
And insane threats of World War Three
By an insane, manic presidency
That is dying, by hatred dead,
His way of being, selfish, broken,
Drying on the vine of misspoken words
And the circle of our prophecy.

Oh the dance, the dream of the dance
That is returning, returning to the ways...!

And once more I see our forefathers
Gathered on the shore,
As an old Asa'teeg sings and cries
– No longer pines or grieves –
Upon the welcome rays of dawn,
Raises up his arms in rattled praise
And rings forth our hoped-for days
When, after four hundred years of scorn,
We can regain his native truth, reborn,
And live in harmony with an earth
Respected as before.

Soon we will meet on that bright and golden shore...

So, what is our destiny, Virginia,
You and I?
What the choices we shall seam

With the needlereams of our tobe?
And what do the ancestors of our soul
Reach out to teach us,
If only we had ears to tell
The retelling of their tale?

Eh, old Virginnie…?

…I ask as I watch,
Unmotioned in my tears,
With you by my side, Virginia,
With you by my side,
My comfort and my pride…

And still upon that sunburst shore,
The Chi-'ka-hom-ini lifts up his arms,
Cries, "Awake, Ke'show-tse, Great Sun! Awake!"
And drifts back those same four hundred years,
Through the stories of his family,
Of Pa-mun'ki, Ra-pa-han-o'k, Ma'ta-po-ni,
Mo-no'kan and Nan-se-mond –
Of how they are still yet ignored, unrecoiled,
Their calls for rights and reservations
Embroiled in fears of gambling joints
And unwillingness to remake those points
That scream of fake humanity –
And so he wonders still, sun-upraised,
Is this a gleaming dawn, or another sun that sets
Upon the history of our dreams?

…As our forefathers cry their cries
Upon
The waning dawn of our skies…

I hope you still feel small
When you stand by the ocean;
Whenever one door closes, I hope one more opens;
Promise me you'll give faith a fighting chance,
And when you get the choice to sit it out or dance,
I hope you dance…

And don't forget to sing…

X

Slowly, slowly, slowly…

Madame Tarot, having tried
Every New Age gimmick, circulating rite,
Every religion, sect and Oriental Way,

Sits down and silent sighs,
Reassesses, and decides
To return to that within spirit,
Arising from her self, her own sweet ways,
Her strength as Mother Healer,
Ergotria, goddess, one-in-three,
Spirit Guide to our confusion
Leading us to some caring place
Where nurturing and being all
Is the pivot of our fame...

Meanwhile, WindTeller, whisperer of the breeze,
Observer of our joys and miseries,
With forefathers in attendance,
Watches a Henry County family,
Wife part-time teacher, husband guard
At a penitentiary,
Travel to sedentary Martinsville
And buy a double-wide,
Brick foundation, appliances,
AC, gravel driveway, fence,
And celebrate their pride and new prosperity...

...As a downy woodpecker ritats
An ancient-tossed black oak tree,
Fallen across a shagbark hickory,
Then flies high to join her nest within
An old-snagged cherry tree...

...While, to redress their pride,
Keep young people in the tribe,
Give employment, retain old ways,
The Pa-mun'ki strive to restock
A shad hatchery
For Virginia's long-mocked riversides...

...Since now, old dams are being blown
And the headwaters once more are home
To sea-going fish, the streams more pure,
Less silted, banks retreed and buffered,
The ecology of our rivers recomforted,
Slowly, slowly, slowly...

...As our forebears call us once again,
To realize and accept
That our environment speaks of all our care
As a joint humanity finally seeks
To share our treatment of the earth...

...and hear the song of the poor whip-poor-will.

Thus I recall, recall,

That light-fallen afternoon when,
On the banks of silent Pa-mun'ki,
Lapping to the marshland grasses
And a misting egret's stutter-stall,
'Neath where the rail tracks rumble
Over the humble river's reeds
Close to the heron's clacking call,
I stood with sacred WindTeller
Before the silent-fallen mound
Of old Pow-ha-'tan, grasséd, bare
Six feet high, a dozen wide,
Buried where his people expend
Their tiny reservation and tend
Their cotton, center, hatchery –
And give respect to his memory…

…For we must remember too,
Recall and venerate,
The yi-ha'kans of bypassed peoples
Whose canoes no longer cut
The James or Rappahannock,
Whose bows and traps lie deep beneath
The bones and sighing blood
Of a dozen crying generations
And the ghosts of their genocide…

…aie, of their genocide.

The ancestors are watching,
Holding to our memory, keeping
Our stiff-hearted history
Safe for final sanctity
Within the temple of the truth
And freedom from all lies –
A time when we will full-encircle
And can, at last, apologize…

Pow'ha-'tan, we greet you!

Oh, let us beg of you our deepest grief
For the unspeakable cruelty we unleashed
Upon your unsuspecting peoples,
And let the rituals of our lives rebloom
In the assumptive rise of all
As we reassume an inner self
That is love, love as one,
Within a unity of all!

Slowly, slowly, slowly
We are learning, burning
The old ways, old laws, mores,
And rediscovering an ancient new…

In downtown Richmond
Tredegar is restored,
The canal basin rejuvenated,
River walk, Belle Isle,
Flood walls built, Shockoe Bottom,
The Capitol repainted and streets relaid,
A new library risen and new plans
For a center of the performing arts...

...Though there yet stew Manchester,
Chamberlayne Avenue,
St Paul and North – hidden scars that remind
Of a deplorable torture we yet inflict
Upon our uneducated and our poor.

Poverty is not their fault –
Oh, listen to the whispers on the breeze,
As sung to the freezing homeless –
"Poverty is not their fault!"

...new housing, schools and Medicare...

So cast the bones, my friends,
Cast the bones upon the stones
Of those ignored in misery...

Oh, Miss American Pie,
No more the miller and the milled,
The dyer and the dyed...

For the tide is slowly rising...

...As we are warned by satellite
Of global warming, ozone layer,
Icecaps melting, violent weather,
Tornadoes, rising seas and hurricanes,
Logging species, habitats,
The world's ecological heart
Ripped through our shuttered doors
On TV screens and Internet,
So that we can no longer ignore
Our impact on the world –
A denuded landscape of deluded dreams
That are in desperate need
Of some new prophecy...

In 2004, the US invades Iraq at the start of Cheney's War. Three years later, we are still embroiled. The so-called 'fight against terrorism' has conveniently replaced the Cold War as an excuse to build up arms, cause fear at home, plunge us into a grave economic crisis, spy into our lives and bully the world abroad. The war in Iraq certainly has nothing to do with fighting terrorism.

Politicians of the élite,
Corporate entrepreneurs of corruption,
Tycoons of over-monied power,
Above taxes, ethics, and the law,
Are now most clearly seen
As morally bankrupt, backward,
No longer our guardians but
Shackles upon all care, compassion,
And decent human development...

They are the new British,
Stripping us of freedoms,
In the name of homeland security...

Too much like The Fatherland...

The Geneva Convention is *de facto* abandoned, Guantanamo Bay a slur on our system of justice, and the executive branch of the federal government seems, at times, to believe itself totally above the law.

Our Founding Fathers
Ride with tears in their eyes
For the way that their state, despite
Constitutional safeguards,
A ban on an standing army,
Is now a secret encampment
From Pentagon to Fort Meade
Of soldiers, sailors and electronic spies...

Oh, there are still dangers, still questions,
Still so many dangerous questions, for
The graves are still dreaming,
Dreaming still,
And the shrouds of mourning do yet steal
Upon the shaded brooks and silent ways
Of our intended path...

...And I wonder at the way
We are ribboned, cut and wrapped
By laws and moral regulations,
Electronic camera eyes,
Extruded, roasted, mass-produced
To fulfill our pre-determined, salted roles,
Melted on miles of toast...

In June 2001, the National D-Day Memorial is dedicated in Bedford County. There are plans to build a National Slavery Museum near Fredericksburg.

When will our lives return to peace,
Our soil to land that's gently free,
And scarce resources wisely spent
To help the poor, the handicapped,

Our schools and arts and inner cities,
Our parks and our forgotten needs?

When will we no longer seek
To impose our strong-armed will
Upon an unwilling, resentful world,
But learn to spread our greatest wealth
In sharing natural blessings
And peaceful, caring amity?

The world waits to see…

…The world waits to see
If James Towne will grow to that dream,
Or be its fateful cemetery…

…As we cast the bones, my friend,
Slowly, slowly, slowly…

And as yet we dance,
You and I, Virginia,
Arms linked in life's embrace,
While we await our circled fate
And listen to the ancestored cry…

XI

In 2005, the population of Virginia surpasses 7,500,000 and is growing rapidly, mainly because of immigration into northern Virginia. The south and west of the state are still largely undeveloped, with little growth. About 80% of Virginians are white, 8% were born abroad, 81% of adults have graduated from high school and 29% have college degrees. The median housing price is $125,000 and the average per capita income is nearly $24,000. However, 9.9% of people still live below the poverty line.[174]

Are you still dreaming,
Dreaming still?

If you are, then bear my hand
And enjoin the Savior Rabbit's paws
As he glory-soars all down the lane,
Black top hat, ragg'd coat and cane,
Skipping to his spritely gait
Along the Road of Cares somehow
That leads us from a distant past
To cast beyond the wear-bared now…

I am still dreaming,
Casting of the bones…

---

[174] Source: US Census Bureau.

Clink-clink, clink-clink...

Let us walk with him along
The fantastic line of Massanutten,
As a groundhog sniffs the air,
Emerges to a trailside verge
Nibbles, tears the grass,
And sweetly breathes the evening sky...

And then let us hike the granite brow
Of Sharp Top, you by my side
In a mid-May mountain fold,
Past yellow lady's slippers,
Spiderworts and trillium, tiny gooseberries
Beneath round-roughed leaves,
New-fledged silvery blues,
Bleeding hearts and hued azaleas
Pink as clouds in a dawning sky...

...And wonder why it is we sit
On vinyl chairs, patent leather,
Polished laminates, in perfumed air,
Unnatural scents, with porcelain,
Nylon carpets, concrete, new-lain cement,
Air-conditioned aluminum, glass meant
To cut us from the wind, when once
We squatted 'mid a self-made life
Determined by the breeze and strife
Of the seasons' gentle whim, within and by
A glow of sentimental harmony...

...clink-clink...

...shlink, shlank, sklink...

...sing and dream and sing...

...For we have tossed from our lives
All ceremony,
Ritually descended to complacency,
Our rites of passage mere pampered guarantees
Of protection, selfishness and need...

Oh, my bones, my bones,
Are we not now
Separated from the consequences
Of the way we act – garbage merely
Wrapped in bags, collected, dumped
Out of sight, as water runs
From faucets to the ground,
Human waste to seas and streams,
Abstract ozone dreams of Antarctica,

A thousand oceans overfished,
– Anything but face the wish or plea
For dialogue, discourse, compromise,
Or change the spurn of our desires
And dire surmise of our consumption…?

…our consumption of our selves…

When will we see the Sufferers three,
Maid Mary, Fla'ed Weaver and The Sadness,
Stop their trance-swept dance around
The pool of endless seeming
And be left to rest at last
Within the peace of dreams
That are our sweeter scheming?

When will we rest in simple need,
And not writhe in others' pressing greed?

Oh, the bones, the bones…
Are they still dreaming,
Dreaming still?

By dwelling on old James Towne ways
We have dazed the earth to crisis,
As we sell our response to others
In taxes, calls to the police,
To teachers, social workers, newspapers,
Au pairs and psychoanalysts…

Or, worse, we live in pure denial,
Global warming refused as fact,
Mere propaganda set about
To destroy the American Way
Of individual liberty,
Since our philosophy still schemes upon
Unlimited resources,
And a superior life of greed
Masquerading as commercial need…

Oh, the bones, the bones…

Where is the sacred in our lives,
The ritual, pride and connection to
The intimacy of the countryside?

Has it been destroyed, along with
The animals and trees, the Indians,
Slavery, segregation and bigotry?
Or does it toil at the margins,
Ready for its time to come
And the circle yet to coil complete?

605

We have struggled four hundred years
For democracy, a free press, to vote,
To love and marry whom we will,
For liberty to speak our minds,
Free trade unions, free assembly,
Fair trials and justice in the courts
– Four hundred years against a state
Overrun by army, militia and police,
By bugs and tapes and endless spies;
Four hundred years of logging,
Deforestation, erosion of our soil,
Pollution of our rivers and our bay;
Four hundred years of élite control,
Of intimidation at the polls, of
Bribery, corruption, and intent
To deny us the right to our consent;
Four hundred years of state-bound lives,
Imposing taxes, laws, bureaucracies
That are beyond our control and say;
Four hundred years of corporate greed
In the rollcall of a dream,
Beyond responsibility or control,
Our laws to suit them, day-by-day,
Until we have lost all power and say;
Four hundred years of communities in decay,
Rotting, unable to compete,
Destroying the very core of that sweet care
Upon which America was built;
Four hundred years of spirit stolen
In a game of righteousness,
One strict God and Christly definition,
Of racism, segregation, eugenics, war,
Women oppressed within the family,
Of poverty and ignorance.

Yet, within those four hundred years,
We have struggled mightily
To drag ourselves from unawareness,
To improve the life of our families,
Fought for rights, conditions and fair pay,
Won democracy,
Challenged those in control, enrolled
In a prosperity and an empowerment
That has fueled resilience and commitment;
We have preserved and restored our culture,
Our heritage and our beliefs,
Have rediscovered the beauty
And wonder of our land
And will regain our lives from a fateful state,
Until we grateful live in health
And a proud and peaceful wealth
Of loving give and of care.

For, never have our liberties
Been more threatened, ever – and never
Has the challenge to reverse the curse,
To find some new stratagem
Of peace and care, community
Been more needed, more urgent,
And also, perhaps, more heeded
By those who hold our future
In the wisdom of their hands.

We must defend our old-won rights,
Our democracy, our liberty,
From these latest cockroach encroachments,
Stand and not submit
To those who stalk our institutions
With the minds of those British
Who ruled us in colonial times...

Click, click, click...
    ...being and belonging,
        ...to the bones, the bones...

Freedom is a constant battle,
Never government given,
But must be guarded and rewon
With every hardy generation.

Oh, how I hear the fiddle and the banjo play!

In the federal Senate election of 2006, George Allen is narrowly defeated by Jim Webb. At the same time, our constitution is amended to deny equal rights to unmarried partners. It is still illegal for unmarried people to reside together, and all sexual positions bar one are still banned. Ridiculous.

– Yet another whip-crack
Of enforced conformity
That smacks too much
Of James Towne's moral tyranny...

...perhaps it will be the last...

...click-click, click-click...

...For Virginia *is* changing,
There are many minor victories
And a more general moral change
That promises to raise us from inequity
To share in liberty and prosperity
– And I can proudly say
That the Commonwealth no longer is
The willing doormat of ex-Nazis,
Pedants, Moral Majority, or the KKK,

But is newly seeking values of
Tolerance, diversity and democracy…

For, in the cities of our strong-grown towns,
Within their temples, mosques and synagogues,
The Horseman sees a bubble,
A quietly stirring mix:
A bar mitzvah of the Jews,
A Muslim Ramadan, Hindu Divali,
A Buddhist Losar, Chinese New Year,
A maypole dance, a Catholic Mass,
A Lent of Mennonites and Afric' rite
That remessages the Middle Passage
– All in a richness he holds dear,
And vows to defend to death our right
To keep freedom's eternal threatened light
Shining on us equally.

…click, click, click…

…Being and belonging
To the ancestral bones…

As, at a crossroads on the night
Of a full moon's doleful tolling,
Madame Tarot dews some drops
Of heaven's kiss upon the soil
And dreams and spells the moment's stop
As the Sufferings sit in solemn toil
And the Callings chant and drum and sing
Some ringed and hummed ancestral light
And our heroes of ancestral past
Join a chanting ring to dawn the night…

Oh, how our ancestors
Fill us all with futured hope!

…zee-zah, zee-zah, zee-zah…

It is to see this hope and the true scope
Of our profoundest change on
The eve of the Quadcentenial
That I park my car and potter-cross
A new-laid parking lot, asphalt, hot,
Then stare in surprise,
Amazed as they materialize,
The Callings and the ancestors,
To lead me through their heroed past
To pay homage to our heritage, mazed
With monumental brick, air-conned
Cases of thick glass,
A fine Elizabethan display,

And watch a heart-jerk film narrate
The Starving Time, buy the tee-shirt,
Pick up flyers for *The New World* movie,
Ma'to'aka still 'playful' Pocahontas,
Anglo-centric, clichéd, counterfeit,
A failure, deeply mired to us Virginians
Who want to progress,
Discover new truths, be reimpressed…

And then, outside,
We pass the flags of fifty states
And ruminate a village veiled
In smoke and cicada zurrs,
Strangely false, inaccurate,
Wrong reeds, wrong site, wrong mats,
But pleasing to the tourist's eye
That knows so little of the fate
Of our harsh-won husbandry,
As it questions unastute
White volunteers in deerhide,
Instead of passéd Indians
Abiding, skinning, chipping 'heads.

Then we stroll, icecream in our palms,
Past a tour guide, school class set,
To a becalmed replica of James Towne's fort,
Though wrongly sited, wrongly built,
Oak-framed houses cramped inside,
A smithy, cruck church, platforms raised
For cannonaded parades and musketry,
Kitchen gardens, chickens, mocked-up well,
Corn swelling by the skiffer's yard
And a few scarred tobacco plants
Down by a new-built pier
Where *Susan Constant*,
Godspeed, and *Discovery*
Slowly bob the James – the always patient
Ancient James' tidal flow.

There, we wheedle information
From an old sailmaker, salt
Needling canvas halting through,
Then walk back, drive south, island-bound,
To the *real* historic site, repark 'round
Behind the Park Museum this time,
"Historic Jamestowne"
Yielding new findings,
Redefining old questions
In this battlefield of myth
That masquerades as history.

Slowly, we follow walkways to

The stray lowland mark
Where archeologists now dig, to
Re-expose the postholes of our mystery,
As masons construct new pathways, repoint
Walls and buildings, cemeteries,
Hasty-plant spring-flowered shrubs,
Bright and temporary borders for
The visit of Her Majesty
To refit, reglitz and re-invent
Old notions of our destiny.

Finally, we are guided through
Real palisades, *real* wells,
Real footings too,
Of early houses, huts and cells,
Of bulwarks, barracks, fortress lines,
Partly sunken now
By the river's constant course,
Eroding slow-enduring veils
That have prevailed four hundred years
Of rewritten past to fit our lies,
Beef up agendas, and delve deep within
The curse of James Towne's innocence,
Our history and our self-belief.

…For we have explored full circle now,
From fortress 'gainst a world of fear,
Through winning entry to a continent,
To seeing the world as terrored foe
Once more, once more, once more…

And I have learned, in my quest
Through centuries of harvest yields
That nothing has been given us,
Everyman, the poor, the wise
– Rather we have had to rise
And, step-by-step, attain the prize.

What *was* real, what *did* breathe
Down the Virgin centuries,
Was resilience, strength, determination
To strive, to stay, to overcome
Every barrier thrown in our way
– Governors, the British,
Slavery and segregation,
Women's social prison,
Gays hidden from their pride…

– *That* is our great heritage…

…As now The Callings peaceful sit
Waiting for the circle to complete,

To miracle and remit,
And ease them final-coursed release...

Oh, play, banjo, play...!

...and sing with me...

...For now we must dance the circle bound,
Sing the round of yesteryear,
And catch our soft immortal tears
In the cradle of our trance...

...As Old Linkum's vengeful sprite
Prances o'er the vales and hills
Of Virginia's ancestral dales,
Happy to freely quit at last,
But with a tap upon our shoulders
To remind us of the past...

Oh, sing with me,
Sing with me forever!

Caring, caring, caring
   ...caring for the bones...

For...
Bliss. There is a bliss around...

I close my eyes and breathe
In the bliss, out the bliss,
In the bliss, out the bliss
Of the oracle of my mind...

...As I halt before a tiny footbridge
And pray to the stream,
Grateful for its giggle
And its eternal dream...

Awake, Ke'show-tse! Great Sun! Awake!

Oh yes, Ke'show-tse, awake,
And make us once more the servants
Of each other, no longer of the self,
And harken to our ancestral hopes
Of a great bespoke tocome to come,
For the descendants of our greatest ones
Are emerging once again,
Resurging and restocking signs
Of circled corn and up'po-woc
To the dawning ring of joinéd hands
That sing re-entry to this land's
Enjoinéd circle, three in one,

611

Finally –
Black and white and Indian.

Oh…

Yes…

I stop and spread my arms,
Refold them to my heart,
For
'Tis time, 'tis time
To close the circle of four hundred years
And mark their passing with
An abundance of our mercied tears,
As we let go the truth of our inheritance
To embrace our future of desire;
'Tis time to sing the earth awake,
To breathe the air and dance the fire
And raise the Sufferers and the MusicMen,
Nine Wefts and Four Abundances,
From their long ancestral rest,
To join with us in our new quest
And caress the sun within the breast
Of our new-nurtured, caring morn,
So that we may final stop our clicking
In the fearful, scorning night
Upon the coming light of dawn…

So sing, my boys, sing,
Reef the canvass in,
Pull the sheets and let new sails
Billow on the wind of change…

Oh, for that dream
And final-ringing prophecy!

I am still dreaming,
Dreaming still…

…click, click… no more…

Come, close ceremony with me,
Thank the spirits and directions,
The energy and love of all,
And repose the circle, now complete,
To hope-enhance our future story,
Replete,
In which we *all* shall dance…

Being, belonging, caring, sharing,
That is all, is all, is all…

…as patient flows the James.

Made in the USA